THE OATMEAL ARK

By the same author

STALIN'S NOSE

RORY MACLEAN

THE OATMEAL ARK

ACROSS CANADA BY WATER

HarperCollins*PublishersLtd*

The author gratefully acknowledges the assistance of the Canada Council.

THE OATMEAL ARK: ACROSS CANADA BY WATER
Copyright © 1996 by Rory MacLean.
For information address HarperCollins Publishers Ltd,
Suite 2900, Hazelton Lanes, 55 Avenue Road,
Toronto, Canada M5R 3L2.

http://www.harpercollins.com/canada

Canadian Cataloguing in Publication Data

MacLean, Rory, 1954-
The oatmeal ark : across Canada by water

ISBN 0-00-255061-X

1. Canada - Description and travel.   2. Inland navigation - Canada.
I. Title.

FC75.M33 1996   917.104   C96-930746-2
F1017.M33 1996

96 97 98 99 ❖ HC 10 9 8 7 6 5 4 3 2

Printed and bound in the United States

to A & J

The Oatmeal Ark weaves invention through true stories, stitches imaginary characters into real events. It is at once a history and a fiction. It tries to reach beyond our tradition of realistic literature, building on the strengths of Susanna Moodie, the *Canadian Vegetable* and the NFB documentary, and to reassert the older mythical dimensions of the land. In my writing I strive to cross the line beyond which fact becomes myth to find a truth that is made sharper in fiction. *The Oatmeal Ark* is a subjective, heartfelt look at Canada, its history and the courageous men and women of all nationalities who struggled — and struggle still — to build this country.

CONTENTS

CUILIDH MHOIRE

Treasury of Mary

CHAPTER I

UNDER GOD'S KILT

WE MET, MY great-grandson and I, more than a century after my death. That is to say I met him; he would not have noticed me had I flapped my wings, danced a reel on his nose and blown Gabriel's trumpet in his ear. His ferry had been delayed by the storm and in his haste to get ashore he did not see me waiting on the pier nor did he recognise me in the Co-op where he bought a bottle of Old Mull to settle his stomach. The crossing from the mainland had been choppy and his face was as pale as a flounder's belly. He hadn't inherited his father's sea-legs, right enough, but the high forehead, grey-green eyes and gestures which rolled from his hands like waves up a beach confirmed that he was kin. There and then I, Hector Gillean, first son and last pastor of the parish of Gualachaolish, thought it would be fine to give him a name. So I called him *Beagan*, which properly means 'a small quantity' in the English, for the paltry boy had lost his moorings and been shipwrecked by death and life.

'WHERE THE HELL can I hire a God–damned cab?' raged Beagan, swaying in the pub doorway. 'Or better still a lifeboat?' A gust of wind howled in behind him and lifted the froth from the top of a dozen pints. Fergus Macaulay downed his dram before the glass was blown off the bar. Billy Munro the landlord blinked at the stranger from under the hood of his anorak. 'Jesus, if I was any wetter I'd take root on this doorstep.'

Archie the Taxi lurched out into the gale, leaving a drink half-finished and a story part-told, while Isaac MacLeod, the harbour master, put on his cap to help carry the antique box trunk off the ship. The rusty Austin Marina sunk on her springs as they heaved it into the boot. Beagan dropped his second-hand copy of *Gaelic Made Easy* into a puddle, swore and kicked the car. Its wing mirror fell off and splashed into the slipway.

'These islands!' Archie enthused with a wave which embraced every kyle and cove. 'It's myself that is as fond of them as a mother of her baby-child.' Sheets of rain swept across russet and honey-coloured hills. Musselshell peaks vanished behind rolling banks of sodden cloud. 'But you'll not have come for the weather, you'll be here looking for your forefathers.'

'I've come to live at the old manse,' blustered Beagan. The twisting Hebridean seas had tied his insides into a double half-hitch knot. 'Unless I drown trying to reach it.' Visitors were a common sight on the island in high summer but come December they were as rare as the winter herring.

'My people went to Toronto,' Archie volunteered. Like everyone else in the bar, he had placed Beagan's accent. 'Maybe you'll be knowing them?'

'Sorry, no joy,' Beagan replied, feeling like hell. 'I grew up on the west coast near Vancouver.'

'Now that's a fine land, all right,' fancied Archie. 'Aye, a man can make good there.'

'Canada killed my father,' snapped Beagan and grimaced, remembering the child's nightmare of his fall, the clutched wounded heart, the brittle knees cracking on a hardwood floor. 'That's why I'm here.'

The taxi swayed into a passing place and gave way to an impatient red Post Office Land-Rover. John the Post was in a temper. He was late for supper and a gust of wind had blown half his letters out into the loch. Beyond the slapping windscreen wipers stood the ruined gables and walls of a dead village. Beagan knew that generations of islanders had left these waters for the backwoods of Ontario, the plantations of Jamaica and the sheep stations of Queensland. He knew too of their descendants returning on pilgrimages to buy tartan in gift shops and climb the earthworks to touch the castle walls. Clansmen from Kentucky were videoed in ancestral graveyards wearing baseball caps which read 'Genealogy is my line'. Whisky-soaked Australians sang 'The Bonnie Banks o' Loch Lomon'' at the Puffer Aground Inn. New Zealanders pinned their family tree to kilts at clan gatherings. To him the tribal tourists seemed ripe for ridicule, their twangs sounding discordant in the deserted hills. He understood that the local residents tolerated them, stuck on the single-track roads behind dawdling rental cars, slipping the dollars into their spurious sporrans, for they themselves were for the most part incomers. Even Archie had moved over from Kintyre. It was the tragedy of the islands; the place was no longer peopled by islanders. Beagan realised that the visitors came in search of a civilisation that had fought for its life and lost.

'Mark you, lad,' said Archie, glancing at the trunk in his rear-view mirror, 'not many bring as much luggage.'

'Those are the family papers,' explained Beagan. 'My inheritance,' he added with a bitter laugh. 'I come from a long line of hoarders. My forebears were too thrifty to throw anything away. Letters, diaries, old ferry tickets, notated napkins, anything of any importance they just dumped in the trunk.' Travel weariness and an aching head had eroded his reserve. 'They haven't been touched since my old man died,' he confided. 'See, he asked our house-keeper, sort of my surrogate grandmother, to give them to me on my twenty-first birthday, but she confused the dates and waited twenty-one years.' Beagan gulped angry breaths of the soft, wet air. 'So when the manse came up for rent at the same time I figured that it was here that the papers were to be read. Finally. This is where it began.'

'You'll be a Gillean, then,' guessed Archie.

His insight surprised Beagan. 'It was my great-grandfather who moved off the island.'

'Hunted off, more likely,' he flashed. History had honed a sharp edge to his tongue.

'I don't know much yet,' confessed Beagan, 'other than his name. The Reverend Hector Gillean. He was minister here about two hundred years ago. My father used to tell me and my brother stories about him, and this place.'

Beagan recalled his father, too big a man to balance on the edge of a child's cot, settling into the willow armchair in the Canadian house. Its weaving had creaked under his weight. Every night beneath pioneer woodcuts and nautical prints his stories had carried the two boys out over dusky waters to sail beside the gaff-rigged smack that had borne Hector out to the New World, away from his beloved Hebrides. The words had warmed them like the Gulf Stream and steered them towards a fine Peterborough lapstrake canoe from which had hailed their long-dead grand-father, the soft-hearted Jamie Gillean. His rag-taggle fleet of coal-burning tugs, leaky scows and puffing paddle-wheelers had once been the largest freshwater flotilla in North America. Their bossy great-uncle Zachary had waved from the first-class salon of the old Royal Mail Ship *Kipper*, tapped his fob-watch then tucked a galley proof of each of his thirty-seven trade newspapers under his arm. At a hundred bedtimes the tales had drawn the boys over black lagoons in a Ditchburn launch counting stars. Their father had switched off the lamp and in the half-light the engraving of the *Good Intent*, the etched palace steamers and water-coloured *canots du nord* had all seemed to break free of their aquatint moorings and sail out of their frames.

'I need to piece it all together,' bristled Beagan. Archie's driving and the winding road had conspired to turn him a bilious green. 'But hey, would you stop the car?' he added. 'I think I'm going to be sick.'

Along the shore the yews bowed to leeward, bruised by the winter wind, and a trawler took refuge in the bay. The taxi stopped and the sound of water was everywhere; beating on the heath, dripping off the gorse and streaming towards the sea which sur-rounded the headland on three sides. 'Mind your step there lad,' advised Archie. 'This place is like chicken wire laid over water. It's a wonder the whole island doesn't sink away.' Beagan stepped from the taxi and sank up to his knees in the wet bog.

'*ÀILTE!*' I HAILED in welcome but he didn't glance up as I opened the door for him. '*Ceud mìle fàilte!*' I repeated but I should have saved my breath to cool my porridge. The boy didn't hear me. After such a wait he could have acknowledged my existence. His behaviour was not only a disappointment, it was discourteous, even in a melancholic man.

The manse felt colder than a forgotten cairn. Its thick stone walls were so damp that the death-watch beetles too had emigrated. The pages of *Oat Cuisine: Cooking in Scotland*, discarded by the summer's last tenant, had curled up on the stone floor like a *mille-feuille* scone. I considered leaving Beagan alone to fester in his rude discontent, respect for his elders appearing to be another virtue which he sadly lacked, but then he dragged the trunk in from the wet, slipped down on to his knees, turned the old key in the rusting lock and released the brass catches. When he pushed back its lid the spirits of the past darted out into the room like fish cut free from a net.

Other families might possess a patch of land, an old house or burial plot but Beagan's heirloom consisted of tracts of my hand-written sermons and caches of Gaelic verse, crudely printed Canadian news pages and packets of his father's lacquer recording disks. It was the trunk full of words that linked him back to a place where he, as one of us, belonged.

In a corner of the trunk under a bundle of ships' logbooks lay a battered leather box. Beagan opened it and eased out the old terrestrial globe. Its painted panels had faded with age. The Indian Ocean, once turquoise, was now a stained verdigris colour. Imperial Russia was dented and torn from Saint Petersburg to Tilsit. Great yellowed swathes of Cathay had rusted away altogether. At the time when my globe was made California's Pacific coast was not yet settled. Livingstone was still to map the African interior. The Arctic regions and much of North America, as yet uncrossed by a white man, were represented as an unbroken land mass and marked 'Unexplored Countries'. The world was portrayed not as it really was but as men then saw it, a place of promised lands awaiting discovery.

Beagan set the globe on the desk from which almost two centuries before I had removed it. He poured an immoderate whisky, raised his glass and addressed the building which he had never before seen. 'Home,' he fumed. 'God-damned home.' The anger startled me and, as I began to sense the measure of his distress, it took me back to my own aimless days.

I belong to the Hebrides, the sweep of islands formed when the Cailleach Bheur, the benevolent giantess of Celtic mythology, let stones fall from the creel carried on her back while wading off the Highlands' western shore. It is a place more of water than land, of wild seas and calm bays, amber burns and white desert sands which surface at the ebb-tide; islands among islands, pools within pools, the indigo skerry at Europe's edge. Ours was a family of mariners; a boatload of sailors and dreamers. The Gilleans had their own ark, or so my father often told me. When the rains came and Noah battened down the hatches against God's flood, the clan crowded into a cockleshell coracle and huddled under a tartan umbrella until the storm had passed. They were used to inclement weather. They were Scots. After forty damp days and nights their leather boat came to rest not on the mountains of Ararat, where the torrents had been stopped, but on a soggy bed of peatmoss beside a silver Caledonian firth. Our forefathers sent forth a curlew, for they had no dove, and it returned with a sprig of heather. The men, their wives, sons and sons' wives took each other in their arms and rejoiced. They had found our home.

But my great-grandson, who seems not to hear that which I tell him, was born in a land where everyone came from somewhere else. Its people had been imported across the sea on sailing ships and ocean liners. No family had lived in his New World for more than seven, at most eight, generations, except the Native people who had been written out of the newcomers' history. No one on his continent could drink from a river that was part of himself or grasp a handful of soil and say, 'I am of this earth.' Its settlers had been washed across the surface of the land only to remain tied to an old country by blood, keepsakes and dog-eared albums of faded photographs.

It was I who, with the idealism of the living, had swept the family from these waters. I had been a man of the Enlightenment. I had believed that thought could renew the life of the world and restore its original purity, energy and justice. Two hundred years ago as an island minister for a congregation of poor fisherwomen and trawlermen I had taken ship west. In the loch below this manse I had boarded my ark. The globe had been tucked under my arm. My luggage was Testaments, Catechisms and the dream of creating a nation of devout individuals bonded by a common idea. The tool with which I hoped to help build this New Jerusalem was neither the axe, plough nor theodolite; it was the Word.

My sons, Beagan's grandfather James and great-uncle Zachary, had inherited the vision. To preach it they had moved from the Atlantic coast to the heart of the optimistic young nation and formed the country's first national publisher. For them the Word was print. Print was the medium of communication and through it they had propagated the settler's belief in a better life, trusting that it would fuse the new land's disparate peoples into a just society.

Beagan's father Sandy had also grown up looking forward towards one ocean and back across another, washed west by the flow yet drawn east to the stream's source. He had pursued his hopes to the Pacific coast. For him words, precious words, had to edify. Canada would be united by radio waves and reason. Sandy had never waited for the world to improve; instead he had set about trying to change it. Like us all he had put his faith in a dream.

'What delivers a man from poverty of Spirit?' asked Beagan aloud, squinting at my copperplate script. I thought for a moment that he was striking up a conversation. That was fine, right enough. The boy seemed to have turned over a new leaf.

'The Word is revelation of Truth for the Salvation of men, also for the Duty of men,' I answered, settling myself down across the desk from him. 'And do you know what Paul tells us of the treasures of wisdom?'

'In the beginning was the Word, and the Word was with God, and the Word was God,' Beagan answered, incorrectly, then turned the page, and I realised that he was only trying to will the words back to life. 'Christ,' he cursed, staring at a detailed homily I'd written on *John*, 'I'll need a bloody microscope to decipher this writing.'

'Hear me,' I commanded, angered by both his incomprehension and his insolence. 'I'll have no blasphemers in this house.' But the boy heard me not.

Beagan continued his disconcerting habit of reading my sermons aloud as he unpacked the Bibles and albums and sorted ribbon-wrapped love letters from dusty broadcast scripts. 'The zeal for preaching God's sacred Word must not slack or go backward,' he stormed while arranging our books in the shelves, 'otherwise we fall into ignorance and darkness.' There were two complete sets of North Atlantic Admiralty charts, a dozen canoe route-maps and the patent papers for thirteen marine inventions. The die of *Red Herring*'s propeller was unearthed from the trunk and placed in a corner. He stacked glass negatives on the kitchen table and bellowed out a psalm: 'I remember the days of old; I meditate on all thy works; I muse on the work of thy hands.'

I paid him little heed, still smarting from his coarseness, but then, it shames me to admit, he flattered my vanity. The silver daguerreotype which he unwrapped remembered a well-made man of fair complexion and steady green eye, bearded, bald and standing some five foot ten in a long black preacher's coat. Beside my photographic likeness he set a snapshot of his father as a boy on the Muskoka Lakes, spanner in hand and tie stained by *Primary*'s greasy bilges. In the distance James's old steamer *Kipper* puffed and wheezed her way around Wigwassan Point.

Beagan laid out the journals, pamphlets and packs of correspondence tied with frayed twine. There was an unused receipt for an Atlantic crossing and a rough sheet of parchment postmarked Nova Scotia and covered with a stranger's hand. 'Thank God,' the forgotten migrant had written three lifetimes ago, 'I am well pleased for coming to this new country.'

Every day he delved deeper into the trunk, perusing our jottings, wading through my writings, until I had to confess that he did possess one virtue, right enough: a passion for memory. He read with a desperate, instinctual hunger that drew the past inside himself. But no matter how much he studied, my clearly articulated principles of right and wrong did not seem to anchor him. It was as if the years of anger and confusion since his father's death had blown him too far off-course and now only the indulgence in ardent spirits could numb him to their winds.

'We are all partial to a dram, but a little temperance

would do you no harm,' I advised, yet Beagan finished the Glenlivet anyway, spun the globe on its axis and stumbled, his face blazing with liquor, out into the night.

'Where the hell am I?' he shouted into the blackness and heard no response. It would have been more useful for him to have asked *who* he might be. The woven folds of the northern lights rustled above our heads. Shooting stars fell from the heavens. The tartan hem of God's kilt blazed a luminous arc across the sky.

BEAGAN BROKE THE surface with a cry, climbed out of the sea, up on to the rocks and ran. He seemed to be on fire, his skin steamed and vapour trailed in his wake, like some primeval amphibian hell-bent on rushing evolution. The blizzard swirled out of his path and he heaved, as the ocean after a high wind, around the sweep of the wild loch, across the rusty waves of heather, towards the blue mist of distance. An icy squall washed him against the manse, into the bathroom, under the shower of scalding needles. He gasped at the humid air, grasped the showerhead in his hands and wept. In his dreams he had again heard his father's stories, sailed once more down the rivers that flowed and carried him on the current. 'It flows far away into the distance and you can never quite see the end,' he had remembered him tell. Beyond an open window the ocean had sighed with the incoming tide. 'And do you hear the water slapping under the bow?' The bedroom had smelt of pine pitch and brine. 'Do you hear it?' Beagan had shaken himself out of the haunted sleep. The freezing swim had flushed away the night's shadows but it could not still the havoc in his heart, the whirlwind of days that had been scattered by the white wings of death. On the earth outside, beneath the wintry clouds, all that remained to recall his passing was the trail of moss footprints across the dusting of snow.

The evening before I had drifted in to him on the wave

of a dream. I had whispered in his ear but he had awoken
with a start and struck out at the darkness crying his
father's name in fear. The rest of his night had passed
uneasily, every gust of wind and creak of stair worrying
him, and I had realised that if he could hear us, how easily
his growing curiosity might be frightened from him. It
became apparent that I needed to take care, to nurture us
in him like the cloudberry in the lee of the croft. I decided
then to dress up guidance as fate, coming to him as coincidence and telling our story through his imagination. My
sons James and Zachary would help me, in time his father
Sandy too, joining us as needed, mapping out his past, his
country's pasts, remaking our worlds in him.

So I stayed there by his side through that first year while
he pored over the brittle volumes. I guided his hand from
Memorandum to Nautical Almanac and when his back was
turned, even leafed on to entries of particular interest. I
showed him that the trunk itself had been passed down from
father to son for three generations. My initials were carved
into its lid. The brass corners and fine-tooled lock had been
added by Zachary. Jamie had restitched the worn leather
handles and Sandy had painted it with a left-over tin of
seashell-blue enamel. Beagan saw that each of us had in
turn worked both to preserve the trunk and to make it his
own. He did not resist my interference, if indeed he sensed
it at all, and my presence no longer seemed to frighten him
for he took less often to intemperate drink.

IT WAS LATE the following January that Beagan noticed the
innocuous brown envelope. It lay sandwiched between a luncheon
menu from the SS *Campana* and a swatch of wedding-dress silk.
More than twenty-one years before, the letter had been shoved
unread into the bulging trunk and forgotten. He opened it and
found it to be a bill. This came as a surprise. It stated that the

family owed back-taxes on land in British Columbia. His father Sandy had once owned a short stretch of Canadian coastline but it had been sold at a loss soon after his death. No property had been mentioned in the will and the deeds, if any, were lost. But bureaucrats never forget and here, in black and white with a red maple leaf in the corner, was confirmation of ownership of a small island off the Pacific coast.

Beagan made some calls. From the manse beside the Atlantic he spoke to his brother in a television studio overlooking the Pacific. The sailboats, Alex said, were out in Vancouver Harbour. 'A whole island? Hey, that's great. It must be in the bay off the old house somewhere.'

'Can you look into it?' asked Beagan.

'You bet, but it's pretty crazy round here.' Hollow voices and ringing telephones echoed down the line. 'It looks like I got my break with the network.'

'That's good news.'

'So why don't you quit travelling and come check it out yourself?' risked Alex. Once every year he tried to persuade Beagan to join his film production company. 'It's nuts that you don't come home.'

Beagan hadn't been back in almost two decades. The New World was the place where a man's dreams were meant to come true but the betrayal of his father's hopes had led him to see the country as a failed nation. It had made an exile of him, travelling without reflection, living as if in a fog, and he had drifted through a miscellany of jobs, letting the current carry him where it pleased like a sailor adrift without a sail.

'There's a real opportunity here now,' added Alex.

'Give me a break, OK?' Beagan told his brother. 'I have to finish going through the papers first.'

'You going through your savings too?'

'They're almost gone, so thanks for sorting out the manse's rent. But I may have an island in the end.'

'What's in the papers? Anything that could make a movie?'

'You know, it's weird,' Beagan admitted. 'These last months

the stories have sort of come alive. With all this reading I don't feel so alone.'

But Alex was distracted by his assistant before Beagan could continue. 'Hey, bro, I've got to go. It's L.A. on the other line.'

'Can you make a few enquiries?'

'No worries,' he said and hung up.

Property in Canada is not sold by name, as Bramble Cottage or the Dunrobin Estate would be, but by number. Newly-weds might set their hearts on picturesque Lot 43 Concession B. A retired couple could pool their lifetimes' savings to buy Island 161A, Township of Georgian Bay.

It was the family lawyer who called Beagan back. There had been a bit of a mix-up, he explained. The problem was with the original transfer document. It seemed that when transcribing the long list of lot and concession numbers his typist, possibly wishing she too was sailing in Vancouver Harbour, had missed one out. A simple mistake, but the lawyers and purchaser had failed to spot it, the transfer had been effected and the sale completed. Until the discovery of the brown envelope no one had known that his father's name had remained on the property rolls attached to the overlooked island. But it had and now it belonged to Beagan, if he cared to settle the matter of two decades' outstanding property tax.

Beagan put down the receiver. On the desk the diaries and half-read letters were piled at wild angles like something washed in by the tide, the jetsam of genealogy. He sensed that his salvation was written between their lines but rather than read the papers he now decided to relive them. He chose to claim his chance inheritance. He would retrace the family's voyage from Scotland, across Canada and through three generations of family history to his promised island. The bulging old trunk would go with him.

The manse was closed, the globe boxed up and the trunk repacked. There was no fatted calf to kill but frozen New Zealand lamb from the Co-op made a rich farewell stew. Archie the Taxi dropped by with a bottle as he had on occasion over the year and, in keeping with tradition, threw the cap into the hearth. It bounced off the Calorgas heater.

'Some days I wouldn't thank you for a dram, but if the crack's good then a bottle won't do,' he confessed, holding his glass of Talisker against the light. 'That trunk of yours looks awful heavy,' he added in jest. 'Are you sure you won't be wanting me to drive you?'

'I'm not travelling by land,' answered Beagan.

'Aye, then it'll be dear to fly with it. There's no way that will fit under an aircraft seat.'

'My father once told me that to understand a country you have to know its waterways,' Beagan said, reaching for the bottle. 'The first fishermen and explorers, map-makers and settlers all travelled to Canada by sea, then went on over it by its lakes and rivers. Did you know that there are more lakes in that country than in the rest of the world put together? Well, that's how I want to cross it, by water, along the channels which connect, communicate and link.'

Archie lowered his glass without draining it, an unusual event in itself. 'I hate to spoil your plans, lad, but you do know that most people go by road nowadays? A Chevrolet's considerably faster than a kayak.'

'I don't know if the water route still exists,' Beagan admitted, 'but I need to try to find out.' He knew that to reach across the country and back into his history, to try to make sense of that which had made him, it was the only way to travel. 'It may sound mad but this feels like the first true decision I've made for a very long time. In any event I've already bought two dozen packs of Kwells seasickness pills.'

'Two dozen packs?' repeated Archie, taking a deep breath and refilling Beagan's glass. 'Well then, that's an investment. So it's ourselves that had better get a move on. You can't go away to the ships until the whisky's finished.'

*   *   *

S SURE AS death Beagan still drinks too much and I would twist his nose were I able. He and that Archie stayed up half the night talking, like two bedevilled soaks, about women and pleasure boats, schooners and malts. It did not please me well.

It was a fine morning with only a wee bit of drizzle and Beagan wore a new shirt as parents of my time would have dressed their children in their first pair of shoes. In his hand he clasped the diary-book which I had held at the same parting all those years ago. I was reluctant to join him on the journey. No one should have to live their life twice. Yet none of us travels alone, there is always an angel by our side, and it seemed only natural that I should be his guardian. In any case the other figments of himself would be with us along the way, right enough, and it was myself who wanted to watch over him at the outset of our second emigration.

My great-grandson and I left the rainy island as black burns drew winter's shroud from the mountain's shoulders. The lonely blue-shadowed hills were wet with tears for absent sons. Above the departing Cal Mac ferry the clouds parted, as they had done when the refugee had been myself, and I half-expected to see my own father at the end of the dabbled beam of sunlight bidding farewell in his soft rhythmic Gaelic.

'Slàn leat, Beagan,' I heard him call. 'Blessings be with you.' And I remembered the hole that my own parting had made in my heart. Then a squall obscured the view and it began to rain so hard that I imagined the mountain to dissolve, the land to break apart and my island to be washed away into the sea.

CHAPTER II

THE GOOD INTENT

I HECTOR GILLEAN, was born the son of a ship-wright, a builder of skiffs and yawls, the maids-of-all-work in the nineteenth century. My mother was a , saillery woman, stitching on her knee the tawny canvas which gave life to her husband's boats. I grew up with the scent of wood and resin, to the laying of keel and sighting of line. At three years old I crawled into the places too small for my father to caulk seams and pick out curly shavings. Aged twelve I built my own *bàta* from off-cuts and flotsam. We called the Atlantic Ocean *Cuilidh Mhoire*, Treasury of Mary, and I rode her swells on shifting decks as if boat and boy and water were one. 'This boat can sail the world,' I imagined and saw myself on the seven seas, steering for Siam and running towards the Carolinas. At night, home from the lobsters in clothes sea-wet, our family ate tatties or kippers cooked in oak ash and listened to tales of Red Rufus of the Minch and the cold green angels that meet drowning fishers who cry, 'I am no more.' My father's story-telling was fine, right enough, and it sustained us when food was scarce but no yarn could ease the hunger that had began to gnaw at our hearts.

My sisters were Una, Meg and Annie, my brothers Iain and Finn. The girls had married crofters and warmed their husbands' hearths in the embrace of the ocean's arms. Una died in childbirth. Meg and Annie raised their bairns, burnt red ware and prickly tang for the kelp trade, grazed their black cattle on the common land until the factor cleared

them out and pulled down their roof and they had to emi-
grate to New South Wales. My father and I stood dumb on
the sands and watched them go, mouths agape like fish fresh
pulled from the loch, little understanding the change being
thrust upon us. Then Finn, a handy seamen, went to sea on
a China-clipper and was never seen again. There had been
no work to keep him at home. Iain, so his story went, fought
at Trafalgar and for his bravery was granted the right to
produce his sword at any time. When the laird's men tried
to evict him he drew his blade and was arrested. The sheriff
demanded an explanation. Iain pulled the King's permission
from his pocket, the sabre from its scabbard and declared,
'If you can no read your head's the first to come off.' I held
fast to his coat-tail as they dragged him to the boat and let
go only when the bailiff bit my fingers.

Scotland in the early nineteenth century was a nation in
ferment. The English sword had butchered the clans and
crushed the Highlanders' spirit. 'I do swear,' my father had
been forced to vow, 'that I shall never use tartan, plaid or
any part of the Highland garb; and if I do so, may I be
cursed, may I never see my wife and children, father, mother
or relations, and lie without Christian burial in a strange
land, far from the graves of my forefathers and my kindred.'
To refuse to submit risked transportation. A thousand years
of tradition were uprooted by Acts of Parliament and the
advance of commerce. The value of an estate was no longer
measured by the number of men that it could raise but by
the profit its land created. Sheep produced more wealth
than crofters so rent was racked from five to twenty pounds
a year and families, unable to pay a figure equivalent to
twice a labourer's annual income, were cast adrift from their
homes.

My heart would sink as one by one the yawls left our bay.
I knew each boat, had helped lay the keels of most, and
held the familiar bows in the water as downcast men spread
their patch of sail above their weeping women. The water

was cold and I wished for shoes. Only one optimistic soul
ventured, 'We will be back before the lifting of the peats,'
but I knew that none would ever see the island again. Above
the broad green landing girls no longer sang on the shielings
and bracken crept into the fields. Iron bedheads rusted in
a tangle of gorse.

The Reverend Hugh McKay McKenzie, a stickit minister
marooned on the island without patron, watched the boats
leave too. In the slate-roofed manse he resolved to give
me the chance that others had been denied. He drilled my
English and favoured me with extra Latin and Greek. From
him I learnt that language could structure the wild spirit of
man, that discipline was essential to survive in the uncertain
world. He turned my love of family into compassion for
men, my passion for stories into a respect for the Word.

McKenzie also taught me the use of globes. There may
have been no other pair in the Highlands, certainly his were
the only ones on the island, and they helped me to see
beyond our sad shore.

'West! West!' he enthused curving his hand from Asia,
across Europe and over the Atlantic. The elbows of his
jacket were worn through and his breath smelt of turnips.
'Listen now, *a bhalaich*.' My boy. 'It was to this fringe that
Caesar pushed the Celts, across these waters that Saint Col-
umba brought Christianity, along this route west that
Brendan the Navigator sailed his leather boat.' He placed
our sorrows in the tide of history. 'And here,' he jabbed a
broken fingernail at the sketchy New World shore. Its
jagged edge scratched Nova Scotia. 'This is where our people
are now going.'

'YOU KNOW,' SHOUTED Beagan across the bustling terminal,
'one in four of the emigrant boats that made this crossing early last
century was lost.' A monstrous orange hull rusting into lobster-red

stripes loomed above him. 'But I would have felt one hell of a lot safer on one of them than I do right now.'

Davey, the tall and wiry Glaswegian first officer, stopped whistling 'For Those in Peril on the Sea' to sidestep a demonic Valmet mobile crane. 'Did you forget your bathing costume then?' he yelled. It was noisy enough on the Felixstowe pier to wake the dead. 'It's my suggestion that when this oary boat starts to sink, you drink a bottle of voddy and let her go down around you. Bugger the survival suit.'

The *Global Trader* was the world's largest baked-bean can, a floating warehouse that shipped twenty-four thousand tons of white beans across the Atlantic to Heinz every month. On her return journey her two thousand containers held a mixed cargo: twelve thousand litres of vodka, eighteen tons of frogs' legs, Chanel perfume, powdered cyanide and a gross of Range-Rovers. A crewman hung from the raked bow slapping anti-corrosion paint on to the hull.

Beagan paused to get a better grip on his trunk. Lugging the papers halfway around the world could prove inconvenient, though he understood that no ship sets sail without its anchor. Except maybe the *Global Trader*.

'Good thinking to bring along something to read,' bellowed Davey, 'cause there'll be no brilliant conversation onboard unless you can natter in Hindi.' His shout brought to mind the cry of a snared animal. 'Apart from the skipper and me, all the officers are Sri Lankan. The company's not training Western masters any more, and the crew is Indian.'

Midshipman Pereira, the Goan steward, helped lift the box trunk over a guard-rail. His smile was pegged on to his face by a solitary tooth. 'Here very good,' he boasted. 'I work on ships ten years. Brother work on ships. Father work on ships. Grandfather, he shoreside working.'

'Pereira, you're a pure waste of space.' Davey led Beagan around a cairn-like stack of containers. 'We've been through the whole jing-bang of cheap labour: Irish navvies steaming on poteen, Red Chinese jigging about the deck doing T'ai chi to Mao's little book, fairy Filipinos and now the bloody industrious Indians. Off-duty Pereira here knocks his pan making toty wee model ships in bottles. He even sent one to the Queen.'

Davey stopped at the foot of the gangway in the middle of a rail line and stabbed a bony finger at Beagan. 'You'll not be a journalist, will you?' His tortoise-like neck extended up from his shoulders and his head twisted as if on a stalk. 'A bloody journalist cost me my job in the navy.'

'Hey, keep your shirt on.' Beagan glanced up and down the track. 'My great-grandfather emigrated to Canada and I'm trying to retrace his route, that's all.' As they climbed up towards the smell of diesel oil he explained about claiming his inheritance – both Pacific island and family history – but Davey couldn't hear above the scream of the gantry cranes. The trunk banged on every step and Beagan tried to remember where the Kwells were packed.

Passage aboard a container ship along the fixed route between Britain and Montreal was not the voyage of a lifetime. Of the great fleets which had once carried passengers and freight across the North Atlantic only the *Global Trader* remained. Romance for the sea had been displaced by the cynicism of routine. The ship would be back from the New World and her crew drinking in the bar of the Hope and Anchor two weeks from Friday. Its monotonous shuttle reminded Beagan of his own drifting years, the dreary round which had eked out a living but wasted half his days, before he had unlocked the trunk and released the spirits of the past.

The owner's cabin had twin beds and a dayroom with two defunct televisions. The drawers were lined with old Admiralty charts. A tub large enough to double as a lifeboat was moored in the *en suite* bathroom. On top of the mini-bar Pereira had placed a model of a square-rigged Indiaman. 'To remember by,' he suggested with a mixture of embarrassment and pride. Beagan set the old globe beside it.

The thump-thump of darts missing a bull's eye drew Beagan to the officers' mess. The officers sat in a long row, left to right in descending order of rank, slouched over the bar, each nursing a bottle of beer. Jagjit, Vijitha and Lakshman were all bearded with hair meticulously groomed and their skin mahogany beneath short-sleeved white uniform shirts.

'Not much in the way of glittering company, I'm afraid,' apologised the captain by way of introduction. He was a soft-spoken and diligent man from Hornsea.

'If he'd wanted glitter he'd have caught a jumbo jet,' crowed Davey, snapping the top off a Beck's and offering it to Beagan. 'This one's on me.'

'I'd accept it,' advised the captain. 'Davey won't offer again.'

'It's the only entertainment you'll get this side of America.'

Beagan looked around the stale, weary mess and wished that he had a boat of his own. 'I've got a lot of papers to go through.'

'Good, because there's no ballroom onboard so dancing is out too,' continued Davey. 'But there is a video. And the wee fairy lights.'

The bar was framed by a string of flashing decorations and flanked by the only two women on board. To the left hung a portrait of Queen Elizabeth II, to the right an under-clad blonde on a Grolsch calendar. 'My officers like them up year round,' explained the captain. The men barely looked up from their beers. Routine seemed to have so dulled them that Beagan almost ran his hand across their faces to sweep the cobwebs from their eyes. 'Jagjit bought them the same Christmas that the Seaman's Mission gave everyone onboard a Montreal Expos baseball cap.'

'I tell you, mate, life at sea is a barrel of laughs.'

Beyond the slouching Sri Lankans three rectangular portholes hung ninety feet above the cavernous hull into which the containers were being swung. To stow the cargo by hand would have taken six weeks. The Valmets took less than twenty-four hours to unload and refill the ship. The *Global Trader* would cast off before midnight. 'Aren't there any other passengers?' asked Beagan.

The captain gestured out into the hold. 'Your only other company might be our uninvited guests.' Since the collapse of communism a stream of frustrated migrants had poured out of

eastern Europe to the Atlantic coast. 'Romanians have been breaking into the terminal at Antwerp and hiding in any container
marked for Canada. One crossing last year we had eight
stowaways.'

'If this was a Greek ship they'd be fed to the sharks,' said Davey.
'Clever buggers those Greeks.'

'The immigration authorities fine the company $5,000 for every
stowaway found on board,' explained the captain.

'How do you catch them?' asked Beagan.

'We don't. They jump overboard in the Saint Lawrence and
the longshoremen find bedding and charred crates where they lit
fires. It gets a little cool at the bottom of the hold in January.'

'Sometimes we just find their bodies,' reported Davey. 'Bit like
your old emigrant boats, eh mate?'

'There was a lot of death then,' confirmed Beagan as his
thoughts reached back to the Reverend's copperplate diary. 'And
hope.'

'The next line of dreamers off to the promised land,' said the
captain in a droll, solemn way. 'Let us know if you hear any
voices.'

I T IS THE waves which I remember. They dipped and
strained and drove us over a pewter sea. I can still
hear their jagged breakers rip along the hull, see curl-
ing billows froth at their crest, ride the deep furrows
which bore the ferry-boat down between monstrous grey
rollers. Each swell wrenched us off our heading. Any wave
taken at the wrong moment could end our days. Yet I loved
to ride them, to taste the salt spray, to feel the surge and
ebb beneath my feet as the ferrymen pulled their round
bonnets low over their eyes and dug their oars into the wild
waters.

My father had sent me away from Gualachaolish. There
was not the money to feed me, let alone to pay for my

studies. He had locked in the cupboard my Almanac and copy of Bunyan and I had left to live with a cousin on the mainland. In the twelve months there I did not read a single book, not even the Scriptures, and lost all scruples about Sabbath-breaking. My free hours were squandered on drink and cards. I had earned my crust and fed my stomach but starved my soul.

Then one Sunday evening with friends I had fallen into conversation of religious matters and sins from which I could not free myself. All of a sudden a terrible fear and trembling had seized me. I saw that evil had come upon me disguised as dissolute days. My life had been wasting away, labour serving no purpose but the spawning of selfish satisfaction. I had to hide myself away, weeping alone and praying. I did not know what had brought on these thoughts. It may have been conscience or the common strivings of the spirit or even Satan but whatever the reason my distress made me see the one field of usefulness which it was in the providence of God to set before me.

Men since Abraham had left their father's house to live in foreign lands and spread the Word of God. I had identified with the tradition and followed across the globe's painted oceans the journeys of missionaries exiled for the sake of Christ. With McKenzie's introduction I had applied for a scholarship at Edinburgh University and studied for the ministry. I had had no wish to be parted from the beloved people whose society was dear to me but there lay overseas opportunities that were denied us at home. I had answered an advertisement for a missionary 'with health and strength of body, the entire possession of the five senses and a vigorous exertion of locomotive powers'. My fluency in both English and the Gaelic had secured an appointment in the province of British North America. I had been preparing to leave Scotland when my father's letter arrived begging me to return home.

The wind tore at our backs and the ferry-boat chased the

whitecaps into our bay. Its oars twisted in the trough of
lofty waves and kind hands seized the bow. A shaft of silver
light shot through the low leaden clouds and illuminated a
great white skeleton lying on the shingle like a beached
whale. An ox dragged logs down from the steading. Sawyers
cut timber into planks. The whale's bleached ribs were larch
moulds. Its spine was an oak keel. The bony frame was the
shell of a ship.

'We are going to find our fortune,' laughed gorbellied
Little Donald, taking my arm. The smith, a man of ample
size and optimism, was unaffected by the stormy air that
whipped the island. On a sinking boat he would have looked
forward to the swim.

'Aye, and the streets of America are paved with gold.'
Duncan, the brogue maker, stood on a stone so as not to
muddy his shoes. His sport was baiting Donald's enthusiasms. 'All men wear silver buttons and buckles too.'

'I have heard tell of it.' Duncan's barbs never snared the
smith. 'And that there are trees which give both soap and
sugar.'

My father lay down his adze and shook my hand. 'We
have been told to leave, Hector,' he said with a dull gesture
along the beach.

'In the name of Providence, not all of you?'

'Aye, one and all right enough.' His eyes had the shade
of the grave. 'It is for this that we are building the *Good
Intent*.' I looked across to the boat.

'Come warm yourself and we will read you the letter.'

The last of my people, hardly twenty souls, left their
labours and followed Donald's stout piggin-jar girth up the
path. Smoke rose from but half the black houses and rotting
barley thatch lay where it had been scattered by the gale.
The laird's sheep grazed on the common ground.

'The factor came ashore this last month and gave us sum-
mons to quit,' Duncan explained, treading on the dry
heather verge. His fine footwear contrasted with a lean face,

dried and cracked like a shrivelled old boot. 'He even denied us the right to fish after Easter Eve.'

'As if any landlord owns the sea,' said my father.

'A cur every inch of him.'

'He is a man who levies tribute on the fish landed.' Ewan Cameron was snouted like a dogfish with pointed nose and a swirling determination to swim free of any net. 'And he cares not a straw for ourselves.'

There had been no burning roofs or dousing of hearths on the island. Bedridden grandmothers had not been thrown out into the rain as they had in Sutherland and on Skye. Estate officers had not hooked up potatoes or dammed mill streams as on Lewis. The crofters had simply been told to go. 'The land is not yours,' the factor had said. It mattered not that their families had lived in the place for a dozen generations. The laird had offered the islanders a stark choice: settle in a remote glen on a bare neck of turf or be transported to the New World.

'That *croit* will not even grow bracken,' snorted Cameron.

'Then your father told him, "We have need of neither charity nor another man's ship, Mr Munro."' Donald recounted the incident with pardonable pride. My father did not lift his head. '"The Gilleans have always had a boat of their own."'

The factor had laughed and turned away but the laird, when he learnt of the plan, had given leave to fell timber in his hills. It was his ox which dragged the logs down to the shore.

'I am certain that he wants to support the wisdom of our decision.' Donald's frank, generous nature had a fine simplicity.

'Or save the cost of our passage,' suggested Duncan.

Inside, the croft was dusky and smoke-dried. The women, hair plaited under white mutches, sheltered children out of the rain. A hook hung from the middle beam with a pot pendent over a grateless fire. Cameron's eldest, the spinster

Kirstie, poured hot water on a handful of oats to make me a brose. She apologised for the lack of butter but it mattered not. I ate with a keen appetite, hunger being the better sauce.

The men gathered around the kettle, sat on stools and waited for the creased letter from a cousin in Nova Scotia to be reopened.

'He writes that there is good land nearby him.' Jewels of raindrops glistened in Donald's eyebrows. He read aloud, 'Thank God I am well pleased for coming to this new country as I find myself quite easy, having occupied land called my own free from all burdens whatsoever. I go out and in my house at my pleasure, no soul living forces me to do a turn against my will, no laird, no factor, nor any toilsome work but I do myself.' Every man and woman present knew the words by heart. The letter had been read a dozen times that month. 'Each man and wife who settles here is granted 150 acres at a cost of one shilling sterling per acre.'

'One hundred and fifty acres.' Duncan stooped to flick a spot of dirt from his shoe buckle. 'See that now, in America we will all be lairds.' An industrious cobbler could make four hundred pairs of shoes in a year. He hadn't sold fifty in the last eighteen months.

'Wait you now, it is certain that the voyage will be hazardous and the life not easy,' I ventured. 'The land must be cleared and I believe the winters are hard.'

'But no winter can be colder than one in a land with tacksmen.' Donald made much of his little knowledge of the New World. His uncle had served with the 78th Highlanders under Wolfe at the capture of Quebec. 'We are sailing ourselves to the Nova Scotia, Hector.'

'God willing, liberty and posterity will reward honest industry.'

'Aye, and it is you that we want to join us.'

The spontaneous agreement of the others embarrassed me. Only my father remained silent.

'It's myself that is for it,' stated Cameron. 'As long as the people are driven from their homes there will be none to buy my fish. I cannot even feed my own.' His daughters no longer followed the herring with their father but were bound instead to work as fisher girls on the mainland.

'I know it as a fact that the waters there are so full of fish that a man might catch one in his hand,' enthused Donald. 'A woman too, sure enough,' he added for Kirstie's sake.

I made my excuses and told them about my appointment. My passage had been arranged and I was to sail from the Clyde at the end of the month. There was urgent work that needed to be done in my new parish.

'But our destinations are not a day's fair wind apart,' rushed Donald. 'I have seen it on McKenzie's globe. Your Cape Breton Island lies hard by Nova Scotia.'

I tried to interrupt but Cameron began to speak. 'Hector, we are too few in number. The ship is wanting of men.'

'We need both a navigator and a pastor,' insisted Donald.

I flushed under their gaze. Even Kirstie met my eyes. 'Guide the *Good Intent* to the New Scotland,' said her father.

As winter turned to spring the ship took shape on the shore. We took from the hills the last tall trees with few branches, for branches mean knots in the wood, and cut them into boards. The men fitted the strakes fore and aft, working from one side of the hull to the other, and ran the line of planking along her length. Grown oak frames were sawn to shape then set into ribs. Extra strength was built into the bow and the hull shaped before laying in the deck. As we were so few there was to be but one cabin below with partitions of canvas dividing bachelor from spinster, family from family. Rough boards would serve as bunks. I did my share of carpentry, setting the garboard strake, hollowing out the rabbet and bending over the wooden plane until it seemed to take on the shape of the timber. My father oversaw the building, the laying of keel and sighting of line, but the eviction had changed him. There were no longer stories on his lips.

In measured steps the children, thin and querulous as hungry birds, moved among us trying to calculate the boat's length from rudder to high curved stem. Amidships they quibbled, lost count and returned to the stern to start again.

'Sixty-two *slat*,' shouted the youngest, his corduroy knickerbockers unfastened at the knee.

'Sixty-two feet,' said Neill Ruadh, who had paid more attention to lessons. Each child ran his hands down the hull, touching the boat as if in blessing, and spoke of it as if about part of Creation.

I made it my duty to instruct them and after they had collected crabs and gulls' eggs from the crag we sat together to read. The curious ones wondered about the journey and Donald would desert his forge to excite them with stories of wild Indians and coconut palms, blue-feathered jays and white polar bears. After our lessons they caulked the seams with thin cedar wedges or clenched the copper nails in the cramped hold, all that is but Neill Ruadh who could never bear to be inside a closed space. In a locked room he would plead for the door to be opened.

The mast that we chose stood on the headland. It was an old Scots pine, not too tall but one which had grown in the wind and storms and so had tension in its wood. We shaved the bark and squared the trunk, then planed its sides to eighths, to sixteenths, to thirty-seconds until the edges curved into an even shaft. The men wedged it up, eased the supports and launched the modest trading smack, a boat far smaller than other emigrant ships, but one made for our people by our own hands.

Sail canvas was stitched across a dozen knees, hemp ropes were spun and oats baked into thin, hard cakes. There was herring to clean, a little salt beef to lay in and whisky enough stowed. The scars on Kirstie Cameron's fingers recalled the tired slip of gutting-knives. Her slow chanting song set the rhythm for the other women milling grain in the quern, turning the upper whinstone with a stick. As she sang I wrote to my sponsor to make my excuses. Any disappointment that the Edinburgh Ladies' Society had felt over my delay in taking up the post was offset by their joy in having more funds to buy Bibles.

We took the Books every morning and nightfall and I led the people in worship. Heads were bowed and hearts raised. We prayed for God to guide us over the ocean, for Jesus to be beside us at the helm, for the Spirit to be with us in every weather and current, each lying down, each rising up, in the trough of the waves, on the crest of the billows, on every step of the journey that we were about to undertake.

On a cold spring morning in my thirtieth year I stood on the wet shingle hearing the cries of children and the screams of birds. Gannets plunged into the water like white hands around the rowing boats which ferried the islanders, their sacks and kists out to the ship. Under my arm I cradled a new diary-book, its crisp pages unmarked by a single pen-stroke, and the terrestrial globe. In the manse the evening before I had sat for the last time beside the Reverend McKenzie. He had decided to remain behind with those few who had chosen not to join the ship. When I had stood to leave him he had given me the globe and the Improved Metallic Memorandum 'found to be of great advantage to Travellers and all persons who wish to preserve their Writing'.

'I won't be coming with you either, Hector,' my father said. He held the oars of my own *bàta* and had neither sack nor kist.

'But there is no life for you here.' I imagined him sitting by the peat fire in a turf bothy with only a scattering of hens and a handkerchief of land. His adze and chisel would rust, his muscles weaken and his eyes grow dim. There would be no sweet flummery of oatmeal. His lot would be the winding-sheet.

'This is my father's island.' His knuckles swelled like great barnacles as he held the oars. 'These waters are part of me, it's their voice which calls to me.' I would have gladly remained for one hundred years if I could have helped save him but he said, 'The voice which you hear calls you away. We have no choice in this matter.' The shingle crunched as we pushed away from shore.

The *Good Intent* had a fine heart in her. Her lines were pleasing and she had a lively keel. The tide was with us and the ship seemed anxious to be underway. Ewan Cameron, who had been elected to take her helm, was in high feather. As the wind freshened he gave the word and we pulled up the anchor, forged by Little Donald from Duncan's metal bedframe, and settled the throat of the mainsail to ease her helm. Our ark shuddered for a moment then lay over and dipped in salute to the sea, rose up and gathered her way. All those around me lay down on the deck and wept knowing that they would never again see their kindred. Their wails swelled my cowardice and I sank to my knees to pray for His guidance and protection 'that Thou wouldst keep my feet from sliding and my eyes from tears and prevent me being a spot on Thy cause'. It was a parting unlike any that we had ever experienced, the start of a journey from which there would be no return in this life, and every one of our number, some fifteen exiles, waved and cried as the familiar isle slipped away to stern.

'*Slàn leat,*' I heard my father call in his soft rhythmic Gaelic. 'Blessings be with you.'

The ship glided on the silver wings of its wake, swept forward by wind and will, barely touching the water, the nearest thing to dreams that hands had ever made. I stood on the bow and flew from trough to crest like a figurehead gone prematurely bald, cloak blown back, arms out-stretched, reaching, rising, falling, twisting, wallowing west. There had never been a more promising prospect; astern lay the sins of man, forward soared his hopes.

In the first fair days no one stayed long below deck. A man named Rankin put on the forbidden kilt as soon as we were out of sight of land. He had brought the pipes too and let their music carry out over the sea, which attracted the attention of a pod of bottle-nosed whales. Donald carried a bag of oats, his pillow at sea and seed for his plot, and entertained us with his fanciful stories.

From the first afternoon each child stared forward hoping to be the first to catch sight of Novia Scotia. 'You can be sure that we will arrive on a sunny day,' argued Neill Ruadh, holding court at the bow. The boy never went down into the hold and even took to sleeping on deck. 'For Little Donald tells me that it is a land of perpetual daylight.'

Each morning I sat with them in the sun beneath the headsail and tried to answer their questions.

'Ah well, *a bhalaich*, this is the way of it,' I explained and we traced our route on the familiar face of the globe, across the curve of ocean, from old home to New World and tried to link past and present with stories. 'We will not be the first to pass this way.'

In the old days, I told them, sometime after Moses had led the Israelites out of slavery to search for honeyed Canaan, our islands had been the repository of Christian learning on the edge of medieval Europe. In the monastery libraries the monks had read Virgil and Solinus. Celtic missionaries, who from Ptolemy had understood the world to be round like a well-formed apple, had come to see it as their duty to spread their knowledge. They had been borne out in small boats alone on the sea, trusting in God to carry them to lands where they could best serve Him.

'But listen now,' I told the children. 'The greatest of these men was Brendan of Clonfert, the navigator saint.' Early in the sixth century God sighed and His breath had blown a currach of oak, ash and leather far into the North Atlantic towards the summer solstice. 'Aboard it were Brendan and his fourteen sailor-monks searching for the Promised Land of the Saints. They visited the Island of Sheep, saw Judas Iscariot cast upon a barren rock and alighted in a paradise where the birds sang Latin hymns and chanted verses at vespers. It is even said that a Gaelic-speaking whale allowed the monks to land on his back to say Mass.'

'But how did they know the route?' asked one child.

'Angels lit candles in the windows of heaven to guide their way,' answered Neill Ruadh. 'Just as they do for us.' He had seen me take our bearings from the stars at night.

'For seven years the exiles suffered great deprivation and maelstroms but they placed their faith in God and survived to penetrate a mighty bank of fog and reach their promised destination. They found the New World, and mark you this, it was four hundred years before the Vikings and almost a thousand years before Columbus.'

The children were quiet. 'And will it take the *Good Intent* seven years to reach the promised land, Mr Gillean?'

'No, Neill Ruadh.' His young friends laughed in relief. 'It will take us four weeks only.' The ship sheered the kind waters in a hissing sound. 'Or maybe three if the wind is good to us.'

'CAN YOU IMAGINE having the faith to cross it alone?' asked Beagan, following the *Global Trader*'s plot across the chart, over the bow, towards his great-grandfather's horizon. He felt the weight of Hector's Memorandum in his jacket pocket. 'You've got radar and gyrocompasses and GPS which can fix our position to within fifty metres but still I'm filled with doubt. Where the hell are we?'

Davey paced back and forth, his trainers squeaking on the rubber flooring of the long, light, glass bridge that swept across the ship's beam. 'This is our certainty,' he said patting the Decca Navigator. 'Sod the rest.' On its screen there were no other vessels, neither brigantines nor oil tankers, only the first growlers and icebergs away to the north-west. No calls crackled from the radio.

'We won't see land for a few days,' the captain volunteered, offering Beagan a mug of stewed tea. 'And if we do we're in trouble.'

The ocean had spread her skirt of seas and the steel ship which at anchor had seemed like a beer-bellied leviathan had shrunk to the size of Pereira's dainty model. Her bulk, so ungainly in port, had found lost grace out on the cold grey waters. Beagan had filled the first morning poring over the contents of the trunk and strolling around the deck, his ear cocked for the cry of a freezing emigrant. Instead of Romanian voices however it was odd snatches of Gaelic which he had heard whispering in the wind. He worried that he had taken too many Kwells.

'I read somewhere that the sea is no friend of man, only an accomplice in his restlessness,' said Beagan, scalding his mouth on the hot tea.

'No one leaves their wife, their children, their home if they don't feel a need,' the captain explained. He had been a sailor all his life. Both his father and grandfather had run away to sea. His family had pleaded with him to become a railway engineer or an airline pilot but it wasn't in the blood. He had joined the merchant marine and earned his Master's Certificate steering ships through the Malacca Straits, around the Cape and for almost three decades across the North Atlantic. 'Things at sea are understood,' he added.

'It's a job, that's what understood,' retorted Davey, lowering the binoculars. 'The romance went out with the ark.'

The *Global Trader* had a reputation for serving the best curries on the North Atlantic. Chief Cook Fernandes was a Catholic from Goa. His assistant, the *bandari*, was Hindu. Colonial history and Empire echoed through their menus: Scotch broth, Bombay curry, China chow chow, Irish stew, roast chicken, cold cuts. Other traditions lingered. Sri Lankan and British officers dined at separate tables. The Indian crew ate on a different deck.

In the galley Davey dished out two double servings of prawn vindaloo and handed the larger one to Beagan. 'I could snaffle this to a band playing.' Jagjit and Lakshman ate in silence at the far end of the airless room. 'Three or four poppadoms?' he asked.

'Better make it three,' hazarded Beagan. 'I'm taking it easy because of the swells.'

'You should eat now before it gets really rough,' Davey advised. 'Later you'll only throw it up.' He lead the way to their table. The linen was stained dapple-grey. The tarnished cutlery had seen service on an Empress liner.

Beagan was reluctant to eat. The motion had unsettled him. 'I suppose it's better than auk.'

'Auk tandoori? Can't say I've tried it.' Davey crumbled the poppadoms over his plate and reached for a tray of condiments.

'In the sixteenth century Spanish whalers came this way to hunt humpbacks and belugas. Their crews lived off freshly slaughtered auk.'

'Have a word with the cook. I don't know how the Hindus will take it, but I'm game to try anything once.'

'The auk is extinct.'

'Then they must have been dead tasty. Mango chutney?'

Beagan dabbed a spoonful beside the ocean of vindaloo. 'I read too that Basque and Breton caravels sailed this route to fish for cod on the Grand Banks.' He picked at a prawn then lay down his fork. 'It's said that the fish were so thick they'd flick the water white like a shower of hailstones. Did you know that European armies lived off salt cod for centuries? The poor too. And every year those whalers shipped home twenty thousand barrels of oil to light the lamps of Europe.'

'You've got a head for facts,' said Davey. His eyes narrowed in suspicion. 'You sure you're no journalist?'

Beagan shook his head. 'It's just history; you know, learning from past mistakes. My mistakes, maybe my family's too. It's why I'm going back to Canada,' he added with a spark of nervous animation. 'The boats that crossed the Atlantic, for example. Do you know what those people all shared? The search for something better.'

'Not on this boat, mate.' Davey poured half a tub of yoghurt on to his plate. 'This is where you end up when you can't get nothing better.'

Beagan swallowed his excitement with a mouthful of curry. 'Did you end up here because of what happened in the navy?'

Davey's expression darkened. 'I told you that we'd get on just fine if you didn't ask questions.'

'Hey, I'm not prying,' Beagan said.

'Just shut it.' Davey ate on in silence. Jagjit and Lakshman finished their meals and discreetly left the galley. Beagan slipped a book from his pocket. The ship had begun to roll. He watched the water rock and shiver in his glass and started to feel queasy. He had decided that it would be best to lie down in his cabin when Davey put down his fork and said, 'I'm telling you this for free.'

Beagan had only little trust in himself but there could be no doubting the effect which he had begun to have on others. His nature seemed now to put people at ease and they confided in him. But as his stomach performed a double somersault he wished for better timing, or a Kwell.

'I joined the navy right out of school, practically before I could tie my own shoelaces.' Davey used a chapati to clean the sauce off his plate. 'I worked my way up above decks and was promoted to officer. I was not too far off having my own command when this mate of mine . . .' He paused to find the right word. 'Let's just say something happened to him.' A jab of the chapati stifled Beagan's question. 'Something bad, all right? Call it a tradition; a little bit of history. Well, the press got hold of it and this journalist came down to Portsmouth, told me that the public had a right to know and convinced me to patter. He said it was my responsibility. The story made headlines. They sold a bundle of newspapers. My mate was pardoned.' He wiped his mouth with the threadbare napkin and dropped it on the plate. 'But me? I got booted off the bloody bridge and out of the service. The journalist misquoted me you see, which was nothing for him, but the navy wouldn't have me. Nobody would have me. It condemned me to a life sentence on this rusty old tug. So don't talk to me about betterment. If you ask me history is best forgot.'

Beagan's glass slid across the table. Davey caught it with a practised hand. 'I'd suggest you get yourself around that curry. Didn't the captain tell you we're heading into bad weather?'

The swells, churned turquoise by the ship's passing, surged deeper, longer, stronger. In mid-Atlantic the wind lifted plumes of spray over the deck that dashed the windows and bent the bulkheads. The *Global Trader* pitched into furrows, bucked through fifteen-metre swells and plunged into the eye of a winter gale. Beagan sat out the storm astern in the accommodation block, watching the reflection of the waves flash across his cabin ceiling, clutching the diary to his churning stomach. The trunk had been lashed to his bedstead. Hector's globe spun on its axis with every roll of the ship.

After Saint Brendan, the Vikings, the Basques and Bretons, explorers and traders had followed along the North Atlantic route, sailing west to reach the east, looking for lands of cinnamon and cloves, greedy for the riches of the Indies. Their charts recorded mountains of gold and fantasy islands named Antiglia and *isola de braçill*. They had mistaken Greenland for Asia and quartz for diamonds. The miserable emigrant hulks that came after them, crammed with the victims of both promise and pogrom, also failed to find that for which they searched.

It wasn't difficult for Beagan to conjure up their memory, to spot a currach or windjammer riding a distant swell. He squinted at the far white horses and fancied catching a glimpse of the *Good Intent*'s sail. Beyond sight of land and without points of reference all sense of time and place was lost. Each day was an echo of the one that preceded it. Admiralty charts showed banks, basins and trenches, a whole world below the surface, but no rock or island above it. The only measure of human scale was provided by the plot. Decca waves and SatNav had replaced the sextant, bearings were now taken from satellites not stars, but the thread of their sightings remained all that strung man across the vastness of the sea. So it was with history, the plot of every individual life marking a moment in time as a navigator's bearings set a position on the globe. Beagan traced the ship's route in the same way that he followed the family's track, each point indicating a course across the ocean, looking at the path of those who had gone before in the faith that it would guide his way.

The *Global Trader* surged over the Celtic Deep, crossed the Porcupine Sea-Bight and rounded King Arthur Canyon as ten thousand vessels had before her. She shuddered in the cross-current. Rollers whipped her amidships. A freak wave, which might have lost her the deck and swept the containers overboard, lunged out of the ferment and crashed astern. Beagan held open the account of Reverend Hector's voyage and read aloud.

'Without,' his great-grandfather had written three lifetimes earlier at about these bearings, 'the expanse of water and sky is our only prospect, unvaried by any object save the distant outline of some vessel at the verge of the horizon, a speck in the immensity of space. Within, as the weather turns against us, an evil wind stirs below decks. We grow sulky and even savage in our privations.'

As the ship rolled in the rude waste of sea Beagan took another Kwell and thought of Davey pacing back and forth in his tiny cabin, caged like an animal, locked in his anger, accepting poor fortune and not acting to change it.

'Last evening three men, armed with sticks and foaming at the mouth, rushed up the hatchway and without a note of warning attacked a group cooking at the sandbox. By chance Ewan Cameron and Little Donald were on deck. They laid about them lustily with their fists and speedily drove the poor souls back down below.'

He imagined the captain watching astern wearing dark glasses and an air of lonely detachment. His vista was empty but for the curl of the exhaust trail.

'As the storms delay our progress the stores become depleted. The prospect of hunger threatens and we are as helpless as infants under suffering. Hope flies beyond the far horizon like the speck of those distant vessels.'

THE SNARED SHROUD unwound fast and the corpse, instead of falling, shot forward into the sea and spun across the swells like a dolphin racing the ship. It skimmed the black waters, dawdled beneath the waves then dived into the deep, the stiff and naked young flesh luminous on its journey from the seen to the unseen world. The mother, with the spume of her child's departure slapped across her raw cheeks, wailed all the louder and tore at my boots. Rankin, the unfortunate piper and poxy himself, was at pains not to swallow his chanter.

'Be to me as a star, be to me as a helm, from my lying down in peace to my rising anew.' Most days, between the tears of the congregation and the rain from heaven, the communion cup was never empty. But that day the cup froze over and the service did not proceed as planned. Little Donald, more for propriety than charity for the bereaved, broke free the frozen end of the winding-sheet from under my foot.

I closed the Book as the assembly swelled about the woman, drowned her solitary sorrow in shared tears and washed her out of the cold in the embrace of a dozen arms. A week before Neill Ruadh had been to all appearances strong and healthy. Now by a stroke of God's justice he was forever released from the fear of confinement.

'Thirty days out of Scotland our frail cargo of hopes and fears lies dying,' I recorded in my diary-book that bitter night. 'The sweet breezes of spring have chilled into wild gusts of winter and stolen the prosperous voyage. The mainsail has been reefed and lashed down and the ship makes no progress against the violent westerlies. Cholera rages among the emigrants and the *Good Intent* has become a floating charnel-house. Our mean rations are all but exhausted and weevils have spoilt the bread.'

The rasp of a raw cough disturbed my writing. I could see little by the dim green flicker of the fish-oil lamp but it sounded like Duncan the cobbler. The air below deck reeked of pitch and urine and I prayed for dawn. Until his fit passed the minutes hung upon me. Then Neill Ruadh's mother cried out in her sleep. I picked up my pen. It had clogged again.

'Yet even worse than the paucity of food is the lack of fresh water. The great Atlantic Ocean, which swirls to the horizon in every direction, holds not one glass to slake a man's thirst. The liquid carried aboard has turned putrid and is palatable only with drops of vinegar. Many refuse to drink it and instead lay canvas sheets on the deck in the hope of catching rain. One family has even turned to whisky. Father and son, mother and daughter mix it into porridge and swill it down after their last husks of oatcake. They laugh and rage, cry and sleep dreaming of the crystal clear stream that will run through their Grant only to awake with throats more parched and burning than ever.'

BEAGAN STARED AND strained but he could not make out the next sentence. The Reverend's pen had started to run dry, scratched a snail's trail across the parchment, then released a blob of viscous ink which had spoiled half a paragraph. It was the inkblot as much as the words which helped Beagan picture his great-grandfather wrapped under a fold of sail in a cold corner of the hold, the diary on his knee, his forefinger stained black. He imagined that it was past midnight. The day of Neill Ruadh's burial had exhausted him. Hector had buoyed the emigrants with his spirit and then in the dark solitude of the night had prayed for strength, attempted to sleep, and when it had not come begun to write with great care on the clean white paper. 'Justice,' he had noted, 'is in all things rigid, inflexible and beyond human comprehension but if for offences committed against God it would better have been me, not the child, whose life . . .' Then there was the blot. The sudden spill from his poor, faulty pen almost made Beagan weep. Hector had bought it at considerable expense not six months before in Edinburgh.

Beagan shivered, even with his thermostat turned to its highest setting, and knew it was improbable that he would die aboard the *Global Trader*, except possibly of gluttony. He was warm and well-fed where his great-grandfather had suffered starvation in a frozen, stinking hold. Yet in the journal there was no word of complaint, no doubt of his duty to keep hope afloat. It made Beagan feel as if his own time had been lived as an observer and not a participant in life. As he rubbed a smudge from its cover he saw himself adrift on the vast and furious ocean, unable to communicate beyond the wave-tossed baked-bean boat, seeking to convey the treasures of his heart yet unable to find the words to express them.

A voice had called out and Hector had laid down his diary, leaving an inky fingerprint on its cover, crossed the heaving cabin and found another young soul dead. A handful of soil clawed from the graveside of his kindred was locked in the stiffened little fist. The hull had groaned in the angry billows of the raging sea. Out on deck the rigging had sung and Ewan Cameron feared that another gust might snap the mast. Beagan read the dull, tired pen-strokes which had concluded the night's entry. 'God in His wisdom has taken three from us this week, called to His side to do higher service. The track of our ship is strewn with dead and the living spend the days watching a shark follow in our wake with great constancy. The gales murder curiosity and the questions of the bairns come no longer. The globe remains in its box.'

THE WEATHER WAS no better by dawn nor by the next. In the creak of the wooden ship women wailed. The men sat on coils of hemp and sang. The tin cup had made its rounds, the grog done its office. Little Donald had told a tale, another story of kind fortune and Indian warriors, and Duncan, who was in his cups, coughed and hawked as he polished the precious shoe buckles that he kept secured in a small cotton sack. Rankin the piper, the most taciturn of them, had let the drink go to his head and song carry him beyond the evil-smelling hold.

Gu ma slan do na fearaibh
Chaidh thairis an cuan.
Gu talamh a' gheallaidh
Far nach fairich iad fuachd;
Gu ma slan do na fearaibh
Chaidh thairis an cuan.

Here's good health to the heroes
Who sail o'er the sea.
To the land of promise
Where they'll not feel the cold.
Here's good health to the heroes
Who sail o'er the sea.

A child had been born to us and I was desirous of baptising him. I passed by the men, ducked into the low byre of the hold and in the gloom struck my head hard on a beam. I felt the wet warmth on my crown and reaching out to steady myself grasped soft locks of hair and a woman's shoulder.

'So you are still flesh and blood,' teased the voice. I could not see her face. She inspected the graze. 'Come into the light, Hector.' I was guided back to the foot of the gangway and felt the sting of whisky clean the wound. 'You wouldn't wish our minister an infection for want of your dram, would you Duncan?' the voice jested. Duncan, no longer dreaming of Nova Scotia, received the now empty cup back in his hand. I thanked him for his trouble.

'It's no the trouble, it's the expense.'

I turned to behold my rescuer and, as my sight adjusted to the shadow, recognised Kirstie. Four decades of toil had fastened in her a fearless and patient faith that had knit her face perhaps too severely, for she smiled little now, though when she did the years were washed away. 'You will have come to see our Mairi,' she said.

In a cubicle of sagging grey canvas on a bed of pine boards lay her sister. 'New sons for a new world, Mr Gillean,' said Mairi and held the baby to her breast.

For two more weary weeks the *Good Intent*, first tossed by storms and then becalmed for a windless eternity, tacked across the Atlantic. Some emigrants begged Cameron to put about and run for home but he showed them no courtesy and bade them to swim back to Scotland if they so wished. My journal remained closed throughout those joyless days. There was no pleasure in recording the ship's suffering. I spent long hours trying to encourage our company and when I could stole short moments to talk with Kirstie and Mairi. But malnutrition and monotony had set in us a deadening lethargy and I prayed most zealously for our aching spirits.

'YOU BELIEVING IN ghosts?' Pereira asked in his elaborate, sing-song English. The Goan steward was silhouetted against the soft green glow of the instruments. 'When I am here at night some-times I thinking there is someone right behind me.' Weird celestial music haunted the dark bridge. A closet of wire coat-hangers tinkled as they rocked with the swells. 'When I turning around there is nobody at all there. Except young Jagjit.' The second officer stood apart from them keeping a silent watch on the empty sea lanes.

'Maybe it's a stowaway?' said Beagan even though the voices that he had heard did not speak Romanian. 'Or someone who has died.'

'No speak of such things.' Pereira seemed shocked. 'If you do they maybe coming true.'

The storm had abated an hour earlier and Beagan had laid down the diary. Lamb korma was on the evening's menu, but the reading had dulled his appetite and instead of descending to the galley he had thrown on an anorak and slipped outside into the night. The air temperature had dropped and fog, thick as the bank which had enveloped Saint Brendan's leather currach, denser than that which had bewildered Beagan's wasted years, clung to a black pearl sea. He had made his way forward, put the noise of steam and steel behind him and paused to listen to the hiss of the ocean seething under the bow. In a matter of days the *Global Trader* would reach Canada and the prospect filled him with trepidation. The ship, Davey had told him over lunch, was on schedule. Nothing unusual was anticipated along the rest of the route. There would be no more bad weather and little other marine traffic, surprises that might upset the smooth operation of the machine and her crew. But neither the high-tech certainties nor the mindless, ping-pong routine had comforted Beagan. The sea through which they plied had absorbed too much suffering; the tears of the tens of thousands who died before reaching the far shore, the most recent tragedy of Vietnamese boat people drowned over the Grand Banks, possibly even now the perished hopes of a frozen stowaway. Maybe there was too much history, as Davey had said, but after years of running from his own past Beagan had begun to prepare to meet old ghosts. The thought of it scared him speechless.

On the bridge Pereira listened to the drone of the engines then glanced over his shoulder. 'On last crossing retired master's ashes burying at sea. Captain order engines stop, say quick prayer and, while *Serang* make photographs, throwing ashes overboard. Old master had designing urn himself, thick and busy in holes so it might fill with water and sink very fast. But lid flying off in a big

way and ashes scatter over the new, damp paintwork.' He listened
to the night. 'Are you thinking it is maybe him?'

'It could be Vijitha's party,' suggested Beagan.

'Maybe,' nodded Pereira with little certainty. 'Maybe. We
going later?'

At the end of the watch Pereira led Beagan down four flights,
deep into the bowels of the ship towards the sound of singing.
The smell of incense hung in the air. Plastic sandals stood on mats
by each cabin door. On the walls hung garish prints of Brahma
and Bombay movie stars. Small studio portraits of sons and daughters were tacked to the head of every bunk. Beagan had met the
Indian crew only when they had emerged from behind watertight
doors or vanished down gangways, their overalls stained with oil,
beaming broad smiles and sharing with him the faulty valve or
pump in their care. Among them only Pereira spoke English. The
others relied on the vast bo'sun, a grinning brown Buddah in
bleached white boilersuit, both to translate and dictate. He was
their *serang*, or boss, and presided over them like a queen bee over
her hive. On his word the crew swabbed and scrubbed and slapped
on another tin of the six thousand gallons of paint applied to the
ship every year.

The crewmen, each with a litre bottle and a shy grin, greeted
Beagan's arrival with applause. Space was made for him on the
front bench. Vijitha from Colombo was celebrating his promotion
to electrical officer and two dozen tired, excited men clustered
around a table laden with duty-free gin and Four Bells rum. Three
trays of onion and hot chilli bhajis were raised on a bed of Coke
tins and beer cases.

'It a lonely life at sea,' Pereira told Beagan. 'We trying to be
cheerful and diligent in our work, doing the needful, but it ten
months long that we being away from our families.' As he paused
to applaud the arrival of a latecomer Beagan recalled Hector's
kindred left behind in the Hebrides. 'I have a little girl. She two
years old. In this life I seeing her once only.'

There was little conversation between the lonely, respectful,
soft-spoken men. Words were not spoken but sung. The Hindu

ballads were about missing home. Every crewman knew the lyrics and all joined in for the chorus. The bo'sun sang a wistful solo. The radio operator tapped out a Morse code rhythm with the fingers of one hand, drummed with a lighter and the heel of the other. Pereira's melancholy lifted and he flashed his single tooth. 'Here very good,' he said.

Away from the cynical huddle of officers Beagan sensed something of the precious hope which sustained life on both ships, but then Davey and the captain arrived, out of uniform, and the crew rose to their feet. Spontaneity drained out of the proceedings. Vijitha made a speech thanking them for their support then sang off-key Elton John's 'Sacrifice', his only English song.

'Not again,' droned Davey and slunk off to the officers' mess to watch a video.

N O MATTER HOW fervent my prayers, no matter how hard I struggled to bring comfort, the islanders took to lying in their bunks for days, awake but unmoving, not caring if they next heard the rasp of keel on shingle or the voice that calls them home. At first I tried to cajole and encourage them but when gentle efforts failed I drove them from their beds with the fear of hell-fire and damnation. Every morning I urged them together and pressed Duncan, 'What is the Chief End of Man?'

The brogue maker's face was thin and anaemic. He had lost a second tooth in the night. 'Man's chief end is to glorify God and enjoy Him forever.'

'What,' I demanded of Kirstie, 'is God?'

She answered with eyes lowered. 'God is a Spirit, infinite, eternal and unchangeable, in His being, wisdom, power, holiness, justice, goodness and truth.'

I prodded them through the Questions and Answers of the Shorter Catechism, the Ten Commandments, the Six

Petitions. My call was for them to be ever more diligent. I bade them to kneel with me. Our psalms filled the hold, drifted out over the becalmed sea and wrapped the body of the ship in an embrace of prayer.

The daily discipline focused tired minds and anchored the drifting hours. But faith alone will not forever hold together body and soul. A man must eat and there was no food. Then Duncan surprised us all by announcing that he would catch fish. The cobbler had never in his life hauled a net yet he began bending his precious leather needles to form hooks and setting them on to laces. His bright buckles were fashioned into lures. He stood on the deck in his stockinged feet and cast the glittering line over the side. The sight of him raised the first laugh heard on board in over a month and before it had died down the cord went taut. Hand over hand he pulled in the laces, the buckles and a great cod. It was the largest that Ewan Cameron had ever seen. But no sooner was the line back in the water than another was caught. The fish were unable to resist his gaudy lures. Duncan hopped from foot to foot and began to land cod by the dozen. The children hung his trophies from the rigging and we gorged ourselves until we could eat no more. Not one to be shy of coming forward Little Donald then turned his hand to making a more efficient rain-gathering system. That evening our parched throats drank the sweet water which fell from heaven.

Later the cats' paws rippled the still surface and the sails filled with a fair south-easterly. I took up again writing my diary at dusk. Astern under a starless sky the piper played a lament, *Cha till mi tuille*. I will not return.

'Our spirits have lifted,' I recorded in good heart, 'with the knowledge that we have drifted over the New-foundland fishing banks. A plentiful catch sustains us as does the certainty that land cannot be too . . .' The pen spluttered and clogged. I shook the wretched instrument and sprayed a trail of clotted ink down my trousers, along the deck and over the piper's left shoe. He failed to notice the offending blot and it seemed churlish to interrupt the music. As I began to clean the nib with a well-stained handkerchief a voice whispered in my ear.

'At your books again?' Kirstie stood at my back smiling. The incident had not escaped her attention.

'One day in New Scotland,' I said while rising to my feet, 'I will buy myself a reliable pen.'

'There are many who will be thankful for that.' She glanced at Rankin, blushed and looked away to sea. If modesty is the ornament of women Kirstie wore hers with a confidence. 'Any sign?' she added.

'No.' We peered forward into the darkness. 'Your father thinks that it will be at least another day.'

Kirstie's cheeks were raw from the winters of wind, and barrels of brine had salted away her lightness of heart, but as she pulled the heavy shawl about her shoulders I noticed the nape of her neck, its skin as fair as cotton grass in the moss. We walked together to the bow of the ship. Patches of sea salt, which had dried on the deck, crunched beneath our feet. 'Tell me about your ministry,' she asked.

I had to admit that I knew very little. 'Cape Breton is, I understand, an island of small settlements divided from one another by inlets of the sea, large lakes and forests. The pioneers there are chiefly from the Western Isles and Hebrides but exist in very poor circumstances. Of the town of Promise itself I know only that many have grown up unbaptised.'

'Can that be true?'

'Aye, I believe that it is so. The country is vast and there are few pastors to spread God's Word.' I lowered my voice. 'In places the Bible is a sealed book.'

'Do these settlers not have their letters?'

'Some of them can neither read nor write,' I confirmed. 'The want for education and religious instruction is so urgent that when a teacher or clergyman comes among the people they flock with great eagerness and in large numbers to hear the Gospel preached to them in their native tongue.'

'Then your services will be in great demand. More even maybe than our own need.'

'I pray that my life may be of some use there.'

Alongside the mast, just beyond the illumination of the ship's lamp, petrels and skuas glided like angels at the edge of man's vision. The sails had been dipped and the night air was cold. Kirstie shivered and we turned to retire below when there appeared in the void, off to port, a single light. In the seven weeks at sea we had seen no other ship at close quarters. Kirstie's excitement, as my own, could not be checked.

'Can you see what she is?' she asked. It was too dark to discern any detail. 'Maybe ... maybe it's a clipper filled with furs making to Europe,' she guessed. 'Or another emigrant ship? There, do you see its mizzen?' I could see no sails.

It was then that another light appeared. Two ships sailing in such proximity was an unusual sight. But when the third and fourth lamp appeared we realised that the lights were not being carried by vessels. A voice called out and Kirstie began to cry yet I heard neither her weeping nor the shouting about our ears. I did not feel the bodies pressed around me. My soul at that moment was alone with God and to Him the only homage I could offer was my own tears. The dozens of lights on the shore glowed as a constellation of stars. The flashing white manes of waves broke on the rocks of the New World.

FIVE DAYS OUT of Felixstowe the radar reached over the horizon and echoed back the coast of Newfoundland. Across the blackness Jerry's Nose peeked above the western shore and Clarke's Head overlooked Gander Bay. A secluded hamlet called Joe Blatt's Arm beckoned from the spot where an English sailor had jumped ship and broken his wrist. Fishing harbours named Leading Tickles and Witless Bay, Come by Chance and Great Paradise clung to the rough, wild shore. The first island of the New World had been made at the end of Creation. God had dumped on it all the refuse of His material: the spare granite from Ur and a job-lot of lava from Harran, the deep inlets, barren plateaux and stunted spruce not wanted in the Garden of Eden.

By daybreak the wind-swept, sea-washed tail of the Appalachians had fallen astern and ice lay about the *Global Trader* like an archipelago of ten thousand silver islands. A blizzard came and went. The harp seals were calving and the captain picked his way through the snow-sheets, passing the vast ship so close to the females that their cries could be heard from the bridge. He steered to avoid the packs of nursing mothers, the ice around them splattered with blood and afterbirth. In the thicker fields the ship lost her momentum. She slowed, shuddered then crunched to a stop. The captain eased astern, back down his track, then ran full ahead into the barrier to punch his way upstream.

As the Gulf narrowed and the banks of the Saint Lawrence drew together the ship regained the proportions of a leviathan. The coast was steep and deeply indented. Red-roofed, white-walled lighthouse hamlets perched on escarpments at the edge of dense forests. A timber-framed summer cottage, wrapped in dawn's mist, gripped on to a rocky ledge. At the foot of the cliffs clapboard villages clustered around the gleaming lead spires of Catholic churches. A serpentine freight train skirted the river's north shore at Point-au-Pic. Its engineer sounded his horn, a long wail of the Prairies, and the ship answered with its whistle.

The long Canadian winter still clung to the late spring and an icebreaker had to clear a channel at Les Escoumins. A jaunty launch darted between the floes and slipped alongside the *Global Trader*. Jean-Louis le Bois, the Saint Lawrence pilot, filled the bridge with the scent of spruce woods and *Eau Sauvage*. His clothes were crisp and stylish. He smoked heavily, ate Fernandes's hearty bacon and samosa breakfast and twanged in nasal Québécois over the VHF radio-telephone.

'This river, she has a long *histoire*,' he told Beagan. Story and history. 'I am a member of *l'Administration de pilotage des Laurentides*, the oldest *corporation* in North America. We know the river before the English, almost before the Indian.'

'It was the French who first found the Saint Lawrence,' acknowledged Beagan. He had unearthed from the depths of the trunk a tattered school history book embossed with proud emigrant ships and puffed sails. 'The English missed the turn-off.'

Five years after Columbus had stumbled on to the West Indies the merchants of Bristol, miffed by the Spanish success and anxious to cut out Moslem middlemen, had sped John Cabot west to buy the goods and spices of the East. They had fancied that he would reach China by sailing around the world. It had not been appreciated that a continent blocked the way. Cabot sighted Baffin Island, the frozen wasteland lying well within the Arctic Circle, and thinking that he had come upon northern Asia headed south to find Japan. But instead of Kyoto he found Newfoundland.

'It didn't much resemble the Orient,' added Beagan. 'Cabot overlooked the mouth of the river and sailed on maybe as far as Florida, reaching the mainland of America before Columbus, the holds of his ships filled with goods for trade, his eyes searching the shore for the golden cities of Cathay.'

A generation passed before Jacques Cartier, a navigator from Saint Malo, became the first European to see the Saint Lawrence. Unlike Cabot, Cartier had come looking for more than just a passage to the East. He had hungered to substantiate the dream of his age: that the discovery of promised lands was rewarded by the possession of their riches. The Native people, whom he called Indians because of Columbus's geographical mistake, had obliged him. They had 'fed and caressed him', even looked upon him as a god and asked him to perform miracles in healing the sick. They had also assured him that, 'A moon distant there is a land producing cinnamon and cloves,' and he decided to follow the river westward. He had anchored his ships below the Charlevoix cliffs and pushed upstream in bark canoes and longboats searching for a paradise 'rich and wealthy in precious stones'. But he had found neither China nor a mythical northern Eldorado; the gold which he discovered was iron pyrites and the so-called diamonds were quartz. Cartier like Cabot had failed to achieve his goal. He is best remembered for his misunderstanding. On reaching a Native settlement at the confluence of the Saint Charles river he had heard his guides call the place Canada and erroneously applied the name to the land. In fact *cannada* is the Huron-Iroquois word for a village.

'No gold. No diamond. *Rien. Alors,* what use is Canada?' asked le Bois and dismissed the country with a Gallic shrug. 'For sixty year nobody care, nobody come, until – *paf!* – Europe fall in love with the beaver hat.'

The first permanent white settlement in Canada was a trading post named *Kebec,* an Algonquin word which meant 'where the river narrows'. The second outpost was established upriver at the foot of an extinct volcano called Mont-Royal.

'Each year one ship come from France,' le Bois explained. 'The first Saint Laurent pilot, *le Pilote du Roi,* was a Breton called Abraham Martin. He row out from Pointe-au-Père – across the river from Les Escoumins – and guide the ship 328 mile to Mon-tréal.' His expansive gestures suggested a thousand miles of frosty wilderness. 'The voyage upriver took maybe four month so the ship, she spend the winter in Montréal. There was not time to reach the sea before the river freeze up, eh? But Martin, he return to Pointe-au-Père by horse to wait for spring and the next ship.'

'It must have been a lonely life.'

'*Ah non.*' Le Bois drew deeply on his Rothman. 'They say he had two wife: in town *une belle française* for summer – someone *propre* and *parfumée* – and at home *une Indienne* – dark and a little smoky – to keep him warm through the winter. *Pas mal,* eh?'

'So the Plains of Abraham,' observed Beagan, recalling the field where in 1759 the French dream of an American empire had died, 'were named after a bigamous river pilot.'

Le Bois gave him a long sideways look. 'It's all that bloody reading he does,' said Davey. 'It gets up my nose too.'

Martin's sons had become pilots as had their sons after them. His family had remained the river's navigators for generations, even after the British had defeated the French and renamed the *corporation* Trinity House, until traffic on the river had multiplied faster than his offspring and new blood had to be recruited. Le Bois was one of the seventy-three pilots who each led 120 ships along the Saint Lawrence every year. The journey which had once lasted four months now took eighteen hours.

'All the *histoire* is in Québec,' laughed le Bois. '*Et le future aussi. Maîtres chez-nous.*' That morning the *Global Trader* passed a dozen ships: snub-nosed American Lakers, scruffy Egyptian freighters, a Russian cruise liner. The commerce of nations rode out to the sea from the continent's heart. The Seaway linked the Atlantic to the Great Lakes and made ocean ports of cities 2,600 miles inland.

The Charlevoix cliffs levelled into pretty hills with strip fields running up from the shore. Barns crowned the heights and the older farmhouses, with the steep pitched roofs and overhanging eaves of Normandy, betrayed the first settlers' origins. Poplars lined the roads as they might in the Loire. Out of the mists rose the snow-capped turrets of Québec City, flanked by the industrial cranes of Levis and Beauport. The ship, which only days before had been in the emptiness of the ocean, was downtown, with ferries and *bateaux-pilotes* scuttling about her. The copper-peaked Château Frontenac dominated the stern skyline as surely as the battlements above Carcassonne. Beneath the grey rock Citadel, whose ramparts had challenged the power of Britain for control of the continent, nestled a place more European than American. Its narrow streets echoed with the solemn psalms of Mass and the smell of fresh *brioche*. Horse-drawn *calèches* rattled over uneven cobblestones, past zinc-bar bistros and snug cafés where students mapped out their lives on paper table napkins.

It was night when the *Global Trader* slipped beneath the canti-levered *Pont de Québec*, an Eiffel Tower laid on its side and the first bridge west of Europe. On the south shore, high on a lofty point called Cap Charles, a Union Jack was run up a spotlit mast and the river boomed with a chorus of 'God Save the Queen'.

For twenty-five years Delphis Duhamel had followed the Marine Traffic List, listened to Coast Guard radio and hailed every passing ship by raising its national flag and playing its anthem. Two vast loudspeakers built into the cliff and powered by a 1300-watt amplifier broadcast his welcome. His collection of 140 flags included the colours of the Czech Republic, Togo and Vanuatu.

'North Korea was the most difficult one for him to get, eh?' le Bois told Beagan. Davey seemed to ignore them and studied the river charts. 'He ask the Embassy but they think maybe he is a spy and send nothing. So he find a nun who go there to work in a mission. She bring him back the flag.'

Beagan speculated aloud that Duhamel must be a retired mariner who missed the life at sea. Davey looked up from the map and rolled his eyes. 'Mate, did you come up the Clyde on a bicycle?'

'*Pas du tout*,' corrected le Bois. 'He is a furniture salesman. He do it for his children, so they grow up to know the world from the ships passing their garden. They stick pins in a big map in the living room. But now his children leave home and he cannot stop. Night and day he is out there with his Labrador, blowing each ship to blazes.'

'At least he looks further than his own backyard,' said Beagan. Along the waterway he had noticed far more blue *fleurs-de-lys* than red maple leafs and the observation had rattled him.

'This is an important year for us. In October we Québécois vote for the right to run our own country.'

'You mean Québec, or Canada?' asked Beagan, perplexed by the flush of emotion.

'The old Canada, she is a lost cause. *Tout a changé*.' Le Bois turned to Davey. 'Duhamel tell me there was a time when he play "God Save the Queen" – *les deux versions, vocal et instrumental* – three or four time a day. Now he only play it once a week.'

'Gie the horn a wee pamp,' ordered Davey. The *Global Trader* blew her whistle and dipped her red ensign.

*　　　*　　　*

Beagan awoke when the movement stopped. The ship no longer swayed. The fans and boilers were silent. Instead of the roar of high-pressure air and the thump of diesel engines, electric gantry cranes whirred overhead. They jerked the containers off their hasps and lowered them on to waiting flatbeds. A freight train shunted in a siding. Tractor trailers idled on the tarmac outside the Racine Terminal, anxious to collect their loads and move on west.

In the mess the officers sat in a long row, left to right in descending order of rank, drinking beer. Beagan's bar bill dangled from a fairy light. The captain had kept a meticulous record. Neither the Queen nor the Grolsch calendar girl waved goodbye. But below decks Pereira's single-tooth smile flashed beneath the cowl of his parka. 'Cheerio, young man,' he said, giving him a handmade model of a Scottish yawl. 'Good shoreside luck.' In twenty-four hours the travelling warehouse would be back on the sea lanes. In a week Davey might wonder, over a plate of chicken tikka masala and chips, if Beagan had ever been aboard.

Beagan packed the globe and books back into his trunk. He slipped the bottled model in between the loose diary pages and a leather-bound address book. Outside the air was freezing. There was not a Romanian in sight. Beagan clambered down the gang-way to find no saluting Mountie or welcoming brass band. He hesitated on the last rung, took a deep breath then stepped on to the concrete pier. No thunderbolt struck him down. The earth did not open up and swallow him. 'So far so good,' he thought. He decided that it would be a fine idea not to kiss the ground and went to call a cab.

CHAPTER III

PROMISED LAND

WE CAME IN with the tide, to the chuckle and snigger of pebbles in the swells. The mantle of rainclouds muffled the cold April dawn. The silent forest soared above us, looming so close to the water as to offer only a mean edge to which to cling. I fell to my knees to thank God for our deliverance but before the words were formed my prayers were interrupted by shrill cries ringing through the dark groves of pine.

'Savages,' guessed Little Donald and raised his fists to fight. But the strangers who fell upon us brandished handshakes not tomahawks. One fair-skinned ruffian, his tattered greatcoat concealing want of other garments, embraced Duncan like a brother. In the ensuing scuffle he lost a shoe in the mire. Another slapped me so hard on the back that the globe flew from my hands. The fall dented the Iberian peninsula. A third man shook Kirstie Cameron's hand with an enthusiasm which threatened to dislocate her shoulder. Then the scallywag tried to kiss her.

'Gather your tail,' barked Cameron, sweeping them back with his dogfish snout. 'Was there ever a more brazen welcome?'

'What is the name of this place?' I asked but their yells were more bestial than human and I did not comprehend the answer. 'The light shines in the dark and the dark understands it not,' I added.

'It might be that we *have* landed in China,' suggested Duncan.

The ruffians bade us follow them from the strip of beach, through the curtain of trees, deep into the hushed woods. They ran ahead leaving us trailing alone beneath a dense canopy. The frowning trees, black and ominous, closed in and shut out the sky. The sun did not penetrate the narrow passage. No light dispelled the sombre gloom. No sound disturbed the vast silence. The women whispered in small voices and held hands. The men fell quiet treading on the unfamiliar pine-needle earth. Nothing had prepared us for either the great loneliness of the forest or the unholy din towards which we were then drawn.

In a clearing a wild woman with loose red hair danced barefoot on a stump and wailed. Grimy children whirled about her, howling like young wolves, stretching their limbs, testing their new-found freedom. A knot of young men clad in tartan trousers lurched forward, seized the siren and carried her off. Their empty bottle was trampled underfoot. Packs of boys kicked a bundle of books until, to cries of disappointment, the spines cracked and the pages took flight like swallows along the shore. A hundred women, with petticoats tucked above their knees, cackled as they trampled clean their bedding in tidal rockholes. Beyond them close-packed sailing boats, their masts like a great forest stripped of limbs, ferried more emigrants ashore. The newcomers fell on to the beach, spilt into the shallows, flung sand into their faces and squealed. 'What is this Babel?' asked Little Donald in disbelief.

Cameron seized an agitated juvenile by the arm. 'Friend, what is the name of this place?' he asked in the Gaelic.

'The books are mine! Mine!' he shouted and struggled to break from his grip.

'In the name of Providence where are we?' I repeated in English.

'Where are you?' he replied shaking himself free. 'The

gateway to the promised land, sirrah.' He ran off laughing so loud that I thought he must be deaf. 'They call this place Ship Harbour.'

We bunched together around the globe, turned it in our hands and scoured the unfamiliar seaboard. 'There it is. Here,' said Kirstie curving her finger along the coast. Ship Harbour was a port on the southern shore of Cape Breton Island, separated from mainland Nova Scotia by the narrow Gut of Canso. We had missed the harbour's mouth and anchored the *Good Intent* over the lonely headland.

The thin blue smoke of wood fires rose from log cabins set in stump-cluttered yards. We skirted the compound, trying not to step on the crisp white pages alighting in the muck and went in search of an authority. A stevedore stopped Little Donald to offer him work and a tavern-keeper hailed us from an open door. Stray whelps sniffed at our heels. A milch cow watched us pass. At the centre of a cluster of painted frame houses, next to the wooden stores, stood the clapboard inn. The sounds of argument assailed us from within.

'Damn your blood, you bounder.'

'Then clear off out of here. I am pig-sick and tired of your hum-ha tongue-tied talk.'

Inside two men faced each other from opposite sides of the table, leaning forward so their noses touched yet yelling for all British North America to hear.

'May I remind you that it is only through my efforts that you secured this position?'

'Only through the sweat of my brow, toady. I owe no man nothin.'

At our entrance they broke off and I asked for directions to the Emigrant Office. The Englishman, the shorter of the two combatants and dressed in the fashion of years long past, bowed then sneezed. His once fine clothes were worn so thin that he kept warm only by wrapping a blanket around his shoulders. 'Sir, I am at your service.' Duncan noticed that his shoes needed new soles.

'This ain't no office and he's fixin to leave,' interrupted the American, dispensing with pleasantries. 'And if you're friends of his then you boys can git too.' He shooed us away with a shapeless palmetto hat as if we were chickens.

The emigrant officer took the opportunity to explain the nature of the disagreement. 'It has been the custom, long before the arrival of this Vermonter, for this establishment to serve as my bureau.' He fussed with his whiskers. 'Now Goodenough here, as the new landlord, has doubled the fee.'

Goodenough took a different view of tradition. 'Your customs ain't worth shucks. I told you my price. Pay up or make tracks.'

'Sir, you bite the hand which has fed you. My teeth are on edge.' The officer again addressed our party. 'This Yankee drank up a good farm in the United States then thought he could do no better than to turn loyal and get one here for nothing.' At the end of the War of Independence one in every five Americans had remained true to the Crown. The price of allegiance for many was exile. But among the fifty thousand Loyalists who had fled the United States were some not drawn north by patriotism alone. Canada had given free land to all comers.

'And I don't give a red cent for your King of England,' he laughed, hitching up his leather leggings and pointing at his feet. 'I'd kick him, his queen and all you Englishers out of my house. Now I said git.' A violent gesture flipped off his deer moccasin which hit Duncan in the eye. Little Donald raised his fists and cursed in Gaelic for the second time that morning. He was not a man to let an insult go unanswered.

'I can out-holler you too,' challenged the American and let loose a tirade of profanities.

The officer held up his sheaf of papers as a shield and retreated shouting, 'God's blood.'

I ended the contretemps by asking where we might obtain

provisions. 'You got money?' came the swift reply. I confirmed that we had limited resources. 'Then why didn't you say so, Reverend?' Goodenough called for his wife and ushered us back over the threshold. 'We'll fix you up.' Then he added, 'You're Scottish, ain't you?' He slapped Donald on the shoulder. 'My grandma was Scots so no hard feelings.' Donald, not understanding the English, did not respond. Goodenough chuckled and whispered, 'And don't tell a soul but my pa was an Englishman.'

As the others carried the over-priced supplies back to the ship Cameron and I rejoined the hapless officer. He crouched on a log surrounded by a band of emigrants. In the bay beyond, the brigs were being fitted out for the more profitable return voyage. Their ballast was jettisoned, bunks cast aside and cargoes of white pine timber for the home market dragged on board.

'Faugh, how this place stinks,' the officer said, turning from the babble. He tried to fasten his waistcoat but finding an absence of buttons instead pulled the blanket around him. 'I've had my fill of New Worlds.' He was the third son of a landed family, forced to seek his fortune in the colonies when their estate in Rutland was seized for gambling debts. His first destination had been Australia but an attempt to domesticate the kangaroo had failed and his convict servants had robbed him. India too had proved to be unsuitable. While there he had contracted a sinus complaint and lost the remains of his fortune in the jute trade. His most recent plan to homestead in Upper Canada foundered when, having insufficient money to complete the journey, he was thrown off the ship in Cape Breton. A sinecure saved him from starvation but the maritime damp irritated his joints and after a lifetime away from England he dreamt of going home, even though no home remained to which he might return.

Yet in spite of his misfortune he was generous to us. I translated Little Donald's letter for him and he directed Cameron to the location of the settlement, a few hours' sailing down the coast. 'But my destination, the town called Promise, doesn't seem to be marked on the globe,' I observed, showing him the sphere.

'Nor will it be for a long time, sir.' He explained to me that my congregation lay two days' walk north on the shore of saltwater Bras d'Or Lake, the golden arm of the sea which cleaved the island. 'But may I advise you to delay your journey for a fortnight and ride with the mail? The road is rascally beyond any conception.'

Although I agreed that my baggage could travel in such a manner, I was determined to leave the following morning.

'Odsooks, sir,' the officer warned, 'this land is so intersected by water that in many places you would be better advised to travel by turtle than on foot.'

'But today is only Wednesday,' I insisted, not wishing to appear ungrateful. 'Please understand that it is my ardent desire to reach by this coming Sabbath those who have waited so long for my arrival.'

Goodenough offered to accompany me 'a piece of the way' but the charge for the pleasure of his company was exorbitant. We took our leave of him, and Ship Harbour, to return to the *Good Intent*.

At dawn a cold silver moon rose out of the sea and hung above the melancholy forests. To sustain me on my walk I had a small loaf, some cheese and the Shorter Catechism. Under my arm I carried the globe. As Cameron made ready to sail I rowed ashore and waved the last farewell. I turned inland and entered a verdant corridor cut between the deep woods. The earth was wet underfoot and the logs, where laid over gullies and streams to make a corduroy road, were covered in thick moss. I slipped and only through the fortuitous position of a stump saved the globe from spinning off into a mudhole. I was on the road to Promise.

*　　　*　　　*

'WELCOME TO YESTERYEAR.' The sodden banner drooped over the parking lot. 'There are no trash cans in Pioneer Village.' Beagan dropped his Fillet o' Fish wrapper in the bin and hurried out of the Atlantic sleet into the Interpretation Centre. 'Follow the Fish' signs directed him to a shoal of spring tourists swathed in luminous wet-weather gear. The children and cameras were wrapped in plastic. 'Let's take a walk back into history,' shivered a freckle-faced, red-haired Dalhousie student in long tartan skirt and windcheater. 'Let's see how our forefathers lived and discover old Scotland in New Scotland.'

'Hey, do you sell those cute bagpipe-shaped air fresheners here?' asked a holiday-maker from Ohio.

In Montreal the day before, the immigration officer hadn't understood why Beagan had stayed away from Canada for so long. 'You are no longer a resident,' he had declared in a crisp German accent. 'You are a visitor.' The passport had been stamped 'Admission valid for six months' and his sense of belonging had been replaced by the curiosity of an outsider.

Beagan had rented a car from a woman wearing a sari and driven back east towards Nova Scotia. Along the *autoroute* pine-needles had lain browning on the hard shoulder, their white covering of frost blown away by passing trucks, and the smell of skunk hung in the air. Headlights had played across the faces of diners eating blueberry pancakes in roadside restaurants. A lone jogger ran up a suburban strip of Burger Kings and Japanese car dealerships, past billboards which assured '*VOUS êtes important.*' A few miles further, across the border in the Maritimes, the same poster read 'We appreciate *YOU.*' There were no signs in Gaelic.

In Halifax faded grand hotels waited to receive the Queens and Empresses which sailed no more. Beagan, like the trans-Atlantic jets passing overhead, had skirted the city and headed up the coast along highways as straight as Roman roads, through marshlands of stunted pine, into the glens of Antigonish County. The lush orchards and ploughlands of the mainland had fallen away behind him and he had driven across the Canso Causeway straight to Cape Breton's Yesteryear Pioneer Village. 'Make a day of it . . .

fantasy fun for all the family.' The site was his starting point, not so he could watch the multi-screen Highland Pioneer Experience or eat Ma McIntosh's Real Down Home Baked Apple Pie but because it was to this place that the Reverend Hector's church had been moved. The old building had become a relic in a museum.

The waterlogged tourists waddled past empty drying racks and the sail-loft exhibition. They watched nets being tanned and photographed the cooper fashioning barrels. Children helped churn butter in cottage kitchens as their parents asked for directions to the nearest McDonald's. Wannabe actors spun sea-dog yarns at the dockside between video shows. From beneath her umbrella the guide spoke in a quiet Canadian way, so anxious not to offend that she seemed to swallow her words. 'Pioneer Village is a living museum to the maritime heritage of Nova Scotia,' she recited, 'a one-of-a-kind seaside treasure in Canada's Ocean Playground.' But there were no boats in the water. Grass had grown over the gunwales of dories beached on the shore. The schooners along the wharf were no longer seaworthy and survived only to house the fish-filleting display. Over-fishing, predatory seals and a change in water temperature had all but eliminated cod from the Grand Banks and the two-year fishing ban announced by the government had been extended. Some mariners feared that the flounder and haddock might never return.

Few of the visitors bothered to look at the church as it boasted no 'rural heritage' demonstration. Their passing interest was limited to the building's relocation. They glanced at the photographs of the timbers being dismantled, the numbered logs being stacked on low-loaders and driven halfway across the province. As the tourists swam on to the souvenir shop Beagan paused at the door of the church. His coat dripped water over the threshold. He slipped up the aisle, stroked the worn pews and stood by the pulpit. There lay a Bible which fell open at *John* and on a whim he read aloud, 'I am the voice of one crying in the wilderness, make straight the way of the Lord.' Beagan stood and waited. He seemed to want something dramatic to happen. He half-expected to hear a blast of Gabriel's trumpet and to see Hector appear before him saying, 'It's good of you to come laddie, but could you no have wiped your boots at the door?' But instead of a heavenly fanfare the only sound which he heard was the patter of rain on the roof.

'Damn it,' he sighed and turned away.

At The Pedlar's Curios Shop the lurid crowd bought salt cod imported from Spain and Olde English beeswax candles. Garish plastic lobsters with spring-loaded claws were the most popular item. An American paid in US dollars and argued over the exchange rate. In the cafeteria young families huddled over steamy bowls of Crofter's Highland Soup. 'What do we do next?' an eager tourist asked her tour guide. 'The Ceilidh Trail or the Great Hall of the Clans?' Beagan nursed a cup of tea beneath the pickled pouting alewives and stuffed silver eels. He wiped the condensation from the window and watched a solitary wooden canoe slide through the shallows towards the village. It didn't surprise him that the church had felt empty. The dislocated building was like a body after death, a shell. The move had separated it from the Reverend's spirit. To find it he needed to go to the place where the church had stood, to where his great-grandfather had lived, to where Hector's sons Zachary and Jamie had been born. He spread the road map on the table to look for Promise and noticed that the canoeist had vanished from the bay.

'**F**ATHER!' CRIED JAMIE laying his paddle across the thwarts and catching the pier. 'Hello, F-F-Father.'

I stood up and struck my head on the overhanging church eave. '*Ist!*' My first day back in the New World with Beagan had left me a little overwrought. 'And botheration.' The modern felicity of phrase had its attraction but little else had met with my approval. 'Mark you this, James,' I shouted, clutching my bald pate and pointing at the wall. 'They have used nails. Nails.' I waved him forward. 'Dear God, as if we had the resources to buy nails.' Jamie pulled his Peterborough lapstrake ashore and joined me by the church. New steel bolts had been hammered into the old logs to secure the dovetailed corners. 'I tell you, James, this is worse than inaccurate, it is wasteful.'

'Maybe the Lord's Will alone no longer holds the building together,' suggested Jamie.

I straightened my long black preacher's coat and struck my head again. 'I'll tolerate no impiety; one desecrator in the family is terrible enough.' Beagan may have begun to engage my affections during the crossing, yet the boy remained soft and cowardly like a crab after casting its shell.

'It's simply a modern precaution, Father,' explained Jamie. 'People today are very concerned for ph-ph-physical safety.'

'It is their spiritual well-being that should concern them.' I tried to pry free a nail with my fingers. 'When I first arrived in Cape Breton I expected some parishioners to be destitute of the ordinances of the Gospel. I did not expect to find it so three generations later.' My fingernail split. 'And where is your brother? Is he not with you?'

Jamie shook his head. 'He who made time made plenty of it, you used to say; but still not enough for Zachary.'

'He agreed to meet us here. I am disappointed.' My displeasure mounted as I inspected my second son. 'And what on earth is that costume you are wearing?'

Jamie was dressed in britches and a worn striped cap. His suspenders were frayed and tatty. 'It's my sporting outfit, Father. After your death I became an avid recreational canoeist.'

'In my day there was little time for recreation,' I recalled. 'He that will not sow on a cold day will not reap on a warm one. But from what I have seen here it is apparent that I took too much leisure. Much too much. At what are you smiling, James?'

Tireless principles can at times be exhausting but the

crusty, dour tenets warmed Jamie's heart. 'It is very good to see you again, Father.'

I too saw the humour in it and spread both my arms and wings. 'My boy, forgive your ungrateful progenitor.' We embraced, which for spirits is something between mortal laughter and a blending of gases, then I added, 'Is it not fine to see our old kirk again?'

'Yes,' hesitated Jamie. 'Yes, because it was here that I always remember you, standing at our head like the captain of a ship, with me quaking in f-f-fear of the Questions.'

'Zachary learnt his Shorter Catechism but the mischief was always coming over you. As I recall you never studied hard enough,' I admonished as we slipped into the building. 'And you will have forgotten your Gaelic too, but *crannag* means both a ship and the pulpit.'

Jamie dawdled at the door. The mention of his elder brother's name unnerved him and his stutter grew worse. 'The ch-ch-church was to have been built in Promise in time f-f-for your arrival,' he said.

'And soon thereafter the schoolhouse.' I laughed at the memory. 'Aye, as I walked through the forest I saw a wide, important and most useful field of labour awaiting me. I looked forward too to the handsome stipend of eighty pounds per annum. Eighty pounds, *a bhalaich*. In those days a man could live a comfortable life on that.' I took my place behind the pulpit. 'Was it not old McKinlay who sat there in the front pew?'

'You always sat us next to him,' Jamie nodded. 'I wanted to hide here at the back with Fisher MacFie.'

'Mark you, it was many years before I was paid anything at all. Not that it mattered, no one had any money, but I hadn't known that at the outset. As for the building of the church itself . . . oh but wait you now. This just will not do.' I had turned the pages of the Book. 'Is this not in English? Where is the Gaelic Bible?' Together we looked under the pulpit and in the cupboard but found only a pornographic magazine and a stash of empty beer bottles. 'Carnality and sin,' I hissed with indignation. 'Carnality and sin.'

'Maybe it's in the old trunk?' suggested Jamie. 'That's the last place I saw it.'

'Right enough. Good, then the blasphemous Beagan will bring it along with him. Well, come you now, I will show you my route to Promise.'

'But what about Beagan?'

'The boy is still swilling tea in the cafeteria,' which I had to admit was preferable to frequenting a tavern. 'He will not be too far behind us when he begins to look at his own map. It and the globe are in the trunk too.' I stood at the door and pointed northwards. 'If I recollect aright this was the direction.' My memory reached out beyond the litter bins and The Pedlar's Curios Shop. The parking lot turned into a rough mail road and the sodden banner became the evergreen cloak which wrapped grey granite hills. 'There had never been a forest the like of it, James. You cannot imagine it.'

I walked through great pine cathedrals and intimate beech chapels where finches and blackbirds celebrated their praises in song. The frosty spring light flicked the tips of trees and filtered down to the forest floor. Wild meadows embraced the track of ice-blue lakes which stepped away to the horizon like footprints left by God. I paused for lunch, a communion of bread and water, and watched a doe drink by the shining stream. But my progress was slower than I had anticipated and not long into the afternoon the corridor sank back into shadow. It narrowed then split and, as advised by Goodenough, I took the right fork to follow a trail of uncertain blazes. The air cooled and I began to wonder where I might lay my head when from behind a confused mass of felled timber a log cabin came into view.

The quick stroke of an axe echoed in the clearing. I climbed over the bush-fence and tried to hail its inhabitant. The axe chopped on and a vicious dog bounded forward. I retreated up a nearby maple tree, lodged the globe on a broad bough and clung to the trunk. It was not a pleasant reception. The hound growled and snapped at my heels. My attempt to calm the animal with kind words only incensed it further and I was forced to scramble to a higher perch. But the racket did flush out the woodsman who, when the dog failed to obey his orders, resorted to a cuff across the ear to silence it.

'For sure yous'll be looking for a place to sleep,' he said, his Irish brogue pinched by an American twang. 'I's keeping the tavern here.' He gestured at the shanty. 'Yous welcome to stop over.'

The so-called tavern was dark, dirty and cramped. Its floor was made of loose split logs and the chimney was a simple square hole in the roof. Snowshoes hung on the wall. The only light came from a hearth burning on bare soil. Its flames flared up as the wind stole through chinks in the walls.

'Yous'll be heading for Promise, I calculate,' guessed my host. His face, rosy and plump, was impressed with a lattice of scars and lines from fifty fights and as many years. As there was no chair he offered me a stool. There was no table either. The only other furniture in the house was a finely inlaid oak closet inside which was an old-fashioned couch-bed. 'Theys'll be right pleased to see your face, Father.'

'You know the town then?' I asked, anxious to learn something of my destination. 'I have heard very little about it.'

'For sure it's a grand place. Good land. Honourable folk. Yes siree, theys always pay their bills on the nail.'

'And the church? Is it a fine building?'

'Well now, Father, that I cannot say for certain. I'd be lying to yous if I said that it was and that wouldn't do. Nope, not you being a parson. Truth is it's been a fair old spell since I was there. But I knows for sure that theys expecting yous. In fact I heard tell theys were expecting yous last month.'

His knowledge of my arrival intrigued me. 'And how in this great wilderness did you come by such intelligence?'

'I like to be at the centre of things.' I could imagine no place less near a centre. 'That's how come I built the inn here.' The Irishman leaned forward, eyes wide with excitement, and stabbed the floor with a crooked finger. 'Here, right here, yous be exactly halfway 'tween Ship Harbour and Promise.' A boy's optimism bubbled through the veins of an old man. 'Any idiot sees that everything is going forward in this country. It's not possible for trade, agriculture and manufactures to get set back. The whole caboodle keeps advancing. So I calculate that this road will get mighty busy. Folks will pass along, see the inn and say, "Hell," sorry Father I mean theys'll say, "Hurrah, we's halfway there. Let's stop for tea and grits or sandwiches and potatoes." We'll feed them up good so that theys'll spend the night and eat breakfast too and pay us well and I'll be as rich as Midas. That's for sure what's to happen.' He leaned back on his haunches proud of his plan. 'Wasn't it a grand thought Columbus had to find out America?'

Over coffee made of dried roasted dandelion roots he talked of his years in Virginia and the family feud which drove him north. 'I've no axe to grind. Here a man can do good. Any settler can reckon in one year having potatoes enough and in the next twelve month grain aplenty. In the third year theys'll see food to spare.' He shook his head in wonder. 'No man goes hungry here. For sure this'll be *tír na nóg*.' The Irish promised land of eternal youth. I asked him how long he had been at the halfway inn. 'Going on five year,' he replied.

Once the fire had burnt low we retired as there were no candles. My host, fully clad, made a nest of odd rugs in the couch-bed. I lay down on blankets by the dying embers.

'This is my first night here in the New World,' I told him.

'God willing it won't be your last, Father.'

I tried to sleep but the cries of unknown animals disturbed me. The bush rustled and mysterious feet padded across the pine shingles. I awoke dreaming that a bear had broken into the cabin. The night was so black and starless that I could not make out the window frame and groped in the darkness for the door. Then the beast belched and I recognised the grizzly snores as those of the Irishman.

We rose before dawn and broke our fast with scarcely palatable milk fresh from the cow which fed on wild garlic. The Irishman, the globe nestled in the crook of his arm, guided me back to the trail, all but invisible in the dim glimmer of morning, and readily accepted payment for his hospitality. 'Yes siree, one day this here spot will be marked on your globe,' he said handing it back to me. 'But 'til then yous won't be needing it, Father. Yous'll be in Promise by dinnertime.' He then vanished into the woods with his axe. The sound of chopping chased me away down the path.

All day I followed the dark line of lofty pines expecting at every turn to see a cluster of houses or catch sight of the silhouette of the church but by nightfall I had still not reached my destination. As twilight descended on the land the forest dressed in crêpe. A chaos of dead timber was cast like matchsticks on the forest floor. The old firs fell, rotted and fed the saplings which sprouted on their corpses. Wind and worms reduced the great trunks to dust. The cycle had not changed since the waters of Noah's flood had receded. The wilderness remained untracked, unmapped and virtually untouched by the mark of man. Like Adam cast from the Garden I too was afraid. At the base of grey granite cliffs I lit a fire. The flames shrugged off the cowl of night by raising above me a gilded green canopy embellished here and there with jewels of stars. Within the dome of light I ate my cheese and bread but the sound of a nearby stream forever rolling by filled my heart with a strange melancholy.

By the end of the next day I knew that I was lost. The blazes, which had been few and far between at best, had now vanished altogether. Tangled undergrowth obscured the path. Roots snatched at my feet. I took my bearing from the sun and tried to steer a straight course but at every step a dozen possible tracks snaked off between the beeches and spring-green hemlocks. My food was finished and, as it was too early in the year for berries, I lay down hungry but with faith that the morning would bring me to my destination.

It was not until late afternoon on the sixth day that I smelt the wood ash. The forest, through which I had imagined that no man had before walked, revealed the suggestion of a path. Fearful of missing a fellow traveller I hurried along the trail, marked by now with fresh footprints, and slipped in my excitement, cutting my lip. My shouts startled a grouse which flew across the path. I ran on, pushed through a stand of sugar maples and crashed into the clearing. But instead of a man with hand raised in greeting there waited by the melancholy stream only the smothered fire which I recognised as my own. My route had described a circle. I slumped against the grey granite cliffs and wept, famished and sickened by my weakness.

The next morning, as I tried to retrace my steps back to the halfway inn, I realised that the angel Raphael walked beside me. He carried a pilgrim's staff and accompanied me as he had Tobias on the road into Media. He was a talkative soul, well versed on the manner of driving away wicked spirits, and I enjoyed his company. After we had travelled some miles together he said, 'You will agree then that you are lost.' I could not fault his observation. 'Well, you can navigate. Why not turn back into the forest and head north?'

'Into the unknown?' I asked. Raphael nodded. I had comforted myself with thoughts of platefuls of fried Irish flat cakes. 'But do you have a map to guide my way?'

'Go out into the wilderness and put your hand in the Hand of God,' he replied. 'That shall be better than a known way.'

Some days later I lost track of time. I had not slept. The long cold nights passed like inky sacks of infinite weight dragged across the sky by a weary old man. Strange visions kept me awake. In the shadows I saw faces. I imagined conversations in the sigh of the wind. The fancies infuriated me and I tried to focus my tired and confused mind. I came on a river swollen by the spring run-off and, though my hunger had waned, tried to scoop a trout from the water. The undertaking succeeded only in dampening both my spirit and my clothes. A single speckled egg, stolen from a grassy bank, tasted so bitter that I retched it up.

At night racoons scavenged about my camp, their black masks giving them the look of highwaymen, and a flying squirrel chattered as it leapt from spruce to larch. I lit a fire and raised the golden dome into the trees. Sleep came with bad grace and brought dreams. The woods fell quiet and I thought, 'An angel must be passing overhead.' I opened my eyes and beheld her standing over me, her long white robes billowing in the night breeze. Above her the canopy had become a giltwood library ringed with pine-needle books. The angel took my hand and led me up a spiral stair. Below, my body slept beside the fire. We paused at a shelf to select a volume and I read about riding the swells in clothes sea-wet and coming home from the lobsters. A pamphlet remembered the *Good Intent*, the laying of keel and sighting of line. There were volumes about my childhood, tomes on my father, a worn French grammar and a leaf from the *Christian Instructor Advertiser* which called for 'a missionary with Evangelical zeal, a love for souls and good health equal to the requirements of the calling. Free passage and outfit provided'. Every book in the library touched on my life, on past, present and future. I climbed further up the steps reading, spiralling upwards, until my head pressed against the apex of the dome, the boughs parted and the dark shroud of the night sky rose over me and encompassed me. I started and reached out for the angel's hand but clutched only leaves. I tried to speak aloud but the words stuck in my throat. Then I remembered that even in the deepest forest the Lord was with me and saw that the north star glittered above me. It changed into the angel who glowed and burnt as the fire at my feet. I laughed with the joy of recognition.

'*Slàn leat*,' she called in the Gaelic. 'Blessings be with you.'

I awoke laughing, blinded by the sun, with a stranger standing above me. In the glare I discerned deep mica eyes, a broad nose and face. His skin glistened with bear grease beneath a simple blue cloth garment tied at the waist by a root belt. He held a hatchet in his hand. The Indian pointed with his weapon and spoke in an unknown tongue. My end had come. I rose to my knees and prepared to meet my maker.

'*Seul?*' he asked in French.

'I am not alone. My Master is here with me,' I replied, breaking off my prayers.

He laid down his hatchet, pointed at the globe and said, '*Écossais, jouez pìob.*' Play the pipes. *Pìob* was the Gaelic word for bagpipe. His request took me by surprise. My life appeared not to be in danger. I stood up. '*Jouez pìob*,' the Indian repeated in his mélange of languages and pranced back and forth, his long black hair swaying, blowing into an imaginary bagpipe and bellowing an awful wail. I picked up the globe. '*Oui, oui.*' His smile revealed remarkably white teeth. '*Maintenant*,' he said and again mewed like a love-sick cat. When I failed to act he took the globe from my hand and blew at Greenland. No sound emerged. He looked disappointed and said, '*Cassé.*' Broken. '*C'est dommage.*' He picked up his weapon and turned to go.

'Please,' I managed to say. '*S'il vous plaît, où est Promise?*'

'*Comment?*'

'*Je suis perdu.*' I am not alone but I am lost. '*Où est le village de Promise?*'

'*Ah, village Écossais? Pas loin.*' He pointed away to the north-west and flashed an affable smile as if I had overlooked an obvious signpost. '*Un jour.*' A day's travel.

'*Et j'ai faim.*' I am hungry. '*Beaucoup faim.*'

He made me nettle soup. The exquisite hot liquid scorched my throat. As I ate, the Indian sat on a carpet of moss and examined the globe's printed panels. He was of yellow complexion, stout and well-made, and I guessed that he was Micmac, a nomadic tribe of the coast which had allied itself with the French in the eighteenth century. '*Belle, mais cassée,*' he sighed after blowing at the subcontinent.

'*C'est le monde.*' I tried to explain by pointing at the eastern seaboard of America. '*Nous sommes ici.*' He did not understand. '*Il est comme une carte.*'

'*Une carte?*' He nodded and scratched a map in the sand: a forest, a line of hills, inlets of the sea. '*Voilà; c'est facile.*' But I could not picture the route.

'*Est-ce qu'il y a un chemin?*' Is there a path?

The man laughed easily and shook his head. It was difficult to relate my gentle rescuer to Little Donald's stories of brutal savages. '*Vous venez avec moi.*' You'd better come with me. '*En canôt.*'

His canoe was ingeniously made without nails, leather or hemp. The birchbark had been sewn together with the dried roots of trees and sealed with pitch. The Micmac, who called himself Gogo, taught me to kneel in the bow and to hold a paddle. At first I found the vessel, which is sharp at each end, unstable but I gained confidence as we followed the black curve of a river. It moved with good speed and grace, riding through the fast rapids and skirting the innumerable fallen trees.

On the water I began again to appreciate the beauty of my surroundings. The oppressive pines fell away and my lungs filled with the salt smell of an inland sea. Pools and lagoons, brooks and burns etched the banks of golden Bras d'Or Lake. Channels reached far into the bush and clear springs splashed out into the bays where young loons preened and fished. A turtle sunning itself on a deadhead watched our passing. A flash of black ducks took flight. Gogo set the course, cast a disappointed look at the mute globe and began to sing in his Algonquin dialect. Deep glens gouged down between the highlands to the water. The mists rose up from bogs and meadows, curled through the dark aisles of forest and wrapped the shore.

I didn't notice the town. It was the movement of a fisherman in a dugout which caught my eye. As we neared the headland he drew up beside our canoe, doffed his cap and sneezed. 'Thanks to God you have come,' he said in Gaelic then wiped his nose with a sleeve. As we cleaved the saltgrass shallows grazing cattle stirred in the bush. A Highlander hobbled across a stumpy field with his *cas chrom*, lay down the turfing spade to help his wife reach the beach. Two scruffy ginger urchins scrambled down the bank. Eager hands grasped the gunwales. McKinlay, the elder and storekeeper, strode into the water with arm outstretched and shook my hand.

'We feared for your life, sir. Your baggage arrived two days ago.'

'I feel as if I have walked from Dan to Beersheba.' I gestured to the Indian. 'And I would still be lost were it not for this good Samaritan.'

McKinlay spoke to Gogo in Algonquin but his thanks was drowned out by the wail of the pipes. Red McNeil, clad in a tattered kilt, sounded the welcome. His wife led him forward followed by their freckle-faced twin daughters. Gogo tapped my shoulder and nodded at Red. '*Ça c'est bon.*' He was content to be relieved of the globe.

The cluster of mean timber huts was all but indistinguishable from the trees. 'Where is the town?' I asked.

'There's no town but what you see,' replied McKinlay. 'This is Promise.'

A swirl of duckdown wafted over the path out of the wood. Anne McNeil wailed and chased through the flurry of feathers into the clearing of spruce-thatched tents. Children as wild as bear-cubs took refuge in the hovels. Their faces pressed against attic windows as their mothers bagged the birds left part-plucked in the excitement. Other women ran after the pinions which floated through doors, settled on stretched deer hides and sailed over split-pine shingle roofs, then stuffed them into homespun pillowcases. One plume settled on the nose of a cow observing the commotion. Others landed on the cod fillers which dried on clotheslines. 'There are those among us,' confessed McKinlay as a way of explanation, 'who never before saw the face of a clergyman.'

'The Good Lord has blessed us this day,' exulted Anne then gave her husband a look which left him no choice but to agree.

The few young people gathered in from the fields so that they might obtain the rare exhibition of a stranger, turning their backs on Gogo as if he were not there. They scanned my appearance with such eagerness that I blushed and with head down strode across the town. In under a minute I had walked through its centre and out the other side. Promise consisted of more salmon-curing racks than houses. 'I understood that well on one hundred families resided here.'

'Aye, that they do, but spread over the country not in the town,' said McKinlay.

'Some folk, sir, live on the backland and come to Promise only to buy flour and rum,' volunteered McNeil, then added with a hint of envy, 'One of them has two wives.'

'It's law that is needed to keep them in order and gospel to give them some better ideas than they have now,' dictated his wife. Her jaw jutted out with every word spoken.

'They say that they cannot meet you for want of clothes but I fear it is more for a want of heart,' lamented McKinlay. 'This stubborn forest has driven many men to despair.'

'And the church?' I asked, my voice strained. 'Where is the church?'

Red McNeil's twins, as headstrong as their mother, each took a hand to lead me up the brow of a hill. Our small group stopped within a thicket of larch. Underfoot was black granite and through the tangle of brush I glimpsed the sparkle of water but there was no church to be seen.

'We chose this spot,' said McKinlay. 'For certain it's the finest on Cape Breton.'

'It's ourselves that had intended to erect the building in time for your arrival,' said McNeil at his wife's insistence. 'But, well, sir, we had a terrible winter.'

'That's right enough,' she added.

It might have been because of the exhaustion of the journey or perhaps as a reaction to the arrival but standing on the hill I felt a great wave of sadness wash over me. I had left my home and family, travelled for months, lost dear friends and arrived in a poor, lonely place to find no manse, no school, no church. The work demanded by my calling did not daunt me nor did the absence of physical comforts depress me. The warmth of the welcome was not lacking for I could see that the settlers were gladdened by my coming. They were resolute, cheerful and diligent in a situation that was both difficult and novel. But even as I resolved to give myself heart and soul to them and the place, there swelled within me a nagging, nebulous sensation that something had been lost.

'We shall build a church here, on this spot, where we will worship together.' I turned to include in prayer all those gathered in the forest and saw that my Micmac rescuer had vanished. 'By faith,' I quoted from *Hebrews*, 'Abraham, when he was called, obeyed to go out unto a place which he was to receive for an inheritance; and he went out not knowing whither he went. He became a sojourner in the land of promise, as in a land not his own: for he looked for a city which hath foundations, whose builder and maker is God.'

THERE WAS NO Promise marked on the new Nova Scotia highways map so Beagan dug deep into the box trunk and unearthed an original, hand-drawn Township Plan. 'Scale: 40 Chains to an Inch,' read the legend. 'Mining Rights Forfeited.' A rigid, right-angled grid pattern had been imposed on the irregular shore. Concession lines struck through the bush unimpeded by rivers or hills, subjugating nature to the plan. His great-grandfather's wilderness had been tamed by tape measures, the unknown banished with the stroke of a surveyor's pen. In each boxy lot the Crown Land Officer had recorded a settler's name: McNeil, Red; McKinlay, Isaac; MacFie, Hamish. In one corner plot a clerk had written, 'Site reserved for Promise Presbyterian Church.'

Beagan drove north away from Pioneer Village and the Highlands of the New World rose across his path. He had made no attempt to walk the Reverend's circuitous trek through the bush. That trail had been followed through the diary's pages. Instead he sped up Highway 105 past deserted farms and tried to imagine the unbroken forests that had confronted the first Scottish settlers. His back began to ache, not from the rental car's uncomfortable seats, but from thinking of the labour needed to wrestle a single field from the bush.

The once wild land had for a single generation lain smooth with meadows ditched and pastures cleared but it was now being reclaimed by nature. The trees pressed in on derelict homesteads. Powder-blue paint peeled from rotting walls. On the car radio listeners rang a phone-in programme for advice on tracing their ancestors from Lewis, Uist and Eigg. Beagan heard in their voices something so plaintive that he had to stop and check the road map for fear of losing his way.

Above a town named Dunvegan stormclouds rumbled across the steel sky. A tear in the firmament released a gleam of vermilion dusk. The first drops of cold rain turned the earth iron red. At Glencoe a sorry herd of cattle sauntered under cover around a beaver-dam lake. Plastic ducks paid no heed, petrified mid-waddle on verdant lawns, but the sleet drove the locals indoors. Apart from the disembodied radio voices there seemed to be no one on Cape Breton. The few other cars on the road drifted out of the haze, lifting waves of slush over Beagan's windshield, but he saw no faces behind the wheels.

He pulled into a neon-lit pizzeria to order a take-away. 'Hawaiian Crab-Meat Special' cheered a poster but the oven hadn't been switched on so he settled for spaghetti and tinned meatballs. The black and white television on the counter played a government Prosperity Initiative commercial. 'Can Canada compete?' demanded the announcer. 'Yes we can,' enthused the orchestrated reply, 'here at the centre of things.'

As his supper warmed in the microwave the owner ground his teeth. 'It's not worth my while heating up the oven, eh? Just for one pizza.'

Beagan sat on a stool shivering and wondered what Hector would have made of it, this New Jerusalem which left him feeling cheated, even deceived. 'Where is everyone?' he asked. He was the first customer that night and the owner had no change.

'Gone away.' The owner gestured out the window at the weather. 'Wouldn't you?'

A damp Canadian flag washed into view. The Clansman Motel was a horseshoe of pale mint clapboard cabins curved around a dirt track on the edge of Bras d'Or. The single picnic table turned its back on a barbecue fashioned from a wheel hub. 'Cabin 11 empty. Pay tomorrow' read the scribbled notice stuck to the office window. The screen door creaked open on to a room of fern-green plasterboard walls and an air of transience. The sagging double bed brought to mind travelling salesmen, nights of foamy beer and roughly fondled breasts. On the coffee table lay the previous month's *Inverness Oran*. It advertised jobs in Australia. 'A fantastic challenge is waiting for you on a farm overseas.'

Beagan dragged the trunk in from the wet and ate a mouthful of tepid spaghetti. He leafed through the sermons and Sustentation Fund accounts. In an envelope lay an edge of sail canvas. He picked up Hector's Memorandum, turned its onion-skin yellow pages and read, 'We laid the foundations of our church. With axe and scythe we cut away the bush, spiralling round and round the centre, pushing back the wild wood. Stumps were burnt or torn from their roots by oxen, boulders split and levered aside. Our foothold on the brow of the hill was enlarged, a plateau cleared where a man could stand and look out, his sight not hemmed in by a barrier of trees but open to the broad vista of water.'

Beagan paused to finish the last meatball. It was cool in the cabin and he wrapped a blanket around his shoulders. The rain blowing off the lake bubbled through the cracked panes and formed a puddle beneath the window sill. He felt his great-grandfather's isolation, a man forever separated from home and family, then with a little less gravity began to wonder if there were any single women alone and cold in an adjoining cabin. He would have enjoyed the company. They could share the warmth of his blow-heater. But when he plugged it in the fuse blew out and he turned with a sigh back to the diary.

'We beat trails like animals between town and quarry and our legs were torn by underbrush and brambles,' the journal continued. 'Isaac McKinlay and MacFie the fisher built two of the corners. To make the others the shore farmers assembled in a bee, as is the custom here when clearing land or raising barns. They felled the spruce and cut the lumber by whip-saw, then rolled the logs over a pit where, with one man above and another below, a drag-saw sliced them from end to end. The logs were mortised or notched so that they locked at the corners of the building. Shingles of cedar were fashioned with an axe and pine planks cut for the floor. Around the rising walls another acre of ground has been cleared to be the sacred resting place of the departed dead.'

A small lead Communion token slipped out from between the leaves and fell into Beagan's lap. He felt its weight in his hand then pulled back the brown cloth drapes and gazed out at the headland. The view promptly vanished behind a curtain of mist. Promise lay beyond the clouds.

'NO ONE WHO ever dwelt in a body worked so hard as did they.' I sat bolt upright, collar tightly fastened and Bible in hand. Jamie perched beside me on the bedstead looking over Beagan's shoulder. 'It was every board that had to be cut by hand. There was not a sawmill in fifty miles. Even the children helped by filling the chinks between the logs with moss and wet clay.' As Beagan lay down on the bed I nodded at the memory. 'Aye, and those good men worked still in the fields and at their nets.'

'Beagan read somewhere,' said Jamie, 'that a naked man standing outside in winter would have f-f-frostbite in twenty seconds and in summer be sucked dry of blood by mosquitoes in six minutes.'

'That may well be, James, but we did not uncase ourselves outdoors,' I reminded my son. 'Except when we bathed. It was the one physical pleasure of those days, swimming in Bras d'Or. The men washed at the foot of the cliff path most evenings. I remember the pale white skin of the tired bodies seemed luminous against the dark green wood.' I held out my hands. The callused tip of my forefinger was smudged ink black. 'We were building something where there had been nothing, right enough.'

'It was the labour that brought you together.'

'It was faith, James. As hard as oak, as lasting as pine.'

In the plasterboard room Beagan's eyes drooped, his head fell and the diary dropped on to the pillow. I spread my cape and raised above us an evergreen cathedral. The sagging bed stood in the glade which was the nave. Around it McKinlay and MacFie, the McNeils and their twins bowed their heads in extempore prayer.

'Before the church was completed our services were held out in the open.' I stretched out further and conjured up old Promise around Beagan's sleeping head. Unshod children sat on the motel coffee table. Men dressed in best black fingered the pages of their Bibles with earth-stained hands. The women wore clean muslin handkerchiefs knotted under their chins. Anne McNeil flaunted a bonnet as a personal extravagance. 'It is myself that would have no kneeling or genuflexion, no candles or crucifixes, no pomp or trappings to stand between man and God,' I recalled. The precentor stepped in front of the broken television set and intoned a psalm. It was sung by the congregation. 'Our words of praise rose into the air and He came among us and blessed us with His presence.'

The town looked as it had before Jamie's birth, the spruce-thatched tents, salmon-curing racks and McKinlay's store. 'Gosh, how clever,' he said, laughing at the trick. It was still Sunday. Families settled under the pines at the end of the first service to eat lunches of squirrel pie, cheese and bread. The men drank from jugs of West India rum, which they had traded for fish, before assembling for the second sermon. 'Can I learn to do that?' asked Jamie.

'It is simply a matter of concentration,' I explained as we walked among the worshippers. 'Now pay attention.' Before our eyes dormant plants came into bud, fruit trees flowered and birds called for their mates. 'In that first difficult year,' I continued, 'the blessings of spring were spoilt by a bedevilled summer. The mosquitoes descended on us like a plague of locust and, worse still, the potatoes rotted in the field. Aye well, the farms on the shore could cope with the blight, their rich soil produced a good variety of crops, but the disease ravaged the families on the backlands. Their poor, rocky plots could grow little else and to fend off starvation the men were forced away from home to dig coal at Sydney Mines. Some took work as gutters on American saltbankers fishing in the Gulf.'

Beyond the cracked window panes and far across the island Jamie saw the paupers frequent the wharves at Ship Harbour. They begged for handouts of Indian meal and flour from every trading schooner.

'Would you be remembering the old canoe?' I asked. Jamie nodded. It was in the canoe that MacFie had found my body. 'It took me out to those who could not come to our tabernacle in the wilderness. In log hovels I preached to congregations of broken men and suspicious neighbours. I read them the Word of the Gospel by the light of my own candle, which I carried so as not to tax their meagre resources. In the presence of God I married couples who had lived as man and wife for decades and baptised their middle-aged children. They wept afterwards over suppers of sooty porridge.' Jamie winced at an unpalatable memory, unable to forget the practice of burning the head of grain before winnowing.

I wore my shepherd's tartan plaid and knelt back in my birchbark canoe. The motel bed drifted alongside me, its counterpane inflated like a hovercraft's skirt. Jamie perched on the headboard. When Beagan began to snore I reached over to turn out the bedside lamp.

'Aye but there was a fearful intransigence too. It was myself that attributed much of it to the excess of tea drinking,' I said. 'They drank slushes of that boiled black liquid. It dulled the appetite, right enough.' Beagan mumbled in his dreams and I lowered my voice. 'So instead of wallowing in paucity I enjoined them to improve their material condition. The Shorter Catechism makes a bold virtue of getting along in the world. A man with an empty stomach worries little about feeding his soul so the duties of my station were not only to nurture neglected spirits.'

'Mother told us that you mediated in quarrels, prescribed

and provided medicine, even advised on crop rotation and drainage.' A summer breeze caught the bedhead and Jamie grabbed hold of the canoe's thwart. 'And there were always widows to be consoled.'

'It was hard on the women, James. A horse's work was taken out of them. They were made to harrow, gather and carry crop, knit and spin with distaff and spindle as they walked, even when with child. There was butter to churn and bread to bake. In any spare moment they turned their hands to the loom to weave blankets or cloth. For most a bit of gay ribbon was a luxury beyond their purse. And when the women lost their brothers or husbands there were never any savings. It is hard to keep a house with empty cupboards.'

Beneath leg-o'-mutton sails a trap skiff rode up to Saint George's Channel and hauled aboard a swelling, silvery catch. Between the spreading and lifting of the nets its crew hailed other passing fishers: Acadian French, Newfoundland Irish and the ubiquitous American Loyalist. Men who had taken their rent from the sea in Scotland continued here to live from the point of the hook.

'We collected alms to help buy seed for the less fortunate and provide books for those in need. Some settlers had bartered their Bibles for cheap spirits but many who were before abandoned found purpose in the true Word. It brought them knowledge, and without knowledge people can be neither good Christians nor good citizens. They began to toil with strength renewed, to spend as little as possible, to live on the commonest fare until a sum of money was saved either to buy an adjoining tract or to send a child away to be schooled.'

With a sleight of wing another season slipped away before our eyes. The waters of Bras d'Or were burnished crimson and gold. Skeins of geese flew south as cold white fingers etched the autumn leaves. They floated on the wind and landed on Beagan's bed. A gentle rain began to fall and he shivered in his sleep. As Jamie tucked the blanket around him the sound of praying reached our ears.

'I recollect standing in the nave of the church, watching the last beams and ribs rise above me, seeing that the roof resembled an upturned boat. Sure enough, its ridge was the keel, its apse curved like a stern, its gable cloven as the bow.' I nodded towards the headland in approval. 'It was a fine *bàta*, a finer ark than any I had built. The ship of the Lord, James.'

In a moment Jamie stood beside me inside the newly completed church. 'It would be a Sabbath-day in October that the long table was run from prow to stern and decked in white cloths for the first Holy Communion. I preached in the Gaelic then in English. We sang from the Psalms of David, the communicants sat at the table and the elders passed among them the goblet of spruce beer – it was not wine that we had – and great chunks of bread which they took and broke and ate and said, "This do in remembrance of me." God's faithful gave thanks for their blessings and worshipped Him in sincerity and in truth. "Glory to Thee forever, Thou bright moon this night. There is no speech nor language where Thy voice is not heard."'

We gazed at my old congregation then I folded my cape and the fern-green cabin walls of the motel closed in around us. The church and its brethren vanished. A passing car's headlights flashed across the brown cloth curtains. Jamie perched beside me again on the bedstead. I turned towards him and said, 'It was a time when there was no doubt.' Then our eyes fell on Beagan who groaned, his rest disturbed by the journey, and together we wrapped gentle dreams around him to soothe the uneasy sleep.

BY DAWN THE rain had lifted. A cool breeze blew off the water, over the yard of sycamore shade and through the screen door.

The motel sat on a wide grassy strip between dark pine cliffs and the shore. Beagan awoke strangely refreshed. His head was so full of images of the land as it had been in his great-grandfather's day that he decided to walk the last mile to Promise and crossed a clover field to reach Bras d'Or. He strode over rocks wrapped in linguine seaweed, past tomato-red fishermen's shacks and around green gunwaled dories with high van Gogh prows. Seagulls squatted on the shingled roofs and crabs scuttled away into the swells. In his pocket was the old Township Plan and the Memorandum.

As he walked it was easy for him to picture the past. Little seemed to have changed around the bay. In his imagination the emaciated settler set foot on the virgin shore. He could see Gogo's canoe slipping through the saltgrass shallows to deliver both Reverend and globe to the parish. He heard the chop of axes and hymn of voices sparkle over the water. Hector's head bobbed above the surface, bathing at the foot of the cliff path, then before his eyes it sprouted a seal's whiskers and dived out of sight. As he rounded the point he conjured up a vision of trap skiffs and Cape boats tacking home ahead of the first blizzard.

'Frost clings to the morning and makes rigid armour of long johns hanging from the line,' his great-grandfather had written during the long, cold December. 'Winter proclaims her arrival with gale winds and horizontal snow. I enter the pulpit in heavy coat, woollen mittens and skull cap carrying a bucket of live coals to warm my feet. No trousers do any good without two pairs of stockings.' Beagan imagined the still waters frozen into sheet ice and felt the bitter wind wail down from the Arctic. 'The men busy themselves cutting wood and hunting moose. They drive the beasts into deep snow then butcher them. Their wives make moccasins from the legs and wear the hide, hair and all, stripped straight from the carcass. The gamy smell lingers about them in church.' The writing became scratchy and indistinct. The pen had run dry and Beagan pictured Hector refilling it while blowing on cold blue fingers.

'Those who do not remain active are sped to higher service above. During Christmas week Alistair MacQuarie lost his arthritic cow, lame horse and wife. I found him weeping before his five children and reading the Gaelic Bible. "This," he said, stroking the Testament, "is my sole comfort." But the dead cannot be buried as the ground is too hard to dig. They are placed on a handsleigh and hauled to the village by relays of mourners wearing snowshoes. Their tears freeze on their beards. The coffins are laid in a cellar, sealed so squirrels can not steal in to bite off ears and nose, until the thaw.'

Beagan pictured a cabin fall vacant, its owner having died or moved on to Upper Canada, and the Reverend take up residence. Anne McNeil brought him steaming dishes of salt pork and *colcannon*, boiled cabbage and potatoes pounded with milk. As he waited to eat, his stomach growling with hunger, she complained about a neighbour's overindulgence in ardent spirits. Her twin daughters cleaned for him, whispering and giggling with every polish and sweep. MacFie stopped by with a few fresh smelt or gaspereaux caught through an ice hole. His nose dripped from the cold which he could not throw off. He never accepted the offer of a chair but turned his beaver hat in his hands and apologised after a few brief minutes, 'Would you forgive me, Mr Gillean, for so overstaying my welcome?' Hector was forever writing, making notes, accounting for the alms, but all too soon the lonely winter evenings closed in and the fire burnt low. No warmth remained in the empty house. Beagan felt his blood run cold as he read that the ink in Hector's vest pocket had frozen during February's bitter nights.

His heart thawed with a diary entry scribbled in late April. 'All winter the woods have remained without voice. A great coldness has silenced the earth. But this last month the murmur of water under the thinning ice whispered of spring. The frozen bay groaned and strained then snapped. Now children clatter between the hissing floes before their mothers, hands wringing, scold them back. Icicles drip from the eaves then drop into muddy drifts. Snowbanks tumble down shingles, slide off roofs and thud on to doorsteps. On the beach the fishers talk of full nets and bellies while sorting their killicks, grapples and buoys.'

Beagan listened to hear the newcomers curse and crash their way through the bush from Ship Harbour. They laughed as they embraced old friends and cried for those lost to the cold. Their axes bit into the virgin forest and seeds were sown between the hemlock stumps and girdled pines. Logs were chopped and heaved and dovetailed into cabins. The whole village seemed to moan with growing pains. Song echoed from the new tavern and the blacksmith's anvil rang under the hammer. The congregation swelled and the fresh voices filled the settlement with prayer.

Beagan's fancies were deafened by a great Mack truck thundering past, 'Snap! Crackle! Pop!' scrolled down its trailer. The driver of a camper van dribbled bits of Big Mac down his Toronto Maple Leafs hockey shirt. A police car screamed after a speeding scarlet Pontiac. The old shore had met a modern wall of crushed stone. Beagan scrambled up the incline and on to a new highway. According to his dated map Promise lay beneath it.

He could not spot the foundations of the church from the hard shoulder and followed a rough path into the bush in search of them. Away from the asphalt ribbon, around the place where McKinlay's store had once stood, he lost his way among the chestnuts. Saplings sprung from the husks of old oaks. Wild spring iris pushed up through the blanket of autumn leaves. Instead of the jighooks and communion tokens which he had hoped to discover he found Coke cans and disposed nappies. There was no manse, no walls, no commemorative plaque. The plots had been reclaimed by the wilderness. The houses had rotted back into the earth. Beagan realised that the town was gone, buried by time and hidden by progress, and the heavy fog of despair closed in around him again.

Guided by the drone of traffic Beagan turned back towards the road, tripped on a moss-covered float and fell against a rusty Studebaker. He stood up and bruised his shin on a sheared propeller. A startled chicken flapped off its fish-flake roost and scuttled away into the undergrowth. In place of fields of golden corn and laden squid racks Beagan had stumbled upon acres of old bathtubs, rotten hulls and decrepit threshers. He picked his way across the

yard of cast-offs, through a wall with a holed rowing boat as its
gate, towards a building. Beagan knocked at the door and, when
no answer came, stepped over the threshold and on to the fore-
court of a petrol station. 'Old Church Texaco' read the sign. 'Last
Gas for 50 miles.' The red-haired attendant, who was filling up
an ancient Newfoundland-registered station wagon, was undis-
turbed by Beagan's unorthodox entrance. 'How's she going?' he
asked, scratching the downy growth of his first beard.

'I'm looking for Promise,' said Beagan.

'Excuse me?'

'The old town. The map says it should be around here.'

'Sorry, mister. Don't know any place by that name.' The dated
gas pump chimed like a clock with every litre delivered. 'Except
the ghost town, eh?'

'A pioneer town?'

'Search me.' The attendant began to clean the windscreen,
pausing to itch his chin with the rubber end of the squeegee,
confident that his past was not worth knowing. 'It was history
even before I was a kid.'

An Acadian Lines coach whistled past the station. Beagan examined his Plan. 'This road doesn't seem to be marked on here.'

'Hey, it's new,' counselled the boy, his tone deepening to
emphasise the importance of the development. 'Three hours to
Halifax. Eighteen hours to Toronto.' He threw his arm westward
with a gesture to illustrate speed. 'Man, that's moving.'

'You going down the road too, bud?' asked the driver of the
station wagon. He, his pregnant wife and two quibbling kids
carried cardboard mugs of complimentary coffee and jam-filled
doughnuts back to their car.

'Yes,' replied Beagan. 'Sort of passing through.'

'We're heading for Ontario,' he volunteered. Newfoundlanders
have the gift of the gab; they can talk a lobster into its pot. 'My
brother says there's jobs going at General Motors.' He untucked
a pack of Camels from his T-shirt sleeve. 'I'd offer you a lift but
we're kinda full up.' The car sank on its springs as the family
clambered aboard. 'You hit your sister again I'll belt you good,'

he told his son as the woman counted the notes twice before paying for the fuel. 'At home it's real bad now, eh?' he told Beagan. 'The wife got laid off from the fishplant. The two of us gotta work to make a go of it so we're going west.' The engine roared into life, spitting a thin slick of oil over the asphalt. 'Hey listen bud, don't stay around here too long. You know what they call a Cape Bretoner? A Newfie who ran out of money on the way to Toronto.'

The station wagon shuddered into gear and lurched on to the highway, its muffler scraping the pavement with a shower of sparks. The attendant pocketed the dollars. 'Stupid Newfies.' His curse betrayed a touch of envy, as if he felt himself dislocated without ever having left home. He slunk off towards the office then turned to direct Beagan up the road. 'You could try talking to my granddad. His hearing's none too good but his memory's okay.'

The shack had once commanded an uninterrupted view of the water but the highway had cut it off from Bras d'Or. Its windows rattled with every passing truck. A dog on a chain barked as Beagan approached. The front door opened and a voice yelled, 'What day is it today?'

'Saturday,' replied Beagan.

'Can't hear you.'

'Today is Saturday.'

'Hallelujah,' declared the obese old man. 'Pension day.' His hearing may have ebbed away with the years but his eyes, which settled on Beagan, gleamed like quicksilver. 'I knows ya,' he hollered. 'I knows your father.' It seemed unlikely. Neither Beagan nor his father had ever been to the east coast. 'I never forget a face and you and your father looked as alike as two cod in a salt bucket.' He leaned his head to one side, eased a fat finger into a bushy ear and talked as if to himself. 'I remember the day Jamie left. He done good in Toronto, your dad.' His chins wobbled as he raised his voice. 'Yes sir, he done good. Now where's me cap?'

'James was my grandfather,' clarified Beagan. He had often been told that the Gilleans had a strong family resemblance.

'I would have gone with your dad but I had Mother to look after.' He found his cap in the electric cooker. It was a gift from relatives and he had left it on the porch to rust. He preferred his old cast-iron stove.

'My grandfather,' repeated Beagan a little louder. Another truck roared past, all but shaking him off the doorstep.

'You looks good for your age, I'll say that. Must be the easy city life. What you doing back here anyways?'

'I've been looking for Promise,' sighed Beagan, glancing around as if he'd overlooked the village.

'Well you found it,' he chuckled and turned back indoors. His heavy tread was like a bear's lumber. He looked as if he'd be happier walking on all fours. As an afterthought he added, 'Come on in while I get my stick.'

Inside, the walls had been painted canary yellow. The worn checkerboard linoleum recorded the years of passage: table to sink, door to armchair. A porcupine-quill box was stuffed with screws, nails and curled photographs of a young woman. Above the television, with its aerial fashioned from a lobster pot, hung an engraving of fishing boats at Portree. A family Bible rested on the sideboard.

'I'm a Macleod of Skye,' said the old man as if he and his kind had been away from Scotland for only a few years. 'My people came out in 1791. It's them that knewed your granddad.'

'My great-grandfather,' corrected Beagan. The old man's distorted sense of time irritated him. 'I can't find much evidence of him.'

'Nothing left of him or nobody else.' Macleod poured coffee thick as molasses into chipped mugs. Beagan refused the offering. 'My people were the first on this stretch of coast so they settled the best land. The latecomers who came after us had to make do with the lots behind, in them highland places you know. Nothing grows up there so they were the first to move on. Then when the shipyard closed and the town's future hung on a fish-hook everybody started to go, eh? Young folks got lazy. They let the land get growed over and the nets rot.' A transport roared past the cracked window, 'Love that Crunch!' printed on its side. His voice rose in anger. 'When I was a boy I was brought up on porridge and the Bible. Now all I see is corn flakes and Nintendo games. Everyone's gone,' Macleod cried above the scream of an Irving Petroleum tanker. 'They even moved the old church to pave a road so folks could get out quicker. Ain't nothing left of Promise except me and the dead and we ain't going nowhere. No sir.'

Macleod found his stick and set off up a pine-needle path, stomped across the highway without a glance to left or right and sidled down the bank to the shore. Beagan scurried behind, darting between two logging trucks. The old man untied the painter and slipped a rowing boat out of its hiding place in a culvert. Beagan hesitated on the shore. He had forgotten his Kwells.

'Don't just stand there, help me push.' Macleod took the oars as Beagan launched the boat out into the bay. He turned the bow back towards the Clansman Motel and against a cacophony of thunderous lorries began to sing. 'Bet in the city you never heard the Gaelic. It was the language of Adam in the Garden. In your granddad's day it was Canada's third most common language. Now there's maybe eight hundred speakers left in the whole damn Maritimes, if you'll pardon my French.' The stroke of the oars left a trail of twisting whirlpools in the wake. 'Used to be that a man from this island was Scottish first and foremost. Second, he was Cape Bretoner. Third, he was a Nova Scotian. And fourth, if at all, he was Canuck.' A guillemot circled overhead and the cry of an air horn echoed across the bay. 'Don't know now what nobody is no more.'

I balanced on the bow behind the splendid fellow and looked back at the receding headland, the tartan cloak cast around my shoulders. Jamie wore a look of disappointment. 'I had hoped at least to see the old manse,' he sighed. 'I can't believe that there is nothing left.'

'Nothing physical,' I corrected sharply. The fate of Promise had distressed me too but doubt tended to strengthen my certainties. 'It is memory alone that endures. We saw that last night.'

'But I can't conjure it up like that,' Jamie complained. 'I haven't the knack.' He sighed too deeply for my liking. 'I would have just liked to touch the old walls.'

'Sentimentality does not become you, James,' I stated, then added with a hint of sarcasm, 'Is it yourself that hankers after your old body?'

'No. I was never particularly f-f-fond of it. There was that bandy limp and, of course, my stutter.'

'The finest thing in life, right enough, is growing older. The back goes, the hair falls out, the muscles sag and that's a disappointment but only a fleeting, physical concern. We die, yes, and that is sad for those left behind, yet the spirit lives on to glean the rich experience and wisdom of living.' I dismissed mortality with a wave. 'Promise is like a corpse, the discarded shell. But its spirit, its history, is alive.'

'Only as long as someone living bothers to remember it.'

'That is why he is here.' I gestured at my great-grandson. 'To grasp that which made him.' Beagan glanced uneasily towards the bow. I leaned close to Jamie and whispered as if Beagan and Macleod might overhear. 'But that apart I tell you this, he may be of our flesh and blood yet he is a person too fond of the fireside.' I sensed myself growing over-excited. 'In my time no man would be caught whistling on the Sabbath. Your mother used to peel Sunday's potatoes on a Saturday night. But in the name of Providence this Beagan contemplates fornication out of wedlock and reads newspapers on the Lord's Day.'

Jamie leaned back against the gunwale and put his hands behind his head. 'Tell me about Mother,' he coaxed. 'It was, what, the second summer when you met again?'

'That was a year of many blessings,' I relented. 'Within the space of twelve months I gained a wife, a home and a son.'

'Tell me,' encouraged Jamie.

'You will recollect my concern for personal hygiene.'

'Cleanliness is next to godliness,' he quoted. 'You were as careful as an Egyptian about your linen.'

'In those days I maintained the discipline of immersing myself every morning. I only succumbed to the bathtub when Bras d'Or froze over.' The recollection brought Jamie out in goose-bumps. He shivered and the boat rocked as if caught by a keen gust of crosswind. Beagan grabbed a lifejacket while Macleod cast a weather eye at the sky. 'It was my custom to swim far out into the bay before rising for air. But one day when I surfaced it wasn't the cold which took my breath away. A trading smack had gybed around the headland and heaved to in our cove. I heard familiar voices shout my name. They spoke the Gaelic and I fancied for a moment that I had traversed the whole Atlantic and swum back to the Hebrides.' I blinked the salt from my eyes. 'It was then that I recognised the *Good Intent*. Ewan Cameron had brought her to Promise for the timber. We had braw woods, right enough.'

'And Mother?'

'Kirstie was with him, yes. It was fine to see her gentle face.' Jamie waited for me to share my affections but none were forthcoming, it simply wasn't part of my vocabulary. Instead I said plainly, 'I can recollect her bridal dress, a grey material with deep blue stripes. The stricter members of the wedding party had thought it rather too gay. I myself found it to be very handsome.'

'There's a piece of it in the trunk,' said Jamie, nodding towards Beagan. 'At least I remember Mother putting one there.'

'Would you know that it rained that whole year from the day we were wed to the night Zachary was born?' I glanced up at a bank of snowclouds rolling in from the Atlantic. 'I caught the drips of rain leaking through the roof in pots splashed across the cabin floor as she wept in her labour. And mark you this, that sweet water doubled our blessings. No one had expected such a bountiful harvest, not from the earth nor from a woman of your mother's age, and the congregation, enriched in soul and substance, bestirred themselves to erect us a manse.' My grip tightened on the Bible. 'To this day I have never yet seen a finer building and sure I am that I never will.'

Jamie remembered the plain, simple house; its kitchen with a black cast-iron stove, the bedroom where he and his brother had been born, the study with the few precious books shipped from Scotland. The globe had been set in pride of place on my writing table. The box trunk had been arranged underneath it as a footrest. Apart from a few letters from home the trunk was all but empty; I was a man who scattered words like seed, it was Jamie who would come to hoard them.

'Kirstie's father laboured too, organising the fishers then dressing, salting and shipping their catches in tierces to the West Indies,' I continued. 'The *Good Intent* traded our salmon and cod for cargoes of sugar, molasses and rum. Then when winter returned he stopped the men leaving for Sydney Mines by starting the shipbuilding. Aye, he constructed a workshop and moulding loft beside his salt store and fish shed. The cooper's yard was extended for a blacksmith. A forge with two fires was added. They felled timber to supply masts for Her Majesty's Navy – he had secured a profitable contract – and his first New World ship took shape on the shore.'

A delivery van down-geared to climb away from the coast highway and distracted me. 'They're g-r-r-eat!' was emblazoned along its length. I found it difficult to correlate the modern world's bold assertions with the sin of its lost belief.

'You can't get away from it, James; Ewan worked like the spring-tide. He had the three qualities necessary for success – judgement, industry and health – and it brought prosperity to Promise. Cabins began to be replaced by farmhouses. There was clapboard instead of squared logs. And

Red McNeil, well now, he built his wife a stone lodge with fretwork on the eaves. Not in Promise itself mind you but there across the bay.' I pointed forward beyond the Clansman Motel. 'Anne felt that stone lent a manorial air and told all comers that the pioneer days had passed. Here, she used to say, is genteel and civilised society. The best corner of the promised land, she called it.' I stroked my whiskers. 'Anne McNeil was a good soul, but as full of boasting as the egg is of meat.'

The rowing boat followed the direction of my finger. 'My responsibilities grew too. The kind and zealous ministry they dubbed it. It was as many as five sermons that I preached on the Sabbath, canoeing to the far reaches of the parish. And there were so few clergymen on the island that more and more people came from far afield to our church. They filled the pews, stood by the windows and crowded the gallery. At one point a hundred young adults and almost as many children, among them Zachary, waited to be baptised. I could not accommodate them all at the font and called for *am Baisteadh Mòr*, a great summer baptism.'

A storm-beaten dredger chugged past and in its swell, in the reflection of Beagan on the water, I saw fleets of small boats converge on the bay. The McLeods rowed their children across West Bay. Barra men coasted down from Iona. Lewis families sailed around Cape Dauphin. The McNabs tacked over from the Loch Lomond shore. 'We gathered together on the beach, plunged ourselves into the glimmering brine and praised God, calling for repentance, for a break with the sinful past. We washed ourselves clean in the name of the Father, the Son and the Holy Spirit.'

'And I was christened then with Zachary?' asked Jamie.

'You, *a bhalaich*, were baptised one bitterly cold February. I performed the sacrament with you in my arms. "I will give unto him who has thirst the fountain of the water of life." I reached into the font and touched cold ice. The holy water had frozen solid so I struck the surface.'

'As I recall your arm was always strong to smite.'

'Forget you not James, the devil does not beguile the disciplined,' I answered. 'The ice shattered into splinters but each shard was bone dry. There was not one drop of liquid between them. So I turned from the font and led the congregation out into the weather, down the winding path to the edge of the bay. There I knelt down, dipped my hand into the sea and anointed your brow.' I reached over the side of the boat. 'With this living water, my boy.'

As if by intuition Beagan's gaze dropped from the horizon and alighted at that moment on the ripple. It was for all appearances a splash from the boat's wake or the cold flop of a hungry fish, and not the touch of the hand of an angel that it seemed to be in his imagination.

THE TOWN WHICH had grown around the McNeil house clung to the end of a point like a clinch of limpets. Keith and Elie's Jingle Restaurant was up for sale. At the Caledonia Co-op a lone couple hovered by the meat counter comparing prices of individual chicken breasts. The United Church appeared to be as forgotten as its faded sign: 'Fight Truth decay, brush up on your Bible.' Broken beer bottles lay splintered on the overgrown playground and yellowed posters pleaded 'Save Our School' from grimy classroom windows. In the post office, where Macleod cashed his pension cheque, an unhappy freckle-faced boy swam in a vast hand-me-down baseball uniform. 'If it's too large you can change it with MacCodrum. Or is it MacCrimmon?' His mother hesitated. 'Who's the first baseman?'

The resident minister bought a lottery ticket and refused to be drawn into criticism of a lapsed parishioner. 'I don't speak disrespectfully of any people. She's a dear soul, drive anyone crazy.' He reminded Beagan more of a jovial game-show host than a God-fearing clergyman. When the postmistress added her voice to the litany he blathered more vapid pleasantries. 'I never heard a woman turn down the opportunity to speak. Especially you Aberdeen girls. You're good at it.'

'Where's that no good son of yours?' Macleod yelled at him. 'Gone to the city?'

'I am the son, Mr Macleod,' the minister replied. 'It's my father whom you knew.' He then noticed Beagan. 'And who is this young feller?'

'He turned up on my doorstep looking for Promise, if you can beat that,' answered Macleod. Beagan introduced himself. He hadn't felt seasick in the rowing boat, possibly because of the company, and wished he were back on the water.

'We don't know how the Lord works but His ways are wonderful.' The minister's laugh was like a fox's bark. 'That's why you're here today.'

'What did he say?' shouted the old man while stocking up on Crunchie bars and Maxwell House.

'That there's a parish concert this lunchtime,' Beagan bawled back.

'Cape Breton is an island of fiddlers,' the minister declared as he led them up the damp empty street. 'The music lifts people's spirits, stops them thinking about unemployment for a time. Did you know that the singing and step-dancing which live on here disappeared from Scotland with the Clearances?'

Beagan found it hard to believe that any performers lived on lonely Cape Breton but there were fiddlers aplenty in the steamy Parish Memorial Centre. The islanders had emerged from behind the closed doors of their scattered farms and gathered together for the Kinettes' concert. They swept in from the wet, stamped the cold out of their boots and shook themselves dry. Daughters swirled their tartan plaids and mothers wore high-necked blouses. The pizzeria owner practised a medley on the piano. At the bar the old men were speaking Gaelic. The minister gossiped with great good humour, paused to inspect the Bake Sale and bought a ticket for the quilt raffle. A handbell rang as he made for the stage. Fiddles and guitars were tuned. Grandparents took their seats between their great-nieces and -nephews. A slender boy with a ponytail darted into the dressing room to wish luck to his parents. The minister's welcome was short and familiar. Entertainers and spectators alike all lived within a dozen miles of each other. Beagan spotted no waterlogged day-trippers who had wandered in off the Ceilidh Trail.

'And to start us off here's young Carrie Macaulay, Libby's daughter, to sing "Sleep Sleep Bonnie Baby".' A voice whispered from the wings. The onlookers chuckled. The minister barked, 'Oh bless my soul, wrong again.' Life and his own jokes amused him equally. 'To sing *Mo rùn Geal, Dileas.*'

Thirteen-year-old Carrie stood off the stage's centre. The spotlight had fused but no one missed its illumination. Her gentle Gaelic air hushed the audience, its sad music washing away their chatter. Her mother's Polaroid flashed and cranked out a picture. There followed a dozen costumed performers with laments about emigration, ballads of mist-covered mountains and shanties for fishermen's fathers and fishermen's sons. All the songs were about Scotland and the pain of diaspora, providing solace in a place that had been economically depressed for generations. Everyone knew the words and joined in for each chorus.

> These are my mountains and this is my glen,
> The braes of my childhood will call me again.
> No lands ever claimed me though far did I roam,
> For these are my mountains and I'm going home.

As they shuffled on stage a troupe of seven MacAskills, shy and soft-spoken, seemed unlikely dancers until the music lightened their feet. The driving rhythm of the step-dance was in the fiddler's bow, in the piano player's right hand, in their lively footwork. A spinster schoolmistress sitting alone at the back of the hall, her torso rigid and face devoid of expression, tapped out the steps on the worn plywood floor beneath her chair. The quiet man beside Beagan introduced himself as a McKinlay. He had grown up away from the island and didn't know his great-grandfather's Christian name. 'But I always knew the day would come when I'd come back to Cape Breton,' he confessed. His tie was stuffed in his suit pocket. 'I love the hills and sea, to hear the Gaelic; it's like falling in love. How do you explain falling in love with a girl?' Beagan asked how long he had been back. 'Oh no, I still live in Ottawa,' he explained. 'I've got a good job with the government and I'm married, eh?'

The audience raised their styrofoam coffee cups and cheered as two sisters from Margaree Harbour sang 'Mairi's Wedding'. Beagan fancied, incorrectly, that the song might have been heard at Hector's wedding.

> Plenty herring plenty meal
> Plenty peat to fill her creel
> Plenty bonnie bairns as well
> That's the toast to Mairi.

'Watch your shins!' shouted the schoolmistress as she took to her feet, and Beagan realised that he had never before seen people so enjoy dancing.

Only Macleod remained silent. Once he cast a cynical look towards the stage then tried to polish away half a century's dirt from a yellowed fingernail. He seemed oblivious to the joy around the hall and grumbled to himself. At the end of the concert the minister took the stage, asked the flushed congregation to bow their heads and thanked God for making them stewards of this land.

Outside it had begun to snow. A spring flurry laid powdery flakes on the islanders' hair and coats. As they crossed the parking lot and climbed down to the water Macleod complained, 'What a waste of a morning.'

Beagan, cheered by the strathspeys and reels, pointed out that there had been a good crowd at the concert. 'And the minister said that most of them listen to the daily Ceilidh radio hour on CJFX.'

'Them that are left. All the others are in Ontario. Every summer they load up their big cars and drive up here for the Homecoming

Crab and Corn Boil on Belle Côte beach. They spend an evening at the Glenora distillery then drive away for another year.' He dropped on to the seat and his weight sent waves rolling down the beach.

'But they remember. They come home.'

'They do hell. The old folks die off and the young get educated until they know enough to leave.' Macleod swore as he took the oars. 'I should never have stayed home with my mother.' Beagan waited to step aboard. 'Come on,' shouted the old man. 'Come on and I'll show you something you won't forget.'

They rowed back across the bay towards the roar of traffic and beached the boat further up the coast. Macleod led the way through the bush, trudged along an overgrown path and emerged on to a small escarpment. 'They're mostly drownings,' he said. 'Drownings and women who died in labour.'

Two dozen gravestones, worn by weather and stained by the years, were hemmed in by the encroaching thicket. Beagan swept away the snow to reveal an elaborate carving of two entwined hands and a chiselled 'Memory'. Beneath the powder blanket the stone of Katie McNeil, 'the beloved wife of Donald Macdonald of Skye', told the living not to weep. 'She is not dead but sleepeth.' Meg Morrison was buried beside her only child. 'Born at Uist, North Britain,' the mason had recorded in stone. 'Life how short eternity how long.' Beagan brushed down the plain marker of a Hamish MacFie of Mull. 'Gone to a better place,' he uncovered. Annie Rankin of Loch Linnhe lay beneath the words, 'Three times a wife but never a mother.'

'Is your mother here?' asked Beagan.

Macleod shook his head. He had nursed her through thirty years of old age. 'My brother took her away to a hospital in Toronto. Said she would be more comfortable. She went and died anyway. So he buried her there.' Beneath his quicksilver eyes, in the folds of heavy skin, dwelt the sadness of the bereaved. 'This place were never no Canaan,' he sighed, 'but it was home. I'll wait for you by the boat.'

'I'll come with you.'

Macleod pointed to a corner of the cemetery. 'That's where they laid your granddad.'

Beagan stopped in his tracks. 'My great-grandfather?'

The old man groaned and heaved himself towards a single grave standing apart from the rest.

Beagan smoothed the snow off the inscription. 'Who's this?' he asked. The name carved on the stone was James MacGillvery.

'How many times do I have to tell you? It's your granddad.'

'My great-grandfather was Hector Gillean. He was the first minister here.'

'Gillean? I thought you said MacGillvery.' Macleod leaned forward and studied Beagan's face. 'You sure look like a MacGillvery.'

'My name is Gillean,' Beagan assured him.

The old man knotted his brow and reached back through the years. 'That was before my time.' He searched his memory and scratched his head. 'I never knew him,' he said then walked away.

Beagan slumped down on a tomb and wished for a drink. The island seemed to have been severed from its past, like the dead from the living, and the trauma of the split had left behind only bitterness, incuriosity and prettified theme parks. The Kinettes concert had been the single exception. In the box trunk there lay reams and reams of records, but as for finding any physical remains of his family's history in Nova Scotia, too many years had passed. He saw that only his memory, the fine, vital thread stretching back through time, could hold and embrace his heritage of the Word.

Beagan shoved his hands into his pockets and found the Improved Metallic Memorandum. He sighed, stood to leave, and then his eyes fell on the old stone. It read 'The Reverend Hector Gillean.' The marker hadn't aged well. A grey blemish ran down over the carved hand, with index finger pointing heavenward, and into the inscription 'Yonder is my home.' Beagan touched the stone, felt the chill of a sea breeze and shivered. He toyed with his great-grandfather's diary and for a moment it seemed that he might read a sermon aloud. Instead he closed the book and whispered, 'Are you there?'

'Is it himself that expects me to rise up out of the earth like a spectre in a Hollywood movie?' I asked Jamie, who had never been as slow-witted as his grandson. 'Who else was he thinking it would be? Aye, it is me that's beside you,' I replied and Beagan heard my voice in his head. He stepped away in shock, stumbled over his big feet and landed flat on his back.

SLIGH' AN UISGE

—— ◆ ——

Waterways

CHAPTER IV

THICKER THAN INK

MOTHER'S TEARS SPILT down her powdered cheeks and dropped dusty clouds into the crystal waters of Bras d'Or. She sat rigid on the seat between Zachary and me, looking neither left nor right, not speaking, not even appearing to draw breath. All movement within her seemed to be suspended, as if her heartbeat had been clenched by the hand of grief. The skin on her face was taut and I felt the stiffness of her spine through the mourning crêpe. But when she released the gunwale to dab an eye, I saw her fingers tremble like winter herring trapped and dying in a fisherman's net.

The pall-bearers pulled on their oars and our cortège grieved across the empty bay, past the silent shipyard, to landfall beneath the headland. They hoisted the pale pine box on to their black flannel shoulders and staggered like a piebald spider through the twists of upturned roots which wreathed the shore. Mother did not take Grandfather Cameron's arm but stepped into the water and on to the beach. 'Has F-F-Father gone to heaven?' I whispered.

'He has gone home, Jamie,' she replied.

'He is dead,' stated Zachary.

She took us by the hand and followed the coffin up the steep, winding path to the graveyard in the wilderness. The bearers lowered it into the dark earth. A paper-white headstone lay on the tangled brushwood like a discarded book which had lost its cover.

Old McKinlay the Elder spoke without notes. He had

broken his reading spectacles. 'Though we are deprived now of his presence do not fail to remember the Word that our departed brother, husband and father has spoken but let it be a living influence in our hearts.'

My new shoes pinched my toes. I felt the bones in mother's hand as she squeezed my own. Fisher MacFie wiped his nose and picked up a spade. The first shovelful of soil landed with a hollow echo and I supposed that the casket was empty, that if I ran down to the village Father would be there making notes on the pier or standing at our doorway eating his bowl of porridge and gazing out over the water. I imagined that come evening the post would bring the month's copy of the *Island Reporter* or *Mac-Talla*. I saw the candles being lit, the neighbours gathered in and Father reading the newspaper aloud from the first to the last page. He would pause between each article to reach for his antiquated globe and point out the location of the towns and cities of our new Dominion. 'This is Muddy York, the place that they now call Toronto,' he might say, or trail his finger across the continent explaining, 'It is here that they are building the railroad.' But when Macfie's second shovel-load struck the coffin with a deadening thud I knew that I would never see him again.

Zachary held back his tears. I knew that it was not done for a boy to cry but I could not control my heart and sobbed like a baby girl. The mourners either whispered tender Gaelic sympathies to Mother or boomed in English that the sorrows of the Lord Himself exceed those of His creatures. Red MacNeil's daughters patted my shoulder and walked away down the slope back to their home.

After the funeral our dark house was full of Mother's silence. She hung her veil over the mirror so its reflection would not trap his spirit. We ate a little cold cod with *colcannon* for supper. As had been our custom we sat before the evening fire around Father's chair. I turned the globe around and around on its axis. The following morning we lay late in bed watching a beam of sunlight creep across the wall and over his bookshelf.

When my father had stood up in church and preached it was as if God Himself was speaking. To him the Scriptures were gospel, literal truths, not allegories. The Sabbath, the pulpit, the Bible, all were the pillars of civilisation, the pillars on which a better world would be built. He had brought this certainty to a doubting, disordered society. He, like many missionaries, had offered its dispossessed people continuity and reason by speaking plainly and clearly of good and evil, heaven and hell. Upon the settlers' changeable present he had fixed the regular pattern of religious ritual: early morning and evening prayers, grace before and after meals, a Sabbath devoted to church worship. His positive assertion of faith had restored their steady self-control. It had affirmed the belief that honest industry brought an abundant tomorrow. The Word focused the hearts and minds of the New World.

As a child I had thought my father to be like the Lord: tireless, all-seeing, immortal. But the relentless patriarch had not been infallible. New times had demanded new measures and new men. During the first half of the nineteenth century the population of North America had quadrupled. The industrial production of the old colonies had surpassed that of Great Britain. By 1867 the new continent had been spanned by thirty thousand miles of railroad, more track than had been laid in all the rest of the globe, and Canada had declared itself to be a nation. The confederation of the provinces had not been universally desired. In Halifax the occasion had been marked by the hanging of crêpe in store windows and the flying of black flags at half-staff. The New Brunswick government had fallen over the issue. Independent politicians in Newfoundland had warned voters that if the province joined the Dominion their homes would be sold off to pay taxes to Ottawa. But within twenty-five years the young nation had built the fourth-largest merchant marine to sail the seas. Man had triumphed over the obstacles of nature and by the end of the century millions of Europeans had turned their backs on the past and ventured west to embrace the present with a certain belief in the success of the future.

On the island windjammers were launched, coal was mined and timber cut. The steamer *Banshee* plied Bras d'Or, called at Boularderie and Wycocomagh, brought in imports and took away a more precious commodity. Cape Breton's greatest export came to be not her trees or minerals but her people. The exodus changed the community. Migrants pinned their hopes on tomorrow and neglected the duties of the present. The envy of those left behind festered into bitterness. My father had no sympathy with those who shirked responsibility. The selfishness of man could not be tolerated and he was not slow to reveal his feelings in unmistakable language. He continued to preach for evangelical obedience, chiding us for our sins, encouraging us to let the Word be a living influence in our hearts. But for many the ambition for earthly success came to exceed their faith in heavenly rewards. It would have been contrary to human nature to expect anything less in a promised land.

The changes brought him into conflict with members of his congregation. Some families withdrew from the church. Others fell into indifference. A few traders took to working on the Fast Day and after one wholesome reproof for sinful conduct Moody the publican began to cross to the other side of the street when meeting Father out walking. But those who strayed from the flock only increased his resolve. One disaffected parishioner came to church chewing Pictou twist tobacco. Another, who had been accused of taking money out of the collection plate, interrupted a sermon. Father banged the pulpit and raged, 'God hath put me here and the Devil will not put me out.'

He delivered over a hundred sermons between his last March and September. Each was charged with fire and wit.

He dismissed as poppycock Darwin's hypothesis that there was no Divine order, that God was irrelevant to Creation, that man was a talking ape. Man, he preached, was not at the service of his species, responsible only for its pro-creation, a novelty dangling on a limb of evolution. He was a noble work, created in God's own image, formed of the dust of the ground and given the breath of life by the Lord. He was a painter, a poet, a shipwright, a linguist, a maker of wonders for the greater glory of God Almighty. But many parishioners no longer listened. In the month before my father's death I asked him why he continued to lecture to the dwindling congregation. 'I used to think that I could change them, James,' he acknowledged. 'Now I keep preaching so that they won't change us.'

Father had been blessed with vigorous health. He took his physical well-being for granted. Then, almost overnight, it deserted him. He began to suffer from pain in his loins and a rise in body temperature. He passed blood and albumen in his urine. Doctor MacKay advised him to rest his kidneys but he paid little heed and went about his business. On a return trip from Sydney where he had bought a set of Communion Elements (for which he had given a dollar him-self and paid for the rest with thirty-two donated quarters) the mailgig was caught in a storm. The wet cold sapped his remaining strength. He took ill and had to stay at home. Headaches plagued him and his nights passed with aching torpor. Old age came as a deep tiredness which blurred his sight, sapped his concentration and rendered him incapable of writing.

As the maples shed their crimson coats it pained him to see the people gather at the church and not to be able to preach to them. He hated idleness. There was so much work that remained undone. One September Sabbath he ignored Mother's protestations and went to the congregation to read the Scriptures. Though not strong his voice remained good and clear but it was his vision which began to fail him. He found it difficult to focus on the text. Before his eyes the printed letters seemed to shiver then come unstuck and slip one by one out of line. He placed his hand beneath the words as if to hold them in place but still they peeled away and fell off the page in a jumble which landed at his feet, a meaningless chaos of symbols. He bent down to grasp them but the letters slipped through his fingers like water through a sieve and vanished in the gaps between the floorboards. He stood up and saw that no word remained on the page. The Bible had been rendered blank. Betraying nothing he completed the reading from memory, closed the Book and returned to the manse. There he excused himself from lunch and lay down for a rest.

Later that afternoon Father began to complain about the untidiness of his room. He seemed to see a great deal of dust and, worse still, mites.

'There Kirstie,' he said, pointing at the floor before his chair, 'tiny, tiny mites. Dear God, there are dozens of them.' Mother explained that he was seeing only a flake or two of dry paint and suggested that his eyes might be tired. The week before she and Red MacNeil's daughters had distempered the walls to bring a little cheer to his room. He dismissed her sympathy. 'Those are mites and they are moving. Was there ever paint that moved? Kirstie, we must stop them from spreading.' I had a flake in my hand and took it to him. 'See that now, how quickly they run. James, put it down,' he ordered then insisted to Mother, 'I am not seeing things.' He became stern when roused. 'You'll not like it when they reach the foot of your bed.'

'Look F-F-Father.' I placed the speck in his palm. 'It is only paint.'

He tried to squash it once then twice then let out a gasp. In his mind the dust, his mites, had become letters. Words untangled at his feet scattering ciphers about the room. The alphabet crawled across the carpet. Sentences unravelled behind the chair. A web of characters, almost a whole psalm, spun apart in furious rupture then crept away into crevices. Columns of symbols slid out of the Hebrew Bible and swarmed over Young's *Concordance* then ran away down the legs of the bookcase. Phrases wormed into cracks in the wall and a dozen vowels took flight. He cried for me to hurry for the broom and I rushed to sweep away the shapes from the floor.

'There,' he shouted, 'and over there.' Father brushed the script off his hands, from his trousers, away from mother's skirts as she held him to her breast. Zachary stared in silence and I beheld the terror in Father's eyes as all that had been order descended into chaos.

By evening, after the doctor had given him a draught to encourage sleep, he was calmer. The letters had risen in a swarm and become motes of light which hovered before him like a cloud of silver dust. Father stared into space and the doctor waved his arm across his line of sight.

'You've put your hand right through them,' he complained then added sternly, 'Wait you now, MacKay, it is not my imagination. I am not going mad.' He then revealed himself as he seldom did even to his most intimate friends. The letters had converged into a single, resplendent beacon. He asked the doctor to look above the door where their light had become the eye of the All-Seeing One. Only a faded engraving of a Scottish loch hung there but MacKay believed that the radiance was upon the minister. There was no longer fear in his eyes. My father spoke of the presence of God. He had no doubt that this was the fulfilment of the promise of His presence through the Dark Valley.

In all my life my father had touched me no more than a dozen times, half of which were hidings, yet in that last night lying on the horsehair mattress he took my hand and held it as if the force of his grip might anchor an ascendant spirit. 'God gave a promise to Noah so that the world might be started anew,' he told my brother and me. 'He gave His promise to Abraham, "Get thee out of thy country, and from thy kindred and from thy father's house unto a land that I will show thee."' His ink-stained finger left a smudge on my palm.

When we awoke the next morning his room was empty. In the night he had tossed aside the blankets and left the house. The bed was still warm and damp from his fever. Every corner of Promise was searched before Fisher MacFie noticed that his canoe was not on the shore. They found Father on the water later that day. His complaint had assumed the character of dropsy and sometime before dawn the hour of his departure had come. He had heard the voice that called him home.

In the old box trunk there is a photograph, a family portrait taken not long after Father's death. Mother sits before the camera wearing a solemn face and a worsted wool dress, its skirts ballooning beneath the Bible on her lap. Zachary stands at her side in the centre of the group, his hand posed on her shoulder and collar button snapped tight around his neck. His long thin features give him a puritanical look. He appears more concerned with the need to uphold rigid morals than to enjoy a little carefree fun. 'There's not a devil in Hell that'll pluck a pin-feather from you,' Grandfather Cameron had often told him.

I had been set on a stool to his left and told not to fidget. The face which looks out from the portrait is round, even chubby, and wears like book-ends the enormous ears which I had inherited from Mother. My cock-eyed collar, well, it had popped undone just before the flash of the photographer's powder, but I had managed to hide from the lens the gravy stain on my cuff.

Father had enriched our souls but not our purse. The few

dollars that he had saved had been loaned to the needy without record or receipt. In the days following the funeral many repaid his generosity with their honesty. Strangers knocked at our door and returned the loans to Mother. To help I busied myself with beanpoles and pea vines, tending to our rows of onions and cabbages. Still there was barely enough to see us rehoused, so at the age of fourteen years Zachary left Promise. His great wish had been to join the army and pursue a military career, but without the money to buy a commission he chose instead to become a teacher. He gave Mother a single goodbye kiss then shook her hand. He was frugal too with time; not an idle minute slipped through his net, and he quickly earned his matriculation certificate, the first vital step on the road to financial success. His first post was at the little red schoolhouse over Cape Breton's Skye mountains. Every Friday evening he walked home with a single silver dollar in his pocket.

'Facts,' he would instruct me while reading a borrowed copy of *Mac-Talla* by the coal-lamp, 'are what one needs to get by in this life. Facts dispel ignorance and darkness.' Zachary studied the reports on commodity prices while I whispered to myself the newspaper's Gaelic stories.

It was some fact which he read that convinced him that my future lay in mechanical engineering. He secured for me an apprenticeship two dozen miles away in Sydney, and at the ripe old age of thirteen I was sent to work for Hiram Whistle, Manufacturer of Steam Engines, Gas Machines and Compression Boilers. The devices that Whistle produced were noisy, noxious and temperamental. His 'Lark' Vertical Steam Engine puffed and wheezed and once spat a comet of flaming coals clear across the yard into the privy. It burst into flames and caused Mrs Whistle to have an attack of neuralgia. His 'Nightingale' Silent Gas Motor tended to overheat and shriek more like a tortured tern than a songbird. It later blew a six-foot hole through the iron hull of the only steamship ever built in the region. There was pleasure in crafting sheets of tin and casting iron pistons but within a year I was sick tired of the trade. The dirty dark workshop with singeing forge gave me a headache every day. The cheap metal tinged my hands with a gleaming silver sheen that could not be washed away.

I tried to explain my unhappiness to Mother but could never find the right words. It was my failing, not hers. I was unable to unlock my heart and let words speak the truth like Father. In the months after his death we had been forbidden to enter his study. Mother slipped in alone at night when she thought we were asleep. We heard the lock click open and the door sigh closed. The key was hidden in a brick behind the stove. One day when the house was empty I took the key, opened the door and stole inside. I stood in the half-light ringed round and round by the shelves of books. I took down a volume of sermons, ran my finger over the spines of pamphlets, breathed in dust and memory and felt a deep sense of contentment well up within me. The library surrounded me with his words.

But Mother came home early from a Presbyterian Society meeting and found me. I expected my disobedience to earn me a beating but instead she knelt down beside me, her black silk of mourning rustling with the movement, touched my hair and whispered, 'When I come here I feel that he is still with us. I feel him near.'

I searched for the right words, grappled to communicate the secrets of my heart, tried to speak with his clarity and eloquence, but my lips were drawn shut like window blinds on the Sabbath and I could only utter a crabbed babble of ugly sound and untruth. 'No. He's not here,' I lied. 'I don't f-f-feel him.' I too was frightened. I too missed him. And I never deranged the papers as Zachary later accused.

My dissatisfaction was not eased when the Dominion

government withdrew shipbuilding bounties to promote
the westward expansion of the nation. Canada wanted
silver rails not wooden boats. Whistle closed his workshop,
mounted a 'Lark' Vertical on a barge and steamed south to
Boston. The change of policy meant that even Grandfather
Cameron could offer me no employment. His yard too was
threatened with closure. I was of little use at home, helping
Mother to put up twenty quarts of beans only to be
rewarded with a length of Zachary's tongue for growing a
single, unprofitable sunflower. I felt myself to be an ideal
candidate for the cutty, the kirk stool reserved below the
pulpit for delinquents. My brother instructed me to join the
newly-formed Dominion Coal Company but I remembered
Father's guidance. 'Much has been given to you and much
will be expected of you,' he had said and every night I
prayed for his blessing.

In spring after planting the early potatoes I boarded the
Quebec Steamship Company's SS *Campana* at Pictou Harbour for passage up the Saint Lawrence River. I had never
before sailed in a real steamboat and she seemed to be a
very fine one. The snow had melted and the blossoms swirled
around the wharf in great pink clouds of petals. Beyond
Montreal the new province of Ontario stretched a thousand
miles from east to west with all the Great Lakes in between.
There were polar bears and tundra in its north, peaches and
industry in the south. I felt the draw of its rich, thriving
capital, Toronto.

I could not afford a berth but found a protected corner
on deck out of the wind. My father's globe was tucked under
my arm. Mother had reached into his study and out of her
grief to give it to me, though I cannot think why as Zachary
had the greater ambition and industry. Maybe she knew
that it made me feel close to him. As dusk fell the sky wore
a string of red rubies. Among my fellow passengers there
was a party of Scots who sang through the night. Their
enthusiasm did little to help my sleep but it didn't matter

for my hopes glowed like the luminous trail of embers flung
into the clear air from the steamer's funnel.

> We're sailing west, we're sailing west
> To prairie lands sunkissed and blest –
> The crofter's trail of happiness.

EVERYTHING IN CANADA moves from east to west: the sun,
waterways and postal codes, explorers, history and hopes. Beagan
would be no exception, provided he could get out of Pictou. He
sat on his trunk at the waterfront looking west, past the unemployed
youths playing volleyball, out towards the Gulf of Saint Lawrence
and sensed something of the vastness of the country. It brought to
his mind the story of an expanding English firm which established
its first overseas bureau in Vancouver. One day the head office
cabled the west coast with news of a prospective client in Nova
Scotia. 'Can you go and meet him?' asked London.

'You go,' replied Vancouver, 'you're nearer.'

There seemed to be no reason for Beagan to dawdle in Pictou.
He had been in town only a morning and its main attraction was
a svelte, underclad volleyball player. The shops along Water Street
seemed tired, their windows were empty. A Native woman
slumped in an alcoholic haze on the steps of the Highland Beverage
Room. The harbourside park petered out into a vacant lot of
rough stone and quarrelsome gulls. Apart from the Heritage Quay,
a fine museum which commemorated the province's first Highland settlers, the only vibrant part of the sleepy port seemed to
be Smiley's Video Shop. It was doing a lively trade in Nintendo
games as Macleod had forewarned.

The meeting at the grave had unsettled Beagan. It was difficult
enough to communicate with the living; one did not expect the
dead to strike up conversations too. The flood of readings, discoveries and fancies sloshed about his head like spring run-off in
a brimming lake. He wanted out of Nova Scotia and scanned the

harbour looking for a boat, any boat. His 'Doers and Dreamers' Official Guidebook could suggest no ferries, no freighters and certainly no passenger ships which might follow in the wake of the SS *Campana*. It seemed that none existed. Only a small catch of lobster skiffs and an erstwhile summer holiday cruiser moved on the water.

He stopped by the office of Scotty's Taxis to ask for advice. The sign above the door read 'We're not here to make a mint, we're here for the business.' The young, tam-o'-shantered owner had a Walkman wired to his ears. 'What do you know for sure?' he said in greeting.

'I beg your pardon?' replied Beagan, looking blank.

Expressions had changed in the last two decades. Scotty translated, 'I mean, like, what's happening, eh?' Beagan's answer caused him to snap off his earphones and fill the little room with the high-pitched hiss of Led Zeppelin. 'Say, you crazy or what?'

'I'm following the route that my grandfather took late last century,' Beagan explained, having decided that blunt confession was the only way to confront his distress. 'His name was Jamie Gillean and he travelled by water so that's the way I'm going too.'

'All the way to Vancouver?'

'Eventually, yes. But Toronto will do for now.'

The tam-o'-shanter shook in disbelief. 'Get out of town.'

'I'm trying to but there don't seem to be any boats.'

'The only way is by road, eh? You want a cab?' When Beagan's spirits slumped Scotty added, 'Looks like you need a drink.' It struck him as a fine idea. 'Come have a swish and we'll talk her over.' Beagan hadn't noticed the matching pairs of half-barrel flowertubs in every front garden. 'Hey, you never heard tell of swish before?' Scotty exclaimed and invited him into the backroom.

Alcohol in Canada is heavily taxed; a bottle of spirits can cost more than twice its American price, so enterprising Maritimers took to buying the empty fifty-gallon oak casks which had been used to import liquor.

'We put into 'em ten gallons of water, five of sugar, then seal 'em up and swish 'em – turn 'em – every day for a month,' explained Scotty while drawing two paper cups of amber liquid from an unsevered barrel. 'Like, spirits are shipped at 100 proof so the wood is real saturated with Bacardi, Johnny Walker, Hennessy, whatever. What we get out after four weeks' swishing is a mean 40 proof. Go figure!' He laughed and raised his cup. 'And not only can you do each barrel twice, but then you cut her in half and give it to a girlfriend to plant flowers. Makes a nice birthday present.' Beagan tasted the smoky peat of a fine malt. 'Trouble came when everybody started doing it and stopped buying their drink at the liquor store. The government don't like losing the revenue so they went and put a tax on empty barrels, if you can believe it. Stopped the whole thing dead.' Scotty removed the tattered cap as a mark of respect and patted his cask, 'This here's the last swish barrel in Pictou County.'

Egg-white meringues of cloud, their bases flat as if dropped on to a great glass baking sheet in the sky, stretched away to the west. A seagull scuttled up Water Street in a sideways crab-like run. Beagan might not have found a route out of town but as he wove back to the pier it seemed to be a less urgent concern. He slumped down on his trunk and into the whisky's numbing warmth. He smiled in the general direction of the svelte volleyball player before noticing the frothing white bow wave of an approaching boat. He rubbed his eyes. 'The third glass is always the killer,' he thought, looked again then tumbled off the edge of the pier.

'F-F-Father, what on earth are you doing?' cried Jamie.

The Reverend Hector set down the end of the trunk. 'That boy is intoxicated. Again,' Beagan heard as he fell, fancying that Hector had tipped him off his seat and into the harbour. 'This behaviour will make the very stones shed tears,' the Reverend added as his great-grandson flailed his arms and spouted water like a manic fountain.

'It looks to me more like he's drowning. And anyway, Beagan only really took to drink again after your melo-dramatic visitation at the burial ground,' accused Jamie. 'Your conduct there was, if you'll f-f-forgive me, quite unnecessary.'

'The boy called for me. It would have been faint-hearted not to reply.' A lick of water splashed Hector's shoes. A gurgling cry reached their ears.

'He hasn't had a wink of sleep since leaving Promise. All night he sits up in bed expecting to see your face appear before him.' In response to the shouts Jamie kicked a life ring off the pier. 'To my mind it would have been more prudent to wait.'

'There's many a slip between ship and quay, James. Mark my words.'

Scotty and the volleyball players bolted down the pier, 'Stairway to Heaven' hissing in their wake. Scotty dropped a line to haul Beagan and the ring on to dry land. The others, seeing him soaked but safe, watched his mirage transform into an approaching thirty-five-foot Bayliner motor yacht. The streamlined bow and moulded decks gave the ship the look of a silver submarine. Her bridge bristled with antennae and aerials, the horn sounded and somewhere a small dog barked.

The splendid craft throttled back and swung broadside to the Pictou gas bar. On her stern beneath a fluttering maple leaf was her name: *Szerencsès*. Two stocky boys wearing baggy shorts and 'Save the Whales' T-shirts appeared on deck holding the rope like a coiled snake. They cast it out suddenly as if the serpent had hissed and licked their fingertips with a cool forked tongue. The volleyball players ran to catch the painter but it fell short into the water. 'Jeez, how stupid,' said the elder boy. 'Mum, it was Randy's fault.'

'Try again and this time concentrate,' advised a gentle voice from the bridge. The twin Volvo Penta diesels reversed to avoid hitting the breakwater.

As the two boys began to retrieve the rope a terrified, auburn-haired hamster darted between their legs. It was followed by a yapping, shaggy mongrel. 'Oh man, Tufty's going to eat him alive,' wailed Randy. The boys dropped the line to chase their pets. As the Bayliner drifted astern they yelped and shouted over the foredeck and around a hatchway. 'If your dog eats Sniffy you're dead meat.' But the hamster had no intention of being anyone's supper. He vanished down a small porthole. Tufty tried to follow but became stuck halfway. His muffled bark echoed out of the air vents. During the commotion a young woman descended from the bridge and coiled the rope. Her throw was so accurate that Beagan had only to bend to pick it up from the damp pool at his feet.

'Fill her up, please.'

As the boys set upon a plate of baloney sandwiches a small crowd gathered to admire *Szerencsès*. 'It means "lucky" in Hungarian,' explained the woman. Her accent was as mellow as eight-year-old Tokaj.

'You can say that again,' observed Scotty.

'She's not that big,' she said with genuine modesty, then added, 'But she is ours.' The young family seemed to be unlikely owners of an expensive yacht. They gave themselves no airs. The boys were even prevented from buying doughnuts from the nearby Tim Horton's as they hadn't earned the treat.

As Beagan looked around the pier for a place to change into dry clothes they offered him the spare cabin. It wasn't hard to engage them in conversation. 'We're going to see the belugas,' enthused Joel, the elder brother.

'The boys are crazy about whales,' confirmed Piri, their mother, while doling out another round of sandwiches. She wore a maple leaf badge on her cardigan. 'I wanted them to see the Saguenay breeding ground before it was too late.' Her movements were fluid and considered. When Beagan explained a little of his plans her invitation was spontaneous and sincere. 'I don't know much about the Pacific but you can come along as far as Lake Ontario.' Her features seemed to be softened by kindness. 'I could do with another pair of eyes on the bridge.'

'I'd be pleased to help,' he replied.

His smile faltered when she added, 'My husband had to fly back to Toronto this morning. Hey, you don't speak French, do you?'

'Some.'

'In Hungary when I grew up French was considered to be a capitalist language. It wasn't taught at school. As a result on the way downriver I nearly ran into a Haitian freighter.' She looked up the pier towards Beagan's bulging trunk. 'You can have the third bedroom, but I don't know where we'll put your luggage.'

'She is a beautiful boat,' confessed Beagan.

'We won it,' said Joel.

No Canadian could ever resist a lottery. The federal, provincial and local governments all operated dozens of games – Wintario, Lotto 6/49, *Le Millionaire*, Scratch 'n Win – and most people almost always had a ticket for an impending draw. It had been suggested that the dream of winning had come to compensate for disappointment in the promised land. That didn't seem to be the case for Piri.

Szerencsès cleared Pictou Harbour and sprinted across the Northumberland Strait. In the picture-window bridge Sniffy the hamster dozed beside the throttle while Piri steered north-west across the waves. 'Before I came to Canada I never thought I'd even learn to drive a car.' Her lips curved into a gentle smile. 'So this is a real thrill.'

'I can imagine,' replied Beagan. He had taken a hot shower, changed and stuffed his wet clothes into the onboard washer-dryer. 'It would have been for my grandfather too. He followed this same heading aboard a steamboat called the *Campana*, though not at quite this speed.' A spume of spray slapped over the deck. Piri switched on the three all-weather windscreen wipers. 'I think he'd only ever been out in a canoe before.'

'When was this?'

'In the late 1870s.'

'Gosh, a long time ago.'

'He was a tireless correspondent. After he left home he wrote a letter to his mother every week for over thirty years. That's what's in the trunk,' Beagan said, gesturing below-decks.

'Wow,' enthused Piri. 'And you've still got them.'

Beagan had begun to feel at ease, though not because of the swish. In Piri he sensed a need to share both family and the experience of emigration. 'It's almost like having him – and his father – travelling with me.'

'That's neat.'

'In one of the letters Jamie – that's my grandfather – mentions a pod of small white whales that encircled his ship and entertained the ladies until someone onboard opened fire with a shotgun. The sportsman, as Jamie called him, killed two before the others vanished beneath the surface. It upset him.'

'It would me too,' she shivered. 'The Gulf must have changed a lot since then.'

'Yes. For a start there weren't ten thousand ships passing through it every season. The great auks would have been gone by then. The last colony had been bludgeoned into extinction about the time Jamie's father arrived from Scotland. But he would have seen the last big herds of walrus. And some Eskimo curlews.'

'Like the boys and me seeing the last of the belugas?'

'Maybe the end of another species,' replied Beagan and caught his reflection in the windscreen.

The Nova Scotian shore was ironbound with moist green sweeps of fertile farmland descending to a silver estuary and tidal mudbanks. *Szerencsès* sliced through the top of the waves and cast great swirling billows in her wake. Piri's confident control and the electronic stabilisers ensured a smooth, comfortable ride. 'She's quite something to have won,' admired Beagan.

'And it's not the best thing that's happened to me.' Piri's eyes seemed to glow with excitement. 'My luckiest day was Monday 18 August 1975.' The exactness touched Beagan and he laughed. 'That was the day when I met a wonderful man, a photography student from Toronto.'

'When you were in Hungary?'

Piri nodded. 'It was the last morning of his holiday and he stopped at the restaurant where I worked as a waitress. He ordered seven cups of coffee just so he could speak to me. Later I learnt that he hates coffee. We wrote each other too, every day for twelve months, then he came back and asked me to marry him.'

As the Maritimes dropped away below the horizon a little of

Beagan's despair went with it. Piri's trusting nature and confidence strengthened his sense of well-being. 'You know I admire your grandfather, leaving home like that,' she said. 'Of all my siblings I was the homebody. We lived in a tiny village. The only time that I travelled to Budapest I got train-sick.'

'Jamie wrote that he felt queasy aboard the *Campana*.'

'Our family was very close, very loving. It had never occurred to me to live anywhere else. But there I was one week after the wedding hugging and crying and asking my parents to forgive me for leaving them. It was the hardest thing I ever had to do.'

'Did you know much about Canada?' Beagan asked.

'I knew that it was far away and very cold, that there were big houses for everyone and big cars. I knew that the people spoke English and French and wondered how the heck I was going to communicate with them. I didn't speak English either back then.' The radio crackled and Piri reported their position to the Coast Guard. 'I'd never been in an airplane before, a bit like your grandfather in the steamboat, so Peter held my hand through the whole flight. He didn't let go once. You see I was only eighteen years old at the time and filled with a lot of insecurity. I worried that his parents wouldn't like me, that I'd never see my family again. But then I remembered the belugas. We'd done a school project on whales and I thought that they were so beautiful. I realised that belugas bred in the Saint Lawrence and asked Peter if one day we might be able to see them. He promised me that we would.

'Although the flight hadn't upset my stomach the drive to his parent's apartment made me really nauseous. I wasn't used to such big cars, or any car for that matter, and going up in the elevator I started to feel sicker and sicker. Peter's parents welcomed us with a wonderful dinner of chicken soup, cabbage rolls, the works. They'd even baked a "Welcome Home" cake. I tried to eat, I didn't want to insult my mother-in-law, only after two spoonfuls I had to run to the bathroom to throw up. "Holy cow," I thought, "I really blew it this time." I hadn't of course. They saw how much Peter and I loved each other and made me feel at home.

'We rented an apartment in the building opposite. We didn't even need a moving truck, just walked across the street with all our stuff. I couldn't believe it; I'd been in Canada only three weeks and already had a place of my own. I thought, "What a great country." But you know it was kind of scary too. In our building lived more people than in the whole village back home and Peter had to leave me with them to go to work.' Piri eased back on the throttle as a surge of cross-waves reared their angry heads. 'He gave up his photography and got a job in Mississauga at the Bay, you know, the department store?'

'It used to be called the Hudson's Bay Company,' explained Beagan. 'It's the oldest company in Canada.'

'Older than Woolco?' asked Piri. Beagan nodded. 'I ask because my mother-in-law helped me apply for work there. They invited me in for an interview and I wasn't sure if I could handle it. What should I say? How should I respond if they asked when I wanted to start? Peter taught me to say, "As soon as possible." I rehearsed the line in the bath, on the bus, over and over again. In her office the manager, Mrs Singh, asked me a few questions, seemed satisfied then really said, "When can you start?"

'"As soon as possible." I said it without a mistake.

'"Be here tomorrow morning at eight o'clock," she replied. I nearly fell off my chair.

'I started as a sales clerk at the fast food counter; you know, candies, burgers, milkshakes, that sort of thing. At the store opening I was so scared that I thought my legs were going to give out on me. My workmates encouraged me to serve the first customer. "Go ahead. You'll be fine," they said.

'"I'm sorry, this is my first day," I told the man, "and I don't speak English very well." I didn't know the name of anything but he kept on pointing and pointing until I got it right. He was very patient. Other customers weren't so nice. They made fun of my accent and I had to sneak away a few times to cry in the toilet but I got by. Six months later I was chatting with a customer who wanted some chocolates.

'"Your English is very good now," he said. I hadn't recognised him. "Don't you remember me? I was your first customer." I was so happy. It made me realise that I was starting to have a history in Canada.'

The lines of cliff and pine wrapped themselves in the ultramarine veil of dusk. Sea and sky entwined into a weave of single hue and the stars came out like diamonds across a black velvet heaven. *Szerencsès* dropped anchor below Rocher Percé, the pierced rock behind which explorers' caravels and emigrant tubs had once weathered the Gulf's storms.

'Do you like whales too?' asked Randy while leading Beagan on a tour below-decks. There was a beechwood cocktail bar and ice machine, three cabins and a hot tub. The yacht's custom-built interior had been fitted out by Finnish chandlers. The cutlery was David Mellor, the china came from Delft and the video had a Dolby Pro-Logic Surround Sound System manufactured by Sony.

Beagan noticed the photographs of fin-backs and great blues hanging around the galley. 'Did your mother take these?'

'Joel did.' He showed off the underwater camera outfit. 'We think whales are the greatest.'

Piri cooked a spicy Hungarian *gulyás* for supper. The side dish was a cool cucumber salad. For dessert she served a honeyed *strudel* of cherries and raisins wrapped in translucent pastry. 'I'm sorry that I bored you with my story,' she apologised as they loaded the dishwasher. 'It was real dumb.'

'You didn't bore me,' insisted Beagan. The boys had settled down to watch a Jacques Cousteau video. 'I'm interested why people leave home and what they find in their new country. You know, the search for a promised land? I feel very bitter towards Canada; it's wasted too many opportunities and broken too many hearts.'

'It didn't break my heart. No way.'

'I see that,' he acknowledged.

Piri stacked away the last of the plates then pulled a small bottle from the cupboard. 'I've a soft spot for apricot brandy,' she confessed. 'Would you like a glass?'

They folded themselves around the galley table. 'A few months later I was transferred to the stationery department. It was a big challenge and the supervisor gave me a huge order book.' Piri hesitated, 'Are you sure you're interested in this?'

Beagan nodded. 'My grandfather once published a journal for the stationery trade.'

'Really? Well, maybe my supervisor should have read it. She talked fast and I was too embarrassed to tell her that I didn't understand. So of course after a few weeks of people buying pens and paper clips and whatever I ran out of stock. The supervisor was really upset and told the store manager that I didn't want to learn. I was totally humiliated. I thought that he would fire me there and then. "There is no stock," he said, turning on the supervisor, "because you didn't teach Piri properly." He made her explain it all over again and from then on I worked really hard. I couldn't let the manager down and everything was soon under control. In fact at the end of my first year some visiting big shots told me that I had the best-organised department of all the Woolco stores in Canada.' Piri blushed. 'Not to brag or anything, but I felt such a sense of accomplishment. I can't really put it into words. I was no longer some Hungarian girl who hardly spoke English but the Canadian who put together a great stationery department.' She beamed with pride. 'I even started to beat Peter at Scrabble.'

'How long did you stay at the store?' asked Beagan, reaching for the brandy. The sudden, loud slap of a wave against the hull made him jump.

Piri put a hand over her glass. 'Not for me, thanks. Five years, hardships and all, and Peter kept his promise, driving us up to the Saguenay every summer to see the whales. At first it made me a little sad, the belugas reminded me of leaving my family, but with the birth of the boys my life really did come to be here. That's why it's important for them to see them. It's funny, when I visit Hungary now I feel that I'm going home, but when I fly back to Canada I am home again.'

'I lived in Scotland all last year on an island that I'd never seen before, eating oatmeal for breakfast, walking in the rain along the seashore, and I felt like I was a part of it. And it was part of me. But here, in the country where I was born, well I can't say that this is home,' Beagan sighed, 'but it is.' He pushed the glass away from him and added, 'Tell me about your other good fortune?'

'Do you mean the lottery?' she asked. 'People say that winning a lottery changes your life, and I guess it does but I was kind of used to change. I was so lucky to meet Peter, to move to this beautiful country, to be blessed with the boys. The money was like icing on the cake. Peter could give up his job at the Bay and take up photography again. We could treat the boys to real special holidays. I could help my parents. People think that there's a science to it. When we won one reporter asked me what system I used. I told him that all I had done was choose the right ticket. It's only a question of luck.'

The next morning *Szerencsès* cut across to the north shore and made for the mouth of the Saguenay, last breeding ground of the beluga whale. A kittiwake veered across the bow then swooped up a cliff chasing its shadow. The valleys and peaks of the Charlevoix, moulded by millennia of rain and wind, had the look of sleeping giants. Their hips and shoulders wore crests of caribou moss. Over their waists and between their toes rushed clear blue streams. For thousands of years they had watched the beluga migrate down the icy Labrador Current to feed, mate and calve between their outstretched arms. Then in the last century the giants had felt their rivers being dammed, smelled the dumped mercury and heard the cries of fisherman as the whales were butchered. At Rivière Ouelle during the 1870s as many as five hundred belugas were slain in a single tide, more than the total number that remained alive in the Saint Lawrence today.

Piri heaved to and let the Bayliner wallow on the deep black waters of the Saguenay fjord alongside tourist steamers and hotel boats. Majestic capes jutted out into the river, their cliffs towering high above the hopeful flotilla. Camera lenses flashed in the sun. Joel and Randy helped their mother lower the photographic apparatus into position. The whale-watchers waited patiently, expectantly, fruitlessly. No pure white tail broke the surface. No dolphin-like face crossed Piri's viewfinder. At the end of a long, empty afternoon the sleeping giants watched *Szerencsès* pull up its sea anchor and slip away from the fjord.

After Piri had put the boys to bed she joined Beagan on the bridge. 'It's a shame,' she kept repeating. 'I've watched their numbers shrink over the years but there's never been a summer when we haven't seen any at all.' Disappointment weighed on her like a heavy cloak. 'Would you mind if we cruised through the night?' she asked Beagan. 'If we take it in shifts we might make Montreal by morning.'

Szerencsès chased the sunset west up the Saint Lawrence. Navigation lights glittered on blunt-nosed Lakers. Buoys blinked and clanged on either side of the channel. Piri turned up the stereo and filled the bridge with Bartók's Magyar folk songs. The river rolled in inky blackness beneath the towering crags. The Bayliner passed Québec City long after the *calèches* had been locked away and the last horse clip-clopped into its stall. Delphis Duhamel was still awake and noted their passing with a vocal rendition of 'O Canada', but it was a *fleur-de-lys* that fluttered on his flagpole. Above them starlight flashed and strobed through the struts of the Pont de Québec.

Szerencsès's custom-built bridge also twinkled and glittered, though it was lit by diodes rather than heavenly bodies. On board were radar, weatherfax and a depth sounder. The Raystar Chartplotter glowed with the vaporous outline of channel and shore. Beagan brought up from his cabin Hector's old terrestrial globe. Piri gazed at its faded panels and pointed at the Austrian Empire.

'There's Hungary, and look, Sopron is marked too.'

'I like Budapest,' he said, recalling an earlier trip to gather material for a guide book. 'All those curves and colonnades and crescents. And the smell of violets.'

'Peter says this machine can track eight satellites simultaneously.' Her Furuno plotter pinned their position on the real globe. 'I guess it's good to know that we can never get lost.'

A tremble in her voice reminded Beagan of the first maps of Nouvelle France which had marked the great wilds of trackless unknown with the inscription, '*On ne connaît point le Cours de toutes ces Rivières.*' The course of these rivers is completely unknown. 'You know, sometimes in Canada,' he whispered, 'gazing out over the bow or looking through the darkened windows of a night train, I'm overawed by a feeling of unimaginable vastness, a sense that out there is wilderness without end.'

The morning was warm and everyone in Montréal looked as if they were off to a beach party. They wore shorts, floppy tops and muscle shirts covered with slogans: 'Peace through Unity', 'White North Hockey Club', 'Je me Souviens'. The only exception appeared to be an anglophone businessman who, admiring his reflection in spit-polish patent leather shoes, stormed up and down the river walk shouting into his mobile telephone, 'Are you still there? Can you hear me?'

In New World cities one needs only to scratch the surface to find the original reason for settlement. As Piri veered *Szerencsès* past the container terminal Beagan gestured above the island city's glass and steel towers to whale-backed Mont Royal. 'That's the hill which Jacques Cartier climbed. You know, the French explorer who named Canada.'

'I'm sorry, but our version of history never included him,' confessed Piri. She eased back on the throttle to give way to a nippy harbour tug. 'But I can tell you the name of the first Russian dog to be launched into space.'

'Cartier was the first European to sail upstream,' persisted Beagan, anxious to tell her their shared history. 'We're a thousand kilometres from the sea and the Saint Lawrence is still, what, a mile wide here. He reasoned that such a broad expanse of water could hardly be a river. To him it had to be the promised passage to the Orient.'

'What made him stop?'

Beagan pointed forward towards the first Seaway lock. 'That rough water there. It blocked the river and his ship could go no further. His search for China ended and he wistfully named the rapids Lachine.'

Piri swung the boat towards a vacant slip. 'Could you look after the bowline, please?' She wrapped an arm around Joel and Randy as they climbed on to the bridge.

'He was looking for a western waterway,' explained Beagan, raising his voice while walking forward, 'a dream inherited by Samuel de Champlain, the father of New France and history's most travelled explorer.' Beagan coiled three loops of rope in his right hand. 'Champlain established Canada's first permanent white settlement and set out by canoe over Lachine. In 1614 his voyageurs paddled west as far as Lake Huron looking for the legendary "*Mer de l'Ouest*".'

Piri spun the wheel and went hard astern. 'Did he find it?'

'It wasn't there to be found, even though it's marked on many of the early maps,' he replied. 'But the energy and faith of those first *habitants* was remarkable, surviving terrible conditions, the bitter cold, complete isolation. It nurtured in them a savage love for the land.' Piri slipped the engine into neutral and *Szerencsès* drifted alongside the petrol dock. 'Champlain traced the lineaments of half the continent. His discoveries opened the interior, laid the basis of the fur trade and gave Britain and France a reason to go to war.'

As Beagan tied up, a middle-aged attendant idled towards the pumps. Montréal was the second-largest French-speaking city in the world and Piri was anxious not to cause offence. She asked Beagan to order the fuel.

'Don't speak to me in French,' snapped the attendant as he tugged at the hose and clanked the nozzle into the tank. 'I'm Greek. Speak to me in English.' He wore a nylon short-sleeved shirt and a scowl. His silver-olive eyes seemed to shimmer and dance in the rising diesel vapours.

Beagan watched the irrepressible Canadian urge to diffuse aggression swell up in Piri. 'You sure are lucky living in this beautiful province,' she said, trying to make conversation. 'We've been right up to the Gulf and back again.'

'Québec has been ruined by the politicians,' retorted the Greek.

'Hey, *calmes-toi*, Andreas.' A second attendant had overheard the conversation. It seemed not to be the first time that he had tried to pacify the Greek. 'They just getting us a better deal, eh? The idea of Canada still moves most of us, except for the hardliners.'

'What? A tolerant land of opportunity away from old world prejudice?' snarled the Greek. 'Tell me about it.'

'Isn't that the ideal which brought the French and English – and Greek – settlers?' suggested Beagan.

'Yeah, sure,' nodded the Québécois attendant.

Unable to restrain herself, Piri chatted about Beagan's interest in emigration. The Greek scoffed and glared at him. 'You want to hear a good story, do you? I came here twenty-five years ago and stayed too long. Now it's too late to move. I'm stuck here. My life is wasted. End of story.'

His anger disturbed Piri. It subdued the boys who slunk back below-deck to watch television. When the tanks were filled Beagan cast off and they drifted past Île Notre Dame. 'We were just trying to be friendly,' Piri said.

'He's frightened of being stranded,' replied Beagan, catching sight of a referendum billboard which translated as 'We have the right to be different.' In a handful of months the province was to vote whether it wished to remain part of Canada. 'You know it's not Québec that is distinct but its French-speakers. The separatists prefer to overlook the fact that one in five Québécois isn't *pure laine*, or pure wool as those of old French stock call themselves.'

'It sounds arrogant. I thought this was the country where different people were meant to get on?'

'That's what the majority want. But then the new populist version of history already omits those who transformed Montréal from a small mission and military post into the commercial capital of Canada,' remembered Beagan. 'After the defeat of Nouvelle France it was British entrepreneurs who came here looking for riches not in the Orient but along the road towards it. Their fervent search for pelts, and later for timber, gold and hydroelectric power, enabled the wilderness to be developed.'

By the 1890s about a hundred Montrealers, most of them Scots, had come to own the wealth of more than half the nation. On the hill from which Cartier had gazed west they had built High Victorian homes with Romanesque arcades and fairytale towers. They had constructed so many banks, universities, hospitals and places of worship that Mark Twain had observed that Montréal was a city where a boy could not throw a stone without breaking a church window. Throughout those years the French, grand-children of the first pioneers who had rooted themselves in the soil, were excluded from the boardrooms and clubs of the élite.

'Now only a century later the old Scottish families are gone, driven out by improvidence and French nationalism,' continued Beagan. 'Since the election in 1976 of the Parti Québécois, 150,000 English-speakers have moved away from the province. Even many new emigrants have voted with their feet.'

'Shifting the country's economic centre three hundred miles west to Toronto.'

'And providing the separatists with a scapegoat,' added Beagan. 'The years of British domination are portrayed as an era of exploi-tation rather than enrichment. Partisan politics promoted this false perception, telling the francophones what they wanted to hear to win their votes, setting them at odds with other Canadians.'

'Nationalists distorting the past?' said Piri. 'That's something I'm familiar with. It reminds me of Yugoslavia without guns.'

'This does not please me well,' sighed Hector. It was not in his nature to succumb to despondency, but the incident with the attendant had affected him too. 'Noah, Abraham and Jacob all died in faith, not having received the promises, the place which they should receive as an inherit-ance. But here I see no faith, no charity, neither on the left hand nor on the right.' He and Jamie sat astern as *Szerencsès* slid into the concrete canyon of a Seaway lock. The heavy steel doors closed behind them and cut out the morning sun.

'It's all down to geography,' suggested Jamie, anxious to lift his father's spirits. He had removed his shoes and his feet dangled above the boat's wake. 'It was Lachine which hindered the inward development of Canada for more than three hundred years. Without it France alone might have dominated the great white north. *"La belle province"* could have been *"le beau pays"*.'

'That may yet be the way of it,' replied Hector, remaining grave, 'and it is not to my liking.' The surface frothed beneath Jamie's toes as the boat was lifted to the upper river level. 'If I recollect aright, the two defining elements of nationality are a wish to be governed together and a common sympathy; that is, shared language and beliefs. You'd see that here as soon as a mote in an oystercatcher's eye.'

'F-F-Forgive me, Father, but you're missing something. When you settled in Promise the land was very young. There was no past, only a present. Now there is a shared history.'

'I see nothing shared here but distrust and delusion. Your grandson has reason on his side.'

Szerencsès plied the channel which skirted the turbulent rapids. A jetboat kicked up plumes of spray as it ran joy-riders over the swift, choppy waters.

'Take Lachine,' suggested Jamie. 'It prevented the French from colonising the interior and made Canada a f-f-fractured nation. That history unites us. The rapids can even be blamed for inciting the American War of Independence.' Hector frowned in disbelief. 'Really,' continued his son. 'In the last half of the eighteenth century the American colonies were reaching west over the Appalachians. The expansion was driven for the most part by land speculators, among them George Washington.'

'James, you are as great a liar as a cat is a thief.'

'It's true,' insisted Jamie. 'In the trunk is a copy of his advertisement from the *Maryland Journal* of 20 August 1773.'

'In our trunk? How on God's good earth did that come to be in there?'

'How did any of it come to be there?' Jamie answered

with a shrug. 'Please, hear me out. Washington's sales pitch enthused, as I recall, that no lands exceeded his on the Ohio "in luxuriance of soil, or convenience of situation. They abound," he boasted, "with fine f-f-fish and wild fowl of various kinds, as also in most excellent meadows, many of which are, in their present state, almost fit for the scythe." I read it again over Beagan's shoulder only yesterday,' he explained. 'Well, the advertisement went on to assure prospective settlers that they "may cultivate and enjoy the lands in peace and safety". But that was the problem, the land was still Indian territory, so Washington and his fellow speculators could guarantee their customers safety only by demanding British military protection.'

'He asked England to protect his speculation?'

'And London tried to oblige. The Saint Lawrence was the best route for shipping troops into the expanding colonies, but with the need to cross the Lachine rapids, the operation was very expensive. The British public had become less and less willing to shoulder both war costs and the colonial burden, so Parliament chose for the first time to tax Americans for the protection which they demanded. The introduction of this levy inf-f-furiated them and when it was extended to a tax on tea they – led by Washington himself – rose up in revolt.' Jamie leaned back against the stern staff. 'It's this sort of story, these events and choices, which made the country. The one element which unites Canada is its history.'

'That's fine in theory, James,' replied the Reverend, his heart still chafed, 'providing someone remembers it.' On *Szerencsès*'s stern the maple leaf flag flapped in the wind, was caught by an updraught and wrapped itself twice around Jamie. Beagan watched its motion out of the corner of his eye.

*   *   *

BEYOND MONTREAL THE alluvial plain was dotted with the isolated mountains of the Monteregian Hills. The shore rose in sweeping slopes to ridges crowned by lush woods. The boys had exhausted their library of videos and were restless during supper. Beagan tried to entertain them with stories about the explorers who had once canoed along the same gentle banks. As they paddled, he told them, Champlain's voyageurs had sung, '*Youpe! Youpe! Sur la Rivière*'. He recalled the open immigrant bateaux and broad, pony-drawn Durham boats that had followed them. Their settlers had camped at night on the shore dreaming of a glad arrival in Belleville or Port Hope, fearing an impoverished landing in Port Credit.

'Is that where they invented credit cards?' asked Randy, holding Sniffy the hamster in his lap.

'No, stupid,' said Joel, excited by the sense of adventure. 'Just shut up and listen to the story.'

At the Long Sault rapids, where *Szerencsès* climbed through another lock, Beagan told them of later migrants who had paused to eat at a weatherboarded wayside tavern. They had stolen apples from orchards skirting the towpath while awaiting the double-hulled steamer *Iroquois*. Later still travellers had boarded the *Rapids Queen*, whose shallow draught enabled her to navigate the wild chutes, and the grand paddle-wheeled *Kingston*, with her potted palms and carpets in three shades of crimson, to ride up the waterway which funnelled settlers from the Atlantic to the Great Lakes.

'In the old days there was so much competition along this route that the navigation companies needed to fight for trade,' Beagan recounted as Piri whisked a chocolate mousse. 'In 1857 two steamboats, the *Montréal* and the *Napoleon*, challenged each other to a race. Each claimed to be the fastest boat and each stoked its boiler with boosters of colophonium and barrels of grease.'

'Wicked,' said Joel.

'They set off to the cheers of passengers and the wail of bagpipes,' Beagan continued. 'There were lots of Scots aboard among the migrants. But twelve miles into the contest the *Montréal* burst into flames. The crew tried to contain the fire with a single hose. The travellers helped out with water jugs. Only the flames spread too quickly and the captain turned the ship to shore. Eight hundred feet from the bank she ran aground with the tide running downstream. The blaze drove all the passengers towards the bow. One of the two lifeboats capsized while the other became overcrowded and sank. People jumped overboard, fell on top of one another, drowned holding their infants in their arms. In fifteen minutes the 253 immigrants who had come in search of a promised land on earth found instead their paradise in heaven.'

'Man, I guess they just weren't lucky,' said Randy, tucking into his dessert.

As *Szerencsès* lay at anchor beyond the last Saint Lawrence lock on the north shore of Lake Ontario, Beagan sat cross-legged in his cabin, the contents of the trunk spread around him on the floor. By his side there was a child's pouch of cat's-eyes marbles, love notes wrapped in hair ribbon and a well-thumbed book of elegies. He lay down the fragile copy of the *Maryland Journal* and picked up a bundle of his grandfather's letters. Piri had put the boys to bed and appeared at the door with two tumblers of apricot brandy. A breath of jasmine followed her as she settled beside him on the thick pile carpet. 'What sort of man was Jamie?' she asked, nodding at the papers.

'Well, good,' Beagan replied. 'Relentless in promoting the good.' He handed her the family portrait taken after Hector's death. 'Much like his own father, though Jamie's definition of it was more liberal. That's him on the right.'

Piri saw two lonely boys and their widowed mother frozen in Victorian formality. She sensed too the loneliness in Beagan. 'It's difficult to know what he thought, or felt, but I like him; look, he's trying to hide a stain on his cuff.'

'This is the first letter he wrote home. It's dated 16 May 1879.' Beagan unfolded a sheet of creased paper and read, 'I arrived early

Saturday morning and our steamer appeared to float through the thick fog into Toronto harbour.'

Piri stretched to look over his shoulder. The page was covered with a neat hand but without paragraphs. 'The writing is so dense.'

'Paper would have been expensive for him.' Beagan read on, pleased to have a sympathetic listener. 'The shoreline was obscured by mist and the buildings seemed to soar above the earth like enchanted castles. Churches shot their spires towards heaven, the Saint Lawrence Hall lifted its copper dome like a hot-air balloon, even the roughcast Parliament appeared to break free of both gravity and civic burden to levitate into the firmament.'

'It can still look like that today, if the pollution's bad. Sometimes you just can't breathe downtown.'

'I don't know if I'll recognise it. I've been away so long and cities change so quickly. I saw that when I lived in Australia. I worked there as a travel agent for a time.' He winced, recalling his attempts to make a home in Brisbane. No sooner had he settled into an apartment and hung his pictures on the wall than the building was demolished and a modern development constructed in its place. It happened three times in as many years. 'So you'll know Toronto better than me now. The new office blocks and roads and all that.'

'Maybe, but you know who made it.'

'The noise of sawmills and smell of distilleries' corn mash assaulted my senses,' Beagan continued to read. 'A cloud of white dust drifted over Gooderham and Worts' flour mill then swirled skywards with the steam from a puffing Grand Trunk locomotive. The steamer whistled its arrival. Baggage porters cried, armfuls of babies wailed and mothers wept on seeing their husbands ashore. An Irishman slipped and fell into the water between the wharf and ship's hull. His friends hooted until they saw him go under a second time. They then lowered ropes that were tied to barrels and other impossible life-preservers before a strong fellow jumped into the water and pulled the drowning man to safety. The rescuer swung lightly on to the wharf, shook himself as if he had been a

Newfoundland dog and walked off into the crowd. Toronto has over a hundred miles of streets, most of cedar-block planking with long-board sidewalks, so every corner of the town resounds with the sound of hooves and boots on wood. Everywhere there is, as Father would have said, so much of a bustle and a stir.'

'It must have felt so busy to him. I'd never seen a shopping mall before I came to Toronto. They were so big that they made me feel a little sick at first. There were so many things to look at, so much choice.'

Beagan shuffled through odd-sized printed sheets and tightly-written cards. 'He had thought that his first week would be spent tramping every board-foot of the town looking for work, but by lunchtime on the first day he had a job.'

'Even faster than me.'

'Here we are.' He showed Piri a Niagara Navigation Company timetable. Across the top Jamie had inscribed in red pencil, 'My First Assignment.' On the back of the leaflet he had noted, 'I am employed as a printer's devil, making rollers and setting type in a small newspaper office on Bay Street. I enjoy the work but my weekly pay is only $3.00. Accommodation costs $2.50.'

'His room backed on to a slaughterhouse,' Beagan explained, looking up from the page. 'He says somewhere that the lows of the cattle ensured he was never late for work. But he had to pawn his overcoat and live off biscuits for a week. In the end he wrote to home for help. His mother sent him money on the condition that he spend it "in a right way". She worried that life in the city would lead him to sin.'

Beagan handed Piri his great-grandmother's letter. Six single dollar bills had once been pinned to its corner. 'Be sure you go regular to church and attend Bible classes. The Lord will be with you; lay hold of Him for He will guide you.' She read out the careful hand then took another sip of brandy.

'Kirstie had grown up as a herring girl in Scotland. I like to remember her as a child gathering tangle for the kelp-making, following the fisherwives home, their scaly creels shining like silver in the moonlight. Later she and her sister followed the herring, seizing and sorting their father's freight of fish. The music of their cries, as they chaffered their wares, would have rung through streets of towns down the length of the west coast. But the years of living with a stern moralist like Hector took away a part of herself.'

'Not her love for her sons,' observed Piri. 'Did Jamie have any friends in Toronto?' Beagan shook his head as he refilled her glass. 'When I first arrived I spent a lot of time alone too,' she said. 'I remember our first Christmas. We had a small artificial tree but I wanted a huge pine with tons of chocolate ornaments on it like back home. Peter really tried to make me happy and bought some *szaloncukor*, the traditional Hungarian candy, to hang in the tree, but then he had to work right up to Christmas Eve. I stayed in the apartment missing my family, crying my eyes out.'

'I think Jamie was lonely,' acknowledged Beagan. 'He worked five and a half days a week in the print shop. Sunday was set aside for worship. Only Saturday afternoons were free, and he took to paddling a borrowed canoe around the island.' Beagan passed her a flyer announcing a public demonstration of Edison's incandescent electric light. On the back Jamie had written, 'The harbour is protected by an arc of flat islands which lie so level with the water that they appear to be half-submerged. It is a place apart from the city with deserted bays, scattered raggle-taggle homes and lakeside cottages. At dusk I like to come ashore on an empty beach, make a driftwood fire and cook a sausage for supper. Sometimes if I'm feeling bold I sing "One More River to Cross" or "The Canadian Boat Song". Last weekend the sound of a piano and a woman's voice reached me from across the water and not long afterwards, although it filled me with guilt, I treated myself to a straw hat as my Scotch cap looks shabby. Cost $1.00.'

'Here his mother writes back asking him not to be too bold on the water,' laughed Piri. She read aloud, 'I enclose a camping quilt of cloth similar to a Paisley shawl so you can spend the occasional night sleeping under the stars away from the clatter of town and the bellow of condemned cows.' She turned the letter on to its side. 'What's this in the margin?'

Beagan leaned close to her. 'That's his brother. Zachary liked to give orders to everyone, especially Jamie.'

'You must decide on the course of your career. Be precise in your objective. I have been informed by an associate that, if you are not too lazy to study, you should attend the School of Practical Science. On taking a course there you can obtain an excellent situation as a Mechanical Engineer.' Piri looked up from the page. 'He sounds a bit like a sergeant major.'

'Zachary had a gift for organisation.'

'Did Jamie listen to his advice?'

Beagan shook his head. 'He had already chosen his career. Both the brothers had.'

Hector glanced over Beagan's shoulder as he reached for a photograph album. On its cover was a snapshot of Jamie standing by a canoe with paddle in hand, his britches held up by a braid belt and sporting the straw hat. 'As I recall a dollar was not an insignificant sum,' chided Hector. 'I hope that garment was not bought with the money your mother sent.'

Jamie removed the hat from his head and suspended it in space between them. 'Even if I had had the inclination to be thriftless there was never the time to spend my wages on anything other than essentials. I watched my money carefully, F-F-Father. In two years I did not once allow myself to take the street cars home, even though I was tired and the road was muddy.'

Hector examined the boater then spun it away towards the *en suite* bathroom. It hit the mirror and knocked Beagan's toothbrush into the sink. He and Piri looked up from the album. 'Your headgear smacks of ostentation,' Hector told Jamie.

'I was no city swell, nor had I ever any intention of becoming one.'

'Nor did you intend joining the ministry. It disappointed me that you did not hear the call.'

'I heard a different voice. In the newspaper office I found

a deep satisfaction in f-f-forming the words letter by letter in the compositor's hand-type. It excited me hearing the lick of ink on the plate and transforming a blank white sheet into thoughts, information, communication. I could find the right words, set them in type, press, preserve and prevent them from ever slipping away. My stutter didn't matter, F-F-Father. I could hold an idea in my hand and share it with another, send it to Mother at home, broadcast it like seed to ten thousand readers.'

Jamie sat up and drifted Buddha-like across the cabin. 'Canada was then a young land of scattered communities. The new railway, reaching west mile by mile towards the Pacific, would soon carry newspapers to every farm, mine and lumber camp in the Dominion. Print was the means of communication. Words could fuse the disparate people into a united nation. It made me determined that I would become a publisher.'

'I am glad, James, that you saw fit to work with your brother.'

'And I too, despite all that happened. You can read of my pleasure at Zachary's decision to move to Toronto.' Jamie gestured at the trunkful of letters. 'There was little love in him but he was a man of great devotion. I looked forward to sharing his company. Yet even in our most optimistic moments neither of us foresaw the fullness of expansion that would grow from our f-f-fine f-f-folly of enthusiasm and ideals.' He pointed down at the album. 'Look there, Father.' Beneath them in the darkened cabin Beagan and Piri were leafing through the black and white photographs. A youthful Jamie and Zachary stood together on Bay Street pier. Their cheeks were clean-shaven and their eyes bright. 'It was you who made it possible.'

'Providence was good to you, right enough,' admitted Hector, who would have flushed had blood still pumped in his veins.

Piri flicked through a dozen pages and two lifetimes. In an early colour print Jamie paused to catch his breath aboard the RMS *Kipper* as she steamed up the Muskoka lakes. By the album's last leaves his hair had thinned and he had taken to wearing a trilby. Slip-knot ties had replaced black satin stocks. He acquired a ruddy complexion, maybe from the trials of the first years, and grew portly. Zachary, on the other hand, maintained his agile wiriness on page after page. His moustache, which in the span of the album had been transformed from copper brown to snow white, always remained neatly trimmed. Jamie's whiskers tended towards the unruly.

'Look here, they are getting too far ahead of themselves,' said Jamie as Piri turned over another decade of pages. 'Don't you find, Father, that clock-locked linear time, with its ticking off of days, is a pattern only the living follow with ease? For me it is like a swallow trying to keep track of a turtle's progress. I want to let go of the eph-ph-phemeral moment, to soar away and to ride the winds and currents of time.' But Hector was not listening to his son. Instead his zealous eye glared at Beagan.

The rocking of the boat and the brandy had conspired to relax the couple. Beagan and Piri imagined voices in the drone of the engine. Its rhythm conjured up the unheard music of the belugas' serenade and Jamie's song to the stars on Toronto Island. In the warm cabin Beagan reached forward to take a bundle of letters from Piri's lap, then laid his hand on her knee. But as his body shifted towards her there was a sudden cry. Randy had woken from the depths of a nightmare. Piri pulled back, stood up and left the cabin.

Jamie put his hands on his hips and turned towards the Reverend. 'Father, what are you doing?'

'If a man looks at a woman with lust then he commits adultery in his heart,' hissed Hector. 'O Lord, lead us not into temptation but deliver us from evil,' he prayed, wrestling in travail with the Holy Spirit, then added, 'This boy seems determined to be a wisp in every bed.'

For a moment Beagan did not move. He took a long, deep breath, looked right and left, then gazed into the empty air around him.

CHAPTER V

WRITING ON WATER

'HOW DOES A poor man enrich the w-w-world?' By hard work, by improving himself, by self-trust. 'Concentration,' I quoted from Emerson, 'is the secret of strength in politics, in war, in trade, in short, in all the management of human affairs.' It matters not if a man is rich or poor, only that he has discipline. Capital and good connections may help to begin a career but they alone will not secure the future. Zachary and I were fortunate to have inherited a zeal for productive labour and a belief in honest industry. We aspired to make our own success by helping other people to prosper.

If I stood on a chair balanced on my bed I could glimpse the glint of blue water across the rooftops. I found comfort in its sight, remembering that it was little more than a century since white men had first sailed around the island and into the sheltered harbour. The early settlers had cleared the oak from the mainland and planted red Fife wheat, as in Promise. In late summer the ripe russet heads of grain had bowed and swayed in the balmy breeze. They had eaten the dense flocks of wild pigeons which roosted so low on the trees that they could be knocked off the branch with a stick.

'F-F-Fisher MacFie and I caught sea-salmon at home,' I enthused to my landlady, her cheeks slashed with rouge bought from my rent money, 'just as the pioneers used to do here on the Humber River.'

'Pigeon pie tastes dandiest with crab-apple jelly,' she replied.

John Graves Simcoe, the first lieutenant governor of the new province of Upper Canada, had led the colonists to the site in 1793. In a canvas house which had originally belonged to Captain Cook, he had laid out his grandiose plan for a great capital city. His surveyor, Captain Gotherman, had then attempted to transform the limitless wilds into an orderly town of geometric splendour. The central business section was to be a precise grid of 121 regular blocks surrounded by a noble common. But the magnificent plan had utterly ignored the terrain and with the first spring run-off the new capital turned into a swamp. The resulting swarms of mosquitoes had brought with them the danger of malaria.

As I trudged around the puddles between my boarding house and the print shop I understood how Simcoe's Muddy York had come to be dubbed Hogtown. His tight-buttoned, tight-lipped gentlemen in uniform, among them the young aide Arthur Wellesley who was destined to become the Duke of Wellington and defeat Napoleon at Waterloo, had sung 'God Save the King' then lain down on their blankets in the mire to sleep. One day, they had foretold, Hogtown would be a cosmopolitan metropolis. But this was still some time off when the province's attorney-general, John White, was mortally wounded in a duel with John Small, clerk of the Executive Council.

The first families, anxious to rise above the common pioneer life, assumed airs and graces and renamed the quaggy city. Toronto, they claimed, was the Huron word for 'meeting place'. Others maintained that the Indian name meant 'trees in the bog'. The discrepancy between how things really were and how Old Toronto wished them to appear to be ruffled me no end.

This disparity spawned newspapers that were a strange

hotch-potch of politics, religion and abuse. Few column inches were ever set aside for accurate and detailed information. The titles of the first broadsheets proclaimed both their allegiance and their attitude: the *Royal Standard*, the *Church*, the *Porcupine*. The publisher of the radical *Colonial Advocate* was William Lyon Mackenzie, a wild wiry Scot who covered his baldness with a flame-red wig and led an unsuccessful armed rebellion against British colonial rule. Tory bully-boys once threw his printing press into Toronto Bay. The second editor of the *Toronto Telegram* was a staunch Royalist. 'Black Jack' Robinson won cheers and circulation when he announced the eleventh Commandment: 'Thou shalt not bear false witness against the British Empire.' Even the political parties themselves launched newspapers. 'We must start the *Empire*,' wrote Conservatives to their prime minister John A. Macdonald, 'or prepare for defeat at the next general election.' In Upper Canada the press was committed not to freedom of expression but to the manipulation of public perception.

In a small society that is stable and not in flux, the line between truth and falsehood is sharp. Words are rooted in a known and knowable context. On Cape Breton, Father as parish minister was heard and trusted. We all knew that old McKinlay would sooner play fiddle for the devil than tell a lie. But as society grows its citizens are obliged to accept information without evidence. Each fact cannot be verified by first-hand experience and language is subjected to the pressure of a changing environment. Words taken on trust may be corrupted by those bent on self-interest. Politicians collect information by secret means and withhold details that do not serve them. Businesses can distort statistics to influence their investors and customers. As words are devalued people begin to lose faith in what they hear, as Promise's parishioners had ceased to listen to Father's sermons. Individuals become confused and start to mistrust their institutions. Society begins to unravel, scattering its parts like the letters of a nightmare alphabet. It was to my mind only an independent press that could counter this descent into confusion by obtaining accurate intelligence and disclosing it to the public. The responsibility of newspapers is to make truth the common property of the nation.

When I met Zachary at the pier he wore a new, natty bow tie. He shook my hand and said, 'You should trim your moustache. Speed on the road to success depends on appearance as well as substance.' His arrival was a day later than expected because Mother had asked him not to travel on a Sunday. As I collected his valise he trotted out her fond saying, 'There is no blessing in the gain made on the Sabbath.' My brother turned his back on the lake, looked up towards the heights of Deer Park and marched inland. He had inherited some of Father's missionary spirit. He too was a man of vision, exiled for the sake of the Word, but instead of the Lord's Commandments the tenet which he strove to impart was the gospel of fact. 'Facts,' he would say, 'are all that a man can depend upon. Words are everybody's business.' In the uncertain world after Darwin, when the Bible had come to be seen less as a literal truth and more as an allegory, irrefutable facts were my brother's certainty.

We walked the city streets all afternoon so Zachary could orient himself. He inspected the business district as a soldier might survey the field of battle, looking for the high ground and taking particular interest in the location of newspaper offices. I made a point of taking him to the intersection of King and Simcoe Streets. On its four corners stood a handsome set of buildings: Upper Canada College, Government House, a tavern and Saint Andrew's church. Education, legislation, damnation and salvation were gathered together at one crossroads. Zachary was unimpressed until I mentioned that the editor of the *Telegram* was an old boy of the college. At suppertime I suggested that we might like to indulge in a celebratory Tom-and-Jerry at Clancey's but he declined. Instead we had a quiet meal at home. Zachary professed little need of physical comforts. Nevertheless he readily accepted my offer of the bed, which left me sleeping on the floor. The next morning he set off early to begin his career.

In Cape Breton he had admired the *Mail* and so he now secured himself employment on the commercial page. Almost at once he deemed its market reports to be unsatisfactory. Inadequate space, he judged, was provided for trade information. The sporting section was his page's main competitor, and in the battle for column inches the Amateur Golf Championships took precedence over the collapse of the Panama Canal Company. Pork belly prices, claimed the editor, never did a damn to increase circulation.

Zachary's frustration only stiffened our resolve to establish an independent trade newspaper. 'Shared knowledge is the foundation of modern civilisation,' he told me over a dinner of fried potatoes. There were two slices of bacon. He ate the larger piece. 'The propagation of accurate information dispels ignorance and darkness.'

The commercial press of the time offered little that was worthy of emulation. Publications lacked independence; their reports read like advertisements and their statistics like fairytales. All the facts were out of date. Paper stock too was of a low standard. Print density was inconsistent and in winter ink froze on the plate in unheated printshops. We calculated that a reliable journal devoted to the interests of the grocery and kindred trades could provide a useful public service. Storekeepers could improve their sales with knowledge of public tastes and manufacturers' wares. Farmers could plan, plant and trade with greater efficiency. It became our ambition to produce a paper of an editorial quality and typographic art then unknown in Canada.

Zachary gave up his post at the *Mail* and we became the brother publishers; proprietor, editor, advertisement solicitor, book-keeper and office-boy of the Gillean Publishing Company Limited. Our days began on foot. One of us walked to the east, the other to the west, first to the abattoir and then to the King Street Produce Market, to reconnoitre for prices, facts and trends. We quizzed traders at the Saint Lawrence Market and questioned dealers at the Exchange. At lunch we hurried back to the office to write up the copy, neither of us dawdling long behind the desk in our nine- by twelve-foot office as we had been able to afford only a single chair. We devoted the afternoon to canvassing for advertisers. Within two months the first number of the *Canadian Vegetable* made its appearance as a monthly periodical. Ten thousand copies were sent out to general storekeepers across the Dominion. It was the intention to show that our new concern would provide them with a proper vehicle for the conveyance of reliable market reports. Our first editorial declared, 'The *Vegetable* is entirely independent and will state facts and express opinions regarding topics of importance to the trade in a fearless and independent manner. We will also pay our bills promptly.'

But the appeal for support which accompanied the initial copy met with little success. One solitary subscriber was the result of the mountains of labour. We were disappointed but not disheartened and tried again, collecting and distilling facts, then distributing another ten thousand free copies to merchants. This time our reward was a mere five further subscribers. Our enterprise was flawed. The *Canadian Vegetable* was not a going concern.

'Old facts don't pass muster,' proclaimed Zachary. It occurred to us that in the ever-fluctuating grocery market a monthly paper was a poor guide to prices. One day's bargain broccoli could be sold at a premium after a spell of drought. Information had to reach the trade promptly.

'Pigeons,' I said in a flash of inspiration. 'It's a pigeon that we need.'

'Don't be sassy with me, chap,' Zachary replied.

We invested in a single homing pigeon with fine white wing patches and a rusty breast. I named her Harriet. Zachary called her Bird No. 1. Every morning I carried her away to the markets, scribbled the latest prices on a tiny roll of paper and released her to carry it back to the office. Zachary, who did not like to be seen with the bird, then updated the produce report. With the last of our borrowed capital we printed a third number and this time issued it as a weekly. The trade appreciated the change and their response was immediate. The requests for subscriptions arrived by the postbag and circulation grew at a remarkable rate.

The alteration also appealed to advertisers. It was the practice of the day for advertisements to appear only in the large daily and commercial newspapers, where not one quarter of the circulation reached the people who were interested in the goods on offer. This approach scattered much seed upon stony ground. Our innovation was to guarantee advertisers direct access to interested readers. In addition it had been the established custom to revise notices only once every six months. We encouraged our clients to update their insertions every week. 'Let your advertisements speak to your customers as your travellers would talk to them,' prompted our handbills. The Gillean Publishing Company applied itself to making advertisers' space, no matter how large or small, profitable.

Our ideal was to conduct business on honest principles, to be independent of any clique, house association or other guild. We strove to resort to no schemes nor use undue influences to secure advertising patronage. As a result a vista stretched before us, an ever-widening avenue of ambitious service.

The formula enabled us to extend ourselves and to

purchase *Paper Fancies*. The official organ of the book, stationery and fancy goods trades had been reduced to a sad, tatty pamphlet. We infused the periodical with energy and, dare I say it, merit, determined to make it an ornament to journalism, and produced it too as a weekly. Modern photo-engraving replaced woodcut illustrations. *Paper Fancies* became a satisfactory index for its patrons and in the first year made a profit of $1,100 after the payment of all expenses. Zachary calculated that we could double the figure in twelve more months. We did.

The key to the success of any venture, with or without pigeons, is good timing. As I reached the age of majority Canada stood at the threshold of a period of remarkable growth. Capital poured into the young Dominion from the London money markets. Investments were repaid with wheat from Manitoba and the riches of the Canadian Shield. Eastern factories manufactured goods as fast as foundries cast the rails to carry them west. Settlers from every corner of Europe swarmed off fast Atlantic steamships and crammed aboard trains bound for new homesteads across North America. Our population began to increase by 10 per cent every decade. Alexander Graham Bell invented his telephone. The Statue of Liberty rose at the entrance to New York harbour and we bought six more birds. The New World spirit was transforming the wilderness into an industrial nation.

We worked hard to expand our papers and did well under the increased responsibility. Each week we met our local customers and tried to understand their requirements better. Our canvassers travelled with a pigeon under their arms to see the more distant merchants. Many of our patrons were general dealers, handlers of hardware and dry goods who made frequent representations to us to serve their branch of commerce. In response to their demands we launched our third venture. The *Hardwareman's Nuts & Notions* met with appreciation and its success required us to move to larger offices. Our advertising patronage increased and brought large additions to the subscription list. Within three years the Gillean Publishing Company was free of debt. We hired two full-time journalists and a girl as a shorthand writer. She set her desk alongside the cages and relieved us of a great deal of letter writing. She also fed the birds. Her pay was four dollars each week, a salary at which I felt her well able to afford a new hat.

The novelty of profit enabled us each to draw ten dollars every week from the company. All our income had before been spent on improving the papers. Zachary deposited his salary in the bank. 'Come what may it goes there,' he declared. 'With this money I will form the nucleus of a fortune.' My deposits in the Home Savings and Loan Company were less frequent, but I did manage to economise enough to buy a fine Peterborough lapstrake canoe. When weather and work permitted I paddled it around the island or sailed under a spread of standing canvas as far as the Etobicoke River. Some evenings I didn't return home until ten or eleven o'clock.

One summer when all the giddy people had gone down to the beach and the cloying heat prevented even Zachary from working I proposed that we take a week's canoe trip together. At first he was suspicious of the luxury – we had never before indulged ourselves in a holiday – but I convinced him that the rest would improve our concentration.

Muskoka is a lake district of lonely pines and pastel pink granite that lies a hundred miles to the north of Toronto. The train dropped us at the Gravenhurst railhead and we paddled the Peterborough towards Shadow River. We dived off blueberry islands, swam through the embrace of cool black currents and dried ourselves within the canoe's cocoon. In late afternoon we slipped through sun-warmed shallows and pulled our boat over sandy beds ridged like a mackerel sky. At dusk we pan-fried fresh trout for supper. The lonely call of the loon echoed across the waters and we fell asleep listening to the flip flop of waves on the shore. Although Zachary spoke of nothing but work we shared the week there, watching deer step out from behind bleached white birches and cross black rocks to drink, drifting shirtless across the lazy afternoons and sheltered bays. It was all too soon that we had to return to the city's noise, hustle and bustle. Zachary was anxious to get back. He missed the work. His skin had also taken on a brilliant red tinge from the scalding sun and I needed to apply an oatmeal powder poultice to his face every morning.

As our train rattled south the thickly-wooded hills became seamed with roads and clearings. Here and there fields appeared dotted with huge pine stumps. We passed a threshing machine and a horseless carriage. Zachary's excitement rose as I sank into disappointment. The fair pastureland around Lake Ontario was fertile but too flat to please me. I knew then that I lived too much right inside myself but, even if I had managed to cobble together the words to explain my feelings, Zachary would not have listened. He was looking forward, trying to catch sight of the city over the cornfields. He got a cinder in his eye. I sat with my back towards the locomotive, gaze fixed on the northern woods, and soothed my sadness by daydreaming of canoe trips around Toronto harbour, unaware that its island was about to change my life.

The island had long been a sanctuary from the rigid conformity of mainland society. Once it had been connected to the mainland by an isthmus and revellers had cavorted in the merry-go-rounds, bowling alleys and abundant taverns of the Peninsula Pleasure Grounds. The amusements and arcades catered for the worst sort of new immigrant, the more prudish Old Torontonians had claimed, and there were calls from the pulpit for authorities to curb the intemperance. In 1858 the prayers of the pious were answered when divine judgement came in the form of a great storm which washed away the landbridge and destroyed the most notorious of the island saloons, Quinn's Hotel.

Thirty years later it was the absence of a regimented grid pattern which drew the less conventional citizens to build simple summer cottages along the winding, leafy lanes. Every June families left their solid Victorian townhouses and moved across the bay to casual wooden homes with open front doors and broad verandahs cluttered by wobbly armchairs. They feasted on watermelon in picket-fenced gardens of lavender and fragrant grey-green mignonette. The girls bathed in the lake, dried their hair in the sun and walked to the Baths to have a little lunch at the pavilion. Afterwards they dawdled at the table to read each other's fortunes in the tea leaves. Their brothers paddled to Hanlan's Point to see a strong man perform, then met their sisters on the beach for a taffy pull. Their mothers called on friends or shopped at Walker's for new blouses while their fathers finished work early and caught the puffing ferry back to the serpentine streets of the summer place apart.

It was the head of such a family, Eden Prosper Goode, who as the Invention & Progress Correspondent of the *Toronto Globe* had provided the capital to launch the *Canadian Vegetable*. He was a man of great enthusiasms, although his technical knowledge was at best hazy. He had been born in the Bishop of Kerry's palace in Ireland where his mother had taken shelter after her Catholic neighbours had burnt down her house. They hadn't been keen on having an Irish Protestant living in the vicinity. Later he and his young parents had been shipwrecked in the West Indies and reached Toronto by way of New Orleans and Boston where his father, who could not spell, had held an editorial position on the *Farmer's Advocate*.

Goode first invited us to the island one humid Saturday

afternoon soon after our return from Muskoka. His summer house nestled in a grove beneath a clump of stately pines. Hammocks and geraniums hung between the trees. A caged canary sang along with a piano playing inside the cottage. Zachary and I mounted the wooden front steps and, the door being ajar, knocked on its frame. A terrier lying in the shade barked once, rolled over and went back to sleep. A child, her hair waved in curls, peeked out from behind a lace curtain and ran away. The piano stopped playing.

'Lizzie,' a woman called from within the house. 'Lizzie?' A breath of cool air wafted out from the shadowy front room. We were dressed in our three-piece suits and it was hot on the verandah. The child reappeared at the window and stared. Zachary knocked again which evoked a third call, this time more insistent. 'Lizzie!'

The child turned and addressed the voice. 'Lizzie is making cocoa-nut cake.' She returned her gaze to us and added, 'I am having mine with raspberry syrup.'

'It is Mr Zachary Gillean to see Mr Goode,' announced my brother, ignoring the child and clearing his throat in an impatient gesture. 'Is Mr Eden Goode at home?'

Footsteps padded across the hardwood floor and a gentle sweet face appeared at the door. Its owner had fair ruffled hair, blue eyes and a graceful figure clad in a spotted cotton blouse and serge dress. 'I'm sorry,' apologised Bessie, Goode's eldest daughter, 'but I thought Lizzie would come.' She stepped into the sunlight and we saw that she wore neither shoes or stockings. Zachary bowed and introduced himself. I had never before seen a young woman's feet and blushed.

'Well, the pigeon publishing brothers,' said Bessie, making us sound like a circus trapeze act. 'But aren't you awfully hot in your suits?' She was as startled by the state of our dress as we were by her undress. 'It is real warm today.'

'Our appointment with your father is to discuss business, Miss Goode,' explained Zachary with due formality. Her lack of respect had irked him.

She raised a hand to cover a smile. 'I am sorry. I try to be quite good-natured but ... but it just comes out all wrong.' She shrugged her shoulders and laughed brightly. The planks of the verandah were painted grey and the shadows of the lattice created by the sun criss-crossed the floor. Bessie skipped from cool shadow to shadow, past the potted palms and on to the grass to avoid burning her soles. 'Father has been experimenting with his photo-camera all day,' she explained, then, catching me looking at her feet, blushed too. 'He is out back, gentlemen, if you would care to follow me.'

We followed her skipping run behind the house to where her sister Daisy was suspended by her feet from a tree. An intricate web of fine supporting wires upheld both her skirts and her modesty. Their brother Arthur was attempting to fasten a hat to her head but it kept falling off. 'We could use a dab of molasses, Pa,' he suggested, at which point Daisy shrieked.

'Just retie the ribbon, Art,' instructed Goode. 'And remember the parasol.' A new Kodak was mounted upside-down on a tripod beside him. He tried to keep apace of innovation, indeed he had encouraged his publishing friend George Brown not to turn down the offer of exclusive British Empire rights to the telephone. Brown, unlike Goode, did not think that they were worth the $150 price asked by Bell.

Goode caught sight of us. 'Excellent; the Messrs Gillean. You're just in time to witness an experiment to prove that the truth is not the facts. Come quickly.' We stepped forward and shook hands. In the sunlight Goode's balding head gleamed like newly polished rosewood. A forgetful house-maid appeared to have left a small chamois of blond hair on his crown. Zachary pointed out his mispositioning of the camera. 'Ah, there you are wrong,' Goode informed him. 'It is just where I want it to be.'

'But the subject recorded will be upside-down.'

'Not so,' said Goode, turning away from his family. 'You will agree that the camera cannot lie.' We nodded our assent. 'Then you must also accept that it preserves an individual perspective.'

'Not individual, no,' disagreed Zachary. 'It records a scene objectively, without interpretation.'

'But I as the camera-man choose where to point the apparatus. I decide what facts are to be included in and excluded from the field of vision. My selection is my interpretation. Yet you maintain that the resulting photograph will be objective. What then if you take a photograph, composing it with whatever facts and elements you choose. Will it be any less true?'

Rather than agree that both perspectives would be valid Zachary said, 'No, but there is always the accepted view. The facts should be allowed to speak for themselves.'

'Facts don't speak, Zachary, they are spoken. An accepted view only comes about because it is preached to or held by the majority, not because it is objective. And in any case it does not negate the individual perspective. Look at Daisy. There can be no such thing as an objective view, not in photographs or paintings, books or journalism.'

Bessie climbed up the ladder as Daisy's skirt slipped loose from an ankle wire. Her flushed and inverted face brought to mind the new red tulips that Dutch florists on Yonge Street had begun to sell. Zachary gestured to the family set-piece. 'But this is a manipulated truth.' I thought it looked like fun.

'It is my truth,' replied Goode. His domed pate coloured as he grew excited. 'The photograph will portray my daughter as the only right-minded lady in a topsy-turvy world. And who is to say that isn't the case? It is the way that I see it.'

'But is that useful?' asked my brother.

'I have an abhorrence of pursuits which are useful and profitable alone. Our family excelled because we liked doing something and not because of any ulterior motive such as making money.'

Arthur passed Daisy the handle of an open parasol. She held it beneath her head and leaves shaken from the tree sailed down into its canopy. 'Father?' she breathed.

'I hope your support of our enterprise,' said Zachary, 'came about because as well as liking it you believed in its usefulness.'

'Every time I see a spark of vision I water it. I nurture the flames of dreams. The Goodes have always done that. Fernando Espero Goode supported Dias de Novais, the Portuguese explorer, and was honoured in the naming of the Cape of Good Hope.'

'Father, we are ready.'

'The English poet Barnabe Googe, who spelt the name in his individual way, inspired Good Queen Bess with his "Cupid Conquered" and became one of her gentlemen-pensioners.'

'Daisy is turning quite red, Father,' said Arthur.

'Think too of Goode's *School Atlas* and *Good Housekeeping*. And consider George Brown Goode, the zoologist, who encouraged the National Museum of Natural History to open its doors to the general public. He also recorded 156 new species of fish.'

Daisy rested her hand on her sister's head and whispered, 'I think that I shall be sick.'

'I don't see what this has to do with facts,' interrupted Zachary.

'The fact is that it's my true story. You will find a Goode in every port of the world and for all of them the means are always the end.' He waved an arm as if encompassing them and the world in his grasp. 'I like pigeons too.'

'Father, Daisy is feeling unwell,' said Bessie. She had taken charge of her younger siblings all her life.

'I am with you, my child.' Arthur removed the ladder. Goode studied his tableau. Daisy's feet appeared to perch on the underside of a branch. Her skirts, held up by the wires, seemed to billow in an imaginary breeze. The book open in her hand completed the impression. Goode clicked the shutter to preserve his vision. A woman of calm countenance stood reading beneath a parasol in an upside-down world.

With a flick of his hand the subject was released and fell groaning to the ground. Bessie took her sister into her arms and comforted her, a spontaneous physical compassion the like of which I had never seen. At Goode's invitation we retired to the parlour to discuss business. Later Bessie stole in to our meeting and left us each a peeled snow apple, its flesh white and cool, and a smile.

The following weeks found me often at the cottage on the pretence of discussing business. I tended to arrive in a rush, declaring that I could only stop by for a minute, then stay all afternoon. Bessie's bright sunny ways drew many young people to her and together we sailed to Victoria Park and played pig on the verandah. I knew no card games and so found myself at somewhat of a disadvantage, especially as Bessie cheated outrageously. She threw back her head and laughed at my endeavours, her face overflowing with such pleasure that it seemed her whole being existed only to share joy. I took pleasure in teaching her how to ride a bicycle but she needed no lessons in canoeing. At the Grand Aquatic Regatta she won the silver medal in the skiff race. She insisted that the prize had really been awarded for her irrepressible chatter. 'I am such a desperate talker,' she told me, and when we stayed up late gathered under the porch's red light playing charades and shouting proverbs, I believed her. Bessie had a kind word for everyone and there was always a story poised to trip off her tongue.

We began to correspond with each other on the days when business kept me in the office. At that time a letter written in the city at breakfast would reach the island by lunchtime and a response could be on my desk before the end of the working day. If we used a pigeon our messages could be exchanged in an even shorter time.

'Go thou in well-doing,' she preached in the morning after a meeting had forced me to cancel our canoe paddle around the island. 'I am quoting scripture today as I suppose you notice.' But it was her Irish heart which spoke in that afternoon's letter. 'Oh do run over here and quarrel with me or find fault with me. I do get so tired of people who always say the right things. You let me scold and grumble at the world and in return explain things as to make me good-natured. I don't have to talk to you unless I have something to say and then you talk to me as if I was a sensible girl instead of flattering me up as if I were a spoiled lady. You are so good to me and I would be awfully glad to see you.'

One Sunday the island church was too crowded and we sang our hymns under the trees on the lakefront. The coots and green-headed mallards paddling around us added their peeps and quacks to our prayers. On the long walk home Zachary talked about social conditions. Although not fond of the extravagance myself I brought her a box of chocolates and took the liberty of addressing her as Miss Bessie. 'It is not good for man to be alone,' I managed to tell her without a stutter.

'Or woman either I think,' she replied.

The days grew shorter and the nights cooled. Even Arthur stopped bathing every morning. The cottages were closed at the end of September. Weatherboards were fastened over the windows and dust-sheets laid over furniture for off-season ghosts. Field mice made their nests in the upholstery. Water pipes were drained before the freeze-up. As families sailed back across the harbour to the confines of city life the launch of a new paper, the *Lumberjack*, stole all my free hours. Zachary and I set up camping beds in the office to enable us to work through the night. The soft cooing drove him back to the boarding house before the end of the week, but it was not the birds that disturbed my sleep.

Bessie spent the autumn calling on friends with her mother, doing her needlework and dancing at society balls in a mauve silk party dress with pearl bead trimming. She went home to a hot footbath and a glass of punch. Yet the social season disappointed her. The rich coat of gold and red which adorned the trees meant the coming of winter. Her spirit seemed to shrink. It curled up in a dark corner to hibernate until spring.

It was in early November that I found both the time and the courage to invite Bessie to the Grocers' Ball, a gala dinner-dance which was renowned for the finest fare and entertainment, but when the evening arrived a spanner in the press prevented my attendance. The junior printer had knocked over his bag of jelly babies and it took me all night to ungum the works. My letter of apology arrived too late and Bessie's feelings were wounded.

'When a girl crimps up for about two hours, arrays herself in silken sheen, soaks herself in *Highland Heather* perfume, it gives one the idea that she rather intends going some-where,' she wrote. 'But when she sits all muffled up for three hours or so, keeps assuring her family that she knows he will come for her and all the time knows he won't, it rather means that, that, well, that matters are a little mixed.'

The hurt which I had caused distressed me. It seemed selfish folly to toy with Bessie's feelings and I resolved that my time would be better employed in productive labour. But despite great application I could not concentrate on my work. Indeed I could hardly eat, playing with my break-fast at the lunch counter, and an absence of appetite had never been one of my failings. Zachary's just criticism of the lapse of discipline increased both my sense of guilt and my misery.

The first snow fell, settled in the carriage ruts and turned the roads into a quagmire. On Front Street my boot stuck in the mud and was trampled beneath the hooves of a Baker Carpet Cleaning cart. That evening I rode home aboard a flying demon of the Toronto Street Railway. The high-voltage flashes crackled from the overhead wire and transformed the bare wayside trees into beheaded corpses. Their broken and twisted limbs swayed to the discordant music of steel wheels on frozen rails. I closed my eyes, pulled my coat around me and forced my thoughts back to summer. The tram jerked and bucked and shook me out of my reverie but not away from the realisation that my life had become joyless without Bessie. It was my timidity which had prevented me from embracing her affection and, aware that I would never be able to say the words to express my feelings, I resolved to write to her that night.

I sat up until dawn spoiling half a ream of good paper and breaking the nib of my pen. My landlady knocked at the door twice. She worried that I suffered from delirium or had a fever in the head. In an attempt to make myself understood I wrote about the three books on my shelf: *The Reveries of a Bachelor*, *Les Misérables* and *Grandfather Grey*. 'What I am trying to get at,' I scrawled, 'is more than I can explain.' It was as if I had taken a crazy fit but somewhere in the scribbles I asked Bessie to marry me. The writing was so bad that she would hardly be able to make it out. I drank six cups of tea and did not sleep. The envelope was too heavy to be carried by a single bird so I made a cat's-cradle of fine string and suspended it between the feet of my two favourite pigeons.

Her response was with me by dinnertime. 'Your letter tells me that you love me but please Jamie tell me with your lips. Make me understand.'

Bessie drew me out of myself and unlocked my heart. At

our wedding she wore myrtle and carried a shower bouquet of white bridal roses. Her dress was simply made, heavy corded silk trimmed with Brussels lace and the orthodox veil of tulle. An orchestra of mandolins and guitars played at the reception. A buffet of dainties was served. I wore a red geranium and small green leaf in my buttonhole. My bride held on to my arm through the whole afternoon.

The success of the firm enabled us to buy our own cottage on the island. Every evening I returned home from work to find a peeled snow apple set beside Father's old globe. We traced the journeys which had made our families, by way of Promise and a West Indies shipwreck, and brought us together. After supper Bessie played Irish airs on the piano and I sang Scottish songs. If we felt daring we risked a duet of 'Seeing Nelly Home'.

She had our bedroom painted blue. 'Now James,' she said as I reached to turn down the lights, 'you are getting bold again.' I picked at the lace trim of her night gown. 'Shall I take it off?' she offered.

'Oh yes; well, if you don't mind.'

'I don't mind.' She pulled the shift up over her head and I held her sweet beauty.

We were never far from each other's touch. On Saturday afternoons the breeze carried our canoe along the lakeshore. Bessie lay on a bed of cushions, a slender arm curled around the bow, her fingers dabbling in the water. The material of her skirt clung to her thigh. In the autumn we went to *Joseph* at the Strand and saw the Robin Hood Opera Company. Some days she did feel poorly and stayed in bed. When I had to travel away from home we wrote to each other every day. On my return she once welcomed me in a feather boa which had been discovered at Walker's. 'Don't you think it makes me covetous?' she asked. Nine months later Claire was born.

The child lay in cotton tucks and pleats on the butternut *chaise longue* chattering at her mother. Bessie stretched out above her as if she were an angel about to take flight. My girls were both desperate talkers. When they grew over-excited I cooled them with a fan and whispered them gentle lullabies. Bessie threw her hands behind her head and laughed and laughed.

Aged eight months Claire died of cholera infantum, a constant diarrhoea which prevented her from keeping food in her stomach. I could never again bear to hear a child cry. Bessie gripped me in her arms and made love like an animal, wailing and sobbing out the terrible sadness. She took to visiting a neighbour's house and begging to hold their baby. She felt her arms so empty.

Sandy was born the next November. In time he would father Beagan. But the Boy was not six months old when Bessie lay down for an afternoon nap in the blue bedroom and did not wake up. On our bed I embraced her with all my strength, gripped her skin, tried to break through to the unbeating heart but the flesh which had brought us close lay cold between us. Bessie was twenty-five years old. Her eyes were closed, her tongue was silent, the silver cord had been loosened and the golden bowl was broken. I wrapped her letters in waxed paper and tied up the package with string. The sealing wax dripped and burnt my hand. I locked it away in the old box trunk with her wedding veil, white satin slippers and the spotted cotton blouse which she had worn. Half an hour after the funeral the Boy was baptised. The funeral boat was crowded and Toronto harbour covered by fog. As the cortège made for the mainland all the steamers in the bay whistled for guidance.

My losses heightened the importance of letters. I began to save all my records. I sorted Mother's correspondence. I filed away my journals. I cherished Father's sermons. The books and papers became my greatest possession. Without the continuity of a family village or old comfortable home all that linked me back to a shared life were words.

I threw myself into work, trying to find distraction in activity and routine. The devil chased me for his copy, the foreman insisted on new type, a subscriber wanted to stop his paper because we had omitted his name from a list of businessmen. Pigeons were replaced by telephones, Bell's not Brown's, and our publications continued to expand. New editors, circulation managers and a corps of correspondents helped strengthen the papers' columns. I oversaw the building of a new plant on the broad boulevard which approached Ontario's Parliament Building.

Zachary came more and more to be influenced by – and influence – the opinions and tastes of society. He enjoyed the power that money brought. He also found reward in the discipline of the militia. All his spare hours were spent with the regiment. He rose to the rank of honorary colonel and in the process learnt to manage people, to delegate responsibility and to direct the corporate attack. His life too came to be run more like a military operation, a well-organised affair of business trips and social engagements, hard work and daily horseriding. There was little room for spontaneity and none for emotion. He never commented on my bereavements. It was not in his nature.

At the opening of the new City Hall with its three-hundred-foot clock tower Zachary stood beneath the Union of Commerce and Industry stained-glass window. His thick, confident moustache and splendid dress, worn with a precision that touched on the pompous, set him apart from the other dignitaries. The evening before, he had been elected by acclamation to the Presidency of the Canadian Newspaper Association. In his acceptance speech he had spoken of the fourth estate usurping the position once occupied by the Church.

'It is powerful and reverenced as a force to help everything good and do justice to everything evil.' He no longer tried to reflect thought but instead aspired to mould opinion. 'It is my aim and hope,' he had told the Old Toronto audience, 'that our publications will provide leadership for the promotion of common interests and help to build up a great nation within the British Empire and in alliance with the United States.'

But Zachary's ambition and our success were no longer enough to inspire me. I needed to mourn. I took to walking through the city at night. The anonymous movement comforted me and I found vicarious pleasure in glimpsing intimate moments through half-opened windows: a couple dining by candlelight, the silhouette of a woman washing her hair, a husband drawing the bedroom curtains. The city had begun to introduce electric street lighting at main intersections and the great arc lamps hissed and spat much like the local politicians who declared that night had been banished. 'There is no more darkness in Toronto,' they lied. The electric glare obscured more and more of the sky. I missed seeing the stars. I seemed to have lost the firmament.

I sold the island cottage, let go of the townhouse and asked Zachary to buy my share of Gillean Publishing. I took to travel and moved west to start trade papers in Guelph and Windsor. The boy Sandy was left behind, placed temporarily in the care of the Goode maiden aunts. I had no other choice. It pained me to look upon the face which remembered his mother's. When he saw me put on my hat and pick up a bag he spoke his first sentence. 'Papa no go,' said my son.

I was once again a wanderer but in time there came to be one place where I could immerse my loneliness. With the settlement from the firm I bought a rag-taggle fleet of coal-burning tugs and supply boats, pinewood scows and puffing steamships which carried freight, mail, passengers and newspapers through a land of thirteen hundred lakes. The Muskoka & Magnetawan Steamship Company was the largest freshwater flotilla in North America. Every summer I travelled north to the pink granite waterland and relaxed into a sort of family life. The Boy was sent up to join me. We paddled my canoe and let the Irish terriers run free. I bought him toy bagpipes and he filled the lakes with his raucous music. At night we cut the motor of my Ditchburn launch and drifted over the black waters counting stars. I never stayed with him for long or explained why I had to go away but I did tell him a story, a story that one day he would tell to his own son, Beagan.

CHAPTER VI

MOSQUITO FLEET

'I HATED GOING to bed on nights like that,' recalled Jamie, gazing up into the heavens. Twilit waves lapped against the side of his canoe. 'I liked to stay up listening to the crickets and waiting for the morning star.' A breath of wind ruffled his thin strands of red hair. 'Look, F-F-Father; there's the Big Dipper. And aren't those the Pleiades?'

'It was the ancient Greeks who considered navigation safe at the rising of that constellation, *a bhalaich*,' said Hector, his celestial reflection shimmering in the moonlight. He trailed his fingers in the cool water. 'They've helped a good many navigators, including the *Good Intent*, right enough.'

'The Boy, Sandy, loved looking at the stars. He always sat with me there, where you're sitting, until he grew bored of his moody old man and got a boat of his own.'

'A stiff measure of discipline would have served him well. As would an absence of that Muscat woman.'

'Rosa was a fine photographer, F-F-Father. No one else managed to capture Pike and the steamships in their prime. That passion for preservation made up for any other failing.'

'There would have been little succour for her in my congregation,' dismissed Hector. 'Look you how her story affected your Beagan. He has all but dismantled the box trunk looking for her photographs.' He was wary of unbridled affection. 'All this feeling can only lead to mishap.'

'It is rather a mystery that, the disappearance I mean,' said Jamie, glancing again at the Pleiades.

'It would have been best had she herself never appeared.'

'No, F-F-Father, you're wrong, because of the love in it, even you cannot deny that. She and Pike are part of the story and Beagan needs to hear it, only, well, I can't do it myself. So would you, please?'

With a theatrical flourish Hector raised his wings above him. Before their eyes night became day, the setting moon transformed into a rising sun and the cluster of stars were bound into red ruby sparks puffing out of a sooty funnel. Captain Pike sounded his two-tone whistle as the RMS *Kipper* rounded Wigwassan Point. In the crickets' chirp Jamie heard the wheeze of the Doty engine and to his delight a little gasoline-powered motorboat sliced through the tossing, rocking swells to catch the old ship's wake.

'I REMEMBER IT,' said Beagan aloud, leafing through the albums again, the contents of the trunk spread around him, every envelope and file emptied out on to Gravenhurst's deserted town pier. 'In the photograph my father is laughing.' He had left Piri and the *Szerencsès* in Toronto harbour, skirted the city and driven north to Muskoka. 'I can see his skiff skimming over the water. I can picture his hair glistening, his eyes sparkling, I can even hear his laugh.' Beagan looked out on blueberry islands and lonely pines. He tasted spindrift on his tongue. 'We cherished that photograph but it has disappeared.'

The photograph was signed Rosa, Rosa Muscat. With her Kodak and a small canvas bag she roamed the Muskoka lakes during the last summer of her short life. Before the First World War her camera drew her into the green dark forests, the wheelhouses of ships, the northern hotels where guests sipped iced tea and lounged in wicker chairs. She travelled alone because her parents were dead. They had been performers who had emigrated from the Azores to Canada. Their speciality had been synchronised swimming. At the Toronto Summer Show Colonel MacKenzie's diving horse – the star attraction – had missed its cue and dived on top of Mr and Mrs Muscat during their popular 'Fallen Angel' routine. The tragedy had closed the show for the day but Rosa had been orphaned for life. She was alone. 'My life is like a piece of old bread, dry and hard, and the sun shines meanly on me,' she had said. So when she fell in love with the captain of the *Kipper* she knew that it was a gift from God. But the Daughters of the Empire (Gravenhurst Chapter) didn't see it that way. God's gifts were reserved for the afterlife, not for common harlots who laughed in church and enticed respected citizens into sin. Society cut her dead. There were no invitations to the Port Carling Water Carnival or Victoria Day picnics on Browning Island. Yet Rosa was used to it. She believed in miracles and had always been either loved or feared for it.

Theodore Pike, the captain, had puffed, whistled and wheezed ships up the lakes since the first logging days. He knew every shoal, every hidden rock, the call of each loon in every bay. He'd seen the old *Nipissing* burn at its moorings. He'd walked on the water of Gravenhurst Bay – from shore to shore, from sawmill to sawmill – across a boom of logs. Like many immigrants he had come to the middle of the vast continent – far from the Atlantic, far from the Pacific – to escape. But Pike wasn't running from persecution or poverty or even failure. He was running from the terror in his heart. On the day he had sailed from Glasgow forty years before he locked it away behind a wall of stone.

It was the lakes which drew Pike to Muskoka. The clear blue-black waters and untamed maple hills helped him forget the inner wilderness. Other settlers were enticed from Muddy York up the Muskoka Colonization Road by free land grants, but the topsoil was too thin to farm so they cut down trees instead. The great oaks and pines were felled on the upper lakes and rivers, lashed together and punted downstream. At the wild rapids the vast rafts were often sucked underwater by the cross-current, their rough cabins swept away in the backwash, and the raftsmen either held on tight to their red pine oars or stayed beneath the waves. They drove the logs down the waterways to the mills and tanneries of

Gravenhurst, then dubbed 'Sawdust City'. The pioneer woods-
men named their townships Watt, Stephenson and Brunel in
honour of engineers who had harnessed nature but they called
the waters Fairy, Otter and Moon.

The steamboats came so migrants could reach the great stretches
of fertile land that lay beyond the lakes. A. P. Cockburn's first
boat, the paddle-wheeled *Wenonah*, was made of planks cut from
the finest timber on Sparrow Lake. Her massive keel was hewn
with broadaxes from a single white oak. Her name was the Ojib-
way word for 'first-born daughter' and Pike worked aboard her
as a stoker, wooding up the roaring sweating boiler and polishing
her gleaming brass valves. His formal manner and taciturnity won
the respect of the locals and he grew with the Navigation Company. He became a deckhand on the iron-hulled *Nipissing*, with
her ornate paddle-boxes and pagoda pilothouse, helped crew the
elfin *Oriole* and was promoted to mate on the *Medora*. On hot
summer nights when the crew took turns cooling themselves
in the Cockburn's Phillips Perfect Refrigerator, Pike sat on the
hurricane deck teaching himself to navigate by the stars. He earned
his Master's Certificate and by his sixtieth year was the senior
officer of the freshwater flotilla. The company's fine new palace
steamer, which Jamie named the *Kipper* in salty memory of Kirstie's
herring days, was placed under his command. Her high razor-shell
bow cleaved the waves. Two full-length decks curved around her
fantail stern. An erect red and black single stack mounted her
amidships. She had a Doty triple expansion engine, two Scotch
marine boilers and a handsome circular dining lounge finished in
weathered oak and burlap. Pike steered her around drifting logs
and surly lumbermen, carried the mail and, as her luxurious
interior appointments had not been built for the penniless immigrant, prepared for the arrival of a new type of traveller.

At dinner parties in Toronto, Pittsburgh and Cleveland the talk
was of the lake district. Its soft healing waters were said to lower
blood pressure and alleviate heart disease. When the rails of the
Grand Trunk reached Muskoka the optimism of the age transformed the backwoods into a fashionable waterland.

The Muskoka Midnight Special, its brass bell clanging sleeping passengers awake, arrived at Gravenhurst from Buffalo and Toronto every summer morning. Young men in white ducks and striped blazers crossed the wharf to the waiting steamers. A moustached banker took his wife's gloved hand as a gust of wind dislodged her broad-brimmed hat. Jamie often sat alone at the end of the pier, watching not speaking, as the crew rolled up their shirtsleeves to load the wicker baskets and leather trunks, buckets of fishing worms and bundles of Gillean newspapers. A blond boy in a sailor suit chased his sister. Her ponytail swung like a pendulum. Their footfalls beat a tattoo on the wooden dock. The purser checked his manifests. A yachting cap blew into the water. 'This steamer,' announced the blackboard, 'is for Windermere.' The chalked destinations read Beaumaris, Rostrevor and the Royal Muskoka Hotel.

The rich holiday-makers cruised up the lakes to the new luxury wilderness resorts. Their gables, turrets and wide sweeping verandahs towered above sandy bathing beaches. The rocky terrain and mossy spruce bogs hindered the construction of roads so the only way to explore the miles of broken shoreline was by water. The hotels organised steamboat outings for the mornings, shuffleboard and croquet matches in the afternoons. Dinner was served by uniformed waitresses in picture-window dining rooms. In the evening guests danced on waxed hardwood floors and drank chilled claret from punch bowls.

The very wealthy moved on from the resorts to build private summer cottages in intimate hidden bays. Their cook, maid, family silver and linen were all transported north on the annual trek from city to country. Their fortunes financed a forty-year flourish of skilled boat-building. Long, sleek motor launches were fashioned from teak and Honduras mahogany. Sweeping windscreens edged in chrome, silver running lights and morocco upholstery set off the varnished decks. The more ostentatious cottagers rode astern and employed a uniformed pilot to attend to the wheel. The handsome pleasure cruisers shuttled between cottages and hotels, meeting trains at Lake Joseph Station and Bala, exchanging passengers in mid-lake transfers. They snubbed together with Jamie's steamers then, while music wafted on the breeze, secured lines and gangways for a moment's coupling. On the *Kipper's* aft deck two members of the company orchestra played a medley of popular airs on the xylophone.

It was in the spring when young deer lick maple sugar from the lower branches that Pike met Rosa. He thrust a boathook down her dress, snared her corset and saved her from drowning. It was long after midnight and Rosa could not swim. As soon as he had lifted her aboard she dived back into the lake to rescue her camera. The snow had only just melted and the waves snapped the thin ice around the hull. Pike took her back to his cabin to warm by the stove. In the lamplight he saw the honey-pale hair of her forearms then noticed that her fingers had turned blue. She shivered and cast a gentle shower of rain over the deck. A tin tub sat full and steaming by the stove. Pike divided the room with a screen, found a clean towel and offered her his bath. As she wrung out her skirt the water ran across the floor to gather in a pool around his feet. Rosa lowered herself into the warm water and startled the minnows in the tub. They had been sucked up by the pump when Pike had drawn his water from the lake.

The cabin was his home. He hadn't slept on dry land since the nineteenth century, and around her she saw his collection of memorabilia: a carved whalebone, the golden toe of a Burmese Buddha, a Pomo coiled boat basket decorated with clam-shell beads and tufts of red woodpecker feathers. A shard of marble from the Great Pyramid served as the soap dish. His towel rail was the bronze censer from a German monastery. Through the course of his seafaring youth Pike had gathered curios and relics from around the world. There were dinosaur bones and petrified eggs, two Roman amphorae filled with American copper pennies and a fleet of schooners in a dozen bottles. Beneath a Saracen scimitar between two sheets of glass was a minute fragment of manuscript, its Greek letters faded and edges singed, the only page to survive when the books of the library at Alexandria were burnt to heat the city. Beside his bed was a tennis racquet used for expelling bats.

'This is my ark,' Pike explained as he passed a dram of whisky around the side of the screen. Rosa was encircled by flashes of silver. The bodies of the minnows were so translucent that they seemed to be more a suggestion of life than its substance.

'It was one of those moments,' she said later, 'when you can no longer put on the shoes that you thought you would wear all your life.'

The drying clothes filled the cabin with her scent. Pike sat in his cane armchair and tried not to watch the young woman's shadow dance over his nautical prints and Chilean engravings. Rosa did not stay. She was anxious to develop the photograph which had almost cost her life. The Kodak sat in a puddle on the deck. After she departed all that remained of her was a damp handprint on his sleeve.

It was her photographs which next touched him. They seemed to see below the surface and capture the essence behind the image. The sensation was so powerful that Pike had to turn over the pictures and look behind them for the perceived depth. His long fine fingers stroked his white walrus moustache but the mosquitoes buzzed around his ears. Women were portrayed without hats. Labouring men were photographed in their shirtsleeves. The Daughters of the Empire didn't approve. Public morals were at risk.

As spring blossomed into summer Rosa discovered the lakes from the bridge of the *Kipper*. She photographed the puffing ships, the belching mills, the prosperous cottagers. Her camera followed their caretakers as they took down the snow shutters and let the cool May sunlight flood into the chalets. Her broom helped sweep away the clam shells discarded by scavenging racoons and the carcasses of dead mice frozen during the winter. She photographed pearl-white boathouses on emerald curved bays and watched the sleek Ditchburn launches being lowered from the rafters into their slips. Through her lens the supply steamers *Mink* and *Newminko* plied the lakes to stock the cottages. Their crew of four – captain, engineer, butcher and grocer – brought staples and gossip to kitchen maids. Fillet steaks and roasts were supplied by McCulley's

Meat Market. Hardware, clothing and shoes were carried on special order. Every week the *Smelt* brought Pike his newspapers and a dollar pot of Quick Cure, a patented remedy used with success in curing colds. He had never shaken off the cough contracted on rounding the Horn and a teaspoon heated on a piece of old tin filled his cabin with fumes which eased sleep. Every Sunday the long-bowed, canvas-canopied church boat nosed from dock to dock gathering the faithful. The *Spray* from Orgill's Point collected and delivered laundry. Bill Campbell peddled fresh farm produce from his tug *Ida*. Private yellow pine launches, their fly-wheels spinning amidships, spat smoke and sparks into the sweet air. The diminutive *Gypsy* from Clark's Mill took more than a day to tow its log boom the few miles from Skelton Bay to Snug Harbour. She often blocked the waterway leaving no passage clear and the other boats whistled their irritation at the sawmill's pointers.

'In my heart there are clouds and thunderstorms,' Rosa told Pike when the days warmed and the air filled with the drone of insects. On a stormy night in June she returned to his cabin and took him as her lover without fuss or formality. As the sway of the ship rocked them to sleep he called her his angel.

'You know how angels behave, don't you?' Rosa replied. 'They always go back to where they came from.' Then she anchored herself to the bed, one foot locked over the edge, the other thrust between their two mattresses and wrapped the sheet around them like the spirals of a conch shell. The great stone wall around Pike's heart cracked and miracles became possible. The prophets had walked on water. Jonah did live in the stomach of a whale. Saul was blind and then could see. Pike was forty years her senior and Rosa had faith.

AS THE *KIPPER* whistled for the *Gypsy* to clear a passage Hector strode from shore to shore, though not across the boom, beside himself with indignation. 'No angel that I've ever met wears lipstick, especially cherry red. And that Pike runs too much from his own doubts and demons, just as does Beagan.'

Jamie followed behind, leaping cat-like over the loose logs. 'Maybe if you stopped attacking her vice you might begin to appreciate her virtue.'

'It was not myself that laboured all those years to tolerate such undirected, unbridled passion.'

'Isn't it better than just being dull and decent?'

Hector stopped in mid-stride, starboard of the *Kipper*'s bow, and the swells lapped over his shoes. 'My role is saving souls, not condoning sin. This sort of behaviour unstitches the fabric of society, right enough. Your brother understood that.' A light laugh sparked across the water and Hector stared up at the ship. 'Bless my soul, is it herself onboard?'

'It is, F-F-Father,' said Jamie. 'And we do need to continue the story for Beagan.'

'That we will. There is responsibility in this memory and that, at long last, he begins to appreciate, though devil enough remains in him to damn a dozen sinners. Now stand aside James, it is time to call your brother.' Hector looked over his shoulder, spread his cape then shouted at the trees, 'Zachary!' A clutch of startled chickadees took flight. 'Zachary!' The *Kipper*'s Union Jack rustled in the breeze. 'Where on God's good earth is he?'

AT FIRST THE Daughters of the Empire (Gravenhurst Chapter) tried to ignore the liaison, but as it was the juiciest gossip since Amanda Dung had eloped with the snakebite–elixir salesman they couldn't restrain themselves for long. Word of the scandal spread through the community, up the lakes and portages, from Bent

River to Swampy Bay. The more prudish citizens who lacked anything better to do refused to travel on the *Kipper* so the town council became concerned, especially as the mayor was married to the chairwoman of the Daughters of the Empire.

One afternoon in late July on her way south through Lake Rosseau the *Kipper* called for passengers at Windermere House. The Daughters of the Empire stepped aboard to find Rosa with her captain on the bridge. Winifred Stubbs suggested that they refuse to travel but, as the chairwoman's bunions were aching, they agreed to compromise their principles. The mosquitoes joined Rosa, the Reverend MacGill and Blossom, Ed Kingshott's prize heifer, on the *Kipper*.

On the approach to Port Carling the *Kipper* hit a deadhead, a submerged log, and the force of the blow snapped the drive shaft clean in two. The current was very strong where the waters of Rosseau rushed towards the Indian River rapids and the steamer was dragged towards ruin.

The women screamed. The Reverend prayed. Blossom mooed. The captain leaned on the wheel but without her engine the elegant ship became sluggish and refused to respond. He pulled the lanyard and a plaintive steam whistle wailed for help. The first mate, an old lumberman with arms tattooed, distributed lifejackets and whispered of demons. It seemed that all hope was lost until Rosa removed her corset. The Daughters of the Empire recognised her as the Jezebel whom they had always feared but Pike saw her corset, the one from which he had released her on a dozen summer nights, as their only chance of salvation.

Together the lovers descended to the bilges. Soaked in grease and oil they crawled forward of the thrust bearing, beyond the pistons and cranks, to locate the break. They fashioned a splint and wrapped the corset around the join. Back on deck the Reverend had lost faith. He prayed aloud while Pike engaged the engine with infinite gentleness. The whalebone stays gripped. The propeller turned. The *Kipper* held its ground against the current and edged back upstream to the pier. Blossom, the prize heifer, never realised her luck. In her excitement and in full view of the passengers Rosa embraced Pike. 'You are the best of men in the world,' she laughed. 'Now kiss me without breathing for one minute.'

In Ontario no one says thank you to a whore. Evil disguised as the common good can spread like a forest fire in August. Mosquitoes bite and the incident fabricated substance to claims of negligence. The council revoked Pike's licence. They would allow no fornicators at the wheel. They barred him from the ship, evicted him from his cabin, banished him from the ark. Pike and Rosa didn't give a porcupine's fart for the Daughters of the Empire (Gravenhurst Chapter) and settled into a hotel. 'Life is a cake full of stones but hope is my motto,' she insisted as September's gusts blew through the open window. But their money was limited and at night Pike hung his cap over the lightbulb to save electricity. The dark room stood still and the air was heavy with the smell of stale beer from the tavern below. After so many years afloat Pike awoke sweating and crying that the wind had changed direction and the bow line snapped. In the grounded sawdust hotel he grappled with imaginary ropes before falling exhausted back to bed.

The townspeople who owed their lives to the unlacing of a corset shunned the lovers. Shopkeepers, farmers, even Blossom's owner refused to serve them. A rumour was spread about that Rosa was pregnant. Winifred Stubbs claimed to have overheard the couple talking. 'We will name him after a river or a lake,' Rosa had whispered. Winifred had to sneak up close to hear their conversation. 'A name not bound to anything just as water isn't bound to anything.' Then the days grew colder, the leaves turned crimson and Pike bought a canoe. He boxed up the Buddha's toe and dinosaur bones, the pyramid soap dish and the Alexandria library parchment. One autumn morning while the mist clung to the surface of the lake they slipped out of town never to be seen again.

'It was shortly before they disappeared that Rosa took the photograph of my father,' remembered Beagan, alone on the pier. 'Years later, after he died, the print was mislaid. I'd always hoped that the negative would be in the trunk, but I've looked right through it and it's not here.' On the strip of negative where the image had once been there was only blank emulsion. The photographs taken before and after it were perfectly preserved but the laughing boy had vanished.

CHAPTER VII

TREES IN THE BOG

'PIKE?' FUSSED ZACHARY. 'I don't remember anyone called Pike.' He straddled the roof of the wheelhouse like a cocksure phoenix, adjusted his splendid evening dress and brushed a fleck of dust off his lapel. The plume of his silk scarf snapped in the breeze. 'Bally fool of a name anyway.'

The ship's bell rang and the whistle sprouted a moustache of steam which curled and wrapped itself around the stack. A trail of smoke spiralled away over the stern of the RMS *Segwun*, the sole survivor of the Mosquito Fleet. Jamie sailed along beside the bridge, paddling the air in an ersatz sidestroke and kicking his feet as if under water.

'I'm not surprised that you have f-f-forgotten him. You hardly ever left the office, except for society soirées.' He tightened the shoulder strap of his bathing costume. 'You never had time to visit me.'

'In all labour there is profit,' spouted Zachary. He was in a particularly pedantic mood. 'And the Lord rewards him according to his works.'

'I will not have the Apostles quoted in vain,' snapped Hector as a guffaw of irreverent laughter chased him up on to the bridge. His inspection of the relaxed holiday-makers on the lower decks had put him in a severe humour. 'Were there ever two boys who forgot so fearfully much learning?'

'James always lacked concentration, Father. He confused the business of work with the matter of life.'

'Be that as it may, you are not the highest tree in the

orchard, Zachary,' reproached Hector. He cast his critical gaze about the modern lakeland. A water-skier slalomed past the steamer, kicked an arc of spray over the dockside satellite dishes and took a spill below a garish billboard which advertised Great North Log Homes. 'That trollop should be in church, like all the other lie-abeds down below.' The ski-boat cut across the *Segwun*'s bow, its passengers raising their beer bottles in salute, but before Hector could pass judgement his attention was distracted by Jamie's aerial ballet. 'And what would it be that you are now doing, James?'

'Swimming, F-F-Father.' Jamie rolled over and flailed his limbs about in an erratic backstroke. 'Or at least trying to remember how to. It's been a long time.'

'It would seem that both memory and elegance have deserted you.'

'Not memory, no.' A startled seagull squawked and swooped away from the foremast. 'I remember that this is the very bay where Zachary and I began our f-f-first holiday together.'

'Our only holiday together,' corrected his elder brother, his back as rigid as the red and black funnel. 'Vacations never agreed with me; all that excessive sun and wasted time.'

'It is not laziness that ever built anything worthwhile, especially a good ship.' Hector paused to consider the *Segwun*'s lines, handsome enough to please the most fastidious sailor, then nodded in approval at the trail of steam. 'Right enough, she has a lively sheer, James. You should feel justifiably proud.'

Zachary stamped his foot on the roof and startled the captain, who looked up from the nickel-plated hand controls. 'I never understood what James saw in old boats. I would have sold out and been shot of Muskoka years earlier.'

'I grew fond of them,' confessed Jamie, breaking into a

back-crawl. 'They were like a f-f-family: little *Mildred*, the busy *Newminko*, grouchy old *Cherokee*.'

'A decidedly unreliable family in my opinion,' tut-tutted his brother. 'The *Mildred* blew a gasket and ran aground. The *Newminko* sank in the Port Carling locks and the *Cherokee* impaled itself on a shoal.' He did not share a love of boats. 'She sheared her propeller blades and was left to rot. The wreckers smashed her wooden superstructure to remove the engines. I warned you that the new highways would stop people travelling by water but you didn't listen. So you lost a fortune.'

'I sold my share in the Navigation Company for a modest sum.'

'Maybe a quarter of its real value. And you gave away the *Sagamo*.'

'Her name meant "Big Chief", and she once carried eight hundred passengers,' Jamie explained to their father. Hector had sat himself in the restored cedar-strip lifeboat and begun pulling on imaginary oars.

'The new owners removed her boilers to convert her into a floating restaurant but a heater exploded and set her ablaze. I heard a rumour that the Fire Department couldn't be bothered to save her and let her burn.'

Hector stopped rowing, scandalised. 'It is only a fool who squanders his inheritance.'

'The whole business was a bad investment,' pronounced Zachary.

Jamie sighed, drank in the clear clean air as deep as his breath would permit then held it as if diving under water. He counted to ten. His brother's zealotry tested his patience but he was determined not to show irritation. 'The *Kipper* didn't sink or run aground. It was bureaucracy which wrecked her,' he recalled. 'Do you remember that fire aboard the SS *Noronic*, the pleasure cruiser on Lake Ontario?'

'Of course. We were the first to have a reporter on the

scene. The tragedy had a considerable impact on marine insurance premiums.'

'One hundred and eighteen excursionists were killed in one tragic night.'

'A sad event but it brought about changes that were good for both the public and business. The Ministry of Transport reacted by imposing exacting regulations on all passenger vessels. Safer ships were built. Insurance companies prospered. Two of my papers, *Great Lakes Shipping* and *Insurance Digest*, had very profitable years.'

'But under the new rules wooden ships never sailed again,' stressed Jamie. He had stopped his thrashing and glided alongside the wheelhouse. 'The *Kipper* was condemned as unfit, stripped down to her main deck and converted into a barge. Muskoka Wharf station was also dismantled, the rails torn up and the trim building replaced by aluminium-clad boathouses. The f-f-fleet simply wasted away.'

'The price of progress, James. I told you to sell your interest.'

'Progress?' said Hector, stroking the lifeboat's caned black-cherry seats. 'Did you say progress?' The further he travelled from his islands the more the lyricism left him. 'It is the old days that I understood better, you can't get away from it.'

'No one can hold back the tide, Father. The successful man goes with it, directs it.' Zachary peered over the heads to spot Beagan's balding pate among the tourists on the foredeck. 'And talking about inefficiency, what is your grandson doing here on this relic, James, other than wasting my time?'

'I suppose he's looking for me,' blushed Jamie.

'He could have saved us all a great deal of bother and stayed in Scotland with the trunk.' Zachary pulled a fob-watch from his waistcoat and gave it a testy shake. Timepieces do not run in the hereafter, yet he could not break the habit of a lifetime. 'There's nothing for him to find here.

Your halcyon retreat now looks like suburbia and you are forgotten.'

'That's a bit unf-f-fair.'

'You left no monuments. Why didn't you donate a ward to the local hospital or establish a Chair of Journalism at some small university as I advised? At the time it was not beyond your means.' Zachary tapped the crystal of his stopped watch. 'But now it's too late to do anything at all,' he added with a flash of bitterness. 'Is that sluggard going to get a move on or what?'

IN GRAVENHURST NO one could remember Beagan's grandfather. Jamie's cottage had been sold and the new owners couldn't be bothered to sail over to the public wharf to pick him up. The *Kipper* was gone and nobody had heard of Rosa or Pike. At the town pier Beagan had opened the trunk and searched for the missing photograph, stretching his memory back to embrace his father's stories. He had then joined the queue of holiday-makers and boarded the oldest operating steamboat on the continent for a two-hour 'fun, romance and history' cruise up the lake. There had been no concessionary fare for the grandson of a past owner.

The RMS *Segwun* slipped through the Narrows and summer-brown children waved from the sweeping sundecks of plush pine residences. Replica Coca-Cola signs hung behind their broad windows. A trained dog scampered out of a cottage, rang a bell with its muzzle and the captain replied with another whistle.

On deck families unpacked their picnics and laughed in the sunshine. Older passengers ordered Ship's Champagne and sat down to lunch in the Royal Muskoka Salon. A lean, bow-legged man sporting a kerchief and worn leather boots swaggered fists first into the lounge. He dropped into a chair, suspended his Ray-Bans from his collar and asked for coffee, black.

'Yes sir, this is a great place in the summer,' he said to a friend up from the city for the weekend, 'but you can't beat the winter.'

He leaned forward to make his point. 'Four busloads of divorcees at Hidden Valley every week. You don't even have time to go skiing.' He thought the waves lapping against the hull sounded like applause. 'Like last year there was this girl who was rectifying her life with her husband, eh? She came up at Christmas, my own little elf.' The coffee arrived. 'But every time I did it to her she said, "You only want me for my body." You know, I like to think I'm more into spiritual growth.' Behind them a tanned, bored day-tripper read his ketchup bottle. His date straightened her shorts. 'So one time she comes up and finds me poking this other chicken and she goes crazy and starts breaking up the place and grabs my snowshoes and takes off.' He swallowed his coffee. 'One week later I'm here in town at the post office getting my mail, you know, and she comes in and she's got the snowshoes and she starts hitting me with them.'

'She still around?' asked the friend.

'Yup.'

'She still got the snowshoes?'

'Nope, I got them back.'

At the next table Beagan ordered a slice of blueberry pie and waited for the president of the company. He had agreed to give him an hour of his time but had been delayed inspecting the new electronic fire-detection system. Beyond the window a towboat pulled forward and another skier rose up out of the water. The outboard's whine drowned out the shrill call of a tree frog. It was somewhere beyond the rotating Kentucky Fried Chicken bucket that, according to the story, Rosa had saved the *Kipper*.

The waitress noticed him staring out at Indian River. 'The best place in the world,' she said and meant it. Her T-shirt read 'Muskoka: The Greatest Lakes'. She tucked a tip into her cut-off jeans and balanced half a dozen plates on her arm. 'I've been coming up every summer for longer than I can remember.' Her family had owned a cottage on Echo Point for over a century. 'It's sort of our touchstone.' She placed a frosty glass in front of Beagan. 'Hey, don't worry, you can drink the water. It comes out of a bottle, not the lake.'

The president could rave all afternoon about hull plates and retubed boilers. His kind, pudgy face was dominated by the wide, rabbit-like eyes of an enthusiast. He talked to Beagan about the history of the line and the coming of the automobile. 'If your grand-dad were alive today,' he said, 'I'd sure like to enquire why he didn't cut the larger ships, forget about serving the distant cottages and run pleasure cruises only?'

'I guess he didn't want to let anyone down,' replied Beagan. He asked about the company records, which had been lost, then added, 'Is there anyone around who knew my grandfather?'

The president leaned back and thought. 'Didn't old Doris Pilch work for him?'

'Sure, for most of her life. But, well, I'm really quite angry at her. My father left her this trunk to give to me on my twenty-first birthday, but she got the timing wrong and waited twenty-one years instead.' His eyes flashed with a moment's bitterness and he gripped the edge of the table.

'So she's gone a bit soft in the head,' shrugged the president. 'Big deal. We had her hundredth birthday party on board last year and she spent the afternoon wandering all over the ship looking for your grand-dad. That's how I remembered that she worked for him.' His eyes widened as if caught in a car's headlights. 'The only thing that keeps her going is the determination to outlive her daughter. Cheryl's spent the last twenty-five years trying to kill her off, waiting for the inheritance.' The president chuckled. 'You should go see them. They live like cat and dog up at old Tobermory House.' Beagan tried to picture the summer resort. 'You know, up on Lake Rosseau, across the bay from your grand-dad's old place.'

North of Port Carling knots of cow parsley, excited by the breeze, nodded their heads in a frenzy like dizzy blonde teenagers, or even après-ski divorcees. The earth's crust erupted through the topsoil. The thin ribbon of highway was hemmed in by great pink outcrops of the Precambrian Canadian Shield. The blueberry pie too was like granite, although Beagan's indigestion was more due to nerves. Doris Pilch had known his grandfather and raised his father, sailed aboard the *Kipper* and watched the Mosquito Fleet rot away. His stomach grumbled and he fished in a pocket for a Kwell when something in the rear-view mirror caught his eye.

His forefathers crammed behind him in a row along the car's back seat and argued. 'Twenty-one years wasted,' repeated Zachary, who had measured out his life in annual reports and inter-office memos. He commandeered the centre of the back seat like a pompous pasha. 'A man makes his own opportunities, James. Fate does not hand them out in turn to all and sundry.'

Hector paid his sons little attention, preferring to sit in silence. A truck accelerated by his window, 'Simply the Best for Less' emblazoned along its trailer. 'Progress,' he reflected then watched Beagan glance again into the empty mirror.

'Who is this Pilch woman then?' demanded Zachary from his throne. 'Another irresponsible friend of that Pike, I dare say.'

'Doris Pilch was my housekeeper; a gentle, mild, diminutive Scot,' explained Jamie.

'Not the one who wore those ridiculous flapper hats?'

'She wore sensible shoes, spoke French and F-F-Flemish, travelled across Europe as a governess and came to Canada to marry the Gravenhurst postmaster. They lived together under the town hall clock but it rang all night and drove him to an early death.'

'May he have found his peace in heaven,' said Hector as Beagan again pulled on to the hard shoulder.

'Why does your Beagan need to check that confounded map so often?' flared Zachary.

'Other side,' whispered Hector into their descendant's ear.

'I wish you wouldn't do that, F-F-Father,' sighed Jamie.

'Look now the two of you, it's well enough that he's coping with it,' insisted Hector.

Beagan turned over the road map and located the route. He took another long sideways look in his mirror then pulled back on to the highway. The acceleration was slow, as if the car was somehow overloaded.

'And yes, Zachary, it was Pike who suggested that Doris might like to be my housekeeper,' continued Jamie. 'She arrived at the cottage by steamer and after a short interview said, "Mr Gillean, it is most extravagant of you to keep the boat waiting. Am I to dismiss the *Kipper* or do you no want me to stay?" I hired her on the spot.'

'It was she who attended to your Sandy?'

'She cared for the Boy as if he were her own, then looked after me until my death.' The car lurched on to a side road kicking up a swirling trail of chalky pink dust. 'I never f-f-forgot her.'

IT WASN'T INCOMPETENT map-reading alone which hindered Beagan's search for the resort. The once grand Tobermory House Hotel had been closed for a decade. The forest had advanced on to the earthen drive, throwing out creepers and reducing it to the width of a footpath. Brambles screeched against the side of the rental car like fingernails drawn across slate. The parking lot was so overgrown that he mistook it for pasture. Bulrushes and marsh flowers had taken root on the beach. Weeds had split the patios and shuffleboard court. The tally of the last match was rusted on to the players' scoreboard.

A weather-worn 'For Sale' sign swung against the central rotunda. In the office lay a dozen table tennis nets, spools of unravelled adding-machine paper and a single flip-flop. The chapel was empty save for a discarded auctioneer's catalogue: '25 oak high chairs, 170 beds, 6 stags heads, 1 row boat (no oars)'. The corral of wood-beamed cottages which surrounded the central building had been ravaged by time and drunken boaters. Rags of curtains blew through jagged window frames. Rat-chewed guidebooks rotted on moulding carpets. Swallows nested under the eaves. The stone chimneys which had been cracked by the frost reminded Beagan of the cleared crofts of Scotland. He remembered the rusting iron bedheads lost in a tangle of gorse, a widow's smashed quern, a child's shattered cup, and shivered at the thought of another generation being cast out from their bay.

Beagan waded through the waist-high grass to the buckled steamer dock. Its spine had been broken by ice floes and the cribs spilt stones on to the lake floor. He knocked at the boathouse door. Seagulls rose in excited white flocks. A woodpecker tap-tapped on a maple, tree frogs sang in the pines and an indignant toad, its sleep disturbed, hopped under a birch branch. Dragonflies mated on the lakeside lamp-posts, their bases eroded and collapsed on the fine white sand. He knocked again and as an afterthought shouted. His voice sounded out of place, as if mankind no longer belonged. Above him a window creaked open and a television jingle drowned out the sound of the waves. 'How do you handle a hungry man? The Man-handlers; bah bah boom boom bah bah.'

'Who's there?' cried a shrill tongue. A head appeared against the sky and though he couldn't make out the face Beagan recognised the voice. He almost heard the electrostatic swish of the acrylic pant-suit. 'Oh, it's you. I guess you'd better come up.'

He climbed the dark stairs towards the announcer urging him to succumb to the temptation of tinned sauces – 'Mix the sauce with your cooked chicken, some mushrooms, peas, parsley, top it with puff pastry and in half an hour, real home-baked chicken pot pie' – and into the apartment over the boat slips.

'You've come to see Mom,' moaned Cheryl. She seemed to distend the compact sitting room. Like many country people she ate a traditional diet, one heavy on bread, fried potatoes and pies, and her metabolism hadn't adapted to a modern, sedentary life. Instead of labouring in winter fields she eased power-steered cars to heated shopping malls and grew obese. Her body had the exaggerated proportions of a plasticine figure lumped together by a schoolboy in art class. The neon pink outfit didn't help disguise her excesses. 'Mom's been poorly and a bit forgetful.' The towered boathouse seemed to sway with Cheryl's movement. 'I doubt she'll remember you.'

While he waited Beagan watched an episode of *The Waltons* sandwiched between ads for antacid tablets and chocolate bars. 'I still remember getting my first candy from my grandfather,' prattled an actor. 'I'll never forget that first taste; sweet and creamy and just plain good. I felt I was really somebody special.' He wondered if the chime of the town hall clock had been more restful than the racket of the television and stood up to turn down the volume. A corn dolly on a paper doily adorned the set. The lampshade was wrapped in store cellophane. Prints of kittens torn from an old calendar and hundreds of losing lottery tickets were tacked all over the chipboard walls. Unlike Piri, Cheryl had never chosen the right ticket. In contrast Doris's few possessions were crammed into one corner of the room. The sheets of used wrapping paper, carefully ironed and refolded, matchbooks and bars of soap from hotels long ago demolished reflected her Scottish frugality.

Beagan peered around the drawn curtains and out across the waters which Jamie and Sandy had shared until he heard the soft shuffle of slippers behind him. 'Oh, you look wonderful,' Doris rolled in her Highland burr. Her slender frame had shrunk in the years since their last meeting. She had the bones of a bird and it seemed that a breath of wind might blow her out of the window and away towards Wigwassan Point. Her frailty so moved Beagan that he forgave her the lost years as she fluttered in his embrace. 'You look just like your grandfather.'

'You're not the first person to tell me that.'

She took his hand and they sat on the sofa. A ghost would have made more of an impression on the cushions than did her featherweight. 'I had pneumonia,' she told him.

'That was two years ago, Ma,' said Cheryl, who had parked herself behind a plastic asparagus fern.

'Was it?' asked Doris and twittered like a sparrow. 'I lose track of the time.'

'She was sick and wouldn't go to hospital.'

'I'll not leave this old bay until the death watch is in my ear.'

'Then why won't you take your cyanide?' jested Cheryl. 'Ma, don't look at me with those beady little eyes.'

'I wish you wouldn't say that.'

'Me too,' said Beagan.

'Great price, friendly advice,' chimed the television.

Cheryl rose to her feet and Beagan imagined her care combined with sudden bursts of impotent rage: incurious, unmotivated and imprisoned by avarice. 'At least you didn't bring her candies.' She stabbed a thumb towards the spare room. 'There are boxes and boxes back there.'

'I never much cared for sweets.' A wrap of medical tape still repaired the bridge of her spectacles broken before the last war. 'Too improvident.'

'Birthday after birthday they've been stacked up in there, unopened, wasted. She won't let me touch them . . . luxuries.' Cheryl picked up a dog-eared scrapbook, dropped it on to her mother's lap and kissed her head. 'She hits me sometimes,' she told Beagan.

'I'm not surprised.'

'Oh, don't hit me again, Ma,' she added, playing the child. 'Bet you didn't hit his dad.'

'You do look so much like your grandfather now,' Doris repeated to Beagan as she examined the tatty leaves one by one. The glue had dried out and all the photographs slipped on to her lap. She remounted each before turning the page. There were pictures of her family home on Loch Fyne and her grandfather's ship, the *Ossian*. Her husband stood beneath the Gravenhurst clock and a brother posed in merchant marine uniform. There were postcards of all the Mosquito steamships. 'What a strong family resemblance.' She lay a finger on Jamie's portrait. 'You know he was a gentleman of the old times.'

'Why not give it to him now, Ma?' proposed Cheryl. 'You'll never look at them again.'

'I might.'

'Then put it in an envelope with his name and address on. It'll be easier to mail after you've gone.' Beagan felt her resist the temptation to ask for a dollar to cover the postage.

'Didn't I already send you something?' asked Doris, her brow knotted with the strain of recall. 'A letter? No, your father's box trunk.'

'You did,' sighed Beagan. 'Eventually.'

'I was glad to get shot of the dusty old thing,' said Cheryl.

'It seemed a long time to hold on to it but your father always had his own way of doing things. Is everything there?'

'Almost. I'm going through it now, trying to follow the family through the papers, and for my trouble getting soaked in Scotland, seasick on the Atlantic, even spooked in Cape Breton.' In the familiar company of the forgetful Beagan laughed suddenly, unexpectedly, as he hadn't done for years. 'It's funny, but it has sort of anchored me, at the same time as guiding me right across the country. By following them I'm finding something that was missing in me.'

'Here he is.' Doris's hand hovered over a snapshot of Sandy as a boy then turned the page. 'And here you are. Or is that his father?'

'It's my brother Alex.'

Doris became confused by the overlapping generations and started to address Beagan with his grandfather's name. 'Did you bring some pictures with you then, Mr Gillean?'

'I've brought back the trunk.'

Beagan ran out to the car and drove it through the tall grass to the boathouse. He eased the trunk upstairs, its memories scraping on every step. They spread the contents over the floor while Cheryl went off to get a Coke and some pie. 'Call this number now for your free personal involvement kit,' instructed another earnest advertiser. 'An operator is standing by to take your order.'

The photographs of bentwood chairs, potted palms and corn-flower-blue china eggcups transported Doris back to Tobermory House's golden days. There were Navigation Company timetables and a blank envelope containing a single lock of red hair. She picked up Hector's globe and wrapped a slender arm around it as a mother would cradle a lost child. Together they turned over a decade's worth of letters from the Boy to Jamie. Beagan read his father's words aloud. 'My dear Dad: I had a fine birthday. I got from Nan a toll set.'

'I was Nan,' interrupted Doris. 'Master Sandy's nanny.'

'The tolls are dandy like this: a fine screwdriver, a fine saw (big one), a dandy plane, a great big stell hamer.' He had added, 'I spalt this myself,' and concluded, as all his letters had concluded, 'Please Dad come home soon.'

'He was very good with his hands. He used the tools to build his first boat,' remembered Doris. 'What was it called . . . ?' She strained to name the shapes in her cloudy memory. '*Maud*, that was it; a log raft with a hole cut in the middle. He covered the hole with a tea-chest cabin and a stovepipe funnel and hid inside burning damp leaves in a McVitie and Price biscuit tin while walking along the lake bottom.' She perched on the edge of the sofa. 'Smoke belched out both the funnel and cabin's eyeholes and he came in covered in soot. He was filthy.'

In a sepia print the Boy beamed at Rosa's Kodak, a spanner clutched in his hand, standing chest-high to the engineer aboard the *Kipper*. Doris's voice took on a disciplinary tone. 'No, not clean enough, Master Sandy. Wash those hands again and this time use the nail brush.' She then asked Beagan how his father was getting on at school.

'Please do not expect another long letter this term,' he recited from Sandy's postcard. 'The exams really start on Friday and I shall be fearfully busy, that is if I want to pass them all.'

'Of course he must pass,' insisted Doris. 'And he can't go on getting minuses.'

Beagan studied the headmaster's comment on the term's report card. 'Sandy has taken a keen interest in machinery and has a practical knowledge of internal combustion engines probably unsurpassed by anyone of his age.'

The Boy wore a folded paper hat and rowed two woolly dogs across the bay which lay beyond Doris's window. 'Yesterday,' Sandy had written and Beagan read, 'I was looking over the

Scripps gasoline engine catalogue. A price list is enclosed giving full particulars. These Scripps seem to be a very straight bunch and their Reliability Engine is the plain, sensible motor with no freaks that powered the little launch *Detroit* across the Atlantic.'

'He promised to meet Mr Gillean off the *Kipper* at Port Carling on Saturday night,' Doris scolded. 'But his wee *Primary* had been in three speedboat races and was much too dirty.' Sandy's first motorboat had been named *Primary*. She had been powered by a Kermath four-cylinder four-cycle engine with reverse gear which produced twelve horsepower. He had fastened a shelf from the cottage refrigerator to the boat's transom at an angle that gave extra lift and she made a good ten miles per hour.

Cheryl had no interest in reminiscences and sat back down in front of the television. 'Years ago it was just vast, open space but then Canadian National opened the way,' blethered a railway commercial. 'Towns sprang up, business boomed across this country.' Doris was distracted by the sound and pointed at the flickering screen. 'Look at that child's posture. It's disgraceful.'

Beagan's hand fell on to an envelope addressed in Jamie's neat script. It was postmarked four months before his wedding. 'If you think you could get those feet of yours to work properly,' he had proposed to Bessie, 'I should be delighted to accompany you to the Grocers' Ball. It promises to be a splendid evening. Will you honour me?' A dusting of a scented powder settled on to Beagan's palm.

Doris fell silent for a moment. She ran a length of silk ribbon through her fingers then reached into the trunk and drew out a small leather album of honeymoon photographs: Montreal in a thunderstorm from the Windsor Hotel, the good ship *Sardinian*, a glimpse of York from a flying train, the ruins of Duart Castle. In a snapshot captioned 'Mother's happy island home' Bessie threw her hands behind her head and laughed. Doris looked up, took Beagan's hand in two of her own and spoke with sudden clarity to his grandfather. 'I think that I know something of the great love you keep for some locked up in your heart.'

Beagan remained silent. Cheryl switched to another channel and turned up the volume. 'Once upon a time in the land of Great Canadian Cheeses was a mighty cheddar bursting with flavour, a mild melting mozzarella and, imagine, delightful parmesan.'

'You live so much alone in so many ways and in her you found one who had the key to your heart,' affirmed Doris. 'Well she is gone and your life is empty.'

'Ma, don't tire yourself out,' said Cheryl without taking her eyes off the screen, then added, '*Lassie*'s on next.'

'Not tired,' snapped Doris, who had used up all her mothering with Sandy only then to give birth to complaint through genetics. 'I sleep all day in this cage and I'm so bored.' The programme's opening credits began and a collie performed a trick. 'Look at that dog, he's put all the rubbish in the bin. What a clever dog.' Beagan started to move away but Doris gripped his hand with sudden force. 'Your life but not your heart for she is with you still,' she continued. Her cheeks were flushed. 'Dear Mr Gillean, she is still alive in your memory, helping you be good and true, still standing by your side. But the Boy,' she pleaded. 'You must not forget your boy.'

Cheryl sniffed the air, sighed and put down her plate. 'Ma, do you want to go to the little girls' room?' Doris looked away as her daughter took her arm. Her lower lip was quivering. 'She wears a diaper now,' confided Cheryl.

During the thirty minutes that it took Doris to clean herself Cheryl harangued Beagan about the Queen. Was she the wealthiest woman in the world? Wasn't it unfair? Beagan said little as he repacked the trunk. 'There's a million dollars in total cash prizes available to be won,' chirped the TV. 'Don't let somebody beat you to the really big money.' When Doris shuffled back into the room her flannel housecoat was buttoned up to the chin. The excitement had exhausted her and she began to repeat herself. 'The first time I came to the cottage the *Kipper* waited for me. There wasn't a soul about so I opened the door and shouted "Hello!" Your grandfather came out of his study and said, "Oh that Fred Flintstone is a cheeky devil."' She had been distracted again by the television and laughed with Cheryl at the cartoon's antics. Beagan closed the trunk. 'Are you leaving so soon?' she asked him.

'I thought I might go for a swim.'

'Will you come back to see me?'

'Not this summer. No.' He explained about his journey west and the inheritance of the Pacific island.

'You mean there was more than just old papers in the trunk?' asked Cheryl from her chair. 'Like valuable stuff?'

'Oh yes.'

'I knew you'd get something. You always got something.'

'But next year? Will you come back next summer?' appealed Doris. 'With the trunk?' Beagan smiled and promised to do his best. She watched him nurse the family papers down the dark stairs. A jingle chased him out to the car. 'You need Fluff Fluff Fluff to make a Fluffernutter, Fluff Fluff Fluff and lots of peanut butter.' Cheryl pulled her mother away from the window and closed the curtains.

Beagan hung his jacket and towel on a tree, lay his clothes on a rock and pushed through the bulrushes on to the beach. He waded into the flip–flop waves then launched himself into the fresh water's embrace. As the gentle currents caressed and tugged him the memory of an entry in his father's notebooks sprang to mind. 'We had for many summers come to these parts and it was here that the love of water and of ships enmeshed us willingly.' Across the lake he heard the laughter of children diving from a dock and floating in rubber inner tubes. Somewhere far away a screen door squeaked and slammed. 'The family's love of words and water was by no means developed in a single generation,' continued the thought. 'It was hereditary.' Beagan felt that he recognised the curve of the bay, the lie of the land and the smell of jack pine which wafted through the dark woods down to the shore. The sun came out from behind a cloud and its glare dazzled him. Two figures were reflected on the rippled surface. He looked up but the shore was deserted. The line of the beach was broken only by the tree on which he had hung his jacket and towel. Yet in the mirror image of the sparkling water Beagan glimpsed a father and a son. Jamie's hand was on Sandy's small shoulder as they heard the two-tone whistle and waited for the Mosquito Fleet to round Wigwassan Point.

On Highway 400 Southbound the cars slowed to a crawl. A truck had overturned and shed its load of flags. The wind lifted them and they soared like rays along the asphalt. Tricolours flew between the lines of traffic. The Mexican eagle swooped above a Lebanese cedar. The colours of Poland, Trinidad and Tanzania flipped and flashed through the warm currents. A motorist tried to grab a Turkish crescent but it slipped through his fingers and skimmed away over the hard-tops. The ensigns became a school of extra-ordinary flying fish swimming free from a net, excited by their new freedom. For a moment the multicoloured beasts cast a spell over the roadway but then, as they crumpled to the ground, the horns started blaring and frustrated drivers became anxious to move on. Like the flags, they and Beagan were destined for the most ethnically diverse city in the world.

Canada is the country of the American counter-revolution. In the late eighteenth century the losers of the War of Independence moved north across the border. Many of the so-called Empire Loyalists were government officers, surveyors and tax collectors who owed their livelihood, and hence allegiance, to the Crown. Between 1783 and 1788 their numbers trebled the existing popu-lation of Novia Scotia and New Brunswick, and formed the nucleus of the future province of Ontario. Britain rewarded their patriotism with grants of free land and positions in the colonial administration. In turn their conservative influence and abiding distaste for republican democracy ensured that the orderly hand of government disciplined the rugged pioneer individualism for generations.

As late as 1910, 90 per cent of Toronto's citizens were still of British origin. Their city was renowned for being good and dull;

an ambitious town of strict churches and virtuous labour. On the waterfront, down the Spadina sewer and up in sewing lofts its citizens aspired to prosper. In mills and factories they produced the goods which built the nation. Their Model–T Fords spluttered along the streets which only a decade before had echoed with the clip-clop of milkmen's carts. On the Sabbath Eaton's, their dry goods and department store, drew reverent black blinds over its display windows. Their magistrates fined sportsmen five dollars for playing golf. The streetcars did not run for fear that their operation might lead to Sunday papers, saloons and theatres. Their city was law-abiding, God-fearing and conformist.

But the Toronto that Beagan found one Sunday in June was neither good nor dull; it was disparate. The city had grown into a conurbation of ethnic enclaves. Little India bristled against the Pakistani community. Chinatown expanded west into Polish Roncesvalles. Along the Bridle Path successful Slavs built ostentatious mansions and pushed out rich Greeks. The old Commonwealth Club had been renamed the Multi-Culti Drop-In Centre. Eden Goode's imposing townhouse in Rosedale had been bought by a Jewish property developer, razed to the ground and replaced by terraced condominiums. Its resident film-makers and lawyers, the great-grandchildren of Empire Loyalists, got together for barbeques and self-congratulation or to visit their parents in Forest Hill, the Anglo-Saxon neighbourhood which smelt of freshly cut grass and two-stroke exhaust. The hum of lawnmowers lulled the warm afternoon air as Russian gardeners manicured the wide verdant lawns bordering streets named Dunvegan, Kilbarry and Strathearn.

'The typical Torontonian has always been the new Torontonian,' pronounced Zachary from his back seat dais in Beagan's car. It pleased him to be in the city again, for he cared little for the world beyond its limits. Clean, modern streets flashed past the car's open windows. Electrum skyscrapers glittered beneath the CN Tower, the world's tallest free-standing structure. The United Brotherhood of Black Educators shared offices with Elusions Cypriot Dinner Dance Club. Next door the Saigon Village restaurant offered a special smorgasbord buffet lunch ('Today only: Surf 'n Turf *à la carte*').

'It was the Europeans who came here after the British,' he explained to his father. 'The Irish arrived looking for work. The Germans came after the shame of defeat. When the Saint Lawrence Seaway opened the port to ocean commerce every other nationality on earth followed them. The Jews migrated to escape pogroms and genocide. West Indians and Asians came in search of economic prosperity. Newcomer followed newcomer year after year.'

Hector stared wide-eyed at the passing scene. He had only once met a black man, a freed slave who had migrated with the Loyalists to Nova Scotia, but never before had he set eyes on an Oriental. Yet outside the Big Land Chinese Supermarket there wasn't a single white face to be seen. 'See that now, Celestials,' he said, pointing at the throng of shoppers buying fresh fungi and crisp *bok choi*. 'I would not be so sure that it wasn't Cathay that Cabot discovered after all.'

'The city is home to almost half a million Chinese, Father,' stated Zachary. 'Also to fifty thousand Somali refugees and thousands of Greeks.' The facts reassured his own sense of authority. 'More Italians live in Toronto than in Venice. Why, in the last thirty years the city's population has doubled, and one resident in three speaks a mother tongue other than English.'

'What then of the first residents? I see no Native faces like the Micmac Gogo who saved my life.'

'The Indians,' dismissed Zachary, 'are mostly dead, drunk or driven west. They won't bother you here.'

In a single block of Bayview Avenue Hector counted two synagogues, a mosque and a Buddhist temple. It was not until they passed south of Steeles Avenue that he saw the first church. 'What would it be that bonds these people together?' Moishe's Kosher Meats nestled beside the Curl Up & Dye Afro Hair Salon. 'What do they all share?'

'Common values,' volunteered his elder son. 'Tolerance, not judging their neighbours, the acceptance that one man's meat is another's poison.'

'There is honey on your lips though there should be a blister on your tongue,' said Hector. He did not understand such an attitude. 'What would it be that you are saying, my boy? That the drunkard is tolerated? Or a father who deserts his family?'

'Today the individual's rights are valued above all else. It is the state which offers help to those in need.'

'But the state would be certain to tell the drunkard to be ashamed of himself, would it not?' asked Hector. 'You would not be saying that it sanctions these values?'

'No man can judge another. It is a matter of freedom of choice.'

Hector was confounded by Zachary's response and began to pray. 'Be Thou a smooth way before me, be Thou a guiding star above me, be Thou a keen eye behind me, this day, this night, forever.'

The car cruised past a vast shopping centre. Listless gangs of youths idled outside the store windows while their parents wound through the acres of parked cars clutching bag-loads of shiny plastic purchases. At the edge of the mall an old woman danced alone around a park bench talking to herself and holding an imaginary partner. 'This is a terrible becoming,' whispered Hector. He stared at his descendants with incomprehension. 'The wind shall subside before I embrace these easy values. Where are the absolute virtues – thrift, self-reliance, respect for the law – the rocks that are not to be compromised? Where is the self-discipline and hard work that launched Jamie's *Segwun* and began your newspapers?' he asked. 'A man cannot improve himself without a moral authority.'

'Torontonians do respect the law, Father; indeed for most the government has replaced the Church,' said Zachary. Hector was too shocked to reply. 'And they share the belief that labour today is rewarded by their children's success tomorrow.'

'They also hold in common a disregard of yesterday,' observed Jamie.

On the drive downtown smoked-glass limousines glided beneath pristine skyscrapers. On every block there seemed to be a homeless person. Some were Cree or Ojibwa. The traffic was bad and Beagan asked a Sikh Mountie in a turban for directions to the ferry pier. He was sent to a parking lot three miles away beside the Daily Bread Food Bank, one of the 'assistance centres' which helped to feed the poor in 174 communities across the province. A recent Department of Public Health survey pinned to its front door warned that 59 per cent of the city's senior citizens were at risk of illness due to malnutrition.

It was the last day of Caravan, the city's annual cultural carnival, and the streets bustled with people in festive mood. Fifty different 'ethnic pavilions' had been set up in civic gardens and squares. In the Jamaican tent revellers bought synthetic rum-flavour cakes then bumped and ground to high-volume reggae. Across the road in the Hungarian pavilion goulash and instant Viennese coffee were on offer. Beagan tried to spot Piri in the crowd but only managed to attract the attention of a gay gypsy musician circulating among the tables and serenading all the young men. Behind the Japanese marquee a geisha girl on her lunch break listened to a Walkman and ate pot noodles.

In the Mexican tent a Rastafarian crowned by a great white stovepipe hat swallowed and laughed, 'Man, I just love tacos.' He took another mouthful of refried beans. 'That's why I come to Canada, to make me life better.'

'We're not as colourful as the Ukrainians,' explained an ex-New Yorker to Beagan while dishing out lashings of cabbage rolls and potato *ponchiks*. A brigade of draft-dodgers had come north in the sixties to avoid fighting in the Vietnam War. 'Like, we don't reminisce about the New Jersey Turnpike.'

'Thai food is crucial,' enthused an anorexic tank-topped woman over her uneaten chicken satays, 'but actually I don't eat salt.'

Entry to each pavilion was by 'passport', a ticket which was stamped at the door as proof of the visit, and the urban globe-trotters rode rickshaws between events. In an afternoon a spectator could take in a dozen pre-packaged cultures, each carefully laid out on a map, and still ride the subway home for supper.

At the foot of Bay Street Beagan caught a double-wheelhouse ferry across the harbour to the island. Under the trees where Bessie had learnt to ride a bicycle a young Malay mother with walnut skin sang to her child. 'Row row row your boat, gently down the stream . . .' Near to the place where Eden Goode had taught himself photography Cantonese students in designer T-shirts and black Bermudas took turns videoing a family picnic. On the sands where Jamie had once beached his canoe an albino Indian family, with skin of translucent silver and long almond eyes, sat in saris on an embroidered mat and nibbled at bhajis.

An amusement park had been built where bulldozers had cleared away the old island homes. A Filipino boy whooped from the Log Flume Ride ('No pregnant riders please'). His optimistic 'My Canada includes Quebec' T-shirt further distressed Beagan, know-ing as he did that the English-speaking child would not be wel-come in the province itself. Beagan rode the Centreville B. & B.R. miniature railway around the farmyard zoo and through Kermit's Frog Bog. He was not surprised by the scarcity of north-ern European faces but rather by the dearth of mixed groups. It seemed to him that Caravan and the island fun fair were Toronto's earnest, superficial response to its own dynamic metamorphosis; an ethnic Plato's Cave where residents preferred the shadow of their city's myriad nationalities to the reality of the neighbourhood next door. He half-expected to find a Quebec pavilion full of jolly *habitants* and back-slapping voyageurs. Then a blond-haired man arrived with popsicles for his Malaysian wife and child. '. . . merrily merrily merrily merrily, life is like ice cream.' They began to play together and when their frisbee spun away Beagan retrieved it and struck up a conversation.

'We in Toronto,' said Glen, pointing across the island, 'this is something we're really proud of.' A tribe of Africans in luminous

baseball caps camped around a picnic table. A bewhiskered mandarin lounged in a deck chair reading the *Sing Tao* Chinese daily.
'When Katelynn was born our parents were pleased as pie. My
mother said, "Isn't it nice that her skin is so dark."'

'My mother said, "Isn't it nice that her skin's so light,"'
murmured Salbiah, his shy, diminutive wife.

'The trouble only started when I lost my job.'

Salbiah lowered her eyes. 'My mother wrote, "It's not right
that you have to work. If your husband cannot provide for you
then you should come home. You are losing your culture and
you're not even getting rich."'

'But can you see her back in Malaysia now?' gloated Glen.
'There's no way that she'll sit below men at table or keep quiet
all the time. No, sir.'

Beagan remembered a pair of gregarious Egyptians who had
opened a corner shop in dour Halifax. They only did good business
when Arab ships were in port. He asked Salbiah about the difficulties of assimilation.

'It's no problem,' replied Glen. 'My friends love Salbiah.'
Beagan heard no trace of doubt in his voice. 'Hey, we're Canadians. We get on.'

Little Katelynn slipped and fell and Salbiah scooped her up in
her arms. She didn't answer the question but clutched her child
to her breast. 'I don't talk to her in Malay but I do sing the old
lullabies that I still remember.'

H ECTOR, ZACHARY AND Jamie sat in a circle
under a broad weeping willow and stared back
across the harbour. Clean-lined sailing boats and
ultra-modern gin palaces glided across the city's
gilded façade. On the beach below the ghosts Beagan
skipped pebbles across the water's surface.

'What a f-f-fine f-f-folly,' laughed Jamie in sad wonder
at their aspiration. 'The communities that we tried to draw

together in our day were diverse enough. But now,' he said with a humility that sprang from loss, 'well, I doubt that the printed word still has such power.'

'Open your eyes and look around you,' insisted Zachary with a preacher's zeal. He considered Jamie's disillusion to be out of place. 'It has been done.'

'Not with Quebec or between these neighbours,' insisted Jamie, his broad gesture trying to gather the diverse people in his arms. 'Our ideal seems f-f-fragmented; small is now beautiful.'

'The newspapers helped set in motion trends which brought these good people considerable gains in material goods, social mobility, racial and sexual equality,' persisted Zachary.

'Yes, but at what cost?' asked Hector, laying down his Bible. The absence of pious devotions in the city tormented him. He had turned to the Word for comfort. 'It is their moral well-being which distresses me.' He watched a replica paddle-wheeler splashing in the bay. 'And how is it that anyone can be going hungry in this rich land? A man with an empty stomach worries neither about feeding his neighbour nor about his soul,' he recalled from Promise.

Zachary did not want to be distracted by his father's concerns so ignored him. 'Maybe even more could have been done if you had rejoined the firm and not wasted away your time,' he told his brother. 'I offered you a generous salary.'

'And I thanked you. But I preferred to paddle my own canoe rather than ride as second officer on another's yacht.'

'That's your damnable pride.'

'My pride?' retorted Jamie. 'You forget that my success was a modest affair. When I returned from Windsor in 1910, and pried the Boy away from his boats, I owned a mere fifteen trade papers. They were designed to complement your thirty-seven titles. Don't you remember that you and I and Sandy met every week to discuss new acquisitions, to share circulation figures and to avoid our journals coming into competition? The only pride that I ever f-f-felt was for you. You made a great success of the b-b-business. You outgrew office and plant capacity f-f-four times.'

'Five times,' corrected Zachary.

'No group of publications under single control anywhere in the world surpassed Gillean for breadth of readership proportionate to population. I always admired your achievement. But wasn't expansion achieved at the expense of publishing's service obligations?'

'The growth of the Dominion made it necessary for local and regional industries to merge and form national companies. You should not have resisted the tide.' Zachary was disappointed with his younger brother. 'Your mistake was not to amalgamate your papers with mine.'

'It was your insensitivity which made that impossible,' flashed Jamie in sudden anger. 'Our history would have been very different had you just once laid your hand on my shoulder and said, "I'm sorry."'

'Sorry?' The bitter accusation startled Zachary. 'But I have nothing to be sorry about, other than being dead,' he puffed. He stabbed an ethereal finger at the willow. It passed clear through the trunk. 'This is my only regret.'

Jamie held his breath and tried to regain his composure. While he counted to ten the ferry *Sam McBride* disgorged another load of day-trippers. Young families of every colour and hue carried picnic baskets across the trim lawns to claim a patch of grass. Tupperware pots of spiced okra, trays of baklava and litre bottles of home-made chianti were laid out on their respective tartan travel rugs. 'It's a curious thing,' he observed, nodding towards Beagan. 'But in Muskoka when he went swimming did you notice his skin?'

'I can't say that I paid much attention.' Zachary had taken a pique against his brother.

'Its colour struck me,' recalled Jamie. 'Pale clay with a sheen like eggshells. And that fine tracery of life.' He paused to remember. 'I hadn't noticed before but it is just like hers.

Like Bessie's. Beagan inherited his grandmother's skin.'

'What of it?' shrugged Zachary. 'He has Father's high forehead and down-turned eyes.'

'His great-great-grandfather's eyes,' corrected Hector. 'The grey-green. It is the gestures that would be his too.'

'It is genetics, Father,' Zachary explained. 'The science of generations, the heredity and variation in plants and animals. It is fact.'

Jamie interrupted them before an argument could develop. 'The point is Zachary that you never said that you f-f-felt for me,' he accused. 'After Bessie's death. Or that of her first child.'

'Of course I did. I expressed my regrets in the proper manner.'

'No,' said Jamie firmly. 'No, you didn't. And well, I think I can say it now that we're dead, your lack of compassion never ceased to distress me.'

'You are certainly mistaken,' Zachary asserted. Hector lay his hand on Jamie's arm. Zachary ignored the gesture. 'In any event, I better expressed my compassion in the care of the living. In the early twenties I repeated my wish that on our deaths the companies should be united and control passed to Sandy. It wasn't my fault that he turned down the opportunity. You never thanked me for that generosity.'

'But by then outsiders had begun to slip the wedge between us. They brought two of our papers into conflict knowing that Sandy was too f-f-forthright for his own good and that you would defend your mission. They exploited our differences with calculated patience and our firms became estranged. The control of Gillean Publishing slipped out of family hands.'

'Hush-up-with-you, chap,' ordered Zachary. 'I don't remember it happening that way.'

'But you do remember that they circulated stories in the trade about our quarrels. We always had our differences but we never argued back then. It was those lies which widened the gulf between us. You came to see your employees as your only f-f-family. They in turn treated you as a patriarch, the venerable father who throughout his life remained true to his ambition, even as your partners came more and more to emphasise profit margins.'

'And what does it matter now?' snapped Zachary, bristling his thick, snow-white moustache. 'We were old and I was dying. It's history now. We can't affect it.' He hated the impotence of death as much as the loss of time.

'It matters because the end of our co-operation was a grave blow to me,' replied Jamie. 'Not because of any hindrance to earthly success, I didn't care two hoots that my titles would never f-f-flourish in the shadow of such powerful competition, but because of the evil of the deceit.' He shivered as if someone had walked over his grave. 'It haunted Sandy too. That's why he set up on his own. He launched the *Toronto Mirror*, Canada's first picture newspaper, in an attempt to distance himself from the iniquity. "Reflecting the truth" was his watchword. The paper was a success but too heavy a drain on our limited capital, and when he came to you for help, your partners advised you not to become involved. The enterprise collapsed. Sandy packed his bags, took F-F-Father's old globe and, like us before him, went west in search of a promised land.'

Zachary examined his watch then struck it with his knuckle. His patience had worn as thin as Jamie's tweeds. 'What is that grandson of yours doing now?' he blurted as if noticing Beagan for the first time.

Hector watched him throwing rocks for a moment, then twisted his wrist and began mimicking Beagan's movement. 'See that now,' he smiled. 'It is myself that skipped stones in that manner when I was a boy.'

'He would be better employed going back to Scotland and growing oats.'

'It is a vanity to speak of our traditions in a deprecating manner,' Hector snapped at his son.

'He's too reflective to live in a progressive country,' replied Zachary, anxious as always to move on. 'There's not been the time for looking back in the New World.'

Beagan threw a last stone towards the gilded façade then turned his back on the city. He began to walk to the ferry landing but stopped and instead stepped under the willow. He stood among them, his forefathers at his feet, and it seemed for a moment that he was going to speak. Then a breeze blew off the water and he shivered. He put his hands in his pockets and walked away.

Beagan didn't visit Gillean Communication's hi-tech editorial offices or vast new printing plant. It wasn't among the Apple Macintoshes and Quark XPress DTP software that he would find a trace of his grandfather or great-uncle. Nor did he see them on the island. He caught the ferry back to the mainland and drove west along Lakeshore Boulevard to Sunnyside Beach. He sat at the mouth of the Humber River beneath the concrete pillars of the Gardiner Expressway and felt waves of loneliness wash over him. He tried to ignore the roar of the traffic and to imagine the Huron warriors paddling down the river with Étienne Brûlé, Champlain's prime scout and the first white man to look upon Lake Ontario. Beyond the ranks of apartment blocks he tried to see John Graves Simcoe coasting along the shore, erecting Captain Cook's canvas tent and establishing a settlement. He wanted to count the bateaux and steamers as they tacked around the flat swampy island bearing the settlers who transformed the oak-covered plain into Canada's metropolis. He tried too to conjure up the boats skimming across Bras d'Or, their paddlers and rowers drawn by Reverend Hector's words, and the puffing Mosquito steamers loaded with newspapers and mailbags carrying the printed word away from Jamie. But from his noisy vantage point Beagan could not summon the past. He saw no trace of the first immigrants' arrival. There was no bay marked by a solitary Celtic cross, no landing beach scored by the keels of ships, no quarantine islet haunted by the spirits of typhus-infected travellers who had lost the battle for life. Instead he saw a history had been forgotten. It had been erased beneath public swimming pools, highway over-passes and civic incinerators.

AN CUAN SÈIMH

The Western Sea

CHAPTER VIII

BACKWATERS

I COULDN'T FIND the spanner anywhere. It wasn't in the tool box, in the bilge or under either of the dogs. I looked behind the cowling and in with the charts. Under the cushions there were only old spark plugs and one squashed chocolate biscuit. It was very soggy but still lovely and sweet. The engine had fouled and I needed the spanner to blow out the carb, at least I did if the problem was with the carb. It might have been water in the fuel line. I would have flushed that out instead had I been able to put my hands on the needle-nose pliers. They seemed to be missing too. *Primary* wallowed in Lake Erie's swells off the end of the Nanticoke pier and I lay my head on the sleeping Samoyed to wait. My feet rested against Brendan, my scruffy mongrel setter. The late summer sun was warm and I found the spanner in my pocket.

I was proud of my old Dad, uncle Zach too for all his faults. They started with nothing, no contacts or friends, and made good. Two quiet, honest sons of the manse created a publishing empire that in their time was maybe the biggest in the Commonwealth. They devoted themselves to encouraging home industry and reducing the dependence on imported goods. The legacy that they left was a knowledge, a confidence in the achievement and potential of Canada and her people. That optimism could never have taken root had the country been served only by English periodicals and American magazines. Without it we would have remained a colonial appendage or even sooner become the fifty-first state of the United States.

It's funny though, the brothers who worked to bring people together lived so much apart. In the tangled web of memory I retain the clear picture of a single Muskoka morning. Dad was inside the cottage. He had arrived the evening before on one of his rare visits. I had readied my boat to take him for a ride around Bohemia Island. Nan was at the dock, insisting that the *Mink*'s butcher cut away the fat before weighing the chops. She and I were climbing up the pine-needle path, me chattering all the while about the Kermath's overheating gearbox, when the sound of singing echoed down to us through the trees. At first I didn't recognise the voice. I had never before heard Dad so much as whistle and his full, deep baritone startled me. He thought himself to be alone in the big empty house and in the privacy of the pine bathroom waved his straight razor like a baton and piped, 'O ye'll tak' the high road and I'll tak' the low road'. My instinct was to run to him, to bury myself in his arms and to feel the tickle of the twisting rust-red moustache but instead I let go of Nan's hand, turned away and slipped back to the boat. For I knew then that he was singing to Bessie.

Only my mother ever found the key to his heart and it went with her to the grave. Dad stayed away from home for months on end but his letters to me arrived every week. He wrote from Atlantic liners and lake steamers and grand hotels on richly embossed stationery.

'My room is on the seventh floor,' he enthused on his first trip to New York. I was eighteen months old at the time. 'When going up to my room a gentleman asked the elevator boy to let him off at the seventeenth floor.' He had underlined the word twice. 'You can quite imagine what a high building this is.'

The envelopes were postmarked Edinburgh, Assiniboia and Bermuda. They were filled with reports on the growth of western trade and the operation of his Muskoka fleet. He wrote as if to an adult, noting the cost of taxis in Naples (two lire from the customs wharf to the Hotel Bristol) and describing his ship's wait in Halifax for the trans-continental train that brought the China mail.

'This is the country of the crocodile,' explained his letter from the Royal Poinciana in Palm Beach, then the world's most expensive hotel at fifteen dollars per day. 'The negroes do a thriving business in catching the young ones and taming them. If it is not too cold I will bring one home for you.' Nan sat by my bedside and read his words aloud.

'Hundreds of people were on the wharf to see friends off,' he had written aboard the Dominion Line's SS *Vancouver* while *en route* to Southampton. 'I seemed to be about the only passenger without a friend to say "*bon voyage*" and I felt decidedly blue.' Nan's tears pattered on the waxy leaves like the first drops of autumn rain. 'Oh how I miss your mother, my boy.'

He understood my loss too. His letters reached out to me year after year in Muskoka, at Upper Canada College and aboard HMS *Chatham* in the Mediterranean during the Great War. In them he scolded me for my shoddily-written replies and reminded me of duty. 'You are a privileged boy. In your short life not only have you never known hunger, not only have you had a large share of good things, but you have never had any real wish ungratified.' His script was simple, bold and sincere. 'Do you realise that in return for these gifts you must give something back to the world? It is you, and boys like you with the advantage of education and background, who must maintain the standards of speech and manners, of integrity, in personal and public life. If you are satisfied with the second-rate, if you let money, material pleasures and superficialities become all-important, then you forsake all that we have worked for, you betray me and break your mother's heart.'

As the waves rocked *Primary* I remembered his letters that had tried to fill the void left by death, the words which my son Beagan carried with him in the family trunk. 'When you grow to be a man I want you to know her. I want you to read all her letters and the papers which I have put away for you. They will give you a faint idea of her sweet life and dear love. Then after they have planted me away in a bone-yard you will have them – and these words which I write from time to time – to guide you.'

THE PICK-UP TRUCK writhed down Slag Pot Captive Road and cut behind No. 1 Blowdown Treatment Plant. 'I come. You come. He comes.' Carlo, a young uniformed security guard with ink-black curls, conjugated verbs as he steered around the coke oven and ore piles. 'I will come. You will come. They will come. Is good, no? Super good.' Beagan nodded in agreement. He sat in the passenger seat, the trunk rattling behind him in the back, and watched Stelco Steel's Lake Erie Works flash by the window. Pavarotti sang *Tosca* on the radio. Carlo glanced at his watch and turned right at the hot-strip mill. 'I have language class now.' He quoted from memory, 'English skill help you communicate at work, better your career opportunity and ensure an open line of communication with younger generation growing up in Canada.' Most of the employees at the hundred-acre works were Italian or Portuguese. Some were newcomers, other families had been with Stelco for two or three generations, all spoke their mother tongue both to co-workers and at home. 'The union and company they offer teach English.' The pick-up skirted coal heaps and followed the mile-long conveyor belt towards the lake. Along it swept twenty-six thousand metric tons of iron pellets, each the size of a blueberry, from a ship's hold to the mill's furnaces. 'You go during regular shift and company pay for all classroom time.' Carlo crunched to a stop and kicked up a cloud of grit. 'I lift. You lift. We both lift.' They heaved the trunk out of the back and on to the pier. 'I go. You go. We all go. *Buon viaggio*,' he chanted and drove back towards the training centre.

The MV *Tadoussac*, a blunt-nosed, self-loading laker, had the look of a vast aquatic caterpillar. Her slinky body stretched from the raised head of the forward bridge to the steaming engine-room tail. Like all Great Lakes bulk carriers she had been built to move not through the waves as an ocean-going ship but with them, and her passage over swells could be traced by the ripple down her deck; the wheelhouse rose on a roller, amidships she arched while the after-house dropped away into the curl of a trough. The lanky proportions enabled her to crawl through the narrow Seaway locks.

The pier was coated in iron dust and Beagan dragged the trunk around the auburn pools of rusty rainwater. 'Fore!' A golf ball shot by his left ear, ricocheted off the hull and splashed into the lake. 'Bloody hell, sorry about that, mate.' The *Tadoussac*'s chief engineer, his eyes crinkled by light and laughter, appeared from behind a coal heap. He wore Bermuda shorts, white socks, sandals and carried a golf bag on his shoulder. 'I was practising my chipping.'

'Here?' asked Beagan, looking back at the black acres of coal.

'Nowhere better. There's loads of space and you just can't lose your balls.' He glanced into the water and added, 'Most of the time.' He held out his hand. 'William Wellfit's the name. You must be our passenger; welcome aboard.' Wellfit took hold of a trunk handle, pointed at the ship's twin stacks and said, 'Do you like my smoke?'

'*Mensch*, Bill,' cried his wife from the forward deck. Gabi Wellfit was as round as a Prussian prune pudding. 'The last time you asked someone that it got you into real trouble.' Wellfit smiled and rolled his eyes. 'You will excuse my husband please,' she shouted, lifting the drooping brim of her sunhat. 'This is his last trip and he's gone soft in the head.'

Beagan and Wellfit carried the trunk over the gangway and Beagan asked if, like the *Global Trader*, the ship had a foreign company. 'The *Tadoussac* has a hyphenated-Canadian crew,' explained Wellfit. 'I'm English-Canadian from Hartlepool and my junior engineer is Kazakhi-Canadian. Dai, the third officer up there on the bridge, he's a Welsh-Canadian. The cook Eddie Palladini is Italian-Canadian and Ruby over there is Jamaican-Canadian.' A bosomy black woman leaned on the starboard rail dreaming of the Caribbean. 'We used to employ cheap labour on board, Poles and Russians who had jumped ship in Halifax, but no more. Now all the foreigners have become Canadians and earn four times their old pay.' He took a swing with an imaginary club. 'That's why the line is in trouble.'

Wellfit paused at one of the open hatches. In the cavernous belly four crewmen used shovels to ease the last few tons of pellets off the saddlebacks and through the chute gates. Three conveyor belts running between the hulls carried the load aft and up the boom to spill into the pier-side hopper. 'Our only Canadian-Canadians are Buddy, Mark and Luke there. They joined us when the fishing died out in Newfoundland. Barry too. He's from Cape Breton and came on when the Sydney steelmills were closed.' Here and there the sooty hold was daubed with flecks of green. Grains of wheat from a previous cargo had taken root between the bulkheads and begun to grow. The *Tadoussac* had been designed to carry iron ore, a million bushels of grain or enough coal to feed a power station for a week but on this trip up to the head of the lakes she was sailing empty.

'Not much goes up the lakes anymore, at least on this ship, and only wheat comes down, most of which is sent to Russia.' Wellfit led Beagan up a flight of steps and into the forward super-structure. 'And when the Ukraine starts feeding Russia again there will be nowhere to sell that wheat.' He shook his head. 'Shipping on the Great Lakes will be dead for us in ten years. We've had the good days and, I tell you, I'm glad my time's up.'

The cabin, grandly named the First Stateroom, had a double bed, shower and porthole view over the bow. Ruby ambled in with a stainless steel mixing bowl overflowing with fresh fruit. A handful of kumquats rolled away under the video recorder. Wellfit pointed out the well-stocked larder and second galley. 'Come and join us aft for dinner when we're underway.'

A vermilion sun dropped beneath the surface and cast a band

of copper across the horizon. A passing laker smeared a smoky smudge along the mauve American shore. As dusk gathered the *Tadoussac* eased astern and swung west around the black silhouette of Long Point. The trip into the heart of the continent would take her across three of the Great Lakes and reach 2,260 miles inland from the Atlantic. A breeze blew up, fretting Erie's surface with a fine pattern of fish scales, while the clear night sky filled with constellations of aircraft landing lights making for Detroit, Toledo and Toronto. The half-moon lay on its back and smiled like a Cheshire cat.

'You look like a ten-pounder,' said Ed. The *Tadoussac*'s cook had mischievous chocolate-brown eyes, fingers the size of Somerset sausages and a deep yearning to satiate appetite. His chins wobbled as he nodded, 'Yup, ten pounds minimum.'

'Ten pounds of what?' asked Beagan.

'Every time someone new comes aboard,' replied Wellfit from across the table, 'Eddie sizes up how much weight he can put on them.' He thumbed a well-worn copy of *Golf Illustrated*.

'But it only takes three days to reach Thunder Bay.'

'Ten pounds,' repeated Ed. He rolled up his sleeves to reveal leg-of-mutton forearms. 'Tonight you can have chicken cacciatore, steak and mushrooms, chilli con carne with cheese or a home-made sausage submarine sandwich.'

'*Ja*, the steak is delicious,' said Gabi, who ate with a determination that would make her a fifteen-pounder.

'It's all delicious,' corrected Ed. 'If you can't find something to eat on this ship you're not hungry. So what's it to be?' Beagan felt spoilt for choice. 'Tell you what,' the cook suggested. 'I'll give you a sample taste of everything, then you can decide.' Before Beagan could object Ed had slipped back in his galley like a whale into a fjord.

'On some ships the crew wouldn't eat if the cook lost his can-opener,' joked Gabi through a mouthful of prime beef. 'Eddie is not a can-opener cook.'

'So what brings you onboard?' asked Wellfit. 'We don't get many passengers.'

'I'm trying to travel to Vancouver by water,' replied Beagan. 'I'm following the family history and my father lived there.'

'Vancouver?' he said in disbelief. 'You know the lakes stop at Thunder Bay? After that it's just prairies and mountains.'

'And rivers all the way to the Pacific. The waterways used to be the only route west.'

'Wouldn't it have been easier to buy a bus ticket?'

Gabi groaned as she put down her knife and fork. '*Ach, das war lecker.* Delicious.'

Ed reappeared at the doorway with a plate in his hand. 'Another helping, Gabi?'

'Well, maybe just a little taste.' He placed a second porterhouse steak before her. 'Eddie, are you crazy? I can't eat all this.'

'Now don't disappoint me.'

'Oh what the hell. I enjoy a challenge,' said Gabi picking up her utensils with renewed gusto. Her enthusiasm for supper revealed a great joy for life. 'Do you know why I eat so much?' she asked Beagan. 'It's the same reason that I came to Canada.'

'I wouldn't encourage her if I were you,' advised her husband, retreating behind his magazine.

'For crying out loud, honey, I was just trying to tell him a story.' Gabi turned back to Beagan. 'At the end of that *furchtbarer Krieg*' – she never used the noun 'war' without the adjective 'terrible' – 'I weighed eighty-six pounds. *Ja*, I know it's hard to believe now that I'm a little *pummelig*, that's chubby, but there was nothing to eat in Berlin. We lost our vegetable patch during an air raid. I had to jump into the Spree to avoid the phosphorus bombs and the last turnips just floated away. My girlfriends in the *Landarmee* were shot by the Russians for stealing food and I watched my mother die of typhoid. In Germany there was no future for me and, *mein Gott*, everyone was so hungry.'

Gabi paused to dab a little mustard on her plate. The aroma of frying onions wafted in from the galley. 'I started walking west on wooden-soled shoes with only the clothes on my back and one extra pair of panties. I washed them every day but in the camp in Bremen someone stole one pair from the line. It was terrible but they had nothing and, *Mensch*, I was lucky. I spoke some English and Canada offered me a job and passage.'

In the galley Ruby crashed between sink and cooker, dropped pots and pans and called on the good Lord for strength. Some crewmen came in for coffee while others took submarine sandwiches back to their cabins and watched television.

'Everything was organised and I was due to sail on a ship called the *Samaria* but it was changed at the last moment,' Gabi continued. 'I cried and cried but that was my fate you see.' She looked at Wellfit concentrating on his magazine. 'Come on honey, tell him.'

'Gabi, he's not interested in ancient history.' Beagan said that he wanted to hear their story, it had already begun to counter the bitter after-taste of Toronto, and when Wellfit relented Gabi returned to her steak. 'I spent the war in the merchant navy, stepping into dead men's shoes. Ten ships were torpedoed out from under me in six years. In 1949 I was engineering officer on the *Scythia*, a twin-screw geared turbine built for five hundred passengers. We were going home to Liverpool when we were diverted to Bremen to take on a thousand DPs, displaced persons, bound for Canada.

'There were only two huge cabins,' interrupted Gabi, 'one for men and one for women, with bunks on top of bunks and no air conditioning and everyone being sick.'

'Everyone except you.

'*Mensch*, no. I never stayed below decks. I was up in the dining room. There was so much food that I stuffed myself like a goose. A steward taught me how to eat grapefruit and I learnt right away. I also rediscovered ice cream. I just couldn't get enough of it and after every meal I would sit out on deck taking deep breaths and feeling sick.' Gabi re-enacted each stage of her story: she puffed up her cheeks with imaginary ice cream, distended her stomach and even tried to turn a bilious shade of green. She didn't so much recount events as relive them. 'One day when I was especially full a sailor approached me and I told him to leave me alone. They weren't supposed to fraternise with the passengers but, you know,

I felt bad for sending him away. He was just trying to be friendly. So when an officer came up behind me and said . . . and said . . .' Gabi paused until Wellfit looked up and met her eye. 'Come on honey, are you going to help me tell the story or not?'

'I said,' sighed Wellfit, '"Are you feeling unwell, miss?"'

'*Ja*, and I was, from the ice cream or the motion I don't know, and I told him so. He gave me some pills. Then he pointed up at the chimney and asked . . .'

'"Do you like my smoke?"' Wellfit blushed then explained, 'The *Scythia* was steam powered and she made that lovely rushing sound of wind and water. Nothing like the rattle from these modern, metallic diesels.'

Gabi did not let technicalities divert her from the story. 'The next day during lifeboat drill Bill made a special point of checking my lifejacket. He inspected the straps two or three times then asked if I would meet him. I agreed and we sat together on the boat deck beneath the half-painted funnel.'

'The *Scythia* was still battleship grey. The lads had just started painting her back in the Cunard colours, the old red and black.'

'I was a displaced person. Do you think I was in the mood to fall in love?'

'You were only in the mood to eat ice cream.'

'*Ach, ich kann nicht mehr.* I'm stuffed.' Gabi pushed the steak away from her. 'Falling in love put me off my food. I couldn't even eat my lovely ice cream. And Bill, his friends told me later, was off his beer. Then all of a sudden we arrived in Quebec and I had to catch a train to my job in Hamilton. For crying out loud we only had an hour together, one hour. Bill threw me to the ground and kissed me and kissed me and promised to write and gave me a dollar bill.'

'I wouldn't have given you a whole dollar,' he teased.

'A dollar was a lot of money. It was my only money. I remember oranges cost four cents apiece. Two months later his letter arrived, thrown off the ship to the dock crew with money tied to it for postage, and Bill had written, "If we follow our hearts with our hands and heads we can make it."'

'I handed in my ration cards at the pierhead in Liverpool, bought my passage to Canada and we were married in Toronto.'

'In a Lutheran church . . .'

'I didn't mind. I like Martin Luther.'

'. . . with organ music because my father had played the organ at church in Germany. We had ice cream at the reception and I got back my appetite.'

'We bought a caravan and a plot of land on the outskirts of the city. I found a job on lakers. Then over the winters and on my weeks off we built our house together; the walls, the roof, even the plumbing and the electrics. No time for playing golf then.'

'We made it with our hands and our heads. We've earned our retirement.'

'It's the only house we've ever owned, and now that the city has grown up around us it's worth a bomb. Ontario has been good to us but it's time to sell up and move on.'

'Where will you go?' asked Beagan, his hope restored by their faith.

'West. End of this season I'll collect my gold Rolex, put an oar on my shoulder and we'll walk inland. First place someone asks me what I'm carrying that's where we'll stay.'

'That will be the day.' Gabi shook her head in disbelief as Beagan thought of Pike and Rosa paddling away from their sawdust hotel. 'Bill, you'll never leave boats behind you.'

Ruby appeared bearing a platter of food. Instead of serving up a small sample of each dish Ed had arranged four full entrées on the plate. The meal would set Beagan well on the way to becoming a ten-pounder. 'And the Word became flesh,' said Ruby.

'*Guten Appetit*,' chirped Gabi.

Beagan awoke at dawn to the low of a foghorn. Along the misty channel the rising sun gilded navigation buoys with golden light. The Detroit River looked like the Nile lined by white picket fences. It was broad, flat and calm but instead of feluccas plying between dusty docks, flotillas of open outboards lay off leafy islands. Yawning sportsmen lounged in deck chairs fishing for perch and bass. A Chris-Craft flying the Italian *tricolore* bounced across the wake. Grebes and coots fed in the shallows. Red-winged blackbirds clucked among the willows. The river narrowed and the *Tadoussac*'s shadow fell across the immaculate lawns of grand Colonial estates. Along backyard canals the luxurious cruisers of the car-making élite lay moored beside the fibreglass pleasure boats of their employees. The five Great Lakes contain 20 per cent of the world's fresh water but past Grosse Île the morning haze took on a tarnished hue. A whiff of sulphur wafted on the breeze. The clouds became fetid and stained as the chimneys of the Great Lakes Steel Mill loomed out of the smog. A line of grimy lakers disgorged black hillocks of coal to feed the furnaces of the Allied Chemical Corporation. The River Rouge ran russet, its waters discoloured by the Ford Motor Company's effluent. The bulk carrier *Algowest* made ten knots downstream *en route* to papermills on the Cuyahoga. Not long ago the river had caught fire. A spill of hot slag had ignited a stream more awash with oil, chemicals and debris than water. Buddy, the Newfoundland mechanic, appeared on deck wearing a T-shirt: 'Detroit: where the weak are killed and eaten', and Beagan's heart sank like a drum of toxic waste. The forty million people who lived along the Great Lakes, including one in three of all Canadians, were exposed to more poisonous chemicals than those inhabiting any comparable area of North America. Pregnant women and nursing mothers were warned not to eat the fish that their husbands and brothers caught downriver.

As well as being a shared transportation network the world's largest inland waterway also delineated the border. Across from Detroit's belching smokestacks and neo-Gothic Renaissance Center lay a sleepy provincial town of wooden buildings and low-rise office blocks. On Saturday morning Windsor's residents, when not driving over the Ambassador Bridge to do a little trans-border shopping, strolled along the river walk watching the bustle on the American side. Their unpretentious houses occupied large gardens, in contrast to the imposing Michigan homes squeezed on to small lots. Life on the Canadian shore appeared to be comfortable, self-satisfied and safe, revealing a people of lazy ambition who settled for half of that to which their materialistic southern neighbours aspired.

At Sarnia the land fell astern and Huron, the second-largest Great Lake, spread her waters before the ship. Ed rustled up a simple breakfast of grilled ham, fried eggs and pancakes as the wheelman adjusted the heading for true north. Only routine maintenance occupied the crew so Mark and Luke relaxed in the sun. Wellfit also took a break from the engine room and strolled on to the deck with his golf bag. He was determined to practise his swing. 'This is how I'm spending the rest of my days,' he announced. An Algerian grain carrier passed to starboard on its way to the sea. 'Did you know that in the first decade of this century the value of this country's wheat production doubled?' he asked.

'And the population grew by a third. Everyone thought that it would be Canada's century,' nodded Beagan. He had been reading back-issues of the Gillean trade journals. 'It started out to be that way too. The country was so optimistic. People believed in possibilities. They had faith in their potential.'

Wellfit admired his ship's fine lines. 'The men who started this company dreamed of creating the largest inland shipping line in the world. And they did it. Up until twenty years ago there were three hundred ships on the lakes. But today there are less than one hundred.'

'What went wrong?'

'I don't know for sure,' said Wellfit as he selected a club from his bag, 'but, well, do you know what I earn?' Beagan shook his head. 'Sixty dollars.'

'A day?'

'An hour. And on top of that there's what we call the Newfie lottery: work on ships for twenty weeks, collect welfare for the other thirty-two. It makes for an easy life all right, but it doesn't seem right.'

'There was no unemployment benefit when we started out,' said Gabi from under the brim of her sunhat. On her lap rested a plate of home-made brownies to tide her over until lunch. '*Mensch*, we didn't want government hand-outs, we didn't want to be a burden on anyone.'

Wellfit pointed at the Algerian *Nea Tyhi*. 'The chief aboard that saltie will bless his lucky stars if he gets a dollar a day. It costs ten times more to run a laker with a Canadian crew than it does to run a foreign ocean-going ship three times the size.'

The red-hulled bulk of an American ore carrier heaved into view. Wellfit fished out a tethered ball and tied it to a hatchway. 'And there are still too many ships on the lakes today.' He took a few practice swings aimed at the leviathan. 'Just watch, some day soon lakers will start having accidents. The *Tadoussac* cost three million dollars to build in 1969. She's insured for her replacement cost; that's sixty million dollars.' Wellfit swung at the ball and missed. 'They had a dream, you know, and something or somebody shattered it.' He tried again and managed to hit the ball but the elastic snapped. It struck the railing, bounced back and almost knocked off his head. 'Golf is a dangerous game,' he declared.

For the rest of the day the *Tadoussac* ran north beyond the sight of land and Beagan walked the deck trying to digest his tortellini Piedmontese and two bowlfuls of tiramisù. There was no doubt that he was gaining weight. Ed promised to serve only a light supper but the fresh blueberry pie was too tempting for anyone on board to resist. Beagan eased his down with two scoops of ice cream.

The following morning found the ship in a timbered archipelago. Retired lakers with sheared propellers or cracked hulls were laid up behind rugged headlands in the De Tour Passage. Across from Frying Pan Island the bleached wooden ribs of an old passenger paddle-wheeler rose out of the shallows. Beyond Manitoulin the *Tadoussac* zigzagged up channels and down narrows, between low, pine-clad islands uninhabited but for the odd isolated cabin tucked into a settler's clearing. The stern swung left then right as the ship rounded buoys and markers. A lofty orange navigation range erected beside an oversize church guided her past Sailor's Encampment, the deserted waystation where west-bound ships of an earlier age had pooled to await a tug tow up Lake Nicolet's fast waters. Nothing remained of the once bustling piers, hotels and mariners' bars. The church looked locked. In the bay where fleets of steamers had laid at anchor a lone Cree fisherman cast for king salmon.

In the wheelhouse the radar reflected the orderly column of lakers queued along the shipping lane. A faint blip caught the eye of Dai, the third officer. It suggested that a small motorboat hugged the ship's stern. He glanced aft over his shoulder and, seeing nothing, adjusted the sensitivity control until the ghostly echo vanished from the screen.

The *Tadoussac* turned into the Saint Mary's River and was thrust out of the wilds into downtown Sault Ste Marie. At the height of the last war more tonnage went through 'the Soo' than through the Suez and Panama canals combined. Now the International Bridge reached across the waterway between the twin American and Canadian cities. Townsfolk dawdled in shops and wandered around Republic Steel's graceful *Valley Camp* floating museum. The ship sailed along West Portage Avenue, close enough to shore for Beagan to watch the flickering television screens in the Seven Seas Motel and to read the take-away menu at the drive-in Dairy Queen. Three crewmen abseiled down the freeboard on to the dock to guide the ship into the lock. The great five-hundred-ton doors closed behind her and, with the beam leaving only a foot of clearance, the ship was eased seven metres up above Lake Huron.

Ed noticed a farmer selling bushels of sweetcorn off the back of a truck and sent out for three dozen ears. Beagan asked him about the wire mesh suspended over the grassy banks. 'The lock-keepers used to get downstream lakers to donate a bag of grain to give to the migrating Canada geese,' he explained. 'But the birds got to be real well fed and stopped flying south, settled down on the islands and became pests. So the authorities decided to introduce pigs on to the lawns to eat their eggs. The scheme worked a treat until someone stole the pigs.'

'Sounds to me a bit like an allegory,' jested Wellfit.

'My pork's all raised on barley-meal,' retorted Ed. He had misheard 'allegation'. 'I never touched those pigs.' The western lock opened and the ship slipped out into the largest freshwater lake in the world.

SUPERIOR SHONE LIKE burnished silver, possibly from the mercury that had been pumped into it by the pulp mills and chlor-alkali plants. I tucked *Primary* in behind the laker, using her bulk as a windbreak and riding in the smooth waters of her slipstream. A breeze blew up from the south and flicked frothy tufts off the wave tops. The Kermath ticked over well enough but, as she only made ten miles per hour at full throttle, it needed all my imagination to keep up with the *Tadoussac*.

Like grand-dad Hector before me I have always liked to take the measure of a place from the water, and nowhere in Canada is one further from land than on Superior. The lake is shaped liked a giant wolf's head biting into the country's geographic centre. Its volume is so great, some 2,900 cubic miles, that if God took umbrage against America and poured out its waters they would cover the whole continent to a depth of ten feet. It is so long that the *Tadoussac*, even with her Sulzer 9600 supercharged diesel, would take more than a day and night to cross its length. It was no wonder then that the first explorers had mistaken it for the legendary Sea of the West.

Long before our time Étienne Brûlé became the first white man to see the lake which the Ojibwa called *Gitche Gumee*, Big-Sea-Water. His discovery so convinced Champlain's scouts of their proximity to the lantern-lit cities of Cathay that Jean Nicolet, who followed Brûlé in 1634, stepped ashore near Green Bay in ceremonial damask robes. He fired a salute with his pistols and advanced upon a band of astonished Native Winnebagos. It was a disappointment that they didn't welcome him in Chinese. Although Lakes Michigan and Superior proved not to be the explorers' fabled sea, their cartographers did note the hundreds of rivers that led still further west. In 1671 the French crown claimed 'all the countries, streams, lakes and rivers contiguous and adjacent, discovered and undiscovered'. Louis Jolliet and Father Jacques Marquette, a Jesuit missionary, then pushed on beyond the Great Lakes to reach the upper Mississippi. The belief that 'the great river of Canada' flowed like Herodotus' Nile in two directions from its source and across the continent persisted for more than another century. As late as 1782 Janvier's map of North America illustrated a vast *'Mer ou Baye de l'Ouest'*, a great body of ocean which gouged deep into the Pacific mainland.

The first voyageurs may not have discovered the North-West Passage but they did find that there were fortunes to be made in the *pays d'en haut*. The 'up country' was filled with beaver and the felt hats which could be made from their fur were enormously fashionable in the seventeenth and eighteenth centuries. 'The Honourable Company of Adventurers of England Trading into Hudson's Bay' was established to acquire pelts in the north. Its rival the North West Company fused French zest with Scots loyalty to reach west up the Saint Lawrence. Every spring the Nor'Westers' big birchbark *canots de maître* raced from Montreal to the western tip of Superior. They followed the barren north shore, traversed wild bays and paddled in close line astern under pitch-pine torches when fog blanketed the lake. Their destination was a summer rendezvous with the beaver-laden *canots du nord* from the interior. It was a trade so valuable that without it, without this whim of fashion, Canada would have been ditched by Europe and absorbed into the United

States. The forty-ninth parallel, the border which stretches almost two thousand miles west from the Great Lakes to the Pacific, was only surveyed to stop American traders poaching Canadian pelts. It was the beaver that created Canada.

I had told all this to my boys, Beagan and Alex, tucked into their cots in the Pacific house, and the stories had carried them out over the dusky waters to sleep. If he remembered his history then Beagan would know that to continue west he had to travel as the voyageurs. No ship could navigate the rapids and shallows of the western rivers. A canoe might be slow but it would speed him on his interior journey faster than any speedboat. It would be easier too for me to keep up with him. I had grown tired of staring up the *Tadoussac*'s backside.

'BEAR PAWS, ROAST porcupine and moose's muzzle were their delicacies,' noted Beagan. Ed had proposed preparing him a farewell voyageur feast and Beagan had reached back to claim the bequest. 'Though out in the bush they tended to survive on strips of dried pemmican.'

'I'm fresh out of buffalo,' said Ed as they leafed through a dusty French tome unearthed from the depths of the box trunk, 'but I figure I can rustle up something tasty.'

That evening the galley was bathed in candlelight. Beagan asked the Wellfits to imagine that they were in a great banqueting room and that outside four hundred *hommes du nord*, the élite voyageurs who paddled the northern waterways, were camped with their Native wives.

'*Ja, ja,*' enthused Gabi. 'I can hear them shouting. *Mensch*, what a racket.'

'That must be the *mangeurs de lard*, the pork-eaters,' suggested Beagan. The sound of shouting in fact came from Buddy's television set. 'The Northmen taunted them for leading a soft life. They only canoed up from Montreal.'

'That's hardly a thousand miles,' said Wellfit in his wry, gentle humour. 'No wonder you didn't bother catching a bus.'

In his excitement Beagan reached for his great-grandfather's globe. He traced the waterways west, then felt sadness that modern, secessionist Quebec might cut itself off from its nationwide legacy. He pointed out the fictitious western sea. 'A Frenchman named Bonne drew a map in 1781 which not only records this fancy but puts a town on its south-east shore, a place he called Quivira.'

'That sounds like Spanish, eh honey?' Gabi said to Wellfit. '*Quivira*. Maybe it means "Who has seen?"'

'Or "Who will see?"'

'I don't know about that,' answered Beagan, wondering for a moment if the separatists like their voyageur forebears were still striving for a fictional destination. 'But according to Indian tales Quivira contained fabulous wealth in gold and silver. A Spanish explorer called Coronado is said to have reached it, God knows how, considering it lay on an imaginary sea, but he found there only rich black soil.'

'Then again, maybe it means "What truth?"' speculated Gabi.

Ruby stood in for a mixed-blood *Métis* serving girl and ladled out soup of beef. Ed followed the appetiser with hotch-potch, or salmagundi, a dish of chopped meat, eggs, onions and seasoning. As an alternative to beaver tails he produced a haunch of venison. Its taste was rich and gamy.

'It's larded with fat salt-pork, marinated in cognac and rolled in powdered herbs,' he explained. 'One of my secret recipes.'

Gabi risked a taste of every dish but in the end asked Ed for a steak. Retirement meant not having to eat buffalo tongues. She and her husband raised their goblets, which contained Dr Pepper instead of claret, to wish Beagan a safe journey.

'May you find your *Mer de l'Ouest*,' said Wellfit.

'*Ja*, but watch out for bears in the woods,' advised Gabi. 'And wild Indians too.'

*   *   *

Beagan smelt Thunder Bay before he saw it. The winds, which had blown heady wafts of pine resin twenty miles out into the lake, brought with them the acrid stench of pulp. It was pungent enough to bring tears to his eyes. The ripe odour of fermenting prairie wheat followed as the slender grain silos sprouted above the horizon. The *Tadoussac* eased herself into the Keefer Terminal and made fast beside the Saskatchewan Wheat Pool elevators. Beagan had not finished repacking the trunk, wrapping the family papers in waterproof plastic, before the loading pipes had been dropped over the open hatches and durum wheat poured into the hold.

Freight trains shunted back and forth along cat's-cradle rail lines spilling iron-ore pellets and potash. Grain took root between the ties. Beagan stepped ashore feeling restored, well fed by the Wellfits and, thanks to Ed, at least ten pounds heavier. He rented a room overlooking the port in a ubiquitous Mariner's Motel. The window had been welded shut to lock out the screech of the hopper cars' steel wheels. He didn't visit the site of the old trading post, which now lay under a railway marshalling yard, or catch the tourist ship *Welcome* to the replica Fort William at Pointe de Meuron. Instead he bought a six-pack of Miller Lite and watched a western on television. Outside the motel a trio of drunken Indians crumpled on to a park bench as if shot by a Hollywood cowboy. At the restaurant the waitress wore an off-the-shoulder dress with wired-hoop skirt and took orders for over-easy eggs. French fries were served with a tiny paper cup of ketchup. In the morning when he opened the bedroom curtains the *Tadoussac* had gone.

Beagan didn't stay long in the world's largest grain-handling port, but travelled the few miles south to the American border and Grand Portage. It was over this Great Carrying Place that Pierre Gaultier, the Sieur de la Vérendye, had climbed in 1731 in search of the Sea of the West. The thousands of voyageurs who had followed in his wake, hauling pelts and trade goods between the Great Lakes and the rivers of the western watershed, made Grand Portage the Nor'Westers' most thriving trading post. In contrast modern travellers tended to venture no further than the screens of the audio-visual presentation. They idled around the rebuilt stockade before driving up the hill to the Grand Portage Lodge. There they played slot machines and tried their hands at blackjack. The thriving casino had been built by the Chippewa and, being on their reservation, was exempt from state gambling laws. Big Bucks Bingo offered a $500,000 grand prize. Every morning a hopeful queue formed outside the gleaming glass doors. It was an opportunistic use of the white man's world to reclaim a subjugated culture. The profit enabled the Indian band to build Native schools and buy back the ancestral lands expropriated from their forefathers.

The climb was steep and the path overgrown but Beagan followed the snaking nine-mile portage past the Lodge, across Highway 61 and around the rapids to reach the lowest navigable section of the Pigeon River. There the wilderness outfitter met him and they slid the aluminium canoe into the waters of *Le Beau Pays*. They lowered the family trunk between the gunwales. As the pick-up drove back up the trail Beagan felt for a moment deserted, the silence he misconstrued as emptiness, the peace as paucity, but then the spirit of the woods gathered around him and he sensed that he was no longer alone.

T HE WATER'S DARK mirror, oily black and polished bright, reflected earth and sky, drawing together the jack pine lands and the reeds of the riverbed. A flush of wood ducks fused into a shoal of fish. Clouds merged with polished rocks. Copper spruce boughs sighed in the breeze like a mermaid's hair adrift on the current. The canoe slipped across the burnished glass, paired with its reflection and became two dancers moving through intricate steps. Beagan knelt at the curved stern, rolled on the gentle swells, paddled with an inside flick of the blade and left with every stroke a trail of twisting whirlpools behind him. Waterbeetles skated across the surface like minute balls of mercury. A crow's caw echoed through a valley of wild blue iris. Around a curve of crimson waterlilies my son waded the sparkling shallows and lined along rapids. At a portage, marked in autumn by the conspicuous yellow leaves of the black ash, he hauled his canoe up on to the beach. The carrying trails often followed the small streams that ran between lakes and ash, red maple and white elm grew in the rich soil. He hiked along the tunnels through the woods, making three trips back and forth for canoe, pack and trunk, at ten places in the fifty miles between Superior and the Divide. At the Height of Land Portage Beagan crossed between North and South Lakes, from the Great Lakes to the Hudson's Bay watershed, and let the current draw him downstream towards the western sea.

It was water not earth which was the dominant element between Superior and muddy Lake Winnipeg. From the divide an intricate labyrinth of interconnected waterways flowed east to the Atlantic, west and north to the Arctic, south down the Mississippi to the Gulf of Mexico. The ridge-pole of the continent rose at an 1800-square-mile wilderness park of six hundred lakes, a thousand tangled rivers and countless unnamed streams. Quetico was an unchanging sanctuary of deep quiet, a place where angels flew overhead and the past could be easily felt.

'Its name,' stuttered my dad Jamie, 'is said to be an old Cree word.' He dug his paddle into the water and lifted up a splash of spray. 'It describes a benevolent spirit who dwelt in a place of great beauty.' He and the others had caught up with us after dawdling behind in Toronto to watch the caber-tossing finals at Caravan's Scottish pavilion. The contest had been won by a Pole named MacTier.

'I think you will find that it is an acronym for the Quebec Timber Company, James,' asserted uncle Zachary, his paddle lying across his lap. He sat in the bow of grand-dad

Hector's slender birchbark canoe dabbing the water off his evening dress. The apparel appeared somewhat incongruous against a mossy hillside of old firs.

The Reverend sat bolt upright at the stern, his legs folded beneath him Indian-style, collar tightly fastened and tartan cloak around his shoulders in spite of the heat. 'Quetico,' he said in his soft Gaelic accent, 'is a kind of Native pidgin for the French phrase *la quête de la côte*, the search for the coast. It is true enough that along these channels passed nearly every explorer looking for China.'

'Whatever the word means, the number one thing that I think about is its people,' I said, bringing up the rear in a rowing boat. The pulling of an oar was better suited to the bush than the putter of mechanical propulsion, so I had left *Primary* tied up to a mirage in Thunder Bay. 'Those Northmen for example, wiry little men dressed in breech-cloth and moccasins with a belted shirt and beaded tobacco pipe, ran all but the most dangerous rapids. What did they feel as their canoes plunged down some thundering shoot?'

'F-F-Fearful,' answered Jamie as we slipped into single file behind Beagan. 'Any jagged edge could tear the thin birchbark skin and suck the voyageurs into a watery grave. No fewer than thirty wooden crosses stood beside some rapids where their *camarades* had drowned.'

'Faithful,' pronounced Hector. 'Every Sabbath-day Alexander Mackenzie, the Scot who first crossed the continent by water, assembled his voyageurs beside their upturned canoes to listen to the Scriptures. In the most extraordinarily pronounced French he would convey three chapters out of the Old Testament and as many out of the New, adding explanation as seemed to him suitable. I read that over Beagan's shoulder, right enough.'

'If you will forgive me, Father, what they were most thankful for was their salary,' contested Zachary. 'It was the thought of money which sustained them through the eighteen-hour days and along the portages when each man carried a 180-pound load of trade goods with tump line and broad leather harness.'

'The devil has beguiled you, Zachary,' scolded Hector.

'They sang *chansons* as they paddled too,' volunteered Jamie, anxious as always to smooth over disagreement. 'Each verse was launched in solo then repeated in chorus North West f-f-fashion, timed to the rhythm of fifty strokes every minute. Somewhat faster than our pace today.'

'Their route was guided by memory and lob pines, tall spruces on high promontories which had been stripped of lower branches.' I pointed up to the evenly pinnacled tree-line. 'Back then the bristly tops stood out like destination signs along a highway. Next exit Lac la Croix, this lane only Lake of the Woods, turn left for the Rockies via the Saskatchewan River.'

'Isn't it grand to feel the world about you from a canoe, to hear the wind in the trees, to notice the shape of islands?' laughed Jamie as we sailed over silver spouts of white horses in the isolated and empty land.

'It is hard to believe now that the volume of early-nineteenth-century canoe traffic made Quetico one of the busiest regions of interior North America,' I said.

'Would that be true?' asked Hector without breaking his stroke.

'Quite true,' I replied. 'I used to tell Beagan and Alex that in 1821, after decades of vicious rivalry, the Nor'Westers amalgamated with the Hudson's Bay Company to create a fur trade empire which encompassed nearly three million square miles of territory.'

'It was a mercantile colony that spanned the continent from Labrador to Nootka Sound,' confirmed Zachary.

'There were trading posts as far south as San Francisco and above the Arctic Circle,' I added. 'And the vast empire was under the mastery of one man.'

'Sir George Simpson,' noted Zachary with a hint of envy

in his voice. 'He had been born in a manse on the Moray Firth and rose to become "head of the most extended Dominions in the known world – the Emperor of Russia, the Queen of England and the President of the United States excepted".'

'Didn't he inspect his domain in the f-f-finest canoe paddled by the most stalwart voyageurs?' asked Dad as we passed beneath glaciated humpback hills. 'I seem to recall that was one of your stories, Sandy. And that he was accompanied by a Scotch piper to herald his arrival at the scattered posts?'

'He was called "the little emperor", a shrewd, despotic, avaricious master of an almost uninhabited land,' I answered. 'But his monopoly over the waterways and beaver swamps ended with a change in fashion. Canada had been opened in a failed attempt to find a route to the Orient. It was a paradox that when the object of that quest reached Europe two centuries later it killed the enthusiasm for pelts.'

'I may say that I preferred the silk topper to a fur hat,' opined Uncle Zach.

'The trade collapsed and the beaver, which had been adopted as the national emblem, was replaced by the maple leaf.'

OF THE THOUSANDS of explorers and voyageurs who had paddled along Quetico's waterways, pausing to gum their canoes and breakfast on a sandy beach, only memory remained. The crosses and lob pines had gone. But it was said that ghosts stalked the portages and phantom brigades still moved across the lakes. In the slap of waves against a rocky shore Beagan heard the splash of paddles. A jay's cry became a voice in the next bay. The wind carried mellow voices singing *La Belle Rosier*. He made camp on a ledge scarred by the last ice age and shaped like the bow of a ship. He scrambled eggs, boiled up a pouch of freeze-dried scal-loped potatoes and, after hoisting the food pack into a tree to deter inquisitive bears, opened the trunk to read by the firelight.

'They were hurled down with surprising velocity through three successive cascades,' the Nor'Wester Duncan McGillivray had written in his log-book. 'The canoe was several times over-whelmed with water and threatened every moment with being dashed to pieces in the windings of the rocks.' The words helped Beagan grasp at the past. 'It remained a considerable time under water. At length however the current drove it toward shore, with the men still hanging on after it, and though they at first seemed insensible, yet they recovered their strength and before night renewed their labours with as much alacrity as if nothing had happened to them.'

The intricate labyrinth of the waterway twisted through Crooked Lake, skipped across Thursday, Friday and Saturday Bays then wound into Lac la Croix. Its crystal waters reflected a shore-line of brooding spruce and silvery birch. Beagan met no other travellers along the looking-glass route so to keep himself company he tried to imagine that his mirror image was a fellow canoeist. But it wasn't Champlain or Brûlé whom he saw paddling beside him, it was the Reverend Hector. After a long moment of synchronous movement his great-grandfather turned towards him and bowed his head. Beagan nodded in return. With a great splash of spray the Peterborough lapstrake sprinted between them. Jamie wore his striped cap and britches and stretched forward with each stroke, splashing great showers of spray in his wake. 'Come on, you old men,' Beagan imagined him shouting from the next river-bend. 'Put a little effort into it.'

Beagan's picture of me was conjured up from an old photograph that he had found in the trunk. I was a boy under a folded paper hat, in sopping wet dockside shoes, with blisters on palm and inside fingers. My light cedar skiff was steered by rudder and tiller ropes rigged up with three electric bells to order the 'engine' ahead, astern or stopped. The two dogs rode with me; the mongrel at the bow and the snoozing Samoyed astern. My shirtsleeves were rolled up and my tie was splattered with grease. It always insisted on dangling in the bilges.

We fell into a line behind Beagan and rode the Namakan's first rapid of long, easy riffles then descended the froth of white water to the lower river. At High Falls and Lady Rapids, where sturgeon lay in the shallow bays, he turned around as if to check that we had not fallen behind or capsized in the swells, but we never strayed far from his trail. In fact the canoes seemed to be tethered to Beagan's stern as Zachary had lain back to read a newspaper and Reverend Hector had lost interest in the passing scene and began to study his Bible.

'Look F-F-Father, there's a moose,' called Jamie as an ungainly brown male raised its broad muzzle from a waterlily-root feed. 'Its name means "twig eater" in Algonquin.'

'"*Alces alces*" in the Latin,' said Hector.

'I shot one on Lake Temagami,' added Zachary, turning to the financial page.

A hen merganser with her chicks on her back shuttled across placid Rainy River, the misnomer for the old voyageur name *la Reine des Rivières*, Queen of Rivers. Our family flotilla eased down its broad brown waters, slipping between tall stands of bulrushes and golden rows of wild rice. Fat black ducks, heavy and sluggish from their gorging, rose reluctantly as we slid past. Their wings whispered over the boats.

'What did Canada promise you?' Beagan asked aloud. He had become accustomed to talking to himself but was unprepared to hear a response.

'In my day it was a promised land that we dreamed of building,' replied the Reverend without looking up from his reading.

Zachary put down his paper and shook his head. 'With all due respect, Father, you still speak as if the world were what you would have it to be, as if the ideal were real. Canada never promised a star-spangled dream.'

'But it was an admirable society, Zachary,' insisted Jamie. 'Why, any immigrant could buy a plot of land and become a home-owner within a generation.'

'It offered a place to work, no more no less,' continued Zachary. 'Any fool could succeed here.' He met my eye then raised the newspaper again to cut me out. 'Almost any fool.'

Beagan knew these thoughts. He had read them in our diaries and letters, yet it surprised him how loudly the words now echoed in his head.

'Hector is right: it *was* a promised land for the newcomer,' he heard me say, 'though only because emigration was for most a matter of necessity. A settler takes what he can get.'

'And thanks the good Lord for it.'

'The country provided a sanctuary, Sandy, and the value of that cannot be underestimated,' emphasised Jamie.

'I don't deny that, but what about her subsequent generations? How does the settled descendant fit into a place that changes to accommodate every newcomer, that becomes a land of the displaced?' I hoped that Beagan didn't detect the cynicism in my voice. 'I became a stranger in my own country.'

'Canada offered the same opportunities to one and all,' stuttered Jamie. 'And everyone came here f-f-for that same reason.'

'Everyone except the Scots,' interrupted Hector.

'What then brought the Scots?' hazarded Beagan. He was convinced that he was dreaming.

'We came looking for something more,' Hector answered. 'This was to be the land that Scotland could have been.'

'But this is no new Scotland,' I said.

'We dreamt of promised lands in a land which promised nothing.'

Beagan stared at us as if he didn't believe his own imagination, then turned and without another word paddled away.

It rained so heavily in the night that at dawn Beagan expected to see a dove fly past the tent, a maple leaf clamped in its beak, but instead swarms of mosquitoes rose up from the rockpools. A heavy mist veiled the far shore in half-colours. Columns of vapour rose out of the forest like the smoke from bonfires. Blue holes pierced the grey clouds as if poked out by divine fingers. He tried to make a pot of tea but there were no dry pine-needles to start a fire. The camping gas wouldn't light either. He sat on a stump and listened to the sough of the wind through the trees. As the mist lifted off the lake and extended our horizon beyond the edge of the island Beagan pushed away from shore.

We kept our distance over the next few days, lagging behind as he navigated through the maze of the Lake of the Woods, dragged his canoe over sandbars and made the short, easy carry from Portage Bay on to the Winnipeg. Once the river had been the grandest and most spectacular on the voyageurs' route to the west. Its waters had surged through tortured rock and dropped fast over roaring falls. But beyond the protective boundary of Quetico modern man had harnessed the wild grandeur and built six hydro-electric dams along the river's length. At Whitedog new channels had been blasted out and the old watercourse was a forlorn and stony emptiness. The Seven Sisters Dam had reduced tumbling rapids and green whirlpools to an idle narrows. Turbines whined within Pointe du Bois's concrete curtain and high-voltage pylons marched away to the city. The dancing river had been drowned beneath headponds and reservoirs and only beyond Pine Falls' reeking pulp mills did Nature reassert itself.

It was there at the edge between two worlds that we realised something too had changed in Beagan. Dad saw it first in his paddling. He dug the blade into the water, thrust the canoe forward and finished each stroke with a strong inside flick. Even Zachary noticed the new confidence, and complained at having to paddle harder to keep up with his great-nephew. After the power and material luxuries of his prosperous life he found the levelling nature of immortality to be a bit of a comedown. 'At least,' he puffed, 'he's no longer wasting time.'

It seemed that in the solitude of the woods Beagan had realised that he was not alone. He might not have felt a sense of belonging but he had understood the value of the journey. He had found the renewed strength too in knowing that we travelled beside him. We closed in upon him and he wrapped us around his shoulders as one would a coat in winter. The river broadened out and at the low misty line of Elk Island spilt into the coffee-coloured lake that the Cree called *Winnipee*.

IN THE OPEN prairie towns of arrow-straight streets and wind-swept bungalows visitors were welcomed with a wary question. 'You going any further?'

'I'm heading for the Pacific,' Beagan answered.

'Oh, you'll love the mountains,' the locals sighed, relieved that their town was not someone's final destination.

Everyone in Manitoba was on the way to somewhere else. Winnipeg had always been a place through which travellers passed. The Native people had long paused to trade at the junction of the Red and Assiniboine rivers. The French explorers had paddled through the Forks *en route* to *le Mer de l'Ouest*. The Scots were the first migrants mad enough to try to settle the wide, sleepy banks. They endured plagues of locusts and winter starvation in hipped-roof houses of rigid symmetry. When the trans-continental railway passed by in 1881 it brought with it an illusion of permanence. A million settlers poured through Union Station, agriculture became the backbone of the economy and citizens bragged that Winnipeg was destined to be 'the Chicago of the Prairies'. At the turn of the century no other Canadian city boasted a greater value of building permits. The Electric Railway Chambers glittered above the skyline, its Italianate exterior columns illuminated by six thousand lightbulbs. The lofty Lindsay Building was decorated with bulging cornucopias of English roses, Scotch thistles and Irish shamrocks. On Portage Avenue the elegant Paris Tower soared eleven stories high to elaborate cornice motifs of teeming immigrant galleons. But Winnipeg's fleeting fortune ended with the First World War. Newcomers stopped homesteading on the plains. The Panama Canal enabled eastern goods to bypass the railway and reach western markets by sea. The crash of 1929 preceded an intense drought which ruined farmers. The grounds of the neo-classical Legislative Building were ploughed for vegetable gardens to feed the city's poor. After forty optimistic years winsome Winnipeg returned to being a stopping place; people came, stayed for a while then moved on.

'I never knew a Kristjanson who wasn't a fisherman,' shouted Marvin Kristjanson above the hiss of his diesel. He gestured at the dozen blond children playing on the deck of the *Hekla*. 'They'll all be fishermen too if there are any fish left.' Across Lake Winnipeg's horizon the peaks of whitecaps looked like the furls of distant sails. The broad-beamed, steel-plated whitefish boat churned north through the caramel swells towards a funeral.

In town that morning Beagan had freighted the canoe back to the Thunder Bay outfitter and gone looking for a boat. At first he hadn't found one. In the tourist bureau he learnt that the passenger steamers and shipping lines had been replaced by eight-wheeled tractor trailers and provincial highways. Commercial vessels no longer plied the world's twelfth-largest lake. His only option had been the sightseeing riverboat MS *Paddlewheel Queen* which ran the few miles downriver to Selkirk. It at least headed in the right direction. There, at the end of the line and behind a giant 'Chuck the Channel Catfish' statue, he had found the Marine Museum of Manitoba. Five beached ships lay on the grass beside a parking lot. None of them would be puffing him up the lake to Grand Rapids. Beagan had bought a hot dog from the A&W on Main Street and eaten it in the shade of the SS *Keenora*. As he considered his next move a blond boy with hooded sky-blue eyes appeared beside him bearing a slice of *vinaterta*, a rich multi-layered Icelandic prune cake. 'Grandpa's gone to heaven,' he announced by way of introduction. 'And now we're sailing there too in his old boat.'

Towards the end of the last century a series of severe earthquakes and volcanic eruptions laid waste parts of Iceland. Hundreds of refugees were forced to leave the island and look for a better life in the New World. On the western shore of Lake Winnipeg they founded Gimli, or heavenly abode. The site offered an abundance of heavy timber, good farmland and, most importantly, fish. The Native people taught them how to set nets under the ice and in summer they built fishing stations around the lake. In 1878 'New Iceland' was officially established and for twenty years no other nationality was permitted to settle within the reserve. The community thrived, until there were more people of Icelandic descent living around Winnipeg than in Reykjavik. But overfishing depleted the stocks on which their prosperity had been built. Mercury pollution poisoned the waters. Wall-eye and pickerel no longer enriched the heavenly abode.

The slice of *vinaterta* drew Beagan to a picnic wake. On his father's death Marvin Kristjanson had gathered together his scattered siblings and their children. At the Marine Museum they ate peanut butter and jelly sandwiches and then clambered over the old man's boat. Little Inga, her hair tied into plaits, tugged at her uncle's hand. 'You said that Opa's gone to heaven.' Kristjanson had been trying to explain death to the children. 'Is heaven near Gimli?'

He introduced Beagan to his family. 'This here is Inga and those are her brothers Thor, Gusti and Stefan. Gusti's the one who brought you the cake. Magnus and Johanna are in the wheelhouse. Over there are my three: Dayna, Brett and Tom. Bjorgvin has gone to the little boys' room and Geiri has as usual disappeared.'

Kristjanson's sister was attempting to rub a grape-jelly stain out of Thor's shirt.

'And will Gusti die?' the five-year-old asked his mother.

'Yes, dear,' she replied, dabbing the cloth in water.

'And will Johanna die?'

'Yes, she will too.'

'Will I die, Mummy?'

'Yes, Thor.'

'When?'

'In about sixty or seventy years.'

Thor knotted his brow. 'Will you die, Mummy?'

'Yes, me too.'

'When?' he persisted.

'In about forty or fifty years.'

'Is that a longer time?'

'No, shorter.'

'But when we've all died who will sail in Opa's boat?'

The hull was well suited to the lake's fickle weather. It was deep and long and reminded Beagan of his own father's last boat and the final, fiery journey aboard her. 'Going together to the funeral by boat is to honour him,' Kristjanson explained as they stowed the box trunk in the hold among the children's sleeping bags. There were no old lottery tickets pinned to the cabin wall. 'I'm sure he'd be happy if we took you along with us to Grand Rapids too.'

The *Hekla* cruised up the low-lying shore past Hnausa, Calder's Dock and Fisher Bay. Anvil-headed kingfishers perched above driftwood beaches and sandy coves. Crows as big as Christmas turkeys cast great black cloaks high on their backs. On board the children drew crayon pictures of a lake filled with fish. Johanna felt sick and Bjorgvin asked if grandfather was alone in heaven.

'No, Oma is with him,' answered his mother.

'My father used to say, "If he's a good fisherman, he's a good man."' Kristjanson gestured away to the north-east and told Beagan, 'He and his brothers came this way every May. They'd spend the summer at their station on George Island, living in a bunkhouse, gill-netting from catboats. The *Lady of the Lake* called in every other week to freight the fish back to Gimli. Now the few of us that are left don't go out for more than a day at a time.'

From his wallet Kristjanson produced a frayed photograph of a bright-eyed old man wrapped in a hooded snowsuit. His thick moustache was silvered by frost. On his feet he wore ice creepers, galoshes inset with steel blades which enabled walking during a winter gale. 'My father made the best damn ice jiggers on the lake. An Indian taught him. You lever the jigger under the ice then set the net. He and his brothers would haul the catch on sleighs to Riverton – 225 boxes in a load, each box with 140 pounds of fish. It was hard work but he loved it. He loved what he could make. "If you want your dreams to come true," he used to say to me, "first you have to wake up." Most folks now just stay asleep.' Kristjanson laughed and waved his hand over the sea of blond heads. 'But look at us. He made us all.'

Brett wanted to know where Opa had gone. 'Well,' said Kristjanson, 'he's moved on. He's gone to the next room.' Brett looked confused. Kristjanson tried to explain. 'You know that you and Dayna and Tom live in a big apartment block with people on the floors above and below.' The child nodded. 'Let's pretend that you have magic powers and can see through the walls and floors and ceilings. You can see me in the kitchen, Tom playing in his bedroom . . .'

'Mummy on the toilet?' said Brett and giggled.

'Old Mr Sigurdson upstairs and Oma . . .'

'But Oma's dead.'

'Yes, that's right Brett,' said Kristjanson, 'but with your magic powers you can see her – and Opa too – in the next room.'

'Telling stories?'

'Probably.' He smiled. 'Now can you imagine that all our family, everyone here and everyone who has died, lives there in our building?'

'Someone flushed the toilet last night and I thought it might be Opa,' said Tom.

'Well, it might have been. And just because we can't really see through walls doesn't mean that it wasn't Opa, does it? He's probably in the next room now, talking to Oma and *his* Opa, watching you, making sure that you're good and waiting to come and help you whenever you need him.' A hint of a smile played on Beagan's lips.

North of Dancing Point sheer rockfaces rose up from the water-line. Spires of pine stretched away beyond the horizon. *Hekla* tramped past isolated villages that clung to the shore, strung together by freight canoes. Telephones were so few and far between that they were marked on provincial maps. Beagan turned on his portable radio but heard only static. Beneath the high blue sky he felt again the immensity of the vast northland where a thousand miles can lie between settlements and there are tracts of tundra on which no man will ever stand.

'Most days the lake's like a spoiled child in tantrums,' said Kristjanson, casting his eye over the placid waters. 'We're lucky, the weather's good today. Winnipeg's shallow, which makes for steep-fronted, choppy waves, and there're almost no islands to break the prairie winds.'

Beagan had noticed that the few small islands along their route were uninhabited, yet were spanned by wide gravel highways. The roads appeared to come up out of the water, strike straight across to the far shore then plunge back beneath the waves. It was as if the world had been flooded and only the highest mac-adamed hilltops showed above the surface. Kristjanson explained that as no roads penetrated the lake's wild eastern shore many communities had been cut off after the demise of shipping. To supply them the government had decided to build winter highways across the ice. Every December huge graders, great roaring Cyclopses with single flashing blue eyes, ploughed aside cascades of snow like a northern Moses dividing the frozen waters of a white sea. In their wake sped oil tankers and heavy transports laden with a year's provisions. In the spring break-up the ice roads melted away and left only the traversed islands.

Two great rivers meet at the head of Lake Winnipeg: the wild

Nelson flowing north-east into Hudson's Bay and the now sedate Saskatchewan which meanders down from the Rockies, across three prairie provinces and drains a watershed twice the size of Britain. The *Hekla* tacked into her wide, smiling mouth and disturbed a regal procession of waterbirds. A dozen cormorants took off as one, lifting themselves up on to the surface then running into flight. The pelicans followed, their black wingtips beating out semaphore signals as they lumbered into an elegant glide.

The whitefish boat came ashore at Lover's Point Park, once Hudson's Bay Wharf, the lower terminal of the derelict Grand Rapids tramway. The first railway in western Canada had been built around the gorge in 1877 to carry passengers and freight in horse-drawn cars between the lake steamers and Saskatchewan paddle-wheelers. But modern travellers preferred the southern highways and the thundering river had been silenced by a great curtain of broken stone and concrete. The rapids over which canoes and fur-traders' cumbersome York boats had been dragged hummed at sixty cycles per second. Manitoba Hydro's dam had rendered meaningless the waterway's original Cree name *Kis-is-ska-tche-wan*, 'the river which flows swiftly'.

In the tail-race terns and shags, their wings dipping below their bodies, swooped into the froth to scoop up beakfuls of fish. Gulls paddled on the surface, lifted now and again by the swells washed out from the generators. Kristjanson cut his engine and the parents who had driven north caught hold of the lines. The children jumped on to the dock, excited by the memory of holidays with Grandfather. Every summer vacation he had led them down moose-track trails, over shining white sands and built match-stick Viking longboats. He had tied to their waists two-quart jars which they filled with raspberries, blueberries and sweet pear Saskatoons. But their laughter stilled to a hush at the sight of the old man laid out in a tired, shuttered bungalow.

'Death is not an end,' Kristjanson reassured Beagan. 'We have split life into two parts far too drastically. It is important that the children understand that the dead don't leave us, they precede us.'

'When I die,' Bjorgvin asked his uncle, 'can I be buried with Hoppy?' The boy clutched his one-eared, fluffy toy rabbit to his chest.

Beagan left the family to their mourning and followed the sound of digging to the small cemetery. Two young Crees had opened up a new plot for the old fisherman but had left the graveyard grass uncut. Beagan sat on a boulder dislodged during the blasting of the power station and saw the boys' high cheekbones, crescent-moon eyes and small pointed chins. To his shame he realised that apart from Gogo, whose compassion lived on in the pages of Hector's journal, the only Native people whom he knew were the primped squaw adorning summer-blue packs of Land o' Lakes unsalted butter and the befeathered chief logo of the Red Indian Mini-Cab Company ('We're no cowboys'). The painted names on the wooden crosses told him too of his arrival at a new frontier. Beneath the willows rested Cyril Mamageesick, Angus Ducharme, Donty Holowachuk and Rusty Vigfusson, names part-immigrant, part-indigenous in a borderland where European influence waned. Away to the north and west lay an ancient land with traditions and customs which stretched back thousands of years. The modern nation-state that had been threaded over it was like a tenuous spider's web through which the wind whispered.

CHAPTER IX

WHERE ANGELS BATHE

'CALL ME AL,' said Corporal Alan Sutherland and let go of the patrol boat's wheel to shake Beagan's hand. He was a slender, soft-spoken Mounted Policeman from The Pas detachment a hundred miles upstream. 'I'm glad I could help out.' His curls, so red that they would clash with the cochineal RCMP dress uniform, were flattened by the breeze. 'Grand Rapids is outside our division but I had to come down to look for Harold Finn – again.' He gestured at the black Avon inflatable raft tugging at the end of a tow rope. Its intoxicated owner lay asleep on the patrol boat's deck with his head craned over the trunk. 'Third time he's got lost this season, but, hey,' Al confided with a boyish smile, 'anything's better than office paperwork.'

The lip of the dam dropped away behind them as the outboard sped west across the headpond. Silver driftwood from the drowned forest cluttered the swampy shore. Rotting branches reached above the surface. Cedar Lake was a shallow, man-made reservoir of dead-end channels and switchback passages but Al knew the route and followed the Saskatchewan's current as it wound beneath the surface.

Beagan had recognised the Scottish surname and asked if Al knew his family's history.

'We go way back,' enthused the Mountie. 'My grandmother came out from Leeds to run the school and teach the Indians how to use a knife and fork. It was my father's people who came from Scotland,' he confirmed. 'You heard about the Red River Settlement?'

'Yes,' answered Beagan. 'In 1811 the Scottish peer Lord Selkirk was granted land to establish the North-West's first colony. About ninety people, mostly Highland crofters from Sutherland and some emigrants from the west of Ireland, were sent here by way of Hudson's Bay.'

'My folks came over on the second ship. They took one look at the blue swamp, the spruce and tamarack and decided to head south before freeze-up. They weren't going to spend the winter in log tents at York Factory.' Al eased back on the throttle to skirt a deadhead. The drunk groaned in his sleep. 'So they just started walking, pulling their boats up the Nelson, hauling their freight over the thirty-four portages and going near on seven hundred miles. Well sir, it was one cruel journey. They lost most of the old people. Then, just north of here at Cross Lake, they turned right instead of left and got lost. The snows came, their food ran out and they started to starve. If it hadn't been for the Moose Lake Indians they would all have died. The tribe's hunters heard the weeping of the women and children and helped them to survive the winter.' Al swung the boat out of the marshland and into the river. A flush of teals scattered out of its path. A beaver slapped his tail and vanished into the swirling water. 'I went up one weekend to the place where they were found. They still call it Crying Island.'

Nine years after the Highlanders' arrival John West, the newly-appointed Hudson's Bay Company chaplain, had followed to establish the Church of England in Rupert's Land, the richest fur region in the Empire. 'Thousands are involved in worse than Egyptian darkness around me, wandering in ignorance and perishing through lack of knowledge,' he had written. 'When will this wide waste of howling wilderness blossom as the rose in the desert and become a fruitful field?' West had prayed for his struggling colony of Kildonan settlers and dispossessed fur traders who, while living on pemmican and hope, aspired to establish a farming community. 'May a gracious God hear their cry and raise them up as heralds of His salvation in this truly benighted and barbarous part of the world.'

Beagan glanced astern and tried to catch sight of Hector's canoe.

He could imagine him pausing to wrap his Bible in oilcloth, reflecting for a moment on similar histories.

'They were terrible years,' confessed Al. 'But having lived through them is something we're real proud of.'

'But didn't you want to move on?' asked Beagan, shivering at the memory of the bucket of live coals that had warmed his great-grandfather's pulpit.

'Nope. The experience taught my family to respect the land, and even to learn to love it.'

Ashen trunks clung to white dolomite cliffs. In places forest fires had charred the shore and toppled copses of hoary trees like a giant's spillikins. The patrol boat glided over the silty waters, described a wide arc and slid under the metal-grid bridge into The Pas. The town had grown up at the confluence of the Sas-katchewan and Pasquia rivers where migrating geese had paused to feed and travellers found a sheltered berth. The birds still came every autumn, filling the delta with their cackle and hiss, but Beagan was the first stranger to arrive by water in a year. There were no vessels to be seen, nothing to carry him further up the Saskatchewan, unless the flat-bottomed riverboat *Skippy L* could be unbolted from its concrete plinth in Kelsey Park and relaunched.

A good policeman can sense people's thoughts and as Al eased up to the dock he nodded at the drunk. 'Harold here came down the river a few years ago. He's the only person I know who's done it.' He secured the painter then pulled the inflatable up on the shore. 'You should discuss your trip with him – when he's sober. Rise and shine, Mr Finn,' said the Mountie, shaking Harold's shoulder. 'You're back home.'

A single bloodshot eye strained open and gazed over the gun-wale. 'As sure as there's shit in a dead cat that ain't Fortune.' The eye snapped shut. The accent sounded like Irish that had been soaked by four centuries of bad weather. Harold Finn was from Newfoundland.

'No, Harold, it's The Pas. You're home in The Pas.'

'Oh Lord jeez, will I never get off this damn prairie?' His eyes sprung open and started at Beagan. 'I've been here so long looks like I'm becoming a tourist attraction,' he moaned. 'What you doing here, b'y? You lost?' Al explained that the two men had a journey in common, all be it back to front, and asked Harold to help put Beagan on the right track. The drunk heaved himself up on to his feet and swayed to port. 'Anybody who don't listen to Al here is three sandwiches short of a picnic.' Beagan looked at the wizened face, the scruff of hair and the beef-red nose swollen like a dory's bow and concluded that all he would learn from the whiplash-thin Newfie were the directions to the nearest liquor store. 'You'd better come home with me then, b'y. We'll talk while Lily rustles us up some supper.'

As they carried the trunk along Fischer Avenue Beagan asked if any craft still went up the Saskatchewan. 'Upstream?' exclaimed Harold, talking at the speed of a force-nine gale. 'You can't go upstream no more.' They turned into a side street and veered through a back gate. 'There used to be one heck of a lot of boats on the river – packets, tubs, queen and tramp steamers that sailed all the way to Edmonton – but only local fishers use the river now. They run their outboards up aways to a favourite fishing hole then hurry back home for supper. Natives use it for sure, but only on social visits to nearby reserves. Hydro went and built a dam on every babbling brook and the old ships, hell, they been dragged around to the far side of the island and dynamited. Anybody wants to go upriver nowadays he gets in a car and drives.'

The back door was open but the bungalow felt empty. Harold breezed along the corridor, called out a woman's name and pulled two bottles of Labatt's from the cooler. 'Forget about going west, b'y,' he advised, leaning so close that Beagan could smell stale breath. 'Come down east with me. It's clear sailing all the way to the Bay and home to Newfoundland.'

'Isn't it a bit late in the year to cross Hudson's Bay?' asked Beagan. Churchill, the country's main northern port, and Polar Bear Capital of the World, was frozen in for all but the few months of high summer.

'Got to get back soon, eh? I got no passport. So if Quebec up and separates I'll be stuck here for good, and I don't belong here in this dustbowl. B'y, when we get down home we'll put into a cove with a flat of beer, jig a fish and drop it in a boiler with some potatoes.' He leaned back in his chair and sighed. 'That's where I was heading just now, until I went and got lost in the Cedar delta. Third damn time this year.'

The mention of food reminded Harold that he was hungry. He set to work making Jiggs dinner, pulling foil-wrapped salt and roast beef from the refrigerator, peeling turnip, carrot, cabbage and potatoes, throwing the lot into a cast-iron pot.

'I been trying to get back to Fortune Harbour for as long as I can remember. I'm a plumber, eh? There weren't no work in Newfoundland so I got a job up in the Arctic. I was the only plumber in a thousand miles but, I tell you, it was some cold. Eskimos say that there are only two seasons in the north: winter and the first of July. Houses up there, they got two big tanks: one for water, the other for waste. If the heating packs in the sewer tank freezes up, and where do you go for a crap in the tundra? Ain't no trees to hide behind.' Harold grabbed two more beers from the fridge. 'One time I got a call to fix this leaking bath in an Inuit house. The government built them new housing and there were always an odd nut wanting tightening, eh? Well, I turned up to find that this Eskimo had killed a caribou and while chopping it up in the tub had axed clean through the fibreglass.' Harold laughed as the house filled with the rich aroma of cooking. He enjoyed the sound of his own stories. 'The money was good but it weren't home, so I hitched a ride to Hay River, bought the inflatable and started to work my way back. When I reached The Pas I met Lily. She was as welcome as a flower in May and, b'y, I got her some pregnant. So now it seems the good Lord won't let me leave.' Harold emptied his bottle in one swallow and reached for another. 'Don't get me wrong, this is a nice town. The people are friendly and I like to watch them bringing in the wheat, but most mornings when I come out and look up at the sky I think, "Another grey day." I sort of wish my cake was still dough.'

It took a dozen beers for Beagan to convince Harold of his need to continue the westward journey. 'Maybe it's too late to go east this year anyways,' Harold admitted. 'For sure I'd end up getting frozen in at Churchill.' He wandered away for a moment, blew open the other doors in his bungalow, dawdled outside the bedroom, then returned. 'Tell you what, b'y. Seems Lily has gone off to her folks' place, not that I can blame her. If you buy gas and the beer I'll run you upriver in the inflatable. It won't take no time to get to Edmonton, and I could do some shopping.' As Harold warmed to his theme his voice began to boom. 'We'll drink lots of brew and tell a few yarns. It'll be great crack.' It was an offer that Beagan could hardly refuse. Six hundred long, wet, ferry-free miles lay between him and the city at the edge of the Rockies. 'But there's one condition, eh?' added Harold.

'What's that?'

'No wisecracks.' Newfoundlanders were to other North Americans what the Irish were to the English and the people of Kerry to other Irishmen. 'Except this one: what's black and blue and floats in the bay?' Beagan shook his head. 'A mainlander after telling a Newfie joke.'

At dawn iron stormclouds weighed on the horizon. The sky was a cold, thin winter blue. A skein of geese rippled south calling to each other as they flew. Harold and Beagan carried the supplies down to the dock and smelt frost in the air. They bolted the Evinrude on to the Avon. A gaudy bumper sticker dangling from its stern read, 'Don't follow me – I'm going to Hell.' Harold yanked the cord but the outboard refused to start. 'This damn motor's two days older than God,' he complained then hit it with a boot. It still wouldn't start. Harold checked that the fuel line was clear and the plugs were clean. He pulled on the starting cord until he broke into a sweat. The Newfoundlander paused to catch his breath then embraced the Evinrude and whispered endearments into its carburettor. It started first pull. 'Just like a woman,' Harold confided to Beagan. 'You got to treat her right.'

The Saskatchewan cut a broad arc across the northern prairies, twisting and turning through the rich alluvial soil. Its brown current babbled over sandy shoals, shifted gravel bars overnight and washed away muddy islands in a season. A red-tailed hawk peered from a lazy willow. Wood ducks nested in old woodpecker holes. For the first hundred miles there were no houses along the shore, apart from the odd cluster of tarpaper shacks used by passing moose hunters, and the inflatable ran easily alongside the secluded banks of aspen and blood-red sumach. Jamie will have to raise a spread of sail above the Peterborough to keep up, thought Beagan, anxious that his imagined companions not fall too far behind. But across the unmarked provincial border the silty river opened into the marshland of Cumberland Lake and the Avon's swift progress faultered.

'Hey b'y,' Harold shouted above the drone of the motor, 'Why is Canada like Christopher Columbus?' The blustery Newfoundlander had stopped singing shanties to concentrate on navigating between the weed beds. 'Because he didn't know where he was going, didn't know where he was when he got there, didn't know where he'd been when he got home, and all the time he was paid by the government.' Harold roared at his joke. 'That's us for sure, except you're not collecting unemployment.' The outboard screamed. 'Well sod me rigid,' he yelled. 'This Evinrude is as useless as tits on a nun.' Every few moments he had to tilt his outboard. 'The big trouble is that box of yours,' Harold complained as he cleared off the propeller. 'Makes us too low in the water and we snare all these frigging weeds. What's in the damn thing? Gold bars?'

'Papers,' said Beagan. He snapped open the trunk and after digging among the plastic sacks extracted his father's naval tin hat and a box of fold-back clips. 'Family papers.'

'Can you tip any of them out? We'd sure make some good speed then.'

'If they go, I go,' replied Beagan. He attached the clips around

the edge of the helmet to fashion a sort of bomb-proof colander.
'There,' he said handing it to Harold.

'You expecting trouble, b'y?' Harold scanned the sky for a stray
Messerschmidt.

'It's a prop guard,' explained Beagan. 'Tie it in front of the
propeller. It should deflect the grasses.'

Through the long afternoon the Avon twisted and turned
around the dense fields of reeds. In places they grew as tall as
walls and divided the waters into channels like unmarked streets.
The shadows began to lengthen and Harold's humour sank with
the sun. Beagan too was quiet, listening to the rustle of the grasses.
'Are we lost?' he asked.

'Hell no,' chirped Harold. 'There'll be a bus along any minute.'
His bravado sounded hollow.

A narrow passage opened up between the beds and the reeds
whispered in the breeze. 'I think we should turn left here.'

'You been down this way before, b'y?' cracked Harold as he
cruised past the entrance. 'The main channel goes straight on.'

'My great-grandfather was handy with a sextant,' said Beagan.
'And I have a hunch.'

'Maybe he went and left us a compass in the box too?' Harold
had left his charts on top of the refrigerator in The Pas, and they
had been forced to navigate from a voyageur canoe map which
Beagan had found in the bottom of the trunk. 'At least it'd be
newer than this old thing.' He steered on in silence for a moment,
then turned the outboard so suddenly that the propeller broke the
surface and lifted a rainbow of spray over the boat. 'Oh Lord
jeez,' cursed Harold as he doubled back and slipped into the
passage. 'What I wouldn't give now to drown myself in a beery
bucket of brew.' A minute later a line of low buildings rose up
beyond the flats. 'For sure that's Cumberland House,' he declared,
his spirits restored by the thought of a drink. 'It's been here since
Noah was an oakum picker.'

Cumberland House, the oldest permanent settlement in the
west, had been the Hudson's Bay Company's first inland trading
post. Established on Pine Island in 1774 it lay at the crossroads of

the fur-trade waterways; to the east ran the routes to York Factory
and Montreal, from the north down the Churchill came the fine
pelts of Athabasca and to the west out along the Saskatchewan
were the great plains which supplied the dried bison meat on
which the voyageurs depended for their subsistence. Tribes were
drawn in from the surrounding lands to live around the post which
at its peak stored and distributed furs and food for half a continent.
But with the collapse of the trade and the departure of the white
man the outside world forgot Cumberland House. Until 1945 the
Natives had no permanent government representative, other than
a nurse. It was 1967 before a road reached the village. The first
telephone wasn't installed until 1971.

Beagan and Harold came ashore on a boggy marsh and walked
inland past the old wharf. With the construction of the E. B.
Campbell Dam the lake level had dropped and boats had to be
moored away from the village in the myriad of shifting channels.
On the dusty main street the windowless brick blockhouse Northern store sold silk plants and shotgun shells, plastic picnic sets and
double leg-hold muskrat traps, fluorescent bingo markers and
Deep Woods insect repellent. Two boys tried to choose a birthday
card. Should it be the Indian Heritage series or Teenage Mutant
Ninja Turtle? At the counter the manager and a slight, dark man
in a baseball cap bartered a few steaks for a load of gravel. Outside
the shop the town's residents perched on benches in the sun. Most
were *Métis*, the offspring of Cree women and the original white
traders who had been joined in *mariage à la façon du pays*.

'My name's McKay,' said a tawny-skinned red-haired fisherman, introducing himself to Beagan. 'My cousin over there he's
a Macaulay, and that's Hilyard McKenzie who operates the cable
ferry over the river. There are a lot of McKenzies in Cumberland.'
The explorer Alexander Mackenzie had passed through the post
in 1793 on his way to the Pacific. 'We don't know exactly what
he got up to here, but we can guess,' added McKay. A chuckle
rolled down the benches like a wave along a beach.

One would have expected the years of isolation to have made
Cumberland House a desolate place adrift in the weed beds but

it wasn't the case. The children emerged from Charlebois School filling the street with bustle and games. Jessie McKenzie led Harold through the throng to buy fuel at the Hems and McKenzie Gas Bar. Beagan was passed on to Virginia McKay, the town's amateur historian. She and the recreation director, Cyril Goulet, talked in Cree and laughed softly as they led him down a path in the bush to a clearing among the birches.

'The experts in Regina wouldn't believe me,' she said, recalling her discovery of the site of the original fort. 'They said I had only found a church and that it was not important. So I filled a pail full of old glass and china to send to them, you know, but my husband left it in the office and the janitor threw it out thinking it was junk.' Nevertheless Virginia had hounded the archaeologists until they agreed to examine the compound. Beneath the mounds of mossy stones they had found the old stockade, crumbled fireplaces, moose bones and Hudson's Bay Company buttons. 'Not only didn't they thank us but they took all the artefacts away with them for dating. They only left our museum a barrel of bullets and a snowshoe needle. Maybe I should have just kept quiet about the fort.' On the walk back to Cyril's pick-up Beagan asked Virginia what the Native people had called the land before the arrival of the white man. 'Ours,' she replied.

In town they stopped to collect Harold and their supplies. The Newfoundlander looked crestfallen. 'There's no beer in town, b'y,' he whispered to Beagan during the drive out to the boat. 'Not even Molson's.'

'THE NEW ELDORADO, that's what they called it,' I said as we slipped through dawn's will-o'-the-wisp. 'Do you remember? "The Last Best West".'

'"This is your opportunity, why not embrace it?" is what the old immigration posters used to say,' added Jamie. He was tucked out of the wind beside Beagan, his hand on his shoulder, reading my book on the early homesteaders. The Peterborough tugged behind us on a fanciful towline. Hector stood on the bow and threw up his sextant for sights while Uncle Zach wrestled with the lunar tables. Harold Finn sat astern at the engine scratching a mosquito bite and humming 'Hurrah for Our Own Native Isle', a near-forgotten Newfoundland anti-confederation song.

The night had been dry not only because of the lack of alcohol. The volume of water released by the Campbell Dam varied considerably and travellers had been known to wake in the morning to find that their canoe had been carried away by a rising river. So Harold had pitched the tent well up the shore but the precaution hadn't given Beagan any extra sleep. My son had been awoken long before daybreak by the screech of fervent singing. Like his forefathers he preferred mornings when the Newfie had a hangover. They tended to be quieter.

'Do you remember the fear that America would seize the western provinces?' I asked Dad. The inflatable spun the rising river mist into a twisting, conical funnel. 'They called it their Manifest Destiny, the God-given right to occupy the whole continent.'

'Yes, that was in my day,' recalled Jamie. 'The prime minister John A. Macdonald said of the Prairies, "I would be quite willing to leave that whole country a wilderness for the next half-century, but I f-f-fear that if English men do not go there, Yankees will."'

'Sir John A. Yes; I met him in Ottawa,' said Zachary. 'An energetic man.' He laid down the tables then leaned against the inflatable's rubber freeboard, letting grains of sand slip through his fingers. With his other hand he tried to catch them before they fell into the water. 'He would have preferred to develop the east first, building up industry there, concentration being Emerson's secret of strength in politics and trade.'

Along the shore the vast undernourished forest resembled

the stubble on an old man's chin. As the sun rose above the treetops it burned through the haze and Harold stopped humming and began to sing.

> 'Ye brave Newfoundlanders who plough the salt sea
> With hearts like the eagle so bold and so free,
> The time is at hand when you'll all have to say
> If Con-fed-eration will carry the day.'

'It was the Americans who least relished a united Canada,' I said, raising my voice to be heard above the din, 'even less than the insular Newfoundlanders.'

'It would have been f-f-far simpler for the Yanks to annex the disunited parts one by one.'

'Sir John and his ministers, the Fathers of Confederation as they call them now, saw the need to people the uninhabited interior. They led the call for the "stalwart peasant in a sheepskin coat with a stout wife and a half-dozen chickens". Quite right too; the need was urgent, even if the drive west did dilute our resources.'

'Listen to this, Harold,' said Beagan, interrupting both his great-uncle's reminiscences and the Newfie's singing. 'The government gave every homesteader who came west a quarter section – that's 160 acres – for only ten dollars.'

'B'y, you can't buy a sixpack of cold ones for that these days. Hand me that rope there, will you? I think I'll go hang myself.'

'That's how the river came to be opened up, so the settlers could reach the virgin prairie.' Beagan stabbed at the book that he had found in the trunk. 'That's why they built the river-boats.'

'Jeez,' blustered Harold, 'there's a thought.'

'In the decade before the completion of the promised trans-continental railroad,' Beagan read aloud, 'a fleet of spark-belching, twin-stacked paddle-wheelers plied the Saskatchewan. This would fascinate my father.'

'And his f-f-father too.'

'They were lovely puffing leviathans,' I agreed with Jamie, indulging our shared enthusiasm. 'Swirling steam and wood smoke, ferrying settlers, forges and church organs upriver.'

'And bringing down wheat, timber and furs for trade,' added Zachary. 'They established the essential commercial infrastructure of the west.'

'They blew the whistle so loud that they made the very cattle rear up their heels and take to full gallop.' Beagan recited the observations of the Reverend Henry Budd, missionary at The Pas, which had been written in 1874 on the maiden voyage of the *Northcote*. 'Not only the cattle but people of all ages and sexes were no less excited by the sight of the boat, the first boat of the kind to be seen by them all their life; in fact, the first steamboat going in this river since the Creation.'

'Aye, true enough,' said Hector, not lowering his eye from the sextant. 'There were none before it.'

'The Native people called them *Ku* ... *Kuska Pah* ...,' struggled Beagan.

'*Kuska Pahtewoosi*,' corrected Harold. 'It means fire canoes, b'y. Lily taught me the word, eh?' He chuckled a raunchy rumble. 'Along with a few others that would make your hair curl. If you had more that is.'

'To what is this sea-dog sinner referring?' asked Hector, his worst suspicions aroused.

'To the tortuous route up from Grand Rapids to the Rocky Mountain foothills,' I suggested as Harold narrowly avoided a shifting bank, his mind distracted by tender thoughts of Lily. 'There were twenty separate sets of rapids, dozens of sandbars and innumerable horseshoe bends. Each boat was equipped with hawsers to winch it up stubborn currents and stout crutch-like spars to lever it through shallows.'

'I may say that they weren't particularly reliable,' affirmed Zachary. 'You couldn't set your watch by them.'

'Time?' barked Hector, taking his sight and consulting

the almanac. 'Come along, Zachary, it is difficult enough without having a rotator log towed astern.'

Zachary shook his pocket watch. 'Two minutes past six,' answered Jamie, peeking at Beagan's wristwatch.

'During spring run-off the *Northcote* could carry fifty passengers and 150 tons of cargo up to Fort Edmonton in two weeks. But at drier times,' I conceded, 'the schedule did tend to be irregular. On some journeys wing dams had to be built on the spot to raise the water level and passengers were ordered overboard to push the vessel around hairpin turns. To lighten the load cargo might be left behind. It wouldn't then be delivered until the following year.'

'What an extraordinary way to travel,' said Beagan as his celestial entourage rocked over the waves. 'It says here that the elegant *Marquette* was loved for her shallow draft. Her captain bragged that she could "navigate on a light dew". The steel-hulled *Lilly* was built on the Clyde and the plush *North West* boasted a strolling deck, two bridal suites and a $5,000 piano.'

'The fleet lasted only twelve years,' I lamented. 'The year after the railway was finished they laid them up and let them rot away.'

Zachary was intolerant of excessive sensibility. 'They served their purpose, Sandy. They – and the overland trails to the south – prevented America from seizing the land at that time. The boats were instruments of economic development, not something to put your heart into.'

'In any event the Americans didn't need to seize the country,' said Jamie. 'It was surrendered to them later, without a f-f-fight.'

'James,' snapped the elder brother, 'I am disappointed in your continued confusion of matters economic and emotional.' He dropped the handful of sand into the river. The splash distracted Harold. 'The nations' convergence is simply a matter of shared values and objectives, a process of maturing realism.'

Before I could form my reply the inflatable lurched up

on its side, sailed into the air then slapped back down on the water.

'In the name of Providence, what was that?'

'Shall I take over for a bit?' offered Beagan, picking himself up from the deck. As Harold's attention had wandered the Avon had grazed a sandbar.

'That's some kind of you, b'y, but you don't know the river, eh?' replied the Newfoundlander. The outboard had stalled during his aerobatic manoeuvre. He reprimed and balanced the fuel tanks then pulled the starter cord. The engine coughed back into life. 'These waters can be trickier than a single woman turning thirty. You stick to your books, I'll handle the boat.'

'Thanks to the blessings of the Good One above us we are on course,' Hector acknowledged with a stern eye on Harold. The rising sun had given him his reading. He could have conjured up the position in his imagination but he preferred to do things the old way. 'Only this Arcadian is not to be thinking that he's brought the ship into harbour yet.'

'There's a town round the next bend. We'll take a break there and get in some beer and grub,' proposed Harold. As the boat regained its speed, he resumed his singing.

'Cheap tea and molasses they say they will give,
All taxes take off that the old man may live;
Cheap nails and cheap lumber our coffins to make,
And homespun to mend our old clothes when they break.'

West of the Campbell Dam the river looped south and the scenery changed. The unshaven Land of Little Sticks fell away and opened on to a bright, clean prairie of primary hues. Yellow wheat fields soared towards blue horizons which red railside grain elevators anchored to the earth. As the inflatable raced across the Tobin Lake reservoir Beagan imagined Polish and Ruthenian immigrants standing on the *Marquette*'s hurricane deck looking out over the golden virgin land, dreaming of a home in the promised west. Men-nonites had settled on the river's south bank between French farmers and a German Catholic colony. Every Sunday the district's dusty roads filled with spade-bearded men driving horse-drawn buggies to church. On the north shore the Doukhobors cultivated broad acres of barley and flax. The pacifist sect had fled Tsarist Russia in the company of Tolstoy's son in their search for religious tolerance. They had arrived with neither money nor oxen and in their early communal villages the women had been yoked to ploughs while the men worked away from home on the railroad. As their farms prospered they abandoned the communes but never strayed far from the community. Behind a single windbreak of trees Beagan saw a grandfather's collapsed sod dugout, a father's first cabin of mud and wattle and the son's proud clapboard frame-house.

'Down home,' announced Harold, 'no one pays much attention to the wind until they see whitecaps in their bathwater.' A cool breeze had blown up, plucking autumn orange leaves from the trees and scattering them on the choppy waves. Beagan had retrieved his father's tin hat from under the outboard and jammed it over a thick woolly scarf which he wrapped around his head. Harold had tired of steering around the sandbars and rather than slow down he now tended to accelerate through the shallows and plough over any obstacle. It made for a faster passage but more than once they had had to step into the cold stream after the inflatable had run aground. 'Never seen anything like it,' Harold exclaimed after avoiding one deep trench by grabbing on to Beagan's scarf. 'If Moses had been here he'd have gone in right up to his tits.'

All too soon Harold decided that his seamanship enabled him to ignore rocky shoals too. He was singing above the whine of the Evinrude, a robust song about the squid-jiggin' ground, when the boat hit the outcrop. The force of the impact punctured the starboard flotation bladder and the jet of escaping air spun the Avon around like a hysterical merry-go-round. The trunk sailed out over the deflating side and Beagan splashed into the water after it.

'Save the Labatt's first,' instructed Harold as the cardboard case fell open and the brown beer-bottles bobbed away in the current.

But Beagan was more concerned with rescuing his papers. He swam hard and managed to catch the trunk at the head of a small set of rapids. It hit a log, turned over on itself and struck him on the head. Both Beagan and the box trunk were sucked under by the cross-current.

'How you getting on there, b'y?' yelled Harold from the shrinking vessel. 'Quit horsing around, eh?

The trunk broke surface below the rapids with Beagan astride it like Arion on his dolphin. He sailed across the whirlpool using the helmet as a rudder and guided himself towards the shore.

Harold ran down the bank and helped pull the unlikely ark ashore. 'Jeez, you all right? You had me worried there.' Beagan managed a damp smile then displayed half a dozen rescued bottles of beer. 'Oh Lord, couldn't you do no better than that? There were a full twenty-four in that case.'

A hundred yards upriver there sprouted from behind a copse of autumn trees the onion domes and slanting crosses of a Ukrainian Greek Orthodox church. 'Did I ever tell you about the time I was called out to fix the plumbing at a church?' Harold asked Beagan as they dragged the deflated inflatable towards the town. The story had already been told . . . three times. ' "Hello Father," I says to the priest, "Is it the holy water again?" ' Harold cackled at his wit then sneezed. 'You know there are three faucets in a church: hot, cold and holy.'

A broad-beamed petrol attendant in an embroidered blouse laughed as she sold Harold a puncture repair kit. While he mended the hole Beagan checked the box trunk's contents. The plastic bags had kept the papers dry and none of the glass negatives seemed to have been broken. Even Hector's globe had survived the dunking intact.

Beagan changed his clothes in a lace-curtained rest room and accepted the woman's generous invitation to lunch. Over the century three great waves of Ukrainians had descended on the province and their colony had grown to be twice the size of the Native Indian population. Her *borshch* was rich and hot and he asked her what had brought her family to the Prairies. 'Why did we choose Canada?' she answered, fluttering her blonde bovine eyelashes like the Blue Ribbon winner at the Royal Winter Fair. 'Because it is a safe, pure country. Because we could work hard, save money, buy an encyclopedia for boys and a piano for girls.' Her solid frame was filled with pride and *pyrohy*. 'All my children are now university graduates.'

The town's general store where they replenished their supplies was owned by a Slovak. 'When in 1968 Soviet tanks invade our country I escape to Austria,' he explained while slicing thick wedges of fatty sausage. 'From refugee camp I apply to come to Canada and they fly me and others twelve hours through the night. The airplane, it land in a blizzard. The doors opened and big men in fur coats step on board. The men, they speak Russian not English and we all know immediately that we are tricked, that we have never leave Czechoslovakia, that the KGB have fly us to Siberia. The women cry, the men not leave aircraft, we all frightened until a Mountie in a red coat come and tell us, "This is Edmonton. Russians emigrated here after the war. Look at me, my name is Shavrov. You are in Canada."'

The Saskatchewan swung north-west to run through an undulating grassland. The earth was the colour of burnt umber and dotted with beehives. Cattle grazed on the crests of wooded knolls and picked their way down the steep slopes to drink. They dislodged divots of turf which rolled off the path and slapped into the water. The dappled reflection of a woman on horseback played on the mackerel riffles. She led a damp setter and stray calf along a line of mustard-coloured oaks. On the roads beyond her, Kubota tractors towed threshing machines past signs for Livelong, Goodsoil, Paradise Hill and Jensen's Alfalfa Seed Cleaning Service.

Oil rigs began to appear over the Alberta border. Their seesaw pivots pumped the ebony crude that had transformed the province from dirt–farm poverty to petro–dollar fortune. There were seven thousand wells operating within a hundred–mile radius of Edmonton. The new wealth grew not only from oil and gas deposits but from the vast reserves of coal, silver, gold and uranium. On lawns the size of football pitches antique traction engines were displayed beside sleek modern combine harvesters. Even the wrecked cars dumped on the riverbank appeared to be newer than those rusting away in Manitoba and Saskatchewan.

The greasy waterway snaked beneath highway flyovers and powerlines, between refineries and factories into the oil capital of Canada. Under the graffiti–trimmed arches cliff swallows built their muddy nests. Beagan had hoped to arrive in time to watch the Kiwanis Club Duck Challenge when rubber ducks were raced between the city's bridges but the shore was deserted. There were no boats on the river or wall-eye fishermen at Whitemud Park. 'They'll all be at the mall, eh?' explained Harold, skirting a gravel bar and running the inflatable on to the Laurier Park launch site. 'So what do you say you and me do a little shopping too?'

Beagan had no desire to visit a store. He was anxious to get on to the Pacific. 'I'm due to meet my brother in Vancouver in less than a week.'

'Hey, it's no ordinary shopping centre,' Harold stressed, itching for some conspicuous consumption. 'The West Edmonton Mall is the biggest damn retail complex in all Creation.' Beagan stared upriver and couldn't make up his mind. 'Come on, b'y, fish or cut bait. Listen, we'll do some shopping, play a little roulette, knock back a two-four of Labatt's and be back on the river in twenty-four hours. Then we'll swim like a dog up to Rocky Mountain House in no time flat. And hey, if you're crossing Canada by boat for sure you got to go some of the way by submarine.'

'Submarine?'

The mall looked like a monstrous moon-base colony dropped on to suburbia. It straddled the equivalent of forty-eight city blocks. Beneath its glass domes and illuminated cupolas were crammed eight hundred stores, 110 restaurants, a children's zoo and an amusement park with a thirteen-storey high 'Drop of Doom' rollercoaster ride. At the Ice Palace the Edmonton Oilers held their hockey practices while four Atlantic bottle-nose dolphins performed throughout the day in a 300,000-gallon tropical lagoon. In the five-acre indoor Waterpark shoppers donned bikinis or trunks to bask on the Caribbean blue beach, to body surf on five-foot waves and to learn how to scuba dive. Throughout summer and winter the Waterpark temperature was maintained at a constant 86° fahrenheit.

The taxi dropped Harold and Beagan outside the Fantasyland Hotel. There was a seven-foot-high carved ivory pagoda in the gilded foyer. Harold wanted to rent a theme room but couldn't decide between Roman and Hollywood. 'The Victorian Coach Suite is real popular, sir,' advised the blonde receptionist. She wore thick blue eyeliner and had perfectly aligned teeth. Harold went upstairs to have a look. The bed was an ornamented carriage driven by a plaster coachman and drawn by two fibreglass steeds.

'I don't like the idea of sleeping behind some horse's arse,' he told the woman. 'You got an Arabian room left? We've got kind of used to sleeping in tents.'

'I'm sorry; the Arabian, the Truck and the Canadian Rail suites are all occupied. But I do have one Polynesian still available.'

The bellhop lay the trunk under a plastic palm tree at the foot of the catamaran-shaped bed. Beagan asked for his roll-away to be made up on the other side of the waterfall whirlpool bath. In Edmonton it was said that one could stand on a sardine can and see the Rockies. Further west still, they said, one didn't need the can. Looking out the window Beagan believed that he could discern snowy peaks. Harold was studying a mall map. 'So what's it to be first?' he said, clapping his hands. 'A round of golf at Pebble Beach, a brew on Bourbon Street or a ride in a sub?'

Harold led the way past Lady Evelyne Lingerie, Cookies by George and the full-scale replica of Columbus's *Santa Maria*, its aquarium hull containing two hundred species of tropical fish. Outside Dawn's House of Fashion he shouted over his shoulder, 'They got four submarines here; that's more than the whole

Canadian Navy.' A broad, rocky lido stretched along the length of the atrium. Suspension bridges reached between the shores and stores. Harold bustled around the coconut trees and down a walkway to the Deep Sea Adventure departure deck. As he and Beagan followed twenty-two other shopping-mall submariners past the yellow conning tower and down the metallic hatch the Newfoundlander yelled, 'Never had any of these back in Fortune Harbour.' The captain secured the hatch, the ballast tanks blew and the submarine dived beneath Ikea and the Body Shop. 'Holy jeez, b'y, it's a shark.' Through portholes and on television monitors the passengers followed their voyage past stingrays, barracudas and around a dwarf replica of the Great Barrier Reef to discover a sunken shipwreck. Lights flashed, whistles blew, the sonar pinged and when it was all over Harold wanted to go again. 'I sure wish Lily was here to see this. She'd be as chuffed as a clam in chowder.'

In between mugs of beer Harold tried to take in all the mall's attractions. He rode the bumper cars, admired the replica Crown Jewels, ate a chilli dog in the mouth of a bronze whale and tried his luck at Caesar's Bingo. 'I'm busier than a one-armed coathanger with crabs,' he told Beagan over a plate of Café Orleans oysters. 'You got a lady friend, b'y?' he asked with the arrival of the third frosty jug of Labatt's.

'No; something – or someone – always gets in the way.'

'Well my Lily, she's a big girl,' continued the Newfoundlander. His expansive gesture brought to mind the Abominable Snowman's sister. 'She turns over in the night and the whole damn bed shakes. You wake up from a dream holding on to the headboard thinking that your dinghy's going down in a storm.' Harold laughed at the memory and sloshed beer all over the table. 'Loving her is sort of like docking an ocean liner – the various bits have to be eased into position, eh?'

In the late afternoon Harold decided to buy Lily a pair of dancing shoes but as he didn't know her size the matter became rather complicated. At Sole Comfort a compliant clerk let him hold her foot and they agreed that Lily was about size six. 'Better make it a seven so she can grow into it,' he hollered into the storeroom, then added to Beagan, 'She can always wear a second pair of socks.' Later in the Carlos O'Grady saloon he told Beagan, 'You know, when Lily and me are really close, like all excited, eh?, I like to lick her neck. Yes sir, the saltiness makes me think of the sea.'

They couldn't decide which film to see in the mall's nineteen cinemas so settled instead for a few frames of billiards at the Master's Club. After steak and kidney pie with French fries and a couple of more pints at the Elephant and Castle Olde English Pub Harold and Beagan stumbled back to the hotel. In the Jacuzzi Beagan's headache and nightmare visions of shoe stores receded until Harold found a dubbed version of *Grease* playing on the Univision Spanish cable channel. Although he didn't understand the dialogue the songs unfortunately remained in English, and Harold sang along at the top of his voice until the night manager hammered on the door and Beagan passed out beneath the Kon-Tiki bed.

'B'y, your face would stop an eight-day clock.' It was not long after dawn. Harold was packed and ready to go. 'Better let go a shotgun in here to wake you up. Come on, the day's awasting.' Another taxi ran them back to the inflatable. The morning was cold. As soon as they were underway Beagan was sick over the side. He was surprised by Harold's strong constitution and asked if he felt all right. 'If I was any better I'd be too good,' replied the Newfoundlander, taking in a deep breath of the crisp autumnal air. 'In a day or two I'll be dropping you off and heading home to Lily. I was stunned as me arse leaving her alone in The Pas. And, no offence, but you snore. Kept me awake half the damn night.'

Above Edmonton the water grew clearer and the current strengthened. Harold ran his boat up the inside of bends, avoiding rollers and haystack waves, skirting sandy islands and the low gravel shore. Around a corner the soft pumice-grey horizon of clouds found sharp contours and the mountains defined themselves. They rose at the end of the prairie, beyond the last chocolate-box grain elevator, silhouetted by the morning's apricot sky. A calm backwater mirrored the peaks until a single ripple broke them into spots and tones like a pointillist painting.

'You know, Lily makes the best bannock bread this side of the Rockies,' reminisced Harold above the whine of the motor. 'Serves it up hot with bakeapple jam, just like I had when I was a kid.' He licked his lips. 'I could do with a slice now for sure.'

Above Buck Creek the glacier-fed river flowed two-tone. The crystal-clear waters of the Brazeau ran alongside the Saskatchewan's familiar silty brown. Dense stands of aspen with bark like tarnished silver huddled along the banks. Their saffron canopy was pierced by the blue tips of spruce and the occasional bald sandstone cliff. The last fairy-skirted harebells flirted around unbowed bull thistles. Iron-red buffalo rye and foxtail barley swayed in the clearings. The inflatable cut across the current, avoided a white eddy and at the Clearwater confluence found Rocky Mountain House.

The town had once been the last fur-trading post before the Rockies. At the start of the nineteenth century the Scots cartographer David Thompson had made the post his base while searching for the western sea. Later, mining and logging camps had thrived in the surrounding Clearwater district. Finns and Swedes had cut trees in Nordegg. Welsh miners had been settled in a hamlet called Harlech. Every Friday night the lumberjacks, coal-miners and men from an unnamed railhead mill had ridden into Rocky for weekend relaxation. Often they failed to return to work before Tuesday or Wednesday, so to improve productivity the owners decided to bring Rocky's pleasures to the mill. A hotel was built, a bar was opened and certain compliant ladies were invited to take up residence. The settlement had grown into a town known as Horburg. But when the mills and mines closed the whores had departed and Rocky had become a forgotten gateway ringed by ghost towns at the edge of the mountains.

Harold ran his Avon ashore below the railway bridge. 'All

change for the Pacific. This is the end of the line, b'y.' Upriver the white water appeared to run colder and wilder. Beagan thought he could hear the roar of rapids. 'The Continental Divide's just a gunshot away.'

'How far is a gunshot?'

'Oh, about a city block.'

It was in fact about a hundred miles to the Height of Land, but between Rocky Mountain House and the Saskatchewan Glacier lay eighteen sets of rapids up which no boat had been tracked in over a hundred years. 'Them canoeists may shoot downstream singing a merry ditty but a man'd be crazy to try going up them,' Harold explained as they carried the trunk in to town. Beagan took a room in 'Rocky's Finer Place To Be', the Walking Eagle Motor Inn. In the parking lot a wrinkled old man snored under his cap in the cab of a Dodge Ram pick-up truck. An elegant cast-iron bathtub was lashed on to its flat-bed back.

Harold dawdled in town only long enough to refuel. Beagan bought him three cases of beer and a waterproof compass. At the landing Harold pumped his hand. 'Got to get back to my Lily before freeze-up.' His eyes glistened at the thought of docking his ocean liner. Beagan asked if he had decided not to return to Newfoundland. 'No man should spend the winter alone. It gets too damn cold.' He laughed as they slipped the Avon into the river. 'But come spring, for sure I don't know. You just might find me looking for that channel out of the Cedar again.'

'I hope you won't need that passport.'

'Too right by a half, b'y.' The Evinrude started on the first pull and with a wave Harold was gone.

Beagan saw no Peterborough lapstrake or cedar skiff along the shore so dragged his feet back to the motel. He felt in need of a long hot bath and an even longer sleep. Tomorrow he could decide how to reach the Divide. Over a Denver sandwich in the Eagle's Nest Lounge he fell into conversation with a young woman. Her thick hair brought to mind a beaver pelt, a rich warm fur pulled across her forehead and over her ears. The bathtub and pick-up, she explained in a soothing voice, were hers. 'I'm a marine biologist,' said Elsie Faithful with quiet confidence. A puppy dozed at her feet. 'I work over on Vancouver Island netting and tagging sturgeon.' Her crescent-moon eyes were coloured tawny lion yellow.

'I don't know much about sturgeon.'

'Do you know that they have been all but exterminated within the lifetime of a single fish?'

'But how long do they live?' asked Beagan, grateful that he hadn't ordered fishcakes.

'On average 135 years. It takes them eighteen years to reach sexual maturity. That's longer than you and me.' He offered to buy her a drink. She shook her head. 'I'm pregnant.' He hadn't noticed. 'And anyway, sturgeon are the only creature that I'd leave my boyfriend for. That's him in the cab.' Beagan thought of the fossil asleep in the Dodge. 'The love and burden of my life. The bath is my luxury.'

BEAGAN LAY BACK in his tub and tried to relax. Even nominal Canadians felt morally reprehensible if more than three days passed between baths. After so long afloat he retained the sensation of movement. The whine of the outboard still buzzed in his ears. The vessel seemed to rock and sway and he half-expected to see whitecaps blow across the bathwater. We settled ourselves down around him in the dim, pine-clad room. Dad dozed under a mildewed map of mountain trails and passes. Hector lacked the strength to read, the mayhem of the mall and the raw consumerism having sapped his celestial concentration. 'I never wish to ride a roller-coaster again,' he groaned. Even Zachary was quiet after the long, weary trip.

The last hundred miles up over the Rockies had always been the most difficult section of the waterway. The mountains had defeated the early French explorers. Alexander

Mackenzie had tried to skirt them by paddling north along the Peace and Parsnip rivers yet even then he still had to line his canoes down the Blackwater and trek over the Rainbow Range to Bella Coola on the other side. But David Thompson, the Nor'Westers' map-maker, had been told by the Natives of a great southern river which led to the Lake of Salt. In 1801 he had followed their trails to the headwaters of the Saskatchewan, only to choose the wrong fork. For over a month he had battled up the Ram, dragging the canoes through black shale canyons, wading in fast glacial water so cold that it 'was known to give the goitres'. When he had given up and turned downstream the savage current had hurled him back to Rocky in six hours. It would take six more years for Thompson to find the Howse Pass through the mountains and follow the Blaeberry River down to the Columbia and the sea. The Blackfoot named him *Koo-Koo-Sint*, 'the man who looked at the stars', after the sextant with which he had charted 1½ million acres of wilderness. His surveys remained the basis for all cartography of the north-west until the 1940s.

'To the Westward Hills and Rocks rose to our view covered with snow, here rising, there subsiding, but their Tops nearly of an equal height everywhere,' Thompson had written on first sighting the Rockies. 'Never before did I behold so just, so perfect a resemblance to the waves of the Ocean in the wintry storm. When looking upon them and attentively considering their wild order and appearance, the imagination is apt to say, these must once have been Liquid, and in that state when swelled to its greatest agitation, suddenly congealed and made Solid by Power Omnipotent.'

Beagan had fallen asleep in the bath and in his dreams the rocking tub began to skim up the Saskatchewan. It swept over the flurries of Fisher's Rapid and skirted the Old Stoney boulder. At Devil's Elbow, an inverted U–bend downstream of Horburg, it surfed around the inside curve and sloshed some suds over the side. Beagan grabbed the rim as the bath picked up speed. It ran past the mouth of Thompson's Ram and up the narrow braided channel above Deep Creek. His face-cloth blew away into the frothing wake. He dropped the soap. Above Dutch Creek the Saskatchewan swirled in a whirlpool and the Bighorn Dam towered above him. Beagan ducked beneath the surface as the bath lifted clear of the sluice-way and sailed up on to Abraham Lake. In his dream passing cars stopped and drivers stared as the tub aquaplaned beneath Mount Mitchener.

On the Kootenay Plain the spruce were iced with snow. Criss-crossed branches gave the tamaracks a crazed look. Eroded sand-stone arches and drumlins fretted the shore. Beyond the fold of a charcoal cliff a moose stepped out of Beagan's way while a fearless grey jay chattered and chased off the water-borne intruder. The balneary projectile skimmed over eddies and chutes, skipped alongside the broad stone pebble banks and shot like a cast-iron bullet under the highway bridge at Saskatchewan Crossing.

As the bath climbed up into the mountains the temperature dropped. The river ran dove-grey and peacock, the colour of icebergs, and Beagan began to shiver. He looked for a towel but found none. The force of the wind prevented him from sitting up so he tried instead to turn on the hot tap with his toes. He succeeded only in releasing a cloud of steam. A lofty stream cas-caded tears down the Weeping Wall. Streaks of morraine ran stone fingers across snow-shrouded slopes. Above Rampart Creek the river split into a maze of channels. The course became shallow and sinuous, in places all but running dry, and the tub's feet scraped along the riverbed, scattering stones dusted grey with glacial silt and knocking rotted logs up on to the gravel banks.

The turquoise tongue of the Saskatchewan Glacier slipped between mountains, licked their peaks and scarred the rock face with countless time lines. Immense icicles hung from the exposed ledges. The river whispered like voices heard in half-sleep. With a shudder the bath lifted above the frozen fount and flew up over the Columbia Icefield. The great glacier's melt ran to three oceans: back along the North Saskatchewan into Hudson's Bay and the Atlantic, down the Athabasca, the Slave and Mackenzie to the Arctic, and out the Columbia into the Pacific.

Soapy water spilt over the rim, splashed down on the icy surface that was wrinkled like an albino elephant's hide, rained on to the rental cars and tour buses motoring in the furrows. A soaked Austrian tourist wearing the badge 'Hallo I am Klaus!' shook his fist at the airborne tub. A Japanese holiday-maker switched on her video. A frill of material tickled Beagan's nose. He looked up to see Reverend Hector, his cape flapping wildly in the breeze, carrying the bath. His sons Zachary and Jamie were on the other side balancing the load, flying their descendant over the Height of Land. Zachary was dressed in tails. Jamie wore a shabby suit with a gravy stain on its cuff. He whistled as the wind swept back his thin red hair. Beagan felt like laughing but it was too cold and he sneezed instead.

It was then that he felt a presence on his right. He turned and fixed his eyes on me. Below us the mountains fell away and the Pacific rivers plunged down to the western sea. My son lifted a frozen arm from the bathwater, reached out his hand to touch me and heard a sharp knock at the motel room door.

CHAPTER X

WAVES' END

BEAGAN OPENED THE door on to the white morning and Elsie. Her Labrador puppy barked at the snowflakes which settled on his nose. 'I thought you might like a ride, what with the storm coming,' she said. The pick-up was running with its heater on. Hotel guests were scraping ice off their car windshields.

'Yes,' Beagan smiled, pulling the towel around him. 'Yes, please.' He was blue with cold and shivering. 'But I've got a trunk.'

Elsie looked past him into the room. 'You must have been a tortoise in a previous life.' She nodded. 'That's okay. It can go in the back. I'll wait in the truck.' The fresh snow crunched underfoot as she walked to the cab. 'Are you all right?' she asked, looking back at his wild grin.

'I fell asleep in the bath.'

As he tried to work his icy fingers to dress himself Beagan could not stop chuckling. The night's encounter had left him elated, and with his trousers half on he stumbled against the trunk, rolled on to the floor and laughed until tears filled his eyes. He almost kissed the chambermaid when he checked out of the room.

A braided ring of sweet grass, its ends burnt as a palliative smudge, hung on the rear-view mirror. Beagan sat with the dog on his lap between Elsie and her still sleeping boyfriend. The old man hadn't washed and his breath was stale with alcohol. An empty rye bottle rolled back and forth under the seat. 'So where's your car?' asked Elsie.

'I don't have one,' said Beagan through chattering teeth. He had drunk two cups of scalding tea but they had not warmed him. 'I've been travelling to Vancouver by water. It's sort of a homecoming. I grew up on the Pacific.'

'You got relatives there?'

'Just my brother. The rest of the family are riding in the back,' he said, pointing over his shoulder. Elsie took a long look in her rear-view mirror. 'My past is in the trunk.'

The advancing blizzard obscured the valley behind and hurried the Dodge up the David Thompson Highway. 'I guess travelling across Canada you get to thinking that it's a young country,' she said, and Beagan leaned closer to hear her soft voice above the sound of the engine. 'The Maritimes have been settled for, what, nine generations. Ontario for six. Pioneers only reached the Prairies late last century and it's not much more than a single lifetime since the Pacific was the frontier.' Along the autumn amber riverbank the spruce were crowned with astrakhan crows' nests. 'On the radio the other day someone asked if Canada had any history,' she remembered. 'It made me so mad. It assumed that time only began when the white man arrived.'

Beagan's smile ebbed away like a wave back into the sea. 'Faithful doesn't sound much like a Native name,' he said.

'It's not. It used to be government policy to adopt First Nations children off the reserves into white families,' Elsie explained. 'Some tribes had eight out of ten of their kids taken away from them. There were no restrictions, even a single man could adopt a child. Me – and Noah –' she gestured to her boyfriend, 'we were given away when we were real small to a couple in a place called Peachland. We didn't even know that we were Native until after Ma Faithful died. Her sister told us the truth.'

'I'm sorry,' said Beagan, sensing himself culpable.

Elsie shrugged her shoulders. 'It must be kind of nice for you knowing your folks.'

'Yes, it's a strength, as long as they don't try to run your life.' The boyfriend began to snore until Elsie asked Beagan his surname. 'Gillean,' he replied. 'It's Scottish.'

She took another look in her mirror. 'Can you trace them far back?'

'About four generations.' In Elsie's curiosity he sensed a compassionate, if not kindred, spirit, and he told her about his journey
from the Hebrides and across Canada, about his search for the
displaced Reverend Hector, about the publishing brothers and the
betrayal of the dream of his ever-optimistic father. 'It's not even
two hundred years of history but, well, beginning to know them
teaches me something about myself and about this country.' They
drove on in a silence broken only by the sound of snoring. 'You
know in Gaelic one doesn't say to a stranger, "Where are you
from?" One asks, "To what place do you belong?"' He grabbed
an imaginary fistful of earth in his hand. 'I guess your ancestry
must give you a sense of belonging. Like, this is me. I am of this
place.'

'In theory, but when I tried to trace my family all I found was
that the adoption papers had been lost. There are over seven
hundred tribes in Canada, you know.' She cast him a sad smile.
'It's funny; I might be Squamish or Shuswap, Haida or
Nuu'chah'nulth. The North-West Coast tribes have the world's
longest tradition of handing down names and I don't know what
mine is.'

As they climbed up on to the continent's spine they left the
storm behind them on the plains. The mountains rose solid, silent,
from the mantle of close dark pine. 'The Blackfoot call them
Backbone-of-the-World,' said Elsie. At Saskatchewan Crossing
the pick-up turned away from the river up which the bathtub
had flown and headed south down the narrow canyon of Bow
Pass.

'It seems extraordinary that Thompson should have stumbled
on any pass through here,' said Beagan.

'The Kootenais showed him the way,' she replied, looking
straight ahead, her eyes on the road. 'The Kootenay Plain was a
trading place, the neutral ground where the Peigan, Blackfoot and
other northern plains tribes met every autumn. The rivers and
passes over the mountains had been known for a hundred generations before Europeans "discovered" them.'

Craggy cliffs crowded and jostled up against the frosty highway.

Beagan tried to imagine the centuries of unchanging migration across the cedar-green plateau. The Sarcee had arrived by canoe. The Blood had dragged their trade goods up the ancient trails by pony and travois. Dressed in buffalo skin, the Blackfoot had smoked pipes of sage over the packs of bark and rawhide and bartered maple sugar for smoked trout. But with the coming of the voyageurs the pelts and pemmican had instead been traded for blankets, knives and guns. Men had no longer hunted for what they needed but for all they could sell. Beyond the steamy window Beagan pictured a Peigan warrior flaunting a prized umbrella. His wife paraded her gleaming copper pot. The first tribes to trade for European weaponry had defeated their enemies and driven the survivors into others' territories. Smallpox had beaten victor and vanquished alike, decimating three-quarters of the Blackfoot nation in one winter alone. When Cabot and Columbus landed in the New World there had been maybe ten million Native Americans on the continent. Today only 360,000 remained, their nations decimated by the disease and famine, alcohol and guns imported by Europeans.

Noah groaned and Beagan asked Elsie if he was unwell. 'He got into a fight yesterday,' she replied. 'It happens every time some wiseguy calls him Chief. He hates that.'

'The Native people who I've seen these past months,' hazarded Beagan, 'have been in a terrible state.'

'And it surprises you?' She spoke with such venom that he had to turn away to watch Noah sleep. 'We gave away our lands, our valleys full of game and herds of buffalo, and what did we receive in return? Rum and trinkets and a grave.'

Elsie stopped abruptly for a lone big-horn sheep and a flock of tourists at Lake Louise. Tour buses paused for a shutter's snap beside glacial lagoons, beneath dogtooth mountains, between a 'Snocoach' icefield adventure and Devil's Gap boat cruise.

'I'm sorry,' Beagan repeated, feeling remorse as a white person for what had happened to the first Canadians.

'I heard somewhere that history is the study of lost alternatives. You know, the "What if . . . ?" school of thought.'

'Like, what if Columbus hadn't reached the West Indies?' he suggested.

Elsie nodded, sensing his discomfort. 'Sure. Or, what if American diseases had been more virulent than the European ones, and those first encounters had killed settlers, not Natives? Or, what if the early immigrants had recognised the culture that they were entering?'

'My great-grandfather's life was saved by a Micmac named Gogo.'

'What if he hadn't bothered?' she asked, understanding then that she too could help.

'I wouldn't be here,' he replied, and considered the dispossessed nurturing the displaced, one tragedy of Canada's terrible becoming. 'I wouldn't be.'

'Nor me, I suppose,' stuttered Jamie, the thought having never before occurred to him. He sat beside Hector on the cast-iron bath as the pick-up ran west out of Banff National Park, over the Great Divide and into British Columbia.

'There's a clipping somewhere here from the *Bismarck Tribune*,' I said, leafing through a file marked 'Intolerance (Examples of)'. A dusty copy of a treaty was snatched from my hand by the wind. 'Here it is. "This is God's country,"' I read aloud from the century-old newspaper. '"He peopled it with red men, and planted it with wild grasses, but as the wild grasses disappear, so the Indians disappear before the advances of the white men. Their prayers, their entreaties, cannot arrest the causes which are carrying them on to their ultimate destiny – extinction."'

'That does vex me, right enough,' admitted Hector.

'Few societies have ever grown at the pace of BC,' Zachary announced while enjoying the view. He sat at the head of the bath and hadn't been listening either to us or to Beagan and Elsie's conversation. His head was too full of facts. 'Why, in 1856 on the whole of the Pacific mainland there lived only 150 men.'

'White men,' I corrected. I sat on the trunk with my

back against the cab and the globe in my lap. My feet were balanced on the rim of the tub.

'Who else?' asked Zachary.

'The Native inhabitants,' replied Hector.

'I chose not to include them because no census did so, Father. It was a different matter once Christian values and Protestant thrift had been impressed upon them. Even if that attempt to make them responsible citizens didn't, I may say, pass muster.'

'It was another opportunity lost, Uncle Zach; a whole race locked away out of sight and out of mind on reservations.' For a generation or more the Native people hadn't existed for other Canadians.

'Forget about them,' said Zachary, his impatience directed at me. 'We are trying to concentrate on the year that gold was discovered on the Fraser.'

'What matters in life doesn't have much to do with money, Uncle Zach.'

'Oh no? If it wasn't for the gold your west coast might still be Indian territory, and then where would you be?'

'Building boats in Muskoka?'

'Don't be sassy with me, chap,' answered Zachary, then continued, 'One sunny Sunday afternoon in 1856 a ship out of San Francisco, the SS *Commodore*, put in to Vancouver Island and doubled the region's population. By the end of that same summer twenty thousand prospectors had sailed north from California. Gold fever drove them up the canyons and opened the interior of the province. It heralded the start of a period of remarkable growth.'

'One successful miner called William Smith changed his name to Amor De Cosmos and was elected premier,' added Jamie. He had been watching a mule deer with oversized ears, white rump and black-tip tail vanish behind a line of rowan trees.

'The Overlanders came across the plains from eastern Canada and down the Thompson, the province's second river, in cedar rafts and cottonwood dug-outs,' recounted Zachary, ignoring his brother. 'Golden City was built at the head of the third river, the Columbia, to serve them, the miners, loggers and traders. Gillean Publishing began distributing its periodicals as soon as the road and rail lines opened the country to business.'

'There were f-f-fine boats to get the news through,' recalled Jamie. 'Lovely, flat-bottomed river-steamers with blunt foredecks that tramped through the locks at Canal Flats. Why, the highest shipyard in the Americas was built just up the road here at Nakusp.'

'But the geology ensured that it was always a place apart, Dad,' I pointed out. 'The Rockies not only impeded easy access to and from the rest of the continent but also between its own communities.' The Dodge ran through a sedimentary pass where shells and fossils littered the roadside. The province had been shaped by its majestic and insular terrain. 'So there was a better medium than newspapers for holding the place together, for fostering a common spirit.'

'The province's isolation did breed an independent cast of mind,' admitted Zachary. 'But I'll have you know that my publications did very well here, very well indeed. In fact if you can stir yourself I'll show you. The figures are here in the trunk, assuming your Beagan hasn't mislaid them.' I swung myself into the bath as he began to leaf through the papers. 'They were filed alongside the company's annual reports. What the blazes is that racket?'

In the cab Elsie had turned on the radio. A brassy signature tune introduced the local evening news. The lead item was about fishing rights. The province's streams frothed with red Kokanee salmon battling upriver to spawn. She changed to a country station and then a religious programme. When the preacher called the faithful to prayer Hector knelt down in the tub.

'Bless our boatmen and our boat,' he recited for Native and newcomer alike, 'bless our anchors and our oars, each stay and halyard and traveller, our mainsail to a tall mast keep, oh King of the Elements, in its place so we may reach our haven in peace.'

On another band the commercials were all in Chinese. In years gone by Elsie might have spun the dial and found one of my stations but instead, today, she tuned to an impassioned report on Quebec.

'It's the referendum on Monday, isn't it?' said Beagan, listening to three French-Canadians debate the possible birth of one country and the break-up of another. The east coast felt a long way away.

'But why should we part?' demanded a lawyer from Lachine. 'This beautiful land was entrusted to us by our ancestors.'

'Because of those ancestors,' argued a university lecturer from Quebec City, his voice choked with feeling. 'Because this wintry cold federalism cannot be maintained. We have to have the guts to fend for ourselves.'

The third, undecided, speaker was dissatisfied with both camps. 'Do we really need to split to be separate?'

'Yes,' insisted the lecturer. His nationalism was an affair of the heart. 'This dysfunctional Canada belittles our identity, allies us with neighbours with whom we have no affinity. We can only truly pursue our destiny alone.'

'The referendum seems to have become a focus for all manner of discontent,' said Beagan, shaken by the debate.

'Many people feel out of control of their lives,' suggested Elsie.

'But I wonder how much this outpouring of emotion is due to real political grievances.'

She shook her head. 'Very little. Separatism is a persuasive placebo.'

'They used to say that BC stands for Beyond Canada,' I sighed, turning the old globe on its axis and running my finger from sea to sea. 'Maybe that's why I moved here, to a new world, for the chance to begin again.'

*   *   *

For me, hard work would make dreams a reality. I trusted in the triumph of good faith. A love of radio took hold of me at the Muskoka cottage. Dad was so often away from the island on business that I filled the empty summer days by stretching a telegraphy line from cottage to boathouse. I wired it up to an oscillating electromagnet, a queer anvil and the best fifty-cent outfit ever produced. On a cloudless July afternoon I touched the key and sent a message out from my bedroom, across the lawn, over the dogs and down to the shore. In an instant a signal came back to me. I didn't understand a word of it but it was a response, a lovely, loud, clear click. At first I thought that my lack of comprehension was the fault of the apparatus but soon realised that the problem lay in my correspondent. Nan had little enthusiasm for idling time away at the boathouse and in any event refused to study Morse. Dad bought her a Codegraph code-learning device but the only message she ever managed to send was 'Brush your hair it's time for church.'

I graduated to wireless with a crystal set. Copper wire was wrapped around an old salt container and the radio tuned with a 'cat whisker' probe on the galena crystal. I rigged one end of a long aerial to the top of a jack pine and trailed the other from *Primary*'s stern out over the lake. The line went taut and music crackled into the headphones from XWA of Montreal and KDKA in Pittsburgh. Brendan the mongrel setter howled like a high-pitched heterodyne. The Samoyed jumped overboard and swam ashore. In my excitement I stopped working the oars, let the antenna dip in the water and the line went dead.

The world touched my lake and I reached back out to it. I taught myself to speed transmit Morse messages with a Ford spark coil and an old boat windshield wrapped in tin foil as the capacitor. The spark gap was made from battery zinc rods. I established regular contact with amateur stations in nearby Bracebridge and Burke's Falls. I even tried to persuade my father to install a set in his Toronto office so we could send each other messages at the end of the day: Did you have chocolate pudding for lunch again? When are you coming home, Dad? Although he understood the principle of telegraphy, radio mystified him. He examined my spark transmitter and crystal receiver and shook his head in wonder. I tried to explain. 'If you have a dachshund long enough to reach from Bent River to Bala and pinch his tail in Bent River he'll bark in Bala. That's the telegraph,' I said. 'If you take away the dog that's wireless.'

Radio transformed the mundane and brought magic to my life. At school I slipped an antenna between the bars of the boarding house window, disguised it as a clothesline and slung it across the headmaster's garden. Through the squeaks and static a voice far-off in the distance said, 'Good evening from KPO San Francisco.' In those days the airwaves were all but empty and on a clear night stations from across the continent could be heard. One midnight in April the duty master found me under my bed listening to a London amateur reporting the *Titanic* disaster. He confiscated the Audion valve set and caned me with 'six of the best'. Two years later as a Leading Telegraphist in the Great War my day on HMS *Chatham* was determined by orders flashed from the Admiralty, across Europe to the Dardanelles. Aboard the SS *Victorian* sailing home from Southampton I danced to the music of an orchestra playing a thousand miles away. The ship was carrying the British delegation to the 1920 Imperial Press Conference and to mark the occasion the Marconi Company had fitted onboard their most powerful marine wireless. We marvelled at the wonder of singing 'God Save the King' together with a choir in Essex. Jamie used the ship's radio-telephone to call Zachary at the office and we laughed together through the ether. He told him that the onboard edition of the *North Atlantic Times* had more current Maritimes news than the Toronto papers. Zachary was not amused.

The novelty captured the public imagination and by the

end of the decade every home in North America seemed
to have a wireless. There were four-tube sets in woodwork
consoles, Radiolas, Parlophones and high-fidelity Atwater-
Kents. On hot Muskoka summer days when the screen doors
were on and the windows open I often walked through
Gravenhurst following a concert, not missing a single note,
the receivers in every house being tuned to the only station.
Many of the country's few transmitters had been set up by
hardware stores. For them radio was no more than a means
of promoting the sale of their receivers by playing the latest
dance bands. The manufacturers themselves, RCA and
Westinghouse, went on air too to expand the market for
their product. As listeners came to talk more of the Creole
Jazz Band and *Amos 'n' Andy* than they did about their
neighbours, the influence of radio became apparent. *Fibber
McGee* and *The Fireside Hour* may have provided a popular
diversion but they did little else.

Wireless had the potential both to bring people together
and to enlarge the world. Its magic could do good by stealth,
raising the consciousness of the listener, pushing back the
boundaries of ignorance and intolerance. I came to believe
that a broadcaster's responsibility was not simply to supply
his listeners with music and baseball, the limited role of
entertainment utility as espoused across the border, but to
provide a public service. While the Charleston and the
World Series might bind together Americans, Canada would
be united by the spoken word.

'Crannag,' announced Hector, laying down his letter tiles
one by one. 'C-r-a-n-n-a-g. You will remember that it means
pulpit in the Gaelic.' Zachary hadn't been able to find the
circulation figures in the trunk but Jamie, who had only
been trying to be helpful, had happened upon a box of
Scrabble. He had suggested playing a match even though

our games tended to descend into argument as Hector used Gaelic words, Zachary technical terms and my spelling wasn't up to much.

'You told me before that it translates as ship,' said Jamie, with his letter rack suspended before him.

'Aye and it does. Pulpit and ship, the same word.'

'That's one bit of Gaelic that Sandy understands,' cracked Zachary while tallying the score. 'Radio was his pulpit.' His temper, short at the best of times, had been taxed by drawing seven consonants from the letter bag. 'I imagine you thought you were fulfilling a popular demand?'

'There is no point in trying to satisfy the public,' I replied. 'Few of us know what we want and even fewer what we need. I never presumed to preach but I did make a habit of overestimating the listeners' mentality. How else can man's reach exceed his grasp?'

'I must admit, Sandy, I hadn't seen the pedagogue in you,' stammered Jamie.

'And from whom did I inherit it?'

'Don't look at me,' answered Hector.

'What's bred in the bone will come out,' added Jamie with half a proverb. 'Whose go is it anyway?'

'It's time enough for Sandy to have his turn.'

'Well, I came out here after the collapse of the *Mirror*,' I explained while juggling my letter tiles. 'Toronto had become too stale, too restrictive for me. Muskoka would have been a good place to set up my first station...'

'It is a fine part of the country, right enough. With the finest boats, too.'

'... but it was sparsely populated,' I told Hector. 'The west, on the other hand, was young and unformed and hadn't succumbed to the moneyed prejudice of the east. And I thought, well, to be honest, I thought that here I had a better chance of doing something worthwhile.'

A great hissing Continental had pulled the train of upholstered sleepers, silver-service dining cars and immigrant coaches with boards for beds and iron stoves for cooking. Over seven days and nights the locomotive had strained around Superior's north shore, darted arrow-straight across the prairies and snaked through the Rockies to carry me down to the sea. 'Direct and Quickest Route to all Points East, West and South,' the line's publicity had boasted. At Kicking Horse Pass Swiss engineers, hundreds of Chinese coolies and seventy-five carloads of dynamite had built a pair of spiral tunnels that twisted down through the mountains. The drivers of long freights could emerge from one end and look back up the Big Hill to see their caboose vanish into the other.

'Vancouver in the early thirties was little more than the place where the rails ended,' I recalled, 'an isolated, fleshpot port of timber mills and trader houses hankering for respectability. Well, the morning after my train arrived I found an office on Water Street. I bought a licence, settled on my call-sign, CUAN, strung a flat-top antenna between two poles on the roof and started broadcasting. It was that easy,' I laughed then laid out seven letters on the Scrabble board. 'Look, I'm on a double-letter square.'

'What might the word be, Sandy?' asked Dad.

'Spinaker. Our studio was in the loft,' I continued with a smile. 'We had a piano, two music stands and three microphones, one of which was a telephone mouthpiece. I'd built the breadboard transmitter myself on the kitchen table following the instructions of the Amateur Radio Relay League handbook.'

'Do you mean spinnaker?' asked Zachary. 'A racing sail?' I nodded, too excited to be distracted from my story. 'Spinnaker is spelt with two "n"s.'

'I don't have a second "n".'

'You'll recall, Zachary, that Sandy went in for the spoken and not the written word,' said Jamie with a smile.

'Our hundred-watt signal covered the whole Lower Mainland,' I remembered, 'reached ships in the Straits and on good nights was picked up right across Vancouver Island. It was all live, there were no devices to pre-record programmes back then, so every voice and sound had to be brought into the office. I invited in teachers, experts, anyone who held a strong belief for on-air discussions. The presenters, singers, actors and George the newsreader – who wore tweeds and a snap-brimmed trilby – all squeezed in with them in the single studio.' The memory of the early days delighted me. 'A river of words flowed out from our loft-room.'

Hector looked up from his letters and recalled the alphabet unravelling over the floor in Promise. Zachary remembered it too and shivered. 'Can we get on with the game, please Sandy?'

'I could do spinach but I don't have an "h" either,' I said, examining the letter rack. 'Tell you what, I'll put down the second "n" next time round.' I turned back to Hector and Jamie. 'So we broadcast farming news and school lessons in the morning, women's talks in the afternoon and Continental concerts in the evening. We played records too, of course, slipping educational programmes in between the popular series. But the area I concentrated on was the news. There's a tendency to favour local events, especially in a place separated from the rest of the world. You may remember the Scottish newspaper which reported the sinking of the *Titanic* with the headline "Aberdeen Man Lost at Sea"? Well, we tried to bring our listeners a broader outlook. Items were not just clipped from the Vancouver papers but gathered from various sources and presented in unbiased, balanced reports.'

'But it made no money,' said Zachary, nudging the floating board away from him. 'Wireless was not accepted as an advertising medium. Merchants preferred to put ads in newspapers which they could read when they came home from work. They didn't want to pay for announcements that went out while they were busy in their shops.'

'A minute spot earned at best five dollars and every thermionic valve which blew out cost me fifty to replace.'

'Cost *me* f-f-fifty dollars,' corrected Jamie, slipping the missing "n" into "spinnaker". He and Hector had grown tired of waiting and began spelling words out of turn.

'But radio grew nevertheless; CKFC formed their own orchestra, CRCV introduced domestic situation comedy and CNRV tied up with stations across the country to transmit to trans-continental trains. By 1939 Vancouver had more radio stations than any other Canadian city. CUAN – thanks to Dad – increased its power to twelve amps.' I chortled, thinking of the night when blue sparks crackled off the antenna and the building's metal railing gave passers-by an electric shock. 'The new signal was a little too strong. The frequency transformed all the cookers in a nearby apartment block into receivers. Their metal frames acted as aerials, the leaves of boiling cabbages rectified the signal and the saucepans amplified it.'

'I dare say that might have put some husbands off their wives' cooking.'

'When the war came, news became even more important. There were brothers, husbands, fathers and sons at sea, in the air, dug into trenches risking their lives. It was our responsibility to bring word of them home to their families. A million Canadians joined up, forty-two thousand never came back. During the Normandy landings one soldier from West Vancouver was reported missing, presumed dead but then, a few weeks later, his wife heard him on the radio. We often relayed reports from the BBC, recorded on lacquer disks at the front, and in one the correspondent had interviewed the injured at a field hospital. The wife, almost five thousand miles away from France, heard her husband's voice and knew that he was alive.'

'War transformed the country,' noted Zachary. He had lost interest in the game when Hector began adding abbreviated psalms in Latin. 'Canada entered it as a producer of raw materials and came out as a manufacturer. We built the world's third-largest navy.'

'In 1945 no country was more optimistic,' added Jamie, emptying the last letters around the board, 'or had better cause to be.'

'There was such confidence then and, it seemed, infinite abundance and promise. So we expanded into bigger premises. I loved watching the construction of the station's acoustic studios and control rooms. The newsroom was equipped with both Trans-Radio News and Canadian Press wire services. We bought record player turntables, RCA wire recorders and Model 'Y' acetate machines for field work. Cables were laid to relay stations in the Interior.' I turned the sphere on my lap. 'On the desk in my new office I had Grand-dad's globe . . .'

'On which your Vancouver is not marked,' Hector observed. 'Of it no man had dreamt when I was a boy.'

'. . . and I set beside it a framed saying: "According to the laws of aerodynamics a bumblebee cannot fly but a bumblebee . . ."' Jamie joined with me to finish the maxim: '". . . being unaware of this fact goes ahead and flies anyway."'

'It's in the trunk,' he said and we chuckled together.

'When we went on air the signal radiated from Salmon Arm to Scotch Creek, Telegraph Cove to Desolation Sound. Our low-powered rebroadcast transmitters reached out to the valleys, the far harbours, bringing the world into every living room.'

'And you stayed true to the Word?' asked Hector. He had used all his letters except for a single 'Q'.

'Yes,' I replied. 'Speech remained the core of our programming, although we did concede something towards the postwar enthusiasm for swing music. A *Jitterbug Hour* was introduced and listeners requested their favourite dance tune in exchange for a donation to charity. The songs were often dedicated to relatives or friends. I remember once the presenter misread an announcement. "And congratulations to Vernon Chipchase who is 111 years old today," he enthused, and started to play "Knees up, Mother Brown". After only a few bars the music faded and the presenter apologised. "I'm sorry but I've just reread the dedication and Mr Chipchase is not 111, he is ill." An embarrassed silence followed. "Get well soon, Vern."'

"I enjoyed the swing era dances,' recalled Jamie, roaring with laughter. 'The Lindy Hop, Pecking and the Suzy-Q; a bit too energetic for me at that age but great f-f-fun.'

'Suzy-Q?' asked Hector in sudden interest. 'Is that a proper word?'

'I don't see why that should bother you now,' complained Zachary. He still had five tiles in his letter rack and the flouting of the rules had annoyed him.

'That same energy built an underground railway in Toronto, the Saint Lawrence Seaway, new ref-f-fineries, aluminium smelters and nickel mines.'

'Few of which were financed by Canadians,' said Zachary. 'All that the war generation wanted were secure jobs, big cars and suburban bungalows with picture windows and basement recreation rooms. They stepped out of uniform and into bed, produced six million baby-boomers in fifteen years and deposited their savings in the bank. It was the Americans who had the foresight to invest in our economy.'

'You and I didn't f-f-fight in the war, Zachary. Those who did, well they felt that they had earned the right to a good life.'

'I am not belittling their sacrifice, not for one second,' snapped Zachary, 'or the value of the ensuing economic boom. But something, somewhere fostered a new complacency. Somehow I . . . I . . .' As he strained to find the words his confidence faltered. For a moment the only sound was the hum of tyres on asphalt. 'I only know that duties lost their value and everyone began to question and contest.'

'Would it be that after this war the demand for rights

became separated from the performance of duties?' asked Hector, rearranging a prayer for deliverance to spell 'Suzy Q'. 'It's myself that has seen people begin to care more and more for what they can take from society and less for what they give to it.'

'Not at the station,' I replied. 'At least, not at first.'

'It is a thousand pities but I fear that the Church may be to blame. It was our mission to maintain the vocabulary of morality.'

'No, F-F-Father,' said Jamie, inadvertently knocking over the Scrabble board and sending the letters spinning above the Dodge. Zachary's doubt had astonished him. 'We took on that responsibility. The press tried to inform and empower through words.'

'And I worked to foster that common spirit too,' I insisted. 'I shared the company stock with all senior staff. I tried to hear every voice at board meetings.'

'That is fine, right enough, but did it work, Sandy?' asked Hector, sadness in his voice.

'The commitment to high standards increased our costs but not our audience share,' I admitted. 'Commercial stations which played only music grew in popularity and, as advertisers turned to them to reach more listeners, our income suffered. My staff began to worry that our public service obligations put the company at risk. Less talk and more music, they said, would increase revenue and secure our future. I demonstrated my faith in the company by investing my inheritance in programming. Our fortunes improved for a time, we wooed listeners away from CKLC's *Dance Favourites* and *Hockey Night in Canada* with our *World Report*, but then . . .'

'Then, *a bhalaich*?'

'Then it was 1954, the year when the change came which none of us had foreseen.'

*   *   *

RADIO WAVES HAD washed over the waters and wound across the land. The spoken word had rippled over the high river terraces, surged across the pine plateaux and curled through arid valleys of mauve and pollen yellow. Elsie's pick-up truck rolled down from the mountains alongside the last miles of the Thompson River and in the whirr of the wheels Beagan heard voices.

'Did you know your father well?' asked Elsie, turning their collective sorrow to thoughts of individual loss.

'No, not really,' replied Beagan, clicking off the radio. Hereford cattle dozed beside juniper bushes. A rancher yawned under his stetson. 'I grew up too shy to ask questions and then, when I realised that I needed to, it was too late. He died when I was twelve.'

'One time an elder who I met told me I have the look of the Senijextee, something to do with my gait and cheekbones.' The puppy pawed its way across Beagan's lap and settled itself on Elsie. 'They were a modest tribe who used to fish round here from sturgeon-nosed canoes.' She picked up the dog and placed it on Noah. 'They're extinct now.'

Beagan winced before he answered, his slow deliberation not escaping Elsie's attention. 'I have my father's forehead. I've seen it in the photographs,' he said, nodding back at the trunk. 'But not his body. I remember that he was rather . . . roly-poly.'

'You mean fat?'

'He had an ample belly and long spindly legs,' Beagan admitted, 'but was too light on his feet to be considered heavy. He always seemed about to break into a jig, especially in boatyards.' Above the roadside a hand-painted billboard offered relaxed country living on the Golden Age River Estate. 'You see, his other great love was the water. He wanted to sail my family away across the Pacific.' A wistful smile crossed his lips. 'He threatened to have his ear pierced and wear a gold earring like a plump pirate.'

'Fat often means happy. Pa Faithful was thin as a rake and it made him mean. I only once remember him laughing. I'd wanted to learn how to ride and saved up for the lessons, without his help. But the first time I tried it I fell off. He rolled around on the ground laughing his guts out. It made me climb right back on the horse.'

Beagan felt the anger rise in her voice but detected no trace of bitterness. 'Heaven blessed my father with a happier spirit, lighter even than his step. It lifted him above day-to-day worries. He owned a couple of radio stations,' he volunteered, 'but he was a poor businessman.'

'They closed down, did they?'

'Not exactly, no. But he was too trusting and maybe too much of a dreamer. And too kind as well. I grew up in the Gulf Islands just off Vancouver. Once my father refused to burn a log because there was a woodworm in it. The stump sat by the fireplace all winter and he grew as fond of the beetle's tapping call as if it were a pet dog's bark. Of course the larvae got into the house timbers and infested the building. My mother wasn't amused when we had to call in the exterminators.'

Beyond the sweet resin smell of the Savona sawmill the hills crowded together and the drowsy river awoke in the twists and turns of the narrowed channel. It swelled over stones and elbowed at sandbanks. By Spences Bridge the river fumed across rapids, grabbed at an inflatable raftload of revellers and tossed it down the white water between wet black boulders. Pink rock scars rose up out of the torrent at Goldpan and tumbledown wooden cabins rotted away where Cariboo prospectors had lost their faith. The Thompson churned into the Fraser's deep-wooded gorge and the lines of rail, road and power jostled for footholds along the canyon's sheer cliffs. The khaki current boiled between crags and outcrops, frothed against mossy banks and gushed into a livid whirlpool.

'I've come home to see what killed him,' Beagan confessed suddenly as hundreds of bats descended from shaggy Great Pacific cedars to skim the waters and feed on moths. 'To see how he was betrayed.'

'This country broke a lot of promises.'

'I've always believed that Canada killed my father,' he said, and Elsie didn't add a word.

After Hope the mountains slumped back into the earth and the waters calmed. In the Upper Fraser Valley logs moved in booms and Native fishermen cast for salmon. Ochre autumn leaves blew across a placid delta and the gentle rain which washed their faces tasted of the sea.

Dragon banners fluttered from maple-leaf lamp-posts. A cruise liner's whistle echoed off glass office towers. Russian seamen dragged shopping bags stuffed with digital watches back to their freighters. At the continent's edge high-rise buildings stepped down from the wooded mountains to working wharves in a protected harbour. Vancouver, the largest Pacific port in all the Americas, was reminiscent less of other Canadian cities than of Hong Kong. Its street signs were written in Chinese. Its Star Ferry-like Seabus linked the downtown core with the Kowloon-side north shore. Its markets smelt of durian and its cafés click-clacked with the snap of *mah-jong* tiles. Yet beneath all the superficial similarities Hongcouver, as the locals called it, was unique.

A pristine white Rolls-Royce cruised past the Balmoral Hotel and turned into Keefer Street to spill a tittering Chinese family into the On On Tea Garden. Along East Hastings petite Thai prostitutes lounged on stretched silver Lincolns. Japanese tourists bowed to one another and snapped photographs of totem poles. At the Royal Vancouver Yacht Club the forest of masts rose from boats with Haida names. There were seaplanes and salmon seiners moored to the piers. The Oriental busker outside the Marine Building played 'Scotland the Brave' on the bagpipes.

Beagan recognised the sturdy mansions in Shaughnessy, the strip joints on Granville Street, the busy quays of Saskatchewan potash and prairie grain. He remembered summer Sundays with his father watching the ocean-bound container ships sail past the Stanley Park cricket pitch. Sometimes if a good batsman was at the wicket the ships were hit by sixes. Behind him he saw the Rockies enfold the city, before him its waters ran out into the oceans of the world. Tokyo, Sydney, Shanghai and San Francisco were just a boat ride away.

'A hundred or so years ago this was all coastal cedar forest,' said Elsie as the Dodge rolled along the Grandview Highway. Across from a 7−11 convenience store a homeowner trimmed his corner of paradise with a lawnmower. 'The Tsleilwaututh hunted white-tailed deer around where the airport is now.' A hoarding announced the development of dream apartments on False Creek's prime real estate. Above the sign Mohawk construction workers bolted together high-rise girders, as they had done on skyscrapers throughout North America, while at its foot a Musqueam brave slept, crumpled and drunk. 'His grandfather would have steamed mussels in their shells at the mouth of the Fraser.'

'Maybe yours and Noah's too.'

'Sure,' acknowledged Elsie.

'It's different now,' observed Beagan, her pain now his own, the country's own. 'For us both.'

'For us all.'

Vancouver's population had quadrupled in fifty years, Pacific Rim business-immigrants bought citizenship in exchange for government-approved investment and half the city's children now spoke a language other than English at home. Elementary schools offered Mandarin immersion courses aimed at making the anglophones bilingual. Local estate agents boasted resident geom-ancers, experts in the Chinese art of *feng shui* which predicates a building's design and orientation.

'But cross the Lions Gate Bridge and beyond Capilano,' Elsie gestured out over the yachts and bulk carriers in English Bay, 'a man can still walk all the way to the North Pole and not meet another human being.'

She dropped Beagan and the trunk by a hedged garden at the end of his brother's drive. She and Noah had a ferry to catch and she asked Beagan to visit them when he reached Vancouver Island. 'Come over for a meal, for a bath too if you fancy another ride,' she added without a smile. 'Mind you, the tub'll be plumbed in by then.' They shook hands and Noah slept on. Beagan watched the pick-up drive away until it disappeared out of sight.

He carried the trunk down to the beach-house of wooden shingles. Its weathered shutters glistened silver-grey in the autumn sunshine. The windows looked out over the sound and had no curtains. Alex had left him a note on the table. It read, 'The kayak is on the lawn and crabmeat's in the fridge. Meet me at North Shore at six.' Beagan's brother was at the studio. On the kitchen wall Bartlett's *Timber Slides on the Ottawa* hung beside a map of canoe routes through Nouvelle France. Etched steamers crossed Toronto harbour above a wooden model of a Scottish *bàta*. Captain Lecky's *Wrinkles of Practical Navigation* was shelved with *Cook's Voyages*. In crisp monochrome gentle Doris Pilch wore a flapper hat and stood by Sandy on the *Kipper*'s hurricane deck. The building was unfamiliar to Beagan but the family possessions welcomed him as an old friend's embrace. He made a sandwich then carried the kayak over the rocks to the shore. Shells crunched under his feet and he slipped on a mane of seaweed. The salt from a splash of cold water tightened on his skin. He launched the canoe away from the beach, out into the bay and felt the surface swell beneath him with the incoming tide.

The ghosts sensed it too. No bathtub was as comfortable as a boat and it felt good to be back on the sea. '*Sàl is bùrn*,' twinkled Hector. Salt water and fresh water. Chalk and cheese. He dipped his hand in the brine then, for the sake of a little devilment, splashed Beagan. His great-grandson hardly reacted to the soaking; he had grown used to the presence of his forefathers and trailed them behind him like a cloud of argumentative midges.

Sandy was laughing, lying on his back at the kayak's bow, recounting a radio story to Jamie. 'During the war we hired a new studio manager. It was hard to get good people then as the finest men had gone overseas. Well, one evening while we were on air this fellow telephoned his mother for a chat. "I'm sorry dear, I can't hear you," she said. In the background he heard the sound of our programme. "I'll just turn down the radio."

'"Don't worry, Mother," volunteered the manager. "I'll do it from here." So he lowered the studio's main output control and shut us down right across the province.'

Father and son chortled together but Zachary, who had been admiring the slick yachts in the bay, sighed and asked, 'So what happened?'

'Pardon, Uncle?' chuckled Sandy.

'What was the change that you failed to foresee?'

Sandy stopped laughing and sat up on his haunches. The kayak shivered with a passing wave. 'Television,' he said.

'Television?' scoffed Zachary.

'In 1954 CBUT-TV Vancouver came on air,' nodded Sandy. 'Almost overnight all the Lower Mainland's radio listeners became television viewers. Their Bakelite wire-lesses were stowed away and new General Electric receivers with veneer cabinets stood in place of honour by family sofas. Fathers settled into their easy chairs, mothers put down their knitting and children stopped chattering. Within two years the whole nation was sitting bug-eyed and passive in front of a million sets.'

'I f-f-found television to be very educational,' recalled Jamie. 'Every time someone turned it on I went into the next room to read a good book.'

'And missed the opportunity, chap,' exclaimed Zachary. 'It was the start of a revolution, the electronic age. I can tell you, Gillean Publishing was prepared for it.'

'It was quite a novelty. Audiences watched anything: Don Messer and his Islanders, Bob Hope, Jack Benny, even the test pattern. Hypnotic, it was.'

'Radio had to search for a new role and most stations found it in easing the monotony of household chores and soothing the drive to work,' lamented Sandy. 'It no longer aspired to stimulate thought but instead numbed the listener with non-stop music, local news flashes and the phone-in chat-show. The scenery might well be better on radio but it took less imagination to picture it on TV.'

'So much changed after the war.'

'I died,' reported Zachary.

'We all did, but there was something else,' mused Jamie. 'This, the finest of countries, prosperous and at peace, lost faith in its potential. The blessèd good people f-f-forsook their resources, their inventiveness, their bounty of land and water. And I don't know why.'

'People like moral absolutes. They like to be told what to do and to ignore it,' said Zachary. 'It is a matter of self-assertion.'

'It is a selfishness that I see,' observed Hector, pointing towards the shore, 'behind this mild-mannered exterior. A spoiled people are unlikely to work for the common good.'

'F-F-Fewer cared about service, that's true enough. Principles changed.'

'Not all of them,' Sandy reminded his father.

Zachary dismissed the argument with a wave of his hand. 'But you cannot blame television for all these ills.'

'Well, no, of course not.'

'I'm not suggesting that,' answered Sandy. 'Television didn't close my radio network. I lost it. I resisted the call to change from speech to music output and my managers pooled their shares to vote me off the board. They maintained that our stations had to provide what the audience wanted, not what I, in their words, "ordained".'

'It is your failing then,' snapped Zachary. There was no emotion in his voice. 'You admit it.'

Sandy's laugh had a lost, hollow sound. 'Times had changed. Radio, they said, was entertainment not education. Information to them meant news flashes on traffic jams and lottery winners. There wasn't the airtime to explain issues and to put complex events into perspective.' He lay back on his son's kayak and shut his eyes. 'I gave my partners the opportunity that I expected Canada to offer me. They repaid me by asking me to empty my desk and leave the building. They didn't even have the courtesy to forward my mail.'

'I may say again that a successful man does not try to stop the tide,' advised Zachary. 'He moves with it, redirects it.'

'Is that why Gillean Publishing came to stray from the discipline of the Word?' asked Sandy.

'Yes,' replied Zachary with a sidelong glance at his father, 'but only after my death. It diversified first into local radio and then into the emerging field of cable television. A very sound financial move, you'll no doubt agree.'

'The acquisitions reshaped the firm into a multi-media conglomerate,' confirmed Sandy. 'The huge profits of the new movie and sport channels proved to be irresistible.'

'The company also established lucrative financial information services for traders on nationwide telephone line links,' added Zachary with pride. 'Yet Gillean Communications' core business remained publishing.'

'Until last year,' said Jamie. Hector had laid down his Bible to listen.

'The firm was bought out, Father,' explained Zachary. 'For many billions of dollars. We started it with what, James, a few hundred?'

'But the paradox is that the aggressive corporate raider who stalked the company wanted it for its cable assets alone.'

'He didn't play by the rules, that's quite true,' admitted Zachary, who believed in the adherence to sound business ethics. 'Stock was amassed in secret and multiple voting shares used to seize control.'

'And the new owner has already dissected the company,' said Sandy. 'He has begun overbuilding the existing copper cable system into a broadband fibre-optic digital super-highway to provide national entertainment packaging and telephony services.'

'I heard English right on the start of my existence but in

the old days I understood it better,' confessed Hector. 'It would be fine if you would please tell me what all this means?'

'It means that Canadians from sea to sea will now be served by twenty-four-hour shopping channels and interactive advertising, that the nation will be united on quiz shows and in video games.'

'A f-f-funny thing that; as the new technology reduces distance, people want more space between themselves.'

'It means, Grand-dad, that after 150 years, this is what has become of our work.'

'The new owner has no interest in the press, F-F-Father,' added Jamie. 'The trade magazines and newspapers which accompanied the sale are of limited use to him.'

'And the fate of the Word?' asked Hector, his voice unusually quiet.

'Uncertain,' answered Sandy. 'As is that of our own. We become foreigners in our own land.'

'CUT!'

'Check the gate,' barked the assistant director.

The clapper–loader released the lens and examined the film track for dust. The actors and crew stood stock still, suspended like a celluloid image. 'Gate's clear.'

'Thank you people, that's a wrap.' The lights went out. The director embraced the lead actress and smudged stage blood on his bomber jacket. The boom operator coiled her mike cable and the make–up man checked his blusher. Everyone on the studio floor relaxed except the assistant director. 'Eight a.m. call tomorrow,' he ordered. 'Scenes 12 to 16 inclusive. That's low-loader and high–hats, grips. Wardrobe; see me before you go.'

'We got to end more upbeat. Give it more hope.' The US network co-producer strode out of the shadows. 'I told you that we can't go out on a downer.' A script–writer worried behind him, tugged at a thin lock of hair and dropped his notes. 'Can you handle it, or do we fax it to Willy?' The writer made a transparent gesture of confidence.

The sturdy figure beside them had Sandy's walk, Zachary's athletic frame and a trim version of Hector's beard. Beagan saw in his brother's face his own grey-green eyes and felt a stab of recognition, as if all the trunk's photographs had been fused into a single composite and come to life. Alex embraced him, a brawny bearhug with ursine grunt, and said, 'It's great to see you, bro. How was the trip?'

'A lot of water,' he replied with a smile.

The American co-producer introduced himself. 'Edgar Jumper Junior. How you doing?'

'Edgar's up from L. A. He's joining us for dinner,' explained Alex.

'Great,' lied Beagan.

'We'll take my car,' said Jumper.

In a black and red sushi restaurant Japanese diners were welcomed by '*Irashaimase*' and replete Westerners sung away with 'Thanyouvelimush.' Jumper ate tempura and talked deals. A weak Canadian dollar, tax concessions and the variety of locations had lured Hollywood producers north of the border. Canada, he said, was a damn good place to shoot pictures. The red postboxes were painted US blue, the street signs changed to Pennsylvania Avenue, and Vancouver made into America's second-biggest television production centre.

'Talent love working up here,' said Jumper, emphasising the point with a jab of his chopsticks. 'The crews are friendly and there's a real let's-do-a-good-show-together feeling.' Beagan asked about the necessity of disguising Vancouver as a faceless Anycity. 'Hey, if all the world's a stage then Canada is the theatre's auditorium, the safest place in a dramatic world. This is the country where anxiety's been reduced to an acceptable level. There's no drama here.'

Alex took exception to Jumper's comments, even though the American was giving him his 'big break'. He had worked for years building up a reputation as an independent producer. His small-budget pictures, all of which had been set in British Columbia, had achieved a minor success and been shortlisted for the Critics' Award at Cannes.

'Hey Alex, don't get me wrong. This is a great country if you like a quiet life. It's like Kansas with mountains. But, really, who cares what happens in Moose Jaw?' He poured out three glasses of Kirin beer. 'Come on, let's drink to free trade. We're all Americans at heart. We all share the same dream.'

'Which dream is that, Edgar?' asked Beagan.

'You have been away a long time,' said Jumper. He thought it was a dumb question. 'The pursuit of happiness, OK? What else drove those emigrants out of Europe and across America? The search for a better life. They chased it to the west coast and then, whammo, they couldn't go no further.'

'So California is the promised land?'

'Yeah, but only in the mind,' mumbled Jumper. He was gnawing on a prawn the size of a croissant. 'And that's where we come in. We're the inheritors of generations of hope. Movies are the manifestation of dreams.' Alex rolled his eyes heavenward. 'Hey, no, guys, I really believe it. Hollywood gives the audience that promised land for ninety minutes then takes it away and leaves them wanting more. It's no wonder movies are our top export. They're universal.'

'I saw their influence near Singapore,' volunteered Beagan. 'I was drifting around Asia and got a construction job with BP.' He poured from the fresh pot of green tea. 'There was a really beautiful tropical atoll on which a refinery was to be built. The island had a natural amphitheatre and on Saturday nights the company would put up a movie screen for the locals. At dusk sampans and junks came across the sea from the surrounding archipelago. The families laid out picnics under the palms and as the sun set the projector was switched on. It was free, so the films were all oldies – *Babes on Broadway, Stagecoach, The Wizard of Oz* – and the islanders loved them. Here they were living in paradise but by the end of every movie they didn't want to be there. They wanted to be in New York or Cheyenne or the Emerald City.'

'Hey, I never heard that,' responded Jumper. He gulped his miso soup and signalled at the waitress. 'It's a great scene. We could use it.'

Alex asked, 'What happened to the island?'

Beagan shook his head. 'It's a floating factory now. The refinery covered it. There are no trees, no valley, no cinema.'

'Yeah it's tough,' said Jumper, paying with his gold American Express card. 'But at least they can still rent them on video.'

It was late when the American dropped them off at his hotel. The faded script-writer, his skin colourless and hair thinner still, was asleep in a foyer armchair, the rewritten pink pages spilling off his lap and on to the marble floor. On the way home Alex stopped to buy a 6/49 lottery ticket. 'The world is full of bastards and most of them are in this Filofax,' he said, fishing in his organiser for a ten-dollar bill. 'At least if I win I won't have to do co-ventures with one of them.'

'So is this the biggest dream then?' asked Beagan, selecting his seven numbers. The slogan printed on the game card read 'Imagine the Freedom'. He shook the ticket. 'Is this what Canada has become?'

'Hey, not just Canada. And if you win you won't knock it.'

At the beach-house Beagan wanted to lay his trip out on the kitchen table, to introduce Alex to Piri, Harold and Elsie. He hoped that his brother would share the Reverend and his *Good Intent*, Jamie and the *Kipper*, Zachary and the *Canadian Vegetable*. He tried to tell him something about Quetico and his companions on the journey but Alex was too much of a pragmatist to believe in spirits. He had inherited Zachary's realism as well as his drive. So instead they opened the trunk and together looked through its contents. Beagan uncovered the papers for the inherited island. 'I thought all that land was long gone,' said Alex. 'I'd really love to see it with you but the network's got us under a lot of pressure. I can't get away this month.'

At the bottom of the trunk were buried a few of their father's dusty broadcast tapes. The brothers dug out a reel-to-reel machine and wired it into the stereo. They laughed at the old school lessons and dated women's talks then heard a play on the life and death of Mary Queen of Scots.

'Do you remember how he made the execution effects?' asked Beagan. Sandy had revelled in creating the on-air sounds, proving like Eden Prosper Goode that truth was not the facts. 'He cut a cabbage with an axe, let it fall into a wicker basket then squirted a hot-water bottle full of baked beans on to the straw — all in two seconds flat.' Alex laughed with Beagan but there was no spark in his eyes. 'Don't you remember? The crinkling cellophane that sounded like campfire? The half coconuts for horses' hooves and gossamer ladies' gloves for the wings of small birds?'

'No,' admitted Alex. 'I guess I was too young.'

Deeper still in the trunk there was a copy of *Tapestry*, CUAN's weekly programme for listeners who were not of British descent, and a Continental concert. They threaded the last tape on to the player and listened in silence. It was a recording of Sandy's obituary.

'We grow up thinking that our parents will be with us forever because they always were there,' said Alex, 'but then they're gone.'

'In a way our old man still is with us.'

'Sure, in a way,' acknowledged Alex. 'But it's difficult to ask his advice or chat about the weather.' Alex leafed through a sheaf of photographs of island cottages, lacquer disk recorders and old boats. He dwelt over a staff portrait taken six weeks before CBUT-TV came on air.

'Did I tell you that I want to go to the old station tomorrow?'

'Forget it, there's nothing there,' advised Alex. 'They tore down the building years ago. It's now a YMCA or something.' He dropped the photographs back in the trunk and closed the lid on its history. 'You know, our family had one great failing. We always looked for the best in people. We gave strangers the benefit of the doubt, at least that was the old man's downfall. All my life I've tried to fight against that instinct.'

'He didn't fail,' asserted Beagan. 'Canada failed him. It deserted him.'

'I don't buy that,' said Alex, shaking his head. 'He should have seen the place as it was, not as he wanted it to be.'

'He lost his country without ever leaving its borders.'

'Because he didn't adapt to its changes.'

'But why should he have? It was his Canada. His family, our family, had helped make it. The Scots really did believe that they could build a promised land here, that thought would restore purity and justice. The tragedy is that the country wasn't up to his faith in it.'

'Canada, for better or for worse, has always been open to all comers: Italian peasants, Jewish intellectuals, American business-men, you name it,' said Alex. 'Sure, successive immigrants have been more practical in their ambitions but what of it? Each new-comer changes the society and everyone else has to adapt.'

'It's not the newcomers that I'm talking about; new blood has always enriched the country. No, it's the balance between the old and the new. I just can't get over the feeling that there's something missing here now,' said Beagan, 'something to do with the re-sponsibility of continuity. You know, continuity keeping the possibilities open, keeping alive hope and vision. The Church used to provide that vocabulary, then it was the press and, for a time, radio too. But today, I don't know, it's as if the words have been lost.'

'I'm sorry,' yawned Alex, 'but the only vision I can deal with now is television. Can we talk this through tomorrow night? It's an early call and I'm so bushed I can't think straight.'

While his brother caught the last minutes of *Entertainment Tonight* on the bedside portable Beagan cupped Hector's old globe in his hands and squeezed it as if the force of will alone could hold together the yellowed panels and faded land marked 'Unexplored Countries'.

In the morning Beagan drove Alex's Mercedes through Stanley Park, across False Creek and south down Cambie Street. A seal sunned itself on Siwash Rock. Two Korean bankers in yellow gumboots fished off Prospect Point. Beyond the sari and spice shops of Little India he found the site of his father's station. But there was no familiar old oak tree for him to climb, no crystal-watered bay in which he could swim, no reminiscent skyline to admire. In the same way that the great stands of Douglas firs had first been supplanted by tidy rows of cabbages, that those allot-ments had then been ploughed under clapboard neighbourhoods and shopping malls mushroomed atop the swelling city, the breeze-block radio building had been replaced by a sports hall. It in turn had been converted into a modern Chinese Presbyterian church. Each episode was layered beneath another like the skins of an onion.

The Reverend 'Rocky' Poon Ho Sing was out jogging in Pacific Spirit Park so Beagan passed an hour driving around the neigh-bourhood and stopping for petrol.

'$17.89,' said the student behind the till and handed Beagan his change. 'The first Chinese were brought to BC.'

'I beg your pardon,' said Beagan. He had filled the tank and given the petrol attendant a twenty-dollar bill.

'You put in $17.89 worth of gas. 1789 was the year the first Chinese labourers were imported to Canada. They built John Meares's ship the *North American*,' explained the student. 'It's a game I play so this job doesn't drive me crazy. I'm studying Chinese-Canadian History at UBC.' His textbooks lay on the counter between the Milky Way bars and packets of automobile air-freshener. A 'Proud to be Canadian' sticker adorned the top volume.

'What if I'd spent more? Say $18.85?' asked Beagan.

'1881 to 1885.' The student swept his fine black hair off his brow. 'Seventeen thousand men from Kwantung, the Pearl River delta, are brought over to build the Canadian Pacific railway. It's they who named Vancouver *Hahm-sui-fau*, the Saltwater City.'

'How about $19.49?'

'Chinese-Canadians are given the vote.' Beagan was surprised. 'There's a long history of prejudice on the west coast. The 1923

Immigration Act excluded Asiatics from settling here. In the following twenty years only eight Chinese were admitted into
Canada. Chinese immigration wasn't placed on an equal basis with
other nationalities until 1967.' The student didn't smile. 'The
game helps sharpen my memory.'

Beagan shook his head and took two Danishes and a coffee
from the food bar. The bill came to $4.58 including sales tax.
'458,' he hazarded. 'Surely nothing happened here in the year
458.'

'Oh, it certainly did. Hwui Shan, the Buddhist priest, discovered
America. He and four fellow missionaries sailed a junk across the
North Pacific. His narrative records the accurate distance of the
journey, describes the west coast redwoods and the unwalled cities
of Mexico.' The student counted out a few coins and pushed
them across the counter. 'Wasn't that about the time that Rome
was being pillaged by Vandals?'

'I regret that I do not know anything about your father,' said the
Reverend Poon, folding his strong hands together like a muscular
Manchu mandarin. He wore a clerical collar with his king-size
tracksuit. 'There are sixty-five Chinese churches in Vancouver.
Maybe his radio station was in one of our other buildings.'

'No,' said Beagan, hurrying to keep up with the Reverend's
energetic tour of the church. 'It was definitely here.'

'One of our elders is an architect,' Poon explained, striding
into the chapel. 'He adapted the sports hall's facilities to suit our
needs. The gymnasium was transformed into the nave. The shower
became the choir. The locker room was redressed as the vestry.
This building is a living testimony to the miracle of God's will.'
He twisted himself into a standing back-stretch then added, 'The
Lord also ensured that we were the first church to have an underground parking garage.'

Beagan admired the vaulting-horse altar and pulpit, the donated
pews and exercise-mat carpet. The cross seemed to be made up

from climbing ropes and parallel bars. He thanked Poon for his time but there was disappointment in his voice. 'Coming back here after so long I thought that I'd find a sense of belonging. Instead everything is unfamiliar. I feel torn,' Beagan admitted. 'I'm pulled back towards an old country yet still reaching out for the new to the west.'

'Or to the east.' Poon lowered himself on to a bench and rolled his shoulders. Beagan expected him to do a dozen sit-ups but instead he said, 'The first Chinese felt displaced too.'

'It seems that every Canadian has two countries. Except the Native people, of course.'

'To our forefathers America had always been the Land of Fusang, an earthly paradise where everything grew to supernatural size. They called it "the Mountains of Gold". You know, that's what the modern ideograph for North America still means in the literal sense.' He sketched the characters on the back of a parish newsletter. 'Last century thousands of Chinese sailed east across the Pacific dreaming of great riches. It wasn't any wonder, in Kwantung a hundred dollars could buy a man both a wife and a house. But instead of discovering a golden mountain they only found work in salmon canneries or down the mines. They were sold like piglets into forced labour, toiled like slaves on the railway, lived above wash-houses and opium dens, tolerated racism. Most had no settlement papers and the Church took pity on them. The mission gave classes in the Bible, English and hope. The first generation is all up there,' said Poon, pointing beyond the basketball hoops and the steel-beamed roof, 'but the second, third, fourth and fifth generations participate in our fellowship and worship. Our role hasn't changed in a hundred years, except today it's Cantonese not English that is taught. We don't want the younger generation to lose their mother tongue.'

'It was the same on the Atlantic coast,' recalled Beagan. 'The Church kept the newcomers' dreams alive. It helped them cope.'

Poon stood up, flexed his hamstring and strode into the presbytery. 'I was an eighteen-year-old weakling when I heard the call to be God's servant,' he said. 'I was a tutor of marine welding in

Canton.' On a wall-map behind him Canada brought to mind a
ship sailing east. Its bow was the Saint Lawrence, Labrador looked
like a jib and the north was its mainsail. The southern border was
the water-line. 'I tried and tried but I could not ignore the call.
In secret I organised a church group disguised as the shipyard
gymnastic team.' He shook his head as if trying to dislodge a
jammed clot of memory. 'Of course the authorities saw through
it. I could no more walk on water than do a handstand then.
They arrested me and separated me from my family for a year. I
was paraded through the streets wearing a conical hat that read
"Reactionary Revolutionary". But in my humiliation was the mysterious guiding hand of God. We escaped to Hong Kong and I
enrolled both in theological college and a sports club.' A shy
woman and a serious young man stood before a running track in
the photograph by the desktop computer. 'As soon as I was fit
enough I applied to come here.'

When Reverend Poon was appointed minister the church's
membership had numbered less than one hundred souls. It was
his athletic faith coupled with the Pacific Rim's rising prosperity
which had nurtured the congregation's confidence. 'You cannot
just sit back and pray to God for a new church,' he had preached
in fund-raising sermons. 'You each have to push yourself hard so
that we may achieve this goal together.' Over the century since
the arrival of the first Chinese their community had swelled to
comprise 20 per cent of Vancouver's population. Its sons had
grown wealthier than the men who had imported their fathers as
labourers. Its studious daughters challenged white children for
the limited university places. Chinese had become Canada's third
most-spoken language.

'There are those who say that there is no God. But without God
where does the widow go for comfort? Without God where do the
weak find strength? Without God man has only himself to blame
for his woes and lacking the courage to do so blames everyone else.
It creates a selfish, lonely society. The mission tried to help by giving
its parishioners a sense both of place and continuity.'

'My great-grandfather shared that ambition,' said Beagan,

looking away from Poon's Cantonese Bible. 'But maybe what is important is not His existence but people's belief in His existence. Having faith in possibilities.'

'I want to fill our church with hope,' replied Poon, then stole a glance at the clock. 'And today is a special day.'

'Because of the referendum?' asked Beagan, aware that the vote on secession had begun in Quebec.

'No, because today my son is becoming Canadian.' Quebec seemed too distant to concern Poon. 'Maybe you would like to join me for the ceremony?' He looked at his running shoes. 'After I've changed.'

Ten minutes later Poon took his fedora from the hat-stand and led the way to the lift. 'Why is your son only now taking up citizenship?' asked Beagan. Beside an exercise bicycle hung a map of Christian missionaries in Africa: sons of China, raised in Canada, preaching the Word in Zaire. 'Was he a missionary?'

'Lord no,' laughed Poon. 'Stanley stayed behind in Hong Kong. He wanted the best of both worlds, the security of Canada and the excitement of Asia.' The elevator descended into the basement garage. 'My wife and I call him *juk-kat*. That translates as a short segment of bamboo, you know, one that doesn't reach one end of the pole or the other. He was neither here nor there, always somewhere in between.' Poon started the engine with a flourish and slammed the car into gear. It leapt up the ramp, dawdled at a stop sign then sped downtown. 'To be honest, Stanley thinks Canadians are lazy. For him every hour of the day is made for work, time used for enjoyment is wasted money.'

'I think he would have got on with my great-uncle.'

An open-top Lotus nipped passed them, its young Chinese driver and passenger both doing property deals on their portable phones. 'But when life gets hard Stanley's attitude has always been to move, to bend like bamboo. It's Hong Kong's unstable political situation that finally convinced him to settle here.'

*　　　*　　　*

'Indivisible' was embossed on the bronze-alloy maple leaf. A middle-aged woman, the sort who writes complaining letters about subway riders' feet on seats, guided Beagan, Poon and fifty other people from twenty nations into the panelled Citizenship Court. The immigrants sat in alphabetical rows and studied the words of the national anthem. Children wriggled in stiff new clothes and relatives took photographs. The clerk, who was of Taiwanese origin, introduced the RCMP officer. Corporal Marina Morazzoni wore a resplendent dress uniform. The Somalis, Colombians, Iranians and Chinese all rose as Judge Jerzy Opolski took his seat between a gold-tasselled flag and the portrait of the Queen. Stanley winked at his father.

The flash pictures stopped during the Oath of Citizenship. With right hands raised the assembly repeated their pledge line by line in English and then, with embarrassed smiles, in halting French. The clerk called out the unfamiliar surnames with equal difficulty. One by one they stepped forward to receive their certificate and shake the judge's hand. 'This is a special day for you, your family and the twenty-nine million other Canadians who welcome you,' said Opolski, maybe wondering if the country would exist the following morning. 'Canada is a diversity of various cultures woven into a harmonious whole.'

Corporal Morazzoni snapped to attention as the room swelled with optimism and a recording of 'O Canada'. A young Vietnamese bride began to cry. A Jamaican matron offered to photograph a Bangladeshi couple. Poon embraced his son. Stanley looked at his watch. The judge wished one and all 'a happy and peaceful life in Canada' as a determined woman holding a child by one hand and her certificate in the other argued with the clerk.

'This paper says I am Yugoslav.' She jabbed a finger at the offending word and forgot her vow of allegiance. 'I am Croatian, not Yugoslav. Yugoslavia does not exist.'

Beagan looked across the proud faces and realised that not one of the newcomers was of western European descent. The only representatives of the founding races in the court were himself and the portrait of the Queen.

It had always been hoped that Canada would mature without nationalism, that the French would live next to the English and Serbs work alongside Croats. In the same way that movies had propagated the American dream, Canada's leaders had created their own myths as a national glue. They had perpetrated the Empire Loyalist fable and the British Empire ideal. They had maintained that a ribbon of steel bound together the Inuit hunter and the Chinese washerwoman, the Newfie fisherman and the cigar-smoking Macedonian used-car salesman. The multi-culturalism myth too was an opportunistic illusion. It had been created by political necessity both to cope with multiracial immigration and to try to obscure Quebec's claims for special status by emphasising unity in diversity. But rather than nurturing that which was shared the policy had drawn attention to the differences. Canada had always welcomed newcomers in the belief that their children would understand the country, but each second generation had been swamped under the successive waves of even newer immigrants. The myths were a poor glue, and no substitute for a philosophy powerful enough to bind together disparate peoples.

As Beagan had seen on Toronto Island and at Caravan, Canadians had retreated into ethnic enclaves rather than assimilate. There was no American melting pot, no continuity to prevent the country from fracturing into competing nationalities, only a common desire for a quiet life with free health care. Less and less cultural knowledge came to be shared. School-age youngsters from Asia could not learn about the voyageurs if they had never seen a canoe. Russian pensioners at the Daily Bread Food Bank did not know that Ukrainian settlers had planted the first prairie wheat. 'I'm a hyphenated-Canadian,' said the owner of the deli where Beagan treated the Reverend to coffee and Black Forest cake. Her divided loyalty reminded him of Gabi Wellfit aboard the *Tadoussac*. 'I'm really German.' Canada had matured into a land of many solitudes.

FTER THE LOSS of CUAN there was only one
direction for me to go. I stepped off the edge of
the continent and crossed the Strait of Georgia
to a pine-clad archipelago adrift in the sea. On
the Gulf Islands with my wife and the boys I made an
attempt at retirement but the idleness frustrated me. I soon
found myself tracing across the surface of Reverend Hector's globe a thousand fanciful routes across the Pacific,
through the Mediterranean, back to Scotland's Western
Isles. Over time my enquiries uncovered a bounty of lovely
ships that were for sale. Bristol Marine had a barge suitable
for fitting out as a verandah-type houseboat, Cantiere
Dell'Argentario offered a staunch twin-screw cruiser to
explore the Adriatic, and the Paddle Steamer Preservation
Society suggested any of a dozen sea-going puffers that lay
unloved in Highland lochs. But instead of buying a Norwegian troll, Greek caïque or modified Fifer I decided to
build my own ark. After all, I had been designing her in my
head for a lifetime, sighting the clean fair lines, and now I
imagined her carrying the family away to sea.

Her white-oak keel was laid in a pebble-floored workshop.
We planed it by hand and set the moulds across its length.
Green spruce ribbands curved around them fore and aft,
were balanced by upright braces then replaced with oak
ribs. She was planked in cedar, cotton caulked and sanded
to a smooth even hull. My two boys crawled around the
low-part, as Reverend Hector had three lifetimes before,
scrubbing the bottom and picking out shavings from places
too small for an adult to reach.

The small trawler yacht with auxiliary sail took form on
the shore and when we launched her she rode the waves
as I had always imagined she would, as if our hands had
hewn her from dreams. She was named *Red Herring* and
in the lee of Vancouver Island we ran her from Saltspring
to Otter Bay, Boot Cove to Tsawwassen. Through that last
summer my family explored the myriad islands and secluded

anchorages of the coastal waterways. In the Sansum Narrows curious harbour seals swam alongside us. On August nights too hot for sleep the boys skinny-dipped in the cool Gulf current.

As the season changed and the colour and warmth drained from the land we laid down plans to cruise south-west. We selected our route, stowed supplies and secured spares for the journey. Then one wet September morning I put in to Long Harbour to refuel. The family had gone ashore to buy lunch when an unknown seiner made port. It steered for the pumps. The dock hands boomed me off from the wharf and I turned over the engine. *Red Herring* was powered by a Parsons Pike 56 horse, a fine diesel that could be heard coming forever, but that morning she sounded all wrong. She coughed, wheezed then sighed into silence. Flames leapt up from the engine cowling. In seconds they spread over the hull and into the wheelhouse, licking the mast and scorching the paintwork. The electrics continued to pump fuel into the fire. The attendant had left the glass filter-bulb disconnected. I switched off but it was too late. Charts turned yellow, curled at the edges and burst into flames. The compass crystal cracked. Varnish bubbled on the deck. The fire curled around my legs like an incensed tom-cat then wrapped me in its fury. On the shore the family ran screaming from the restaurant. Beagan dropped his ice cream. At the water's edge they reached out their arms and tried to stretch across the infinite distance of thirty feet. My nostrils filled with the reek of singed hair and blistering skin. I stepped back and fell overboard into the cool embrace of the sea.

I didn't die. The dock hands launched a skiff, rescued me and saved the boat. Their blanket of extinguisher foam transformed her into a water-borne cocoon. The attendant was contrite but our plans were put back. The voyage had to be delayed.

The grafts took well and I soon began to mend. In a month

I was out of hospital. At home I took it easy, walking with
a cane, watching the boys flip the canoe and dive underneath to play games in the air pocket. They stayed in the
water until their skin turned blue and we warmed them
around the great stone fireplace with the old stories.

I read a lot, sorting through reams of family papers and
packing them away into the old box trunk. There were
sermons and charts, press galleys and the *Kipper*'s hand-
stitched Union Jack, Bessie's wedding veil and honeymoon
album crammed with photographs of Dad. I found his ridiculous, pom-pommed Tam-o'-shanter, set it on my head
and smelt him in its wool. It brought his memory so vividly
to mind: red hair, chubby face, his fine folly of ideals, the
song to her as he shaved, 'O you tak' the high road and I'll
tak' the low road and I'll be in Scotland afore ye.' It made
me want to laugh, the love in it all, and I did but it hurt,
dear God it hurt. I clutched my chest as I fell crashing
against the table, knocking over a bookcase, hardly feeling
the bumps against my ribs and thigh. I landed on all fours
and cracked my knee on the hardwood floor. The footsteps
came running but I heard no breath through my lips and
then as if a silver cord had been fastened to me my life was
eased like a butterfly up out of its chrysalis. Beneath me
lay a body collapsed, lifeless and released from pain. My
wife wailed and held me and cried out my name. I tried to
touch her, to tell her that it was all right, only the words
were muffled, all sound was deadened, until I heard a clear
voice call to me. I did not want to turn from the sad scene
but a brilliant white light drew me away and I drifted, no
flew, up through the roof filled with such joy and a sense
of new beginnings that I thought I might die.

CHAPTER XI

PARADISE SUBMERGED

THE SILVERY ROPES went slack, the gangway withdrew and the seamless white liner cast off like a shrouded body released from earth's hold. Her parting whistle echoed off the ivory sail-towers of the Cruise Ship Terminal.

'Don't forget us,' cried a voice from the shore.

'Bye Grandma,' shouted a twelve-year-old, 'This Bitch Bites Back' printed across her lycra vest.

The white-haired passengers crowded the decks to wave fare-well. Their tears were caught by the flash of a dozen cameras. Florid streamers spilled down the hull and laced strangers together. Retired couples inspected lifeboats that were broader than my grandfather's Peterborough lapstrake had been long. On one ocean-going balcony a pensioner flaunted his complimentary champagne, popped the cork and drank from the bottle. A blue-rinsed widow in an orange lifejacket threw macaroons at the shrieking gulls. They dived towards the swells where seals fed on fish stunned by the propellers' wash. In the harbour the *Regal Princess* turned her bow towards the sea, slipped beneath the Lions Gate Bridge and a boy at my side said, 'She's gone.' Husbands folded weeping daughters into their arms. Families shuffled away down the pier back to emptier lives. But the sense of loss was not in the ship. It was in us. Beyond Prospect Point the liner was no smaller, no less beautiful, no less buoyant than she had been when lashed to the land. At the very moment that she vanished from our eyes someone somewhere watched her sail into view.

'Here she comes,' they cheered.

I, Beagan Gillean, turned away from the ocean terminal too.

It was not yet time for me to travel so far. My destination, as that of those who accompanied me, lay closer to home.

At Horseshoe Bay the Nanaimo ferry glided away from the rocky mainland, past islands enfolded in mist, towards my promised land. Tugs heaved barges of containers up the coast. Seaplanes kicked up rainbows of spray in their dash to northern outposts. In the bow cafeteria the four ghosts seemed to have settled themselves around my table. I imagined Zachary to be displeased; he wanted fresh coffee, not instant, but the maple syrup muffins caught my father's eye. To placate Hector I restrained myself from ordering a beer and drank instead a single mug of tepid tea while listening to two islanders argue with an official from the Loyal Nanaimo Bathtub Society.

'It ain't right. He notched the flywheel,' accused the local man. 'Made his eight-horse go like a ten.'

'We were on Kits Beach, everything was fine,' fumed his friend. 'Now this screws up the whole race.'

Every summer, I told my grandfather, a howling swarm of outboard-powered bathtubs buzzed thirty miles across the Strait of Georgia between Nanaimo and Vancouver. Half the entrants tended to sink before they cleared the harbour. Others ran aground on the Spanish Banks. I wondered aloud if Elsie had raced her tub across the strait before plumbing it into her house.

'I hit a great big mother of a wave,' claimed the local, interrupting my speculation, 'and it just about twisted the motor-mount right off.'

The first tubber to reach the mainland, to stagger up Kitsilano Beach and to ring a bell became the World Champion Bathtubber. The event had been declared 'an epic saga of raw courage and true bathtub seamanship'. Jamie, I decided, would have loved to enter the race.

Departure Bay was the first place-name I encountered that referred to leaving in the land of arrivals. I drove south from the ferry terminal and hopped across the Stuart Channel to the Gulf Islands. Saltspring had changed in the twenty-two years since my father's death. The new waterfront shopping mall was filled with

Japanese tourists, American yachtsmen and deconstructionist poets
on sabbatical from eastern universities. Holiday-makers from
Hong Kong ordered desserts and sides in 'casual grazing' restaurants. The Everlasting Summer Dried Herb Farm was owned
by a band of greying hippies. They had driven their VW campers
out from Toronto at the dawning of the Age of Aquarius then
cashed in on the property boom and, in a manner of which
Zachary would have approved, invested their windfall in health
shops and 'natural' souvenir stores. At Flashback Nick-Nacks day-
trippers bought 'treasures and icons' and a wilting flower-child
named Tina told me, 'I really like your camera. I bought mine
in London in the sixties.' When she stopped toying with her beads
to finger my lens I felt Hector breathing hell-fire down my neck.
Her daughter wore a sheer white cotton dress and giggled behind
a copy of *Drying Flowers with Your Microwave*, an island best-seller.
'We have a little row-boat on Vesuvius Bay,' added Tina as if to
enflame the Reverend's wrath. 'It's just right for two.'

But down the road nothing had altered at the Quarter Deck
Coffee Shop. The familiar screen door swung open blowing in
sawdust, boat-builders and the smell of sap. Sloops and smacks,
skiffs and salmon seiners were mirrored in the glassy water beyond
the window. Oak keels and cold moulded hulls lay in the yard.
The coat of arms of the Worshipful Company of Shipwrights still
hung behind the hissing, spitting tea urn. A carved dove perched
on a bowed hulk set atop a green mound panel. 'Within the Ark
Safe for Ever' read the chiselled motto. I took a chair on to the
familiar porch and waited for my ride.

After the fire my mother had decided to move us away from
the islands. The lawyer had sold our property and we parted with
the boat. A chapter had closed and we tried to begin anew. But
my father's death had left me both displaced and embittered. As
I grew older I seemed to belong to no single place, had called no
harbour my own and for years had let the current carry me where
it pleased. I had cruised across America, coasted about Europe,
run to Australia and in every port cast my need like an anchor in
the hope that it might tether me to some town or infatuation or

society. It never did and I drifted on without a sail until a storm shipwrecked me on a Scottish island, twenty-one years late and two hundred years later, with the trunk by my side. There, in the dusty pages and wild wet winds, I began to understand that my roots were not in a landscape or even in a country but rather in my memories.

It was the remembrance of things that brought me a sensation of sorrow as *Red Herring* tied up at the Government Wharf. I had traced her new owner through the old boatyard and he had agreed to meet me. Yet even though our cruiser had been refurbished and painted in different colours, I was unprepared for the sight of her haunting lines. They took me back to the cold, mourning dawn in the old house. My brother and I had laid late in bed without joy and eaten breakfast without taste. In the afternoon my mother had taken us to the radio station to sit on stools in an editing booth and watch a producer assemble our father's obituary. Snatches of his voice had echoed through the loudspeaker. Reel after reel had preserved his broadcasts. The producer had cut out words and hesitations, hung whole sentences around his neck and cast the out-takes over his shoulder. The clips of recording tape, the record of our father's thoughts and laughter, had spiralled down on to the floor and been ground underfoot. As the memorial was aired the janitor had swept up the trims and dumped them into the bin. All, that is, but the one that I had slipped into my pocket.

'You heard about the referendum?' asked the new owner as we sailed *Red Herring* out of the harbour and into the islands. 'It was a damn close thing.' The day before Quebec had voted by the narrowest margin to remain part of Canada. The out-going separatist premier had blamed the defeat on the 'ethnic' vote, that is Quebecers not of old French stock. But despite accusations of racism and minority fears that any new state would be founded on chauvinism the Parti Québécois vowed to hold another ballot. Sovereignty remained its fundamental objective. 'They can have their independence for all I care,' said the owner. 'I for one have run out of patience. But I do hate to lose our motto, eh?'

'From Sea to Sea?' I asked as the Parsons Pike diesel putt–putted us around Saltspring. Hector would know the Latin: '*A mari usque ad mare.*'

'Yeah. It won't mean diddley-squat anymore.'

In summers that once seemed to last forever my father had embraced us in this fold of the sea. Beneath the red-barked arbutus tree in a copper-green cove my brother and I had built sandcastles and driftwood rafts. We had disturbed hissing Pisaster sea stars, imagined the fishy breath of passing whales and heard the cough of West Coast trawlers as they dragged their purse-string nets up the Swanson Channel. From *Red Herring*'s bridge I recognised familiar inlets along the broken shore. Behind them I remembered leafy roads that climbed high into the broom. I recalled the alders and cottonwoods and sweet-water streams which ran so clear that they appeared to be pools of vapour, heavier but no less transparent than air. In my mind's eye a red-capped woodpecker tapped at a great cedar and sphagnum beards bristled on shaggy maples. Here and there wisps of mist curled up from valleys dank with the smells of autumn. Yet along the beach were scattered not the solid, moated sandcastles of my childhood but elegant seashell temples and delicate pagodas made of pebbles.

Red Herring navigated around the last promontory, tacked into our old bay and reached the point marked on the chart. The property deed was clutched in my hand. I scanned the channel for my sylvan paradise but saw nothing. I checked the concession numbers and confirmed the co-ordinates. I took another bearing off the headland. We were at the right place yet the cove was empty. There was no island. Then as we drifted on the clear, still waters the tide began to ebb and a swell rippled the surface. A flat black reef broke above the current. The rivulets ran off its surface and the rock revealed itself. A seal would have had trouble finding a dry seat.

'You'd better get a buoy put on that,' suggested *Red Herring*'s owner. 'Otherwise some fool'll run into it and sue you for damages.'

This, then, was my inheritance, my promised island. Paradise was a hazard to navigation. There appeared to be no more new frontiers, no *terra incognita*. The ghosts were silent and in the early evening when the tide turned again the rock vanished below the sea as if it had never existed.

'I can't tell you if the ghosts are really there, if my father's flapping his silver wings and waving a sparkling wand . . .'

'And wearing an earring,' added Elsie Faithful. 'You said he always wanted to wear a gold earring.'

'Probably a crown of curly hair too,' I nodded, glancing over my shoulder. 'Or if their spirit is within, in my mind and genes, sheltering inside my memory.' I took another sip of peppermint tea. 'Whichever it is, I feel they are with me, in everything that I do and see. And that's wonderful. Their presence gives me strength but . . .' I hesitated and looked out of her open windows at the old hills bare as razor-shaved heads. '. . . but some of their views are, well, a little restrictive. It's a bit like still living with your parents when you're thirty-three.' I leaned forward and lowered my voice. 'You see, I can't get to know any women. I can't even have a drink without feeling guilty. It irritates the Reverend.'

It was for the living as much as for the dead that I had travelled the last few hundred miles west from Saltspring to Elsie's clapboard house on the Pacific shore. The narrow waist of Vancouver Island had once contained the greatest weight of living matter per hectare in the world, but that morning, as on many others, the air was thick with chainsaw exhaust fumes. The switchback road wound across the MacKenzie Range, through the scorched glens where fire had followed the loggers' trail of destruction, and I recalled that only three of man's achievements were visible from outer space: the Great Wall of China, the land patterns of Peru's Nazca Indians and the clear-cut forests of British Columbia. An acre of Canadian timber is felled every fifteen seconds.

I had found her small village at the edge of the decimated woodlands, past the 'Forests Forever' signs, beyond Ucluelet's Pioneer Boat Works, and arrived like the fishermen who dropped by to have a shower or phone home, leaving in the sink an armful of salmon as a token of thanks. She had welcomed me as she welcomed them, with tea and fresh bannock bread. There was moose meat in the freezer, bulging stockings of raspberry leaves hanging from the rafters, paintings of sturgeon tacked on to every wall.

'When someone dies and their spirit won't leave the survivors alone we have a last supper for them,' Elsie explained. The taciturn Noah dozed with the Labrador puppy by a broken television behind a thicket of thriving begonias. 'We cook up their favourite food, set them a place at table then send them on their way.'

'But I have four of my forefathers with me.'

'That'll make it a real party. Noah,' she said to her boyfriend, 'go borrow a couple of chairs from next door.'

At the grocery store by the Government Dock I spent a small fortune. It was as if a plague of locust had swept over the shelves and through the freezer. Noah and I lugged half a dozen carrier bags back up the muddy street. The meal that I had chosen would start with finnan haddie, a golden smoked haddock dish, long a family favourite. It would be followed by an entrée of mutton, lamb being too wee a creature for Hector to eat, boiled with carrots and turnips. I would prepare a rich caper sauce to tempt him. We planned to cook stovies and *colcannon* for his sons. They had been partial to potatoes since their earliest, hungry days in Promise, although Zachary preferred his dressed up as *pommes dauphinois*. Elsie even offered to bake a chocolate cake for my father. She had remembered his sweet tooth.

'Ghosts come in three different types,' she explained as I trimmed the gigot. 'First there is the busybody; the curious soul who likes to keep up with things. You know, the long-dead grandmother who appears beside the cot of every new baby born into her family.' She beat the butter to a cream and worked in the sugar. 'Next are the spirits who died with an earthly problem unresolved. They're the Hollywood movies variety who return to the living and redress wrongs.' She whipped the egg whites. 'The third category of ghost sits a little uneasily with Christian beliefs. They're earth-bound spirits who don't know that they're dead and, if confronted, will deny not being alive. "Me dead?" they'll say, "Don't be crazy; I've always lived in this house." They are trapped in an old existence like a long-playing record stuck in a groove.'

I soaked oatmeal then strained it through a fine sieve. The liquid was mixed with Old Mull whisky and heather honey then stirred with a silver spoon to make a potent Athole brose. Even Hector would not refuse a glass. 'So which type are mine?' I asked.

Elsie shrugged. 'Don't know. I guess that's for you to decide.'

As the smells of cooking filled the house I told her about the last days in Vancouver and my watery inheritance. She must have heard the disappointment in my voice for she said, 'You know there are others who found a promised land here and lost it too.' I uncorked a couple of bottles of Bordeaux to let them breathe. 'Have you heard of the Nootka?' I shook my head. 'They were a maritime people who navigated by songline, by snatches of verse.'

'Like the Australian Aborigines did on land?'

'Sure,' said Elsie, laying seven places at the table. 'Their epic poems described every bay and channel and linked together the whole Pacific coast.' There were not seven matching glasses in the cupboard so I collected a mixed batch of tumblers, beakers and toothbrush mugs. Someone would have to drink from a jam-jar. 'Their neighbours were the Squamish, who drew maps that represented water as the positive space, noting sandbars and sea-marks like an Admiralty chart, but left the shore as blank. Then there were the Nanaimos and Kwagewlth, carvers of the finest totem poles, and the Cowichans too, the philosophers of the north-west. They all lived on these waters and followed the runs of salmon along ocean routes so definite that they might be considered the salt-water extensions of rivers. All this was theirs until the white men came.'

Noah had not borrowed enough chairs so we decided to use the trunk as a bench. 'Drake and Cook were looking for the western entrance of the fabled waterway from the Atlantic,' I said, recounting the European version of history. 'And Catherine the Great seized Alaska in a natural extension of Russia's advance across Siberia.' I unearthed Hector's globe, set it at the centre of the table and laid a finger on Mexico. 'Then Carlos III reasserted Spain's title to all the New World's coasts to protect his Central American Empire.'

'The Ahousaht people named all these white sailors *mau mau'l ney*. That means "floating on the water without land". They welcomed George Vancouver and his surveyors and, while their shoreline was plotted, shared salt pork and Salish hospitality.' Elsie laid out the mismatched tin knives, plastic forks and a single silver Haida spoon engraved with a scene of whales and canoes. The spirits would sit between us and a cut wildflower was placed at each setting. Noah fashioned candlesticks from old gin bottles. 'It was the custom of some tribes to give their women to honoured guests. The courtesy spread European diseases through the region and in one year alone a third of the entire Native population on the coast died. Great stretches of Nootka songlines were lost with them.' Outside, the setting sun caught the tops of the last Pacific cedars and arrayed them in cloaks of burnished gold. As dusk gathered around the house Elsie smiled for the first time. 'So your family isn't the first to lose this promised land.'

THE GHOSTS, SMALLER now, floated above Hector's globe on cartographic clouds, looking at this faded panel and that tattered gore, the hemisphere dented by a fall on to *Kipper*'s deck, the frayed edges of Greenland which the Micmac Gogo had blown like a bagpipe's chanter. They eyed the Hebrides and the wide Atlantic, the vast American continent and the Pacific beyond, then ducked their heads as their clouds drifted under the copper bracket. All around them the candles glowed like stars in the night sky.

'It is myself that sees it now as a road to somewhere else,' said Hector, nodding at Canada. 'For the explorers it was an inconvenient obstacle between Europe and Asia, for us a stopping-place between the old world and a promised land.'

'*Une terre conquise, f-f-faute de mieux*,' stuttered Jamie. For want of anything better. 'The voyageurs were after the silk of the Orient, they had to make do with beaver pelts. Homesteaders wanted paradise and settled for Saskatoon.'

'That alone is reason enough for moving on,' laughed Sandy and swallowed the last mouthful of haddock. 'Very good this, but have you seen what's for dessert?'

'Now who would like some mutton?' I asked while carving the roast. The leg was a little tough but the seasoning delicious. 'It seems to me that no other land has had greater hope projected across it than Canada.' I recalled from the diaries that Zachary had a voracious appetite and cut him four thick slices of meat. 'I suppose that after those early dreams were dispelled the country became simply a place of sanctuary, a caring society where the world's oppressed, homeless and fearful could build a new life.'

'At the expense of the Native people,' said Elsie while dishing out vegetables and serving the ghosts. 'Gravy anyone?'

'That's true,' I accepted. 'And it is our responsibility. But for refugees, for the Empire Loyalist, the cleared Highland crofter, Jews who survived the Holocaust and Chinese escaping the Red Guards, it was a place apart from the anger and hatred of the world, a place that wanted no conflicts or arguments.'

'It was a bountiful land,' insisted Zachary, making a point not to speak with his mouth full, 'where any labouring man could make a new start, build a home, raise a family away from the prejudices of the old world.' He tucked into his meal with great gusto. 'And Canada is still all these things; a bridge between west and east, a rich natural resource, a sanctuary . . .'

'But it is no promised land,' said my old man. 'It is not a place that rewards dreams.'

'In the name of Providence, there can not be more?' exclaimed Hector as Elsie set at his place a plate laden with mutton, frozen fiddleheads and stovies. 'I have eaten that fine fish and enough is as good as a feast.'

'Please indulge yourself,' urged Jamie, 'if only for Beagan's sake.'

'It is a generous portion and I have no need of this food,' Hector said and passed on the plate. 'Although I would not say no to a small glass of that fine refreshment.'

Zachary did not complain about the second serving of mutton, even if he would have preferred fresh Muskoka lamb, and the *pommes dauphinois* went down a treat. Sandy skipped the meat course altogether and went straight for the chocolate cake.

I raised my glass to the minister-mariner, the paddle-wheel publishers and the boat-building broadcaster. They had tried to enlarge the world, to push back the boundaries of ignorance and intolerance, to bring people together with holy water, with radio waves and steamships which delivered newspapers. 'I am proud to be your descendant,' I added and downed the glass.

'It is easier to lose a good name than to gain one,' counselled Hector, draining his toothmug of Athole brose. 'Mischief was always coming over you, Beagan, but for all the quirks and quibbles, your like is not to be found in every peat-bank.'

'Pichon-Longueville,' remarked Zachary in approval. 'And a good year. Surely he didn't find this in this outpost?'

'I seem to recall laying down a f-f-few bottles for him in the trunk,' confessed Jamie.

'Did you now? Did you really.' Zachary took a long gulp and rolled the Bordeaux around his palate. 'A fine vintage, James. I had forgotten what good taste you had in wine.'

'Oh, it was usually on your advice.'

'Well, maybe another wee dram.' Hector passed on the

wine but let Sandy indulge him in a third glass of liquor.

'I'm not sure which is the more ardent spirit, Grand-dad; this malt or you.'

'I recollect one particularly severe winter in Promise,' Hector said after taking a deep draft. The whisky had brought a story to mind. 'You will recall that all my parishioners contributed alms. Aye well, the fortunate were most charitable and the poor who had no money were good enough to give butter instead. The verger, Lachie Dunnachie by name, went out one bitter morning to collect the donations and returned at dusk in very good humour but with only half the names ticked off his list. Well now, I asked why he had failed to call on the other brethren and he replied, "Auch Mr Gillean, them's teetotal."' Hector laughed and took another sip. 'My word, I haven't supped this well since the nineteenth century.'

The good food and plentiful drink had mellowed Zachary too. When Hector and Sandy began talking about boats he leaned towards his brother and whispered, 'I'm sorry, James. . . . Bessie. The child.'

The others fell quiet. Jamie smiled then thanked him and after a moment asked, 'Why did you never marry, Zachary?'

'Why?' He lay down his knife and fork and fussed with his bow tie. 'Because I didn't want to admit my mortality, to accept the finite. You know: birth, marriage, children, death.' He patted the stopped watch in his pocket. 'Nothing frightened me more.'

'We are all mortal too soon,' said Sandy.

'But look you now, *a bhalaich*, it is not finite,' insisted Hector, the old Gaelic curl back in his vowels. He was somewhat in his cups. 'Life has its difficulties, its sorrow, its unfairness, but it does not end. Death is only another stage in our existence.'

'Yes,' Zachary admitted with a terrible sadness in his voice. 'Yes, I see that now.'

'I will put a stone on your cairn, Zachary,' said Hector, then hiccoughed.

'I won't f-f-forget you either,' added his brother.

A man remembered never dies. I thought of Icelandic Opa and his descendants, Ewan Cameron's dogfish snout and Theodore Pike's walk on water. The wine had soothed me as well. 'I used to believe that Canada had killed my father,' I told Elsie as an evening breeze washed the smell of the sea into the room. 'Now I think that his dream might have been betrayed anywhere. His view was simply at odds with the prevailing ethos in the world today: choice without variety, quantity without quality, the dominance of the present at the expense of understanding the past.' I spun the globe without thinking and the ghosts were thrown off, scattered like seeds from a dandelion. 'But his tragedy is more conspicuous here because less is shared. It is cast into relief by the vacuum behind it.'

'So where do the Gilleans go now?' asked Elsie.

'If you're asking me where it ends, I don't know. Here on this coast, where western migration meets eastern expansion, feels like the end of space. I'm not even sure where the journey began.'

'It started with the *Global Trader*'s arrival in Montreal,' stated Zachary, picking himself up from the table. He could not change a literal mind.

'I beg to differ,' stuttered Jamie. 'Surely it began when Beagan f-f-first opened the trunk?' The continuity of words was his comfort and strength.

'Or when the Reverend stepped off the shingle and on to the *Good Intent*,' suggested Sandy, remembering the pain and loss of the hopeful voyage.

'Wait you now my boys, it started when the Celts were driven by the Romans into the sea,' proclaimed Hector, waving his hand west across the face of the globe. He paused to reconsider. 'Forgive me, I mean when Moses led the Israelites out of slavery to search for honeyed Canaan.' He hesitated again. It seemed for a moment that the Old Mull and modern age had conspired to muddle his certainty. But then he beamed with sudden clarity, '*M' athair, m' anam.*' My father, my soul. 'You old fool, it began with our own ark, right enough.'

'IT STARTED WITH the great flood,' said Noah so suddenly that the puppy barked. His voice was as rough as scree in a riverbed. 'That was when Raven brought back the promise of life, a sprig of cedar.'

'That's what the Nootka say,' added Elsie.

The candles had burnt low and Noah didn't lift his eyes from his plate. 'There's a story that they tell about Mah Teg Yelah, the wife of Thunderbird. She saved herself and the animals by sealing up a longhouse with pitch so that it floated. When the rains stopped she sent Raven out in search of land. He found a strip of sand stretching north from Naikun. It's called Rose Spit today.'

'Raven was a creature of great appetites: hunger, curiosity, lust and a desire to change things,' Elsie added.

I tried to imagine the hooded eyes, hunched wings and prying beak probing at the debris which the receding water had left behind. His spiked claws left crow's foot patterns on the wet beach.

'He loved playing tricks on the world,' laughed Noah while cutting himself a second slice of cake. 'So Raven, he hadn't eaten for forty days and was real busy feeding himself when a flash of white caught his eye. There, right at his feet, half buried in the sand he saw this gigantic clam shell. Real, real big. Raven looked at it and saw that it was full of little creatures, all naked except for long black hair on their round heads. Luckily he had gorged himself already so he didn't eat them but they were scared anyway, man were they scared, by the size of the sea and the height of the sky and the blackness of the bird.' He licked off a mouthful of chocolate icing. 'Well he used his tongue, ravens got this smooth trickster's tongue you know, and he coaxed them out into his shiny new world.'

'They were the original Haidas, the first humans.'

'So that's where it all began. Up the coast a ways on Rose Spit.'

'As on Mount Ararat,' I said. 'And maybe in the Hebrides.'

'Sure,' replied Noah and fell back into silence.

'The Haidas dominated the coast for almost ten thousand years,' clarified Elsie. 'They built a complex society, filled their long-houses with heraldic carvings, launched great war canoes.' She traced her finger down the western seaboard from the roughly sketched Queen Charlotte Islands to Nootka Sound. 'But it's all gone now. There's only a couple of thousand of them still alive and they've all changed. Most of their villages are abandoned and in ruins. I guess it's a bit like your Highlanders, both in old and New Scotland.' She rubbed her distended stomach then held out a hand. 'Here, give me your shoe.'

'My shoe?' I asked, handing it across the table.

'Native people believe that life is cyclical,' she explained, taking hold of the grubby object. 'The older we grow, the nearer we come to death, the closer we are to the spirits and our rebirth.' She lay the shoe flat on the table and selected a sharp knife. 'That's why children have imaginary friends and senile elders talk to themselves; it's the dead trying to coax them back to the spirit world.'

Elsie raised the knife above her head as I said, 'I don't have a spare pair.' She pierced the sole with a single cut. 'Oh dear,' I sighed.

'A Native child will have a leather wristband or a hole in his shoe,' she continued while enlarging the gash, 'so he can tell the spirit that he cannot travel with him, that he is tied and grounded to the earth.'

She handed back my skewered footwear. A small sturgeon could have swum through the puncture. 'I would have been happy to wear a wristband.'

*   *   *

No one lives their life disassociated from those who have come before them. That night the noises around me in the dark were my forefathers. I slipped out of bed, opened the trunk and leafed through the rustling papers. As I repacked them my eye fell on a dusty copy of the Apocrypha Old Testament. It opened at the passage when Death is sent by God to Abraham which ends with the words: 'Abraham said, "I understand what you are saying; but I will not follow you." And Death was silent and answered him not a word.'

At dawn I closed the lid. I had planned to wake Noah to help me carry the trunk to the car but that morning it felt surprisingly light. I stowed it and the old globe in the boot and walked west towards the thundering surf. The stiff winds had stunted the spruce into tuckamores. I pushed through their battered stands, disturbed a squabble of terns and felt the wave-scalloped sands under my feet. Crabs scurried out of my path, into salty tidal pools, around bull kelp stems like giant spermatozoa. As I strode down to the shore I remembered the plea of the dispossessed Ozette Chief Tse-Kaw-Wootl, 'I want the sea. That is my country.'

'*An Cuan Sèimh*,' said Hector. The Gaels' Western Sea. 'It is long enough that I have wished to see it.'

'As did the French voyageurs, F-F-Father,' yawned Jamie. He would have preferred an extra hour in bed and his creased shirt-tail hung down over his sporting britches. 'It is their promised *Mer de l'Ouest*.'

'To the Chinese it is the Great Peaceful Ocean,' noted Zachary. He was dressed again in splendid evening dress, and prepared for the journey. 'I may say that the future is there over the horizon; in terms of trade at least.'

'I could look at the sea all day,' said my father Sandy, staring out over the Salish's rich *Shkwen*. 'Not that I can ever see out that far but, well, it's the prospect of those uncharted waters that draws me.'

'And was there ever a better watch to keep?'

The ghosts turned back to look at me, watching them watch the sea. 'Come you now, my boys,' sighed Hector, 'it is no more that he needs us. He has found the love in it.'

'Is it time?' asked Zachary without checking his watch.

'It is, right enough, and for sure we are all a little while from home.' Hector enfolded them in the embrace that was something between mortal laughter and a blending of gases, and I heard them call, '*Slàn leat*, Beagan.' Blessings be with you.

THE PAST WAS like the foam on the crest of a wave, rolling up the beach, stretching over the shingle. I reached to grasp the ephemeral froth but it sighed away whispering half-heard words, slipped through my fingers and out of my palm, away into the sand. There was no longer the need for anger and confusion. Instead I sensed that which everyone feels, that something is eternal: words and water, love and reconciliation, the circle almost circled. On the edge of the Pacific I felt Hector's clothes sea-wet on the shifting *bàta* deck, saw the New World's lamps glow as a constellation of stars, smelt print-shop ink, heard the two-tone whistle echo around Wigwassan Point and remembered my father laugh, laugh as he spoke into the microphone. The tide advanced again, swelled over my shoes, soaked my feet, and I knew that we shared the hope and responsibility of dreams.

ACKNOWLEDGEMENTS

An afterword of thanks to Sir Lachlan and Lady Maclean of Duart for safe harbour on the dark headland and to Allister Campbell for the brimming vessels of Old Mull. May bottletops forever bounce off his Calorgas heater. Rody Gorman of Sabhal Mor Ostaig, Isle of Skye and C. S. Paterson CBE of Caledonian MacBrayne eased the passage through the Hebrides. Angus Macdonald caulked the *Good Intent*'s leaky seams. Tim Sheppard and Ian Matheson of Communications Partnership made possible the Atlantic crossing. Maison du Québec, London, gave warning of navigational hazards along the route to a new world.

In Canada Susan and the late J. G. Crean, Rick Salutin, H. J. P. Schaffter and Bruce Litteljohn helped me trim the sails and set the course. Raymond Johnson of Canada Steamship Lines provided the culinary cruise to the head of the lakes. W. L. and Ruth Boynton, Rita and Peter Kent, Moira Farr, Valorie Crate, Harold Critch, Francine Holowachuk, Chief Simon Baker, the Cree community in Cumberland House, the Ukrainian Cultural Heritage Village, the Reverend Rinson T. K. Lin and the Muskoka, Prince Albert and Nakusp Steamship Historical Societies steered me from Ontario to the Pacific.

JoAnne Robertson's keen eye and handy sextant guided me through particularly treacherous waters; without her the ark would have been lost with all hands. I would have been completely at sea without the support of Rachel Calder, my top-gallant editor Michael Fishwick, Robert Lacey, Annie Robertson and Marina Cianfanelli. The assistance of the Canada Council and the Authors' Foundation is buoyantly acknowledged. But whether on waterways real or imagined, meandering or metaphoric, the blessing for which I am most grateful is the anchor of Katrin and my family.

Hound

a mystery

Vincent McCaffrey

Small Beer Press
Easthampton, MA

Small Beer Press
150 Pleasant Street #306
Easthampton, MA 01027
www.smallbeerpress.com
info@smallbeerpress.com

Distributed to the trade by Consortium.

Library of Congress Cataloging-in-Publication Data

McCaffrey, Vincent, 1947-
  Hound : a novel / Vincent McCaffrey. -- 1st ed.
     p. cm.
  ISBN 978-1-931520-59-1 (alk. paper)
  I. Books--Fiction. I. Title.
  PS3613.C3435H68 2009
  813'.6--dc22
                              2009016320

First edition 1 2 3 4 5 6 7 8 9

Cover photo "Longfellow Bridge, Boston, Massachusetts, 2000" © 2009 David Fokos (www.davidfokos.net).
Printed on 50# Natures Book Natural FSC Mixed 30% PCR by Thomson-Shore of Dexter, MI.
Text set in Baskerville 12pt.

For my Thais, and the mystery of love

Chapter One

Death was, after all, the way Henry made his living. The books he sold were most often the recent property of people who had died. Book lovers never gave up the good ones without cause. But then, the books which people sold willingly were not the ones Henry really wanted. The monthly public library sales were stacked high with those—the usual titles for a dollar apiece, yesterday's best sellers, last year's hot topics.

But not always. Occasionally, some relative—often the child who never cared much for Dad's preoccupation with medieval history or Mom's obsession with old cookbooks—would drop the burden their parents had so selfishly placed upon them by dying, and there they would be, in great careless mounds on the folding tables in the library basement or conference room. Always dumped too quickly by a "volunteer" from the "friends" committee, with the old dust jackets tearing one against the other.

Like encounters with sin, Henry had occasions of luck at yard sales, though not often enough to waste a weekend which might better be spent at home reading. His favorite haunts were the estate auctions, and the best of these were the ones held at the very house where the old geezer had kicked the bucket. And there was always that thin network of friends who knew Henry was a bookman—who heard of book lots being sold and passed the word on. Albert, of course, had been a regular source for this, simply because his trash-removal business so often involved

houses being sold where the books had accumulated over the years and the dead were recently departed.

Henry had spent the half hour since they had first arrived at the Blue Thorn talking about death. Albert had said nothing in response. He would not be provoked. Tim had busied himself counting receipts.

Henry studied Albert's darker reflection next to his own pale face in the mirror across the bar. There was no visible re-action. Albert's eyes were down on his glass. Henry knew that look from a thousand glances over a chessboard. That stolid brown face might not give much away, but his eyes were his weakness.

Henry pursued, "You know, the end might come too late for some people. They stay too long. All the good is over for them. With others, killing would be a kindness. I've seen them. Dying can be such an ignoble event. I go into their houses afterward. I see the decay of the things that once made them proud. No one really wants to die, I guess, until it's past their time and all the dodging is over. Dying is just the final alternative." Then he moved his thought at an angle, like an overlooked bishop from a neglected corner. "Maybe that's what makes murder the solu-tion to so many problems."

Albert ordered a second pint before heaving an unhappy breath at the subject matter.

Tim wiped up the tale of the glass after he set the ale down, and then stopped, a frown of thought wrinkling his open forehead. Smaller than either Albert or Henry, he leaned over the bar between them, on his forearms, as if suddenly wanting to express a confidence. Henry looked down on the freckles scattered over the bald center of Tim's head and thought of islands on a pink sea.

Tim tapped the counter in front of his nose with his crooked

index finger. "My uncle Jerry died in an accident on the job. Steel beam caught him the wrong way. But get this. Only the day before, he called my Aunt Deirdre into the dining room and asked for a sheet of the special paper they kept for answering invitations and the like. Then he sits down and, out of the blue, he makes out his will. Even calls my cousin Frankie over to notarize it. Can you believe that? He must have had a premonition."

The subject of death had only occurred to Henry because everyone seemed to be dropping dead lately—or nearly everyone. He had heard from his dad last week about Mrs. Levine, a childhood neighbor. She was a large-breasted woman Henry always pictured with half-framed glasses hanging on a silver chain around her neck—the glasses in constant danger of being swallowed in her cleavage. And then "little" Greg Dunne, who had run the Gulf station for as long as Henry could remember, had passed away the week before. People had been telling Greg to lose a hundred pounds or so for years. Now Henry's favorite gas station was closed. Where else was he going to get gas when the book orders were light and he needed credit?

Finally, this morning, Henry had been awakened by a commotion downstairs as they carried away Mrs. Prowder, his landlady. Her arthritis had turned out to be more than just that. In any case, death did not seem like an uncalled-for line of thought while drinking with his friends.

Albert suddenly nudged him with his shoulder and spoke in a scold as Henry fought to keep his balance on the stool. "Mrs. Prowder wouldn't hold with an attitude like yours, Henry. She knew her time was coming. There was no fear in her eyes. She just enjoyed each day's chance to observe whatever came her way. She could see the pattern to things. She cared for the living and let death be damned."

Vincent McCaffrey

To Henry, Mrs. Prowder was now a piece fallen off the table, where the puzzle of his own life was already in disarray. He was being pushed. Shoved. Like a kid in the schoolyard. He was supposed to be more mature. Grown-up. Adult. Even though the slightly out-of-place, off-center, ill-fitting, everyday discomfort he had first felt as a kid in high school was still with him. He was getting close to forty, for Christ's sake.

He looked at Albert in the mirror. "Jeez, that's just like you, Albert. It all makes sense to you. Just a part of life, right? It's like you have this root that goes down into the earth so deep you never get off balance. Why can't I see it that way? To me it's like something was stolen."

He shut up at the whine in his own voice. But it was true. It was something that had gone missing. Something not where it belonged. What was the pattern to that? He'd spent twenty years trying to stay out of the shadow of the frickin' Catholic Church and managed to run right into it again and again. Not that he was going religious. No. Not that. He had just turned around and noticed the empty space there behind him and wondered what the hell he was doing with his own life. Yes. It was as if he were living in a dream world. He played with his books and the years went by. And who cared, anyway? Did anybody actually read the stuff? They just collected it. Most of his clients were damned speculators. They didn't love books, much less what they contained. What good was there in that? His old boss, Barbara, had it all over him on that score. The ones who really loved the books liked to browse, dip into a page here and there, and feel the cloth and smell the paper.

Henry heard the whine in his brain now.

His eye caught Albert's in the mirror. His friend scanned the scene at the bar for anyone who might hear. The stools to either side had emptied since they arrived.

4

Albert spoke in a voice that barely reached Henry's ear. "You remember Patty?"

Henry leaned in. "Your first wife, Patty?"

Albert adjusted himself on the stool. "I got word from her brother that she died last year."

Henry put down his glass, his mouth open.

Tim moved in close again as well, already speaking. "Albert. You never said anything."

Henry said, "I'm sorry."

Albert shook his head. "I had nothing to tell. Alice knows. But I haven't even told Danny and Junior yet. I don't know how to tell them."

Albert sat back on his stool now until the wood popped.

Henry asked, "What happened?"

With Henry's face just over Tim's shoulder in the mirror, Albert looked at Tim. "Drug overdose, probably. You don't want the details. Let me say that…. But that's not the point. I didn't bring it up for that reason. Henry thinks I'm the Rock of Gibraltar. The big guy. He's been coming to me like I'm his stand-in parish priest since we started playing chess together back in the seventies. I've always got all the answers, right?"

Henry studied his glass self-consciously.

Albert nudged him again. "He doesn't remember. Back then it was different. Back then we used to argue politics all the time. I was angry at the world. I was blaming everybody else for what was happening to me. I was a piece of bad work. That was when I was with Patty."

Henry said, "I remember," and offered a smile.

Albert turned to him. "You remember. You remember holding me up when she left. You used to babysit Junior at five in the morning so I could do my rounds with the truck." He wiggled a finger at Henry while looking again at Tim. "This

man changed Junior's stinking diapers. Junior still remembers when Henry walked him to school...." Albert sat forward on his stool again, looking through the mirror, only at Henry now. "You want answers to things you don't even have questions for, son. Hear me? And when I have a problem like that, I go ask Alice.... And she tells me to sit on it."

Tim said, "Alice is a rock."

Albert said, "Alice is the hard place." But he let a smile slip after he said it.

There was more to it, though, for Henry. More even than the passing of Mrs. Prowder.

Henry had just gone to another auction the day before, this one in Connecticut. Mostly furniture, but a fine collection of books as well. He had missed out on several lots of mysteries—Hammetts and Chandlers and Cains. He seldom had that kind of money to spend anyway, but he had gotten what he could realistically have hoped for—three lots of lesser-known authors in dust jackets from the same period. The Mission-style table the books had been stacked on had sold for eight thousand dollars. Henry paid eight hundred for the books.

He should have been satisfied. Reasonably satisfied. Resigned, in any case. He could not easily dismiss from his mind seeing Dashiell Hammett hardcovers in that kind of condition. He had never even seen a first printing of *The Glass Key* in the dust jacket before, much less held it. But the three lots he had gotten were good enough. He was still busy convincing himself of that when he had gotten home the previous evening.

Mrs. Prowder leaned forward from her chair and looked out the open door of her apartment on the first floor as he passed in the hall, the white of her hair like a flag where it had come loose from the comb.

As always, she asked, "You were successful?"

She loved to hear reports of his adventures. She did not care so much for the accounting of books he had found as for descriptions of the homes he had been into and people he had seen.

He had answered, "Not as much as I hoped. Enough, I guess."

She appeared to be tired. She had asked none of her usual questions, but said, "Don't be discouraged. It's more important to keep trying. Sometimes the success is hidden in things, and you only find it out later on."

Henry's mind had been on the books, and he was not sure he had even said good night to her. He would miss that.

"Miz Prowda," as she always introduced herself, owned the narrow four-floor brick on Chestnut Street. It was just one in the row of close single-family town houses built while John Quincy Adams was still president. Henry liked the simple and unpretentious brick faces. They were classic now, but once they were only average in a time when averages were higher. Mrs. Prowder lived alone on the first floor and rented the rooms above to single men. Her door was always open—she had said that the first day—and it was, with a clear view of the front door and the stairs. She appeared to know everything that went on in the lives of her tenants and was not shy with her comments. She was a Yankee, with a touch of Down East in her voice and a no-nonsense approach to any subject.

No more than a week ago she had remarked, "Did Eliot and his acrobatic girl friend disturb you? He's a lot healthier than he looks, isn't he? I wish he was more considerate. He kept me awake all night."

Eliot lived below Henry on the second floor, but thankfully he heard little of that.

Mr. Elwin Prowder had been dead for twenty years but

lived on in continued anecdote as Mrs. Prowder compared observations of her tenants to incidents in her husband's life. Those comments usually involved something small, like a better way to carry the boxes of books Henry was often moving in or out the door to the street where the inclined brick sidewalk passed the bottom of the steep granite steps. The week, years ago, when he first moved in, the comments had started.

Those steps could be a logistical challenge, with Henry's van parked illegally to the side of the narrow street, blinkers on, and nowhere to leave the books in the close passage of the halls above. Every armload had to be carried all the way to his third-floor apartment.

She studied his frenzied unloading and spoke to him as he passed. "My Elwin would make a pile on the sidewalk first, hikers be damned." Then, "My Elwin would put the smaller boxes down first so you can level out those stairs to one side and stack quite a bit all at once." Then, "Once my Elwin used a straight-backed chair to carry up all my mother's china to the attic after she passed. He put his belt through the slats and held the top rung like this against his back." She demonstrated, her arm crooked over her opposite shoulder. This suggestion was ingenious, a kind of rigid backpack that might work for large boxes of books as well, and Henry decided to put a version of it to use on some later occasion.

A few years ago Mrs. Prowder had called to him from her chair as he came in the door. Her arthritis was keeping her from getting up that day, but she adjusted some white strands of hair over her ear in a gesture of civility.

"You know, a young man like yourself should be careful. When you hit your thirties you can get lonely without knowing it, because you're working harder just to keep busy. I know you don't have a girlfriend. You never go out on Saturday

night. You go to the movies alone. If it wasn't for that friend of yours—Albert, is that his name?—you'd never go out at all.... You know, once my Elwin was set upon by an older woman. She wasn't as old as I am now. She was fifty or so, the wife of a State Street banker, and they lived just up the way near where the little grocery used to be on the corner of Revere Street. Elwin was a good-looking fellow, much like yourself. Much like yourself in many ways. Same chocolate hair. Always a little surprise in his eye over what the world was offering. And I was awful big just then with Mary, my youngest, and had to be careful. At that time..." She looked toward the window to find the thought. "Truman was having his hissy fit with MacArthur, I believe. Well, some women can just smell a man who hasn't spent his passion lately. She came to see Elwin at his office. As you know, Elwin was a lawyer and had his office just down on Charles Street, where the liquor store is now. She stopped him in the street on the way to the grocery store to talk, and then she had him in for tea one Saturday afternoon so that he could look at some family papers. She was a marvel. Well, poor Elwin didn't know what hit him. He was the guiltiest man I ever saw. All the while he was giving me more attention than I could handle. He was as sweet as a puppy. But I knew something was wrong. He started to whistle. Do you whistle? Elwin whistled when he had something on his mind. He was whistling up a storm for the short while it lasted." Mrs. Prowder pursed her lips and blew a thin note that became a silent mime before she gave it up. "Well, then it all came out about two years later. There was a scandal. Mrs. Sears—oh, I shouldn't be telling you her name, should I?" She paused with mischief in her eye. "Oh, well. Too late. Mrs. Sears was caught in bed with one of the grocers, by her own husband. It became a scandal because her husband immediately had the grocery shut down for a permit violation.

The grocer fought back, and it got into the papers. I read the story to Elwin out of the newspaper over breakfast and saw him turn a shade of color. I knew my Elwin. It didn't take long to get some details out of him." She held up her hand like a traffic cop. "This is just a bit of caution. You have to watch out for older women. Especially at your age. They will have their way."

This was all said to Henry with no real prompting. She could not have known he had been seeing Morgan Johnson. The Johnsons lived blocks away on Marlborough Street. In any case, he had only gone there to deliver the books Morgan purchased at the auctions. With Mrs. Prowder's caution, Henry could not escape the thought that there was some hidden power possessed by older women—an ability to read a man's mind—which was passed on through the generations and unbeknownst to mere men.

Sitting in the Blue Thorn, staring at their reflections in the mirror across the bar, Henry reviewed much of this in his head as he had done many times since the morning. Now there was the news of Patty. Poor Patty. Lost Patty.

He felt more than slightly maudlin and tried to shake it off by speaking up loudly. "A good pint of ale is worth living for."

Tim shouted, "Hear, hear!" from a table where he was serving someone else.

Albert nudged Henry with his shoulder and spoke in lower tones. "All you need is a woman of your own. All you need is a hug, but I'm not about to give you one. Alice would object—" He stopped short and turned to Henry on the stool. Henry could feel Albert's eyes directly on him. "Shit. This isn't just about old Mrs. Prowder, is it? Does all this have anything to do with a woman? Are you having problems with a woman again?"

Henry opened his mouth and let it hang as he tried to find the right words, knowing Albert would interpret them the way he wanted. "Morgan Johnson called me last night. She wants me to look at her husband's books."

Albert turned to the reflection in the mirror, then heaved another sigh. "You need a younger woman. At least pick on someone your own age. It's healthier."

Henry defended himself. "I'm just looking at the books."

Albert said, "Then stay away from the books in the bedroom."

Chapter Two

The books he had purchased at the auction had cost Henry twice what he had wanted to spend, but then they were still worth a great deal more. He would just have to find a way to get his money back a little faster. There were several ways he could think of to accomplish that in how he presented the goods. He had played with this in his imagination as he unpacked them onto what would be called his kitchen table if he had a kitchen and not a kitchenette. He seldom used the space for eating, and his desk was already occupied with the remains of a previous batch.

He first organized the books in short stacks, faceup, directly below the ceiling light which illuminated the whole of his apartment. He could offer them as a group, as authors of the 1930s. Most were women, like Bess Streeter Aldrich, Vicki Baum, Dorothy Canfield, and Fanny Hurst. He could offer those separately as key figures in twentieth-century women's literature. He could even ignore the content and offer some of them for their Deco dust jackets and design.

He had speculated about this into the late hours, recombining the blunt colors of the covers and the bold typography of the titles for the visual effect that might be most eye-catching on his web site, until he was interrupted by the ringing of his phone.

He had not even said hello before she spoke.

"Henry?"

Her voice was just the same, as if he had spoken to her only the day before.

He managed to say, "Hello."

Her voice lowered with recognition. "Hello."

The moment was short, but many thoughts ran together. "Morgan. How are you?"

She let one of her brief silences go by. She had always been good with silences. "Fine. A little lonely."

He said the obvious. "I heard. I'm sorry."

Her husband, Heber Johnson, had died some months before—was it in the early summer? Henry could not remember in the confusion of the moment. He seldom read the newspapers, and someone had told him after the fact. Heber had been eighty-four; once the most fearsome literary agent in Boston at a time when Boston bank money still financed the films made in Hollywood. A bullish figure in a silk suit and black felt fedora, Heber always had the ever-present cigar in hand, and by the late 1950s he had made the New York writers come to him. Even in his old age, his name had commanded respect. His authors were always published, because his authors always sold well.

She said again, "I'm fine." And then, as if to convince him, "It was a long time coming. How are you?"

"The same. Of course. You sound good." That was not what Henry meant to say. He added, "It's good to hear your voice." But she was not calling for a chat. "Tell me what I can do."

She might be over sixty now. Henry had never known her age. Heber Johnson had married her when she was still in her early twenties.

She answered, "You can look at Heber's books.... I'm not selling them. I'm donating them—to Boston University. But I need them appraised. Honestly appraised. Not to scam the insurance company or the IRS. I need to know what they're

really worth. A fellow from the university was over last week, and they have agreed to keep the collection together. It would be an appropriate memorial to Heber. And I hate those weaselly appraisers. The fellow from the auction house who looked at the furniture yesterday turned my stomach. He was practically begging for me to pay him off for a lower estimate so I could cheat on the estate taxes. You know how it is...." He could hear a weary breath in the pause. "Sure, I'll be taking a tax deduction. Certainly. But we haven't been doing well for some time, so there isn't a lot we need in the deductions department. You know Heber had gotten worse. He was bedridden for the last year."

Henry told the lie. "No. I didn't. I'm sorry."

Of course he had known. Why hadn't he called her? Why hadn't he offered some moral support, at the least? But she let him get by with it.

"I don't know exactly why it matters now. I just thought..." Her voice disappeared again.

He could not remember that voice ever sounding weak. The point was that she wanted his advice. She wanted his help, now.

He said, "If you need the money, you should sell them." He had to say that much. He was pretty sure the money made no difference to her. He waited for her to answer.

Her voice lifted at the thought. "I don't. Not really. I have some family problems to take care of—nothing I can't handle. And my son Arthur is doing well. He's made another film. He's managed to stay off drugs and stay married, and he has two kids now. I'm a grandmother! How unlikely is that! And he wants me to come out there to live. I put the condo up for sale, and I'm going out to California officially for a visit. If I like it, I'll stay. When I've paid all the bills and the government gets through with me, I'll still have more than enough, I think."

Henry had met the son once. More like his father than his mother.

"Okay. Sure. When do you want me to come over?"

Her voice regained the positive control he'd always admired. "Well, that's the problem. I thought I had lots of time. But I received a good offer on the condo last week. That means I'll have to be out of there a little sooner. With the holidays coming, it could be confusing if we wait till next month. I'm guessing it would be best done this coming week. Can you manage that?"

He could. Oddly, the first thought which occurred to him was that he should quit smoking immediately, so she would not be disappointed in him. The thought was broken by the sound of a voice in the background.

Henry said, "Where are you now?" His eyes went to the clock by his bed. It was after ten.

She answered, "In the house on the Cape. I haven't stayed in Boston since Heber died." But he could tell she was distracted by something else.

It was odd how things happen. He had even been thinking about Morgan at the auction that day. But then, he often thought of her.

He had first met her as Mrs. Johnson when he still worked for Barbara at the bookshop. Morgan had come into Alcott & Poe looking for "yards of books" to fill the shelves in Back Bay condominiums owned by people who did not read. Barbara ran the best used bookshop in Boston and understood the need to sell stock in quantity—she was always struggling with the Newbury Street rents—but she hated interior decorators. She called them "furniture dealers" and passed the job of helping Morgan off on him.

Henry had liked Morgan immediately for her forthrightness. She directed him to "Skip the best sellers. I want copies of

the good books by the midlist authors who earn a living, day in, year out, with their typewriters."

Henry liked the arch of her eyebrow, which made her skepticism at some of his choices seem so obvious without a word. He had liked the agate green and brown of her eyes. She used them to see and not just look, and this had made him uncomfortable on a few occasions.

Morgan once asked him, "What kind of books do you keep at home?" after rejecting one of his recommendations.

He had fumbled for the right explanation. "Favorite authors—but only in editions I like. Reference books, of course.... I don't collect, really. I don't care much for the untouchable quality of first editions."

She liked that answer and added, "An untouchable book is worthless. Who do you read? I bet what I'm looking for is exactly what you read."

No. His habits were rather parochial, he knew. But that was that.

He had confessed his orthodoxy. "Mark Twain. Trollope. Yeats. Robert Graves." Then he had told her hesitantly, "I've just begun to read all the Shakespeare plays, first to last. I've always meant to."

She looked at him very seriously, as if her words should not be ignored. "You must read your Shakespeare out loud. It is the only way to understand the brilliance. There is music in the language that gives it meaning. You don't want to miss that. Pretend you're John Gielgud. If it drives your roommate crazy, find a new roommate. Shakespeare is more important."

Like a teacher, he thought.

He defended himself too quickly. "I live alone, so that's not a problem. I'll give it a try. I've actually never thought to read it aloud."

She had backed away then and looked at him from head to toe. "I'm surprised you live alone. You're smart. You're a very handsome man. You shave. I notice you bathe regularly. You stand up straight. You laugh at my little jokes. All you need is someone to show you how to dress. Go to London and live for a year. You'll find a good English girl there who'll fix your wardrobe right up."

Morgan was a lean woman, arms slender with muscle showing instead of loose flesh. She stood very straight herself, almost soldierlike, he had thought before learning that her father had been a career naval officer. She was strong and enjoyed showing it, the same way Henry's sister, Shelagh, used to rebuff his help. Morgan carried her own choices to the register, grasped in stacks between her sagging hands and raised chin. And there was always her voice—her voice so very sure of itself.

The very first day she had explained it all shamelessly. "These people I buy for don't read. They are cretins. But I have to buy good books for them anyway. I have to make it appear that they have taste. I'll give them credit for that. At least they want to appear civilized, and they have an idea what that looks like. So that's my job. If I buy a lot of leather bindings, then everyone will know they're phonies. They really want to be taken for what they are not. They want the books to look used and appear that they've been read, but in a condition that says they take care of them. These are not the intellectual slobs who hold a book with one hand while eating dinner with the other. These are people who buy five-thousand-dollar dresses to go out to fund-raisers for the poor, where they write a check for five hundred bucks so they can congratulate themselves on their generosity.... I'm sorry. I apologize for sounding so cynical. But I need your help. Who knows? Maybe some rainy day,

they'll read one of these books and it will change their lives—or at least make them want to read another. It's possible."

He had gotten to know her then, and on her repeat visits, but not well until several years later. After Henry had left Alcott & Poe and was selling books on his own, he had encountered her at an auction. Then it was like meeting a lost friend on the field of battle.

She immediately made her case. "Your old boss, Barbara, wouldn't help me. She tried, but she doesn't think like you. She started picking out a bunch of classics. I tried to tell her how that would look artificial. I think she took it the wrong way. So now I'm out here trying to buy books just like you."

In fact, she had not really been looking for the same kind of lots. He had no use for the common good books. He only wanted the unusual and uncommon things he could sell in his catalogue to other book dealers. When she started showing up at one of the larger auctions in Northampton, they sat together. They began having dinner together after previewing the lots and before the actual auctions began. The auctions were held at the old hotel there, and often ran late.

It was on a rainy night in January, when Henry had worried out loud about driving back to Boston on icing roads, that she had simply stated the fact.

She said, "I'm staying put. I've rented a room. And I think it would be very nice if you would stay as well." With her eyes fixed on his own.

Because of her style, the way she walked, the words she used, he had assumed she had come from old wealth.

He had known people born and raised in wealth all his life. It was the nature of his hometown, divided as it was between the Village and South Brookline. Growing up in Brookline meant that he had been in the homes of the rich with friends

from high school long before he was a book dealer. And more importantly, he had seen their books. Henry had observed their indulgences and divided them into two types. There were the ones who reacted against their breeding by becoming rude and arrogant slouchers, who assumed too much and expected everything. Morgan was the other type.

She wore clothes he thought were high fashion until a remark he made about a green dress he liked, when he had learned it had been bought in Paris almost twenty years before. She wore jewelry, a diamond ring which had belonged to her grandmother, and sometimes her mother's favorite pearl necklace. She wore no perfumes, but he could not forget the scent of her for days after they had been together.

It was an odd and disquieting relationship, which had only lasted a year. He never really saw her in Boston, but often at the auctions. When she ended it, she had done it in the kindest way.

"I love you. You're a foolish book hound to have gotten involved with an old bitch like me. You're really too innocent for a man your age. But my first love is my husband. I've been selfish enough. Being unfaithful has been a little harder on me than I thought it would.... I'm not saying that to make you feel guilty. This was my doing. I needed you more than you needed me. But it has gotten to be more than I can handle."

Her husband needed her care. He had suffered another stroke. He was incontinent. They had not slept in the same room for years because of his coughing and fitfulness at night, but Heber needed her to be there now.

In fact, it was Henry who had been wrought with guilt.

He had never really thought about marriage. He had, in fact, purposely avoided thinking much about it. His life was simple and peaceful, and he had liked it that way. He had been in love before—passionately enough to want to be with someone all

the time. He had survived those experiences—though he was not really sure he had survived his relationship with Barbara yet. He was still feeling like an escaped prisoner who might be tracked down.

Now he had been responsible for the unfaithfulness of another man's wife. He could not excuse himself for acting out of love. Not love as he wanted it to be. He certainly liked Morgan more than any woman he had met since Barbara. He liked being with her. And he enjoyed her—like a dessert, he thought. One could live without dessert. One should not break moral codes for the pleasure of dessert.

But his feelings for Morgan had been new to him. He might have loved her if she had wanted him to. She was an extraordinary woman. But she had never allowed any real intimacy beyond the physical. She had kept the greater part of her life separate from him, seldom speaking of it more than was necessary. And he was happy to have her companionship. He had not spent time with a woman since leaving Alcott & Poe.

Unfortunately, they had too little time together. She was always rushed. He never saw her when he delivered the books at her apartment building—only Fred, the useless superintendent, who stood and watched while holding the door—except for the last time, when her son, Arthur, had been there visiting and had helped Henry unload. Arthur had been inquisitive about his mother's new profession. Henry had said little and played the part of delivery boy.

Henry drove to the auctions in his rusting blue Ford van, arrived early, and examined each lot in the preview carefully, taking notes even on things he knew he would not buy, if only just to learn a little more about them. Morgan arrived in her Jaguar with little time left, walked around the room at a steady

pace, and took no notes. It was completely a matter of first sight with her.

At dinner they spoke about films or books they liked, or some gossip she had heard about an author. She enjoyed gossip. She seemed to have read everyone. These were untold stories, some she had witnessed, and others from her husband, about writers and other agents and publishers. He had suggested more than once that she should write a book of her own.

Her opinions were far more defined than his, and always had the sound of finality.

Once, she surprised him with "Updike will be forgotten within a few years of his inevitably overblown obituary notices. The term 'a writer's writer' really means he holds little interest for the general public, and I don't even think the high-lit types really like him. For a writer so proud of his stylistic control, he seems to have a limited idea of what he's writing about."

Henry had read no more than a few short stories by Updike and had little luck over the years selling his work. His own judgments were more practical. Because he had not really gone to college, beyond a few night classes at Northeastern, he had never taken any stock in those authors who were the darlings of academia. And over time he had found, without exception, that the writers he was most passionate about were also the ones he sold most easily.

Another time she said, "Who's good?" And he had answered without thinking, because it was the book he was reading then.

"Nick Tosches. Have you read him? He's very good. Edgy."

"Difficult man," she answered. "I've met him."

This had sparked him. "The good ones are all difficult, aren't they? Each in their own way. But they're difficult for a reason. Tom Wolfe. Harlan Ellison. They're not alike. They're fighting

for their lives. Everything is FDA-approved now. Homogenized. Pasteurized."

To Henry's bewilderment, Morgan found this kind of off-the-cuff criticism enchanting. She seldom argued with his pronouncements, especially after encouraging him to talk about the authors he read and to explain the reasons he liked them. To entertain her—to see the curve of amusement in her eyes—he stretched his opinion in hyperbolic flares of dissatisfaction with the current state of literary affairs, making high crime out of lapses in creative effort, and capital offense from a waste of talent.

One night he had brought a bellman to their door because he had spoken too loudly for too long. "Where is our Dickens? Where is our Trollope? What challenge is there to investing supernatural powers in an automobile when the world is in need of explanations and our religions have failed to answer? Where are Tolstoy and Dostoevsky when the dating habits of an airhead sell in the millions? What pleasure is there in a Cold War fantasy about the life and death struggle of a cardboard spy when the intrigue and game of our time needs a Dumas and the upheaval of history cries for a Victor Hugo? Why are we cursed with mediocrity and obsessed with the dissection of literary mice just as we stand on the doorstep of the stars?"

He could bring the smile to a laugh if he worked at it long enough.

At first she appeared surprised that there was a rationale beyond the accepted judgments of the literary establishment. She took his homegrown opinions as interesting vernacular aberrations—even cute. Why was Kipling so underrated and James so favored by the critics? Why was Thornton Wilder so often ignored? Was it impossible to overrate Mark Twain?

Once when they were together, he had stood up on the

mattress above her and posed with his hands in the air as if holding an imaginary book to the light.

> *Study is like the heaven's glorious sun*
> *That will not be deep-search'd with saucy looks,*
> *Small have continual plodders ever won,*
> *Save base authority from others' books.*

He had said it to show off his attention to her sincere advice of long ago. He had finished his set of the *Yale Shakespeare* and had already begun rereading the ones he liked best. *Love's Labour's Lost* had become his favorite. He should have been embarrassed at his poor delivery, but she sat up from the bed, one hand extended dramatically toward him, and hardly missed the beat.

> *These earthly godfathers of heaven's lights*
> *That give a name to every fixed star*
> *Have no more profit of their shining nights*
> *Than those that walk and wot not what they are.*

He took her hand and kissed it. She was so much brighter than he was ever going to be.

His anger had brought him to his knees then. "Then why read? Why care about them? What does it matter what they write? Isn't it just for the little pieces of the puzzle that might be found there? For the little pleasure of another voice? Why do books matter at all? If the godfather's only search is for fame, what does it matter what name they give the stars? It's all a waste of time. We're better off wallowing naked in the grass by day and huddling in caves at night. The light of a television is more than enough to have sex by."

But she had picked up the quote again. "'How well he's read, to reason against reading!'"

He was astonished, as he often was. "It's only wonder, not reason. I'm in awe. I lie on my bed at night and read as if my life depended on it. And it does, even if it's a mundane life—but I'm talking about what goes on in my head. It doesn't matter whether it makes me laugh or cry, so long as it fascinates me. It doesn't even matter if I agree with what the author is saying, so long as I can talk back. There is no conversation with most of them. It's all one way. 'Now listen here. Hear me, and shut up!' But with the good ones, I lie there and wonder at all the things the words have made me think about that I never would have imagined before. I've even thought—once, when I was reading a book by Joseph Conrad, *The End of the Tether*, I think; a dark little story—and suddenly he said something. I can't remember the line exactly, but the old captain sits down with his Bible— no, his dead wife's Bible, with his finger in the leaves, but closed and held on his knee, and begins to remember her.... I had just done that. The very same thing. I had just been reading Yeats and stopped to hear my own mother's voice in my head. It's like having a conversation with someone without the rush of time."

Soon enough, she became intrigued by his explanations, and then fascinated with the connections she could see between Henry's dismissal of New York literary judgment and her husband's dislikes for the people for whom he worked.

She often quoted her husband's words. She called the literary establishment "The Self-Obsessed" because Heber did, and Henry adopted the term as his own. She held her own opinions as only that—opinion—subjective personal reactions. She never defended them afterward and wasted little time in explanation.

Once she told him that, inexplicably, Heber had always liked Westerns, but she had never developed a taste for them.

Henry, who had been introduced to Western fiction by his buddy Albert, tried to convince her to read a few of his favorites, which finally she did, and admitted reluctantly she liked them. Soon he had her reading Elmer Kelton novels, and Clair Huffaker and Jack Schaefer. He had even persuaded her to read Owen Wister's *The Virginian,* and then she wanted to talk about it all night, like a girl with a crush. She had a way of suddenly seeming very young.

She had said, "It's a better world they're in. It's a world of men and women and right and wrong. It's so civilized. It makes me want to cry."

It interested him when it came out that she seldom saw any manuscripts for Westerns these days—probably because so few Western movies were being made.

"Hollywood matters," she answered. "What's good for Hollywood is good for America. The books are not bought for themselves, but because of what they can be used for."

Morgan Brown had started working for Heber Johnson as a reader soon after getting her master's in literature at Boston University. She had worked as his assistant for the rest of his life. It had only been in the last ten years, as Heber's schedule slowed down, that she began to look for other work.

"I really hated being an agent. I hated making decisions about people's lives. Heber depended too much on me. If I said no, he said no. I never negotiated any deals. I just made the decision that made the negotiations necessary. I think Heber started hating the authors, though he never said so. It wasn't like the way I feel about the people who own the homes I decorate. That's more disdain, not hate. Heber simply didn't want to read the work of his clients anymore, with all the complaining and the moneygrubbing afterward. He would get them a hundred thousand dollars more than they had ever made in their

lives, and they would whine about his fifteen percent. Their greed colored his view of them."

Then her face had changed with an urgency, as if she had not said all that she meant and to get it right mattered. "But Heber hated the publishers who encouraged it all even more. 'It's all about the money,' he said. They could be marketing breakfast cereal. They all used nice words to the feature reporters to explain how they loved books and the romance of publishing and then turned around to their desks and signed another author who could churn out thrillers by the half dozen, or a self-help book which just happened to be like one already on the best-seller list, all the while some sap in Poughkeepsie slaves away at night trying to write the next great American novel, never knowing there is no chance in hell it will ever get published without passing muster in the marketing department—you know, the marketing department: where they tell him that the woman Raskolnikov kills has to be young so the story will appeal to the right demographic."

Her voice had wavered with the kind of passion he wanted to hear. He could feel it in his spine when she broke through the reserve and her words came more quickly. She paused as if to contain the memory, but could not. "Though I seldom saw all that. I always loved the other part—not talking with the authors—just reading their work when it was still new and no one but they and I knew yet how wonderful it was…or how bad…." She took a breath, and then another, and the words slowed again. "When he stopped negotiating as often, I had less to read. Getting into a new line of work was natural. And you know, we had moved so often over the years. New York. Beverly Hills. Back to Boston. We even lived in Vermont for two years. I had decorated at least twelve homes just for ourselves. It was the only other thing I knew about. And it has paid so well since."

Henry knew, from very early on, that theirs was not a permanent relationship. But he had ignored the thought. The kind of matter-of-fact affair he had with Morgan seemed almost perfect to him. Until it was over.

The end had been unexpected. Her announcement had come one morning, after little sleep and much talk. He was not sure he truly understood then, even as she drove away.

Afterward, he endured the first bout of depression he had ever known. He had not wanted to get out of bed in the morning, and was too tired to read at night. His appetite for food disappeared. He stopped going to the Blue Thorn and nursed his bottled beer at home. Albert had shown up at Chestnut Street several times—spending more time talking to Mrs. Prowder than to Henry.

Gently mocking, Mrs. Prowder had frowned at Henry as he passed. "You are getting too thin. And you are smoking again. I thought you had given up that nasty habit. You need to find yourself a good Italian girl...I know that Lisa, who works at the Finnian's Drug Store. She's a pharmacist. Very pretty. Very patient. She puts up with me well enough. You must have noticed her. She was dating a doctor, but that's over...."

In time, Henry had solved the problem with a daily walk from Beacon Hill to the Blue Thorn in Inman Square, and a liberal application of fresh ale. He had begun to smoke again, and lingered longer at the book sales.

But the thought had occurred to him often since, that he was living an apparently pointless life. Morgan had gone back to caring for her husband, after years of being instrumental in the publishing of the very books Henry sold—and he would continue selling them, making a basic living with just enough left over for gas.

What did he do that could not be done by others? The

pleasure he felt before in his job was suddenly ephemeral. He liked to think he had some hand in preserving good literature for future generations. A high cause. But this sounded better than it felt. He never blamed his depression directly on his loss of Morgan. He had always thought of her as a catalyst.

Chapter Three

"Don't confuse legal and illegal with right and wrong. The difference is not a detail. It's like water and air. You swim in one and breathe the other."

Uncle Jack tossed his cigarette at the hardened soil beneath the battered garbage cans beside the stairs. He was scowling as much at the sun as at Henry. Still, Jack looked too much like his brother for Henry to speak to him easily about things. It was in the hard edge of bone in his face and the turn of his mouth. But Jack wore a flat tweed cap, while his brother, Matt, went bareheaded in the worst weather. Jack shaved close and smelled freshly of witch hazel while Matt skipped his razor as often as not and usually displayed a rough of graying beard. Jack was not a skeptic, believing Lady Luck was only a disguise for the Virgin Mary, while Matt was positive the human race was lost and all that was left to do was finish the task as best as one could. Jack was the older brother, but few knew it.

Henry tried to keep a poker face. "How much?"

Jack squinted, even with his eyes shadowed by the bill of his cap. "A grand would just about cover it."

Henry squinted enough to give his words the authority of serious consideration. "For how long?"

He would not have denied Jack unless there was no money to be had.

His uncle scuffed at a tuft of grass to help the pretense of negotiation. "I got loans out that are due by the end of the month. Two of the guys will be late. They always are. Say Thanksgiving."

Henry lowered his head to make sure there was no question of the more important matter. "You won't tell Dad."

Jack brushed the air with one hand. "Your dad likes not to be told. He's happier that way. I wouldn't disturb him for the world."

Henry wanted more assurance. "You told him about the car."

Jack bobbed a bit to avoid the jab. "He was on to me. It was in the heat of an argument. It slipped out. I'm sorry about that."

Henry had rented a car for Jack so that his uncle could drive down to the casino in Connecticut. Jack had no credit cards. Henry's father knew that much to begin with. Henry had actually rented cars for his uncle more than a few times. Jack hated buses. He never liked sitting too close to strangers. Besides, if he had a car, he could take his girlfriend along. Sally would not sit on a bus. And then Jack always paid the credit-card bill promptly. This was one of the few times he had ever borrowed money outright.

Henry asked, "What kind of deal is it?"

A scowl erupted, and his uncle's eyes narrowed further. "For a grand I'm not telling you my life story. I'm saving that for the biographer."

Henry relented. "I'll go to the bank later. Come by my apartment after nine."

Jack looked down at something on the ground that needed study and kicked at it.

He said, "That old lady you rent from doesn't like me."

Henry answered, "Mrs. Prowder died."

The scowl in Uncle Jack's face collapsed. "God bless her soul. I didn't see it in the paper."

The obituary column in the *Herald* always got his uncle's first attention.

Henry said, "She didn't rank a column inch. Just a good old lady."

His uncle Jack nodded slightly. "Too few of those. Far too few, and most of them gone now…. She had a good eye for character."

As Jack turned and walked out the driveway with his odd lope, the bottom edge of his tweed overcoat dipping close to the ground, Henry watched with the thought that the step was getting slower, no longer the little dance they once teased him over. Three vertebrae were fused together—to "take the swing out of my boogie," his uncle liked to say—from a time when he was driving trucks for the Marines. Korea was still his favorite topic of conversation after the third beer.

Henry said "Toodle" out loud to himself because Jack had left without his usual parting word. His uncle's mind was already on some other objective.

As his uncle disappeared onto the street, Henry counted the number of cigarette butts on the ground to calculate how long Jack had been waiting. At least an hour.

Because he only needed it about once a week, and rented parking spaces in Boston were at a premium well beyond his budget, Henry had always kept his van at his father's house in Brookline. It was the house Henry had grown up in, and the one he often referred to as home even after being on his own for over twenty years. Nevertheless, he wondered how his uncle guessed he would be there today.

Two strips of broken concrete, tied by knots of grass, passed between the house and the neighbor's at one side, in the direction his uncle had gone. At the end of this was a separate garage of cement block molded to look like stone. His father's truck, emblazoned with Matthew Sullivan Electrical in large gold, gothic lettering was kept within the garage, and Henry's van,

unmarked except by rust, was parked to the side and just in front of the barbecue pit which was made of the same cement block as the garage. The barbecue had not had a fire on weekends since his mother had died so long ago.

With his van parked, Henry always used the back entrance, which was usually unlocked. This door stood in a direct line to the door at the front of the house. The two were so much alike that when two people entered from both ends of the house at the same time, it often appeared to be a mirror image. With his mind on his uncle, the coincidence startled him now as he entered.

The figure at the front end of the hall spoke to him. "Everybody's been lookin' for you. Your dad's been looking for you. He's gone off. Your uncle's been looking for you. He's outside somewhere."

Malcolm Moore turned with the end of his words and headed up the stairs, as heavy-footed for a skinny man as he had ever been.

His father had always taken in boarders. When growing up, Henry usually had someone living in the opposite room down the hall on the third floor. It had been a problem for him more than once—Maureen Williams had caused him his earliest heartache. An exchange student lived there even now. And Malcolm Moore had been occupying Henry's old room for almost the entire twenty years since Henry had moved out. In all that time, Henry had never heard Malcolm say hello or how are you or good-bye. But Malcolm had stayed the longest of all the renters through the years.

Henry said thanks into the empty hall and went to the kitchen, in need of a drink of water. There his father had left a note in that perfect script the old man had learned in the late 1940s at St. Mary's school, before all the world had changed

and handwriting became a lost craft. Henry had gone to Lawrence, the public grammar school, and his own handwriting was always a matter of embarrassment.

Letty Levine is dead. Never paid her bill. Her son said I should take anything I want to cover it. She has avocado curtains and pink pillows. Nothing I can use. But she has a whole lot of the Erle Stanley Gardner books. I said you'd be over to take them. You can give me what you want when you sell them.

Another piece of the puzzle, but at least there were many who would mourn her passing. "She was a fixture," someone had once said. Always at town meetings. Beating up on the school committee for spending too much money every year. A town-council member for decades. She had been a widow for as long as Henry could remember.

Leaning on the kitchen sink, Henry reread his father's note as he considered what he should do. Going to the bank for Jack's money could wait an hour. The thought of picking up a load of Perry Mason novels at Mrs. Levine's did not thrill him, and would be better done and finished with. Then again, lugging them back to Beacon Hill on the trolley did not make sense. Henry imagined the stubby little book-club volumes he saw at every library sale and cursed out loud. Because of the long popularity of the Perry Mason television show in the 1950s, millions of copies had been sold. If they were in perfect condition, he might get two dollars apiece. Why did the old man do things like this to him?

With all her public works, Mrs. Levine had also been a thorn in his father's side nearly forever. He could still remember her calling his father over to fix things at all hours, and never understood why his father put up with it. Henry figured

he might as well pick the books up now and maybe just leave them in his father's kitchen until the next time he came for the van. Maybe the old man would read one or two. At least that would be some form of payment. In any case, he knew his own reluctance was actually the fear of encountering Leona.

The Levine house, up the block and around the corner, was almost an exact copy of his father's and probably built by the same people at the same time—about 1910. All of these houses were three-floor rectangular boxes, smaller versions of the cheap triple-deckers which crowded Boston but with shallow peaking roofs instead of the flattops and planted with just a little more space between. They had been made to house the influx of Irish workers who had previously gained their financial foothold in nineteenth-century slums downtown and were ready to move up to a better life in the "suburbs" of Brookline Village.

Now, as the old timers passed away one by one, even this cheaper housing was being transformed into condominiums by Henry's own generation. A one-floor unit had recently sold just a few doors away for more than what a small palace in South Brookline used to go for when he was a boy.

On hearing the figure, Matt Sullivan had said, "Only lawyers could afford to live in one of those."

His father was right about more than that. Mrs. Levine had not changed the color of her curtains. Henry found her son, Joe, boxing up odd objects in the living room, with the front door open to clear the way to his already well-packed minivan in the driveway. Henry was greeted first with the sound of a breath blown dramatically as Joe turned his head up to look. "Jeez, what a job. She never threw anything away."

Henry looked at the scattering of sorted piles. This was a common sight in his business. He shook his head in sympathy.

"I was sorry to hear about your mother. She used to make a wicked peanut butter and jelly sandwich."

Joe nodded at that. "Thanks. She did, didn't she?"

They shook hands while Joe was still half bent over the box he was filling. Henry had played both basketball and baseball with Joe Levine until they graduated from high school. This was no longer the bony guard who knew how to use his elbows. Joe kept his legs spread wide as he bent, with butt thrust well back to counterbalance the mass of his upper body. His stomach pulled against the buttons of his shirt. Henry had bumped into Joe a number of times through the years. The weight had been added steadily.

Henry said, "If you need help, I know a guy who cleans out houses."

Joe tossed a hand in the direction of the other piles. "Nah. My sisters want most of the stuff. I'm just taking some of the bric-a-brac. My wife, Molly, is doing flea markets lately. You ever do flea markets?"

Henry wondered if he would ever be reduced to that. Could the book business change that much?

"No."

His answer was perhaps a bit too emphatic.

Joe persisted. "She does pretty good. It's only seasonal, of course. But she'll make more than I do on an average day."

Joe was a high-school math teacher now in Newton. Henry might have predicted a future like that. Some things worked out the way they were supposed to.

He thought again of Joe's sister, Leona. The odd green-colored couch which was now shoved to the side had been an important place in Henry's life. He had not even seen Leona for at least twenty years.

"Is Leona here?"

He shouldn't have asked.

Joe turned an eye up at him. "No. Tomorrow. She'll be here tomorrow…. She's divorced, you know."

Ever-helpful Joe. Henry moved to discourage that line of conversation.

"I actually came by for some books. My dad said your mother had some Perry Mason books and he was taking them in some kind of trade."

Joe pointed with another swing of an arm. "Trade. Hell. She never paid him. I told him he could take anything he wanted. He just said he wanted the books. They're in that box in the corner. Take 'em away."

It was an oversize moving-company box, too large to be hauling books around in, and by the weight, it was packed. Scanning the floor for an open space, he could see little room to be looking at them on the spot.

Henry hoisted the box onto his shoulder. "If I miss her tomorrow, say hello to your sister for me."

He had said it to be polite and was sorry as soon as the words were out. Leona's brother knew too much about that high-school romance to let a casual comment get lost. Joe nodded as he left.

Henry carried the box around to the back door of his father's house and put it up on the kitchen table. With the light directly overhead, it was clear to him as soon as the first flap had been turned back that the box was not filled with book-club editions.

Gardner was a Massachusetts boy, born in Malden, who had worked dozens of jobs before training himself in the law and passing the California bar. His great success had been shaped by the writing of hundreds of stories for pulp magazines like *Black Mask* in the 1920s and '30s. For mysteries, Henry had

always been more partial to Raymond Chandler or good old Conan Doyle. Henry had never particularly liked Gardner's style or his sketchy characterization. But the plot twists were always entertaining.

The condition of these were mixed: few truly fine, and several lacking their dust jackets. But they were almost all first printings. There were over forty of them, each published long before the popularity of the television show which had made Perry Mason a household name even to nonreaders.

Had they always belonged to Mrs. Levine? Or were they something left from her long-dead husband? Again Henry stirred the odd thought: he made his living from the death of others. At the very least he had that in common with Erle Stanley Gardner.

The burden of the box of Perry Mason books riding his left shoulder had increased greatly by the time he had carried it up from the Arlington street subway stop and across the Public Garden to Charles Street and headed up the hill.

Mrs. Prowder's narrow brick row house on Chestnut Street was further compressed within by the rise of the stairway to the right, directly in front of the entrance. This left a pinched room at the front on the left, which had once been a parlor. Mrs. Prowder had used this as her living room, with her favorite chair close to the frame of the window for the best view and facing the door she always left open when she was awake. On each of the upper floors there were two studio apartments, one at the back and one at the front. Henry's apartment was at the front on the third floor. Mrs. Prowder had used all of the first floor, with her kitchen and dining room to the rear on one side and her bedroom at the back beneath the stair.

Mrs. Prowder's door was open. Henry took the excuse to set the box beside the stairs and ducked his head in to see what

was happening. It was an apparition of Mrs. Prowder who sat in the chair beside the window now.

The woman who stood up for him was Mrs. Prowder as she might have been thirty years earlier. Her hair, still the bright orange of the fruit, was cut shorter. She was possibly a bit taller, and perhaps heavier. She wore the same rimless bifocals, but instead of a dress, she wore a flannel shirt and jeans.

She spoke first, as Henry stared. "I'm her daughter. I'm Mary. Which one are you?"

Henry smiled unconvincingly. "Henry Sullivan. Third floor."

Her eyes narrowed, as if she had finally caught him. "You're the book guy. Good. I could use your help."

The makeup she had used to darken her eyelashes had been wiped by her sleeve into a gray feather on the pink of her cheeks. He guessed she had been crying.

Mary led him into the dining room, a space Henry had never actually been in before, only seen from the front room. There on the wall, across the table from a glass cabinet full of imitation Blue Delft, were built-in shelves lined floor to ceiling with row after precise row of books exactly equal in height and width. Here was every procrustean Reader's Digest edition ever published, or so it seemed.

She said, "What is the best thing to do with these?" Presenting them with a sweep of her hand.

Henry had always imagined that the editorial staff of the *Reader's Digest* was made up of a menagerie of barely anthropomorphic creatures, missing an arm here, a leg there: this one a hand, that one a foot, some eyeless altogether. Educated by machines in sunless rooms, they must huddle for hours over desks lit by sputtering candles, while fed gruel on paper plates by conveyor belt, the sounds of their own sneezing and coughing absorbed in the hiss of old Muzak tapes from

the 1960s played endlessly. There they took fresh new novels, biographies, and histories and snipped them with the kind of scissors handed out to first-graders, removing any word they thought might offend an imagined public of maroons who would be shocked from their intellectual sleep by too many syllables or a colorful four-letter word; cutting chapters that ran more than eight pages, trimming pictures larger than four-by-six inches, all in order to produce shortened versions of popular books which might fit four at a time in the stubby little uniform volumes they called "condensed."

Henry answered, "You would do the human race a favor by putting these in a dumpster."

She stared at him a moment, not speechless as much as unready to speak. He could not tell if his brutal answer was taken with humor or even understood. He tried to clear up any confusion.

He said, "I'm sorry. It's not a time to be flip, I guess. It's just me. I guess that was rude…. They're not the real books, you understand. They're shortened to sell to people who don't want to take the time to read a whole book. Your mother was a sweetheart, and I know she was sharp right to the end, so I am totally flummoxed as to why she would have these."

Mary Prowder laughed then, loudly. Not a happy laugh. "I'm not hurt. It was my brother, Richard. He gave my parents a subscription every year for Christmas. She never read them. Dad never did, either. You can look. They've never been opened. The jerk never gave them more than three phone calls a year. Rich never visited except during the holidays, and he only lives in Albany, for Christ's sake."

Henry had never heard Mrs. Prowder speak of her son. He was wary of entering into another family dynamic. "That's too bad. Someone should have told him."

Vincent McCaffrey

She laughed again, but this time with more control and a sad shake of her head. "She told him only once—every Christmas. Rich would come for Christmas dinner and leave before dessert because he said he had such a long drive back. He works for the state government. He's a lawyer. Lived at home all the way through Suffolk Law and then left one day for Albany because his buddy had a job for him there, and he hardly ever came back. That's the way he is. An asshole. Now he's left me with this. Says he doesn't have time to help. But you can be damn sure he'll be here to pick up his half of the check when we sell the place. He won't miss out on that."

Henry hoped his nod appeared sympathetic and let her finish before he spoke. "Do you think you'll be selling the building soon?"

Her answer was immediate and said in a flat voice. "Wednesday."

He looked for some sign of humor in her eyes. "You're kidding."

She repeated, "Wednesday. The real-estate guy called me this morning. He already has a buyer. This is Beacon Hill. Every nouveau-riche techie, doctor, lawyer, and politician in town wants a row house on Beacon Hill. No parking—no problem. Historic district restrictions on renovation—no problem. Shortage of reliable and qualified electricians, plumbers, carpenters, and bricklayers who have an honest bone in their body—no problem. Shortage of money—never...."

Henry stood back to answer, "Well, my father is an honest electrician." It seemed like a weak defense.

She shook her head at him. "Tell it to the lawyer who bounces you out of here. I can't keep the place. My brother wants his money. The IRS will be looking for their death tax. I bake bread for a living. I can't afford to keep it. I grew up here.

40

I broke my arm on those front steps when I was twelve. I hid in the attic from my asshole brother until he got old enough to be afraid of girls. It would be nice to keep it, but I have to support my own family, and I can't pay Beacon Hill property taxes." Her voice was changing as her throat closed on her words. Henry looked down at the threadbare carpet.

Henry said, "I understand."

She continued to shake her head. "No, you don't, really. She always kept the rent low for you guys. But the politicians don't give a damn. They raised the taxes every year anyway. You're pissed that you'll have to move, and I don't blame you, but I can't help it any more than I can deal with the rest of this shit." And she was starting to cry again.

He said, "It's okay. I've moved before. I can handle it."

She began to shake.

Henry reached out a hand for her shoulder as she fell toward him. He held her for several minutes before she took a deep breath and pushed herself away. Extracting a wad of tissue from a tight front pocket, she began to blow her nose. She finally spoke with the tissue still at her face.

She said, "I'm divorced. You could have taken liberties."

He answered automatically, "I'm sorry."

She laughed, less painfully this time. "Your face is red," she said through a smile and sniff. "I've embarrassed you. My humor isn't always... The whole thing has been a little more than I can handle. We buried her yesterday. Next to Dad. My brother showed up for five minutes. It was a very moving ceremony. My kids and I all crying and my brother looking at his watch and the priest saying 'Powder' instead of 'Prowder,' and her friends all sitting in lawn chairs and chatting about the color of the leaves this year because the ceremony started an hour late.... My daughter even wrote a poem to read, and they never gave

her a chance because there was another funeral waiting behind us. God, when I die, I want it to be on an ocean liner with icebergs and a band playing. I'm sorry. I just don't have anyone to talk to. You're a good listener...."

Henry backed up. He thought it was a good moment to break away. "I have a friend, Albert, who cleans houses out. He's good—and honest. Let me know if you need help. I have to take care of a few things right now."

She smiled again. She was prettier when she smiled. He had always imagined Mrs. Prowder was a good-looking woman in her time.

The old stairs barked beneath his added weight. The bittersweet smell of marijuana seeped into the half-dark of the hall from Eliot's door along with a Beatles tune he could not remember the name of. Old Mrs. Prowder had always discouraged smoking in the house. Eliot was taking quick advantage of the changing of the guard.

Henry opened his own door on a trim of late sun highlighting his window frame and illuminating the whole small room in an antique glow. He was happy to be home.

When he called his father later, the best of the Erle Stanley Gardner books were spread out on the table ready to be photographed.

His father sounded irritated at his surprise and told him so. "I knew they were good books, or else I wouldn't have offered to take them. Joey was ready to chuck them out on the curb yesterday. But they're yours now. I'll look forward to a check whenever you get around to it."

He always underestimated the old man. His father could still read Latin now almost fifty years beyond his own high-school days. He may not have ever read a mystery novel in his life, but he could recognize a regular edition of a book from a book club.

Henry chastised himself. "I'll drop a check on you when I have another appointment and I come for the van."

The old man grunted before speaking, a habit he had in common with Albert when they had something unpleasant to say. "Jack was by, wasn't he?"

It was best for Henry to keep his answers short. "Yeah. I saw him earlier."

"Needed some money, did he?"

And it was always best to keep everything aboveboard with the old man.

"Yeah. A quick loan."

His father said, "Don't let him get in to you for too much. He still owes me for a bag of marbles I bought for him at Nantasket Beach once. He forgets. He's getting old."

"Yes, sir."

His father's sense of humor never changed. He grunted again. "You know, her daughter called about an hour ago."

But the change of direction left a momentary silence as Henry worked on an answer.

"Leona?"

"The one with the big boobs. Anyway, yes, I believe it was her. The one you got involved with."

What other surprises did the old man have coming?

"How do you know about that?"

The old man grunted yet again.

"Hell, we all knew about that."

Henry remembered the great lengths he had gone to in an attempt to keep it all a secret. Leona had never been shy, but Henry feared his father's wrath. That was how Henry had once broken an arm—trying to climb out his third-floor bedroom window in the dark of night to meet Leona on her porch.

But he had to ask, "What did you know?"

His father did not hesitate in his answer. "I know I was glad to hear from her mother that she was on the pill, that's what I knew. I knew a broken arm wasn't going to keep you two apart."

The broken arm had actually done the trick. Leona made it her job to nurse him through the following weeks.

Henry said, "Jesus. I wonder why we thought it was such a secret."

"It was a different time, my boy. It was your secret. It was something special just between the two of you. It's not the way they do it today. They just do it in the street today...."

He had never spoken with his father about sex. Or, more to the point, his father had never spoken to him. The frankness of his father's words after all these years was another surprise. It made him wish momentarily that they had been able to talk openly long ago.

"What did she say when she called?"

"Nothin' much. I gave her my condolences. I wasn't really wanting to be talking with her about her mother. Then she asked about you, and I gave her your number."

Henry said, "No."

The old man answered back quickly. "Yes. I did. I'm sorry. She asked, and I did. I couldn't say I didn't know your number, now, could I?"

The conversation ended the way most of his talks with the old man always did, somewhere in the timeless air of the past.

Henry resorted the Gardner titles in the best condition to sell them individually while he listened to a recording of the Sibelius Second Symphony he had picked up at a yard sale the day before. The record was pristine and probably never played before. His job was done by the time the doorbell rang.

Uncle Jack stood on the brick of the sidewalk at the bottom of the stone steps, reluctant to come up. A cigarette burned

between his fingers in the dark. Jack's eyes shifted to the light in Mrs. Prowder's window. "My back is bothering me."

Henry looked for odd fears in his uncle's face. "Her daughter's here. Come on up. Let me show you some books."

His uncle shook his head with emphasis and exhaled a cloud around him. "I gotta get going."

Henry half turned and waved him up with a hand. "I've got some Perry Masons. You liked Perry Mason, didn't you?"

Jack squinted. "The lawyer? You're remembering me coming over to watch that old television show when you were a kid. That was just to get a taste of the desserts your mother used to make. I don't like lawyers."

Henry relented and closed the front door behind himself, stepping down far enough on the stoop to sit with his feet planted on the brick.

"Why are you both so contrary? Where did that come from?"

Jack knew he was being compared to his brother.

"Family trait. Your sister has it. You don't. Runs like that in families. Like green eyes.... Did you get the money for me?"

Henry pulled the small fold of hundred-dollar bills from his pocket and passed them to his uncle's hand. They disappeared inside the coat with a single pass.

Henry said, "Mom wasn't contrary."

"Your mom was an angel. She was lucky Matt found her first. I would have broken my back again to marry a girl like your mom."

Henry smiled at the statement of fact, and believed it. "Was it Grandpa, then? Was he the one?"

Jack waved the thought away. "No. He was a good egg. Steady. Worked himself to death. It was your Nana. She was always at the end of something. She pushed until she got her

way. She pulled until the string broke. One eye was always a little wider than the other."

Henry laughed. "She always had mints. I remember the mints."

Jack smiled enough to break his lips apart. "'You always get more with candy,' she'd say. But that wasn't really her way.... Your father isn't so contrary. More like Dad. More like you. It's just that way between dads and sons. He just wants the best for you.... Thanks for the money. Toodle."

It was almost an hour later when Leona called. Henry had begun reading one of the Perry Mason novels, *The Case of the Lucky Legs*. It had surprised him. It was much more lean and hard-boiled than he had imagined it would be, although the prose was still not as alive as the work of Hammett or Chandler. And Leona's voice was huskier than he remembered. He knew she smoked, because she had started him doing it. He wondered what she looked like now. Having seen her brother, he wondered if she had gained weight in the same way. With his mind pulled from the world of crime and detection, he immediately thought of Lauren Bacall in the movie *The Big Sleep*. He knew that Leona looked nothing like Bacall, but the mellow sound of her voice was close.

"I'm sorry I missed you at the house. How long has it been?"

"Maybe twenty years."

"More than maybe. You know, I've thought about you a few times. What are you up to?"

She sounded cheerful.

He said, "Still selling books."

"But your dad says you work for yourself."

"I have a kind of catalogue. I sell on the internet. I sell to other dealers, mostly."

"Does it pay well?"

"Not particularly. I get by."

There was a brief silence. He figured it was his turn.

"What are you doing these days?"

She said, "Real estate. It's what housewives with time on their hands do—real estate."

"I thought you were divorced."

"Well, yes. But I'm still the official guardian of two kids in high school. Ed doesn't do anything he doesn't have to."

Henry said the name aloud. "Ed Quinn."

She said, "You remember Ed? Sure you do."

Henry remembered Ed. He had always imagined that Leona's pill supply had unfortunately run out at the wrong time.

"Yeah. A dentist. Right?"

"Yeah. He got the army to send him to dental school after we got married. It was a good thing."

The story Henry vaguely remembered now was that Leona's mother had cared for the first child while Leona worked and Ed finished his obligations to the army.

He said, "I'm sorry that didn't work out for you."

She answered quickly, as if the thought had been considered a thousand times. "It did. It really did. We had some good years out of it. Ed just couldn't keep his zipper up. I guess looking down the cleavage of all those young girls who didn't floss regularly was too much for him. He started taking other forms of payment for his root canals.... He's already remarried."

Henry's only clear memory of Ed Quinn was a missed foul shot in a basketball game with Brookline High School's great nemesis, Newton North, during their senior year.

He thought he heard some humor in Leona's voice. "You seem to be taking the reversals of life pretty well."

Vincent McCaffrey

"Yeah. Well. That's me. I roll with the punches. So, why aren't you married?"

Right to the meat of the matter.

He tried to keep the answer light. "Haven't found the right girl."

She came back quickly. "Have you looked?"

"Yes."

There was a brief pause before she answered. "Well, I was right there for you."

He knew he should not hesitate now. Saying the right thing would matter.

"You were there. But you weren't the right girl, Leona."

She said, "I guess you'll never know."

He said, "I knew."

It would not be wise to leave any opening at this point.

She said, "Why were you so sure? I never understood why you were so sure."

He remembered that tone in her voice. The implied criticism of it. He thought of half a dozen reasons, but said, "Because you liked to watch *Charlie's Angels*."

There were several seconds of silence before Leona spoke. The first word exploded from the phone. "What...? Because what? What was wrong with *Charlie's Angels*? Everybody liked that show."

"I didn't. I couldn't stand it."

"You changed our whole lives because of a television show?"

The tone of her voice had hardened.

That was another sound he remembered too well.

"No. It's just that I wasn't going to change my life so that I could watch something like that. Don't you remember, Leona? The argument..."

48

The silence was short.

"Yes! Now I do! I remember you wanted me to read that stupid book, and I said I didn't have time because that TV show was coming on—*Charlie's Angels* was coming on. I remember. You went crazy. What was that stupid book?"

"I just wanted you to read the beginning. I was excited. I was filled with the buzz of it. I wanted to share it with someone. And you couldn't take the time."

She repeated, "What was the stupid book?"

"*The Right Stuff.* Tom Wolfe's *The Right Stuff.* I still think the first sixty pages are the best sixty pages I ever read."

There was another long silence. He waited. He had nothing more that he wanted to say.

She said, "You know, you're right! I remember now. You made me cry my eyes out, but you were right. I wasn't the right girl, was I? Your damn books were more important."

He let that go.

"But you were close."

He said it as some kind of conciliation, but it sounded weak. Leona took an extra breath. He had to give her that. She had grown some patience over the years.

She said, "Yeah...I remember. So, how's your arm?"

Her voice had changed, the tone softened again.

He said, "Fine. Works fine."

She had lit a cigarette, and he could hear her inhale and then almost see the words wrapped in smoke. "I do remember. Do you still have that microbus you bought from that old hippie?"

He had never missed it. He had hated the lack of power from the engine and the enervating hesitation every time he tried to enter traffic on a thruway. But then again he remembered their trips out to the Cape. It was a good vehicle in the

Vincent McCaffrey

sand. He especially remembered one evening out on Duxbury Beach.

"No. Traded it for something else. I have an old Ford van now. Better for hauling books around."

"Do you ever sleep in the back, like we used to?"

"No. Never have."

"I remember that."

"I do, too."

As they spoke, he had kept the image of Lauren Bacall in his head. It seemed better that way.

Chapter Four

Albert's voice on the phone was husky with dust. He had awakened Henry from a difficult dream.

"You ought to come over here and take a look at this. I think you'll like it."

Henry could only manage, "What?"

Albert's voice held no patience. "Just come on over. Take my word."

And Albert was not given to pranks.

Henry showered to wash the sleep and sweat away, dressed in the same jeans and shirt he had worn the day before, and dropped down the stairs two at a time in his rush, half expecting to see a scowl on Mrs. Prowder's face for making too much noise as he passed her door. Only when he saw the door closed did he realize he was really just half awake.

He prolonged his breakfast at the Paramount Cafe on Charles Street by drinking an extra cup of coffee. He had not slept well, and the bits and pieces of dreams still floated around his head. Before cutting across the Public Garden to catch a D car at the Arlington subway stop, he had to pause briefly to watch a gathering of children, herded by half a dozen young mothers, around the brass statues of the ducklings along the walkway in the Garden. A regular sight on sunny days, but something that always entertained him. The transit in the trolley was made more brief by the scraps of memories stirred up over the last few days.

Behind his father's house in Brookline, some birds had

51

scattered their droppings over the windshield of the van, and he broke the hose loose from the side of the house to wash it down. He arrived at his destination in Dedham, despite the traffic on Route 1, less than two hours after he had rolled out of bed.

Henry liked Precinct One in Dedham. With all the newer building which had crowded around it over the years, and the Norfolk County Courthouse looming at one side, it still managed to keep some feeling of the New England village it had been since before the American Revolution. The house Henry stood in front of, however, was a white Gothic cottage from about 1850. A steep-pitched slate roof projected in four gables in each direction, diminishing the simple white box of the structure beneath. The house itself was made elegant by tall windows which arched at the top, giving it all the appearance of an enlarged dollhouse. What remained of the original property was cramped by post–World War One neo-colonials. Enormous oaks, still holding on to their leaves late into the season, towered over the house to each side and showered the black slate roof with acorns which popped apart and rolled off onto a trampled garden.

Albert scowled down from an opening at the end of the gable above the narrow porch, where a dark green shutter was broken free.

"What took you so long? I've got guys on wages here."

He was not going to be defensive about getting up so early without explanation. "I stopped to eat. I like to chew my food carefully. That's just the way I am."

Albert was not forgiving. "You ought to get up earlier. I've been up since it was still dark. You can't catch any fish if you get up with the damn sun. Now, come on up here."

The house was cool inside. The rooms on the first floor, al-

ready nearly empty, echoed with his steps. Two of Albert's men greeted him as they passed, coming from a small kitchen, their arms loaded with trash.

The echo of Albert's unhappy voice wafted from above.

"Where the hell are you! Come up the stairs."

Behind a broad hearth with several openings, obviously once used for cooking in a distant time, Henry found the stairs, narrow and walled at both sides. At the top of the stairs, through open doors, he could see three rooms beneath the gables, all of them empty. The reverse shadows of missing furniture left patches of bright wallpaper and the odd outlining contrast of stains from long use. Albert's voice beckoned him again. Around to the front of the chimney, wood and plaster had been broken away and a man-sized hole made. Henry peeked through. There was Albert's large figure, beside a half-shuttered window opened now to daylight, sitting in a chair too small for him. The whole room, little more than eight feet across and perhaps ten feet long, was greatly cut down in size by the slant of the roof as it filled the area beneath the fourth gable overlooking the front porch. Next to the window at Albert's knee was a desk, neatly arranged with writing paper and envelopes, ready to use.

An electric light with a frosted glass shade hung by a cord from the highest point of the ceiling at the center. Low shelves, no more than four feet high, rose to the slant of the plaster wall which sealed the angle of the roof beams.

Albert's lap was full of papers. He did not rise in the cramped space, but he did smile.

"I wanted you to see this before we packed it up. I've already taken pictures. I ran out of film taking pictures. I've got to get me one of your digital cameras. I can't afford the film anymore."

Henry climbed through the broken opening and stood upright, his head close to the slant of the wall. The shadows cast by the glowing filament within the clear glass of the light bulb were weakened by the sun glare from the window.

"Holy moley."

He used the old expression just to compliment Albert's obvious satisfaction with his discovery and then stooped again automatically to better see the titles of the books, trying to avoid his own shadow against the spines. Most were popular authors like Alice Hegan Rice, Ellen Glasgow, and J. M. Barrie. He counted six Gilbert Parker novels together. John Fox and Kate Douglas Wiggin were mixed randomly with Mrs. Humphrey Ward and George Barr McCutcheon and Robert Chambers. A run of dark blue Henry van Dyke volumes filled half a section. These were the popular novels of another era, just after the turn of the twentieth century, all gathered together in the random order of a small library in use.

There was little order among the titles because none was needed. The books had the appearance of being read once and then popped on the shelf. None were especially valuable that he knew of, because all had been best sellers. What made them dear was the condition—read once and put away. Many had dust jackets, a rare thing to find now on books published before the First World War.

The entire room looked as if it had been left one day a hundred years before and never touched again.

"She was an itty-bitty thing." Albert said. "I don't think she was more than five feet tall, or else she would have bumped her head at every turn."

Henry knelt, his knees pressing through his jeans to the coarse weave of the Indian rug spread from side to side over the wide yellow pine boards on the floor. On the opposite side of the

room the shelves were filled with the limp leather of Roycrofter volumes, many of these laid sideways. Above this was a cigar box missing its lid, and partially filled with never-used postcards, collected from xGreece and Italy, France and Spain. A separate gathering of English scenes rested beside the box.

Henry finally asked, "What was her name?"

Albert answered with a tone he reserved for his elders. "Helen Mawson. Quite a traveler. The grand tour. She saw it all."

Henry nodded. "She loved to read. She loved books."

"And looky here." Albert handed him a sheaf of papers from his lap. "These were in the desk drawer. Letters from people she visited. Dozens of them. She wrote everybody she met. She must have been a good writer, too. Listen to this."

Albert pulled a pale sheet from the pile in his lap.

"'Oh, my dear, we have missed you since you have gone. Your letters have made us wonder how we might have wasted precious time when we had you here. I read your description of the little town of Rye to Sophie, and she cried. Please write again soon, and let's plan another visit for the coming year if you are free.'" Albert looked up. "That was from 1911. But all the letters are like that. They all praise her own letters to them. I wish we had one of hers to see what the fuss was about."

Henry said, "I'd like to see her picture."

What did women wear in 1911? Were they still wearing corsets then? Beneath their skirts they wore something called a chemise, he had read. He had always wondered what that might have looked like. And they wore drawers, not panties. And her hair would be long, of course.

Albert shook his head. "I haven't seen any pictures."

Henry looked around again. On the slant of the wall near Albert's head was a map of Europe. There the visual politics was greatly simplified by geographic swaths of color: Germany

ranged in pink from Baltic Russia to the Rhine, the Austro-Hungarian Empire bulged in green from the Adriatic to the Black Sea, and the yellow of the Ottomans reached from the Persian Gulf to well beyond the Aegean. Henry imagined for an instant the young woman—she would be young, wouldn't she?—turning from the letter she was writing on the desk to check the map.

He said, "What do you think happened to her?"

Albert's face fell to a flat expression of resignation. "She must have died. This room was sealed up. Look behind you—where I broke through. That was a door. It's still locked—and whoever locked it was not content with that. They put lathing over the wood and plastered it. I felt like Carter entering the tomb of King Tut. But I knew it was here. I could tell from outside that there had to be a room here. And I figured, if they were going to tear it all down anyway, I might as well see what was in it." Albert's eyes scanned the shelves as he spoke.

Henry asked, "Who owns it all?"

"Well, the house belongs to a fellow named Rogers. But he's not even here. He lives in Florida. Herb Stanley, the builder, hired me to clean it out so they can tear it down. Everything I take out is mine. Only, they start ripping the place apart tomorrow, so we have to get this all out of here today. Pronto. Now."

Henry winced at the thought. "Why tear it down?"

Albert shrugged. "To build a bigger one. It's too small."

Henry said, "It's big enough for me...."

Henry knew Albert was no happier at the thought than he was. Albert's tone hardened again. "Well, if you have three or four hundred thousand dollars handy, you can probably negotiate something."

Henry had little to answer that. "Damn!"

Albert heaved his shoulders again in resignation. "I see it

every week. But not with something like this in it. This is a time capsule. I haven't seen anything like this in all the years I've been hauling trash. You see bits and pieces, but never like this. It's a tiny museum."

Henry took a breath. Behind him, by the break in the door, was a broad chair with wide, flat arms. Henry rose from his knees before sitting there to survey the room.

This was the chair she must have used when she read the books. He turned. A slender brass floor lamp with a flowered shade was directed down at him from behind.

Henry said, "What's your plan?"

Albert sighed unhappily.

"Junior's off getting some boxes at the liquor store now. I figured we'd pack it up as best we can and then load it into your van—it's dry in there, right? No rust holes in the roof yet—and then we can sort it out later. The furniture's not much. The shelves are homemade. Just this little desk and that Morris chair you're sitting in."

Henry's hands gripped the flat oak of the arms. "Morris chair? It has a name?"

Albert nodded. "After William Morris. It's a recliner. I've seen them before. You could drop the back down and take a nap, if you had the space to do it. We can get this room cleared by lunchtime if we get snappy about it, and then you can see if you can sell some of these books. I'll get rid of the furniture on my friend Bernie."

Henry ran his hands over the wood, caressing it, and nestled himself further in the chair.

"I always wanted a chair like this…to read in."

Albert said, "Better to nap in."

Henry squinted at Albert. "I'd like the chair. I'll buy the chair for whatever Bernie will pay."

Albert waved him off. "You've got no room for it where you live."

Henry shook his head and turned. "I'll figure something out—and I want this little lamp, too."

Albert sighed with resignation and then yelled for his helpers. They were both on the front porch smoking, and their voices mingled with the fresh air from the window. Henry was guessing that Albert had his own thoughts about the chair. But Alice did not like him bringing things home. She had put an end to that many years ago.

When Junior returned with the boxes in his father's big truck, Henry began the packing with Albert while the others finished with the downstairs. As they worked, Henry learned that the house had been occupied until recently by an elderly couple who had bought it in the 1940s. Prior to that, Albert knew nothing.

Henry carefully released the map from the plaster and folded it with the letters. The dry inkwell, the pens and the pencils, the hardened gum eraser, and even the small blotter with the name of an English maker of jellies on the back were put into a box together with an assortment of clips, bookends, and a brass letter opener emblazoned with the name of a Boston stationery company now long gone. As Henry packed the books, he resisted the urge to look into the titles he had never seen before. The Roycrofter books were packed separately so that the dried and powdering leather would not mark anything else.

More of the door was broken away to pass the desk and the chair through. Only when the chair was lifted from its dark corner did they see the rosewood box, its lid unclasped over the bulging of its contents. As hands grabbed the chair through the opening, Henry knelt and lifted the box, wary of opening the lid further and spoiling his instant hope for what it contained.

Albert stopped his packing and grunted with impatience. "Go ahead."

Henry raised the lid slowly, enjoying the small drama. The cream yellow of the letter paper appeared new. The blue ink of the handwriting had not faded or darkened.

Albert said, "Attagirl."

Henry asked, "Why here?" His hand waving at the floor.

They both stared at the box as if its contents were inexplicable. Henry used a finger to tip the upper edges of the pages without removing them. A moment passed, with only the sound of the fellows downstairs moving over the old floors.

Henry thought out loud. "Her father… 'Dear Papa,' they all say. He might have placed them there. He might have sat in the chair to read them as they arrived."

Albert muttered, his thoughts on that distant past, "He might have put them there before he sealed the room."

Henry placed the box securely under his arm, pressing the lid shut and closing the clasp. The rug was rolled, baring the wide pine boards and revealing a brighter yellow beneath.

Henry asked, "What about the wood? Can't they save the wood?"

Albert shook his head. "That's up to the contractor. They might save some. My job is the trash."

By noon, the room was as empty as the others. Henry's van was loaded, and he drove back to Brookline in slow traffic with his mind happily lost in the Edwardian Age of Robert Chambers, Ellen Glasgow, and Edith Wharton.

Many years before, still in high school, Henry had read a book by Jack Finney called *Time and Again*. His memory of the book came back strongly as he drove. That book was an account of a time traveler, a passage from the present to the past—from the 1970s to the late–nineteenth century in New York—but the

discovery of the little room beneath the closed gable in Dedham was as near to traveling through time as Henry ever expected to experience. He was happy for the escape. He was happy for the chance just then to be gone from this time he was living in.

When finally he sat alone in the van, behind his father's house with the motor off, he opened the box, unable to wait any longer. The first letter on top, still creased from having been folded square, was dated April 5, 1915. The heavy commercial black lettering which topped the sheet with the name of the Biltmore Hotel in New York City only served to exaggerate the delicate beauty and curve of Helen Mawson's pen line in blue ink.

Dear Papa,

You are still angry. I know. I can see your face as you read this. But it was Mama's wish. The money was for me to spend in just this way. When you are finished scowling, I know you will be happy that I have arrived safely. I am staying at the Biltmore because it is so close to the station.

Please don't worry about the price. They have smaller rooms for butlers and maids, and I have talked my way into one of those. I will be careful with my funds.

There are several shows I want to see before I leave. The Ziegfeld Follies are the biggest sensation just now. And there is a Sherlock Holmes play which I will see for you and tell you all about. The city is just too marvelous for me to find enough words. Imagine, a hundred times over, our puny Washington Street. They build what look like the honeycombs of gothic bees wedged between columns of marble and all pulled like taffy into the sky. And merchant signs sprout everywhere, like a million gaudy flags of every color and size. Conjure a whole city of businesses turned on end so that a citizen never need travel beyond the clink and whir of the

elevator. Then multiply it countless times. Boston is so pitiful by comparison. Why, certainly the automobile cars you hate so much will be obsolete in no time. We will all be taking the elevator!

I went directly to the Woolworth Building, and it is even more incredible than I imagined, not only scraping the sky but piercing the gloom of evening like an ancient sword. The clouds move from its path as it soars, and the earth tilted beneath my feet as I stared in wonder. See the postcard I have enclosed.

You must come, someday, and see this place. You cannot think that you would make Mother happy by staying home. Her spirit is in me. I must fly.

Dearest love,
Helen

Chapter Five

He had expected some difference. He had prepared himself for the moment and assumed there would be some visible mark of the time since he had seen her last. He was not prepared to find Morgan as if he had just left her the day before and she had only changed her outfit. Her honey brown hair was still cut short—to compensate for the "big head," she had once said. The agate brown and gray in her eyes was clear, almost polished. The running shoes she was wearing brought her eyes up almost to his. Morgan had always liked the Kate Hepburn–style pants and loose shirts with wide collars that Henry had only seen before in old movies. He even remembered her saying once that she was born a generation too late.

She opened the door of her apartment as the door of the elevator folded back. There was no hallway necessary because the apartment occupied the entire floor.

She did not hesitate, as he did, and hugged him with more than polite friendship. She was not wearing perfume. She never had, that he could remember. He had always liked that. She smelled sweet to him without it.

"Thanks. Thanks for coming. I just got here myself. The weather has been so good that I stayed on the Cape for a few extra days. I needed the time.... How are you doing?"

As usual, he had little to tell her. His life was far less eventful than her own. It had always been his part to listen to her stories, not the other way around.

She said, "You've been living by yourself too long, you know. Men who live by themselves change in the wrong ways."

He was uncomfortable with one fact he could not escape. He was still very much attracted to her. Time had not altered that.

He said, "Have I changed that much?"

"Yes. You look thin. You aren't eating well enough. You look pale. You need sun. And don't tell me you can't afford to spend weeks on the Cape like I do. You can still get out. Get some fresh air. Exercise. You still have your health. I can see that. You should take advantage of it while it's still yours."

This was the mother in her. It had come up before.

He answered, "I suppose I'm indoors too much."

She would not let the thought go. "You don't have a girlfriend, do you? I can tell. Men look so much healthier when they are spending time with a woman."

That was a fact of life he could only blush over.

The air of the rooms was stale. Morgan pulled back curtains and opened windows to the morning light as she gave him a tour of the books in each room, and he got the pleasure of watching her move again. He had forgotten how graceful she was. Even her small movements had poise.

Because the apartment covered the entire top floor of the building, light seemed to arrive from every direction. The books filled the interior walls. He had always been good at estimating quantity, but his quick count became mired by the size of the collection spread over so many rooms in such a variation of shelving. In the room they called the library alone, the only one without windows because it filled the center of the space, there were over four thousand volumes in oak shelves lining all four walls.

Several times he had to remind himself to breathe as his

Vincent McCaffrey

eyes absorbed the titles and authors. As Morgan pointed out
the last group in a small study by her bedroom, he knew the
total would be well over ten thousand volumes. The majority
were average octavo size in hard cover, and almost all published
after World War Two. The bulk were fiction, which had been
Heber Johnson's specialty. Most astonishing to Henry's eye was
that they all looked brand-new, even a copy of Sloan Wilson's
The Man in the Gray Flannel Suit, which Henry pulled off a shelf
at random, published in 1955. He guessed that nearly all the
books were first editions. A quick check established that those
separated out in the center library were signed, representing
the work of Heber's clients.

It occurred repeatedly to Henry that he could live off the
sales of a collection like this for the rest of his life.

In the past, when he had delivered books from the auctions,
he set the boxes in the vestibule of the building, at Morgan's
request. He wanted to see the apartment, but Heber had been
alive then, and Morgan thought it best to avoid a meeting. Now
he was glad for another reason. He knew he would be dreaming about these shelves for years.

"Please" was the first word he found to use. "Do not donate
these to a library. They'll store them badly in boxes until the
spines are warped. They'll rip off these precious dust jackets
and discard them like wastepaper. They'll mark the spines with
irremovable white labels and then put them out for uncivilized,
unwashed, rude students to paw over as they pick their noses
and sneak Cheez-Its out of plastic bags in their pockets."

Morgan laughed. She had always laughed at his melodra-
matic rants against the "Goths and the Visigoths," as she called
them.

She said, "They'll be in a special collection, catalogued
separately and kept exactly as they are. They're even interested

in the shelving. Heber had it all custom-built by a local wood-worker, and Miss Crist, the librarian, thinks they can install it all together in the space they've made available. I've spent a lot of time negotiating this. Don't worry. You know I wouldn't let Heber down."

She made tea for him as he began to look more closely at the titles. He had brought one of his usual small notebooks and pulled a pencil from his shirt pocket. She handed him a clipboard with a fresh legal pad and a pack of pencils newly sharpened.

By noon he had finished only half of the living room. He had stopped looking for reader's marks. There were none. He had stopped checking the publishers' copyright notices. They were always first editions, unless they were much older titles, and then they were the better reprints from major publishers. Through the years, they had kept no trash.

Remembering the remark she had once made, he thought it was funny that she had what appeared to be a complete collection, up to the 1990s, of the works of John Updike. She shrugged innocently when he pointed this out, as he looked carefully at a copy of *The Poorhouse Fair*, trying to remember the point of difference between the first and second printings.

Thankfully, the books were not in alphabetical order, but rather collected by period and kind, or some other interest. All of George Duggan's books were there, each signed to both Heber and Morgan, with an inscription. When Henry pulled Harper Lee's *To Kill a Mockingbird* off the shelf, he did not expect the signature inside. He had never seen one before.

Was she giving that away as well?

Yes. Everything.

But she had taken the clothbound *Le Morte D'Arthur* by Malory from his hand when he had slipped it down from an upper shelf. It was the Rackham illustrated edition, Henry's

favorite, and was out of place beside an older set of the *Encyclopedia Britannica*.

"Not that. It was Heber's. He received it on his twelfth birthday, from his grandfather. I'll be taking it with me for my son's children."

There was no time to ask if he could sit and leaf through it now. She put it back.

He had taken a short break and become quickly engrossed in the first chapters of Patrick Leigh Fermor's *A Time of Gifts* when she tapped him on the shoulder where he sat on the floor.

"I actually did something like that once," she said. "In 1961, on my summer break in college. The only flight I could afford was to Lisbon. We started hitchhiking there and made it all the way across Spain and France and down the boot of Italy to Sicily. I was a classics major, remember, so I wanted to see it all. It took me the entire three months. At that time, you couldn't go where Fermor had walked back in 1932. Fermor did it before Hitler and Stalin. But now, with the Iron Curtain gone, you could retrace his whole trip."

He asked, "You weren't alone?" Imagining a young Morgan with her thumb out beside an ancient road.

"No. Girls didn't do those things alone then. There were three of us. Two classics majors and a language major."

Henry had never traveled beyond an occasional train ride to New York. The thought occurred that he'd give up twenty years of his life to have been on that journey with Morgan.

She put a plate of neatly divided roast-beef sandwich down on the floor next to him, along with a beer.

"You still drink your beer, I hope."

He had tried to convince her years ago that there was a difference between tap and bottled beer. He had not been successful.

After that she left him alone while he worked. Several times the phone rang and she stood in the kitchen and spoke just beyond his hearing.

Again, he caught sight of her, lying on the couch in the living room with her arm bent and her palm against her cheek with a book open. Henry had always liked the sight of a woman reading a book.

By midafternoon, with the sun glaring lower in the sky, she went from room to room and pulled some of the curtains and opened others. The apartment was on the ninth floor, offering a commanding view over the lower brownstones of Marlborough and Beacon Street, of the Charles River and Cambridge beyond. Henry took the time to look out, then. Morgan stood beside him, close enough that the smell of her warmed the air.

"I'm going to miss this. When there's a breeze, the seagulls float down from the roof and hang in the air just there, swoop like acrobats, changing places, and look back at me as I watch them, as if they want me to applaud, which I do, of course. I know they can't hear me, but they know I'm here."

With nothing so exciting to tell about his own life, he told her then about the mysterious Helen Mawson and the sealed room. She wanted to hear all about it.

At one point Morgan interrupted, "You see, you don't live such a boring life. You have discovered a tragedy. Perhaps a great tragedy. It sounds like Ibsen."

Henry had never developed a taste for such heavy drama.

He answered with his first thought. "I always wondered why the people in those plays stayed together. I never got to like Ibsen because of it. The Russians may be unhappy, but they have dreams of happiness and pursue their dreams. The Scandinavians are just unhappy, and wallow in it."·

She laughed at that.

"Inheritance. They are waiting for their inheritance. The ones who had nothing got up and left and went to America. They were the happy ones. It's just a matter of natural selection, then. The unhappy ones stayed home and waited their turn and bred the next heir in a desperation of boredom."

That comment somehow seemed to be a more negative sort of humor than she used to have. It even sounded a bit like something he might say. It reminded him of the Irish families he had seen at odds with one another at wakes.

"Dad's already told me—when he goes, the house is my sister's. No arguments."

She shrugged. "It's the way it should be. You make a will. It's all settled. No arguments."

He picked on the Scandinavians again. "Of course, now the Scandinavians have ended all that naturally selected unhappiness by having the government confiscate everything when people die so they can redistribute it like good Socialists—now everyone can be unhappy together. No more Ibsens."

Morgan raised an eyebrow. "It's not so different elsewhere. No more Shakespeares," she said. "No more Mark Twains."

He left the more complicated titles in the library as well as those in the smallest room to the second day. The red scar of a setting sun over Cambridge chilled him. He wanted to stay, to hold her hand against his chest the way he had once done. But this was not what she had asked him to come for. And if he asked, he was sure she would—just because he had. Unfairly.

He kissed her quickly on the cheek and left as she pulled her reading glasses away and stood from paperwork at a desk.

That night his dreams of her fit uncomfortably in the bed with him.

The coffee was ready when he arrived early the next

morning. The sun curled in the billow of the curtains shielding open windows. She kissed him again.

That warm impression of her lips was still there through the morning, pulling his mind from his work. He concentrated as best he could, moving from chair to chair around the conference table in the library.

Three low metal filing cabinets were tucked below the center of the conference table at one end. The lack of windows made it unique. With the door closed, all the sound of the world was shut away.

Morgan said, "This was really Heber's room. He spent more time here than anywhere else. The table wasn't for conferences, really. We never had more than two or three people here at a time. It was so he could spread the pages of a manuscript out and look at them all at once. He said it gave him a better sense of a story. He was very good at spotting problems."

She had found a small baked ham and a block of Swiss cheese and cut into the crust of a loaf of French bread for sandwiches at lunch. He was sure she was trying to please him.

She said, "I'm not sorry about the books, really. I am glad to lose them. They've been a weight on me. And the apartment as well. The house on the Cape is my only regret."

Henry knew that loss. The house where he had spent his own summers as a boy was there, at the end of a sandy road in Eastham, and was now long gone—sold—and the memory still fresh.

He said, "That place slows the hours. The Cape gives time itself the feel of passing. It's the sun, I think. You can feel the tilt of it against your skin there."

Morgan said, "Yes!" And the green in her eyes sparked.

He let the thought continue. "And on days when the salt is in the air, it slows your breath as well. Your thoughts spread

out wide on the ocean. That little shack I've told you about was on a dune, just high enough to catch the curve of the earth on a clear day. I used to sit there and read my books and let the scenes play out before my eyes, all the way to the horizon."

The spark of her eyes drowned in the darkening of a shallow frown. "Yes. It's so much more like losing the world, to give up all of that, than to lose all of this." Her eyes searched the walls of books around them.

He turned to her. "Why don't you keep the Cape house, at least?"

He was sorry he had said it. Of course the thought had already hurt her enough.

She looked down. "I can't. There are things that I must take care of."

She spent less time reading that afternoon and stood more at the windows, where he caught sight of her standing in silhouette, still, lost in thoughts he could not know.

The sun was long out of the rooms by the time Henry had finished in the small study off the bedroom. His eyes were tired. He had seldom in his life reached that point when he had looked at too many books, but this was one of those times.

She had come into the room behind him then. He spoke without turning. "I'm afraid I haven't finished. I have a good sense of the collection, but I'd like to check many more of the individual volumes. There are points, you know...."

He was setting the clipboard down on a small stool when he had turned enough to see her bare feet.

Once, inspired by the musk of leaves in the air, and the hard bright light of a cold autumn morning after an auction, she had taken him on a journey to New Hampshire. They had left directly from the hotel in Northampton and driven the old

70

road up the Connecticut River past Greenfield and Brattleboro and across the bridge at Bellows Falls.

Her Jaguar moved quietly and low along the road and never fast. Their passage seemed silent to the point of hearing the leaves stir on the pavement. He never asked her where she was going. He saw the scenery more from her window than his, watching her face in the dapple and splash of the sunlight.

She had told him then about her first memories of childhood, the years late in the war when she and her mother lived near San Diego in a house so small it had only three rooms, including the kitchen, and they had covered one wall with National Geographic maps of the Pacific and tried to guess where her father might be; and of the years afterward spent on military bases in Spain and Turkey, when she had lived in books as the only way to overcome the loneliness; the time at a boarding school in Virginia where the girls spent hours dressing up and talking about their real and imagined boyfriends while she had tried to study her Greek; and then her own discovery of boys at college. Without details, he understood she had fallen in love with a rat and thought her life was ruined until, soon after graduation, she had met Heber Johnson.

"He did not take advantage of me. You must understand. I worked for him for three years before I could get up the courage to tell him I loved him. He was devastated when I said it. I remember he sat down where he was and put his head in his hand. He was balding even then, and it was a sad sight. He did not know how to handle it for weeks.

"He knew his position and what would be thought. But, you see, I knew already that he loved me. He had loved me since the day I had started to work filing correspondence and answering letters. He had hidden it for so long, and I had taken such advantage—such mean advantage of the knowledge. Girls can be

Vincent McCaffrey

so cruel. But in the end, I knew it would be fine, and it was."

Henry recalled now that he had never been uncomfortable the few times she had spoken of Heber. It only seemed a natural part of things as they were.

That day they had driven as far as the Saint-Gaudens museum near Cornish, New Hampshire, and spent the afternoon there walking the grounds and talking amidst the sculpture—talking again about Italy, and Siena, where she had briefly lived and sculpture was a part of everyday life, and about movies, which she did not approve of on the whole.

She had said, "We stand in awe of marble sculpture because it is the truest of arts. A painter can work over his mistake. A writer may change a word used wrongly. But the sculptor cannot take back the blow."

Henry could not find such words to change her opinion of film or convince her that movies were not the beginning of the end of civilization. This was an irony given Heber's success with turning the work of so many of his clients into celluloid.

For the most of that day they were quite alone because it had begun to rain in a slow drizzle, and the enthusiasm of their words fell off into the whisper of dampening leaves, with only stone faces to concur.

That night at an inn run by a woman who was probably the same age as Morgan and had given them a critical eye, they struggled to keep the noisy bed from announcing their every move and had slept little.

Beside the road the next morning, a moist and warm autumn morning with the river overlaid with a bed of mist and creamy light, they had stopped again. They had lain in leaves where a young maple had shed early on a mown field and had made love until a crowd of milk cows had come to investigate. She had raised her bare foot in the air, leg stiff, set against

the sky as if sculpted. He stood then, admired its shape and complimented the artist before he kissed her foot, as the cows watched in placid curiosity.

Chapter Six

Leona Levine did not look like her brother. This left Henry wordless, caught at his father's back door looking down on her as she stood on the top step.

"Henry! I just knew you were over here!"

She stepped up and spread her arms. He had no place else to go when she hugged him. He was thinking about the softness of her body compared to Morgan's as she looked past him into the house.

Behind him were the books from Helen Mawson's room, stacked neatly on a strip of boards laid end to end along the hall, all the way to the front door. This was not the first time his father had indulged him when he needed space for particularly large loads, but it might be the last if he were unable to get them moved soon. The stacks were now organized well-enough for him to begin his research.

"And you brought your books with you," she said.

She had perhaps grown more buxom, but then she had always been that. Her hair was too black to be in its natural state, though she had not gained more weight than she had always carried well. Leona had been never skinny, even as a little girl. Henry had always thought of her as voluptuous. She still filled a pair of jeans with nothing to spare, only now she wore them low, as was the fashion, and at least six inches below the torn bottom of her sweatshirt, so that he could appreciate a small rose tattoo just where the curve of her hip turned away from the empty belt loops. She had driven him crazy during

his high-school years until he had broken his arm.

He finally managed to say hello and ask how she was.

She said, "I'm fine. I just finished with the last of Mom's stuff. Took us all week. I thought I'd take a break and see if you were around. What'cha doin'?'"

Henry shrugged at the obvious. "Sorting books."

She said, "Who'd ever guess? Is your dad here?"

"No. At work…"

She pouted theatrically. "I have something for him."

Leona waited, obviously wanting him to ask.

"What?"

Both of her well-drawn eyebrows arched. "I probably shouldn't tell you. But I will. That is, if you won't tell him I told you."

Henry knew she had every intention of telling him in the first place. His father's van was obviously missing from the open garage.

He tried to cut through the artificial suspense, repeating the word. "What?"

Leona pulled a folded piece of paper from an impossible space in her back pocket.

"A note. Something your dad wrote to my mom—I'd guess about 1979 or '80.…" Henry's mind froze on the last words. He knew immediately what was coming. He supposed he had always known but had ignored the fact of it. She spoke without taking a breath, her voice slowly rising. "We found it when we were cleaning out her room. In her personal copy of the Torah, no less. You know what it says?" Her eyes had widened further beneath the arched eyebrows.

He raised his own voice. "No. I don't want to know. It's private. It was between them."

Leona tilted her head to the side. She was not going to stop. "They were lovers. Did you know that?"

This was something which had crossed his mind only fleetingly through the years, only to be folded away and purposely forgotten. He resigned himself now to the realization. "I guess. I don't think I wanted to know."

She stepped back and jumped now on the top step, just enough for the wood to squeal beneath her as her bosom rose and fell. He motioned her into the kitchen with the fear of neighbors hearing anything more.

She was squealing now. "Isn't that exciting?"

He could not think of any words to describe it. "I don't think we—"

"Isn't that amazing!" She held her hands out in the air, the note clutched in between two fingers like a specimen. "Your father and my mother were lovers. It's like in a movie. You and me making out in your old Volkswagen minibus while our parents were sleeping together back at home…. Wow!"

Wow? Was that the word to use?

He said, "Yeah… More like a made-for-television movie, don't you think?"

Leona shook her head back at him, both eyebrows still up.

"I really shouldn't stay. He might come back, and I wouldn't know what to say to him right now."

Henry said, "Don't say anything. It would mortify him."

"Mortified! You should read his note. It's positively steamy." Her dark eyes gleamed with her found knowledge.

Henry said, "He always wrote well. He was always too shy to speak. He's a very private man. He wouldn't want anyone to know."

She turned her head slowly back and forth, as if Henry did not really understand.

"I was so surprised when I saw him at the funeral. I thought he was just being a good neighbor. Now I understand! Do you

realize! If they had gotten married, you would have been my stepbrother. We could have been committing incest!"

Henry was not so sure.

"I don't think it counts the same. But in any case, maybe it would be better if you go. I don't want him to get upset right now. I've dumped all these books in his hall."

Her face fell, as well as her voice. It was back to Lauren Bacall again.

"Maybe you're right.... But it would be nice to see you again. Are you going to be around?"

He answered, "I live in town. That's where I work." And then thought his voice sounded a bit defensive.

She frowned. "In your apartment? You work in your apartment? Where you live?"

He had to be patient. "Yes."

The bit of skin between her eyes folded even more. "Well, that's why you look a little pale. You ought to get out more. Working at home can be bad for you"—she stepped back and looked at him head to foot—"you know, cardiovascularwise. Do you get any exercise?"

Henry admitted his fault, gladly. "Not much." Almost pleased that the subject of the conversation had switched from his father to himself. But why did women keep giving him instructions for his health? He felt fine!

Leona straightened her back in a full display of womanly posture. "I exercise every morning. I go to a health club. Why don't you join a health club? You could even join mine. I could get you a discount."

He said, "I'm busy."

She turned her head slowly in disapproval again. "You need a push. You need someone to get you out of bed in the morning."

He said, "I get out. That's how I find my books."

She pushed. "I mean, to work out. Make your heart pump a little faster."

Henry did not think that was a serious problem. He was admiring the rose on her hip again as she turned toward the door and then stopped.

Over her shoulder he could see a policeman looking through the glass of the door. Leona, turning to Henry, looked down the hall to the front door instead. The doorbell there rang.

Henry reached and opened the back door.

As Henry spoke, he noticed that there was no pleasantness in the officer's facial expression.

Henry spoke first. "What can I help you with, Officer?"

The policeman's face appeared frozen in place. Only the lips moved.

"Are you Henry Sullivan?"

They were there for him. Something had happened.

He said, "Yes, sir. What's wrong? Did something happen to my father?"

Leona backed away toward the kitchen table as the policeman stepped inside.

"No, sir. I don't think so." Then he looked at Leona. "Could you let the officer in the front door, please?"

Leona popped forward as if wanting the reason to move.

Henry said again, "What's wrong?" His mind raced over possibilities. Was it his sister? "Is Shelagh okay?" His heart was sinking, as if a hole were opening in his middle. He had meant to call her. He had been meaning to speak with her for weeks.

The officer stepped closer to him.

"Who is Shelagh, sir?"

"My sister, Shelagh."

The officer shook his head once. "I don't know, sir. I don't think she's involved."

The policeman who had been at the front door came into the light of the kitchen behind Leona. Leona, looking bewildered, sat down in a chair at the kitchen table for lack of anything else to do.

The second officer frowned at him. "Henry Sullivan? You're the same Henry Sullivan from Brookline High class of 1980, right? You were in my brother's class. Jim Norris…"

"He was our catcher." Henry said it without enthusiasm. He knew the policeman was not there because of his brother's baseball career.

Leona began to speak, before realizing the same thing.

"I knew Jim. He moved to New…York." Her voice trailed.

The second officer nodded at him. "My name is Sergeant Norris. I'm afraid I'm here on behalf of the Boston Police. I regret to be the one to tell you this, but someone has died."

Henry's mind scanned other possibilities. One did not fade. "Who?"

The officer's eyes skated over to where Leona sat in the chair, and then back to him.

"Do you know someone named Morgan Johnson?"

When Henry closed his eyes, he saw her face. She was scolding him, just before he left that morning.

He had stood at the open elevator door.

She was saying, "I have to be going on to California, but you could use the beach house. It's empty now. The pipes and electricity are still turned on there for the real-estate people. And the weather is perfect. You could be swimming right through October if the weather holds."

He had kissed her again. Not a passionate kiss, but not only as a friend. He had told her, "I've got to work. I can't be working on a suntan right now."

She had brushed his cheek with the back of her hand. "You need some color."

Vincent McCaffrey

He smiled with resignation. "I'm fine. I'll e-mail you about the appraisal. Call me soon if you can."

She kept her fingers to his cheek. She wore a green silk scarf—as if to hide some lines of age in her neck. He had never noticed them. The scarf echoed the flecks of green in her eyes.

She said, "Thank you for coming—for being here—for staying. I needed you to be here."

He had repeated, "Make sure to call me." He should have said something more.

The elevator door had closed then. She had been smiling, and as he remembered this, he could see a halo of morning sun from a far window caught in the honey-colored edges of her hair.

After he left, he thought repeatedly of the haloed icons of stained glass at St. Mary's Catholic Church in Brookline, and it troubled him with the thought that he might be drifting back toward the religious fervor he had felt once as a boy. He had rejected the Church after his mother's death, as his father had already done long before, and often worried that some unnoticed ratoon might linger in his subconscious, waiting to sprout unexpectedly in a moment of weakness. He fought back at this now with the thought of Morgan's smile. The icons had never smiled from their high places above the marbled walls at St. Mary's. But the image of her face and of the halo came back to him again and again.

Chapter Seven

Albert leaned in on the bar, resting on his elbows. His inquiry had not been soft, and that seemed right to Henry. He needed someone on his side now who could think clearly.

Albert said, "Did you pick up anything from the way they asked their questions?"

Henry sat back and held the edge of the bar with his fingers. He was tired, his back sore from sitting in hard office chairs and on wooden benches. He had slept badly after he was driven home.

"They have no idea. They thought I did it. That was clear. They were pretty rude. They seemed to know a lot more than they were saying, but their questions were way off base."

Albert said, "How did the killer get in?"

Henry hunched his shoulders. "She must have let them in. It must have been someone she knew. The building is locked and has buzzers. The elevator is keyed. The elevator door wouldn't open unless she opened the door to the apartment."

Was it possible to coldly analyze this? Like a chess move after the fact—like a queen taken by a rook? She was dead. There was no rematch.

Albert seemed to realize that he might be pressing a little too hard. He turned to the mirror across the bar.

His voice dropped. "There would be a stairwell and a fire door for emergencies."

Henry addressed the near-empty ale glass in front of him. "The cops seemed to be interested in that elevator."

Albert asked, "Was anything stolen? That'll be important. There has to be a reason for it. They wouldn't just kill her."

Henry nodded. "There could have been. Maybe that's why the cops searched my apartment."

Her life had been stolen, of course. A theft that could not be returned. So odd. The unexpected. Henry released his grip on the bar, half expecting to fall backward. In a dream he would fall, or float. Instead, the weight of his body sagged forward on the stool.

Albert persisted—the voice of reality. "Do you know if they kept your old friend Leona for long?"

Henry answered, "No. I called her when I got home. She seemed rather excited about getting questioned by the police. I swear, she's as old as I am—she has two kids for Christ's sake—and she acts like she did when we were in high school."

Albert grunted and said, "That could be a good thing."

Henry sagged further. "I don't need that right now."

He did, in fact. He wanted to hold something more than the edge of a bar and a glass of ale.

Albert's tone of voice became apologetic. "Maybe not. But you need your mind off Morgan Johnson. Why don't you read the letters we took out of that little room? Alice wants to read them, you know, and the sooner you finish with them, the sooner she'll stop bothering me about them. She loves to read other people's mail."

That was something. They had already given him a small measure of relief just in their own mystery.

Henry said, "I did. I read a bunch of them last night. I couldn't sleep."

Albert sat back again and looked at Henry as if he had not completed a sentence. "And? Any clue what happened to Miss Mawson?"

Henry tried to change gears. He knew Albert was just trying to divert him, but he had not had time to think about the
letters.

"Maybe. I don't know. They're not all dated. I don't know
half of what they're talking about—mostly about people doing
this or that." Henry swallowed the dregs in his glass. "She seems
to be the friendliest person you can imagine. She made friends
wherever she went. She made friends with a couple in Cornwall, the Wrights, just walking along the road. Next thing, she's
staying at their cottage for a nephew's baptism. A real thatched
cottage! Then she's there again for a visit in the summer, and
they have all the eligible bachelors coming from miles around,
to meet her and she dances with every one. Twelve farm boys in
a row, and her feet are so sore from being stepped on she can't
walk the next day. She must have been a good-looking girl to
get them all to dance.... She sounds like a real sweetheart."

Albert mused, "I wonder how she could afford it. That little
house in Dedham didn't show a lot of money."

Henry had thought a little about that himself. "That's the
thing. I don't think she had a lot of money. Perhaps a small
inheritance from her mother. She was just something of an ad-
venturer. She wanted to write travel articles for the *Herald*. But
they evidently rejected her. I think she wanted to write books
about her journeys, but there is nothing listed on the internet,
so I don't think she ever managed that. I found one reference,
but not to her—to someone I think is her father. He was part
owner of a coal company in Dedham. I was thinking that might
be why she went to Cornwall. There's coal there. She might
have had a contact there through her father. But she spends
most of her time with that couple in that cottage. The wife
was a beekeeper. She liked to hunt mushrooms and had taken
Helen with her on several rainy-morning expeditions. She's the

one who wrote many of the letters. Mr. Wright, the husband, was a retired military gentleman. 'The General,' she calls him. Always properly dressed. Mustache waxed. Erect. Helen is shocked the first time she sees him in work clothes mucking out the enclosure for his prize bull. Real characters. The Wrights had no children of their own and seem to have adopted her. But beyond that, she walked. She had written to one person about the best kind of walking shoes to buy, and they thanked her profusely. It was her intention, I believe, to walk all over England and visit the homes of the great English writers. She had definitely visited Thomas Hardy. There's a reference to visiting him more than once. She called him the 'sad man,' and I suspect she might have even stayed in his house. Mr. Wright did not approve. You can't help wondering what kind of person she must have been."

Albert finished his ale. "But nothing about her getting sick?"

Henry almost grunted at the thought and stopped himself. He did not need any more bad habits. "Nothing. She must have been healthy—even robust for all the walking."

Albert hit the edge of the bar with the flat of his hand. "She might have died of pneumonia from mucking about in all that English weather."

Henry shrugged. "There is nothing in the letters to say. But I was thinking.... Last night, as I was reading, it occurred to me that she might have been murdered."

Now that he said it out loud, he realized how stupid that thought was.

Albert grunted definitively. "That's just your frame of mind," he said and stuck his finger up for Tim to notice.

Tim had lodged himself at the end of the bar, where he had a radio on low and listened to talk shows when business

was slow. He grabbed a fresh glass, pulled another ale, and set it down in front of Albert, but looked at Henry.

"You can tell a lot about people by the books they read.... You said that once, and a guy on the radio just said the same thing."

Henry was always amazed that Tim could listen to two conversations at once and not lose track of either. Henry had already wondered about the books. "She was quite the reader. She seemed to read anything popular at the time. Even Fra Elbertus—old Elbert Hubbard..."

Tim shook his head. "I meant your friend Morgan Johnson.... You looked at her books, right?"

Henry was confused. "Yeah. But they were mostly her husband's books."

Tim pressed forward at his side of the bar. "You said she was practically running the business for the last few years. Maybe you could just say they were all her books, too."

Tim's eyes stopped at Albert, who had leaned forward himself and was staring at Tim purposefully almost nose to nose.

Albert said, "It might be a good idea for Henry to get his mind off all that now. He can't do anything about it."

Tim retreated down Henry's end of the bar, speaking as he went. "You know how many unsolved murders there were in Boston last year? Dozens... It can't hurt if the cops got a few hints."

Albert grunted loudly before making his voice heard anywhere in the room. "People get hurt every day by sticking their noses where they don't belong."

Tim retreated further and answered again. "Henry was the last person to see her, except for one...."

Albert rose from his stool and headed for the door. "I've got better things to do. I could be taking a nap."

Henry stayed where he was, studying the light reflections on his glass. He could see a miniature of Albert there, his body made even wider by the curvature.

Henry said, "See you later."

Albert gave an extra grunt and left.

Henry had another ale and then decided to leave when the after-work crowd started showing up. The subway was already crowded, forcing him to stand too close to a woman who bathed in perfume. By the time he reached the Charles Street station, the sidewalks were thick with people going in both directions but most of them turning toward their apartments up the Hill. He was almost home before he saw the police car, a wide Crown Victoria without markings, parked up over the stone curb onto the brick of the sidewalk to let other cars pass and directly in front of Mrs. Prowder's door. He stooped by the side of the car and interrupted the officer sitting alone in the passenger seat, who was writing something on a pad.

Henry had already seen enough of the cops. He was tired and suddenly raw. "Is there anything I can help you with?"

The cop looked up stone-faced and then went back to writing as he answered. "You can get in the back so we can take a ride."

"Where to?"

"Jack will tell you."

The detective who had questioned him the day before was named John O'Connor. Henry got in. "Where is Jack?"

The cop folded his notepad.

"He's upstairs taking your place apart."

Henry protested, "They already did that."

"Well, they're doing it again."

It had taken Henry a couple of hours the previous night to put things back in order. He did not want to see what it looked like this time. He waited quietly. It was not long.

Detective John O'Connor came out the door at the top of the steps with another man, probably also a plainclothes policeman. When he spotted Henry in the backseat, he smiled and spoke to the other fellow.

"Meet us over there. I have the key."

Henry noticed that the other man was carrying a satchel, but O'Connor's hands were empty as he got in the front seat.

O'Connor slapped his hand on the window frame.

"Just in time. If we make this quick, we might all get home for dinner."

Henry asked, "Where are we going?"

"To the Johnson apartment. I want you to take a look with me."

Henry felt a chill.

O'Connor turned on the warning lights and parted the traffic at the bottom at Charles Street fairly quickly with a couple of short blasts of his siren. They were in front of Morgan's building in minutes, and then sat in the car and waited for the other fellow to show up.

O'Connor turned to Henry. "What's with all of those letters on your bed?"

Henry answered, "Something I'm investigating."

O'Connor's eyes went to the cop beside him. "What would that be?"

"What happened to Helen Mawson."

O'Connor's voice lost any shading of interest. "So who is Helen Mawson, and what happened to her?"

Henry noted the flat tone of the detective's voice. He tried to counter it by answering as dryly as he could.

"We don't know what happened to her yet. She used to own all those books stacked in my apartment that you guys made a mess of. She disappeared"—as he said the words, he realized

how they must have sounded to a cop's ears; he added a detail—
"around 1915. I'm going to be selling her books, and there were
all these letters in the same room where we found the books." He
took a breath. "The room had been sealed up and untouched for
over eighty years. The books all belonged to the young woman
who received those letters. Her name was Helen—"

O'Connor's face began to sag.

"I got it—right…that's very interesting."

Both men got out of the car and led the way into Morgan's
building, with the third fellow carrying the satchel just behind
Henry.

The elevator was barely big enough for four men. The
apartment appeared exactly the same. The quiet seemed amplified. The air was stale again.

"If you open the windows on that side you get a breeze,"
Henry said, not wanting to leave his position by the front door.

O'Connor turned to him.

"How was it when you left the other day? Were the windows open?"

"Yes…They were closed when I arrived the first day—but
she had just arrived, too. She opened those windows first and
said that was where the breeze came from."

O'Connor pointed. "Right…Dave. Check for prints on the
windows over there, will you?"

The fellow who had followed Henry went to the windows.
Henry watched as he opened his case and pulled something
from a plastic tube. Meanwhile, the uniformed policeman had
gone around the apartment and turned on most of the lights.
The late-afternoon sun entered directly into the living room,
making the electric lights seem weak.

O'Connor faced him. "I want you to do me a favor. I want
you to look around. Don't touch anything. Just look. Tell me

what you see. Notice things. Anything. Just say it out loud. If I want to hear more about something, I'll tell you. But just start talking. Walk around."

Henry was hesitant at first. He had no idea what was needed. He understood the detective wanted him to notice something that might be different, that might have importance, but it was difficult to guess what that might be, and most things seemed too unremarkable to mention.

He went around the living room first. Nothing there had changed that he could see. Even a dish towel she had used to dry their breakfast dishes was still where she had tossed it over the back of the couch the moment he had said he had to be going. He mentioned that.

In the kitchen, the breakfast dishes were still stacked neatly in the dish holder by the sink. In the breakfast nook, the Patrick Leigh Fermor book was where he had left it on the counter. He had taken it with him from the bedroom and set it aside when she had put the eggs and toast down on the table. He had spent little time at all in the dining room, one of the few rooms without bookshelves, and had not even remembered the pictures on the wall there. In her bedroom, the bed was made. He thought he remembered her making it while he was in the shower. In the bathroom, the towel he had used was in the hamper. He had left it—he thought—in the bedroom, where he dressed.

In the small room she had called her study, next to the bedroom, he saw no difference, but something she had said came back unbidden—a phrase, "It's just a room of my own," when he asked her what she used it for. He had said she should take Virginia Woolf's direction. She should use it to write a book, just as he had told her long before. She had said, "I have nothing I want to say, and certainly nothing worth reading."

This answer had bothered him at the time and afterward.

He did not mention any of that to the detective.

In her husband's bedroom, everything looked exactly the same. He even found the pencil he had forgotten there as he finished looking at the books, still lying on the floor. Bending for the pencil, he noticed a opening. Three books were missing from one shelf. He noticed this very suddenly. They were part of the Boswell journals. When he mentioned that, the detective smiled and said they were beneath the bed, where he had put them earlier. It was obviously some kind of test. Henry objected. It was impossible for him to remember where all of the books had been.

"Maybe. But I just wanted to see if you'd notice.... And I wanted you to know I wanted you to notice."

Henry proceeded from there to the library. Finally, in that room, some things seemed out of place. He was not sure what exactly had changed, but it seemed more than incidental, and he said this to the detective.

O'Connor answered his observation.

"This is where she was found.... I'm afraid a lot of things were moved in the first rush."

Henry sat in the leather chair by the door and looked around for a moment. He felt suddenly drained.

He said, "Who found her?" He had never asked.

The detective looked at him from where he stood across the expanse of the table. "The cleaning service."

"Where...?"

"There. Just by where you're sitting. On the floor. A Mexican woman. All the cleaning services are using them now. She thought Mrs. Johnson had fallen. She even lifted her up before she realized. Then she ran down the stairwell screaming in Spanish all the way to the street."

Morgan had been strangled in that space beside him, only two days before. And two nights ago they had made love.

"Jesus." The word escaped from his lips.

The detective stopped his nervous circling, and his voice lowered.

"Can you keep going?"

Henry straightened his back and blinked against tears.

"Yeah…"

He stood and walked around the conference table before the question struck him out loud.

"But why was she in here?"

He was still not quite in control of his voice.

O'Connor asked, "Why?"

Henry took a breath for the oxygen to speak. "Just a thought. This is Heber's room. All these are the books of his clients. They kept them here because they used to have small meetings at the apartment with the authors and the lawyers and all that. All the other books in the apartment are their personal books, the ones they read for themselves."

The detective nodded, but he did not answer. He was thin-lipped and flat-cheeked and expressionless except for his eyes, which Henry had begun to watch for some clue of what the man wanted.

Leaving the library, Henry walked again around the living room. The sun was gone now to a red haze above the purple of Cambridge and the liquid black of the Charles River. A faint brush of color danced in the wake of a few small boats.

It was Albert's contention that Morgan had been killed by a thief. And according to the best television cop shows, and the received wisdom of the ages, thieves only kill when they've made a mistake. They are there for the money, or jewels, or whatever, and then run. Morgan was probably in the wrong place at the wrong time. She had been away for months and come home unexpectedly. She was there alone after Henry left.

Albert wondered if the police had checked out the building superintendent. In his own experience as a trashman, the building superintendents were occasionally up to no good. They were often trying to sell goods they had acquired from unsuspecting tenants.

Henry answered Albert's theory skeptically. "Fred. Fred doesn't look very dangerous, He's about sixty-five. He hardly moves."

Albert closed his eyes as if Henry were hopeless and said, "He probably knows everything there is to know."

Henry mentioned Albert's theory of building superintendents to Detective O'Connor as they let themselves out of the building. The super had always been there when Henry had unloaded books in the past. Where was he now?

The detective responded without enthusiasm to the suggestion. It seemed the superintendent's job was only part-time now, in these days of tighter budgets.

"Let me do the wondering. You won't be doing yourself a favor by dwelling on any of it," he was told.

Henry walked home alone. Marlborough Street was relatively quiet now, despite rush hour. There was an audible whisper to the yellowing leaves even above the hiss of traffic, at least until he reached the phalanxes of cars coming off Beacon Street.

The lamps which illuminated the Public Garden above the shadowed walkers on their way home appeared old enough to have been burning in another age. High heels barked at the walkways. Was it really simpler then? Would an adventuress like Helen Mawson have taken any note of a poor, hopeless used-book dealer?

What had happened to Henry had greatly disturbed Albert. That he knew. His friend had been wordless for most of the first account Henry had given him. Then Albert's frequent contention in darker moments, that human beings were all just sav-

ages in designer clothes, was brought out. He noted again that the purpose of civilization was just to distract the savages with trinkets while the innocent made their escape.

"We live our lives with the tacit understanding that our time is borrowed, allotted, and proscribed," Albert had said. "Something terrible like this is everyday in other places. You wouldn't want to live in Sarajevo or Mambasa. Or Detroit, for that matter. Jesus! My uncle used to live in Detroit."

If that were true now, it might have been true in 1915, Henry thought. And, of course, there was a war in Europe at the time. Murdering was sanctioned and made official.

Henry had objected, recalling his own favorite argument. "I've told you—Hobbes was wrong. We don't need kings. A life that's 'solitary, poor, nasty, brutish and short' is only for those who don't read Shakespeare, or care to. We don't need the State. We need Yeats. We need more books and more time to read them."

But then, Morgan had read her Shakespeare, and still she had been caught by a brute.

Albert had sighed loudly with some kind of deeper resignation.

"That's all too complicated. When I go home, there is always one person who's happy to see me. My little Jimmy. He never yells at me. He never complains. He never asks for anything—well, not much, anyway. He doesn't need a new pair of shoes every three months. He never tells me what I should have done. Dogs are more civilized than human beings. What you need, Henry, is a dog."

Walking home alone through the busy shadows of Beacon Street, Henry wished he had a dog.

Chapter Eight

Mrs. Prowder's door was open when he came in, and Mary's head popped forward much as her mother's often had—the red of Mary's hair almost garish.

"Hello…hello. Mr. Sullivan. I was wondering what the police were here for?"

She stood then by the door, and he stopped at the foot of the stairway.

He said, "Just 'Henry' is fine," trying to gather his thoughts for an answer. "They wanted to speak to me.…" He told her as briefly as he could what had happened. Feeling the weight of the lack of sleep, he leaned in the doorway and was instantly aware that old Mrs. Prowder would have objected and advised him to stand up straight.

Mary did not seem surprised by his story. Perhaps she had already heard and only wanted reassurance on the matter.

She said, "I'm sorry. We've both lost someone, then.… I was about to leave, and I was hoping you'd be home. I wanted to give you something." She turned and grabbed a small book from the fireplace mantle facing the door. "You know she mostly read the papers and chatted with her friends. But she did like to read a book now and then, even if she didn't read those 'digest' things. Mostly, she got what she wanted from the library. But this was in the china cabinet. I thought you'd like it. It has someone else's name inside. I figured some tenant left it behind."

Henry knew the book at once. It was a small green leather

and India paper edition of the poems of Tennyson published by Nelson in England and popular in the United States as a Christmas gift at the time of World War One. Not worth a great deal, but with reasonably large type—good to handle and read.

He said, "It's very nice. Have you read Tennyson?"

Mary forced a polite smile. "No. I never read poetry. It's all so very precious and fancy or mean and nasty. Not my thing."

Her distaste for poetry was audible in the tone of her words alone.

He shook his head. "You'd like this, I think. Your mother liked it. She read it through more than once."

This widened her eyes. Henry thought she might be too weary from her own efforts to show more. She held the small book in the palm of her hand with her fingers bent back like it was an exhibit of some kind. "Really? I didn't know she ever read poetry."

Henry put his hands in his pockets, trying to avoid the desire to lean again as he offered more of an explanation.

"She told me once she hated her name. She wouldn't tell me what it was for a long time. Always said she was known as just Mrs. Prowder and happy with that. But then I noticed a letter once from her bank and saw her name on it."

Mary interrupted.

"Enid. She hated it. Enid and Elwin Prowder. She thought it sounded silly."

Henry smiled and took the book in his own hand.

"So I gave her this. *The Idylls of the King*. There is a wonderful part of it called 'Enid.' She even learned a portion of it and recited it back to me a few times. 'Turn, Fortune, turn thy wheel with smile or frown; with that wild wheel we go not up or down; Our hoard is little, but our hearts are great....'"

95

Mary's eyes showed her confusion. "Not really. My mother? Out loud? She was always so practical."

Henry said, "Not always," without being sure of exactly why poetry was not practical.

"Oh. I didn't know…." Her fingers closed on the book in his hand. "I'll keep it, then."

She clasped the small book against her breast and smiled back at him, now obviously pleased. Henry was afraid he might be seeing tears form in her eyes soon, and he quickly said good night.

Eliot opened his door on the landing; the music behind him thickened the mix of yellow light and the smell of cooked food. He was thin to the point of being bony, a wispy beard covering sunken cheeks. Mrs. Prowder had often worried over Eliot's sallow complexion. He was a vegetarian, it seemed, an unnatural religion in Mrs. Prowder's cosmos. His greatest offense, however, was his overweight and overactive girlfriend, Jessica, who often spent the night and seldom slept.

Jessica smiled at Henry from the couch. The light of the apartment gave Eliot's complexion the look of cheese.

Without greeting, Eliot said, "What were the cops about?"

Henry fleetingly considered being cute and saying they were looking for drugs. "Just me. Someone died. They're just checking people out."

Eliot's chin went up, and he studied Henry with half-closed eyes over the beard-stubbled expanse of his cheeks. "Something wrong?"

Henry said, "She was murdered."

This brought the chin back down with a gape. "Mrs. Prowder?"

Eliot's cheeks now rose in a swell below his eyes, and his mouth widened in a grimace.

Henry took a breath against smiling at the facial contortions. "No. Someone else. Don't worry about it."

Behind Eliot, Jessica's smile had vanished in a wide expression of surprise.

She said, "Where?"

Henry needed another breath for that. His own body weight seemed to be doubling as he stood in place.

"A few blocks away. Don't worry about it. I've got to get some sleep. I'm pretty beat. Good night."

Henry made the last flight of stairs one step at a time. There was less to clean up this time from the police visit, and he gathered Helen Mawson's letters to one side and lay down on his bed, intending to close his eyes for only a moment before straightening up. Instead he fell into a pool of sleep, the sinking weight of his own body more than he could hold up. He resurfaced only fitfully to occasional street noise or the odd figment of a fading dream.

"Helen."

In the dark of early morning he awoke thinking of a young woman he did not know. Her hair was long, tied to one side with a turn of blue knitting yarn so that it fell over one shoulder. What was the color of her hair? Brown? Not plain brown. Something more. Her eyes were blue, almost purple, and too big for her face, which made her look very young. Cornflower blue came to mind, though Henry was certain he had never seen a blue cornflower in his life. She was small-boned but large-breasted, and this could not be hidden by the dress she wore, which was ankle-length and began at her throat with a white frill of lace. The dress was a deep blue brilliantine, embroidered with the same white lace. She had been looking directly at him, and he was sure he had spoken her name when he awoke.

The room was not completely dark, and the gaslight from

the streetlamps below cast a film through the flaws in the glass of the window onto his ceiling. The blank plaster directly above, with its small cracks, was now the background to the image of the girl he had seen in his dream.

He knew the dress had been mentioned and complimented in one of the letters. The size of her eyes, and their color, too, had been mentioned in another. He was not certain how his mind had formed the whole of the image, but it fascinated him and brought him wide awake as the image faded beneath the onslaught of his thoughts.

He remembered again the Jack Finney book, and the idea of time travel. Surely, his small room in this house was part of another time. The letters had transported him so easily, so clearly.

When he turned on the light by his bed, the piles of her books stacked in front of the already-full bookcase along the wall presented themselves as an eccentric cityscape in miniature. The matching maroon cloth volumes of Richard Harding Davis and the green of F. Hopkinson Smith towered at one end over shorter stacks of Anthony Hope and Rudyard Kipling. Another tall stack of Winston Churchill rested beside the shorter one of Edward Noyes Westcott. Thick Mary Johnson novels butted against thin ones by Alice Hegan Rice.

His father had brought the books over as some kind of gesture, and Henry was thankful for that much. Henry would have to thank the old man again for it, even if he'd done it just to get them out of his own way.

Henry wanted to catalogue as much as he could before packing them up, and he had not yet found a space that would be best for that.

Still in his underwear, he sat at his desk and pressed the button on his computer before he had actually made the decision to start working.

Closest to him were the five stacks of leather-bound Roy-crofter books, and he pulled off the top volume of these and set it by the keyboard. It was part of a pamphlet series of "Little Journeys" which had been gathered later into a single volume. This one began with Wordsworth. The leather of the cover was brushed to a soft texture and not stiffened with cardboard but left limp, as was the style of many of the other volumes. The paper was the color of dark cream.

All of it was intended to evoke an ancient time, an idealized moment of harmonious human endeavor which had never actually existed outside the minds of those first children of the industrial age who were already despairing of steel and smoke. Henry had read a little of melancholy Ruskin and mad Morris—or was it the other way around?—the Arts and Crafts movement, The Pre-Raphaelite Brotherhood of Dante Gabriel Rossetti and his lovelorn and religiously unhappy sister, Christina. The artifice of it all had always struck Henry as false. A made-up past imposed on a rejected present, and like Christina and her unrequited lovers, barren.

Well, he thought, to be fair, there was the chair. Albert had taken it from the little house in Dedham and was keeping it for Henry in his basement. William Morris had in fact made a good and comfortable reading chair.

Turning the title page of the Wordsworth to read the copy-right, he noticed a penciled comment in a neat script. "Not the way it looks at all. Probably did not go inside as I did. Sounds like one of the Stoddard descriptions." The handwriting was Helen Mawson's.

Henry turned a clump of rough-cut pages and read a paragraph of chatty background biography on Wordsworth. He had never been fond of Elbert Hubbard—his pedantic style or his overplayful use of difficult words—and it did not

take long to make Henry quit and close the book now.

Setting it back, he noticed the edge of something protruding from another of the volumes lower in the stack. He opened this to a batch of thin pamphlets and folded sheets. They were all printed in the same style as the books and bore the Roycrofter heading here or there. On stiffer stock was a printed listing of room rates at the Roycroft Inn at East Aurora, New York. One listing was circled with the date October 12 penciled beside it. The cost was three dollars per night. Breakfast was fifty cents. Dinner was a dollar fifty and included a choice of beef or lamb. The rate card included the date 1912 at the bottom.

Elbert Hubbard had run an amazing operation for many years. In the best American business tradition, he had adopted the aesthetic socialism of the Rossettis' Pre-Raphaelite Brotherhood, and the Arts and Crafts medievalism of William Morris, from England, to the American business credo and the middle-class prosperity of upstate New York—and made it pay. Pamphlets and books were hand-produced by the thousands on letter presses in the shops he had built in the small hamlet of East Aurora, near Buffalo. His short-story pamphlet, *A Message to Garcia*, had sold in the millions after the Spanish-American War.

In a colony-like settlement, Hubbard had encouraged volunteers to come and learn handicraft trades ranging from printing and papermaking to the hand illumination of books, and including the carpentry necessary for building the shops where all the work was done. This for a middle-class market which was only just finding the time to spare for luxuries and home decoration. Hubbard's reinvented aesthetic was a match for his marketing genius.

So it appeared that Helen might have gone to East Aurora. This seemed like a loose end of information to Henry, and he had no idea what use it might be.

Fully awake now, he pulled a container of orange juice from the small refrigerator in the kitchenette and sat back at his desk to begin cataloguing. He set the more difficult Roycrofter books aside and picked from a stack of books by fabulist John Kendrick Bangs to begin. He had finished those, and four by Mary Austin, as the glass of his window had turned gray. Nearly thirty titles were entered by the time his stomach pulled him away to the Paramount Cafe to find some food and coffee.

Henry had long before learned the benefit of concentrating his efforts only on books in the best condition. Almost every entry began with the words "Fine, in dust jacket." He knew it was easier to note a later printing than to fuss over the details of wear and damage. The reason his books sold easily whenever he posted a new catalogue was that his customers could be sure of what they were going to get, and, of course, because they got to determine the price. Not having to think beyond a certain point about accurately pricing each individual volume saved at least half his time. When his customers got the listing, they checked off the ones they wanted and inserted the price they could afford. The highest bidder got the book—in most cases. He had begun to limit the purchases of some of his customers to keep them from totally dominating his list. The more people who had some success in their bids, the more bids he got. Because most books sold at about a third of their potential retail price, he made less than the dealer who bought the book, but he risked less and turned his stock over quickly.

Nearly all of his customers were registered dealers, and most of those dealers ran used-book shops. He had even required the few private individuals who ordered from him to register as dealers in their home states because he did not want to play games with taxes. All his sales were made to resellers and thus were not liable to tax. And each sale was automatically

registered by the computer when he printed out the shipping form. Henry's accountant, Ralph, had designed the program for a computer-software outfit in Cambridge before they went bankrupt in the shakeout of the late nineties, and now Henry used it for all his book sales so that at the end of the year he could file his income forms in a matter of minutes. This one innovation alone, Henry considered a coup, and it pleased him no end when he spoke with Albert, who seemed always to be fighting over some tax problem or other.

But Henry's great secret was in the shipping. He reused corrugated boxes from the liquor store which he cut apart and turned inside out so only the plain brown interior could be seen. Henry could cut a box and refold it in less than a minute. The cost of a brand-new shipping box would be more than a dollar. Thus, Henry calculated he was paying himself over sixty dollars an hour to cut up boxes. He usually packed the orders in the evenings, when he was tired and could listen to the ball game or an old phonograph record as he worked. Most days he received six or seven orders, usually for more than one book per order. Because he was selling the books wholesale, they averaged around twenty dollars apiece. More than twelve years into it, and he was making about seven hundred dollars a week, after expenses.

And he liked his work.

He showered and dressed and put one small Roycrofter volume in his pocket to go. Then, as an afterthought he grabbed his notebook as well.

Passing Mrs. Prowder's closed door now with only a glance, he found himself wondering about what her Elwin would have done under these circumstances. What advice would Mrs. Prowder have passed on to him? There must be a method to such things. Henry was not about to play Sherlock Holmes

or Perry Mason, but something in what he knew might be of importance.

Henry paused at the top of the granite steps and surveyed the empty street.

What could be sufficient motive for someone to kill Morgan? Dear Morgan. What could she have ever done to deserve such a thing? How would the killer benefit from such an act? There could be no possible gain for the loss of her.

At the Paramount Cafe he sat at the counter as he always did and drank his first coffee quickly then finished his eggs before opening his notebook, using the empty space beyond his entries for upcoming library sales and auctions.

Henry was fairly certain O'Connor had finished with him. It was in the tone of the detective's voice the evening before. Henry now followed Tim's lead and made a list of those people who might be suspects in Morgan's murder. Because he knew so little of the life she had been living recently, the list was short.

There was the obvious possibility that it was a thief—a "bungled burglary" as Erle Stanley Gardner might say. He got the sense now that O'Connor was looking in that direction. There was Fred, the building superintendent, even if Henry's suggestion to O'Connor had not been accepted gratefully. And then there was Morgan's son, Arthur, the former drug addict, who lived in California. Henry put Arthur down as the prime suspect. If he had any special dislike for his fellow man, any prejudice he was consciously aware of, it was for druggies who habitually avoided reality by choice. Then there was the voice Henry had heard behind Morgan as she spoke to him late that night from the Cape. It was a man who had spoken, and Henry noted it simply as "the voice." Henry included the weasel from the auction house who had come in to look at the furniture. There had to be a Realtor, too—but then what would a Realtor benefit if

his client was murdered? There was the cleaning service. That would be the motive of theft again. He had never asked if the Mexican woman was alone. He put that down, believing he had covered every possibility he could think of.

Then he added the name Ranulf Richter.

This was an odd thing. He certainly did not remember exactly how the books had been placed on the shelves in the inner-office library. But when he had first come in with O'Connor, he had noticed something, along with the rest of the displacement of chairs and the ashtray at the center of the table. He was fairly certain that those things had been at one end of the table before. And he had noticed a narrow space beside the three books of Ranulf Richter.

Morgan knew Richter better than most of her husband's other clients. There had been some passing mention, but Henry could not remember what. There had been an envelope—when?—the second day—only a few days ago, when she was still very much alive—after he had begun to look at the books. It was in the kitchen on the side with other opened mail when she had given him a glass of water. It was addressed to Morgan, at her Cape house. The return address had been a distinctive signature, simply "Richter" in the corner of the envelope. And then, when he had been appraising the books in the library, he had noticed that even though most of the books were inscribed to Heber Johnson, the inscription in at least one of Richter's books had been "To Morgan."

No. As he thought about it again, that book had not been with the others in the library. He had noticed that book in the small study by Morgan's bedroom.

Henry was fairly certain there was something more between Morgan and Richter, and he could say little else. He had not mentioned this yet to O'Connor, because he wondered if it was

fair to cause that kind of trouble for someone he did not know, and because, at the moment, he felt some small jealousy. He worried that it was Ranulf's voice he had heard behind Morgan when she called from the Cape.

It only made sense that Morgan, in her loneliness, and having not seen Henry for over six years, might have found someone else to comfort her. And it was none of Henry's business, except that now Morgan was dead and someone was responsible.

He began another page in the notebook now. A page for motive. Only one thing occurred to him, however, through his third cup of coffee, and it sat on the page in a single word.

He wished he had a cigarette. He had quit at the wrong time. Too much was going on. He had always been able to think better when he smoked.

Still, only one motive came to mind, to fill an entire page of empty lines: money.

Chapter Nine

Ranulf Richter had the appearance of a savage even in church. In warmer weather, he famously wore a navy blue blazer jacket with no shirt and shorts and sneakers with no socks—to all occasions. It was reported in frequent newspaper coverage that he disdained underwear. Though his body seemed to grow a sufficient mat of red-black hair to keep him warm in cool weather, he did alter his wardrobe in winter to a Harris tweed to replace the blazer and a pair of corduroy pants, but still avoided shirts. He was known to strip naked at parties and swim in whatever pool of water was near at hand. Though he was a professed vegetarian, he had established a reputation for biting photographers, reporters, and presumed girlfriends. Additionally, he was known to have some expertise in martial arts. This was probably useful in his frequent encounters with the enraged boyfriends of his artfully bitten women.

Ranulf, as he was known to all, was the son of a Norwegian diplomat who had served the interests of his government during World War Two, and, as a quisling, been unable to return home. The boy had been raised on the Upper East Side of Manhattan, sent to private schools, and for an uncertain period of time attended the Sorbonne in Paris.

Ranulf had entered the literary world through the New York party scene, on a public challenge, after he had loudly criticized the work of one established New York writer after another, and then written a novel in one month, while not missing a single evening of social events. That book, now justly forgot-

ten by everyone but book collectors of first novels, concerned a famous-for-being-famous social buffoon who could find neither true love nor a good cup of coffee. The critics hailed it as social satire. Some critics said it was infused with Swiftian genius. It sold poorly, so the authorities felt their judgment confirmed.

Ranulf had found his real success with his second book, in a character named Bent. The orphaned son of a Nazi father and a Jewish whore, Bent is an out-of-work circus clown and proto-performance artist whose creative expression is displayed in flamboyant dress and impromptu street theatrics. Bent dwells in the twilight of a New York perpetually shadowed by sky-scrapers, supporting himself by taking from the rich, giving to the poor, and sleeping in whatever bed is offered. Bent steals a Steinway grand piano from the penthouse apartment of a fa-mous concert pianist who had been saved as a boy from the Ho-locaust but would now only play for exorbitant fees, and leaves it in the plaza fountain at Lincoln Center. Bent robs a bank vault of a hundred million dollars in venture-capital bonds only days before a new computer company goes public with a soft-ware device stolen from a young inventor and then drops the paper from a World War I–era biwing over the length of Wall Street during lunch hour. When the mob uses its knowledge of a key player's sexual proclivities, Bent stops play by throwing pink basketballs onto the court at Madison Square Garden dur-ing a fixed New York Knicks game. Bent releases helium-filled party balloons decorated with dollar signs from beneath man-hole covers during mayoral campaign speeches.

Ranulf's conceit is that the poor are always demanding more of his character, and the rich give away their money too readily, to assuage their sins. Bent is never prosecuted for his crimes, no matter how outrageous, simply because his intentions are good. But it is his hyperbolic comment on errant political programs

which caused a new concern among the intelligentsia who cannot bear to have their motives questioned. Over time, Bent falls from favor. Bent's final punishment arrives when he goes virtually unnoticed in a city which has adopted his theatrics into its daily life. His stunts pale beside the reality that has become the norm. On the last page he is drinking a fifty-cent cup of bitter coffee in a greasy spoon in Chelsea, unrecognized, and accepts a card from a Salvation Army worker for a warm place to sleep that night.

This book had sold over a million copies in hardcover and been made into a disastrous movie which badly miscast the character of Bent. The enigmatic thief of the original was now the flesh and blood of a well-known Hollywood actor who lacked even the flare of Bent's author—and all mystery lost in the detail of how the pranks are executed.

Two other less successful satires followed, a Hollywood roman à clef rejoicing in the disdain of film makers toward the written word, and then a gynecologic examination of the feminist art world. Ranulf's fifth novel—a sequel to the second— wherein his hero, Bent, is finally eaten alive by a roving band of starving musicians unable to find an audience willing to pay for the privilege of sitting still for a silent concert of performers refusing to play their instruments—all in protest against world hunger—had failed with critics as well as the public. The resulting stacks of remainders had created a lack of interest in Ranulf's sixth book, for which Heber Johnson was unable to find the right publisher.

This was the man who sat in the second pew on the right, visibly positioned by the center aisle, black silk scarf tied around his neck, thankfully wearing pants and not shorts, as the minister addressed them.

In front of Ranulf were family members Henry had never

seen before, and from their advanced ages, and appearance, he assumed they were Heber's blood relatives. Morgan's son, Arthur, sat in the first row on the left, where Henry could barely see him behind the taller heads. The middle pews on both sides were only half-full, but the faces were familiar. These were the three-dimensional-but-aged representations of dozens of photographs he had seen many times on the dust jackets of countless books.

Henry sat in the last row on the left, just in from the center, alone except for a tall, thin man with an abundance of uncut blond hair. Directly across the center aisle from Henry, Detective O'Connor sat with another man who also looked very much like a cop.

The interior of the church was a single long chamber darkened by the shadowed aisles at the sides behind the arching piers and by the blackened wood of the pews and the soiled stone and stained glass left uncleaned. The echo of voices and the shuffle of feet mimicked the sound of an empty stage, as if a hollow space lay just beneath the marble floor. The small electric lights suspended candle-like in tarnished metal fixtures from above were harsh to look at in the amber of the room.

This was not Morgan's church. It had undoubtedly been chosen for the memorial service because it was close by, and probably selected by her son. Henry knew that Morgan was Episcopalian only because her parents had been. This minister had never known her. The minister's words were spoken with the flat resonance and mechanical modulation appropriate to a classroom reading of chosen boilerplate, obviously taken from a book filled with such words for all occasions. The service had been requested by her brother, Aaron, and Henry assumed it might be a smaller occasion meant only for family and friends. The faces of so many authors Heber Johnson had

once represented made it clear again to Henry the influence of Morgan in that relationship.

Her brother, Aaron, spoke next. He had little to say that was not commonly felt. However, he told a small story from their childhood which appeared to evoke more of his own sense of life than Morgan's. She had camped in the little woods behind their home all night to catalog the nocturnal sounds for a classroom project. Aaron, younger and jealous of his sister's adventure, had gone out repeatedly to check on her, causing an argument about his scaring the night creatures into silence. In her final project she had included Aaron's whispers as one of the catalogued sounds.

After Aaron, several childhood friends spoke, recalling another time and the society of military families trying with difficulty to live normal, everyday lives in extraordinary places marked by incidents of little consequence except to themselves.

Then George Duggan arose, walking with clear reluctance to the pulpit, seeming unsure of his purpose. Henry knew that Heber had been Duggan's agent since his very first book sale in 1982. Duggan's large figure folded over the lectern for support as he spoke, as if the weight of the words were difficult to bear. He was not yet sixty years old, but he had grown a full beard since the photo on his last book jacket, and the gray of it, rather than the short cut of the receding hair on his head, made him appear older.

He took a breath, squinted at the assembled, perhaps trying to find a face in the crowd, and then spoke.

"I was remembering just now my first meeting with Morgan. I had already met Heber. He had asked me to come by to sign something. We were sitting in that windowless room in their apartment that he used as his office—some of you know the

110

one—with the books surrounding us on all four walls. Heber was keen on having me understand the rights I was giving up. It involved a great deal of money, more than I thought I would ever see in a lifetime. I was giddy. I was simply ecstatic about finally selling something to a major publisher. The real amount of the money had not dawned on me."

Duggan hesitated with the memory, his eyes turned downward. "As we were sitting down, Morgan asked how long I had been writing, and I told them that I had started when I was nine and never stopped, like a spigot with the handle busted, and that I really never wanted to do anything else but write stories till the day I died. Heber then began to go over each point of the contract, when abruptly Morgan interrupted. I did not know at the time that she was more than Heber's wife. But at that moment, her face was the face of a mother."

Duggan paused again, the silence suddenly magnified. He cleared his throat. "She said, 'Wait! You must think about this. I can see that you still don't understand. This is not just a matter of serial rights, paperback rights, or movie rights. It's your human rights that are being sold here. Your life will never be the same again. You will be indentured. You will be a slave, owned only in part by George Duggan. Your talent, which makes you feel so powerful and free, will be your chain. You will be writing for the rest of your life just to support a plantation that includes editors and proofreaders, printers and binders, publicists and lawyers, distributors and booksellers—and your agent. And your agent's wife. That spigot you were telling us about will now become a word factory. And if ever you falter or fail, the collapse will be a kind of unforgiving bankruptcy you will never be able to overcome, and it will leave you with debts you'll never be able to repay. Publishing is cruel. Success is a burden. This book will sell. We both think it will sell like crazy, but you will

Vincent McCaffrey

have to write another. And another… We believe in you. We think you can carry that weight. Even though most authors are one-book wonders, we think you are the one to make it beyond. That's why so much money is involved. But is that what you want? You can keep your job as a waiter and write your stories for the rest of your life without any other cause than your own love of it—find a quiet happiness and never fail yourself. You can continue to publish in the little magazines. I can give you the name of a small press that would gladly publish your book.… Are you aware that your soul is involved in this? You will never be happy simply being a waiter again. You think the choice is obvious, but it's not. In a year you will be famous. I predict you will be very famous. And that will mean you are a freak. A sideshow. Your life will be as publicly owned as any corporation."

Duggan took a breath, more than a pause, as if to gather the memory before his eyes and be sure he had told enough.

"I was dumbfounded, of course. I looked at Heber. He smiled and looked at Morgan and shook his head. I said to them, 'Is it my soul I'm selling? Is this man the devil?' But she didn't laugh. She said, 'No, but Faust is within you, like a common virus we all live with. It will rise when you are weak—if you don't take care. I'm only warning you of the danger.'"

Duggan took another and longer breath. In the short silence, there was no shuffling of feet against the marble floor.

"'Faust is within you.' The reverend just said the Lord was within us and it made me think of Morgan's warning to me. It is so difficult to imagine the Lord is within us. We are such small and frail and smelly creatures. Where would the Lord find a place to hide? But Faust! That I easily saw. That I understood.… She was right, of course, this woman who was never famous but known so well by all of us. I have made many mistakes in my life since, but I have always been aware of the Faust

112

within me. That caution has, I hope, kept me from the devil, and I thank Morgan for it."

The words sounded so much like something Morgan might say, Henry could distinctly hear her voice in them. Still, it was an odd memorial to give. But it was not as odd as what came next.

Ranulf Richter had taken Duggan's place, passing the taller man with a touch of his hand on Duggan's shoulder.

Richter sniffed and wiped his sleeve on the stubble of beard that covered his face. His black scarf barely covered the chest hair that peeked from beneath it.

"Morgan was a dear and lovely friend to most of us. And we do not need a service like this to remind us of what we have lost.... I do not need to be reminded. I will think of it each morning when I awake. With due respect to Aaron, she was my sister. We had long since passed that threshold of friendship when the beat of her heart made my blood rush.... And she was killed. She was murdered. She was strangled. The dear, warm life in her was wasted. And my own life has been damaged beyond all repair. Someone is a killer. Someone is a murderer.... Someone here, with us, now.... My God—" He choked, cleared his throat and raised his voice. "My God is a vengeful God, and I am his servant."

The heavy silence of the great room broke into whispers only after Ranulf Richter sat down again. Henry turned to the eyes of Detective O'Connor, who was looking in Henry's direction but beyond him. Henry turned around. The tall, thin blond fellow who had been at the other end of the pew had disappeared.

Chapter Ten

The phone rang persistently, stopped, and rang again. Henry put down his book. It would not be Albert. Albert went to bed early, as did Henry's father. It might be Leona. He was not in the mood to be talking to Leona. Then again it could be Shelagh. Henry picked up the receiver and leaned back in his chair.

The accent of the caller's voice was English, with the quick and precise enunciation achieved by the repetition of Latin verbs in a public school.

"Mr. Sullivan. My name is Peter Johnson. I have been told that you did an appraisal of my father's books."

Henry liked his old phone. It was a fifty-year-old black rotary which still had better sound than any new one he had tried. He liked the weight of the receiver in his hand and the mechanical whir of the dial. One thing he did not like was that strangers could call him, people selling almost anything, and enter his small universe without permission. If he had a new phone, he could see the incoming number and make the choice to answer it. But then, he had often admitted to himself that he liked the unexpected quality of lifting a receiver and not knowing what he was going to get. It was a small element of the unexpected in a day mostly given to routine. Besides, he did like the sound of the old phone better.

"Mr. Sullivan?"

Then again, he did not like to be suddenly presented with problems he could not take the proper time to consider. His mind

was going over everything he had ever known about Morgan Johnson. He had never heard of anyone named Peter.

"Mr. Sullivan?"

Henry said, "Who are you?"

There was a sound of an exasperated breath. "My name is Peter Johnson. Heber Johnson was my father."

Henry spoke deliberately. "I don't think so. Morgan had only one child."

There came the sound of another breath. Audible impatience. "That's correct. Morgan's son is Arthur. My mother's name was Ismay. My mother was married to Heber Johnson after the war—when he was at Oxford. They divorced afterward. It is a matter of public record. A matter of bad judgment in the heat of the moment, you might say. My mother has been dead since 1964. It seems very few people ever knew my father had been previously married."

Henry said, "I guess not," allowing his doubts to linger in the tone of his voice.

The man said, "No. Well, we had little contact. He supported my mother, of course, and then paid for my schooling. None of that matters now. My concern is more immediate. With Morgan dead, I believe I am heir to half of my father's property. The value of that property is of real concern to me. I am not a rich man. I never had the good fortune that blessed my father. I cannot ignore the value of his estate, nor continue as I was."

Henry's thoughts ran together. His first response was not his first thought.

"Morgan has only been dead for a few days. How did you hear about it?"

The caller offered a theatrical sigh. "Sadly, the papers. My wife and I have actually been in Boston for weeks. But I don't believe that is a matter for your concern. In any case, I heard.

I was shocked, of course. And greatly saddened. And my purpose now is to establish some sense of the value of the estate as soon as possible. There are other lives involved. I have my own responsibilities. What I badly need from you is your estimate of the value of the books."

Henry wanted to slow all of this down so that he might comprehend it. "How did you get my number?"

The answer was quick and prepared. "I got your name from Arthur. I got your number from a friend in the book business."

Henry thought to ask, "So you have been to the apartment?"

There was a definite hesitation.

"Yes. More than once. I have been to Boston several times over the years. I came to the apartment to see Heber more than once." The voice hesitated again. "Why are you asking these questions? This is really only a family matter, and not your concern."

Henry answered quickly. It was his turn to set the bidding.

"Morgan was a good friend. I am aware of her hopes concerning the estate. What happens to it matters to me."

The voice altered—just enough for Henry to imagine an adjustment of direction.

"I'm sure you mean well, but as I say, it is not really your concern. I can have no interest in broadcasting private family matters to a total stranger."

Henry said, "But you want my help?"

There was another hesitation.

"You were paid to do a job."

Indeed, he had never asked for his usual payment, but that was known only to one other person, who was now beyond telling.

"One dollar. My customary fee to friends, just to make it legal."

Another pause. The impatience in the voice was clear. "And that estimate of value is now part of the estate. I am asking, as a legitimately interested party, that you give me a copy of your work."

Henry managed his voice. "That's fine. I'll give you a copy on receipt of a letter from Morgan's attorney, Mr. Downes, requesting I comply."

Another pause. The tone changed yet again.

"I need some help in this, Mr. Sullivan. I can't be fighting everyone. I have no money for lawyers.... Can I speak with you privately?"

"I suppose."

"Can we meet for breakfast tomorrow?"

"Where?"

"This is not my town, Mr. Sullivan. You choose the place."

"Charley's Sandwich Shop, on Columbus."

"A cab will know where that is?"

"If he doesn't, get out and find another cab."

After deciding on a time, Peter Johnson hung up, and Henry called the number on the card given him by Detective O'Connor. He got an answering machine and attempted to summarize the conversation while it remained fresh in his mind. There was still little reason to mention Ranulf Richter, but Henry added a new name to his short list.

He turned out his light and lay down on the bed, but there was no drift of sleep for him now, only the near dark punctuated by the sound of Eliot's girlfriend, Jessica, or an occasional car in low gear working its way around the street looking for an open parking space.

The pale film of street light on the ceiling offered few images until hours had passed, and then it was not Morgan or Helen Mawson but his mother he remembered—as she was

before she became sick—as she used to sit in a straight-backed chair on the small front porch on warm mornings and read her books.

When he was a child, he supposed this was part of her work—to read each day before she left for her job at Boston Edison. When she was finished with a book she would leave it on the seat of her favorite chair in the front parlor, and after she left, Henry would pick it up and put it at the end of the row of books that slowly grew in length on the shelves there. Four hundred and thirty-six. He kept count of them from the time he was old enough to do so and told her the number very officially each time she finished one, and his father would say that he was going to grow up to work in a polling place at election time someday. The last count had been four hundred and thirty-six. Excepting a few favorites. Those she placed separately in the china cabinet in the dining room.

A funny thing. Mrs. Prowder had done the same with the Tennyson. But Mrs. Prowder's cabinet had been otherwise full of imitation Blue Delft. There was never any china in his mother's cabinet. They never owned much more china than was dirty in the sink or drying in the rack. It was because she did not arrive home again until after eight that they only had elaborate dinners on the weekends. She never liked to cook in any case, even though she did it so well. His father's cooking had only been adequate for spaghetti, hot dogs, hamburgers, and odd sandwiches made from cold meats and smelly cheeses. His mother enjoyed going out to eat when they could, and they always did that at least once a week, usually on Saturday. Sunday she would cook. With the Betty Crocker cookbook open on the slick tablecloth, she would make something in a quantity which would give them leftovers for at least one more meal.

Her favorite things to make were roasts; lamb and beef and

pork, which she pestered with a spoon, stooping to look in the old oven with one of his father's battered flashlights in one hand and the spoon in the other—the oven light had never worked in Henry's memory. Why had his father never fixed it? The smell of the roasting meat filled the whole house right up to his room, where, because it was Sunday, he would be doing his homework at the last minute, until the odor drove him mad and he came down to watch and talk.

Shelagh was always there first. His sister had helped skin the vegetables, shaved them until they were bright with their own color, onions always and potatoes and carrots, but sometimes turnips, which Henry hated. What he loved the most was the gravy and the thick, fresh rye bread his father picked up at the Jewish bakery.

His mother liked to talk when she cooked—"chatting," she called it. She liked to tell stories about her childhood, about her first job as a sales clerk at Woolworth's, when she was assigned to care for the dead goldfish, or going to the circus when it came to the old Boston Garden, and her first date with his father, and other such things which had no importance except to them.

But he did not want to be remembering all of that just now. Not now. Henry turned on the light in his room; his remembrance vanished within the limits of hard edges.

The line of reference books behind his desk stopped his eyes before they settled on the stack of paper he had left on top—the Helen Mawson letters. He had already read most of them. They would not be a diversion now. The allusions to small events in the lives of strangers would only be more frustrating than his own thoughts.

He pulled a book from the stack of odd titles on the table. It was a lucky choice. *Three Men in a Boat* had the sort of reserved

humor in a distant and foreign world he needed. He read until well after dawn.

Peter Johnson was the man who had been closest to Henry in the pew at the church. He was taller than Henry, and thinner. His blond hair was freshly cut short at the sides and long enough at the top to comb roughly over with a swipe of the hand. He wore small oval glasses. He had large ears, which was at least one characteristic Henry thought he had noticed in a picture of a younger Heber Johnson.

Peter Johnson's tie was loosened because the morning had already turned warm, and his tweed jacket and corduroy pants looked uncomfortable in the close and steamy heat of Charley's. He had taken a seat by the window and already ordered a small stainless-steel pot of tea which gleamed in the sun beside his cup. He seemed to unfold from his chair to stand as Henry entered, saying, "Good morning." The hand he offered was cold.

Henry said, "Good morning," with as cool a tone as he could muster and sat down across the table, with the sun at his back. He asked, "Have you eaten yet?"

Peter Johnson grimaced a smile. "Not as yet. I am fairly famished, though."

They ordered, and Johnson cleared his throat several times on the way to saying something. Henry waited until the man settled on a beginning.

"It's good you came…. I'm a little at a loss, you see. I don't—I'm not sure how to proceed."

The dissembling seemed rehearsed.

Henry said, "What can I help you with?"

Peter Johnson raised his shoulders in a performed shrug.

"The books, certainly. I'm not sure of anything else…. You see, we are in the same profession. I am a book dealer as well. I had a small shop in Hay-on-Wye, in Wales."

This was a place Henry had often heard of, an ancient Welsh farm town converted almost entirely to the book trade, right up to the ancient castle at the center.

"I suppose I shouldn't be surprised. Given your father's interest—"

Johnson interrupted purposefully.

"And my mother. She was a writer, you see. Travel books, mostly. She wrote under the name Ismay Whyte. Her maiden name."

Henry knew the name. He did not think she had ever been popular in the United States.

Henry asked, "What kind of books do you sell?"

Peter Johnson tilted his head, arched a brow, took a breath, and poured more tea in a half-filled cup, all in an ordered sequence.

"Well, travel, naturally—mostly. It's a nice specialty. I've done well with it until lately. Business was pretty bad in Hay-on-Wye after September Eleventh. It's really a tourist town. The number of buses from London are way off and half-filled. It hasn't really recovered. And…it's not your problem, of course, but to add a human interest that matters to me at least, my wife has been ill."

Henry was wary of this. He made his "I'm sorry" as flat in tone as possible. He had always been a sucker for sad stories.

Peter Johnson sighed.

"Getting the right care for Vivienne has put the finances into a bad spin.… I want you to understand—I would not be playing the part of the greedy relative otherwise—I am broke.…"

The choking off of the man's voice made the point that this confession was made out of necessity.

Henry said, "I thought medicine was socialized in England."

Peter Johnson rolled his eyes more than necessary. "Indeed. Very. If your back is hurt or you need a tooth pulled, it's just fine. Cancer is another story. We've come to the States three times already for treatments. She's here now. We've been staying at a very nice rooming house in Brookline. Six treatments this time, over three weeks or so. She has already been in remission twice, but it came back in the spring."

Their food arrived. Henry wondered if he had put too much of an edge in his statement on the phone to Detective O'Connor. This man's dramatics might only be the simple defensive measures of someone unused to speaking of private matters with a complete stranger. Henry said, "Had you gotten help from your father with this?"

Johnson nodded. "Yes. A good bit. Up until last year. He paid all the bills that I couldn't cover.... But I wanted to show some independence, you see. I didn't want to be a total leech. I covered too much myself, and as business fell, we got behind.... This spring, I asked again. Heber was already in pretty bad shape by then himself. He gave me another ten thousand. But it was gone in no time. The doctor—Dr. Shore, wonderful man—he's been holding up his billings, trying to help us out. But it will all have to be paid for, eventually. Most of it involves other specialists and the damned medicines."

Henry felt contrite. He could imagine himself in this. "Did you ask Morgan for help?"

Peter tried to smile. "Yes. Of course. I'd do anything. And she was brilliant. She was doing what she could. She'd put the beach house up for sale and promised us whatever it brought. She had us out there during the summer, you know. But I suppose the market is off.... Nevertheless, Viv was very grateful. I was very grateful."

The picture Henry had imagined was now changed.

He said, "But with Morgan's death, that's all on hold."

Peter nodded again, just enough to answer. "Quite… And Arthur is not interested in my problems. I suppose he has problems of his own. I could be sympathetic, except my situation doesn't allow for it."

Henry looked at the man's eyes. They were small for his face, framed by the lines of squinting below the heavy fold of his brow, and set back above the wide columns of his cheeks. Those eyes looked back at him as if in a plea to say no more.

Henry said, "What was your plan?"

Peter took a slow breath. "I was hoping to get an estimate of the value of the estate, together with a legal statement of my position as an heir, so that I might get a loan. I have spoken to a bank officer, and they are willing to help. It's just a matter of paperwork…and Arthur. Arthur is not cooperating."

"Why?"

Peter shrugged. "Taxes, of course. If the estate is valued to the high side, the taxes will be levied accordingly. This was already a problem. Morgan said she didn't really want to sell the condominium just now, because of the market—because she would get less. Arthur told her to wait, I think. The taxes are going to be so great, he wanted to hold out for a higher price to help cover some of it. In the meantime, the medical bills are mounting…. Now this has happened. Everything's at a stop. I'm afraid the situation can only get worse. I know Arthur wants his rightful share of the estate. Heber's will left everything to Morgan, and I believe she never made a will herself. However, she did speak to me about selling the beach house to raise the funds to help. And, of course, Arthur is her only son. It all becomes a matter for probate."

Henry shook his head. "It doesn't sound like Morgan. She was always more efficient."

Peter answered, "Arthur doesn't want a contest. So here we are. Back to the books. Arthur is willing to sell the books to avoid any added difficulty."

Morgan never exactly planned things. She just always seemed to know what was next. Henry let the thought slip away. He said, "She must have been torn."

Peter said, "I suppose she hadn't the chance to think very much about it, after Heber's death."

Henry nodded. She probably just wanted to escape it all. She had gone to the safe haven of her house on the Cape for just that reason.

Henry said, "You'd better eat."

Peter half smiled at his cold eggs. "Yes."

Peter Johnson's idea of "famished" was not at all what Henry would have experienced. The man ate small bits off his plate and looked uncomfortable doing it.

Henry ate most of his breakfast before going on.

"Well, I'll give you the appraisal, certainly. We don't need Morgan's lawyer's approval for that. Mr. Downes seems like a reasonable fellow to me. But the value is pretty high. I think those ten thousand or so books are worth more than half a million dollars."

Peter Johnson took a breath. His eyes did not rise from his plate as he searched for something small with his fork. After a moment, he said, "I thought as much. With all those signed copies."

Henry had to speak to the facts.

"But"—he paused to gather the thought—"this is my problem. Morgan told me she wanted to donate them. It was for Heber. She wanted something to represent his work. She was hoping that Boston University would set up a small memorial library of late-twentieth-century popular literature along with his papers and things."

Johnson shook his head and exhaled as if in exasperation.

"I know. She explained it all to me. It was a very fine idea. But there are other considerations now. Arthur says he wants to wait until the market rises before selling the condominium or the beach house. He is fine with selling the books. If I can sell the books now, he has told me I can keep that money pending the sale of the rest of the estate, so long as we avoid causing any trouble. It might be enough. It could get us through."

Henry answered, "I see."

He said the words, but he did not see, really. Why had Morgan told him she was selling the condominium this year and needed his appraisal of the books as soon as possible? It was clear that Arthur was in control of the estate now, and whatever Morgan's intentions, her own son would determine the final outcome. But Henry was not sure he should be telling Peter Johnson something that might only cause more worry.

Chapter Eleven

"It's either money or sex, or both. The only other reason people kill is because the commanding officer said so. If you are going to keep putting your nose into this, it's me who's going to present the unpleasant facts to you."

Albert was annoyed.

Henry moved his queen forward into the path of Albert's bishop, and in line with his king.

"Check... I think it's money."

Albert could not resist the bait.

"Slam, bam, thank you, ma'am. I think it's sex."

He took Henry's queen with his bishop. Henry took the bishop with his knight, leaving Albert's king exposed now to Henry's bishop. Henry's knight guarded the escape.

Henry put on his worst imitation English accent. "Thank you, good sir. You are as easy as one of Boswell's threepenny whores."

Albert hung his head in mock shame. "That was sloppy. I can't believe I missed that. We have to play that one over. I was distracted with all this crap about Peter Johnson and Arthur Johnson.... The only Johnson I want to hear about is old Sam. That's the life I'd want—to live like Samuel Johnson. I'd like to live in the Inner Temple and spend my time in coffeehouses discussing the events of the day, going off to Drury Lane in the evenings to see a little Sheridan or Garrick—I've told you I went there with Alice when we were in London on our honeymoon."

Henry said, "More than once."

Albert did not catch the hint. "No, we went only once. A cold and dismal day. Almost everything from Sam Johnson's time is gone. But you can stand at the spot and imagine—if you put your hands over your ears to kill the Fleet Street noise and close your eyes—"

Henry interrupted, "I can do that just as well right here in Boston."

Henry began to put the chess pieces back in their places. The sound of a voice from Tim's radio buzzed with anger from the end of the bar, too low to comprehend.

The tone of Albert's voice changed, the annoyance increasing. "But it's not the same here. You can't imagine that particular past time the same way. The smells are different. I would think a fellow with a nose as sensitive as yours would be more discriminating."

Henry moved a pawn forward. He said, "Did you know what Boswell did the day after he met Samuel Johnson?"

Albert answered, "No," his tone dismissive, as he moved his own pawn into place.

Henry pushed his morsel of knowledge forward with another pawn. "He sallied down the street and picked up a 'fresh, agreeable young girl' named Alice Gibbs."

Albert's eyes opened with greater attention. "Alice…? How do you know that was her name?"

Henry smiled smugly. "He tells us. It's in his journal. No pretense. If he has the urge, he goes out and finds himself a whore."

Albert blew air in a silent whistle and moved his own pawn to confront Henry's.

"I'm glad my Alice didn't know that the cold day I dragged her out of that cozy bed-and-breakfast down by Victoria Station

and walked her all the way up the Strand in her brand-new shoes just so we could stand in front of an ugly soot gray office building in the rain. She had blisters the size of acorns."

"See? You could have done that right here in Boston."

Albert frowned with irritation at such an idea and sat back to consider the board. Henry thought his friend was still pouting about his loss of the previous game, and it came out with Albert's next words.

"I had my eye on that knight. I knew he was there the whole time. Then I lost sight of him."

Henry smiled. It would annoy Albert if he smiled. "It's the sex that distracted you. That's because you're basically just a decent guy, Albert. You have your priorities in the right order. But I think it's the money that attracts most people. They do things just for the money. Even sex."

Albert's chair shifted backward with his weight, the wood groaning painfully. He looked over the empty tables around them before speaking.

"What if someone saw you there...? I'm not trying to put any guilt in your head, understand, but things happen for a reason. Okay? Let's take that approach. What if someone did? And what if he somehow knew she had just spent the night with you? He might be jealous, right? And he'd be afraid he was going to lose his meal ticket, right? If she married you, there goes the inheritance. So, there are two reasons in one."

This had never occurred to Henry. His thoughts overran. "How would he know?"

"She might have told him."

"But why?"

"To get him to leave her alone.... You said you heard another voice on the phone. What if it was the killer's voice? What if he was there when she made the appointment to see you?

What if he already knew she had been involved with you, back years ago…?"

Henry needed time to consider this. He could not dismiss it.

"What if…we get another ale?"

Henry rose from the table and leaned on the bar, with two fingers out as Tim looked his way.

Tim answered as if he had been part of the conversation all along. "There are other reasons to consider. It might have been a matter of love."

Albert grunted and spoke up from the table.

"Tim, you are the most God-awful romantic son of a gun I have ever run into. Why aren't you married with six or seven brats clinging to your heels?"

A silence passed between Tim and Albert so great even the ice machine quieted. Other conversations in the room seemed to pause. Traffic on the street appeared to stop. Tim's love life was a raw subject.

Henry took the opportunity to be glib. "What do you mean, love? That's the same as saying it was sex."

Tim finished pulling the two ales and set them onto the bar. "You don't think you can love without sex?"

But Henry's heart was not in the fun. He considered Tim's rebuke seriously as he took the ales to the table. Possibly in another time. Not now. Not today. Christina Rossetti could have loved without sex. In Helen Mawson's time, perhaps. And, of course, there was the love of a parent and a child.

"I will not so easily fall in love, Father," Helen had written "You have set too difficult an example for that." Henry had read all of the letters now—some several times over, in search of even an inflection of meaning in her words. The letters from her visits to East Aurora were the best. She had found in that small utopian community the intellectual excitement she sought.

Albert was giving Henry the raised eyebrow, waiting for his response.

Henry raised his glass to Tim. "Sure... For love."

That was the element on the great periodic table of life which carried the greatest weight of all. Not gold or lead. If someone had killed Morgan out of some twisted love, wouldn't it be somehow apparent? But then love was the invisible element.

In one letter Helen Mawson had said, "I wish to love, free from chains and shadow. I am sure Mr. Hubbard has found this with his Alice."

Henry sat back in his chair and put an eye on Albert that made both his friend's eyebrows rise in question. Henry teased. "You know, Elbert Hubbard's wife was named Alice, too."

Albert was not impressed.

"Really. So was Ralph Kramden's."

Albert moved a knight's pawn forward. Henry ignored the comment and studied the board as he spoke.

Henry developed his distraction. "It was Hubbard's second marriage. She was from somewhere around Boston, you know. And it was a friend of Alice's who introduced Helen Mawson to the Hubbard community. A neighbor, I think. She was on her way to East Aurora, and Helen tagged along."

He moved his queen's pawn reflexively to gain a center defense.

Albert shook his head at Henry's effort. "Let's move the game along. My Alice wants me home by dinnertime." He brought his queen's bishop out to the space vacated by his own pawn.

But Henry's mind wandered between the pieces in front of him. Helen had been fascinated by another guest at the Roycroft Inn during that first visit. She had mentioned him only twice then. But he was there the second time she visited, as well. Henry imagined her father might have worried over his

daughter's welfare and wished she had not returned to East Aurora. Mentioning a young man could have been an additional worry. Henry moved his king's bishop out behind his queen's pawn. Always counter an aggressive move with aggression. Albert sat back.

Helen had written of a Marcus, a newspaperman who had come from Chicago to interview Hubbard. Marcus had been put off at first by the same glibness in Hubbard's words that bothered Henry.

"Very rude," she had called the fellow, "with the dark eyes of an anarchist." Yet she had taken the trouble to call the fellow by name.

"Marcus Evers stood up at his table, halfway across the room in what they call the Phalanstery, and addressed Mr. Hubbard whilst he was still eating his soup.

"'Do you think they eat so well as this, below the factories in Buffalo or Erie, Mr. Hubbard?' Mr. Hubbard made use of his napkin for the moment to catch his thoughts. The room fell quite silent as heavy utensils were momentarily set aside.

"'I think not, Mr. Evers. Nor perhaps in East London or much of Russia or China, for that matter. Our own starvation will not feed them, in any case. But our effort to set an example for improvement might make a difference to a few, and those thus enlightened may then spread that knowledge to others.'

"Mr. Evers did not seat himself with this response. We had all heard him arguing his points before the meal when Mr. Hubbard arrived. This newspaperman pursued his purpose now without embarrassment.

"'Your hopes for the future, Mr. Hubbard, feed no child tonight. Your pretty copper utensils carry no food to thin lips, or ever shall. Your illuminated pages cannot alight the minds of those in the dark of ignorance for want of good schools.'

Vincent McCaffrey

"Mr. Hubbard stood up at his table in a deliberate fashion now to face his accuser.

"'Your uncivil words, Mr. Evers, offer no hope of true discourse. But let me briefly defend myself in the public place you have chosen for your attack. Our aim here is not to feed the stomachs of the hungry, but to carry the burden of knowledge that it may one day reach their minds. We are not farmers. We are printers and painters, coppersmiths, carpenters, and leatherworkers. By example we show the potential for beauty in everyday things.'

"Mr. Evers attempted to interrupt at that point, but Mr. Hubbard continued. 'You are a guest in my home. Have some manners, or you will be shown the door.... In a world of countless millions, there is no hope possible to any one man except to set an example—unless you advocate the use of force.... You declaim my commercialism. Yet it is through that very salesmanship that we are able to continue our efforts. You assail my motives, yet my life has been quite open to scrutiny for some years. You have come to do a story on your own preconceived idea of what we are about. Why not just stay at home and fabricate? Why come here to show your belligerence? I'll tell you why. Because your own ideas have failed you. Fifty years of German socialism have produced more guns than butter, more bodies than books. Ours is a peaceful way. Your own troubled mind disdains peace. Yet I can wager that you came not because of your political confusion or need to write falsehood about our small efforts here. You came in veiled hope of finding an alternative. You see the cold, dark road you are on and stop at our small inn for some light and warmth. I regret only that we have failed to nourish your soul. Yet I would not have expected such success with someone so religious in their beliefs as yourself. Our audience is with that portion of humanity which

132

has already agreed to the terms of a civil society and wishes to endow it with the grace and beauty it deserves. Such people do not attack their host at dinner with boilerplate arguments better left at the union shop.'"

Albert's voice interrupted the argument Henry had envisioned. "You have to take the pawn. There is no other move."

Henry took the pawn from the board.

He had read the letter more than once. He had looked for something in Hubbard's words to find fault with. He wanted very much to dislike this pompous ass who wore his hair in a style more suited for the age of Benjamin Franklin and had written the single worst essay Henry had ever read, "A Message to Garcia." Now what he liked most came from Helen Mawson's retelling of what Hubbard said. Would she have altered the words...or the content?

Albert intruded again. "I am starting to feel the first pangs of hunger. You've got to make your move."

During the battle for Cuba, a man named Rowan had carried a message from President McKinley to a leader of the insurgents gathered somewhere in remote mountains against the armies of Spain. Rowan had asked no questions and required no other motivation than that his President had asked him to do it. The essay extolled Rowan's act as an example of "Initiative," getting the job done without excuse or complaint. Carrying the "Message to Garcia" was a metaphor in Hubbard's world for the ideal employee. Don't ask why. Don't ask how. Do it, and do it well. The pamphlet which carried Hubbard's essay became one of the most widely distributed pieces of literature of all time. It had firmly established Hubbard's Roycrofters in the public mind and made Fra Elbertus, as he wished to be affectionately known, famous. Henry considered it balderdash.

Vincent McCaffrey

Albert groaned. "We aren't going to get this one finished, buddy. Your mind is not in the game."

Henry looked down at the board. Albert had advanced his queen's bishop across the board to a position threatening Henry's castle and limiting the escape of Henry's king. Henry brought his own queen forward to check Albert's king and force a defensive move before Albert could bring his other bishop out as well. Albert was trying to move the game along, and getting careless again.

Albert moved a pawn forward to block the check.

Henry took the weak defender with his own pawn.

Albert sat forward as if the battle was his.

"I might have to take your traveling queen with my knight." Albert moved the piece into position.

Was Helen taken by the rude newspaperman? No. In her quest for "love, free from chains and shadow," she would not have given her heart so easily—not the girl who had been wooed by twelve farm boys. Her father had "set too difficult an example for that."

Who was her father, then? What kind of man had he been?

Albert lifted his glass. He was looking for a distraction of his own. There was calculation in his voice. "What was Heber Johnson's role in all this, anyway? He is the father of two sons, both anticipating an inheritance. He's only been dead for a few months. How much did Morgan love the old guy?"

Henry said, "Enough. That was where her love was."

Albert seemed satisfied with that. Tim had gone back to his corner by the radio. Henry looked out at the sun-sharpened movement of cars on the street as his thoughts faded.

Albert said, "What's your move?"

The queen could be lost. The bishop was ready. Henry moved his forward pawn again to take the pawn that still

guarded and pinned Albert's castle. Albert could never resist a queen.

Albert took her with his knight, while already working on another distraction. "You said O'Connor didn't give anything away when he called back. That might be a good sign. If he had no questions, it means he already had some answers. They are on to something. Arthur Johnson was in a contest with his mother over the estate. Now this guy, Peter Johnson, is a wild card. Inheritance is a big motivator in this world. It's the money angle all the way. When my brother Daniel's father-in-law died, they found out they had relatives they never heard of. At least a dozen. And that old man didn't bother to marry some of his women. Daniel and Mina had to hire their own lawyer just to stay out of the mess. When it was done, that whole strip of buildings on Washington Street that the old man had put together with his poker money after World War Two was sold just to pay the lawyers. God help me, Alice brings it all up every time we have Daniel and Mina over to dinner."

"And hate," Tim interjected. "Where there's love, there can be hate."

Both Henry and Albert looked toward the end of the bar, where Tim huddled on a stool.

Henry said, "Why aren't you married, Tim?"

His friend answered, "You know why."

Henry raised both arms. "That was almost twenty years ago."

Tim said, "To me, it's just like yesterday."

Albert arose and took the stool at the end of the bar. "I know a sweet little girl who handles my insurance. She's single. She's pretty. She's smart. About thirty years old, I'd say. And she told me the other day she's paying some goddamn dating service just to find the right guy. You know, a guy who brushes

his teeth and changes his underwear at least once a week.... You don't spit. You don't smoke. I seldom hear you cuss. I could get you her number. I could set up a date. I could have you both over for dinner some night. You know Alice would like that. She loves to play matchmaker. She's already trying to find a girl for Junior. How about it?"

Tim put his fist in his cheek and leaned on the bar. "I'm just too old and ugly now. I've got my ways set."

Henry took the next stool. "I know a redhead you'd like. I mean it. I know you go crazy for redheads. And she's as sappy as you are. I've seen her cry."

Tim's eyes looked up. "Is she ugly? False teeth?"

Henry shook his head vigorously. "She's a good-looking woman. She's divorced, with a couple of kids."

Tim said, "She probably snores."

Henry shrugged. "I wouldn't know. You might try to find out."

Tim drew a circle with his finger on the bar top. "You know what happened when I went on that date last year."

Albert protested, "She was a mental case. That's not your fault."

Tim said, "But the worst part was, she snored."

Albert returned to his chair by the chessboard, his face hung with a look of sad resignation for his lovelorn friend. His expression twisted itself into disbelief as he took a new look at what he had done. Henry followed and remained standing as he moved his bishop across to checkmate.

Albert studied the catastrophe, then looked up at Henry, his face blank now—dismissing his own foolishness.

"Who's the redhead?"

Chapter Twelve

"**Y**'ever find money in a book?"

Her black eyes watched him the way pets often did when he was in a house to look at a collection of books.

Henry truncated the top twenty hardcovers from a stack which towered precariously against a wall and set them aside.

He lied because he was sure a positive answer would lead to another question. "No."

Miss Galiano shifted her position from the small couch to a chair, moving closer to where Henry worked. Her eyes went repeatedly to the open door as if worried that her words would be heard by someone else. Henry knew the building was empty now, at midday, except for them.

She said, "I found a hundred dollar bill once."

She was not yet seventy. Robert, her now-sainted brother, had turned seventy shortly before his death, and she was the younger sister. Yet her confidence reminded him of a little girl's whisper.

Henry had made his way through three rooms piled with books as she talked to him incessantly. Every corner had been filled waist-high into embankments of volumes. Most furniture hid clots of books beneath. Henry did not respond to her revelation. He feigned a deeper interest in the titles he scanned now below a table. His knees were already sore from several hours of digging through one cache after another.

Miss Galiano's cheeks pinched backward to expose the perfect fence of her dentures. "I found it in a library book. Robert

said I should keep it. I was afraid. What if they came looking for it, and it was missing? They could find out who borrowed the book and find me."

Henry decided this was a harmless trail of conversation. He had worried she might tell him still more about the funeral and her brother's long illness.

"What did you do?"

She spread her fingers over the fabric of the dress covering her knees. "I gave it to St. Anthony."

She seemed very pleased with her solution to the problem and now folded her hands in her lap. Henry shifted a short pile toward the center of the room so that he could gain a better look at the stacks behind the couch.

He had asked her why her brother had never built shelves. She had answered, "He was claustrophobic. He thought it made the rooms feel too small."

The rooms were, in fact, small, condensed to allow a four-story nineteenth-century brick apartment building to fill the lot of a two-story eighteenth-century merchant's house. The older wood structures of the North End had been replaced to achieve some safety from fires when the moneyed of Boston were moving into the newly created Back Bay. Few of these buildings offered the luxury of extravagant space or the detail of an architect's care.

Robert Galiano's single passion had been films, and the books all related to that subject in some way. Henry had so far ignored the videotapes which puddled on most upper surfaces, lined windowsills, and reached head heights from the surfaces of tables and appliances. The dark, outsized screen of a television set reflected Henry's movements from the opposite side of the room.

Miss Galiano's high voice picked up the strand of her thought as if she were swallowing some amount of pain. "People put things in books.... I found a flower once."

Henry nodded without answering or looking up from his work. Perhaps this line of conversation had its own problems.

She paused, looking for a word. "Sender-ipity. You never know what you might find."

It was apparent that whatever Miss Galiano found in books, it was not on the page. Henry sighed at his own cynicism. Only then did he realize she might be trying to tell him something else.

He asked, "Should I be looking for anything in particular? Are you missing something?"

She shook her head, answering too quickly. "No… Just a picture."

Her eyes went up to the door again. Was this just a habit? Or had she been looking out for her brother's intrusions for so many years that this watchfulness had become a reflex?

He had to ask. "What was the subject? What was the picture of?"

She shrugged, lifting her arms and hands with her shoulders. "Just a picture…. A boy…a boy I knew once…. Robert took it from me and hid it. He said he put it in a book and forgot which one. I never did find it."

What made him curious? Was he bored? Not enough happening in his own life? Still, he had to ask for more. "When was that?"

She spoke quickly again, the answer already in mind. "1959."

This forced Henry to look up at her face again. He could not quite glimpse the twentysomething-year-old woman she had left behind. Perhaps her cheeks had been fuller then, her lips not so narrow. The recessed shadow of her eyes would not have been so deep.

Henry felt compulsive. What good was there in pursuing

this? Why did he want to know? Nevertheless, he asked, "Was he your boyfriend?"

She did not smile at the inquiry or hesitate with her reply. "I had many boyfriends."

She quieted after this, and Henry turned back to his job. He told her, "I'll watch out for it."

He had counted over a thousand titles, mostly oversized picture books from common publishers covering the careers of film stars and the production of film studios. All of them were in fine condition despite being on the floor in most places. The rooms were dry. The sturdy North End brick had been well-built, at the very least.

Her bedroom door was closed, so he had no idea of what might be kept there, but through the other rooms he had found very little trace of this woman. It was if she had been a guest in her brother's house for over forty years.

A large black-and-white photograph in a simple metal frame hung by the entry door. This picture of a young man in dark uniform standing behind a pretty woman in a pale dress sitting in a chair with her hands folded in her lap was the only show of personal history amidst the similarly framed lobby cards from dozens of movies which occupied any open stretch of wall between windows and doors. The uncomfortable poses of long-dead film stars captured in their candy-colored prime beneath glass made Henry think of the butterflies in the Natural History Museum at Harvard.

Henry restacked the last of the books as he had found them. Almost all of it was fairly saleable material, with perhaps a third of the titles in frequent demand, but not the kind Henry could afford to catalogue, with a few exceptions. One book, an oversized limited edition of the Saturday matinee B-movie serials from the thirties and forties, was of significant interest.

The calculation was fairly simple. She wanted all of it removed. He asked to use the phone and called Barbara at Alcott & Poe. This was good shelf stock for an open bookshop, and Barbara would do well with it. Barbara agreed. He told her he would call back in a few minutes.

He said, "I would like to offer you three thousand dollars for the lot."

The woman squinted at him and shifted her teeth in her mouth before speaking. "How about the videotapes?"

He knew it was best to keep it simple. "I'm sorry, we can only buy the books."

Her face showed nothing of her thoughts. "How about thirty-three hundred?"

He had not expected to bargain. To this moment Henry had worried that the sister had been so protected by her dead brother that she might not be able to take care of herself. Miss Galiano's expressionless face changed his opinion. The price was still within range.

"Sure."

He called Barbara back and set up an appointment for her to come by with the store van and pick up the rest of the books.

Miss Galiano took Henry's check for the books he wanted to take with him as a deposit on the remainder. She squinted twice at the check and then back at him before speaking again. "Before you go, I want to know just one thing."

Her voice was suddenly animated by some new interest. She was standing at the front door, half hiding behind it, girl-like, and as if he had just arrived.

Henry shifted the loose books in his hands. "What's that?"

She squinted at him now as she had at his check. "I want the truth, now.... What's the best thing you ever found in a book?"

The true answer to this was too long to give. He shortened it. He said, "A poem."

She shook her head. Her squint becoming a frown of disappointment. "No. I mean the most valuable. *Worth* the most."

He smiled. "Truly. It was a poem."

Her frown deepened to folds in her forehead and cheeks. Loosened dentures slurred her speech.

"That's just words. Words aren't worth anything."

He was trying too hard. He wished there was some way to communicate to this woman what he meant, but he did not see a way to that.

"Sometimes they're all that matter," he answered.

She shook her head and closed the door without saying good-bye.

He was suddenly caught by the sadness of it. This woman had several cousins who lived somewhere—she was not sure where. She had no children and had never married. The father had died sometime long before. The mother had lived on in the apartment with them for years, but she too was long gone. The brother had managed a package store on Hanover Street. The sister had worked in department stores like Stern's and Gilchrist's, finally "retiring" at Jordan Marsh after it was sold to Macy's. All of these facts amounted to far less than a portrait of a human being.

She had not asked what the poem was. She was not at all intrigued by his answer, because it did not involve money. And that, in essence, was what was wrong with his business.

Henry's mother might have been this woman's age just now, had she lived. And she often put things in books as well: newspaper clippings about the death of an author she liked, and bits of magazine stories that must have intrigued her. But Henry had thought before that the most valuable thing he had ever

discovered in a book was a poem, and in those few words he had in fact found his father.

Once, when Henry was still living at home, he had been sitting on the parlor floor, wishing for just a moment that his mother were close by again in her chair. By that time, his sister Shelagh had already run off with Rick, and it was just Henry and his father left. Even their long-time boarder, Maureen Williams, had moved on. It was a day when summer rain beat upon the house with a growl. His mother had often remarked how she especially liked rainy days, and perhaps this had heightened his own sense of it. She had explained how this was her chance to read indoors without the guilt of losing the precious sun.

Because he was never comfortable sitting in her chair, he had found the same place on the hard polish of the wood floor below the shelves as he had always done when she was alive. When she would sit in her chair by the floor lamp and read her Yeats, he would lie near with a pillow from the couch beneath the crook in his arm, elbow to the floor and hand against the side of his head, reading some book of his own. And until that moment long after she was gone, he had not thought to open the blue cloth volume she liked the best. Henry believed that the book had never been moved from the space where he had placed it on the shelf the morning of the funeral four years before.

Henry did not hear his father's approach. He had left the old man in the kitchen boiling an egg for lunch. Avoiding conversation was the habit between them after Shelagh was no longer there to mediate their disputes. Henry had wandered to the front of the house toward the din of sound made by the rain on the roof of the front porch. With the floor light off, the books on the shelf were small, dark ribs, but Henry reached for the Yeats at the instant his eyes met the spine—as if it were about

to fall into a void and needed saving—and his legs buckled beneath him as he opened it.

Henry sat there on the floor and read what opened to him in his hand, a page indelibly marked within the thread of the binding by repeated use. Unconsciously he had begun to read the passage aloud.

Turning and turning in the widening gyre
The falcon cannot hear the falconer...

It was then, just beyond those first lines, that his father's voice cut into the crowding anger of the rain, making a sudden silence about them. Henry looked up.

The old man did not have a reading voice. Henry had never heard him recite anything out loud other than a prayer. But his father said those next words then as if in answer to some hidden question.

Things fall apart; the centre cannot hold;
Mere anarchy is loosed upon the world,
The blood-dimmed tide is loosed, and everywhere
The ceremony of innocence is drowned...

The gray figure in the frame of the door did not move for the time it took the sound of the rain to swallow that strange silence once more, and then he turned back to his chore in the kitchen.

Chapter Thirteen

Fred was leaning against the brick wall that separated the rear parking area of Morgan's building from the one next door. The cigarette perched in the man's mouth allowed him to read the newspaper with both hands. Henry had rung the superintendent's bell at the front several times over the previous week and gotten no answer.

Henry's "Hello" felt awkward, but he could think of no other opening.

The paper dropped a few inches, and the head tilted back to study Henry. Fred did not answer.

Henry started again. "You might remember me. I used to help Mrs. Johnson out with the books."

Fred kept his eyes on Henry as if expecting something more. When he spoke, his lips barely moved the cigarette. "Her boyfriend. I told the cops you were her boyfriend."

Henry nodded, and smiled just enough to seem unconcerned by the revelation. A good offense was needed. "And I told them you were the dishonest superintendent that was probably stealing stuff on the side."

Fred folded his paper, then laughed with a loud "Ha!"

Henry tried to smile a little more broadly. "Would you mind talking to me for a minute? I know you don't have to. I just need a little help."

Fred studied Henry long enough to create some doubt that there would be a reply before finally speaking.

"What do you need to know?"

Vincent McCaffrey

Henry had to be careful with this. He had to make this man want to speak to him. But he could not afford to be coy. "What the cops won't tell me. I need to know who else came by to see Morgan that day."

Fred folded the paper one more time. "No one—when I was here. The elevator never moved when I was here. But I was gone before noon. I wasn't back until four-thirty. I think they said it took place sometime in the middle of the day."

Henry asked, "Did anybody else you know visit her in the days before?"

"Yeah. Sure. You!"

"No one else?"

"No one I saw."

"Somebody you didn't see?"

Fred smiled as if Henry had picked up on a subtlety. He said, "The elevator went up half a dozen times. Could have just been her coming and going. I don't know. They don't pay me to keep a desk log. They pay me to clean, take out the garbage, and call the plumber when he's needed. That's it."

Fred spit out the remainder of his cigarette, unfolded his paper, and lifted it again.

Another effort at playing detective had failed. Fred was not a likable fellow. Though what the man said seemed worth knowing, Henry left with the feeling of understanding even less, unsure of what more he might have asked—especially who else might have known about his relationship with Morgan.

Henry had even been unable to reach Morgan's lawyer, Mr. Downes. He had left his name and number with the secretary twice. The offices of Peals, Burgher, and Downes was a glass fortress in the Hancock Tower. And Ranulf Richter had no known address at present according to his last publisher.

Perhaps it was for that reason that finding Ranulf Richter

lying back on the stone steps at the front of Mrs. Prowder's house when he got home was an even greater surprise. Richter wore the same black silk scarf and dark blue blazer jacket Henry had seen at the church service, but had returned to wearing his shorts.

Richter said, "You are Henry?"

Henry did not answer, but instead stood a short distance from the sprawled figure as if waiting for it to move so that he could get by.

Ranulf sat forward. "I've been waiting for you. Wanted to talk about Morgan a bit.... Could you?" Thick eyebrows rose to a permanently furrowed forehead. "You were fond of her. So was I...." He paused as he searched Henry's face for some understanding. Henry waited. "The coppers don't take me seriously, so I thought I'd talk to you, and maybe you could pass something on."

Ranulf was not a good-looking man. His fashionable four days' growth of beard exaggerated the hollow of his cheeks. His jacket was unbuttoned, revealing that the bloom of dark hair from his chest had become soiled with gray by age. The boniness of his knees below his shorts gave him a malnourished look.

Henry said, "Is there a reason anyone should take you seriously?"

Henry was surprised at himself for expressing this thought out loud. Ranulf's answer was quick.

"Morgan did. You had a good deal of respect for Morgan, I believe. Then you might respect her judgment."

Henry wondered if this answer was prerecorded—the at-the-ready answer to any number of key doubts Henry might have. But it was true. It was the only reason he might give Ranulf the time of day.

Henry stepped closer to the building to let someone pass behind on the narrow brick of the sidewalk before he asked, "What did you want to say?"

Ranulf looked upward at the door. "Can we go in? I need to pee, and there is no good in telling the neighbors more than they already know."

Ranulf moved to let Henry step upward to unlock the door. On the inside stairs, Ranulf stopped repeatedly to look around.

"This is an old one," he said. "Not an imitation."

Henry spoke without looking back. "1820s."

Ranulf said, "It has the feel to it."

Henry had always liked the simplicity of the building—the lack of obvious detail. The character of the structure was in the small scale of things, the narrowness of the staircase and halls, the lower ceilings, as well as the absence of decoration. If Henry had been an inch taller, he would have had to duck to enter his own door.

Henry unlocked that door and pointed the way past the kitchenette to the bathroom. There were only two chairs, and his table was still stacked with Helen Mawson's books, so he pulled the extra chair out from behind the table and set it in the middle of the floor, sitting himself by his desk with the daylight of the window directly behind his head.

Ranulf had washed his hands and stood at the door with the hand towel, surveying the room before he folded the towel and hung it up. Then he turned the chair around backward and straddled it, resting his crossed arms on the back and his unshaved chin on his wrists.

"This is very nice. A good little room. You've managed to get quite a lot of books into it. I take it you eat out a lot."

This made Henry smile. The savage washed his hands after using the toilet and was very observant.

Henry answered, "A lot."

Ranulf studied him. "Me, too. Cooking is too much bother when others can do it better and in less time. Why spoil good food and miss the chance for a great meal?"

Henry was not about to engage in small talk. "Exactly... Tell me about Morgan."

Ranulf's eyes were blue, but too dark to return much color to the light. His large forehead and brow shaded his eyes enough to make them hard to read.

He said, "Well. I can tell you that if I had ever been inclined to marry, she is the woman I would have been looking for."

Henry wondered what the point was going to be. "What did you want to tell me?"

Ranulf tilted his head to the side, pivoting on his chin. "I suppose the reason you seem so unsociable is that you wonder if I might be responsible for Morgan's death. Such thoughts would put me off as well. But I did not kill her. I loved her. It disturbed me more than I can ever tell.... I actually got drunk the day I heard. Despite what you might have heard, I never get drunk. My antics are pure theatre. I have a small talent for overacting, and little else, as my three books have clearly over-exposed to the world.... A lesson in that. If you don't have the talent, don't let them know it. Morgan understood my situation. She told me not to publish the first one. Now the world knows what a fraud I am, and I've had to reinvent myself. Again. I have begun to paint. It's far easier to get past the appointed authorities. Words are so definite, finite, final. But they don't know what to make of my painting. Their standards are so arbitrary, so political. I work very hard to keep any identifiable content out of them. They've been calling the paintings genius. I have a show in Provincetown right now. Big hit. We made the New York papers in August. Admittedly, that's the slow period for

art openings, but it's when everyone from New York is on the Cape. Big hit. Big hit. And Morgan tried to stop me from doing that as well…. And she'll be right again. In time."

Henry slouched in his chair, feeling dislike for the subject. "Why are you telling me all this?"

Ranulf appeared to be pleased by something. "By way of introduction. We don't know each other—well, I suppose I know more about you."

Henry said, "Funny, I was thinking the opposite."

Ranulf smiled. "No. All you know about me is what you hear about from the newspapers. That bullshit is worth every penny I pay for it, which is nothing. It's publicity. On the other hand, what I know about you, I know from Morgan. Morgan and I have been friends for a long time. She talked a great deal about you."

Henry sat up straight again. His sense of the situation was suddenly slipping. Why would Morgan speak of him to Ranulf? What was this man after now, that he should pretend such a thing?

Henry said, "Like what?"

Ranulf lowered his head just enough to look through his own eyebrows, as if hiding.

"She loved you."

What was this man up to?

"Why would she tell you that? She never spoke of anyone else to me. She wasn't that type."

Ranulf lowered his eyes as well now in some respect for the subject. "That's because there wasn't anyone else to talk about. You were the only man she loved, after Heber, of course, and only then after he became ill.… You didn't know that?"

Henry answered reflexively. "I hadn't seen her in four years."

Ranulf said, "Well, that's the case."

Henry felt the hollowness came back, the feeling that there was a hole inside him that was growing even as he sat in his chair. Henry stood and took a breath.

"Why…?"

The word escaped.

Ranulf said, "Why what? Why did she tell me? Because I was her friend. And women can find it easier to talk to a gay man, even more than to another woman. Odd thing, that. But then we were friends. Dear friends, and as you must know, she had few friends."

Henry took another breath to speak. "Why didn't she tell me?"

Ranulf now squinted against the light to see Henry's face better. "I think she did. But she thought you couldn't hear— didn't understand—just then. I suppose she was right about that, too. Her first responsibility was to Heber, and you were stealing her heart. She would not be torn."

Henry sat again, feeling trapped but with no want to escape. Ranulf was not looking at him now, but at the titles of the books, as if avoiding his eyes.

Ranulf's voice lowered, perhaps wanting to hide some other thought. "The literary snows of yesteryear. The drifted best sellers of times past. So very important in their moment. So dead…" Then he turned back to Henry. "I can't really believe she's dead, you know. I haven't accepted it yet. I just saw her a couple of weeks ago.… I was the one who told her to call you. She didn't want to. She didn't think she could handle it. But she needed another friend to help, and I somehow knew you would. It's just so damn stupid that it turned out this way."

Ranulf's eyes sparked. The twisting trail of tears were no longer hidden in the stubble on his cheeks. He looked down

and wiped a darker stain onto the navy blue jacket sleeve.

Henry said, "Thanks."

Ranulf sniffed and shook his head. "For what?"

Henry said, "I'm not sure. Thanks anyway."

Ranulf cleared his throat. "The reason I came here was to talk to you about something else, though." He wiped his cheeks again on the other sleeve of his jacket, sniffing again. "She was murdered. It could have been a burglar, I suppose. I just don't believe it. I tried to tell the police. They thought it was you. Of course. I told them I didn't think so. All they did was check my whereabouts at the time it happened. They think I'm a nut—which of course I am. There is a downside to all that publicity." One short laugh broke his admission. "But I feel rather strongly about it. And I'd like you to press the issue a little for me, if you could. I think she was killed by her son."

The son. Which son? Another thought occurred. "Why were you so sure I didn't do it? I was nearly the last person to see her alive."

Ranulf nodded. "I wasn't actually sure. Not until now."

There seemed to be no center to this. Gravity had lost its hold. Things were falling apart. Henry grabbed at another thought for balance.

Henry had spoken to the acquisitions librarian at Boston University that morning—Miss Crist. The arrangement Morgan had wanted was in writing, but never signed. Their assessment of value had been lower than Henry's. Miss Crist apologized, saying the value of most modern first editions had plummeted in recent years because of the increased availability made possible by the internet. Henry had disagreed and made a point of the association value of books from such a specific source, the signatures and inscriptions, and recalled the condition of the books as extraordinary.

By the time Henry had left the office, Miss Crist appeared more depressed than simply sad at Morgan's death. She wondered out loud if the collection might end up somewhere else. But it was the last thing the librarian said which had hung in Henry's mind.

She had asked, "Were you the fellow who called? Someone called. Said he was a book dealer, and he had examined the collection. He gave me his name, but I didn't know it. And I didn't write it down. He was interested in comparing his evaluation with mine. Seemed to know Morgan and Heber quite well."

Henry had said the name of each of the sons, but the librarian had recognized neither. Henry had asked if they had spoken of actual amounts.

Miss Crist had said, "Yes. I told him it might be worth a quarter of a million dollars. The dealer agreed with me."

Henry looked at Ranulf now, as the man examined the leather cover of a Roycrofter volume. "Did you ever call the acquisitions librarian at B.U.?"

Ranulf answered absently, his eyes studying the illuminated letters of a title page. "No. Why would I do that?"

"Because somebody did. Because somebody was very interested in the value of those books. And because it is the theory of a friend of mine that Morgan was killed for money."

Ranulf looked back at Henry without question.

"Morgan was killed by hate."

Chapter Fourteen

Henry often read his favorite books two and three times. The good ones were to be savored more than once. And for this reason there had never been anything more than fitful curiosity at a library. There was no sense in getting involved with books there. There was no future in it. The first time he discovered a book he loved at the Brookline Public Library, he was twelve years old, and he could not bear to return it. He paid the library the fine for keeping it, in spite of his father's scowl. That copy of *Oliver Twist* was still his, still marked and battered by the careless use of others before him, but safe in his possession now, and treasured.

Henry had bought his first book with his own money—earned shoveling the short sidewalk for a neighbor—when he was eight years old. It was a copy of Robert Lawson's *Mr. Revere and I*, which he still owned as well, and left at his father's house in the bookcase by his mother's chair where he had first placed it years ago. But the first book his mother had bought at a store along with him, or at least the first one he could remember, was found downtown, at the Brattle Book Store, in the autumn of the year he had turned six, after she had taken him to a sale at Filene's Basement. The Brattle was not a large store, but it had seemed enormous to him then. The narrow aisles were often stacked with boxes and the broad tables filling the open center of the floor toward the front had the appearance of overflowing. Old Mr. Gloss, glasses falling low on his nose, sat behind a book-encrusted counter near the door and watched Henry as

154

he explored the edges of a jumbled stack on a table too high.

Gloss had said, "The best ones are at the middle, young man, because they aren't picked over as much." In the nearly empty store, that weekday afternoon, Henry was startled by the voice suddenly directed at him and dropped the book he held in his hand.

Mr. Gloss spoke again.

"You don't want that one, anyway. Use the stool from the corner back there. You'll find something better at the middle."

Mr. Gloss did not smile. Finding the right book was serious business, it seemed.

Henry did just that. A Kipling. A copy of *Just So Stories* illustrated by the author himself which was now on the same shelf at his father's house, near by the Dickens and the Robert Lawson.

He had learned at the Brattle to always check the lowest and highest shelves because most people were too lazy to bend or reach. Most of his first books had come from the bottom.

When, years later, just out of high school, he had taken the job at Alcott & Poe, it was only because of Barbara. He had been waiting for a job opening at the Brattle.

Barbara had looked him over with obvious distrust. Less than six months after opening her own shop, she could not yet afford another employee. He had liked her immediately. He liked the smell of her, which he thought might be the smell of a soap but later learned was simply a passion for licorice. He liked the intense brown of her eyes. He liked the way she took him seriously from the very first. He did not know until later that she was only a few years older than himself.

She had asked, "What kind of experience do you have?"

Why did she ask—even after telling him there was no job open?

He looked about. Her shelves then were widely spaced, still

low, barely head height and sparsely filled with the new titles she had bought on credit and spread face-out in most areas. He had already been into the shop several times out of curiosity, after he had first seen her setting up some months before. It was the girl in front of him who had brought him back to the shop, not the books.

He would not have admitted that at the time.

He said, "Not a lot with these. I can't say I know a lot about the new ones. But it doesn't look like you need much help with what you have. What I can do is buy good used stock and fill your shelves up for less than half what you are paying for this new stuff. You'll make more. And I know the right books to buy. I know what's good. I know what will sell."

He said it as casually as he could. It was only bravado. At that moment he knew nothing more about actually selling books than what he had overheard in shops while browsing for himself. Perhaps a little more. He had long thought that he might want to have his own bookshop one day. Up to that moment, however, he had never actually worked in one. That particular night he was working as a busboy at a restaurant in Harvard Square. All the knowledge he had was gathered from buying used books and reading them. He had begun to collect his favorite authors. He had read the Van Allen Bradley book on collecting, but all that detail seemed too precious. Yet he had made his case, believing for that instant that it was true because he wanted it to be. And she did not answer immediately, as he later learned she was usually so quick to do. She looked him over again.

She said, "I'll tell you what. You go out and buy a hundred dollars' worth of books that you think I should have. I'll put them on the shelf. If a third of them sell in two months, I'll hire you."

Where did such an idea come from? She could not have

planned it. It was one of her inspirations, of course. A hunch. How many times afterward had he seen her give way to such an impulse, and often win? It was a challenge he was unable to resist.

He had answered, "My money, I price them—your money, you price them."

She smiled at that. He knew it was the right thing to say.

She said, "Your money," without saying "of course," though it was obvious.

He had bought more than two hundred dollars' worth of books over the next week—hitting yard sales on the weekend, the Salvation Army, Morgan Memorial, a couple of public libraries with ongoing sales of discards and donations, and several other bookshops where he knew there might be underpriced and overlooked treasures. And then, unhappy at some of his choices on second thought, he had pulled books from his own shelves which he thought might be replaced easily. He still remembered the loss of giving up those titles as he stacked and ordered his selections late into the night, feeling all the while that he was betraying himself by sacrificing his own treasures. In fact, there was a copy of Bram Stoker's *The Lair of the White Worm* among them which he had never been able to replace in all the years since.

She had smiled a little too knowingly when he returned that Monday. He had come in empty-handed, the books boxed and still sitting in his Volkswagen microbus outside.

She said, "Second thoughts?" without a greeting.

He had many, in fact, but he lied readily. "Not yet. Where do I put them?"

When half the books he had brought in and priced had sold within the allotted time, he had admitted his subterfuge rather than accept the credit she heaped on him. He had spent more

than one hundred dollars. He had salted the selection with titles not easily found in a typical sale. He could not guarantee his picks would always be so good…. And he heard her laugh— laughing at him for the first time, and not for the last. Not cruelly. Never meanly. Then she had hired him anyway.

Mixing old and new books on the shelf, often of the same titles, was a new idea in Boston at least. The alternative of choice it offered serious readers created a strong following. The comparative bargain it presented to the budget-conscious persuaded them to more readily part with limited funds.

At the age of eighteen, only a few months removed from the childhood bedroom in his father's house, he was "assistant manager" of a bookshop with only two employees, in charge of purchasing and pricing used books. Most of his time, however, was spent learning how to construct good shelving.

The original three aisles had soon been shifted to make four. The height of the shelves increased to the full length of a standard one-by-ten-inch board—eight feet. In those days, the odor of drying polyurethane often overwhelmed the delicate aroma of decaying paper. The smell of Butcher's Wax announced the last moments before a section was ready for waiting books. The cry of the circular saw proclaimed the start of another unit.

Through that time, she had watched him. She had pestered him with questions that made him find answers. She had questioned his answers enough to help him discover his mistakes before they were too costly. She made him keep a notebook: what he had bought, for how much, and when it sold. Another notebook he used for ideas to investigate, places where he had found books, and even designs for new shelving.

By the third year, Alcott & Poe had a reputation. It had become the first place to go for students hoping to save on books for assignments. Never the largest shop, it was already known

for its depth. Not a carriage-trade antiquarian, hidebound by pricey first editions and leather sets, it became a favorite with readers if not collectors.

Over time, Barbara had taken a true interest in the used books as well. She began to develop specialties in areas neglected by the new-book shops. Small-press limited editions seldom made a profit by themselves but brought in dedicated readers. Genre specialties in areas like fantasy, science fiction, and horror brought the kind of enthusiastic buyers who filled bags with their discoveries. Westerns brought in older readers abandoned by the chain stores aiming at a younger demographic. English authors, like Henry Green and Angela Thirkell and Nevil Shute, otherwise unavailable except for one or two titles per year as the publishers cycled through their backlists, became mainstays. Regional authors, commonly ignored by the Departments of Literature but loved by readers nonetheless, appealed to the independent-minded portion of the quarter-million students from all over the country and even a few of the professors who had migrated to the Boston-area colleges. These were presented side by side with the usual suspects like Atwood and Tyler, Malamud and Mailer. The shop prospered.

It was the shop he had come to love first, even before he realized he had succumbed to the rough charms of his boss. It was the shop which kept him there, sanding shelves or pricing books long after closing time, even when Barbara's edges and quirks wore his patience thin and the daylong necessity of dealing politely with random members of the human race made him want to flee for his life. It was the smell of that shop, perhaps more than Barbara's own warm breath, which overwhelmed him and swallowed him and made him happy and miserable.

They had chosen first to set the shelves in line, only to discover that the old building, once a horse-and-carriage stable

for the Back Bay mansions, was itself not plumb or forgiving of straightness. Over time they had shifted and molded the cases to allow for human passage while permitting the greatest number of books in the least amount of space. The small paperbacks were separated from the rest to make the best use of the geometry of inches and to quickly satisfy the needs of those with the least to spend. Folios and elephantine art books were restrained upright to the narrowest units to keep them from warping and splitting. Most books ranged shelf upon shelf, case after case, so that a customer, upon entering and standing at the door, lost perspective in the converging lines—a visual exaggeration of the stock, with the closeness of the aisle only adding to the contradiction of space. And the height of the shelves, now reaching nine and ten feet toward the nineteenth-century ceiling, creating immediate shock, if not awe, and for the book-minded, an inevitable wonder.

This was the shop, Barbara's "perfect bookshop," dampened by a deeper patina of dust than he had allowed in his own time there, which Henry sought out on this day. His body was directed by habit as his mind doubled down on thoughts he had trampled before.

Barbara sat at the front counter, pencil poised over a catalogue of new titles. Her dark hair was tied back with usual carelessness by a rubber band. Her green vest, bristling with pencils from one pocket, hung open to the rounding of her shirt. She looked up without an immediate greeting—waiting for him to give away his purpose—playing dumb as she pulled her own mind from its favorite task, choosing new books to buy.

He said rhetorically, "Having fun?"

"No," she answered, pulling a fist from one cheek and leaning forward as if hoping for a kiss. He obliged, kissing her cheek instead of her pursed lips.

He said, "I'll bet. How goes the battle?"

Barbara's eyes half closed in resignation. "The Goths are at the gates. Trajan's great work is in danger."

He could not help but smile at her melodrama. He added "As always" to her complaint.

She gave a shake to her head. "Worse than usual. You know it's been three years now since the siege began."

He knew what she meant. He knew it was true and not just a passing comment on the economic weather. He had not actually spoken to her about business for perhaps six months, but all the news had been bad for far too long.

He said, "Need some books?"

She shook her head again. "I wish I did. We're still buying more than we're selling. Now I've just gotten in a few hundred goddamned film books I'm going to have to find a place for. Not good economic behavior…. What brings you in?"

He seldom actually brought her books now. More often, he came just to chat. And now she was, again, the smartest woman he knew.

He told the obvious lie. "Just passing."

She answered, "Not likely. You hate Newbury Street."

He said, "I don't mind the street…."

She looked past him toward the few browsing customers within earshot, realizing she could not correct herself.

She asked him, "How's the internet?"

Small talk about business wasn't really fitting to his mood.

"Slow. Not like this"—he turned to the few customers visible—"but slower than ever. Everybody is complaining. I haven't been hit yet as badly as some."

This kind of talk was old hat. Rote.

She said, "Too many sellers, chasing too few customers."

"I'd say so. It'll shake out. Give it time."

She said, "Trying to. But Sharon's more impatient than I am."

She looked up to the ceiling, toward the second-floor office, where her assistant, Sharon, spent at least half of her time in front of a computer. This was where the rare and unusual books had been moved after Alcott & Poe had taken over the entire building during their steady expansion in Henry's time.

Months after Henry had left so long ago, Barbara finally gave up her hope that he would change his mind and hired Sharon to take his place. Not to replace him, because Barbara had assumed the job of buying the used stock herself, but to fill the void in necessary work hours cataloguing the used stock of special value, and the more basic tasks of restocking shelves, helping customers, and running the register. When the internet had burst on the scene in the mid-1990s, Sharon had taken over that specialty as well. Barbara disliked computers and used them as little as possible.

He lied again. "Business will come back. Just give it time. That's always been my motto. Give it time, and work like hell while you're waiting."

She looked unconvinced by the words. He smiled as sympathetically as he could.

He told her, "What I need is to borrow your Elbert Hubbard Roycrofter bibliography. I'm hoping you have the same one we bought way back when."

She answered, "It's yours. You left it."

He objected to that. "But I bought it for you."

"I haven't used it in years," she said. "Stay here."

She made him wait at the desk as she ran up the stairs to the office. He could not help but pay attention to that. He wished she did not wear jeans all the time. She looked very good in a dress. He always liked it better when she left her hair down, as

much as it annoyed her to have the loose hair in her face when she worked.

The phone rang. On impulse, he reached across the desk and answered it. A publisher was worried about an open invoice. Henry assured them that it would be taken care of soon. They said that was what they'd been told the last time they called. He told them to be patient, and hung up. Barbara was back with the bibliography as he put the phone back.

He said, "Just a bill collector."

She smiled, resignation in the flattening of her lips. "Thanks."

He tapped the loose sheets on the desk with a finger as she handed him the book he had come for. "Is that your Christmas ordering you were doing when I came in?"

She sighed. "Yes. Late. Yes. I still have a few open accounts."

He asked, "How bad is it?"

She simply said, "Bad," and turned away.

He had to ask. "Is your 'perfect bookshop' in danger?"

"Yes. But we still have a few options. There are still things we can do to make it work."

She would, he thought. She always did,

"Let me know. Let me know if I can help."

She said, "I will."

He kissed her on the forehead, like he used to do. It always infuriated her. She clasped his face with both her hands and kissed him on the lips.

Chapter Fifteen

Y ou may remember me. I'm Arthur Johnson."
The man did not extend his hand with his words. He
stood at the bottom of the steps as if blocking them. Sum-
moned by the ringing of his bell, Henry waited in the doorway.
Morgan's son had the stockiness of his father, but his mother's
eyes. He was balding, as his father had been, and hiding the problem by cutting his hair short to the scalp. Henry appreciated the
advantage of standing at the top of the steps before answering.

"What can I do for you?"

Johnson's arms hung at his side as he spoke. "I wanted to
discuss a few things—particularly my father's books."

Henry considered the situation and knew he did not want
the man in his apartment.

"Down the street, on Charles, there's a place called the Paramount. I'll meet you there in ten minutes."

Johnson moved forward a step. "I wanted to talk privately."

"Then get a booth."

Henry closed the door and went back up the stairs to shave.
When he came out again, Arthur Johnson was still there, leaning against the lamppost. He stood straight in some effort to
increase his height.

"Can we begin again? I'm Morgan's son, Arthur."

His hand went out as Henry reached the brick of the sidewalk. Henry took it.

"I'm Henry Sullivan."

Johnson nodded. "Yes. We met, you might remember, some

years ago. I believe you were dropping some books off at the building."

Henry thought Johnson's smile was unconvincing.

"Yes."

"And I saw you at Mother's funeral service. I appreciated your coming. I was happy to see that Mother had so many friends."

Henry turned to begin the walk down the Hill toward Charles Street. Johnson followed reluctantly, as if he still wanted to be invited up to Henry's apartment.

Henry said, "She was a good and lovely lady. I'm sure everyone who knew her, loved her."

Johnson's voice was less certain. "Yes. Perhaps. Funny thing—when Dad died, there weren't half so many. He had a far more difficult personality."

Henry looked back over his shoulder to gauge the distance between them.

"I never knew him."

Arthur Johnson offered an artificial laugh. "Take my word. Everyone was always so surprised that they were married. You could see it in their faces."

Henry turned again to catch Arthur's eyes. "Your father was respected."

Johnson's voice lowered. "Yes. He was respected…. And I know she loved him. I have always known that. In any case, I now have to deal with his books. And I wanted to get your advice. I know my mother trusted you. That's good enough for me."

Henry stopped and turned, with the corner and its added noise and traffic just ahead. "What would you like to know?"

Johnson knew why he was there. "About the appraisal you sent to Mr. Downes. He's a lawyer, not a book person, and wanted to accept it as stated. I'm—I'm whatever I am. Call me a movie producer if you like. I'm not a book person, in any case. But I

have to deal with the tax man. They're going to hit us pretty hard. Between the Commonwealth of Massachusetts and the I.R.S., it's going to be a very costly situation. The appraisal seemed a bit high. I have to make some decisions. I wanted your advice.... You know, I think, what my mother wanted, but it has to be looked at a bit more coldly. The family shouldn't suffer because of wishes which did not take the bigger picture into account."

The question in Henry's mind came out before he realized it should be asked. "Why not?"

Arthur Johnson stood in place, again without gesturing with his hands, and seemed to be gathering some thread of thought before speaking.

"It would break us. It would break me.... I've been broke before. But, truthfully, I've always had Mother and Dad to fall back on. They were always there. Now I have to think about things a little differently. I have a family. If I blow this—if I lose this chance, I'm not going to have another.... The last film I made was a critical success, but it didn't make a dime. The distributor got something, but that's about it. I'm not in debt. Everything is okay really. But I want to make another film, and financing has dried up. There's nothing out there for a guy who hasn't already hit the jackpot at my age. If I was twentysomething it would be different. There's lots of table money for the hot young things. But I'm not hot. I have to put together a deal on my own. I have to have at least a million and a half to get a project going. And I have to do it soon. If I wait, no one will remember the reviews I got last year. I'll be dead in the water."

The only person Henry could remember who avoided moving their arms when they spoke was a jujitsu instructor who had dropped Henry from his class for daydreaming instead of paying attention. That fellow had said again and again, don't waste energy moving your arms unless you intend to use them.

Either way, Henry was unhappy with the observation.

Henry said, "No. I meant, why aren't you a book person? How could you have two parents as devoted to literature as Morgan and Heber were, and not care about books?"

Johnson shook his head as if clearing it. Henry walked on to the corner, stopping for the traffic light.

Johnson said, "Long story. The short of it was basic teenage rebellion.... The shrink says I was jealous of the time they spent with the books instead of with me. I guess that's what happened."

Henry could not help an obvious skepticism in his voice. "I can't believe Morgan was a neglectful mother."

Johnson spoke at Henry's back as they crossed Charles Street. "Neglectful? Hell, no. She gave me everything I wanted. She even let me go—she let me live away at prep school when I wanted to.... It was my father I had problems with. He was such a hard case. Old-school. Like when I got caught with some weed—he went ballistic. You know how kids are. It only made it worse.... In any case. Well. Here we are. Dad left everything to Mother. Mother left everything to me."

They had stopped just outside the restaurant. Henry did not move to open the door.

"What about your brother?"

This brought a collapse of Johnson's facial muscles, and one hand came up stiffly in an unfinished gesture. "You mean Peter? You know about Peter?"

Henry nodded slightly. He had no intention of telling this man what little he actually knew.

Johnson's hand dropped again. "Peter had his. He got his share. He used it up."

Johnson's voice had become louder. Henry still did not reach for the door handle but stood facing the man in the full glare of sun off the window. Two people at a table just inside

turned, obviously aware of their voices.

Henry said, "You mean for the medical expenses."

Johnson's hand moved up stiffly again, this time ending in a dismissive slice to the side. "Whatever. Long before that. Dad paid for that mistake a hundred times over. I mean, he even married that woman after a one-night stand. Dad supported her till the day she died. Dad supported that bastard of hers right to the end. Then Mother even started supporting him.... Peter's not part of this picture. He gets nothing as far as I'm concerned."

Henry tried to keep his voice uncommitted. "Your mother wanted the books to be donated to Boston University to create—"

Arthur Johnson waved the other hand in the air now. "That's all wishful thinking of the past. This is the present. The money is needed elsewhere."

Henry asked, "What about her will?"

Johnson jerked back in an unintentional mime of a blow. Henry had never seen a man react that way, as if he were physically struck by words before. He spoke back at Henry even before he had gained his feet again.

"What do you know about that? You mean my father's will. That left everything to Mother, for me—"

Henry said, "Morgan's will."

Johnson straightened his back and stepped forward again, his face too close to Henry's, twisted in a distortion of disbelief.

"She didn't—Mr. Downes never witnessed a will. Have you ever seen one?"

Henry took a breath without giving ground. It was a guess. It was a terrible guess to make. He only knew it was actually true when the words were spoken aloud.

"She wanted the books to be donated to Boston University. She wanted Peter to have the proceeds from the house on the

Cape. She wanted you to have the sale of the condominium."

Arthur moved closer, spittle white at the corners of his mouth, his eyes squinting painfully into the glare of the sun.

"How do you know that?"

"She told me—most of it."

"She told you there was a will?"

"That's what I understood."

"Then where is it?"

"I can't tell you."

"You won't tell me?"

"I can't. I don't know."

Arthur turned his body around in a near pirouette. Both arms clapped repeatedly at his sides.

"Shit. High holy shit. God damn fucking shit. Why can't anything go right? Have you told Mr. Downes this?"

Mr. Downes had still not returned any of several calls to his office.

Henry answered, "I've never spoken with him."

"Oh…" Arthur's voice lowered to a strained whisper. "He doesn't know about this? Then it doesn't exist. That bow-tied Yankee bum-kisser may be milking his job for everything he can get, but he's not about to hold out a piece of information like that. It doesn't exist. There's no will. She just said it to you. That's all. There is no will!"

Henry was suddenly calmed by the thought. "I think you're wrong."

Johnson's arms flapped upward. A bird without feathers. "Where is it, then?"

Henry thought he knew. Anyone could guess. That was the problem.

Chapter Sixteen

Within the near silence, there was the false sound of memory. Often, only a voice. Not always in the simple quiet of the night, but more often in the sudden still of time after dawn when the sun briefly entered the space of his room in a flat and angled geometry of light. The early noises of the city were easily overcome there between these old walls. He restrained his own movement to listen.

The voices he heard this morning were crisp and close and given to incomplete sentences and single words.

"Why?"

Morgan's voice—he did not answer. He wondered instead if this was the source of the human belief in ghosts.

"Why?" she insisted.

He had not been paying attention, having turned his thoughts to the cause of things. She had often told him he needed to discipline his mind, when he questioned her quickness.

What did he know the "why" of? What else might be the cause of her question?

"My Elwin would never ask why," another voice advised. "He never wanted to know the why of things. He took them as they were and did what he could to deal with them. Lawyers are like that, you know. Too much knowledge can fog their way."

When had Mrs. Prowder ever said those words? It must have been—he could not recall.

"Why?" Morgan's word was a plea now, more than a ques-

tion. She might have asked that of the one who killed her. She would. She would have known what he was there to do. She had always anticipated things that way. It was in the way she moved—her grace. It was in the way she drove her car....

Henry spoke aloud. "Why?"

The sound of his own voice was a shock, an invisible intruder in the room, and made him sit upright in his chair.

Why had she chosen him? What good was he to her, then? Or now?

In the halted time of the room, he found it difficult to grasp all the pieces in his mind.

The letter from the lawyer who was buying the building had come. Mrs. Prowder had always declared her building as a private residence with guests. There were no legal apartments. Henry would soon be moving.

The day before, Mary Prowder had warned him of the situation. She'd been sitting on a box in the empty room by the door when Henry came home. She had been crying, and the pink around her eyes did not match the red of her hair.

"I was hoping you'd come. I wanted to tell you that the sale has gone through."

Henry nodded. Saying thank you did not seem appropriate.

He said, "It's a weight off your shoulders. You should be happy."

There was no happiness in her eyes.

"I suppose—you know. The problem is, there's no one to be happy with. After a while it gets a little boring being happy all by yourself."

Henry looked down at the floor, wishing he was smart enough to avoid feeling some personal attachment where there was nothing he could do.

He said, "Is your brother happy?"

She answered, "I couldn't tell...." Her voice trailing to a whisper.

Old Mrs. Prowder had never spoken of her son, and Henry could not imagine him.

"Tell me. It's none of my business, I know, but tell me if you can. Why didn't your brother ever care as much about your mother as—"

She cut Henry off as if the thought had already been spoken.

"It was because of Dad.... Richard is gay. Dad reacted so badly to it. He just could not accept the idea that his only son was gay. Mom couldn't really, either, but for once in her life, she never said anything. But Dad always had a solution for everything. He kept trying to talk Richard out of it. Things were different then. You know. Dad loved him so much. I can't explain it. They used to spend so much time together. And then—it was like he died."

Henry said, "I'm sorry."

Tears came back to her eyes. "Rich didn't help. He was always so political. Always arguing his points. Always aggressive. Always the lawyer.... But even when he was a kid, he used to run away and hide in the attic. He would put on a big show of being angry and then just disappear." She swallowed a breath. "I'm sorry."

She was crying over a past that was lost to her now. Henry understood that futility too well.

Another thought occurred to Henry then.

"It's all right. Cry if you can. I've never been good at that myself. But, look—I probably won't be seeing you again, and I wanted to mention something.... And, there's no good way to go about this right now...."

172

He had gotten too much of her attention. She appeared frozen in place. How was he going to explain this foolishness?

"But I have a friend…"

Henry had not been prepared. He should have put together a script for this in advance, but it had not been on his mind. She blinked.

She nodded. "It's good to have friends. I don't have enough friends myself."

Her voice was suddenly flat with sarcasm. Henry felt stupid. "That's not exactly what I mean. I have a friend. A good friend. He's single."

Her eyes rolled. "Oh, Christ. Are you trying to get your friend a date?"

Henry shrugged with his embarrassed smile. "He likes red-heads."

Her sarcasm increased. "Is that the only criteria?"

How could he make this work now? He tried to explain. "He's too damn shy, but he's a good guy."

She stepped back. "You're single. Are you shy, too?"

He had no ready answer. "No. I don't think so. I'm just…" He had no finish to the statement that he wanted to say aloud.

She said, "Either you don't like redheads or you already have someone you're serious about."

That was an obvious-enough excuse and only partly a lie.

"Yes. No. Yes…I'm kind of involved right now."

She stared at him with a straight face, waiting for him to add something before she spoke again. "So what's your friend's name?"

"Tim."

She said, "Does Tim have false teeth? The last guy I dated had false teeth. Bad breath."

"He's bald."

"He's old?"

"No. About my age. He's just bald."

"Bald is okay. What does he do for a living?"

"A bartender."

She tilted her head. "An honorable profession."

Henry gave her Tim's number, figuring this was about as much as he could do at the time.

The lawyer who had bought the house was overly solicitous of Henry's welfare and offered to help find him temporary quarters so that the work on the building could begin. Henry assumed his status as Mrs. Prowder's "guest" might be a worry and a source of legal problems. Eliot had even popped his head out to ask how much money the lawyer had offered Henry to move. Henry just shook his head.

Henry wondered that none of this seemed important to him now. Only the past held his attention in the early light of the morning.

"Why?" Morgan insisted again, bringing him to the present.

He could not imagine why. He had not imagined why. He had made a list. That was all. Imagination could not be contained in a list. Knowing was something more than the facts placed and numbered on a page.

Just as he had known where to look for the will.

Detective O'Connor had been reluctant. Oddly, Henry had been forced to persuade him first that Morgan's will might matter—might be evidence in the investigation of her murder. Odd. Wasn't that obvious? Or was Henry's insistence about going back to the apartment somehow alarming? Perhaps they thought he was up to something else. Imagine. Henry had been

the last person they knew of to see Morgan alive. Was he still a suspect?

O'Connor asked, "Why wouldn't she have left the will with her lawyer?"

Henry knew that as well. "She didn't want the lawyer to know what it said. She was being careful, but she did not want to upset her son unless it became necessary."

Henry offered this answer without explanation. O'Connor accepted it.

Two officers accompanied them to the building, as if Henry were under guard.

The stale air of the apartment hit him with a wave of nausea. Not the amount of odor, but the peculiar smell of the place. When the detective opened the door from the elevator, it struck Henry as suddenly as the knowledge of what it was. Books. Just books. As if they inhabited the rooms with their own body odor and cooking smells. The grasp of the sun each day, heating the rooms despite the curtains, and the cooling of the night, became the giving and taking of breath.

He had always enjoyed the smell of books. More. He had craved it. He looked forward to it. Never had it made him sick.

"Where's it at?" O'Connor said, as if irritated by some inconvenience.

The rooms were half-dark within the shield of the curtains, but Henry needed no light to find the book. His worry, the one that had wormed its way through his mind for more than a day, was that the book would be gone—or worse, that the will would have been removed.

But it was there, still beside the old *Britannica*. Though a beautiful copy of the book, he did not pause to look at the Rackham illustrations but cupped the spine in one hand and

Vincent McCaffrey

turned the pages to the last, where the words were set apart: "Here lies Arthur, the once and future King."

The will, a single page written by hand, was folded there.

To my Arthur, I leave all that I can, my final home on Marlborough Street, and my love. To my husband's son, Peter, I leave the small house Heber and I bought in Wellfleet the year we were married. Our small treasure of books, all but this one, I leave to Boston University, according to the terms discussed in August, 2003. This book, Le Morte D'Arthur, *Heber's favorite, I leave to my own Arthur, that he may remember his father's love, and pass it on to his own children. Most of our savings having been spent long ago, little remains but this. All the paintings, furniture, and additional contents of the apartment should be sold at auction and added to the sum in my account at the State Street Bank in Boston to cover the inevitable taxes. Any additional taxes or fees must come from the sale of our Boston home. If, in the unlikely event, anything else remains, it should go to Arthur.*

Her signature at the bottom of the page was notarized by a State Street Bank officer and dated October 13.

Why had Arthur been so reluctant to believe there was a will? Money? Was everything reduced to that? Why would Arthur be so sure there was no will? Because the lawyer, Downes, worked for him now. With Morgan dead, Arthur was his client. Perhaps Arthur had been his client even before Morgan's death. The thought that she had kept her will secret, even from her own lawyer, made sense that way.

Arthur was Morgan's son. How could she have raised someone so lacking in the virtues she had displayed so easily herself? Arthur was his father's son as well—as much in body as soul, perhaps.

But then, how could Morgan have ever loved a man so

176

much, whose soul was bought? Was Heber Johnson ever worth her care? The man Henry knew now from pictures was broadly built, once muscular, and perhaps not actually as tall as she. A large head, handsome perhaps but jowly in his last years, and balding, with yellowing skin spotted from sun and age. An old book.

The man Henry had once imagined in her words, when Morgan spoke of him, had been a scholar, a connoisseur, an authority, a confidant of accomplished people, a master of negotiation, a mannered gentleman of the world. That man was now only in the memory of others and beyond the grasp of Henry's imagination.

Human "being" was ephemeral, of greater weight than the sum of bone and blood and flesh. The being of a person had no time or geography. It was a passage of hope conjured by a single mind, one instant upon another, without math or calculation. Henry had never known Heber Johnson and thus would never know him except in the evidence left of what he had done. Heber had made Morgan love him, and that was enough to know, and for Henry to judge. And Henry had known Morgan.

Chapter Seventeen

The early dark had turned cold with a moist wind by the time Henry crossed the elevated walkway from Charles Street station and descended to the pavement. He did not quicken his pace against the chill. He liked this street, especially in the night, when the phony "antique" store signs approved by the historical commission were faded by shadow, and the yellow light from the windows of the small shops made it easier to imagine the way it might have been a hundred years before. Now Christmas lights softened the glare of fluorescent and halogen. The old gaslights on their cast-iron lampposts, following the curb at either side, gave a steady border of definition to the chaos of illumination and glare.

Stopping momentarily to look upward at the Pinckney Street crossing, he noted the rise of those gaslights hovering in the air all the way to the top of Beacon Hill, their black iron posts invisible in the night. The stern faces of the nineteenth-century brick row houses looked unhappily from behind a barrier of cars parked end to end.

On Charles Street, the sidewalks narrowed around the congestion of parking meters and wastebaskets and black metal rails guarding steps down to lower-level shops, causing him to repeatedly halt his pace to let someone else slip by from the other direction. The street bent here as it turned, as if sagging with the accumulated weight of the brick houses which scaled the modest heights of Beacon Hill above. At Mt. Vernon, the street crossing was clogged by a taxi which had decided to let

go a fare. Horns pressed the air. It reminded Henry to pick up a new bottle of aspirin at Finnian's Drug Store on the corner.

As he waited in line at the register, he watched the pharmacist counting pills on a tray. Mrs. Prowder had told him once that her name was Lisa. Now she seemed familiar, though he could not recall ever noticing her before. How could he have missed her? But then, he was seldom sick.

At that moment, a movement of her left hand caught the light in a small diamond on her finger. Henry paid for the aspirin and shoved the package in his coat pocket as he left. "You snooze, you lose." That was one of Albert's expressions.

But the color of her hair was important. It was the color of the hair in his dream.

Chestnut Street was quiet, as usual, and he took the incline with larger strides to be home sooner. He did not take special notice of the absence of light in his own doorway or see the figure on the steps until the miscalculated swing of a fist just barely caught him on the side of the head.

The guttural rasp of a voice followed the sting. "Son of a bitch. You cost me more than you'll make in a hundred years."

A left hand came at Henry's face in a downward arc and missed his nose only because his body was still reeling backward from the first blow. Henry tried to catch himself on the tilt of the brick sidewalk, but his right foot had not moved far enough, quickly enough, and he fell.

The voiced rasped with an alcoholic slur, "You're gonna need some teeth when I fuckin' finish with you."

Falling, Henry's arm had doubled beneath him with his own weight, his elbow reaching the brick too hard and jolting him with a shock of pain. The sole of a shoe scraped Henry's cheek as it missed his face. Henry rolled. The wheel of a parked car stopped his escape. Another shoe caught him in the ribs, the

padding of his coat taking much of the impact. Henry rolled back beneath his attacker, his free arm numb from the shoulder down, and brought what he hoped were the knuckles of his right hand up into the man's crotch. A short gasp was the answer. Henry rolled away again and gained his feet.

"Fuckin' son of a bitch," came the voice.

The face above the stooped body coming at him again was now clearly Arthur's. Henry kicked upward at the white of it, caught a grasping hand instead. He twisted away. Arthur followed Henry's retreat without a pause. Henry turned as if to run and turned again full circle to bring his left fist at the mouth of the man. The mouth was opened as if to speak again, but the words were lost in Henry's fist. Arthur fell backward to the steps. Henry's knuckles blazed with the cut of Arthur's teeth.

The door above them opened. Eliot stared down at them from the frame of light.

"What's goin' on?"

Arthur turned to look up at Eliot, and Henry took the instant to grab at the collar of the man's jacket and yank it downward at the back. The inner silk lining ripped apart at the shoulder. Arthur tried to twist away, his body still inclined toward the steps. Henry kicked at the supporting foot, and Arthur's body dropped lower, his jacket still pinning his arms enough so that it was his mouth that took the edge of the stone.

Eliot said, "You guy's are really fighting, aren't you? You can get hurt, you know."

Another voice came, "Let me see!" The larger figure of Jessica pushed at Eliot's side and gaped down at them.

Retelling the details the next day, Henry found it difficult to make a victory out of the confrontation. Albert was not impressed, as

he sipped the top from a beer. The afternoon had turned toward dark by the time Henry made it to the Blue Thorn.

Albert asked, "What happened then?" Blandly staring at Henry in the reflection of the mirror. He was not going to show Henry any additional concern.

Henry said, "Jessica screamed. Like in the movies. She saw the blood rising in Arthur's mouth."

Tim leaned close over the bar and grabbed at Henry's right arm. "It's not broken?"

Henry shrugged. "I don't know. I can't bend the elbow."

Tim continued to squeeze, as if hoping to cause pain. The numbness had not yet faded. He said, "You need an X-ray."

Henry shook his head. "I can't afford it. I think it's just bruised. I'm going to give it a couple of days."

Tim said, "Go to the emergency room."

Henry sipped his ale before speaking. "Sure. You pay for it."

Tim backed off. "Okay, give it a couple of days. Then go see my doctor. He'll give you a special rate, but you have to donate your body to science and give blood three times over the next year."

Albert grunted. "They won't want his body. It's damaged goods now. So, what happened after that?"

Henry tilted his head with the thought. "Cops came. Arthur was sitting up on the steps then with a towel on his face from Eliot. I gave the cop a report and filed a complaint. I was pretty pissed…. Arthur wouldn't talk. He broke some teeth. I think he was too embarrassed to drop the towel. They took him away in a cruiser to Mass General. I haven't heard anything else."

Albert's voice dropped to the full low of a bass cello. "Does this mean what I think it means?"

"What?" Tim asked when Henry did not respond.

Henry had thought that question through several times as he fell asleep the night before. He answered, "That it wasn't Arthur."

Albert repeated, "That it wasn't Arthur."

Tim seemed confused. "Why not? Because he's a fool and goes around picking public fights? Because he's not trying to hide the fact that he's greedy? Maybe. Maybe not."

Henry played with the bandage on his left hand. The brown stain was hard where some of the blood had come through.

"Maybe not."

How could someone act that way? Why would someone who had so much lose his mind over relatively little? Why had Arthur attacked him? Henry would be happier if he had a better understanding of how Arthur figured into everything. Or at least if he could grasp this short thread of human nature.

Albert said, "It was probably just the weather." Holding his beer up to the light before he set it down. An amber spark struck Henry's eye.

Henry leaned back. Something more was coming, and he voiced his fear. "Oh, crap."

Albert said, "It makes everyone a little crazy at times. Just like it was in the fifth century. A few of those really cold winters in a row—maybe caused by a couple of volcanic eruptions here or there—and suddenly you had these Germanic tribes marauding about. The Angles, the Saxons, the Frisians, and the Jutes—really just proto-Vikings—tribes that had to move on and find someplace a little more hospitable. The land wouldn't support them all. There was probably a good deal of infighting over who goes and who stays. Better to kill some bloke who couldn't understand your language than to put an ax in the neck of your cousin Fred…. Don't forget, the Huns had just come by, and life was not all that settled for anyone. And these

were small tribes—maybe fifty clans or less each, a few thousand individuals. Why not get up and go? They had the boats. They were coastal people. And they had undoubtedly heard of the green hills of Albion, or even seen them, just as they had grown up hearing tales about the Goths and the Vandals. Their larger Frankish neighbors were being pushed west by the Slavs, who seemed to be endless in number. So an old Roman coin was tossed, and the losers took to their boats and crossed to Albion. And there they confronted the Celtic Britons who had invaded the island in their own quest for safety half a millennium before, when they had displaced those strange dark people, the Druids…. I have a theory about that—"

Henry said, "You have a theory about everything."

Albert was obviously reading another book. That was the way he had always committed things to memory after reading. He retold what he could to Henry. Albert had this method down pat.

Albert nodded and swallowed. "Not yet. I'm working in that direction, though. You know Einstein was a genius, but he couldn't manage to brush his teeth or comb his hair. My mother named me after the smartest man in the world because she had high hopes. But my theories are based on more practical realities. I'm going to call it the Unified Trash Theory…. So they cross the sea, and there is King Arthur. He has brought the clans of Celtic Briton together following the abandonment of the Roman overlords. The Romans, of course, are still busy collapsing beneath the onslaught of all those Goths and Visigoths, Franks and Avars and Vandals. The Britons were a fierce people, mind you. They survived on their ferocity, but their numbers were not much greater than the invaders', and worse, they were broken by their own clans, with their own grudges. An independent people, they were. Still are."

Henry interrupted. "And stubborn." Thinking that the picture was incomplete.

"And stubborn." Albert nodded. "And Arthur brought them together for a while. For maybe fifty years. He must have been a considerable king. He might have rallied the Celtic clans from Ireland and Scotland and even from far-off Brittany to defend against the Viking invaders. A proto-Churchill, if you will. But when he died, just as it happened to the great Alexander, the alliances broke, and the invaders took the good lands and pushed the Britons off to the rock and mist of Scotland and Wales."

Henry had to ask. "So what has this to do with anything?"

Albert answered, "You asked how I thought Arthur figured into the picture."

Henry let a short beat of silence pass. "You know I meant Arthur Johnson."

Henry watched Albert's face in the mirror. Albert stared back innocently. "Didn't I say it was the weather?"

Henry tried not to smile.

Albert stared into the mirror a moment longer, then drank down the remains in his glass and began again.

"Arthur's a questionable character. We don't know much about him.... He could have done it. But why would he take the risk if he had more than half of everything anyway?"

Tim had worked his way down the line of patrons from the end of the bar.

"Greed," Tim said. "Because he was about to lose a part of it. The English invader endangered everything."

Henry leaned against the wood toward Tim. "You're right, you know. The property was going to be divided. If Arthur was in debt, and had already used up a sizable portion of his inheritance fighting his own battles, then he might not want to see what still remained divided further."

Tim added, "And then there's the Viking."

Albert shook his head vigorously. "No, we're talking about Arthur Johnson."

Tim asked, "What about that guy, Ranulf?"

Henry smiled and studied his ale.

Albert pushed his empty glass forward with added unhappiness and silently waited a moment for Tim's attention, then asked, "What about Tim's redhead?"

Tim's head jerked about.

Henry answered first, happy to change the subject. "I was considering the redhead for myself."

A look of irritation wrinkled Tim's brow as he pulled a beer for someone else instead.

Albert said, "I thought you were being pursued by your high-school sweetheart."

Henry explained that his father was unhappy with him. Leona had been by to talk. She was asking about things his father was not in a position to answer for. Henry had apologized. His father then suggested to Henry that she was a good woman, and good-looking, too, and Henry was getting a bit old to be still fooling around. He warned Henry that he was going to end up like his Uncle Jack.

Albert grunted his agreement. Tim looked over from his radio without further comment, still ignoring Albert's glass.

Chapter Eighteen

He had not made the past. He had found it. Orphaned. As if no parent or guardian had survived and all responsibility had been lost. Only a vague history remained—and the books. Though there was no custody over the past, he mused that he might have visitation rights. He could change nothing, but he could choose the portion he wanted to remember. And he could dwell in the shelter of certain moments better than others.

Helen Mawson had gone to New York in the spring of 1915. She clearly intended that to be only the first part of a longer journey. But there was a war in Europe. She could not be going there, and her letters said nothing about her objectives, perhaps because she did not want her father to know. Was her actual destination Chicago? The trains went that way back then, from Boston to Chicago. Everything went through New York.

She had gone so many places before. She had been to Budapest! She had fed the pigeons on the plazas of Venice and stood at the foot of the great columns of the Parthenon. She had watched the clouds above the open top of the Circus in Rome. But she had returned to only two places more than once. She had returned to England, to the Wrights' cottage in Cornwall. Was there a farm boy there who danced better than all the others? She had gone more than once to the Roycrofters in East Aurora. The reporter for the Chicago papers had been there at least two of those times. What coincidence might that be? How was Henry going to step beyond the surviving letters she wrote?

Marcus. What was his last name?

The woman behind the desk at the Boston Public Library was not at all sure the microfiche would be available. Henry filled out the request slip anyway. The *Chicago Times* had long been out of business and its name joined with the *Sun*. The older records were not itemized by the library in Chicago.

Henry visited Barbara again. Alcott & Poe appeared busy with noontime shoppers in the midst of rushed lunch breaks. He recounted his fruitless search for a book at the library which purported to be a history of the *Chicago Times*. She was sympathetic.

Her tone grew more compassionate when she asked why he was using only his left hand to browse. He cut the story short and told her he had fallen and could barely bend his arm. Barbara called one of her part-time staff to watch the desk and then helped him search the journalism section. After a few minutes she had an even better suggestion: biographies. Barbara had an opinion on this as good as any.

"Reporters love nothing better than to write about themselves when they retire. They've flown too close to the flame. They've seen the mortality of the great and recognized themselves in the faces of the notorious. Reporters aren't historians. They sometimes see themselves that way, but it's just a failing. They're too much a part of the history they cover. They can't separate the details for lack of perspective. People close to them seem so much larger than those at a distance. They're often overwhelmed by subjects bigger than they are."

It was Henry who was feeling overwhelmed. "I don't even know if Marcus was a staff reporter, or just a stringer, or maybe an independent working on spec."

Barbara's confidence was daunting. "Staff. I'll bet he was a staff reporter. Elbert Hubbard was not a random subject.

He was as famous then as Ford, and Edison, and Rockefeller. At least one of his books could be found in every middle-class home in America."

Henry returned to the library looking for the biography of an editor of the *Times* prior to World War One. Barbara had found the name in a few minutes by simply doing an internet search. But that book, too, was missing from the library shelves.

The woman at the library desk apologized.

Henry turned and stood, with the length of Bates Hall before him.

As a child he had imagined this to be a playing field raised to the level of the broad oak reading tables. More than the familiar shapes of houses in his neighborhood, this library had first instilled in him a sense of architecture. That was before they had built the crude, lobotomized bulk of the new addition—attached to the old library like half a brain but without aesthetic memory and judgment, much less understanding.

In his youth, this great room had been the center of everything. Now, a few dozen people occupied the hundreds of chairs which were once jealously waited for. Towering windows at one side of the hall arose perhaps fifty feet to arches in support of the ceiling. As if embarrassed by their own height, the windows were made smaller by the bars of thick black muntins. The scale and the clear expanse of the ceiling was visually reduced by enormous plaster-cast rosettes, each set against the shadowed relief of a continuous pattern of squares. This optical contradiction of the actual size of the room had confused Henry even when his mother had brought him there so long ago. Later he wondered what the architects had feared? Was it a joke? Was their pleasure being taken in the visual reduction of what was inherently awesome? Wasn't this a place for the

mind to soar and the eye to wander or rest from the near focus of words on a page?

It was here he had first understood the true smell of books. The peculiar odor of a few pages held open to his nose was already a perfume he had savored. Here, it was the sum of the scent of a million books which once flowed and ebbed on the tide of human inquiry—the aroma mixed with the smell of polished wood, cooled and condensed against the marble floors, arising again around the electric glow of milky orbs in brass bowls, drifting about the green-shaded lights at the tables, and stirred by the brush of wool on the arms of readers lost in a greed for words.

They had not come often when he was young. Perhaps once a month. His mother liked the excuse to be going someplace special. His sister, Shelagh, would be at school then, or off with her friends. The trolley ride alone would have been enough for Henry.

How many times had he climbed around the ledges of stone where crouching marble lions guarded the great inner stairway, hushed by the echoes of his own feet, and been made church-reverent by the dim illumination of the globes of light on their darkened brass pedestals? He had traced with his fingers every name of the Civil War battles won by the Massachusetts Volunteers and the Twentieth Massachusetts Infantry: Ball's Bluff, Mary's Heights, Bristoe Station, Antietam, Chancellorsville, Wilderness, Gettysburg!

The murals on the walls were fabulous cartoons to him then—life-sized—larger-than-life recreations of stories he could only guess at. The names of Sargent and Abbey and Chavannes meant nothing to him. But these things could be found in books! When he had begun to read the Scribner's editions with their Pyle and Wyeth illustrations, he had made a connection which

had brought him back repeatedly to stare and wonder.

In those days the walls between the artwork were darkened and faded from a century of containment. Refurbished now, even the subdued greens and yellows and blues seemed unnaturally bright. But what had disturbed Henry most when he entered the building earlier in the day was the smell of food. A room which had once held nourishment for the mind and soul now offered sandwiches and coffee. A small restaurant had taken the place of books. And worse still, the pernicious smell of food had overwhelmed every fragrance of binding or paper stock or potion of ink.

Henry could smell the pastry and burnt soup even here, in the great vessel of Bates Hall.

Why was all the world he wanted or cared for being destroyed?

His eyes fell down from the rosettes above to a familiar shape at a table nearby. Ranulf Richter reclined at odds with the angle of the chair beneath him. His book rested upright on the surface of the wood and his face nosed closely to the pages, with his chin on one fist. Henry thought to ignore him, and then reconsidered.

Henry said, "Hello."

The eyes looked up, dazed from some inner view. He nodded before finally speaking. "Good day, Mr. Sullivan.… This is fortunate. I've been meaning to speak with you. You're never home, it seems, or your bell doesn't work."

Henry nodded. "Home less these days. Trying to stay busy. What can I help you with?"

Richter looked down the length of the table, which was empty, but then behind to the person closest to him.

"Let's go outside."

Henry said, "The courtyard is good."

And Richter responded immediately, "Yes! A very Italian place. Made for conversation. I like the courtyard."

The chill of the afternoon shadows had left the courtyard empty. They stopped at the edge of the arcade in front of the empty fountain, faced with a joyous bronze nymph clutching a naked child; the statue's nakedness was an affront to the cold.

Richter began as if they were already in the midst of a long dialogue. "No one will speak to me, of course. I can't find Arthur, and he's instructed the lawyer, Downes, not to speak to me. Peter is afraid of me—I think he believes I might have killed Morgan. My little speech in the church that day might have backfired.... You know. In the movies it makes the killer try something foolish. Arthur has done nothing. He is gathering up all the loose ends in a neat little bag, and he'll walk away like a thief on a holiday."

Henry decided it was best not to mention his own encounter with Arthur and studied the geometric balance of small square windows beside windows arched, all scattered on a broad face of yellow brick; here the dimensions exaggerated the height so that the ceiling—a field of open sky above—seemed that much further away.

Henry said, "McKim had fun with all of this."

Ranulf was wholly puzzled by Henry's attempt to change the conversation. "Who?"

Henry played his hand across the air before them. "The fellow who designed all of this. He must have enjoyed life. Planning it all, picking the bits and pieces from everywhere and matching them up in one enormous toy of thought and then making it real."

It occurred to Henry that this space was not so different in size than the center court at the Gardner Museum. The difference—what made the Gardner court seem larger—was

the glassed roof. Here, the depthless sky diminished the span of the walls.

Ranulf's eyes searched the surfaces of the space around them. His mind appeared to focus as he spoke.

"It's a copy of someplace in Rome, I think. I've probably been there. It's whimsy. We once had time for whimsy.... That's the kind of thing Morgan would say. She was always looking for the cause of things. She always knew the why of things. Though she never seemed to care about my foolishness. I think she understood it better than I do myself."

Henry looked at the man's eyes. Wherever he was staying, he was not sleeping well. A blue shadow had spread above his cheeks like color in porcelain.

Henry said, "And she loved Arthur. He loved her. You think he killed his own mother?"

Ranulf turned quickly, like a dog biting a pursuer at its heels. "She did not trust him. She even told me that."

Henry shook his head. This was not going well.

"It's not the same thing. He had gotten himself into some trouble. She knew he needed time to grow out of that. But she still loved him."

Ranulf looked back at Henry, his face empty of intent, his voice held in check. "I've seen her cry over it. He had run away from his father, you know. Not from her."

Henry answered, "He loved her."

Ranulf pulled the lapels of his jacket together over the black scarf. His voice lowered in weariness. "I suppose. But it's the money he cares about now."

Henry asked, "Why do you think he ran away in the first place?"

Richter said, "Why do boys hate their fathers?"

Henry shook his head. "You think it was hate?"

192

At least Ranulf gave that a pause for thought.

"No. I suppose not. I'm projecting, of course. But they couldn't get along."

Henry tried a smile. "Fathers can be difficult."

Ranulf sat down on the stone bench behind them and huddled with his hands in his pockets for warmth. Above Ranulf's head a bronze relief plaque memorialized a hero of a past time. Henry could remember standing on that very bench once to read the words there.

"'Francis Amasa Walker.' Why do they seem like such giants? Why does it feel like we are the children who will never grow up?"

Ranulf's head turn upward toward the weather-darkened image. "I suppose they were."

Henry felt weighted with his mood. "When given the chance, we build something less than mediocre—like the piece of crap on the other side of this. There is no respect. There is no honor. And there is no whimsy."

Ranulf gave a quick laugh of discovery. "She told me you were too critical—too serious.... That's all past now. That world is finished. We've gone disposable. Everything is short-term—postmodern, you know. What comes after postmodern? What oxymoron would fit? They should have known they had an historical problem when they labeled themselves 'modern.' But they couldn't see that far into the future while looking in a mirror. It's a short-sighted world now. And it's run by a gang who never figured to make it much beyond thirty. We never really cared about anything but ourselves. We have no second act, never mind a finish."

Chapter Nineteen

They had arranged to met at Michael's Delicatessen for pastrami. Peter Johnson swore he had never eaten a pastrami sandwich before, and there was only one place Henry thought adequate for such an introduction.

Johnson ordered the half-size and was still working the edges of his sandwich when Henry had finished his whole one and began picking the loose bits from his plate. Conversation about the book trade in England compared with the United States turned to the differences between the customers themselves, and then the continued attraction of Americans to things English—Austen and Dickens and Waugh. Perhaps that was part of what Heber had felt.

Henry asked aloud, "Why do you think they married?"

Peter shook his head without looking up from the dissection of his sandwich.

"That would be me. She was pregnant. He was still a student when he met her. The young medieval scholar. He must have seemed a very romantic figure to her then. I think she was already eccentric. She might even have appeared to be exotic to the American mind, letting her hair grow to her waist. Strawberry red—she only pinned it up for her bath. She was given to wearing robes and cloaks—she had one, a green velvet shawl she wore in autumn for all the years I can remember.... She believed in fairies, you know."

A picture of Ismay Whyte came to mind drawn from a Pre-Raphaelite painting Henry recalled, but he had no ready

comment that seemed politely possible.

"Really?"

"Very much. She believed there were several races of them—very Tolkienesque—living in the woods and dales. She would take me to the woods and sit on a log and say, 'Listen—hear them? They play.' And I would say, "Mother! It's only the leaves. It's only the rustle of the squirrels.' And she would say, 'Be quiet. You must listen. You'll hear them.' She meant it. She was raised to believe it. Her father was a friend of Conan Doyle's. Her mother was a Scot. The Scots are hopeless about such things."

Henry laughed. "Her travel books must have been wonderful."

Peter Johnson's face brightened as he looked up. "Oh, they were. They are. She went to places no one else cared for. Dragged me all over the back roads of Brittany. We went to every one of the chalk circles. We visited each of the great stones. I spoke French like a Breton until I got through school. She liked the Pyrenees. She loved the Basques. And she found fairies everywhere. For a short while, in the mid-fifties, her books became the rage for the educated British on short holiday. You weren't allowed to take much in the way of funds out of the country then, and of course we were all still broke from the war, so the three- and four-day holiday was quite popular."

Henry took a jealous breath. "It must have been fun, tagging along."

Peter actually smiled. "It was, in retrospect. But I made few friends. I had my books, of course. I had my Oxford Classics. I don't know if you had them here, but those little blue books were stuffed in every pocket, wherever I went. I felt like another piece of her luggage at times. She even called me…" Peter hesitated. Henry wondered what revisions he was making to his words, and waited.

Finally the man spoke again, "Once, going across the border from Portugal to Spain, the guards inspected everything we had. It wasn't much. And then the fellow said. Is that all? You have nothing else to declare? And she said, 'Nothing, except for the stolen child.' She said it straight-faced. The guards went crazy. Phone calls were made. We were there for hours. It was a silly joke. Somehow she thought it was all very entertaining. But after that, she often called me her stolen child…and it was the last thing she ever said to me."

Henry heard the words in his head. He knew them by heart and repeated them aloud.

> *Come away, O human child!*
> *To the waters and the wild*
> *With a faery, hand in hand,*
> *For the world's more full of weeping*
> *than you can understand.*

Peter frowned. "You know the poem?"

Henry nodded. "'The Stolen Child,' by Yeats. Something my mother liked."

Peter stopped nibbling, with a genuine look of puzzlement. He said "Really…" in a near whisper before looking away from Henry's eyes to study the edges of his sandwich again. His puzzlement became a frown.

Henry pursued the past. "And you never came to visit your dad?"

Peter said, "No. Not then. I hardly knew him. I was barely four when he left. I had seen several letters. Their correspondence was rather harsh…. Mind you, she never said a bad word about him. In fact, she said very good things about him. But like all children, I was curious. I found the letters…. She still loved him."

Henry followed the line of his own curiosity. "Why did they divorce?"

Peter's back straightened. "He divorced her. Because he did not love her. It was his mistake. No one could have ever loved him more."

Henry could not meet the man's eyes now. He could not tell him that he knew what Morgan's love must have been like. Such comparisons of love were beside the point.

This was the thought he had pushed from his mind only an hour before, when he had met Leona at his father's house. She had called him earlier to talk, and he had told her he would be there on his way to a lunch appointment. But it was a thought he had considered many times before. There was no measure of love.

That meeting had been thankfully brief. Leona had gotten to the point quickly, sitting at the kitchen table and twisting a rubber band in her fingers.

"Did you love me? I mean, back then?"

He was unready for that kind of discussion.

"I think so. We were kids. Do kids really understand things like that?"

She was ready in her own thoughts.

"Better than adults, I think."

He had said, "Everything was much simpler then."

She had answered, "Maybe." Her eyes were attached to his. "But you never said it, you know. I thought about that a hundred times later on. You never really said it."

Had he ever actually said it? To anyone?

He said, "I don't remember."

She heaved her bosom with a breath that seemed enough for both of them.

"But you acted like you did. You were very cute. But you

never said it. And the words matter.... And I was thinking. I remembered. I did say it to you. I wasn't just playing. Do you remember? I meant it. Did you know that?"

He did not know what the answer to that was. The silence as he searched for the words grew painful.

Leona took his right hand and lifted it. She had been there when he broken his arm years ago. He was glad it wasn't broken this time.

"Does it still hurt?"

"Not much. Just a little stiff."

"Stiff can be okay."

"You've got the wrong limb."

"I've got the right limb, but maybe it's attached to the wrong guy."

Avoiding her eyes, so close, meant watching her hand on his.

He said, "You're probably right about that."

She shook her head at him. "Why do things have to be so difficult? Weren't you the one who always said keep it simple?"

"My father says it."

She answered back, "You say it, too."

He looked away. He was lost. "I guess I do."

"You remember the letter your father wrote—the one you wouldn't read?"

He tensed at that. "Yes."

She held his hand between both of hers. Her hands were warm in a way he recalled. "He told Mom that he loved her. He wrote it. He said it was not the same as the only love he had ever known before, but it was love and real nevertheless. He said it very sweetly. I think it must have made my mother very happy."

What other fractures would he find in his world? "The old man is full of surprises."

It had not been the right response. He had no idea what the right response might have been. If he had loved her, he had never been sure enough of it to say the words. And there could be no comparison of love, from one person to another, or even of love from one time to another. Whatever love was, it had no measure.

Leona had been disappointed in him. It was on her face, and she had let go of his hand, and he knew, even more than feeling sympathy for her, he had felt relieved. But it was the thought which he still played with. His father had often surprised him, more because, in most things, he was so predictable.

Now Henry watched Peter Johnson slice another edge of his pastrami away with a knife—perhaps because it appeared to be burned.

Henry said, "It's too bad you never got to know your father."

Peter raised one eyebrow skeptically.

"Perhaps. Perhaps not. I'm not sure I could have ever liked him.... I saw him once again when I was still young. Before I went off to university... after Mother had died. He had offered to cover my expense at school and sent a check, and I used a part of it to buy a ticket to the States. It was quite a surprise to him.... I had not remembered well. I had conjured a picture of the American. Something along the lines of William Holden in *The Bridge on the River Kwai*. I did not expect him to look so— well, you see me. One forms an idea about others based on oneself. Heber was not a thin man."

Henry asked, "Was he unkind?"

Peter tilted his head. "No. Not actually. Rough. That was, I suppose, part of his charm to some. His cigars. The sharkskin suits. But he was civilized. He must have been an odd duck during his Oxford days in any case.... When I arrived, he had his new young wife beside him. He looked very comfortable. And,

as you know, he was already quite successful. I thought he was full of himself."

At the time, Peter would have been the man's only child. Henry could not imagine why Heber would show so little interest. What was in the letters that was so harsh? It seemed like a question he could not fairly ask.

When he told Peter what was in the will, he watched the man's eyes. That was the purpose of their meeting. He wanted Peter to know in case Arthur was not forthcoming. This might be something which a bank would take seriously if Peter needed money right away.

Peter seemed oddly interested, not in what the will said, but where it was kept.

He looked up from the splayed body of his sandwich and said, "And there was Heber, the Arthurian scholar. It says something, don't you think, that she would hide it there, in the Malory, from her own Arthur?"

Henry had to agree.

Chapter Twenty

M arcus Evers was killed on a field in France. The poison of a yellow-green gas had found him where he lay wounded with a dozen others. It was only one loss among many, but made more noteworthy because he did not have to be there. He had chosen his own place in time.

Henry turned the knob on the microfiche machine and refocused on the gray film. A woman nearby complained of something to the librarian at the desk. Henry tried to shut out the distraction.

The first report, on July 24, 1916, had been too short.

Correspondent Killed

Marcus Evers, correspondent for the *Chicago Times*, has been reported killed during the ongoing British military action at the Somme. His timely dispatches have been a constant feature in these pages in recent months.

And a week later.

Reporter's Death Confirmed

The death of *Chicago Times* reporter Marcus Evers has been confirmed by

Vincent McCaffrey

British War Office. Some question has been raised concerning his reason for being on the field of battle. American reporters have often been excluded from field action during the European conflict. Most dispatches are filed from Paris or London, and Berlin. Evers' detailed reports of ongoing hostilities have been the cause of frequent criticism from British authorities.

A month later, the last newspaper story appeared.

Marcus Evers' Father
Makes Donation.

The father of Marcus Evers, the *Times* reporter recently killed in the ongoing military action at Somme, has made a donation to the City of Chicago to be used in part for a memorial plaque.

Evers died in July after suffering wounds received from a shell burst. His death occurred during a German counterattack employing poison gas following a British offensive action when he was unable to move to safety due to his previous injuries. His dispatches have been sorely missed. As an American correspondent, Evers was not officially attached to the British battalion which had become the subject of his reports. His presence had

been a matter of controversy. It appears that Evers' previous friendship with Field Commander Lieutenant General David Wright had served as his pass to the front lines. A letter from General Wright to William Evers, the father, offers further details confirming the death of the *Times* reporter. Evers' sharp eye for detail and his patent disregard for his own safety gave American readers a most revealing look at the ongoing horrors of war. His untimely death has made him a tragic part of the very subject he had so well covered. General Wright's condolence noted Evers' bravery and the reporter's own recent private loss as a source of in-spiration for his brave work. The *Times* has established a scholarship in Marcus Evers' name at the University of Illinois. The memorial plaque will be placed at the Chicago Public Library.

What private loss had Evers suffered? Henry had found the book by Charles Whitman, the former *Chicago Times* editor. He had ordered it from a bookshop in Ann Arbor. Only one paragraph referred to Evers.

Henry reread the passage when he got home. The shadow in the words was not clear—but it was there.

"Several of our reporters were to die in that war. One, because he was the first to go, stands clear in memory. Marcus Evers, always eager, always quick, who had

worked with me in the newsroom fresh out of college, had grown in a few short years to be a featured correspondent. He might have remained at his desk and enjoyed his success, and one day even taken my own chair. But the sting of personal misfortune stole away his care for mundane things. Nothing less than the larger tragedy of our time could quiet his mind. He pulled strings enjoyed by few and placed himself in the forefront of the Great War. He died there, only twenty-nine years old."

What personal misfortune?

Had he lost the woman he loved? Had life become so bleak for him that only the cut and stench of war might be felt?

Who was Lieutenant General David Wright? Certainly he was the same "General" who, with his wife, had befriended Helen Mawson.

Henry ignored the buzz of the doorbell. He wanted to sleep. It felt as if he had only just closed his eyes, but it was the sun that burned now against his eyelids. He thought for a moment, with his eyes held shut against the light, that it was Saturday and he would have to be getting up for the auction in Concord, and then realized it could only be Friday. He had spent his Thursday at the library. The buzz of the doorbell broke the silence again.

Whoever it was wanted to talk, and he was not in the mood for conversation. He rolled over and faced the relative darkness of the wall. His phone rang.

He capitulated and picked up the receiver.

"Good morning, Henry."

It was Leona. The huskiness in her voice was smooth.

He said, "I suppose. I was trying to sleep."

She said, "It's gorgeous out here. You can smell the autumn, and there's just a hint of the ocean."

Henry was afraid to ask, "Where are you?"

She said, "Sitting on your front steps."

He was trapped.

"What did you want?"

"You. I came to get you up and out of your little library. Come have breakfast with me."

He had not eaten the night before. The confrontation with Arthur had come back to him in his dreams. He had awakened twice in the midst of a struggle with his blanket in the dark. Now he was, in fact, very hungry.

He relented. "It'll take a minute. I have to get dressed."

Leona said, "I'll wait. It's a little cold, though. Can I come in?"

He climbed out of bed as he put the phone back in its cradle and took the few steps to the button which unlocked the front door, and then turned the latch on his own door as he went through his kitchenette to the bathroom. He turned on the faucet in the tub and heard his apartment door open as he waited for the hot water to rise to the shower head.

He said, "I'll be out in a minute.... Read a book."

He heard her say, "Which one?"

He said, "Take a chance. Any one."

Her question struck him as funny. For all his critical judgments about books, he would read almost anything given the spare time.

He had just gotten the soap out of his eyes when the bathroom door opened.

She said, "Can I come in? I'm really not in the mood to read right now."

Vincent McCaffrey

Through the break in the shower curtain he could see the red petals of the rose, not far below the dark chocolate bud of her right breast.

Chapter Twenty-One

The street was quiet in the midday sun, dry leaves huddling at curbs and chatting in whispers when cars passed. The rooming house faced the street with its broad side, fronted by a long porch, and even at three floors, including the dormers, it seemed much smaller from the street than the place he was more familiar with from the rear. There the land fell away to the playing fields of Lawrence, Henry's old grammar school. From the back, the brown-shingled Victorian dropped a full four floors, broken by an endless number of windows above a gravel parking area. At one of those windows a very buxom and completely naked woman had screamed at her departing lover in the driveway below as Henry and his teammates stopped playing baseball to watch. It was a fond memory often brought up at reunions.

Henry rang the buzzer. Within, through the door glass, he saw a dark common room, chairs and couches, spread toward an empty fireplace to the left. To the right an oak staircase rose to upper floors.

He rang the bell again.

Squinting through the glass, he could see mail spread on a small table. He tried the handle. The door opened.

He said, "Hello," his voice dying in the still air.

The mail on the table was addressed to half a dozen different people, including Peter Johnson. One of those, from a doctor, also listed the room number as twenty-two.

Henry climbed the stairs, the baritone grunt of the wood

against wood echoing around him. Number twenty-two was the first room at the top. He knocked.

A woman's voice responded, "Hello?"

He answered against his own polished reflection on the door.

"Hello. My name is Henry Sullivan. I was looking for Peter Johnson."

The door opened to a burst of sunlight from the back windows. The woman standing before him was very thin; the gossamer fabric of her robe revealed the dark shadow of her frailty. Her face appeared almost joyous with surprise and delight, as if she had long been expecting him. She wore a hand-made cotton knit cap which only served to accent the absence of hair on her head.

"Hello. I'm Vivienne, Peter's wife. I know you! Peter has told me all about you. Please come in."

She swung her arm in a lanky gesture of welcome toward the bright interior. The paleness of her skin was barely colored by a blush of rouge on her cheeks. Her eyes were large and dark and touched by every glint of color in the room.

He said, "Thanks. I hope I'm not disturbing you."

She shook her head with a girlish laugh. "God, no. I sit here and pray for someone to come that I can talk to. I even spoke to the minister from St. Paul's church yesterday. I usually hate ministers. He was lovely, though."

Henry's eyes scanned the room. It was in perfect order, newspapers stacked square, a short row of books arranged on almost every flat surface. This was a sitting room. A bedroom led off to the side.

He asked, "Will Peter be back soon?"

She shrugged, and the bones of her shoulders poked at the fabric of her dressing gown.

"I don't think so. He's out job hunting. Jobs for middle-aged booksellers are not easy to find, as you probably know too well."

Dressed in the pearl white fabric, he thought she had the appearance of someone in the theatre.

Lacking a more positive response, he mumbled, "I guess so."

She held up a hand. "But can you stay a moment? I'd love the company."

Vivienne tugged at the back of one chair, which did little more than tilt with her hand. Henry moved it and waited for her to sit on the couch which faced the rear windows and the sun.

She said brightly, "It's a very pleasant room, don't you think? I used to sit here and watch the children play in the field, but they've blocked it off now for the construction at the school."

Henry peeked out at his old haunts before he sat down. The playing field was gouged by the tracks of large equipment and divided by temporary fences.

He asked, "How long have you been here?"

She said, "Only a month…this time. But we found this room some years ago when I was here first, and it was so nice, we have arranged to get it each time since."

"It must be difficult on your life at home to be away."

She did not quite shake her head, but angled it back and forth oddly, as if she might be avoiding some pain by the movement. "Only on the pets. But I give them to my mother. They know her house as well as any. Sadly, we've lost the little house we had in Hay-on-Wye. That went with the shop.… But it was a rickety little place with hardly any yard, so I think the pets are better off with Mum."

Henry had not asked Peter more about the business.

"When did you lose the shop?"

She sighed. "The last time. Last year, when we came over. The little ass Peter had found to run things ran off instead with the best books and what little money had come in. Business was terrible, in any case. Half the stores have closed since the internet came along."

Henry nodded at the reiteration of a sad fact. "I'm sorry."

Vivienne smiled instead. "No. We are very fortunate, really. We lost a little, but we got out with something. And Peter will find another job soon enough. He's very good. He's really quite a scholar in his own right. Medieval studies... Do you like medieval history?"

Henry relaxed. Her question seemed genuine and interested. "Yes. I guess Peter and I have that in common. I like the early part, mostly. The 'Dark Ages.'"

She smiled. "King Arthur! Yes? Americans love King Arthur."

Henry grabbed at the subject as something to talk about that might avoid things more obvious.

"I suppose so. In spite of all the books, all the silly fantasies, I still think it's underappreciated. It's part of the mythology that shapes us now, in our own age. And like most mythology, I think it's most often based on fact."

She almost hopped in her seat as she straightened.

"Exactly! Just what Peter thinks. You two should talk about that. I'm trying to get him to write a book about it. He has so many ideas. He was telling me just last night about the monasteries. About all those rules and restrictions. No property, no meat, no company, no sex, and all the rest. Did you realize that those things had little to do with any principles of faith? The rules were simply trials, made to keep out those whose faith was not strong enough. In that time, the monastery

210

was a perfect refuge from the boil of trouble in the real world. Anyone with half a brain would want to be a monk. Did you ever read the Umberto Eco book, *The Name of the Rose?*"

He had ambivalent feelings about Mr. Eco's scholarship, but her enthusiasm was clear.

"I did. The descriptions of the making of the books and the burning of the fire was incredible."

She somehow straightened further. "Peter knows all about that kind of thing. He got it from his father. Heber was a medieval scholar, too, you know."

Henry said simply, "Yes."

Vivienne angled her head once more. "And his mother, Ismay. She was a bit of a nut—pagan spiritualism and all of that, but she loved historical detail. It was probably what attracted Heber to her in the first place. But she was so very kind to Peter. He was her little prince. She spoiled him, really. I think it was because she bought him any book he wanted at a very young age that he became so devoted to books."

Henry found it difficult to imagine—now the man was forced to sell his father's books to save what mattered even more.

Henry wondered, "What kind of jobs has he looked into?"

She answered immediately, the thought already on her lips. "The libraries, mostly. He has a green card because of his father. Library work would be good for him. But nothing's open just now, and he's trying anything. He's had some part-time work, but they want to send him to the worst places. I worry about him. He's so foolish about some things. Naive. He'll be taken advantage of…. He was even mugged once. Last spring. He was an awful mess. Just some drunken bullies."

Henry imagined Peter was too thin to be a match for more than one. He asked, "What was your interest before you became entangled with Peter's book business?"

Vivienne smiled. Her teeth were white and perfectly formed within the curve of her pale lips. Her tongue caught at her teeth in a bit of a tease.

"You'll never guess."

Her eyebrows rose in expectation. He knew she wanted to tell him.

He said, "An actress?" He guessed only because it was his unlikely first thought.

Her face fell to a pout. "He told you."

Henry shook his head defensively. "No. It was just a guess."

Her dark eyes danced with reflected color again. "Nobody ever guesses it...but it's true. I finished the run of a show in Piccadilly one day and decided to take a drive in the country and just kept going. Something made me keep right on. I ended up in Hay-on-Wye. And there was Peter. Looking like the bookworm that he is, all folded up behind his desk. He practically killed himself trying to get up when I came in. I was in love with him before he managed to straighten his tie. What a boy! I gave up the lead in a very promising production of a Terence Rattigan play and asked for a job. And he, without a penny in his pocket, hired me. Just like that. And I would have thought such things never happened."

Chapter Twenty-Two

"Who's to blame?" Jack said. "There's people that go around putting blame to anybody but themselves. And then there's your dad. He takes the blame for all that's happened. It's his way. Always was. Did I ever tell you about how I got into the Marines?"

Jack pulled a cigarette from the pack in his jacket in preparation for a story and offered one to Henry. Henry was not sure he was in the mood for either one, but he said, "Yes."

His uncle ignored him and flicked his lighter, developing a thick circle of smoke in the still air of the room.

"Yes...Well, remember it! Now, there's your dad. When he joined the navy, he looked pretty fine in his whites. The true figure of a man. Poster-worthy. Then they trained him as an electrician, and he thought he was the sharpest knife in the drawer. I couldn't stand to be near him. The same room was unbearable. The same house was too much. When he was stationed at Portsmouth, he used to come around looking for your mother, dressed sharp right down to the shoes. I joined the Marines to get away from him. Not what you heard."

Henry said, "What I heard is what you told me."

Jack hesitated only briefly.

"I lied then. I'm a liar at heart. It's why your dad never wanted me around. He thinks it might be some kind of viral infection and you kids would catch it."

Henry sat down in the chair by the kitchen table, knowing Jack would not sit even if asked. His uncle had awakened him,

and Henry was not prepared to offer him even a cup of coffee. Jack's eyes catalogued the room around them.

He finally said, "Too many books."

Henry's answer was automatic. "You can't have too many books."

His uncle's arm waved the cigarette through the air, leaving a trail of smoke.

"You could put a sofa there and a TV over on that side, if you didn't have so many books. You can't have girls over without a sofa. If you just have chairs, you end up talking too much."

Henry said, "I like to talk."

"Talk just gets people married and divorced. A sofa and a TV will keep things just right."

It was still too early to be listening to his uncle's philosophizing. Henry wiped the sleep from his eyes. "What will you be doing for Thanksgiving?"

His uncle took a breath worthy of Albert. "Sally's taking me to her mother's. Punishment to fit the crime. Her mother is as old as I am. Unbearable. But she's a swell cook."

Henry said, "Good enough. But I've been invited out to Albert's. I was just a little concerned about Dad being alone."

Jack shook his head with a total lack of pity. "Buy him a turkey sandwich at Michael's and go your way. He's not helpless yet."

His uncle pulled a silver money clip from a pocket and counted out brand-new hundred-dollar bills in a neat stack on the kitchen table.

"Thanks." Henry spoke reflexively.

Jack stood back from his task. "Thanks? I borrowed the money from you. Don't be thanking me for returning it. Just be remembering I returned it when I said I would, so you won't be telling wicked stories about me in the years to come."

"I've told a few already." Henry pulled a bill off the top. "You made a mistake. You counted out eleven."

"That's the interest." Jack waved a hand dismissively.

Henry shook his head. "I didn't ask for interest."

Jack frowned with mock disgust. "You're too old to be handing out money with no interest. I got mine. You get yours—told what? What lies have you told about me?"

Henry accepted the responsibility for being too glib. "Like how you used a phony driver's license to get your job driving trucks for the Marines in Korea."

Jack looked away at the window. "It was cold on the ground. My feets don't always like the cold. I only did it to get my feets off the ground."

"So you admit you used the phony license?" Henry raised an eyebrow.

Jack glared in return. "Makes it sound like I never learned to drive. I passed the test. I passed a test in the Marines, as well. They don't take anybody's word in the corps till you earn it. It's what you do that counts. Anyway, if the cops had returned my real one to me, it wouldn't have been necessary."

Henry had to ask, "What did you do to make the cops angry?"

"Drove a truck carrying the wrong goods."

"Stolen goods?"

"Mistaken goods."

"What was that?"

"Bananas."

"Whose mistake?"

"Mine. I had pneumonia at the time. I couldn't smell a thing."

"What were you supposed to drive?"

"Strawberries."

"Were you arrested?"

"No. The union beef tried to beat the crap out of me is all."

"What happened?"

"I had some crap left, so I laid it on the guy's face."

Jack did not exactly smile with the memory, but his eyes looked satisfied.

Henry said, "They must have been unhappy with you about that."

Now Jack smiled just a bit. "They were still looking for me when I joined the Marines."

Henry pursued, "You said you joined because Dad bet you a hundred dollars you wouldn't."

Jack wagged his head back and forth. "Well, I couldn't join the Marines without some folding money in my pocket. I got your dad to make that bet. What would I play poker with? So I set it up. And I got him to pay up."

Henry asked, "How did you do that? Did you have to beat him up, too?"

Jack's face pinched up at the absurdity. "Jesus. Anybody ever beat your dad up? Not to my knowledge. No. I got him to make the bet in front of your mother."

Jack turned and left with a "Toodle."

Henry sat awhile with the thought of those times before checking the weather at the window, which was gray and probably cold. He showered and half dressed enough to sit at his desk with the computer and catalogue rather than go out.

It was afternoon before hunger took the lead. He was tired of staring at a computer screen. He needed to stretch his legs. When he started to walk, his legs took him to Inman Square.

Albert had already arrived at the Blue Thorn. Henry related his most recent thoughts and discoveries as well as his

encounter with Vivienne. Peter Johnson's sad tale prompted Albert to caution Henry about involving himself in other people's problems. Then Albert launched into a lecture concerning the best approach to fighting windmills.

"You cannot simply run at them with your lance. You need a stratagem, or they'll toss you."

Henry lowered his head to avoid eye contact. "If I am unworthy of the role of Don Quixote, then let me be his dog."

Albert dismissed this conjecture after a long sip off the top of his glass of ale.

"He had a horse, Rocinante, not a dog."

Henry tried not to smile. "Rocinante! Yes. But I am satisfied to be his dog."

Albert added, "And a squire."

Henry had to look away toward the street to answer. "Yes, Sancho. And Sancho Panza had an ass by the name of Dapple. But I will play the dog."

Predictably, Albert persisted. "I don't remember a dog."

Henry said, "His name was Flip."

Albert sat back on his stool and raised an eyebrow. "I don't remember that."

Henry shrugged, then asked, "You don't remember his turning somersaults in the air to entertain Dulcinea?"

Leaning forward now on his forearms, Albert cracked a smile and spoke into the hollow of his glass before taking another swallow. "No, but where did that get him?"

Henry said, "Doing somersaults for a woman will get you nowhere. Thus the expression, 'Don't be flip.'"

Albert grunted and then began again with his previous thought. "I wasn't being flip. I was only making the point that you can't play Don Quixote. These are real people, and there is a murderer among them. There are no windmills to battle.

Besides, they burn coal now instead, so we'll have something good to breathe after they've outlawed cigarette smoke. Life is just a series of small indignities which we overcome by feigning ignorance and the government reinforces by passing laws."

Henry said, "Like being overrun by a herd of pigs."

Albert paused in an effort of patience.

"Something like that. And more importantly, there is no Dulcinea."

"There's Alice."

"She's no Dulcinea."

Henry said, "Squint a little."

Henry had opened the gate. Albert took a breath. "Squinting is not the answer. I want to sally forth and do battle. I want to build my own home without permission from the zoning board. I want to plant my garden with flowers and trade a dozen roses for a dozen eggs. But we've replaced tradition with law. Traded our prudence for jurisprudence. And we've replaced simple prejudice with hate. We homogenize and pasteurize, and the milk that used to keep for a week is now bad in three days, and it doesn't taste as good even when it's just bought. I remember sweat. Remember sweat? It was the smell of people who worked hard and bathed every day. Now the only time you smell sweat it's on some poor homeless idiot who should be taken care of, but we've tossed him out on the street to protect his civil right to freeze to death. Heroes used to unhitch the plow, kiss their wives and babies good-bye, and march off to protect their country. Now they use the word for just anybody that does the job they were paid to do. If it breaks, don't bother fixing it, just throw it away. Everything is disposable, including honor."

Henry said, "You're ranting."

Albert raised both hands in the air. "I'm trying to tell you, everything is trash now. There is nothing worth keeping."

Henry objected, "That's not like you. You're the guy with the positive mental attitude. How many times have you lectured me on the meaning of trash? Trash is good. Trash is the simple waste of living. If you don't have trash, then you don't have choices. No mistakes, no risk. No shit, no life. So what's wrong?"

Albert filled his lungs. "What's right? I put in for an adjustment on the increase in my real-estate tax last spring. Well, a guy finally came out and looked at the house a couple of months ago, and now, instead of adjusting it down, they've gone and raised it some more. So now, that two thousand dollars I paid Junior and his friend to paint the house over the summer is going to cost me another fifteen hundred a year. And Junior just lost his weekend job because he told his boss she was full of shit. I asked him if he actually used the word 'shit.' He did. I asked him where he learned to talk like that. He said it was from me. Meanwhile, Alice wants to go on a diet. You know what that means. It means we are all going to have to go on a diet. I told her I liked her the way she was. I been sleeping on the couch since I opened my fat mouth. And Junior has discovered girls, big-time, and they've discovered him. His report card says he's missed a dozen homework assignments in one semester. So my neighbor has filed a petition to keep me from parking my truck in my own driveway. Naturally, I parked it at the curb in front of his house, instead. He knows I go to bed early, so lately he's been turning up the music later at night. He listens to hip-hop. Alice blames me for that, too. There's no heat in the house. The boiler's got a crack in it. The damn thing is only eighty-five years old. I thought things were supposed to be made better back then. Now the guy from the oil company has refused to fix it. Says if I want his service that I've got to buy a new one. Need I continue?"

Some things just broke, Henry figured, but it wasn't worth saying. It did, however, bring up a thought which had not left his mind since it happened.

"My father said something the other day. It was about our stove. I had to ask him—I don't know why; it just occurred again to me out of the blue—I asked him, being that he's an electrician, why he had never fixed the light in the stove. You know Mom was always bending over with a flashlight to see how the pot roast was coming along. He said it was because General Electric was supposed to do it. It was covered under the warranty. So I said the warranty had probably run out forty years ago, and he said he knew that, but now he never used it anyway. They should have fixed it then, like they promised."

Albert did not catch Henry's drift. "That's just like Alice.... You can't promise Alice anything unless you mean to do it. I promised her to get the leaves out of the gutters last week. She has barely talked to me since. We ate takeout three times this week. Then Junior got tired of takeout, and he went and cleaned the gutters himself. But Alice isn't satisfied, because I broke my word. A promise is a vow. Good Lord, she has no mercy."

Henry said, "A vow is a promise."

Albert waved. "You aren't married. You just don't know."

"And promises should never be broken. Not by old Don Quixote. And not by..." Henry paused with the thought. "It's a matter of honor. A knight's honor."

Chapter Twenty-Three

He remembered very well the first time his mother had taken him to the Isabella Stewart Gardner Museum. It was the winter after he had turned nine, and he had loudly objected that he had better things to do. He could not remember now what those things were.

His complaints had turned to pouting and obstinacy. Walking with her from the house, he remained five or ten feet behind. He had taken to refusing to hold her hand, having grown too big for that. But he had always liked the feel of her hand on his. It was his loss forever now.

The outside of the museum building did not impress him— a boxy structure within a black iron fence. There were no fountains, or stone lions, or even flags. Years would pass before he understood that only the treasure inside mattered. He had moaned out loud after they entered, making an ugly echo in the inner courtyard. The tempered light beneath the high glass which enclosed the courtyard intrigued him. He moaned again to hear the change in his voice. He had smuggled a toy in his pocket, a small racing car, and wanted to hold on to it when they checked their coats. For one of the few times he could recall, his mother had lost her patience and told him to stay there, in the exit hall, and wait for her beside a sad figure in a suit of armor. He had folded his own arms in defiance.

There was a door there, across from the coat room. He thought of it often as he passed it afterward. It was plain by comparison to so many of the great and wonderful doors which

had been salvaged by "Mrs. Jack," as they called her. She had brought the doors from castles and palaces across Europe to Boston and preserved them throughout the museum. However, that door just happened to be the one through which Henry passed from his childhood into the difficult years of his youth.

In later times he would often walk up and down the long gallery on the third floor—that high and narrow space of letters and books, paintings, busts, gilded chairs, and the dark menace of wooden church stalls, all of which ended at the salvaged altar of a medieval chapel and the firework of stained glass illuminated by sunlight—as if it were his personal arcade.

How many hours had he watched the still figures of the tapestry there as if waiting for them to move—knights in armor astride their horses, the hounds just ahead, and maids in their funny caps and bright gowns left behind at the castle wall.

But that very first day he had wandered no further than that one small room at the bottom—the Blue Room, they called it—not at all impressive with its poor light and low ceiling. This, Henry came to realize, was the best room of all; an afterthought, crammed with its marvels like the accidental accumulation of a basement. It was a perfect room for the boy he had been and tried now to remember.

There, set high against the wall and at least as large as he was then, another boy stood, forlorn: "The Standard Bearer of the Harvest Festival," forgotten in his task, upholding a staff of tattered flowers and wheat, dressed in the heavy cloth of an un-comfortable costume. Henry immediately knew that boy very well, and knew his thoughts. And below the boy's sandaled feet, beneath the ornate frame with the name of the artist Antonio Mancini, the dark wood of a glass-fronted bookcase secured the space—this not quite as high then as Henry's chest.

A mixed assortment of books, some upright, others on

their sides, a casual presentation, intrigued him. He would have quickly pulled a volume out had the case not been locked to prevent this.

Who was this Henry Adams? What kind of "education" did he get? Henry strained to see the darkened titles through the glare of the glass. There was a name he knew: Omar Khayyam, with gilt decoration on the spine. And another: a plain brown Nathaniel Hawthorne. His mother had read some of the *Tanglewood Tales* to him once, but he had fallen asleep. These books were in the case at home as well—no, not these books: cheaper editions.

Who was Okakura Kakuzo? Was Claudius a name or a place, or perhaps a Latin word for the weather?

He asked the guard. The guard looked at him as the troublesome child he was and did not answer. Henry sat on the polished wood of the floor in response—not unlike the floor in the parlor at home—directly in front of the case of books and read each title, in order, occasionally looking up again at the eyes of the unhappy standard-bearer above, who must be very tired by now from holding that cumbersome staff. Henry imagined that the boy's legs might ache. His fingers would itch where they grasped the bulky decorations bound to the wood of the pole. The boy could switch hands, of course, but in his other hand he held a dark fabric bag—perhaps his regular clothes, which he longed to put on instead of those he wore.

Henry lost his count of the books then, with the thought of what the boy's bag contained, and he stood instead to wander the room. The guard moved with him, a shadow at his left eye, and Henry refused to acknowledge the presence in return for the man's rudeness.

The people in the paintings were, most of them, unhappy, or just sad. Perhaps from waiting. There was a camp in the

woods, the white billow of canvas wrapped on Aspen poles. That seemed a happy place, but abandoned. A woman sat on an omnibus, dressed for a day on the town—or coming home perhaps, a shard of sun on her cheek. She seemed distressed. Another woman stood in flowing white robes over a pot of incense, her veil held out to catch the smoke. Was this self-punishment? The incense Henry knew from the holy days at St. Mary's made him choke.

A sour priest looked over the room from above the door; another woman with white hands and white face seemed buried in the black of mourning clothes. Nearby, a young woman in a white dressing gown brushed the wild fall of her red hair—in privacy perhaps.... Wasn't that the same picture he had imagined when Peter had spoken of his eccentric mother? And wasn't the reason he remembered it so well, that he had once watched at home as Miss Williams, the student boarder across the hall, had combed her hair like that—her door drawn open by the summer air from the window when he had closed his own. She had been naked. The first naked woman he had ever seen from head to foot. She brushed methodically, in quick strokes, eyes closed, her breasts bouncing as the bristles pulled free at the ends. Her unraveled hair, which he had thought was black, as it was usually tied in a tight bun on her head, had transformed in the light of the window and against her pale skin, and he saw that it was really a very dark red, as was the short red nest of hair between her thighs. She had opened her eyes just then, had seen him, and with a smile, had closed the door again. This had stirred him at the time, only months before his visit to the museum, in new ways, and stirred him now with the memory.

The guard had cleared his throat for attention. Henry moved on around the room. In another frame, a woman in a dark dress

holding an umbrella for shelter made her way on a snowy street in old New York. It was a small picture by Childe Hassam, and Henry remembered standing in the spot and imagining the moment in the picture long enough for the guard to again be worried.

A phone rang. Henry started.

Below the half-size reproduction of the *Standard Bearer* on the wall, a light flashed in a small panel above a neat desk. The secretary returned from wherever she had gone at least ten minutes before and answered the phone, speaking while looking critically at Henry where he sat on the couch. She seemed especially unhappy with his jeans. He had worn them a few days longer than he should to avoid doing his laundry. He returned her glance by developing an opinion of her legs, which were bare from above her knee, where the pleats of her gray wool dress stopped short. He could not be so critical of what he saw. He settled on the possibility that she worked out regularly in a gym.

She hung up the phone and turned and then turned again. "It could be a while longer. He's still on the phone with a client."

Henry's eyes went to the buttons on the panel by the phone. None were lit. Her eyes followed his, and then she turned her back and disappeared down the hall.

There were other pictures from the Blue Room which had stayed with him since that first visit. There was a picture of a young man with a bandage on his head by Denman Ross. Henry had always associated it with Ernest Hemingway. Somewhere he had seen a picture of Hemingway bandaged, and even though the author and the subject of the picture were physically different, it was the fellow in the picture who had filled the role of Hemingway's hero in Henry's mind when he had read *A Farewell To Arms*.

The athletic legs suddenly filled the frame made by the small rug on the wood floor. Henry looked up at cold eyes.

The receptionist said, "Mr. Charles is free. You can go in now."

He walked down the hall behind the undulation of indelicate curves which filled the back of the gray dress.

Mr. Charles did not stand. Henry accepted the hint and sat in the chair on the opposite side of the desk without being asked.

The Realtor spoke perfunctorily after looking at Henry's clothes a moment too long.

"What can I do for you?"

The voice was high and nasal, as if bored by routine. The man had a mustache on a thin upper lip which exaggerated a mouth already too wide.

Henry checked the art reproductions on the office wall to see if any others were from the Gardner as he answered, but none were familiar. "You were the broker for Morgan Johnson's condominium on Marlborough Street."

An eyebrow as thin as the mustache rose slightly.

The Realtor said, "I still am."

Henry tried to keep the tone of his own voice disinterested. "Not if Arthur Johnson thinks too much about the fact that the sale was being done without his knowledge."

"Never take disrespect lightly," his father often said. "Respect is the measure of a relationship. If someone shows you a lack of respect, show him something he'll remember for the next time."

Mr. Charles sat just a little bit straighter in his chair. "What business is it of yours?"

Henry studied the copy of a painting of an old man just to the left of the Realtor's head. It was a perfect distraction for the moment.

"I'm a friend of the family. I'm worried that people are being taken advantage of. There's been a murder, as you know. The estate is in probate. It could stay in probate for a long time if the situation is not resolved quickly. You won't be seeing any broker fees if there's a contest."

Mr. Charles's mustache turned down as Henry spoke, and then turned up at each end when Henry sat back in his chair.

"Yes. Well. That would be a pity for everyone concerned, wouldn't it? But what is it I can help you with, Mr.…Sullivan?"

Henry wondered if the man had actually forgotten his name. The realtor's voice had lowered in both tone and octave. Henry tried to look as serious as he could manage.

There was in fact a painting in the Dutch room at the Gardner, near the Rembrandt self-portrait and also painted by the master—*An Old Man in Military Costume.* It would fit Mr. Charles quite well, if the real-estate man's lip had not been so thin.

Henry said, "What was the price Morgan was asking on the condominium?"

This would be public information if Henry knew where to look for it, but more easily had now by asking.

The mustache barely moved with the answer. "Three and a quarter."

Henry asked, "And what was the offer?"

Now, this was more difficult. He was not at all sure the Realtor would tell him this much, but he might as well try.

The mustache moved, stopped, and moved again.

"There … There were two offers. One for that amount, and one for three and a half."

Henry made a guess. "Isn't that a little low?"

"Well, yes. But Mrs. Johnson wanted to sell it before the end of the year. She had some plans."

Henry nodded, and let a beat of time pass before asking, "And why wasn't anything signed?"

The broker's eyes closed too slowly and opened again with some effort.

"We had a verbal agreement...."

Henry smiled. He had tried not to. He had not wanted to. It was reflexive. "You told Arthur you had an agreement."

The Realtor repeated, "A verbal agreement."

Henry said, "Arthur thought otherwise."

"He misunderstood. Nothing was filed."

Henry offered a half-truth. "So we noticed."

The Realtor sat forward. "It was my intention—I had an appointment with Mrs. Johnson the day she was murdered. I was going to have her sign then."

Henry could not help raising an eyebrow. "You were there?"

It was the wrong question.

The Realtor sat back in his chair again. "I arrived in time to spend an hour or two with the police. It was very unpleasant."

Henry tried to turn the conversation back. "I don't imagine Arthur will want to go along with your verbal agreement."

The Realtor bounced just slightly in his seat.

"Mr. Johnson does not seem to be in much of a hurry."

Henry asked, "Have you spoken with him recently?"

"I haven't been able to reach him."

Henry said, "He's been busy."

"Is there a problem?"

Henry said, "The price."

The man's cheeks tucked in slightly between his open teeth, and he came forward again. "But there is an agreement."

Henry said only, "Verbal."

The Realtor shook his head once, "Yes, but—"

Henry was not prepared to argue real-estate law. He interrupted. "What did Detective O'Connor think about it?"

The Realtor sat back now, as if to avoid any sense of confrontation. "He's a very suspicious man. His job, I suppose. But everything was perfectly legal and aboveboard."

Henry answered that quickly enough. "Except for the matter with Arthur."

The man came forward once more, this time with both hands attached to the edge of his desk.

"Well, the property at that time was hers, not his. She had told me not to tell him. Mrs. Johnson seemed very concerned about it. I'm not sure why. She said several times that I should not talk to him about it. I was only following her wishes.... The offer is solid. The buyer is completely legit. He might be willing to go up slightly to get the deal done. He wants to move in by the first of the year if it's at all possible."

Henry shifted his chair back as if to leave. "I'll tell Arthur, but I don't think so."

The Realtor answered quickly, "The buyer might pay a premium if—"

Henry had left the impression he wanted, but if he started negotiating, he might be caught in some level of fraud. "I'll tell Arthur. Don't speak to me about that. But I do want to know what Morgan said. Why did she want to sell so quickly?"

"Taxes. I think it was for tax reasons."

This seemed probable to Henry. It had been suggested before, and he had encountered it many times. People often sold off entire estates at reduced values just to escape the reach of the Internal Revenue Service or reduce the hit of the Massachusetts Department of Revenue. Morgan was facing a large financial loss in the current year with Heber's medical bills and death. A large sum of money had been given to Peter for his

wife's medical care. The donation of the books to Boston University would amount to a considerable deduction. She wanted to sell the condominium while the loss was fresh. With Heber's death in June, a great many things had begun to change very quickly. The will was probably made as a temporary measure. It would be just like Morgan to have all the bases covered.

But the issue remained: she was keeping secrets from her only son.

Chapter Twenty-Four

Both Albert and Henry stared at Tim across the bar. Tim pretended to ignore them. Albert was the first to ask. "How did it go?"

Tim mumbled, "Fine."

They were not convinced. Henry looked at Albert and then back at Tim. "What was fine about it?"

Tim did not meet their eyes. He said, "She's a good cook," and went away to take care of someone else.

Albert shook his head as if in pity. "He missed a damn fine turkey if she wasn't."

Henry agreed. "Alice's best ever."

"Which reminds me…" Albert dug into his coat pocket and pulled out a folded batch of yellowed paper. "You might want these. They're from the Mawson house."

The irregular batch of odd-sized paper was a shock. Henry gaped. "Where in the Mawson house?"

Albert shrugged at him to pass the omission off. "The cookbook. From the kitchen. There was a Fannie Farmer cookbook in the kitchen at the Mawson house. It's what Alice used to make the turkey this year. And the stuffing. Killer stuffing, wasn't it? Well, that old book was pretty stuffed itself, with scraps of recipes. Alice loves that kind of thing. I brought it home. But they weren't all recipes. Some were notes with a mention of food in them. A lot of them were from Helen Mawson to her mom."

Henry's voice raised an octave. "Why didn't you say anything?"

Albert looked at him in total innocence. "I didn't know. She didn't tell me. She's been hoarding them. I found them on the counter when I was doing the dishes after you left. I knew you'd want them."

Henry felt stunned by the very fact of it. "Why didn't she say anything to me?"

Albert took his customary breath when speaking of Alice. "She's jealous. Alice is a jealous woman. All women are jealous, I suppose. It's in their nature.... She knew you'd want them."

Henry carefully opened the folded sheets on the bar and read the neat hand of Helen Mawson again.

Tim came back and twisted his neck to read the writing sideways from across the bar, saying, "What's that?"

Albert snatched them up and held them beneath his hand against his chest.

"Not till you tell us what happened."

Tim backed away, his face like a dog caught after making a mess on the rug.

He repeated, "She can really cook."

Henry said, "It's your third date Tim. Mary had you over for Thanksgiving dinner on your third date. That's impressive."

Tim considered the matter.

"Her kids were there. I'm not sure if they liked me."

Albert asked, "So what did you do?"

Tim said, "I taught them to play chess."

Albert and Henry looked at each other and then back at Tim again.

Albert nodded. "That's good,"

"Impressive," Henry added.

Tim said, "I'm going to take them to the movies tomorrow."

Henry said, "Very impressive."

Albert asked, "So you like her?"

Tim shrugged. "I always like redheads." He said it like it was a foregone conclusion.

"Did she kiss back?" Albert wanted detail.

Tim asked, "When?"

Albert turned to Henry. "*When* the man says. He's kissed her more than once already."

Tim confirmed, "We kissed," with another half shrug.

Albert insisted. "But did she kiss back?"

Tim said, "That's personal."

"Good. She kissed back." Albert gave a single nod of satisfaction.

Henry added, "Very good."

Tim escaped back down the bar.

Albert wiped a spot of water off the counter with his sleeve and put the papers down again and flattened them with both hands.

Henry picked the one off the top.

"Charlotte russe. What's Charlotte russe?"

Albert shook his head. "Kind of souffle-like, I think, only cold. It's good."

Henry recognized the scrap, even without the printed heading. "This is stationery from the Roycroft Inn."

Albert picked the next one from the stack. "Where do you think this is from?"

Henry took the piece between two fingers and held it up to the light above the bar: a small, square, cream-colored sheet with a recipe for a walnut cake. Half of a watermark extended into the frame.

"Liverpool."

Albert lifted the next. "And this one?"

First Henry read the handwritten note at the top aloud.

"Mother always loved ginger. I'll make these when I get home. He says they are his mother's favorite."

Tim asked, "What do they say?" Returning to investigate.

Albert answered, "Orange, ginger, and molasses,"

Henry said, "Who do you think the 'he' is?" Holding the paper up. There was part of a mark which he could not read. "Looks just like the other piece of English paper."

Albert said, "Could be."

There were other notes on other recipes, but not another mention of a "he." Most of the paper was from England, Henry noted, but then, English paper was sold in the United States.

The three of them studied the stack until they were all hungry and wishing they hadn't.

Henry folded the small papers at the original creases and asked for a piece of stiff cardboard from a liquor box and an old envelope so that he could put them away in his coat.

Albert said, "Alice wants them back."

Henry answered, "Only if she makes the cookies."

Albert asked Tim again about Mary Prowder. Tim looked like he needed a break, so Henry changed the topic of conversation and told them about his father's hundred-dollar bet with Jack.

"Dad laughed. I haven't seen a laugh like that out of the old man in memory. He said that was some trick Jack pulled—only he had pulled it on himself. Dad knew the cops had nearly arrested Jack after he wiped the floor with some Union bullyboy. He found it out when three thugs showed up at the door looking for his brother. Dad decided Jack needed to get away. The Marines were recruiting down by the S. S. Pierce building in Coolidge Corner. Dad says he teased Jack into the bet, knowing he couldn't let go of an easy hundred."

Henry did not bring up his latest thought about Morgan's

murder. It was all guess. It was all just a matter of maybe and what-if. But he was not going to sit on what little he knew. There could be no good in letting time pass and police interest wane.

As soon as Albert and Henry had come in the door, Tim had announced to them that there had been another robbery and murder nearby in Inman Square the night before. Only two blocks away. And the cops had not even found the person who had committed the last one yet.

Now, Albert ignored the story about Jack. He finished his ale and turned his head at Tim.

"You better be careful. Don't be trying to save your money if some guy shoves a gun in your face. Let him have the money. You have a girl now. When you've got the girl, you don't need the money."

Chapter Twenty-Five

The snow, which had been suspended in the air as if too light to settle completely to the ground, now began to stir in a sideways roll against his windshield for the last miles along Route 3 before he reached the bridge. The van headlights were absorbed by the gray wool of night, gaining him only a short view of road before the distances became featureless.

The last time he had come to the Cape in the winter was after the great storm of '78. It was the year his father had sold their small shack on the bluff in Eastham. The old man never liked going there after Henry's mother died. He couldn't bear it, and keeping the little house up had become a miserable annual chore. He had wanted to keep it for Henry and his sister, but those were the Carter years: money was tight, and jobs for electricians had dried up. The old man sold it after Shelagh had left home, the same year Henry took his first full-time summer job.

The house Henry was looking for now was no shack, but it would be no more visible in this weather than the dark gaps of shadow which appeared regularly at both sides of the road. Occasional lights distinguished one shadow from another, revealing the presence of other human beings. Cape Cod was a lonely place in winter.

He was thinking he should turn back. It was only five o'clock as he passed the rotary in Orleans, but he might not be able to find the place now in the dark. He should have started earlier. The book auction he had attended that morning had

extended into the afternoon. He should have changed his plans. The weather report had not mentioned snow, but then New England weather reports were useless—worse than useless, they were misleading. He was happy he had worn his boots.

Albert would have known what the weather would be if Henry had bothered to ask. Albert could read the look of the clouds like any good fisherman. But by then Henry had already made the phone call. Whoever had picked up the phone without answering would have heard his voice. Henry had even given his own name in the hope of getting them to speak. Henry was very sure it was Arthur who was staying at Morgan's beach house.

A street sign caught an edge of his headlight. Henry stopped and backed up until he could see it fully, and then checked his map. Only two more intersections.

The sign for the road he wanted was encrusted with snow, but a car had left the highway there and made its tracks. He followed these for over a mile before getting the idea that perhaps they were Arthur's tracks. How many people would be staying in a beach house in early December? Arthur might have gone out to buy some milk or get the paper. Henry only hoped that the tracks were going toward the house and not leaving.

The house was gray shingle and white trim, invisible to the eye but for a yard light by a low rail fence. The tracks Henry had followed led to the dark hulk of a car parked in the driveway in front of a separate garage. The snow burst upon him as he opened his van door. The wind here had a hard edge of salt and the smell of metal.

A steady hiss and moan spoke from the eaves of the house and in the pine boughs that blocked what view of the ocean he might get from the driveway on a good day. There was no light on at the door. A bedroom lamp glowed through a closed

curtain in a dormer above. There were no footprints at this front door, and Henry assumed the preferred entrance was at the rear, but he rang the bell anyway. He could hear the electric trill even through the wind. There was no sound of response. He rang it again.

After the third try, he walked around the side where the garage offered a brief shelter from the blow, probing through the drift of snow for the steps to the deck with his boot before noticing the imprint of someone else. A metallic crack behind made him jerk his head around. It was the cooling of the engine in the car parked there—recently arrived and only just beginning to collect a coat of snow.

In front of him, on the sculpted surface of snow across the deck, there were other footprints. A lamp blazed through the glass of a sliding door. The door was partly open, and snow was beginning to drift through the opening over a small rug onto the wood of a polished floor, where it melted into golden beads of water.

The light caught the footprints on the deck in a moonscape of scrapes and depressions. These were two sets of footprints, mixed. The snow had blown up deeply against the house beside the door, and in that there was the impression of something which had lain there recently—no, had fallen. It was the impression of a body. Across the snow dark pieces of something had been tossed. Henry bent down to pick one up, and realized it was not whole. Bloody snow fell apart in his glove.

Henry went through the opening of the door and closed it behind himself.

"Arthur?"

A momentary silence was slowly replaced by the muffled wind outside. There was no other sound within. He turned away from the glare of the light. A kitchen, close by on the garage side,

suddenly hummed with the sound of a refrigerator. He jerked, then took a deep breath to force a measure of self-control. Away in the other direction stretched a darkened living room. On the wall by the kitchen was a phone. Henry picked it up and dialed for the police. He had to say the address twice. He hung up then, impatiently.

His eyes sought the splatter of more blood. There was none. The house was in neat order, with dish towels stacked in an open pantry and place mats laid on a glass-topped table near the sliding door. The curtains of the living room were open to a flat gray movement of snow—to a view in better weather he could only imagine. A wall of books faced the windows from across the arching back of a couch positioned before the metal hood of an open hearth. Half-burned logs smoldered there.

Behind the wall of books a stairwell rose to the upper floor. Henry called Arthur's name again as he climbed the steps. His voice died in the still air. Two bedroom doors were open, with a bathroom between them. One of the beds was only half-made. There was no sign of anything else.

Downstairs again, Henry opened the sliding doors to the howl and press of the wind—growing now, it seemed. Snow attached to his eyelashes immediately. He wiped his face and looked off the deck in the direction of the ocean. Faintly there, only a few feet away, the tracks of two people broke the flat white surface of the slope between stunted pine.

Henry followed, stopping briefly when he saw again the dark pieces of splattered blood to one side. The footprints fell further apart.

They were running. They were running, one from the other. He followed more quickly. He knew who these men were. He was not sure which one to be fearful for.

Ranulf had called Henry that morning to ask if he had any

Vincent McCaffrey

idea where Arthur might be. He said he wanted only to talk
to him. Arthur had been avoiding Ranulf since the memorial
service. Ranulf thought Arthur had left town until someone
else mentioned seeing him the previous week. Then Henry had
made the mistake.

The Realtor had called to complain about Henry sticking his
nose in where it didn't belong. Henry's pretence of friendship
with Arthur was a fraud. And part of this had come out when
Henry had asked Ranulf if he knew how much debt Heber's
sickness and death had left on Morgan's shoulders. Henry understood that it was at least partially his own stupidity that had
caused this bloody mess now.

The push and shove of the wind took Henry's sense of
balance away. He fell when his boot slipped off what must have
been a board-covered path below the moving surface of the
snow. The sound of the ocean was clear now.

A triangle of darker wooden railing protruded from the
snow and Henry stopped just short of it with the realization that
these were steps and the gauze before him was empty space. He
felt his way blindly downward until the squall passed and the
beach suddenly presented itself in variations of gray.

A steady grind of surf separated into the fall and crash of
individual waves. Blackened ocean parted from the mottled
dark of the sky; the snow emitting its own fluorescence. Wind
carried pellets of ice against the skin of his face, stinging.

He heard a cry. It was a cry. Not a scream.

He stopped and scanned the slope of broken drifts across
the beach for some sign of their movement.

There was another cry.

They were there. Only yards from him. On the covered
sand. One figure twisted away and gained his feet, turning to
run. The other arose in a wave of snow and enveloped him.

Arthur's voice tore from his throat. "Insane...you're insane. I loved her.... I swear I couldn't kill her!"

Henry ran at them headlong, hitting both from the back at once and knocking them to the ground. The black tatters of blood marked the snow around them as they turned on their backs to look up at him. Blood oozed from Arthur's nose with each heave of his chest.

The truth seemed obvious.

"Ranulf. Arthur didn't do it."

The words were simple enough to say.

The two men lay still, their breath blown from their mouths in belches of smoke, until the distant blue of a police light entered the plane between the snow-thickened air and the icy rubble of the beach.

Chapter Twenty-Six

Henry parked his van at the curb in front of the guest house on Longwood Avenue where Peter and Vivienne Johnson had been staying. The snow had turned overnight to rain, and the rain puddled on flat surfaces within boundaries of fallen leaves and frozen remnants; a pathetic end to the first winter storm. He had anticipated awakening from his brief sleep to a clean white cover, with everything frozen in place. He wanted the kind of snow where the whole world stopped and looked in wonder and breathing was slowed.

The dark brown stain of the shingles was blackened with the rain. The door was locked, and his ringing several of the buzzers produced nothing. A single lamp in the entrance hall burned dimly, with no sign of movement through the clouded glass.

Stopping at the top of the driveway as he walked from the house, he noticed a dump truck and a backhoe where grass should be on the school fields below and behind, and walked down to the guest-house parking area to get a better look at his old playgrounds. The parking lot was empty, the unraked leaves clotted against the chain-link fence that marked the end of the property from the lower ball fields of Lawrence School.

Too many good hours of his youth had been spent playing on that field for him to be happy about someone changing it all. The hulking metal bodies of construction equipment parked

aside on the grass disturbed him more now because their very size made the grounds seem smaller than he wanted to remember it in his mind. The school, closed for renovation, appeared abandoned beneath the flat gray sky. A temporary safety fence surrounded the old brick building with the look of containing something more than keeping the curious out.

The white flash of a hand moved.

Below him, on a bench at the edge of the field and nearly obscured by the wet black trunk of an oak, a man huddled with a cigarette, as if watching a game on the sodden grass. Even covered as the figure was by a hat and overcoat, Henry knew this was Peter Johnson.

Henry walked back to the street and then around to the entrance to the field and approached along the walk. He was ignored until he stopped in the man's view, and then the blue eyes searched upward at Henry's face.

Henry said, "Hello, Peter."

There was a frown instead of a greeting. Peter inhaled on his cigarette until it burned red and then flicked it out onto the wet grass. He did not exhale for enough time to make Henry wonder, and then blew a plume of smoke that reached outward like a tongue. The frown remained.

Peter said, "You were looking for me?"

Henry stated the simple fact. "Yes."

"Why?" The frown still had not changed.

It seemed the only heading to take was directly into the storm. Henry said, "I just want to understand...."

Peter leaned forward, shaking his head at the ground. "And you've come to ask me? Of all people. I understand nothing."

Henry tried to frame his words. He did not want a confrontation. He wanted only to understand what had happened. The why.

He said, "You know what happened. You know something of why it happened, even if you may not understand—"

Peter turned to him, a smile twisting the frown on his face. Henry had never seen a smile so unhappy.

The voice which spoke was empty of emotion. "She's dead."

He knew who Peter was speaking of. Henry tried to stop himself from saying he was sorry, or something equally inadequate. He let the odd hollow silence of the weather answer at first. Peter pulled a hand across his face like a mime, and the smile was gone, and his face as emptied as his voice.

"There will be no funeral. No Mass. No flowers...perhaps not even myself."

Henry found himself answering reflexively now. "I'm sorry." All words were inadequate.

The blue of Peter's eyes were gray in the light, as if faded. After a moment, Henry sat down on the bench as well, and stared off across the field at the imprisoned school.

Peter said, "She was a dear, sweet thing. You can't know, of course. Almost no one knew...."

Peter took out his pack of cigarettes and offered one to Henry. Henry took it and the flame of the lighter which Peter offered. He suddenly felt better. Calmer than he had been in weeks. He had finished some great task. The work was behind him. If he ignored the gaps in his knowledge, the pattern at least made some sense to him now.

He felt the need to pay some respect to that woman he had only met once.

"How did you meet?"

Peter face was struck by some inner amusement. "Just as she told you. In my shop. She came in by chance and then pretended she was looking for work. She told me about your visit.

She always told me everything. She took delight in details." As Peter spoke, Henry remembered Vivienne's own words about taking a drive one day and stopping at the shop. A half smile moved Peter's cheeks again. "She knew nothing of books. She never did. She hardly ever read except for the magazines. But she kept the place as neat as a pin and answered all the mail that I always neglected and closed the windows when it rained and made the numbers in the accounts book match up and was sure to lock the door at night. I hired her on the spot because I wanted to sleep with her as soon as possible. I was possessed, all of a sudden, with the need to be inside of her, to hold her, to kiss her.... It's so strange. I even thought I might be queer somehow. I went so long without knowing any other woman well enough. They were always so concerned about foolish things. So worried about stupid things. I had no interest.... My mother was not like that. She never remembered the little things. Practical things were of no importance to her. She was the true Lady of the Lake. What mattered was what was great, and what must be done.... And that was what I had wanted before I met Vivienne—a woman who might give me the sword to slay..." Peter exhaled his smoke slowly in thought. "But sweet Vivienne was so misnamed. She was merely a flower. Not a nymph. She only offered her love...and I loved her so."

Henry thought of it like one of the tapestries at the Gardner Museum, a story on one continuous cloth, this one not large but worked by the needle in a tight design of costumed figures attending to a struggle of armed knights, swords raised or already piercing, with blood spilled in colored thread. And always the hounds were there, standing by for the kill.

Henry voiced his thoughts. "The myth gets mixed in the reality. Arthur is no king. Just another mixed-up fellow looking for

his own fame and fortune. Heber was no Merlin—just a scholar with the talent to make two women love him. And Morgan did love him as well. Isn't that fair enough? Couldn't that be enough? Why did your mother have to be avenged?"

Peter looked at him. The face was slack with misery, but an eyebrow arched in surprise. "Did you figure that out for yourself, or did Ranulf say something?"

Poor Ranulf, wanting to murder Morgan's killer with his own hands, but going after the wrong one—tapestries were like that. Who was the killer, and who the defender? Which was a victim, and which the casualty of war? Frozen in place, the characters could only be identified by their costumes. Not an easy thing to do these days.

"You told me…. Just now, again. I thought you killed Morgan, but I had no reason to attach it to your mother. I thought it might have been just about the money."

Peter turned a grimace of contempt toward Henry. "Of course it was the money. It was always the money."

The dismissal was not convincing.

"I don't think so…. Didn't he always send you something? Didn't he pay for your school?"

Peter seemed irritated at Henry's answer. His voice rose. "She wanted his love. She never wanted the money. The money was a curse."

Henry thought of Tim's conjecture. Was it for love then…and now? He asked, "How did she die?"

Peter seemed startled by the question, both his eyes on Henry. "Who?"

On a tapestry, the stories often began at the far corners of the fabric and worked their way to the middle, with the same character appearing several times.

"Your mother."

Peter turned and scanned the scars on the sodden field for something never there. Finally he said, "She drove to White-haven and swam to the Isle of Glass."

And left her son behind, Henry thought.

He asked, "When? When Heber remarried? When she found out he had married Morgan?"

"Yes." Peter's answer barely slipped his lips.

Henry took a breath. "Then, after all those years, wasn't his dying enough?"

Peter sat straight and rigid for a moment, his lanky slouch absorbed by an inner attention to some detail.

He said, "It might have been."

Henry looked for the next element in the picture and stated what appeared. "But he had helped you so much with Vivienne."

Peter's head shook only slightly—a jerk of objection. "No...I found that out too late. When I went to see him last spring. It wasn't him. He didn't care. He was finished with all of that. It was her. It was Morgan who had given us the money. Heber wanted no part of it. He was angry with her for doing it. He called me a bastard...."

Henry stared through his own confusion. Surely Peter had killed Morgan. But had he killed his father as well?

"But why kill Morgan...? Because she had helped you? Because she had tried to help you? Or was it because she refused to help you any longer?"

An unhappy smile flitted across the thin features of his face. "No... She only asked how much I needed."

Henry took a breath, trying to imagine it.

"What was it, then? What did she say? What made you kill her?"

Peter exhaled—the smoke drifting in front of them both before being caught by some movement of the air.

"The money didn't matter anymore. They said my Vivienne was going to die. There would not be another remission...."

Henry pursued, "But why hurt Morgan? What had she done?"

Peter winced, as if the answer stung. "She had...done nothing."

He was crying, the tears spreading broadly on his cheeks.

Henry asked again, "Why, then?"

Peter spoke to the field. "For everything. For all that had gone wrong."

Henry asked, "And for your mother?"

Peter answered, "My Lady of the Lake..."

Peter turned to him then with the look of a man just possessed of a thought.

"How could she still love that fat old man? She killed herself over him.... I was the only one who ever really loved her. But she left me."

Feeling the sorrow of it, Henry said the obvious aloud.

"And now Vivienne."

Peter coughed and his voice cleared. For the moment, they might have been discussing politics. "I didn't go there to kill her, you know...I was blind. I told Morgan I needed money. We could go to Mexico. The doctors here wouldn't try anything else. They wanted to give up. Morgan tried to tell me—I told her that I would never ask again. I told her it was only my right, as Heber's son. I told her it was only fair. She said I was wrong. Then she went into that room to get a letter—from my mother. She told me I should know something—," Peter's eyes searched upward to the dull grey sky. "And suddenly I already knew. She wouldn't have gone to get the letter if I hadn't said what I did—I had said something about Heber. She thought it was unfair...Unfair to Heber. That stupid man. The stupid

American. I said something like that out loud. He came to Oxford and thought he had conquered the world and my foolish mother fell in love with him. She always loved him. After all those years. I knew that. And Morgan was looking for the letter in his files. She wouldn't stop, and there around us were all those books...I took one down, and then another. They were signed. All signed. They all adored him. The great Heber. What a name! How can one go through life with a name like that. Like a bull, I suppose...And then she had it in her hand. My mother's writing was so affected. So odd. She loved flourishes. She wrote so carefully that all the lines came out almost even at the end ..."

Henry could not imagine it.

"What did the letter say?"

Peter shook his head. "It was an apology. My mother was apologizing to Heber! She said she was sorry.... *She* was sorry."

"For what? Why was she sorry?"

Peter turned to him, his voice momentarily calm again. "You know, she must have written that letter at the same moment she wrote her note for me.... It was on the same paper. From the place she had stayed last—a bed-and-breakfast in Whitehaven. But she didn't apologize to me. She left an instruction for me, like she used to leave taped on the door when she went out before I got home.... She said she had to go away. She would not be back.... She told me to forgive her. She told me I was her stolen child and that I must forgive her."

Henry could not help asking, "Why did she apologize to Heber? What had she done?"

The twisted smile returned. Peter held his face with his hands until the tears found a way through his fingers. With his

elbows on his knees and his face buried in the clutch of his palms, he spoke to the ground.

"I was not Heber's son...."

Henry could smell the metal and the rust of the construction equipment in the air. The smell was plain. The decay was obvious. But he would not have known what it was if the machines were not right there in front of them.

"Your mother had lied to him?"

Peter spoke loudly through his fingers.

"She had lied. But not about her love.... I was just her stolen child."

"How?"

Peter pulled a handkerchief from his pocket and blew his nose. Again the calm returned. "When he graduated, after all the celebrating was done, he left her behind. He just left. He got on an airplane and went his way.... She did not like to drink. She was quite silly when she drank anything. She left her job at Blackwells and went home to her mother's in Glasgow to cry. Unfortunately, a lad she had grown up with was home as well.... His name was Peter. I even met him once when I was still a boy. I don't think he ever knew. Peter was a merchant seaman home for a rest. He had no interest in marriage. And when she found out she was pregnant, she wrote Heber and told him I was his child.... And Heber returned. He married her. As if that could make everything all right. He married her. And she was a happy woman again. A foolish woman again. For a little while.... But she never told him the truth. Not until the end."

Henry said, "But then you knew. From the time he got her letter, he knew."

Peter sat upright again, wiping his hands on the wool of his jacket, his cheeks still wet. "She did it for me. She could

never have earned enough on her own.... You know what the publishers pay. They wouldn't even cover all her expenses. And he had so much. The money did not matter to him.... I was her stolen child. It was a poem she must have liked. She read it in her Scots voice to me once and I never heard the Irish in it. I never knew it was Yeats.... I am sorry. I had never meant to harm Morgan. I was angry. And it was done so easily. She was wearing a scarf."

Henry spoke aloud, "The green scarf."

Peter turned to him, the tone of his voice reduced to a plea. "She turned away, and I took hold of it, and turned it, and it was done. So quickly—"

A slap of metal broke the silence.

They both turned to the sound, the links of the fence up high behind them striking against the metal posts.

Henry stood. "Oh, crap."

Having reached the top of the fence, Ranulf hesitated, only then realizing how great the distance was to the ground and looking ridiculous with his chest bared where the buttons of his jacket had already been torn away—and then he jumped. His black scarf fluttered behind in his descent. Henry moved to break the man's fall, or to simply stop him—the thought was incomplete. Ranulf reached the incline of the earth feet first and came forward in an uncontrolled tumble onto Henry. Henry fell back, the breath forced from him beneath Ranulf's shoulder. Henry's head slapped backward against the pavement of the walkway. His head buzzed.

Rolling awkwardly to his feet, trying to find his balance on the flat surface, Henry looked after Ranulf, already yards away on the path, with Peter gone from sight.

Henry repeated the obvious. "Oh, crap."

Neither man was anywhere to be seen as Henry climbed

into his van. His head ached. Where would Peter go? A train? He had no car, but he might rent one. An airport? But where would he be going?

The ache had faded by the following afternoon.

Tim said, "You had to figure it would be water," leaning in on the wood of the bar.

Albert rested back against the sharp complaint of his chair. "How's he going to get to the ocean from Brookline on foot?"

Tim answered, "The trolley. The Aquarium stop."

Albert said, "Sure. The harbor. A cruise boat in the middle of winter?"

His sarcasm fell flat.

Henry remained quiet until the speculation had ceased. "I didn't know where he might be heading. I took a guess and started driving. Then I saw Ranulf's car crossing Beacon Street a block away at the next intersection and turned to catch up with him. But he was gone. I headed in the general direction, and then turned down Commonwealth Avenue. I called the cops from a phone there outside B.U. That was a waste of time, because I saw Ranulf's car again heading across the B.U. Bridge and I dropped the phone and went down Commonwealth and made the illegal turn. That's what got some cop's attention." He drank what remained in his glass and handed it to Tim.

"Right when I heard the belch of that siren behind me, I look out over the Charles River from the bridge and I could see Peter below me. Right there, for Christ's sake. He's running along the tracks of the railroad bridge that crosses at an angle underneath. And then I could see Ranulf, on foot, coming at him from the Cambridge side. I stopped the van where I was on the bridge, and I got out. The cop got out and was yelling

bloody Jesus at me. I was yelling back at him about Peter being right below us on the tracks. The cop had no idea what I was talking about. But Peter heard me. Peter looks right up at me, and then starts running back, away from Ranulf, who is running down between those tracks, puffing like a train. So I got back in the van to turn around and get to the Boston side. That's when the car hit me. Right in the middle of the U-turn. Blocked all the traffic in both directions. The frame of the van broke apart all the way when the tow truck tried to lift it. Total loss."

Albert reared his head back in frustration. "So what the hell happened?"

Tim pushed a full glass back at him. Henry tried to see the moment.

"Well, the cop, he had finally taken the trouble to look down at what I was making such a fuss over. When the car hit me, I got out again. The cop's face is red now. He wants to shoot me on the spot. I tell him we have to get to Peter before Ranulf kills him. The driver of the car that hit me is coming at me with a fist in the air. The cop says he's going to shoot us both if we move. Then someone yells—there's a little crowd then—and a couple of people have gotten out of their cars. One of them is looking over the rail and sees Peter jump."

Henry took a swallow of his ale to wet his mouth. Tim groaned with disgust.

"I never get to see anything. I just hear about it. That's the crummy part of being a bartender. You hear about stuff you'll never get to see."

Albert spoke while he looked at Tim and pointed at his own empty glass. "So what happened then?"

Henry looked at Albert in the mirror. "I outran the cop to the end of the bridge and down the steps there to the embankment. There wasn't much ice. I've never gone swimming in ice

water before. I guess I hesitated for a second. But I couldn't see any sign of Peter. I thought I could see bubbles. Ranulf was standing up there on the side of the railroad bridge looking down into the water for some sign of him. There was a line of faces up on the B.U. Bridge. Nobody could see where he went. I took off my coat to go in, and that's when the cop put his handcuffs on my wrist.... Peter's body didn't come up again until later."

The stolen child was lost in the man.

Chapter Twenty-Seven

The echoing clop of someone's wooden-soled shoes against the brick of the sidewalk below awakened him. Drawn from his sleep, he thought at first it was the sound of a horse. The Boston police still used horse patrols on occasion, and they sometimes trailed up Charles Street from the Public Garden. The dark of his room felt thickened with the dissolving of his dream.

Leaning from his bed he pushed the gray folds of curtain aside and looked out at the night. A barrier of fragile black lace—thin leafless limbs made electric by the polish of rain—separated him from the closest building across the street. There the owners had set out the traditional single light for Christmas, with the look of candles, in each window.

He was unsure of the dream he had awakened from. But one part of it he was now familiar with. This lingered with him as he sat in the chair by his desk in the dark, his eyes captured by the small window lights as they multiplied in their reflections on the thin wet limbs of the trees. Helen Mawson.

Burnt umber hair, escaping a blue twist of yarn, flowing unfettered over one shoulder—her left shoulder. The collar of her blouse was high, but open at the front, and he imagined a gap of pink white flesh below her neck. The blue of her eyes looked back at him in challenge at his own visual exploration.

Henry wondered if she had ever loved. Certainly she must have. Which one? She had declared no one a favorite in the

letters they had found. Surely, someone in letters lost now. Perhaps Marcus Evers.

All they had, including the scraps from the cookbook, amounted to less than one hundred pages, written in a small and precise hand. She would have written thousands, even in twenty-three short years. She wrote every day. She was not ashamed to speak her mind—even now, to him. How old would she be? One hundred and seven? How sad only a broken fragment of the life she lived still remained.

For a moment he wished he had kept one of her letters for himself. Perhaps the account of her visit to Venice. He had always wanted to go to Venice. Morgan loved Venice and had spoken of it often. But he had given all of the letters back to Albert. Alice wanted them. At least she would take care of them. They were not lost. Alice had even asked for the Roycrofter books which Helen had annotated in the margins. Alice never did anything by halves.

The old thought returned that he would have liked to have known Helen Mawson. What would she have thought of him? She was more courageous. Fearless. Would she have cared for someone who had never escaped the world that was handed to him—never built a better one? Why would she? What quest had he followed? Good books? What grail had he found? There had been that copy of *Connecticut Yankee*...Henry smiled to himself at the pettiness. What dragons had he slain? Never slain, nor a dragon fought, only a sad Englishman. How was he worthy of her? A bookman's worth? What honor was there? A book hound's honor? What honor to defend?

His doorbell rang.

The burnt umber flow of Helen Mawson's hair was erased as he flipped the switch on his desk lamp. It was only six o'clock. Not even dinnertime. On his bed, where he had fallen asleep,

was the closed first-edition copy of *A Connecticut Yankee in King Arthur's Court*, which he had found only a few hours before in Cambridge. He had begun reading it as he rechecked the condition and had fallen into the story until the light had grown too dim and he had drifted to sleep.

The bell rang again. He reached for the button and pressed it as he opened his own door.

He spoke into the well of space between the stairs. "Hello?"

A woman's voice echoed back. "Hello?"

A thin slice of her face looked up at him between the banisters. Her hair was very short and very blond.

She asked, "Is the landlord here?"

Her voice was clear, precise.

He shook his head. "No. Can I help you?" He tucked in his shirt as he spoke, walking down the stairs in his socks.

She spoke back as he descended. "The building seems pretty empty. Do you know if there are any apartments available?"

It was still raining. Large dark blotches marked her coat. She backed away from the stairs as he reached the bottom, looking at him almost directly eye to eye. Brown eyes—hazel brown, he thought. The shoes on her feet could not be responsible for more than an inch of the height.

He shook his head again, but less emphatically. "No. The building has been sold. I'm the last one. They'll be gutting it the week after New Year's."

She was obviously disappointed. "You'd think with the economy supposedly so bad, there would be more places for rent."

He made an expression he hoped was sympathetic. "It'll be too expensive in any case. I have to leave here myself."

She answered quickly. "Everything is too expensive."

She was looking at his shirt. Flannel could look pretty rumpled when you slept in it. What could he say?

"It's worse here in town. Even the North End, especially now with the Big Dig almost done."

She tilted her head to the side. "But I always wanted to live on Beacon Hill. Just once in my life."

He had wanted that once as well. "It's good. It's what little is left of old Boston. I was lucky to be here awhile. The previous owner kept the rent down."

She took an unhappy breath.

She said, "I've been looking for two months. I keep raising my limit. It doesn't do any good."

How was he going to prolong this conversation?

He said, "Team up. Find some roommates. I hear the larger apartments are cheaper per square foot."

That was a bit too officious. She returned a weary smile. "Right. But there are no larger apartments on Beacon Hill. It's all so old. Besides, it gets a little tiring after a few years to be listening to other people's music and cleaning up other people's dishes all the time."

How old was she? he wondered. There was a leanness in her cheeks. Perhaps thirty. She was very pretty. There were no rings on her hands.

He said, "I can't put up with that myself...."

She nodded. As he looked for more words, she studied his face. "What are *you* going to do?"

The thought occurred that perhaps he had made a mistake taking an apartment by himself. He said, "I just found a small place in Cambridge through a friend. That's always the best way. Check with your friends."

She flinched. "I guess I don't have the right friends."

She was turning to go.

"Well..." What more did he have to say? What excuse could he come up with to keep her a moment longer? "My

name is Henry. Let me know if I can help...."

He reached into his shirt pocket. He knew a bent business card was still there, and he handed it to her.

She smiled at him uncertainly and read the card. The hope flitted across his brain that she might just say, "Oh. A bookseller. I just love books." But she didn't.

She said, "I'm Della," and shook his hand before turning again to leave. The grip was firm.

He looked down at his socks and wished he had put on his shoes. When he looked up again, she had the door open. He struggled for something else to say. Then she was gone.

"Merry Christmas," he said to the closed door. The echo of his own voice in the stairwell above him made the words sound hollow. He followed the echoed beat of his own footsteps upward again.

Della. He could remember only one person by that name. Della Street. She had been the helpful secretary in the Perry Mason books.

The bell rang again, startling him, just as he reached his open apartment door. This time he grabbed his shoes as he pressed the button and skipped steps as he went down again.

But it was Leona who faced him there with a wide smile. She was holding a small gift-wrapped box. "Merry Christmas."

He kissed her on the cheek. "Merry Christmas yourself. But I thought you were through with me."

Their last argument had not ended well.

Leona nodded. "Take it as a peace offering, then.... Why are you holding your shoes?"

"I was just about to put them on."

"Going out? Can I come?"

He shrugged. "I haven't eaten."

"Me, either. I was hoping you'd ask."

There was no escape. He would rather not be alone with his thoughts just then in any case.

"Just a minute. I'll get my coat."

She said, "Open your present first!"

Leona bounced where she stood. Her enthusiasms were hard to deny. He took the thin box, pulled at the ribbon, and the top came off by itself. Inside was the gray-riddled brown of a round Irish tweed cap. He watched her expectant face as he put it on. It fit perfectly. She kissed him on the lips before he had time to move to thank her.

She said, "Tell me you like it."

He said, "I like it fine."

"I knew it would fit."

He said, "It fits fine."

Off guard, his amazement must have been obvious.

She confided, her voice lowered, "I knew it would fit because I didn't buy it. My mother bought it. She never bought wrong sizes. She had the eye."

He did not understand. She raised her arms in defense.

"I couldn't throw it away. It was brand-new, still in the box. When we were cleaning the house out, I found it in her closet and I couldn't figure out why it was there. Dad never wore hats like that. Besides, his head was smaller. Then, after I found that letter from your father, I realized. Mom had bought it for him, but he probably wouldn't take it. Anyway, I kept it. I don't know why. Well, I probably knew why. But you made that pretty easy when you complained that your dad was not even willing to wear a hat. I knew it would fit you."

Henry knew he would have to wear it, whether he wanted to or not.

Over hamburgers at the Paramount, Leona told him about her recent struggles as a single parent, including a quest to find

shoes for her oldest son, who had the feet of a basketball player and the coordination of an elephant. Henry recommended Chad Humphrey, their old schoolmate.

She said, "Sad Chad. Always at the back of the band. Always holding his trumpet in one hand and that little handkerchief with the other."

Henry added, "Nice guy. Knows his shoes."

She said, "The 'trembling trumpeter.' Someone called him that once."

Henry remembered. "Never liked to be in front of people. Still plays trumpet."

She said, "Never married?"

Henry smiled at the thought. "Not yet. Used to talk about old horror movies whenever the conversation turned to girls."

She said, "Some subjects are too scary."

Henry said, "Girls are always pretty scary."

She rolled her eyes at that. Women never understood just how scary they could be.

She asked, "So, what did you talk about when you first met a girl?"

Leona knew the answer to that. Why did he have to say it?

"Books. Remember?"

Her smile faded.

"Yes."

There was no sadness left in him for this. She wanted something that was long gone from both their lives. A moment of innocence. Simple love. But there was none of that left in either of them.

He kissed her at the entrance to the subway. With Chanukah already past, he wished her a Merry Christmas once more. It was half a smile she returned, with one lift of her hand for a wave. He tipped his new cap to her. She had come by to be

with him, and he was in fact sorry he was not in the mood for conversation or much else.

Walking back through the Public Garden, he wished it would snow and clean all the darkness away, or at least dress the world again the way it had been when he was young enough to be led by the hand beneath the Christmas lights on the Commons. The colored lights strung there blazed starkly behind the darker silhouettes of the nearer trees of the Garden. He looked for the Swan Boats, as he always did, even when they were gone from the pond for the winter. A glaze of gray-mottled ice trimmed the black water, and this was decorated with a spill of color angled from the distance.

Out loud he said, "Della."

Wasn't it odd that she should still be occupying some space in his mind? He was wrong. Of course! He did want company. But not Della. And not Leona. The person he had wanted to speak to more than once over the last week was Ranulf.

There was some unfinished business there. There was something left to say. What?

That there was no revenge. That there was none to be had. Morgan had been a casualty of life itself. As if she had been taken by an undetected cancer as well. That Ranulf's loss—that Henry's loss as well—was something grown out of the same life that had benefited them all.

Still, it was odd that he was thinking about Della. The mind was a funny place.

Passing Deluca's Market, he stopped impulsively and went in without an aim, bought a carton of eggnog, a bottle of Jamaican rum, and a package of cigarettes and went on home.

After closing out the street noise behind him with the door, a sound wafted from high in the stairwell. Certain it was from within the building, Henry left his package on the floor and

stepped lightly upward. Something was pulled across rough boards. Someone was in the attic.

The last steps were steeper, angling over the stairwell below. He had always hated heights, and looking down gave him a shiver at his spine, even with the hot air at the top. The skylight close by caught the sound of cars from the street and dampened the noises from the open door. He knocked on the frame with his fist.

"Jesus!" came a voice. Someone stumbled. Something fell. Something else fell.

Henry said, "Hello?"

The voice was high-pitched with surprise.

"Who's there?"

"Henry Sullivan."

"Sullivan?"

A face poked around the door frame. The close-cut red hair was receding on a broad pink forehead covered with sweat.

Henry said, "I live on the third floor—until next week."

The man said, "I thought you were gone."

Henry answered, "Nearly. And you're Richard Prowder. Mary's brother."

Richard Prowder took a breath of relief. "Right. Can I help you?"

The irritation in his voice was clear.

Henry had intended to come up sometime during the week to retrieve some of his own things he had stored away. He had to wonder why Richard Prowder would be there now.

"As a matter of fact, I have some books up here. Your mother let me store them."

Prowder shook his head with a jerk of disgust. "Christ. She was worse than my sister."

Henry lowered his voice. "What do you mean?" He stepped

into the low space which diminished into the dark.

Richard Prowder kicked at a box. "Keeping stuff. She kept everything."

The landscape of the attic was a range of various boxes, some marked by red crayon, others not marked at all. When Henry had last been up here, the boxes were still on the shelves that now were in the shadows behind them. Each shelf had been carefully labeled. Henry had thought it the most well-organized attic he had ever been in.

Most of the tops of the scattered boxes were open. Odd corners of cloth protruded in dark tongues beneath the single light by Richard Prowder's head.

Henry asked, "What brings you up here on a rainy Christmas Eve?"

Prowder turned to survey the mess he had made.

"Something…Just something I wanted. With all the crap up here, you'd think the one thing I wanted would still be here."

Despite the mess, it did not appear to Henry that anything had been removed.

He said, "I thought your sister was having it all taken away."

Prowder's disgust returned. "She never finishes anything. It's always up to me."

Henry decided to avoid arguing. "She was pretty wiped out by the downstairs. She probably forgot about this."

The assessment produced a mutter in response, and Henry moved toward the pile of boxes under one empty angle of roof. Broken chairs and cracked flower pots were piled neatly together beside an old radio, the wooden cabinet of a television, and bundles of hangers. The television reminded Henry of a black-and-white model they had still used at home when he was very young.

Prowder suddenly said, "Have you seen a boat up here?" The renewed irritation in Prowder's voice made the question seem comic to Henry.

"A boat?"

"A boat. A big boat. About two feet long. Plastic. Something I built once…with my father."

The hesitant addition of "with my father" reminded Henry of Mary's words about their family discord.

Henry mused, "No…I built a boat with my dad once. A sailboat. Lost it on Jamaica Pond the day the paint dried."

Prowder shook his head and knelt to rip open another box. "It sank?"

Henry smiled at the memory now. "No. It was a windy day. Dad told me not to try it. The fishing line pulled loose, and it headed right away. I think some kids got around to the other side before I did and stole it while I was busy. Dad was giving me an earful."

Prowder said, "That's what fathers were made for."

Henry nodded. "I guess. I guess I wasn't very good at listening."

Prowder waved a hand. "Does it matter? You're just supposed to do what they want you to do. Families are not a democracy."

Henry tried to keep a smile as he answered. This was not a fellow he wanted to be talking with about democracy on Christmas Eve.

"No. Democracy only works with adults. And then they have to want to be cooperative. I wasn't very cooperative when I was a kid."

Prowder stood up and watched as Henry grabbed several of the boxes of books and moved them close to the door. Henry's assessment must have sounded impersonal.

Prowder's voice calmed. "You never knew my father. Everything had to be done right. There was a system for everything. Everything had a purpose.... Look at this." He pointed with a free hand. "Every shelf was labeled. But he was the only one who knew what the labels meant. It was his system. It was his way. Now I can't even find my own crap."

The small plea came in his tone at the very end of the words. Henry set a second box down.

"Maybe I can help?"

Richard Prowder pushed another box aside with his foot. "I don't think so."

Henry said, "I'm not in a rush. Let me see the labels."

Prowder tilted the light in the direction of the shelves. They were lettered and numbered by hand on thin strips of yellowed paper. It was a very familiar-looking code.

Prowder's voice lowered to a hopeless resignation.

"What makes it even harder is that he packed everything in old clothes." He waved at a box by Henry's leg. "That one there is my snowsuit from when I was maybe six years old. You have to unwrap everything to tell what it is. It's filled with glasses. He even used my mother's old brassieres, for heaven's sake."

Remembering Mrs. Prowder's story of her husband's trick with a chair as he carried her mother's china to the attic, Henry pointed to an opened box close to the shelves.

"What was in that box there, dishes?"

"Yes. How did you know?"

"The call number behind it. See? 'NK.' Its the same subject code they use in libraries. At some point when I was a kid I stumbled on the code for china—as in porcelain. It was on a removable label in a brass tag at the end of a row of shelves at the library. I used to switch it over to the 'DS' section, to Chinese History. My idea of stupid fun. Mrs. Smith, the librarian,

would go bananas. She finally caught me. She banned me. She kicked me out of the library for six months. I've always been thankful."

Prowder frowned. "Why thankful?"

Henry said, "Because it made me buy more books. And then I had to sell them to get the money to buy more."

Prowder rolled his eyes. "I forgot. Mary told me you were a bookseller."

Henry said, "So what would your father call a boat—nautical—naval. Look for a code that starts with the letter *v.*"

Prowder wiped the moisture on his forehead with his sleeve.

"A toy. He called it a toy. That's why I left it up here. I told him I was putting away my toys."

Prowder's voice had grown suddenly tense. Even so, that was a memory Henry shared as well.

"Why do you want it so badly just now? You want to give it as a Christmas present to someone?"

Prowder shook his head. "No. No. I just wanted it for myself.... It was probably the last thing we ever really did together."

Henry nodded and scanned the labels. He was not sure of the code for toys. His own father was never too fond of buying toys. Matthew Sullivan gave his son tools for Christmas, and his daughter as well. A set of screwdrivers. Three different types of hammer. But it was true that they had made toys together.

Henry said, "My dad was a pain in the ass, but he left me alone, mostly. I think that's what bothered me more, when I was a kid. He let me roam a little too much. He only had a few rules. No smoking in the house. No girls in the house. No drugs anywhere, and be home by seven in the winter and nine in the summer. Period."

Prowder said, "You had it easy."

Henry answered, "I broke every rule I could get away with."

Prowder asked, "What did your mother say?"

Henry scanned the semidark with a squint.

"She was…gone then. She died when I was twelve."

Prowder's voice sharpened. "Oh…Well, your dad was just trying to make it a little easier on himself that way—trying to keep it simple."

Henry turned.

"Right! That's what he always said. Keep it simple."

Prowder said, "I wish my father had the same idea. My father had rules for when the rules were broken."

Henry ducked to where shelves filled the lowest slant of the roof. His knees cracked as they folded against the wood of the floor. He admitted, "I thought my dad didn't care. I used to think he didn't love me. That's how stupid I was then. It was just his way. He always had trouble expressing himself out loud."

Prowder stood aside to keep the light on Henry.

"Well, my father was a lawyer. He knew the Latin for everything he said in English. He had a motto for everything we should do in life."

Henry strained his eyes into the dark in front of him.

"Does 'TIT' mean anything in Latin? It's not a library code I know of. I would have remembered that for sure."

Richard Prowder fell on his knees and scrambled below the eave.

"*Titanic.* That's it!"

Putting a finger into a flap of the box, Richard Prowder dragged it out, still on his knees and pushing other boxes out of the way as he reached the center beneath the light. The dried tape fell away. With all the flaps open, Prowder removed a bleach-mangled towel and wadded bundles of old socks. Beneath them,

on the bed of a blue dress that might have once belonged to his sister, was a ship.

"The *Titanic*...." Henry repeated. That was something he had never thought of. "When did the *Titanic* sink?"

Prowder answered absently, "April 12, 1912," absorbed with his own memories. The finely detailed ship gently arose from the box in Prowder's hands.

"Too early," Henry said.

Prowder turned. "Too early for what?"

Henry's eyes studied the ship in front of him. "Just something that popped into my head. Someone who disappeared. It would have been very romantic if she had gone down on the *Titanic*."

Prowder asked, "When did she disappear?"

Henry said, "1915...Sometime around April, 1915."

Prowder held the boat at arm's length, the light reflecting on the painted metal work. He said, "How about the *Lusitania*, then? The *Lusitania* sank in May, 1915."

Henry bumped his head rising to his feet.

He would have fallen down the stairs had he tried to land on any one of them. His hand slid on the rail, slowing his descent until the heat of the friction was too hot, and then pushed off as he landed on his feet. His key was out of his pocket by the time he had made it down the next flight to the third floor. He did not bother to close his door. The light from the hall kept him on course to the book by the window.

It would be in the Hubbard bibliography. There was a short biography there. He had breezed through it once. He had seen something there on the *Lusitania!*

On May 7, 1915, the British passenger ship *Lusitania* was sunk off the coast of Ireland by a German torpedo.

One thousand, one hundred and ninety-eight people died, among them Elbert Hubbard, his wife, Alice, and her assistant, Mrs. Evers.

He read the paragraph, just a few words, several times.

When Henry climbed the stairs again, the door to the attic was closed. He had no one to tell. Albert was home with his family. Henry could wish him Merry Christmas and then tell him, but the line was busy. He could not sit. He could not stay. The clock in his room said it was nine. Time to be home, even in the summer. But it was winter. It was Christmas Eve. He had an excuse for being late.

Henry grabbed his coat, and on the way out he grabbed the bag with the eggnog and the rum from the floor beside the front door, removing the package of cigarettes as he walked and burying them deep in his pocket. The old man did not approve of smoking. The old man would be surprised—but he needed a few surprises.

Marcus Evers, the cynic, died in France at the Battle of the Somme, July, 1916. Marcus Evers, the disappointed man, went to cover the war in Europe after finding out that Helen Mawson, the woman he loved, had died on the *Lusitania.* Running off to war must have been a small distraction for a heart so drowned.

"Man has created death." Yeats had said. His mother told him that more than once, so that he might remember, because he was too young then to know what she meant. "Man has created death," he said again, unconsciously, aloud on the trolley to Brookline. A woman ladened with Christmas packages turned to the sound of his voice and moved away. Henry smiled at her, and she shifted further.

When he was twelve, death had been given a name. He had

learned that death could not be halted. The sound of death was the echo of rubber heels in empty halls. The feel of death was cold. The shadow of death was the clear cloud of space separating the darkness in the stiff plastic universe of an X-ray film. He understood that death brought an untouchable emptiness and that the threat of death was what fear was.

It was only now, so many years later, that he asked himself why he did not fear life instead. All the pain and misery was in life. In death there was nothing. All the sorrow and shame was in life. In death there was nothing. What he feared was nothing. Pain was the cut and scrape in pursuit of life. All desire was in life. All hope. And all that he could ever want or lose was in that sweet misery.

About the Author

Vincent McCaffrey (vincentmccaffrey.com) is the owner of the Avenue Victor Hugo Bookshop. For nearly thirty years it was a landmark for book lovers on Boston's Newbury Street. He recently moved the bookshop online and runs it from Abington, MA.

He reports: "I have been paid by others to do lawn work, shovel snow, paint houses, and to be an office-boy, warehouse grunt, dishwasher, waiter, and hotel night clerk. I have since chosen at various times to be a writer, editor, publisher, and bookseller—and managed to pay myself occasionally for that. But the one thing I am sure of is that I was very good at shoveling snow...."

Acknowledgments

I would like to thank the seemingly depthless patience of my family who have always been my encouragement, my first readers, and my most constructive critics. A special thanks goes to Frank M. Robinson who read my early efforts in this series and hit me up-side the head when I needed it (he bears no blame for my misuse of his advice—but I think the first sentence should be dedicated to him). And if they will allow, I must thank Gavin, and Kelly, and Jed, for what they do.

Hound

the key to the golden firebird

the key to the golden firebird

a novel

maureen johnson

HarperCollins*Publishers*

Produced by 17th Street Productions,
an Alloy company
151 West 26th Street, New York, NY 10001

Library of Congress Cataloging-in-Publication Data

Johnson, Maureen, 1973–
The key to the Golden Firebird / Maureen Johnson.—1st ed.
p.   cm.
Summary: As three teenaged sisters struggle to cope with their father's
sudden death, they find they must reexamine friendships, lifelong
dreams, and their relationships with each other and their father.
ISBN 0-06-054138-5 — ISBN 0-06-054139-3 (lib. bdg.)
[1. Grief—Fiction. 2. Sisters—Fiction. 3. Fathers and daughters—Fiction.
4. Automobile driving—Fiction. 5. Alcoholism—Fiction. 6. Softball—
Fiction. 7. Philadelphia (Pa.)—Fiction.] I. Title.
PZ7.J634145Ke 2004
[Fic]—dc22
2003021444

Typography by Christopher Grassi
1 2 3 4 5 6 7 8 9 10
❖
First Edition

*For my dad, Raymond R. Johnson, who gave me the
following piece of advice when I started high school:
"Take it from me, if you're going to sneak out of class through the
window and climb down a drainpipe to the ground, wear
shoes that don't slip." This is a foolproof suggestion,
which only goes to show how smart dads can sometimes be.*

Firebird, golden
(largous automobilus yellowish)

1. A car manufactured by Pontiac. In this particular case, a car painted a color called Signet Gold and built in Lordstown, Ohio, in 1967. Almost sixteen feet long, with extremely poor gas mileage and no modern amenities. Has a cream-colored interior and a black convertible top and belches noxious clouds of instant-cancer fumes whenever started. Attracts an unreasonable amount of attention from car buffs (for its collectability) and others (because it's brightly colored, noisy, and as big as a battleship).

2. A mythical creature prominently featured in Russian folktales. Possesses magical powers. Wherever the Firebird goes, princes, princesses, kings, and mad wizards are sure to follow.

3. Presumably, any golden bird that's on fire.

before

"*Ch*ome on," Palmer said, her words dulled from numb-tongue syndrome caused by the Icee she was slurping. "You haff to admit it *wash* funny."

May, who was sweating profusely and peering longingly through the bottom of the screened window at a swimming pool, turned and stared at her little sister.

"No, I don't," she said.

"It wash . . . ambhishious."

"Ambitious?" May repeated. "Looks like you got a new vocabulary word."

"It *wash*."

"They didn't play 'Wind Beneath My Wings' for *you*," May said. "Just be quiet for a minute, okay? I'm trying to listen."

She turned back to the window.

"I shtill can't believf the Oriole pickhed you up," Palmer went on, grinning at the thought. The Icee had turned her teeth a faint blue, which looked even creepier against her braces. It was as if the disguise was being dropped and thirteen-year-old Palmer was revealing herself to be a monster with blue metal teeth.

May wasn't smiling, because the memory wasn't funny to her. She was here for a reason. She was getting revenge—revenge that had been a long time coming. Peter Camp was going down.

Pete was the son of her father's best friend and had been eleven months old when May was born. There were pictures of him lurking above her as she was swaddled in baby blankets, unable to move. He looked surprisingly the same—brown curly hair, body covered in head-to-toe freckles, a slightly goofy, yet predatory expression as he reached for her stuffed duck.

Right from the beginning, May had been the unwilling straight man in Pete's ever-evolving comedy routine. There was the lick-and-replace sandwich gag from kindergarten. The yo-yo spit trick at the bus stop in third grade. The terrifying "lawn sprinkler" (don't ask) from fifth grade. The dribble holes in her milk, the lab worms in her lunch, the bike-by Supersoaker attacks . . . There was nothing too low, too stupid, too disgusting for him to try. Then Pete had moved on to Grant High, and they'd been separated. The next year May had ended up going to a different high school—to Girls' Academy, in downtown Philadelphia. Aside from the occasional whoopie cushion at holiday gatherings, she believed the menace had ended.

Until last weekend, when the Golds and the Camps had taken their annual trip to Camden Yards.

The Camden Yards trip was one of the major events of the year. Even May, who didn't like baseball, was able to work up some enthusiasm for it—if only because her father and sisters were practically humming with excitement. Also, May's dad always saw to it that she was entertained in one way or another. He'd let her choose some of the music in the car. (Along with the obligatory Bruce Springsteen. Her dad had to blast "Out in the Street" and "Thunder Road" as he tore down I-95 in the Firebird. *Had to.* As if the earth would explode if he didn't—or worse yet, it might rain and the game would be a washout.) He'd glance at her through the rearview mirror and make his "big tooth" face, pulling his lips back in a horselike grimace that always made her laugh. As a reward for sitting through the game, her dad would slip her some cash (he had developed a very slick move, which even Palmer couldn't detect) so that she could buy herself an extra snack from the concessions. So May had come to peace with the event.

On this last trip she had been biding her time during the seventh-inning stretch, staring absently into the depths of her cup of lemonade. The next thing she knew, a pair of huge and fuzzy black wings embraced her. Suddenly she was being lifted out of her seat by someone in a black bird costume and was on her way down to the field. Once there, she was immediately set upon by five members of the Baltimore Orioles, all of whom shook her hand. One gave her a signed ball. The crowd began to cheer her. Then, just when things couldn't get any weirder, she looked up and saw her own face—big as a building— stretched across the Jumbotron.

Underneath it was the caption *May Gold, formerly blind fan.*

She didn't even have time to react before she was escorted back to her seat.

It had taken over an hour to get an explanation because that was how long it had taken for Peter Camp to stop laughing. He revealed at last that he had told one of the public relations staff that May had been born blind, had just been cured by surgery, and was fulfilling her lifelong dream of seeing a live baseball game. It was an incredibly weird story—so weird that they'd actually believed him.

The audacity of the stunt had kept Pete from getting into any trouble; in fact, the Gold-Camp contingent now ranked Pete among mankind's greatest thinkers. May's father had immediately claimed the baseball and held it carefully with both hands for the remainder of the game, as though it were his very own egg that he was protecting until it hatched.

The rest of the night was ruined for May. She flinched whenever anyone came too close—even the waiters at the restaurant they went to for dinner. Her psyche was shot. Pete had finally gone too far.

The Camden Yards stunt had brought May to the pool house at the local swim club that afternoon after school. She and Palmer admitted themselves using keys borrowed from their older sister, Brooks, who was a lifeguard there. This was the day before the Memorial Day opening of the pool, so it was filled and ready but deserted.

Their accomplice was Diana Haverty, a fellow lifeguard and one of Brooks's friends from softball, who was known to be the current object of Pete's desire. Diana had obligingly asked Pete to meet her there for a private swim. Diana was going to dare Pete to disrobe. He would be ambushed by May and Palmer. From there, it was a simple grab-the-clothes-and-run operation, taking as many pictures as possible with May's Polaroid camera in the process. It was a beautifully simple plan.

Except that Diana wasn't there yet. She was fifteen minutes late. This worried May a great deal—even more than the fact that it was over eighty degrees outside and it was even hotter inside the crowded office, which was also the storage area for several vats of pool chemicals. They'd been waiting there for over an hour, crouched on the concrete floor. The hot chlorine vapors invaded all of May's pores. The smell burned her nose, stung her eyes, and infected her taste buds. She wondered if it was possible to die from inhaling chlorine fumes. It would be a stupid way to die.

Palmer drained her cup loudly and launched it across the room at the trash can. Just then May heard the front gate creaking open. There were footsteps in the breezeway. Someone was walking toward the pool. May silenced Palmer by raising her hand, but Palmer had heard it too and was frozen in place. May got a little lower and kept watching out the window.

"Please be Diana," she mumbled under her breath. "Please."

But it wasn't Diana. Pete emerged from the breezeway, looking somewhat baffled. He stopped and looked around, then started patrolling the far side of the pool in his slightly slouchy walk, his crown of finger-length curls bobbing with every step.

"We're dead," May said. "Let's get out of here."

"No, we're not," Palmer replied as she crept across the floor and joined May under the window. "Quick! Take off your shirt."

May's head whipped around in Palm's direction. Her green eyes, so similar to May's, were flashing maniacally. Her fingers were already clawing at one of May's short pink sleeves, trying to tug it down her arm.

"I am not taking off my shirt," May whispered.

"Just the right side," Palmer said. "That's all we'll need."

"What are you talking about?"

"Just do it!"

It was moments like this that May felt that nature had been much too unfair. Palmer, like their older sister, Brooks, had gotten all the enviable physical traits the family gene pool had to offer—the golden blond locks, the endless legs, the slender, boyish hips. It didn't stop there. From their father, an excellent baseball player, Palmer and Brooks had gotten exceptional athletic ability. They were all muscle and blessed with grace and speed.

May had hair that wasn't quite blond and wasn't quite red (she called the shade "anemic strawberry"). From her father, she'd gotten the high arch of her brow that made her look like she always thinking, *Huh?* From some unknown, less-evolved relative, she'd gotten shorter legs, pale, sun-sensitive skin, and a lack of coordination. The consolation prize was that she was supposed to have gotten intelligence, but intelligence doesn't matter when your thirteen-year-old sister can just sit on top of you and take your shirt by force if she decides she needs it for something.

"It's not enough," Palmer said, looking at the shoulder May had just freed from her shirt. "The strap is in the way. The bra has to go."

"Oh my God." May rolled her eyes. "I've wandered into a teen sex comedy."

"Would you shut up and take off your bra?"

"Okay, now you just sound like a scary boyfriend," May said, reaching under her T-shirt to unhook her bra. "Explain. Why am I doing this?"

"Bait."

"Bait? My shoulder is bait?"

"Show more if you want," Palmer said, flashing the blue

teeth again. She really did look like some kind of otherworldly predator when she did that—one that wanted May's bra for some insidious purpose and that now thought of May as "bait."

May yanked off the bra and covered the rest of herself as best she could by clutching her shirt against her chest.

"Is that better?" she asked.

"That's good." Palm nodded. "Now stick your arm out the window so it looks like you're naked. Then wave him into the water."

"*That's* your idea? He'll never fall for that."

"Don't doubt the power of a little suggested sex."

May looked over in disbelief. "Who are you?" she said. "What have you done with Palm?"

"Either you get him to strip and wave him into the pool or we go out there, hold him down, and get the pants. What do you want to do?"

Faced with this dire choice, May sighed. She took a moment to try to invest as much come-hither mojo into her bare arm and shoulder as she could. She imagined Nicole Kidman—how would *she* beckon someone with her bare arm? Slowly, she thought, with a little wrist action. Gracefully. Slight rotation in the shoulder. That's what she would try.

She put out her limb and waved. Her move didn't seem very seductive. It was a bit more ground-crew-guiding-in-the-plane in flavor.

"Diana?" Pete called to the arm.

May looked down at Palmer in panic. Palmer had to shove her fist into her mouth.

"What do I do?" May whispered.

Palmer replied by taking May's bra from the ground and shoving it into her sister's hand.

"Wave it," she said. "Like a flag."

May flapped the bra around. Pete stared at it but did nothing.

"Come on, Camper!" Palmer suddenly shouted in a remarkably good imitation of Diana's high, twangy voice. "Get in the pool!"

"Get in?" he called back.

"Wave the bra again!" Palmer hissed. May shook it around once more. It got stuck in a nearby bush and she had to pull it free.

"See? I'm getting undressed," Palmer yelled, her face turning red from the effort of holding in her laughter. "Come on! Take it off!"

Palmer pulled May down next to her. They waited, just under the window, unable to breathe. May expected Pete to come to the window at any minute. Something awful was definitely about to happen. This was going to end badly.

A very long minute passed.

Splash.

Palmer and May peeked out of the bottom of the window. Pete was in the pool, and his clothes were on a chair.

"I don't believe it," May whispered.

"See?" Palmer said. "Showtime! Come on!"

May pushed her arm back into her shirt, shoved the bra into the pocket of her long khaki shorts, and fumbled for her bag. Palmer was already slipping out the door. May followed her into the breezeway and concealed herself behind the soda machine.

Palm crept to the edge of the breezeway and crouched down to evaluate the situation. She nodded her readiness to May, and May nervously nodded back. Even though Palmer seemed as ready to go as a trained commando, May was not. But she was here, and it was happening.

Palmer counted down from three on her fingers and bolted for the pool. May heard Pete yelling, and Palm barreled back, grinning crazily, with a pile of clothes in her arms.

"Now!" she yelled as she passed.

May readied herself and raised her camera to her eye. Pete was about to come charging right at her, in his *natural state*. Yes, May knew what to expect. Yes, she knew what to look for and where to look for it. Still, she decided to just shoot straight ahead and not focus too much on what she was actually seeing.

And around the corner he came. All of him. May started snapping away.

On seeing May and the camera, Pete had the good sense to immediately turn and run back around the corner to the pool. Faced with the choice of running after him (and possibly being overtaken by a wet, naked nemesis) or running to the car and getting away, May opted for the latter. She turned and ran toward the lot. Brooks had already pulled up in the minivan, and Palm had the door open. May scrambled in, her hands full of still-gray Polaroids. Brooks peeled out of the lot and down the street.

The three Gold sisters were convulsing from laughter in the minivan as they drove away. The images on the Polaroids were blossoming. Many were blurry, a few were interesting studies of the ceiling or the wall, but there were a few promising ones in the bunch. These were examined closely and critically by Palm.

"She-male," she said, holding up a streaky image.

"Cut the guy some slack," May said graciously. "He was just in a very cold pool."

"I don't see any slack to cut," Palm said with a shrug.

"Come off it. These pictures are too blurry to tell. He was moving too fast."

"I saw it."

"You didn't see a thing." May shook her head. "He was in the pool when you saw him. But he ran right at me. I saw it. And it was what you'd expect. Regular."

As she squealed to a stop at a red light, Brooks turned a questioning gaze on May.

"And you're comparing him against . . . what?" Brooks asked, one eyebrow raised.

"I'm . . ." Now Palm had fixed May with a stare as well. Unless May had been withholding important information, they knew she didn't have a clue what she was talking about. "Guesstimating."

Palm snorted and fanned the photos out on the backseat.

"Here's one of his butt that's pretty good," she said, plucking out a picture taken during Pete's hasty retreat. It caught him midrun and was elegant, nearly classical in composition. Pete had the naked flair of an ancient Greek, but his butt was highlighted by the red glow from the Coke machine. Palmer named it *Naked Running Rudolph Butt*, which triggered the laugh attack all over again.

"Okay," May said, catching her breath. "We have five minutes to get home."

"Not a problem," Brooks said.

As Brooks cranked up the music and went into hyperspeed, Palmer and May examined the spoils of war: one pair of jeans (with wallet—that would need to be returned right away), one gray T-shirt, one red-and-white short-sleeved cotton button-down, one pair of boxers imprinted with pictures of chickens (very strange), one pair of gray socks with a thin red stripe. Palm hadn't had enough time to get his shoes, but they could live with that.

Brooks turned down the entrance to their road. The Golds lived in an old suburban development outside of Philadelphia. Back when it was new, it had probably been the neatest, most uniform community in the world, with its six different models of houses randomly and endlessly repeated down meandering tree-lined streets. But in the half century since it had been built, everything had been overgrown, and all of the houses had deteriorated or been altered or rebuilt. Their little corner in particular was the forbidden forest of mismatched additions and sagging garage porticos. They passed the Camps' on the way to their own house and gave a triumphant wave.

As May was in the middle of putting on Pete's shirt, Brooks suddenly turned off the music. May looked up from her buttoning.

"Why did you . . . ?"

May never finished her question because she soon saw what had caused the disturbance. In front of them was a parked police car with a silently pulsing siren light. It was next to an ambulance and a fire truck.

"What's that?" May said.

At first, May would remember, she thought that something had happened to their elderly neighbor, Mrs. Ross. But as they drove closer, they saw that the ambulance was in their driveway and that the fire truck and squad car were in front of their house. But there was no fire.

Though Brooks accelerated toward the house, to May it felt like the minivan was moving slowly. Now she could see the activity in their garage. Her father's Firebird was neatly parked in its spot, richly reflecting the late afternoon sun from its deep gold exterior. Three or four people in blue uniforms were calmly standing around the car. Some of their neighbors were on their front lawns, watching all of this.

Brooks brought the minivan to a jerky stop and killed the engine. Palm and Brooks ran out. May moved more deliberately, gathering her photos, picking up her purse and locking the doors. Then, when she was ready, she turned and walked toward the garage.

There was a large orange kit in the garage entrance. It sat open, revealing white sterile packages and plastic tubes from unseen devices. There was a stretcher set up by the tool bench. As May and her sisters approached, one of the EMTs pulled a sheet over it. One of their neighbors, Bonnie Stark, was in the driveway. She ran toward the girls, ushering them back. Bonnie had been crying.

"Girls," Bonnie was saying, "something happened. . . ."

May never remembered what it was that Bonnie told them; she only recalled that when Bonnie finished speaking, Brooks ran into the house. May looked down and with complete presence of mind counted every single one of the geraniums in the flower box by her feet. There were thirty-six. There was a whistling noise in her ears as she sat down in the driveway. Palm clung to her. Palm was crying—screaming, actually. May absently stroked her hair. It was slightly oily. Her poor little sister. She was so long and skinny, and she was clinging onto May like some violently terrified baby animal grabbing onto its mother's fur. Howling.

May started counting the tiles on the roof of the garage.

The next thing she remembered was walking into the kitchen. This must have only been a few minutes later. Pete's dad, Richard Camp, was there, on the phone. He was tall and thin like Pete and he was slumping a bit when May walked in, so he looked a bit like a drooping plant. He straightened up when he saw her and rapidly finished up his phone call with a curt, "Okay," and, "I'll call you back." She didn't really question why he was in their kitchen, on their phone; instead she wondered whether or not to tell him that Pete was stuck at the pool and that he had no clothes.

He hung up and walked over to her and tried to put his hand on her shoulder.

"May," he said, "I'm so . . ."

She moved away.

"Can you tell me, please," May said, reaching back and holding on to the kitchen counter, "can you tell me what's happening?"

"Your father . . . ," he began. He was speaking in an unnaturally precise manner, and he gripped the top of one of their heavy kitchen chairs until his knuckles were white. "He had a heart attack, May."

"When?"

It was the only thing she could think to ask.

"About forty-five minutes ago."

Forty-five minutes. You could save someone in forty-five minutes. That sounded reasonable. You hit them with the electric paddles or you gave them some medicine. Aspirin. She'd heard that aspirin could save you if you took it while you had a heart attack.

"Where is he?" May asked, surprised to hear the low insistence in her own voice. "Where did this happen? Here?"

"In the garage. In the car. He parked it, and then it must have happened."

"Have they stopped trying to . . ." May didn't know the words. "Those people, are they going to keep trying? You know. To help him?"

Mr. Camp didn't say anything for a moment.

"It was too late when they got here," he finally managed. "Do you understand?"

"Too late?"

"He was already gone, May."

No. He wasn't gone, not literally. He was out in the garage.

"He's dead, May."

May swallowed a few times in an attempt to get the whistling, air-suction noise in her ears to stop. It didn't work.

"Can I go see him?" she asked.

Mr. Camp sighed and ran his hand through his hair. It was straight, unlike Pete's, and turning a steely gray. Her dad had no gray hair.

"I wouldn't. Stay here with me, okay?"

"Where's my mom?"

"She's coming home now."

"Does she know?"

"She knows something is wrong."

"I'll call her." May walked toward the phone.

"She's on her way. She's not at work anymore."

"Cell . . ."

"Why don't you wait?" he asked. "I think that would be better. Safer. She's driving. Is that okay?"

May stopped halfway to the phone and thought about this.

"Safer. Okay. She's driving."

"Right." He nodded.

There was a lull. Neither of them moved.

"May," he finally said, "I'm so sorry."

"I have to go look for Palm," she replied. "I'll come back."

Halfway to the door, May realized that her bra was still dangling out of her front pocket. She yanked it free and threw it on the stairs as she passed. Stepping out the front door, she was shocked at how achingly sunny it was. Somehow she felt like it should have suddenly gotten dark. The paramedics were still there. They gave her sideways glances as she wandered to the quiet street, looked to the left and right, and wandered back toward the house. Another neighbor approached. So many neighbors. They were coming out of the woodwork.

The buzzing in her ears was getting louder.

"Have you seen my sister?" May asked anyone nearby. "Palmer?"

"She's over at the Starks', honey," one of the neighbors replied.

That's right, May thought. Bonnie had taken Palm to her house.

The neighbor was reaching out to her, trying to embrace her.

"Oh, right." May nodded, backing away. "Thanks."

She walked around the house, straight to the back of the yard, to the narrow, secluded space behind a bush that separated her sisters' pitchback and the shed. It was a damp, spidery spot, but it couldn't be seen from the kitchen window. She sank down into the grass and leaned up against a pile of cinder blocks that someone had stacked there six or seven years ago and never bothered to move. She started to laugh. It was completely automatic and spastic and so forceful that she actually gagged once or twice. She wasn't sure how long she sat there. It could have been five minutes or two hours. She didn't hear anyone approaching.

"May?"

May looked up to find Pete, now dry and dressed, standing next to her. He must have followed along to their house with his mother; she would have gotten the message as well. And of course Pete would know to look for her here. This had been a long-standing hiding spot in all kinds of games when they were kids. As for the incident at the pool . . . that had been sometime in the distant past or in another dimension.

Pete watched her. No jokes this time. Somehow having Pete standing next to her with a serious look on his face made the whole thing a little more real. And the real was horrible. The real made her panic. The pressure of his stare caused her laughter to evolve into a different, more logical emotion. She wanted to run, but she knew that she couldn't. Her legs, her arms—she didn't really know how they worked at the moment.

"Hey, Pete," she said as the last of the laughter died out of her voice, "I have your wallet."

next may

Babysitting

1. Since there's a baby in it, you'd think babysitting only meant babies. Then again, it also has a sitting. It's one of those things you can't get too literal about.

2. Something I first offered to do when I was four or five years old. I told my parents that they should go out because I could take care of Pawmer and Bwooks. They laughed and said that was really cute of me. I think they took it seriously on some level, though, because I feel like I've been doing it ever since. So it's also one of those things you have to be careful about volunteering for.

May Gold's actual name was Mayzie. As far as she knew, this was not a real name. It was a made-up, moon-man-language name based on Willie Mays, one of the most famous baseball players of all time.

All of the Gold girls were named after baseball players, a testament to their father's obsessive love of the game. Brooks was named after Brooks Robinson, twenty-two-year veteran of the Baltimore Orioles. Palmer was named after Jim Palmer, who was considered to be the best pitcher in Orioles history. May's sisters' names had relevance in their lives. They played softball. (Palmer was, in fact, a pitcher.) Also, Brooks and Palmer were kind of cool-sounding names. May could imagine a Brooks or a Palmer working in a law firm or becoming a famous artist. Mayzie was someone who had a washing machine on her front porch and turned up on some trashy talk show for the "My Mom Married My Brother!" episode.

So when the driving examiner, a woman with a helmet of tight, steel-gray curls, a state police jacket, and aviator glasses, came across striding across the lot, calling for "Mayzie Gold!" May nodded stiffly and felt the first tingling of nervous perspiration. She hated hearing that name announced in public.

"Get in, please," the woman said. It wasn't a friendly request.

May opened the driver's side door of the green minivan and

took her position behind the wheel. This was just a test, she told herself. An easy little test. And if there was one thing May was good at, it was tests. Okay, so she hadn't exactly prepared for this test so well. Who needed more than three or four sessions behind the wheel, anyway? She tried to relax, tried to release the tension-building death grip she had on the steering wheel, tried to send messages of peace along her arm muscles, tried to tell her eye not to spasm.

The woman got into the car. Now that she was so close, May got the full effect of the glasses and the hair and the jacket, and she saw the ashy gray color of the woman's skin and her purple-blue lips. She had a slight wheeze.

"Windshield wipers," the woman snapped.

May reached for the wiper switch. She had it in hand. Wipers. Definitely the wipers. But flicked the wrong way this switch turned on . . . the *high beams*.

Brain, May begged internally. *Brain. Do not send me bad information. DO NOT TURN ON THE HIGH BEAMS.*

Flick. Wipers squealed their way along the dry windshield. Flick. Wipers off.

The woman nodded.

"Hazards," she said.

Hazards. Yes. The panic button—the one you hit when something was going wrong with the car. She knew that one. May clicked the button with confidence, and the car responded with the comforting ticktocking noise of the flashing lights.

"All right, Miss Gold . . ." She snapped May's learner's permit onto her clipboard. "Hazards off and let's go. Straight ahead."

May turned off the hazards and toed the gas pedal.

"I'd like to finish this test today, Miss Gold. A little faster, please."

May put her foot on the pedal lightly, cranking the car up to about the speed of a casual bicycle ride. The examiner sighed and made a note. May's eyes flashed over to the clipboard. In the process she rolled five feet past the first stop sign. May hit the brakes hard, coming to an abrupt stop.

Well, that was wrong, she thought, easing the car back into motion. *Better keep going.*

May continued on to the serpentine, the pattern of orange traffic cones set up as a winding path. Unfortunately, the serpentine didn't look like any kind of path to May—it looked like a random mass of cones tossed into the road to block her. She dropped the car's speed even more and started trying to pick her way through the mess without hitting anything.

"Speed up," the examiner said.

May ignored this.

"You missed one of the cones," the examiner added as May struggled through the forest of orange.

Only one? May said to herself. *Better than I thought.*

From there, she faced the stall for the three-point turn. This was the dreaded part of the exam where she was supposed to pull the car into a tiny box, then had to figure out how to get out of it by backing the car up and only turning it three times. She pulled in carefully.

"All the way into the stall," the examiner snapped.

"I *am* in," May offered meekly.

"You're barely halfway in."

May blinked and looked around her. The low walls of the pen seemed to be coming in at her. It was like the examiner was saying, "Don't just tap that metal divider May—*ram* it. I want to see spare parts and twisted metal *everywhere.*"

"Pull in!" the examiner repeated.

May pulled another half a foot forward.

"Miss Gold," the woman said with a sigh, "if you don't pull in, you can't complete this part of the exam."

"I'll hit the barrier."

"The barrier is over six feet away."

Six feet? No. It was right in front of her, just over the hood of the car. Any closer and they would be less one minivan. May felt the panic juices start to speed through her system.

Though she would have liked to, she couldn't just leave the car here in the middle of the course. Leave it and run. Off to someplace where cars were not a required feature of life. Maybe Holland, where her mother's parents lived. From what she'd heard, the Dutch had so many trains and trams and boats that no driving was required. She could see the canals and the tulips and try those fries with the weird mayonnaise sauce that her mom said were so good. . . .

"Miss Gold."

"I can't," May said, looking down at her lap. "I'm sorry."

"Back out and turn around."

May managed to recall only one thing from her studies of the art of driving: when facing a collision that is impossible to avoid, relax—the impact is less damaging that way. She let her elbows drop, and her breathing became shallow. She slowly turned the car around and managed to wind her way back to the parking lot in front of the exam building. She stopped the car in the vicinity of the curb and killed the engine. The key stuck in the ignition. She had to wiggle it out.

May was calm through the quiet scribbling on the clipboard. She saw x's being made at what had to be the wrong end of a chart. A slip of thin paper was handed to her, which she grasped in a slightly shaking fist and could not bring herself to read.

"I'm sorry, Miss Gold," the examiner said, not sounding sorry at all. "You'll have to come back."

"Thanks." May nodded. It seemed kind of stupid to thank someone for failing her, but it was an automatic response. The woman wheezed once more and exited, and May slid over to the passenger's seat and stared at herself in the side-view mirror. Apparently she was closer than she appeared. Another mystery of driving that she would never understand.

A minute later her mother's face appeared in the car window. She evaluated May with a quick glance, got into the driver's seat, and quietly started the car. She took her sunglasses from their resting place in the gentle blond spikes and put them over her eyes.

"It's no big deal. I failed the first time too," her mom offered when they were safely up the road.

"Okay."

"You just need a little more practice. Maybe you can take it again in a week or two. . . ."

"Can we talk about this some other time?" May said.

"Sorry."

May stared into the pile of rubble that had pooled in the

console. Coffee rings with change and grit stuck on them. Wrappers from candies and meal-replacement bars. Crumpled receipts from the hospital parking lot. A french fry container dotted with clear congealed grease stains. So gross. For a nurse, her mom could tolerate a pretty disgusting car. Even if May could have gotten through the test, she probably would have failed for poor automotive hygiene.

"Our car is nasty," May said, closing her eyes.

"I know."

Her mom switched on the radio, and they soft-rocked out for a few minutes. Neither of them really liked that kind of music, but it seemed soothing, numbing. One of the other things about May's mom was that she had once been a hard-core punk girl. The spikes in her hair had been harder, stiff with gel, formed into sharp points. Gone forever (but not for-gotten—her father had taken a picture to use as blackmail) were the ripped fishnet stockings, the shock-white face makeup, the black eyeliner that stretched all the way out to the hairline, and the combat boots. Now she was a gentle, soccer-mom kind of punk. But the soft rock was still unacceptable.

"I'm working tonight," her mom finally said. "I asked Brooks if she could take you to work if—"

"If I failed. Which I did."

"I'm sorry I haven't had more time to teach you."

"It's not your fault," May replied. "We're just on opposite schedules."

"Could you make sure Palmer eats some dinner before you go?"

May wanted to say, "She's fourteen. She can feed herself."

But that would be ridiculous. Palmer would survive solely on Doritos and doughnut holes if she could get away with it. May's father, the security systems salesman, had been the great negotiator of the family, coaxing each bite of roast beef or tuna fish into Palmer with offers of softball catches and water ice. But Palmer was too old for that now, and her mom didn't have the time or energy to think about how things should be—she only knew how they were. She knew that Palmer needed to have an actual dinner put in front of her and needed to be watched to make sure she ate it. And that kind of job always fell to May. In fact, May didn't have to say anything at all to her mother's request because her mother knew her answer would always be yes. There was no room to say no anymore.

"I don't want to pressure you, May." Her mom sighed as she turned down the shady entrance of their street. "I'm sorry. You know how much I count on you. Brooks should be more responsible, but we both know she isn't. I need your help. And when you can drive . . ."

"It's no pressure," May lied. "It'll be fine. I just need a little more practice."

"Right. You'll have no problems the next time."

She gave May's ponytail a light tug. May forced a smile.

Inside, Palmer was sprawled all over the sofa, her long limbs draped in every direction. She tipped her head up on their arrival, took one look at May's face, and lowered herself back down and focused on the television again.

"You failed," she said. "Great. Now I still have to ride with Brooks."

May trudged upstairs, threw herself onto her bed, crawled under the quilt, and fell asleep.

It was late in the afternoon by the time that May woke up. Her room was dark and cold. She rolled out from the warm spot under her quilt, slid into her slippers and pulled on a sweatshirt, and made her bleary-eyed way downstairs. The television was blasting from the living room, and her sore head began to pound slightly.

A glance at the clock told her that her mother had already left for the hospital and that she had less than an hour to get ready for work. She headed to the kitchen to get some dinner together. Along the way, she picked up a cup and a coffee mug from the hall table. There were even more dishes scattered around the kitchen. May gathered them up and loaded the dishwasher. She wiped down the counter. She had to scrub hard to get rid of all the sticky juice and soda and coffee rings. The washcloth had a sour, fishy smell.

Dinner prospects were grim. The edible contents of the refrigerator consisted of one bottle of Brooks's spooky blue post-practice Gatorade (strictly off-limits to anyone else), year-old pickles, some tuna fish salad (age unknown), half a piece of fried chicken, and some brown iceberg lettuce. The pantry wasn't much better. There were some boxes of cereal that contained only dry, dusty evidence of their former contents. Some soups that had been around so long, they had become heirlooms. Crisco. Rejected packets of plain instant oatmeal.

May finally settled on a box of macaroni and cheese. She found some freezer-burned ground beef and decided to warm it and cook the two together. This "casserole" was one of the few foods that Palmer was sure to eat. Not the most nutritious meal, but probably better than a handful of chips. At least it was the good kind of macaroni and cheese—the kind that came with the pouch of cheese goo.

After starting the hot water for the macaroni, May sat at the table and pulled over the stack of textbooks she had piled in the corner. She had just enough time to finish up the set of trig problems for class on Monday. Grabbing a mechanical pencil from the fruit bowl, she set to work.

The phone rang immediately.

She stared at the cordless that sat just two feet in front of her, then smothered it with the quilted toaster cover.

"Get that?" May yelled in to Palmer.

No reply. It rang again.

"Palmer! Get that!" May repeated.

"You get it."

"I don't want to talk to anyone!"

"That's *your* mental problem," Palmer replied.

Why did the toaster cover have so many burn marks on it? That couldn't be good.

"What if it's Mom?" May called back.

"What if it is?"

One last ring and the caller was shuttled off to voice mail land.

"Thanks!" May added.

"No problem."

May heard the television volume increase. The kitchen wall began to vibrate. She got up and marched into the living room.

Palmer was huddled close to the television, basking in its glow. She wore her sweats, her fleece jacket, and nasty fuzzy slippers. Additionally, she had draped the old crocheted living room blanket over her head like a hood and was wearing May's chenille gloves. If she'd had a marshmallow on a stick pressed up against the screen, May wouldn't have been completely surprised.

"You know that you're not outdoors, right?" May asked.

A cold stare.

"Could you turn that down a little?"

Palmer turned the volume up another notch.

"Where's Brooks?"

Palmer shrugged.

"She's supposed to be taking me to work in an hour," May said. "Do you know what time her team meeting is over?"

"There's no meeting today."

"Then where did she go?"

"How am I supposed to know?"

"Did she tell you?"

"No. She just left with Dave when you and Mom were asleep."

"Dave?" May repeated. "Oh, great."

Dave had recently come into Brooks's life. He had wide brown eyes, high cheekbones, thick eyebrows, and a fringe of long hair all around his face. He was always smiling a slow, mysterious smile, and he had to lean against something whenever he wasn't sitting down. May begrudgingly admitted to herself that he was handsome—in a lethargic, werewolfy sort of way. She couldn't tell if the two of them were dating, since

Brooks never discussed it. And Dave certainly wasn't shedding any light on the subject. May had exchanged exactly two sentences with him in the three or four months he had been coming by. One was, "I'll go get her." The other was, "She's coming down."

If they were dating, Dave stood in stark contrast to Brooks's last (and only) boyfriend, Brian. Brian was the brother of someone on Brooks's softball team—a pleasant, extremely dull guy, who Palmer had blessed with the nickname "Nipplehead." (There was nothing specifically nipplelike about his head, but the name just seemed to fit. Even their mom, who liked Brian, said, "You know, he really is a Nipplehead.") He'd disappeared sometime during the events of the previous summer, and no one had asked about him since. Dave seemed nothing like Brian. When Brooks went out with Dave, she came back late and usually drunk. This was a new thing for Brooks. May was still getting used to the sound of hearing her come in and stumble around, doing everything too loudly and dropping stuff in the bathroom.

But only one part of this interested May at the moment: Brooks definitely wouldn't be back in time to take her to work.

"Put my gloves back where you found them when you're done." May sighed. "Those are my good ones, from Christmas."

Palmer plunged her gloved hand into the remains of a bag of barbecued potato chips that lay by her side.

"Don't eat those," May said. "I'm making you dinner."

Palmer shoved the chips into her mouth and turned back to the television.

Sighing again, May went back to the kitchen and headed straight to the refrigerator. She pulled out Brooks's bottle of Gatorade, poured herself a small glass, and dumped the rest down the drain. The empty bottle she placed in the middle of the counter. She looked out the kitchen window at the pounding spring shower that had come out of nowhere. This would prohibit her from getting to work on her bike—the trusty Brown Hornet, her dad's twenty-five-year-old brown three speed, complete with "guy bar."

She could call her mom on her cell and tell her what Brooks had done, but there was no point. Her mom would be halfway to downtown Philadelphia by now, weaving her way through Saturday night traffic to get to the hospital. She would sigh and swear in Dutch and say something about having to talk to Brooks, but she wouldn't. Lecturing Brooks was as useful as lecturing a cat.

So May sipped the Gatorade and looked out at the rain.

"Thanks a lot, Brooks," she said to herself.

Brooks had no idea where she was going. She had just gotten in the car when Dave pulled up.

At the moment there were five of them in his Volkswagen, even though it really only held two people comfortably since the front seats were always pushed back to the maximum. Brooks sat in the back with her face pressed up against the window. The rest of her was pressed deeply into Jamie. Jamie was giving off a powerful orangey-jasmine odor, almost candy sweet. Someone else reeked of patchouli incense, cigarette smoke, and fast food. Brooks considered trying to crack open the window a bit for some unfragranced air, but she would be guaranteed a wet head if she did so. The rain was practically coming down sideways.

"Come on!" Jamie yelled over the music pounding from the stereo. "It's pouring. So let's forget it. I want to go to that tattoo place instead, the one off of South, on Fifth."

Dave looked at Jamie in the rearview mirror with a bemused expression.

"For what?" he asked. "So you can stand there in front of the place for an hour again?"

"I'm going to get it this time," Jamie said. "And Brooks wants to go. Right?"

"Sure," Brooks said, barely listening.

Dave smiled at Brooks in the rearview mirror. It was his let's-humor-her smile. Brooks returned the grin.

"We'll go afterward," he said. "Relax."

Small exchanges like this one told Brooks that she was in Dave's inner circle now—the one whose only consistent members were Jamie and Fred. Jamie was an extremely tiny and pale girl with catlike features and black hair cut into a sharp bob. She always wore tight, clubby clothes and three or four necklaces. She waxed her black eyebrows into high, dramatic arches and wore stark red lipstick that never seemed to wear off. She was so strikingly feminine that Brooks occasionally felt like a lumbering guy sitting next to her. Fred always rode in the front seat since he was about six-foot five. He had white-blond hair cut into a little boy's page cut and a tattoo of Snoopy on his forearm.

Along with Jamie and Fred, Dave always had a bunch of guys around him. Different ones every time. Henchmen.

Tonight's random henchman was sitting on the other side of Jamie. He was a weedy guy in a hooded sweatshirt who was interchangeably called "Damage" or "Bob," but Brooks thought she heard that his actual name was Rick. Damage/Bob/Rick didn't speak. He spent the entire ride trying to remove a thread from the back of the driver's seat upholstery.

Fred passed a plastic soda bottle full of orange liquid into the backseat.

"Who wants it?" he asked.

"I'll take it," Brooks said, grabbing the bottle. "Jamie's wasted."

She uncapped the bottle and took a long swig. She shook her head from the force of the strange elixir—it was like gasoline with a little orange added for flavor.

"What is it?" Brooks said, trying to place the sweetness and the hard, burning sensation that came with it. "Rum?"

"King of Pain," Fred said. "It's got 151."

"One fifty-one . . ."

"A hundred-and-fifty-one-proof rum. It makes *really* good fires. You like it?"

"It hurts." She groaned as the burning in her throat stopped. "But I like it." This stuff was *fast.* Faster than anything she'd had before, even grain. She was laughing, and her head was thrumming within seconds.

"Hey, Dave," Fred said. "Can I light it?"

"Not in the car," Dave replied.

"I'll hold it out the window."

"Dude . . . ," Dave sighed. "Relax."

"This one time," Fred went on, "I flamed it, right? I was down the shore and I flamed some 151 on the beach. And I was looking at it. And I totally burned off my eyebrows. Check it out."

He pushed back his hair and tilted his big forehead in Brooks's direction. She saw that his blond eyebrows were very sparse. The skin underneath was all scar tissue, thicker and whiter than the rest of his face.

"That was hilarious," Dave said. Even Damaged Bobrick stopped thread picking for a moment to smile.

Jamie was whispering into Brooks's ear.

"I'm going to get it," she said.

Brooks nodded her approval, even though she couldn't care less if Jamie got a tattoo. She looked out the window at the flag-lined road they were driving down. They were downtown, on the Benjamin Franklin Parkway. In front of them, high above the road and looking like some Greek antiquity, was the Philadelphia Museum of Art.

"The art museum?" Brooks asked. "Is that where we're going?"

Dave smiled into the rearview mirror again. He turned off the parkway onto a smaller road that wound its way up to the art museum. They drove around its base to a small service entrance for emergency vehicles and maintenance crews, cordoned off by a single chain drawn across two poles. Dave stopped the car, and Fred got out and moved the chain so that he could drive through. The path was narrow, just wide enough for the car. The bushes rubbed at its sides as Dave slunk along, lights off.

"Should we be here?" Brooks smiled nervously.

She could see high windows through the greenery—bits of sculptures, walls of shadowy squares that had to be paintings. To

Brooks's amazement, Dave pulled the Volkswagen right up onto the grand plaza in front of the colonnaded central building and the grand fountain. The building's two wings spread out on either side of them, embracing the entire area. The fountains and buildings were lit up with golden spotlights. In front of them was a huge, steep set of stairs that led down to the boulevard. It was intensely bright, but it was so high up that it was also amazingly private.

"Rocky!" Fred screamed.

"Rocky!" everyone else but Brooks yelled back.

There was a scrambling all around Brooks. Doors flew open, and Fred, Jamie, and Bobrick tumbled out onto the brick plaza. They didn't seem to care at all that there was a deluge going on. Fred and Damaged Bobrick were now screaming out the *Rocky* theme and running haphazardly toward the huge steps. Jamie delicately followed them in her little boots.

Brooks noticed that Dave was lingering behind. Something told her to do the same.

"You going?" she said casually.

"No," Dave said. "Come on up."

She slid out of the back and joined him in the front seat, getting fairly drenched in the process. She brought the King of Pain with her.

"Ever see *Rocky*?" he asked.

"No."

"Well, he's this boxer, and he lives in Philly. There's a really huge scene where he runs up these steps. . . ."

Dave pointed to the huge slope of steps directly in front of them, which everyone else was now stumbling down.

"And that song plays."

Everyone else had passed out of sight by this point, but Brooks could still hear them screaming out the song. It grew fainter as they got lower. She took a long swig of the punch.

"We used to come here a lot last year," he said. "They do this every time."

"You don't do it?" She smiled.

"No." He shook his head. "I've never seen the movie."

Brooks laughed. Dave grinned back at her. He had a small scar above his upper lip that stretched when he smiled. Maybe they all had scars on their faces. She would check Jamie's face later.

"So," Dave said, "they don't make you practice softball on Saturdays?"

"During the day they do."

"How many afternoons a week?"

"All of them."

"Harsh."

"It takes up a lot of time," Brooks said, passing him the punch. Her hand brushed against his jacket. It was a heavy, soft corduroy, lined with a knobby wool that peeked out at the collar and the cuffs.

"You've been playing for a long time, right?"

"Since I was four."

"Aren't you sick of it?"

"Sometimes," Brooks said. She leaned against the dashboard and looked down at the view. The dark was dropping lightly, she noticed, like a falling blanket. It caught on the spires of the Liberty Towers first, and they lit up. The yellow clock on top of

City Hall was illuminated. The punch had gummed up all the vessels in Brooks's brain that juiced her nervous reactions. Of course she should be here, in this most illegal of spots.

"I used to dive," Dave said, taking a sip. "That took a lot of time too. I liked it, but—"

"Exactly," Brooks cut in. "I like it, but—"

"So quit," Dave said.

He said it like it was simple, like softball was just something she could give up.

"I can't." She laughed.

"Why?"

"Because . . . ," Brooks said, and then found that she had no concrete reason to give. She knew it had something to do with her dad and never having really known a life outside of softball. Her father had put a bat in her hand the minute she was strong enough to hold it up, and that was that. Afternoons and weekends were for playing. She didn't even know what people who didn't play sports did with their time. But she had to admit, she'd seen less and less of a point in playing in the last year.

"Because why?" Dave said. "You don't sound like you want to do it."

"Sometimes I don't. Lots of times I don't."

"So don't do it."

Maybe it *was* that simple. Maybe the problem was that she'd just never thought about quitting as an actual option.

She heard Dave shift in his seat. Something was happening. Tonight was different from the other nights they'd gone out. She felt like he'd wanted to come here for a reason.

"Yeah," she said, "I guess I *could* quit. . . ."

When Brooks turned her head to face him, Dave kissed her.

A minute or two later Bobrick and Fred reappeared, winded and sopping wet, at the top of the steps. They ran over and threw themselves against the hood of the car. Dave waved them away with one hand, and they disappeared into the scenery, like all good henchmen should.

Pete had the radio blasting when May threw open the door to his old Cutlass Ciera. He'd been letting his hair grow, so now it was similar to the way it had been when they were kids— loose and crazy, sometimes forming perfect corkscrews, some- times just flying out in mad, electrified strands. He was bobbing his head slightly and playing with the zipper on his blue hooded sweatshirt. As May went to sit down, he quickly reached over and grabbed a bunch of papers, plastic bags, unmarked CDs, and wrappers that covered the passenger seat and tossed them into the back of the car.

"I can't control the volume!" he screamed as a greeting. He killed the power so that the radio switched off. "Sorry," he said. "It's a new thing. The volume only goes up to eleven."

The last word was said in some kind of British accent.

"Eleven?"

"It's from . . . nothing. It's a quote. So what happened?"

"Brooks pulled a Brooks," May explained, throwing herself into the seat and shaking off some of the rain. "She knew I needed a ride, but she went somewhere."

"Oh. Well, good thing I was home. Let's go."

He turned the key. Nothing happened.

"Huh," he said, rattling the key in the ignition.

"What?"

Pete flicked the key several times and stomped his foot on the gas. Still nothing.

"It's been doing this," he said, knitting his brows together in concentration. "It usually starts. Eventually."

"In how long?"

"Ten or fifteen minutes. As long as I keep trying. The longest it ever took was like half an hour. Unless it's the transmission."

"The transmission?"

"Well, I had to have mine taken out last week," he said, flicking the key in disgust and shifting through the gears a few times. "They put in a dual battery instead. It was cheaper than getting a new engine, you know? But it's been weird ever since."

May faced straight out and counted the uncollected newspapers on the Starks' front porch. She told herself to be calm as Pete tapped strategically on the dashboard, trying to make the car come back to life.

"Just give me a second," he said, reaching under his seat. May heard a popping noise. "Be right back."

Pete jumped out of the car and disappeared behind the raised hood for a moment. She could hear him banging on something furiously. He came back a moment later, his great mass of hair sending water flying in all directions.

"Yeah, it's the transmission," he said, wiping his hands on his pants. "I don't think I should have let them take it out."

"Does that mean it isn't going to start now?"

"Probably."

May sank her head into her hands. Her desperate gesture must have touched the car because suddenly the engine purred. May refused to look up until it was actually moving for fear of making it stop again.

"Take out the transmission?"

May opened her eyes to see Pete grinning down at her. He was alternately glancing between May and the road, obviously pleased with himself.

"Take out the transmission?" he repeated. "Replace it with a battery?"

Age seventeen, tormenting May with little car pranks. Age seven, tormenting May by sneaking up on her and sticking Cheese Puffs up her nose and then pulling them out and eating them. It was all pretty much the same thing.

"What?" May shot back. "That means nothing to me."

"A *dual battery?*"

"Car isn't my best subject."

"The transmission makes the car go vroooom," he said. "It makes the wheels go round. If anyone offers to take it out of your car for you, say no."

"I'll remember that if I ever drive. But that's probably not going to happen."

"What do you mean?"

"I failed my exam this morning," May said.

"Oh," he said. "Sorry."

"It's fine. I just want to get to work."

"What happened?"

"What did I do wrong?" she said. "You want the list?"

"But you never fail things. You're test girl."

"Well, now I'm failure girl." She sighed.

"Who taught you?" he asked. "Your mom?"

"She tried, but she doesn't have a lot of time."

"What about Brooks?"

"Reliable Brooks? The one who's taking me to work tonight? The one who goes over speed bumps at eighty miles an hour?"

He nodded, understanding this. Pete knew a lot of things about them, including some things May would have preferred to keep private. Like the fact that they were broke, for instance, and that going to a driving school was not really an option.

Soon after May's father's death, an unpleasant fact had had to be faced: Life is not like the movies—you don't just get money when someone dies. Sometimes you lose money. There are strange expenses and taxes. Mike Gold had taken only minimal steps in the way of insurance, so without his income, they were in trouble.

In the summer and the fall, May had sat with her mother and helped work out their budget. They'd canceled her father's subscriptions to his sports magazines, turned off the cell phones, and limited the cable service. Her mother had switched to working nights and bumped up her hours. She'd also accepted a few small family loans—enough to pay for May's tuition and a bit of the mortgage. Still, things were not looking very good.

Pete's dad was an accountant. He did their taxes, and he knew the score. Pete's mom often sent over strange assortments of extralarge items she picked up at the wholesale club—jumbo bottles of dishwasher detergent, twelve-packs of soap, jugs of shampoo with pump dispensers. She'd say, "It was such a good

deal, I couldn't pass it up!" or, "It was two for one, so I just figured I'd give this one to you!" to try to keep the whole thing
from being awkward. It still always was.

They pulled into the shopping center where May worked,
which was between a collection of housing developments and
the access road from I-95. Pete drove up to the brown building
in the far corner of the parking lot, the one that had been born
as a Pizza Hut but had lived through several incarnations since
then.

"Do you need a ride home tonight?" he asked.

May looked out at the rain. She had no other option, aside
from walking through the downpour in the dark.

"I don't want to mess up your plans . . . ," she said.

"I just have to go over to school later and finish hanging
some lights for the show. We're doing *Joseph and the Amazing
Technicolor Dreamcoat.*"

"It sounds like an infomercial."

"It's a musical," Pete clarified. "They're always musicals. So,
what time are you done?"

"Eleven."

"Eleven," he repeated, again in the strange accent. "So, I'll
come back then."

With that settled, May stepped out into the rain and ran to
the door, and the Cutlass rolled out of the parking lot and vanished beyond the gray horizon.

Presto Espresso wanted desperately to look like it was part of
some huge chain of coffee bars. It had the wooden tables, the
wall murals, and the recycled cups. It had drinks with catchy

names, always prefaced with the words *our signature,* as if Presto Espresso made coffee in some special, famous way. It had generic jazz music pumped into the air from hidden speakers. What it didn't have was customers. Working there was a long exercise in killing time—stacking cups and grinding coffee and standing around. Specifically, it was an exercise in killing time with Nell Dodd, the assistant manager.

"My dorm was right near this massive cell phone tower," Nell was saying as she arranged a pile of cups in bowling-pin fashion at the far end of the counter. "And it's a well-known fact that cell phone signals give you brain cancer. So I talked to the residence life staff, but they completely refused to move me."

"Uh-huh," May said.

Nell had started college in September and left after two weeks. She'd been living at home and working at Presto for the last nine months while contemplating her "new direction." May had started working at Presto in December, and she'd heard this story at least fifteen times since then.

"Everything about the place sucked," Nell went on. "Like my roommate. My roommate was this total crypto-fascist sorority-girl wannabe. I mean, pretty much all she wanted from college was to pledge Sigma Whatever Whatever, which is just about the saddest thing I have ever heard. I showed her a book once and she kind of shrank away, like Dracula from garlic or something."

"Uh-huh."

"And my classes were just kind of stupid, you know? All kinds of stuff I didn't need. For my core science class I was tak-ing their highest level of Biology 101, which was for majors, and I wasn't a major. But it was *nothing*. I did *all of that* in high school because we had a completely amazing biology program. My high school was *so* much harder, you know? Because I went to an alternative school, right?"

May was taking seven periods of biology a week, along with an introductory chemistry class to prepare her for the two more years of chemistry she still had to face. She somehow doubted that Nell had ever done the same amount of work, but she said nothing.

"So I'm kind of taking some time to think it all over," Nell continued. "I want to reapply to some really good schools, like Bennington and Smith. You know Bennington and Smith?"

"What? Oh. Uh-huh."

"Bennington is like amazingly cool, but it's really expensive. Sylvia Plath went to Smith, and she totally exposed it for everything it was, but I think it's really cool now. Did you read *The Bell Jar*?"

Actually, May considered, this wasn't the worst of the stories she'd had to endure. Nell had once entertained May with a two-hour saga on how she'd been vegan for two years during high school, but then someone had slipped her some cheese-mushroom ravioli and the whole thing had fallen apart, ending with her decision to revert back to ovo-lacto. There had been another grueling evening in which May had learned all about Nell's eight piercings: the two on her face, the three on her ears, the one on her belly button, and two small rings that she actually called "knocker knockers." Now *that* had been a really bad night.

Nell snapped her fingers in front of May's face.

"What?" May jolted.

"A guy. A guy is here."

May followed Nell's gaze. She was staring out the front windows at Pete. He was getting out of his big gray sedan.

"What?" May said. "Him?"

"You see another guy?"

"That's Pete," May said. She realized as she looked at the clock that Pete was fifteen minutes early.

"Pete?" Nell asked.

"Yeah. That's Pete."

"Right. Got that part. And who is Pete?"

"Oh," May said, "he's kind of like our neighbor. A family friend. Kind of like one of our old friends."

"Boyfriend?" Nell said.

"What? Mine? No." May hastily dusted off her apron. "No."

"Check out that hair. He's got a full-on 'fro. You like him?"

"He's Pete," May said.

"Oh." Nell nodded. "It's like that. Okay."

"Like what?"

Pete came in before Nell could answer and before May could remove the baseball cap with the cartoon of the dancing bean on it. That was probably for the best anyway—Nell would have noticed if she'd taken it off.

As the assistant manager, Nell was able to use her rank to push the uniform to the limit, adding a studded black belt to her ragged cargo pants and wearing a torn black mesh shirt over her white T-shirt. She decorated her fiendishly healthy complexion with a few small bits of metal, including the stud in her nose and the ring through her lower lip. She didn't have to wear the hat, the name tag, or the apron. May did. Nell liked to point this out—as a joke, or so she pretended. Nell had an annoying sense of humor like that.

"You're early," May said. The abruptness of her remark caused Pete to stop in his tracks. Nell snorted. Her nose always whistled a bit when she did that as the air passed by the nose stud.

"If you're busy"—Pete motioned toward his car—"I can go. . . ."

"Are you kidding?" Nell threw herself down on the counter. "A customer! We are at your service!"

Pete stared down at the back of Nell's head, then looked at the pile of cups that she had arranged for her game of bowling for Kona.

"You guys are bored," he deduced.

"Is it that obvious?" Nell asked, looking up from her prone position. "Please stay. We are but two young virgins trapped in this remote outpost, with no men to talk to."

May winced. Okay, maybe Nell could joke around with a word like *virgin*—a description that probably didn't fit her—but May couldn't. She kept a wide berth around that term.

"We have nothing to do," Nell went on. "You know those people whose job it is to paint the Golden Gate Bridge? They start at one end, and it takes them a few years to paint all the way to the other side, and when they finish, they just go back and start over? That's kind of like what we do. No one comes here because this place totally blows. Right, Ape?"

"Ape?" Pete repeated.

"My nickname," May said, without enthusiasm.

"Yeah, when May first started, I had to make her name tag,

and I forgot which month her name was. I thought it was April." Nell reached over and grabbed at the strap of May's apron and flashed Pete the tag for proof. "So I call her Ape."

May silenced Pete with a stern look before he could make any reply. Nell was staring at Pete's chest.

"I like your shirt," she said.

Pete was wearing a T-shirt that read, mysteriously enough, Best Wishes to Your Family.

"Well," May said, quickly untying her apron, "we're pretty much done here, right?"

"Sure," Nell said. "Why don't you two go?"

"Okay, then," she said, before Nell could say anything else. "See you later."

May felt Nell's gaze following them as they left the store.

"So that's where I work," she said, sliding back into Pete's car.

"She's interesting," he said.

"She's a special person," May said, giving Pete a light punch on the shoulder. "Just like you, Camper."

"Not special. Challenged."

"So," she said, "what do you have planned as an encore? Are you going to fake a ten-car pileup or something?"

"Eleven," he said, once again in the weird mockney-Cockney accent.

Pete spent most of the ride back smacking and yelling at the radio dial, trying to convince it to work correctly. This didn't accomplish much. He gave up and switched it off when they pulled up to May's house.

"Listen," he said. "I can teach you, if you want."

"What?"

"Driving?"

"Teach me *driving*?"

"It was my mom's idea," he said. "I went home for dinner after I dropped you off, and she suggested it."

"Your mom wants you to teach me?"

"*I* do," he clarified quickly. "It was her idea, but I think it could be fun. You know. Spreading my knowledge."

More charity from the Camps. She should have realized this would happen. They sent Pete to do everything—cut the grass, deliver the bulk purchases, clean the rain gutters, shovel the snow.

"I don't want to take up all your time."

"It's not a problem," he said. "Besides, someone has to teach you, right?"

May couldn't argue the point, even though it made her sound somewhat pathetic. "I guess I'm on the to-do list," she said.

It took her a minute to figure out why Pete was staring at her so strangely.

"You know what I mean," she added.

"So? What do you think?"

What she thought had nothing to do with it. There was only one answer to give.

"Okay," May said. "Thanks."

Palmer was in the exact same position in front of the television that she'd been in when May left, even though four and a half hours had gone by.

"Brooks come home?" May asked, peeling off her damp jacket.

"No."

"She call?"

"No."

And that was it from Palmer.

May went upstairs to her tiny room. Her wallpaper was covered in pictures of white horses with pink ribbons in their manes. Most of her furniture was unfinished light pine, which tended to splinter a bit along the edges of the drawers. One snagged her favorite sleeping shirt, one of her dad's old University of Maryland shirts, as she pulled it from the drawer. She carefully picked the splinter out of the worn fabric, pulled the shirt over her head, and crawled under the quilt.

She turned off her bedside lamp and stared up at the shadow of her blinds, rippling across the ceiling. Someone drove by in a car with way too much bass, and the room thumped and rattled until it passed by.

"I suck," she said out loud. "How could I fail?"

The phone rang. Probably her mother's midway-through-shift call to check on them. May clawed around next to her bed for the phone and answered it. The person on the other end breathed heavily into the phone. She allowed this to go on for a minute or so.

"What's up, Camper?" she finally asked.

"Do you like scary movies?" the voice whispered.

"Do you like getting hot coffee poured in your lap? Because that's what's going to happen the next time I see you if you don't stop it."

Pete cleared his throat.

"I forgot to ask you when you wanted to start," he said. "Monday?"

"Okay." May yawned. "Monday."

"Six?"

"Fine." After a moment she remembered to add, "Thanks."

"No problem."

"Good night, Camper."

Shaking her head at the great unfairness of it all, May hung up and dropped the phone beside her bed.

Even though Palmer was only a freshman, she was already the pitcher on Grant High's varsity softball team. This would normally be a rare and remarkable accomplishment, but really, no one expected less from the little sister of Brooks "Solid" Gold—shortstop, Grant's record holder for most hits in a season and in a career, two-time All State selection, with the team-best batting average of .692.

Palmer intended to do even better than her sister. Along with the formal daily practice at school, she did a separate workout at home. Her father had helped her design this routine. It was based on his college workout, and he'd modified it carefully for her. She followed it religiously. On Mondays, Wednesdays, and Fridays she worked on her pitching. On Tuesdays, Thursdays, and Saturdays she stretched and ran a few loops around the neighborhood.

Since it was Monday, Palmer slipped on her fleece jacket (which she wore all year round, except in the most excruciating heat, to keep her body warm and prevent injuries), grabbed her small bucket of softballs, and went out into the backyard. First she set her face in her standard pitching grimace—she narrowed her eyes, sucked in her round cheeks, and tipped her head to the side. (It was actually her imitation of Dirty Harry. She thought it made her look a little older and more imposing.)

Then she started to throw.

Twenty wrist-snap pitches close to the pitch back. A series of fastballs, ten inside and ten outside. A few rise balls, a dozen drop balls and screwballs. Last, she worked the changeups, the balls that actually slow down as they travel. These were the hardest, but they were also some of her best. She wrapped the whole thing up with a dozen very fast, very accurate throws, aimed directly at the center of the net.

With the formal practice over, she allowed herself to throw whatever she liked as her brain tried to process the news, which she had gotten along with everyone else, dished out cold at an impromptu team meeting after practice. Brooks had quit the team that morning. In fact, Brooks was completely AWOL. She hadn't even been around to help Palmer get home. She'd had to bum a ride home with one of her teammates.

When she heard the minivan pull into the driveway, she stopped her practice and went inside. Brooks was in the kitchen, staring into the fridge.

"What's going on?" Palmer said bluntly.

"Yeah," Brooks said, "I was going to tell you."

"*Going* to tell me?"

"May made you dinner," Brooks said, pointing inside the fridge. "She says it's meat loaf, but it looks like one of those old Duraflame logs from the garage."

"You were *going* to tell me?"

Brooks let go of the fridge door.

"Look, I've just had enough, all right?" she said. "I've been playing for what, twelve, thirteen years?"

"You could get a scholarship," Palmer said, her lips clenched. "Or try out for WPSL or the Olympic team . . ."

"Palm," Brooks said with a laugh, "I don't want to go pro. And there's no way I'd even make it."

"Yes, you would. You could. Easy."

"It doesn't matter. I don't want to."

"Why didn't you even tell me?" The strain in Palm's voice was clear now.

"I just decided," Brooks said as she played with the fridge magnets.

"So? You should have told me before you quit."

"You're right," Brooks said. "I should have. I was going to."

May ran into the kitchen. Without bothering to greet either of them, she moved Brooks out of the way, opened up the fridge, and grabbed at the meat loaf. She cringed when she saw it—it looked kind of wet, and it was dotted with soft, sick-looking peas. She sliced off a chunk, dropped it on a plate, and tossed it into the microwave. Normally she went right upstairs to remove her school uniform. Today she just pulled off her maroon blazer and threw it on a chair.

"You're in a hurry," Brooks said.

"I have a driving lesson."

"With who?"

"Pete's teaching me," May said, dropping her bag onto a chair.

Brooks gave her a sharp sideways glance.

"Pete Camp?"

May pulled out a book and instantly started reading.

"What are you doing?" Brooks asked.

"Homework," May said, not looking up. "It's work. You do it at home. You take it back to school the next day."

"Ohhh." Brooks nodded, looking over May's shoulder. "*Romeo and Juliet*. How appropriate."

"What are you talking about?"

"Getting in the mood?"

"I'm getting in the mood to wing this book at you," May said, snapping to the next page.

"Touchy, touchy."

Palmer watched this exchange, then sat down next to May and folded her arms over her chest.

"Did she tell you?" she asked.

"Tell me what?" May asked, reaching around to grab the meat loaf from the beeping microwave.

"She quit the team."

"What?" May's mouth dropped open. "You quit softball?"

Brooks didn't reply. Instead she bunched all of the magnets together and then started dividing them into groups—picture frame magnets, fruit magnets, baseball magnets. . . .

"Can you do that?" May asked. "I mean, can you quit in the middle of the season?"

"You can quit anytime," Brooks said.

"But that's not good, right?" May persisted. "If you wanted to play again?"

"No, probably not. But I don't want to."

"Not even in college? I thought you wanted an athletic scholarship."

"Well, I don't anymore."

"A *scholarship*, Brooks. You're going to need it. Think about it."

"I *have* thought about it."

"You couldn't have, or you wouldn't be doing this. How else

are you going to get a scholarship? You're not going to get an academic one, and we can't pay full tuition."

"I'll work."

"And make ten or fifteen or twenty thousand dollars?" May said. "Doing what?"

"Why is this your business?"

"It's all of our business. There's only one pool of money for tuition. We have to figure out how to divide it."

"Like that's up to you," Brooks said. "Besides, you're the only one whose school costs money. Why don't you just go to our school?"

"We don't pay my tuition," May said quickly. "Grandma and Grandpa Gold pay it."

"So? Couldn't we use that money for something? It's what, six thousand dollars? Seven thousand?"

"It's different."

"How?"

"I don't throw it away," May said, her voice rising. "I actually work. If I get a scholarship, it will all be worth it. It'll be worth *more*."

Palmer started chomping furiously at her nails.

"I'm telling Mom," she said.

"Go ahead," Brooks replied, meeting Palmer's gaze.

There was a knock at the front door. May made a move to get up and answer it, but Palmer beat her to it. She had to get up or she would start screaming.

Pete was waiting there when she opened the door, dressed in a loose pair of jeans and a blue T-shirt that said 100% Hawaiian Pure.

"Hey," he said. "Is May here?"

He looked just over her head, in the direction of the kitchen. Palmer waited a minute before answering, trying to figure out a way to get him to come in and join the conversation. Maybe *he* could talk some sense into Brooks. Before she could think of anything, May came up behind them.

"I'm ready," she said, stepping around both Palmer and Pete and out the door.

"You can come in," Palmer said to Pete, even though it seemed like the wrong time to finally say this.

"That's all right," he said. He looked over his shoulder at May. "We're just going to go, I think."

"Uh-huh," May said, folding her arms over her chest. "Definitely."

She walked across the lawn toward Pete's car.

"See you later," Pete said, smiling at Palmer.

"Later."

Palmer watched Pete follow May. When she turned around, she saw Brooks coming up behind her and heading for the stairs.

"I'll tell Mom myself," she said.

Palmer shut the door.

"Whatever," she said. But Brooks was already gone.

Pete's car was saunalike. Waves of heated air came blasting from the vents.

"Sorry," he said. He threw his arm over her seat and craned his neck around to back out of the driveway. "My radiator is leaking."

"What?"

"My radiator. I have to keep the heat on so the car doesn't overheat."

"You have to turn on the heat to keep the heat down?" May asked. "That makes no sense."

"It pulls the heat out of the engine and pushes it inside the car. That's how heaters work."

"Is this a joke? Like the one from the other night?"

"No," he said. "This just sucks."

May noticed that his skin was flushed and he'd stripped off his sweatshirt, so he probably wasn't kidding. Pete tried to turn on the radio, but the stations drifted wildly every time he turned the steering wheel, so he had to switch it off.

"I think my car's possessed," he said. "And I just finished paying it off, too."

"Didn't your parents buy it?"

"Yeah, but I've been paying them back. It was fifteen hundred bucks."

"I didn't know you were working."

"Yeah, I am," he said, running the back of his hand over his forehead. "I work for this place in New Hope that rents theatrical equipment. Lights and stuff. I only help out when they're busy or behind, so it's really off and on. I need something more regular for the summer. More hours."

They stopped talking for a minute to lean out their windows and catch a breath of air.

"So, that's your uniform?" Pete asked, glancing over.

May looked down at the mass of maroon that was herself. She was so used to wearing her uniform now that she forgot how strange it had to look to other people. It was kind of severe—a plain, straight skirt with a single pleat, a white oxford-cloth shirt, maroon kneesocks, and loafers. The blazer, which she had tossed into the backseat, completed the look, which was kind of a cross between a stewardess and Thelma from Scooby-Doo.

"It's ugly," she said.

"No. It's . . . I've just never seen you in it," he said. "It says *academy*, you know? It's kind of serious looking."

"It's kind of polyester."

"Okay . . ."

"Sorry. I'm just irritated. And hot." She leaned out and took another breath of air. "Is it ever legal to kill your sister? If you had a really good reason?"

"I guess it depends. What's the reason?"

"Forget it. It's too annoying to even discuss."

"Brooks or Palmer?"

"Really, forget it."

"I'm guessing Brooks."

"Camper . . ."

"Ve can fix zees problems, you know. Ve hav ways of fixing ze peoples."

"Camper," she said sharply, "forget it. Where are we going anyway?"

"I'm psyched. I found the perfect place."

The perfect place turned out to be a deserted housing development still under construction. The roads were just laid, there were backhoes and cement trucks parked against the shiny new white curbs, and the streetlights weren't on.

"It's dark," May said, squinting.

"There's some light."

"From the moon."

"Driver's ed by moonlight." He grinned. "Come on—that's cool."

"I guess. It's your car."

May spent about fifteen minutes going over all of the controls in Pete's car. It wasn't that they were hard to understand, but she was nervous about practicing with his most valuable possession. She tried to relax and get the news about Brooks out of her head, but that didn't really work.

"So," Pete said, rubbing his hands together, "I guess you should just start driving around."

"You want me to just . . . drive? Around? What, in circles?"

"No, just normally. Like this was a real street. Just for practice. Let's see what you need to work on. We'll try the three-point turn, parking, all of that."

The first discovery they made was that May only seemed able to drive at five miles an hour or fifty—and she usually alternated between the two rather abruptly. The second was that she seemed to think things were much closer than they actually were. As a result, she drove down the center of the road.

"A little closer to the curb," Pete said, looking out the window.

"I'm going to hit it."

"No, you're not. Ease it in a little."

Pete watched for another minute.

"A little closer, May," he repeated.

"I just moved it closer!"

"We're still in the middle of the street. A little more."

May pushed harder on the gas.

"Not faster," Pete said. "Closer."

In frustration she slammed on the brakes, sending them both pitching forward. She ran her hands through her hair and grabbed two big handfuls.

"Okay," Pete said, pushing himself back off the dashboard. "So, I guess we'll kind of start at the beginning."

"I think I need to get out for a second." May sighed and wiped some of the perspiration from her face. She put the car in park and turned off the engine. They both got out of the car, leaving their doors hanging open to air it out. May sat on the brand-new curb and rubbed her eyes.

"How did you learn how to drive?" she asked.

"My dad. And driver's ed."

"You passed the first time, didn't you?"

"I had more practice."

Somehow May didn't think that was it.

"Things come easier to you," she said.

"I'm not even going there," he replied, shaking his head.

"What?"

"You know what."

"School stuff doesn't count," she said.

"Since when? I've always been way behind you. This is the only thing I've done better at first."

The flattery lifted May's spirits a bit, but she didn't want this to show.

"The only reason I have to learn is because my mom has all

these jobs she needs me to do," she said.

"That doesn't matter," Pete replied. "The best part about driving is that you can just sit and think or play music. Whatever you want. You're totally on your own."

May turned to him. He was too tall to sit with his knees tucked up, like hers were. He had to stretch them out.

"I want that," she said seriously.

"So, come on. Back in."

The car was slightly cooler when they got in, but this didn't last long.

"I've got an idea," Pete said. "We're going to play 'let's pretend we're in England.' This is how it works: You drive on the left side of the road. That way you can see how close you are to the curb."

"So I watch out the window?"

"Bloody right."

Pete was using the same strange voice that he'd been trying out on Saturday.

"We're going to do this without the accent, okay, Pete?"

"You got it," he said, again with the accent.

It took about an hour of going back and forth between the left and right sides, but she eventually managed to drive on the correct side at the correct distance from the curb. But an hour in the punishing heat of the car drained them both, and they turned around and headed back to May's house.

"So, what do you think?" he asked. "Want to do this again?"

"Yeah," May said. "It was good. I think I almost got it."

"You did get it. You were fine."

"So what's the catch?" May asked.

"Catch?"

"I'm just waiting," she said. "I know you have something planned. I know I'm walking into some plot of yours."

Pete snickered. "Just wait and see."

"Yeah," May said, getting out of the car. "I can hardly wait."

One of May's ultimate pet peeves was when people said to her, "Your dad's in a better place now." Like he had moved. May always wanted to say, "Yes. He loves it in North Carolina." Or, "He says Spain is amazing."

May resented the idea of anyone else thinking they knew where her dad had gone. She didn't know where her dad was. Not even physically. His body had been cremated, and the ashes were being stored somewhere. She had never asked where because she didn't want to know. As for the spiritual part (which was what the "better placers" were talking about), she got the impression they were talking about a heaven where he was floating around in the clouds, consorting with famous dead people.

The other thing they seemed to be saying was that death was a great thing. That was probably the part that made her so angry. It was like they were telling her she should be happy that her father had dropped dead because he ate too much fat and didn't exercise enough and clogged up his arteries. That was what her mom had explained to her, anyway. She said it could have been heredity or stress, but May had seen her father eat enough chili cheese dogs to know the truth.

On some level, she blamed him for it. He'd been a big guy to start with, and he'd just let himself get bigger. Mike Gold was definitely not a dieter. He was the kind of guy who just liked to let things go and have a good time. That was probably why he'd liked Brooks most of all and allowed her to do whatever she wanted. That Brooks was lazy, that she did the minimum amount of work at school or at home—her father never seemed to notice. As long as she could hit a ball with a stick, she was a wonderful human being. So Brooks coasted by, and May picked up her slack or dealt with the consequences.

For example, here May was at five thirty-five on Thursday morning without a single pair of clean underwear to her name. And why? Because in the week and a half since Brooks had quit the softball team, she had yet to actually complete any of the newly assigned chores that their mom had given her, including laundry. This meant May had to sneak into Brooks's room (she didn't make much effort to be quiet) to try to find some clean underwear.

Under ideal conditions, the ride from the Northeast Philadelphia suburbs to Girls' should have taken only half an hour. But May's bus served another private school on the edge of the city, so there were other stops to make, and there was rush-hour traffic to take into account. In the end, she had to be at her bus stop just after six.

As her bus rumbled through downtown Philadelphia, over the Schuylkill River and down into University City, past the dignified stretches of the University of Pennsylvania buildings, May was fast asleep with her head against the window. Her bus hit a huge pothole at Thirty-third and Chestnut, causing May's head to smack into the window, waking her. She didn't mind. She counted on that pothole to be her alarm clock.

Linda Fan, May's best friend and her constant companion

since day one of her freshman year at Girls', was sitting on the stone bench by May's bus stop, where they met every morning. Linda lived twenty blocks north and a few tree streets over from Girls', in a condo on Locust Street. She usually just woke up a half hour before school, threw on her uniform, and hopped on the subway.

Linda's parents could afford to live where they did because they were both doctors at Jefferson Hospital and Linda was an only child. She never had to worry about having enough underwear in the morning, because her family had a woman who came in three times a week to straighten up the house and take care of the chores, like the laundry. The only bad part of the deal was that her cousin Frank was living with them while he went to Drexel University, which was very close to their house. Frank was an engineering student with five pet snakes. Unfortunately, snakes terrified Linda, so she missed a lot of sleep.

"I'm dead," Linda said as May approached. "Very, very dead. I'm not even done with my history paper. I'll have to finish it and print it out at lunch. I would have gotten it done last night, but Frank was letting Harvey out for his weekly crawl, so I couldn't even think."

"Which one is Harvey?"

"The Burmese python," Linda said, getting up. She was almost a full head shorter than May, so May always had to look down when they were talking. It was an unusual experience since May was the runt of the Tall, Blond, and Wonderful family. "Anyway, I had ten minutes on the subway this morning to work, but Aubrey had to re-create this entire conversation she had with her boyfriend last night so I could analyze it. You know, because I'm a licensed psychologist, right? Do I wear a sign on my back that says Overshare with Me?"

"Yeah. A really little one."

"I thought so," Linda said. "So, do you have any personal information you want to share with me?"

"I'm wearing Brooks's underwear."

"Again?"

"She's supposed to do the laundry—but it's been over a week. You know Brooks. She doesn't do anything."

"Is she still seeing that guy?"

"Dave?" May said. "Yeah. More than ever now."

They walked up the front steps and in through the ornate doorway of the school. Herds of maroon-suited girls hurried in all directions.

"What about you?" Linda asked.

"What about me?"

"Aren't you getting lessons from Pete?"

May nodded.

"So?" Linda said. "How's that?"

"We've only gone once, a week ago on Monday. It was fine."

"You haven't complained about it at all. You always complain when you see Pete."

"He's behaving."

Linda hmmmed.

"Don't do that," May said.

"Do what?"

"Make that noise."

Linda smiled innocently.

"Anyway, I don't even know what's going to happen when I do get my license," May went on. "We only have the one car, really, and it's not like I'll suddenly have this amazing life even if I *can* drive."

"*When* you can."

"Whatever. The only reason I'm getting my license at all is because my mom can't count on Brooks to do things. We can't afford the extra insurance right now."

"But it will help," Linda said, "with getting a life."

"How do you get a life?" May asked. "I mean, does it just show up someday?"

"Getting outside of your house for something other than school or work is probably a good place to start."

"Well, that isn't going to happen," May said.

Palmer was happy out on the field, with the dirt, the grass, the blinding sun. Heat, cold, sweat—no problem. Outside, it wasn't quite so obvious that every part of her body was weirdly *long*, like she was actually a short person who had been stretched out of shape. It didn't matter that she had no chest or that she had the gangly walk of a girl who really only knows how to run. On the field these were advantages. On the field she was the pitcher—the star.

Here in the locker room, though, with the gels and lotions that smelled of peach and coconut, the body buffs, the blow-dryers, the exfoliant scrubs, the intense conditioners—this was where it all fell apart. This was where it was all too clear that Palmer was fourteen and flat, with perennially oily hair, chewed-up nails, and skin that was always either windburned or sunburned. In here, Palmer was just a gawky freshman. It had been different when Brooks was here. Brooks had always been so popular, so loud. She was the shortstop and the talker, and Palmer was the quiet, intense pitcher. That was how Palmer liked it.

Now she was just Palmer, naked, struggling to pull a scratchy towel around herself. The towels she brought were always too small, so she had to hunch to cover herself up.

Diana Haverty was sprawled out over most of the bench behind Palmer's locker, wrapped snugly in the thickest red towel Palmer had ever seen. She was examining her toes, which were tiny and cute. Her toenails were painted an Easter-egg blue.

"I don't know if I like this color," Diana said to no one in particular.

"I think it's nice." Emma, the third-base player, turned from her locker to join in the examination of the adorable digits. "Who makes it?"

"Hard Candy."

"Stila makes a color kind of like that, but it's a little glossier."

"Really?" Diana said. "I need to pick something for my prom pedicure, and that's what I want: a light gloss, but sort of like this."

Palmer looked down at her own big feet. She quickly threw on her grocery-store flip-flops and hurried to the shower with her little basket. She preferred being the first one in and out. As she dripped and flip-flopped her way back, she stopped short when she heard Diana say Brooks's name.

"Is she really dating Vatiman?" Emma was asking.

"That's what I heard. I don't know. She doesn't call me anymore."

"Isn't Vatiman a dealer?"

"Something like that," Diana said. "That girl Jamie I always see them with . . . psycho. Seriously. I had four classes with her last year. She's a total head case."

"I heard that."

"But you know Brooks," Diana said. "It was just a matter of time."

One of them mumbled something. Palmer knew instinctively that it must have been about her.

"I know," Diana said. "It's a shame. I really wish I could help."

Palmer stood there, unsure of what to do. It wasn't like she could just turn around and leave. Quietly she came back over. As she'd expected, Diana and Emma pretended like nothing had been going on. Diana looked over as Palmer tried to dry herself without removing the towel.

"That was an amazing curve today, Palmer," she said. "Really good. Are you going to a pitching coach?"

"No," Palmer said.

"Your arm is getting stronger."

"Thanks." Palmer hastily pulled on her shorts and her fleece top. She pulled her wet hair back into a heavy ponytail. Within a minute she was hefting her bag over her shoulder, ready to go.

"See you tomorrow," she said softly.

"Do you need a ride today?" Diana asked.

"No." Palmer shook her head. "My mom is coming for me."

"Hey," Emma said. "Palmer."

Palmer stopped and turned around.

"Is Brooks really dating Dave Vatiman?"

"I guess."

Diana and Emma exchanged a look.

"I have to go," Palmer said.

Her mother was waiting for her in the parking lot. Palmer climbed inside the minivan, roughly tossing her bags into the backseat. She didn't speak for the first few minutes of the trip, prompting a few quick glances from her mother.

"What are you going to do?" Palmer finally asked.

"About what?"

"About Brooks."

"What about Brooks?"

"About softball."

"What do you want me to do, Palm?" her mother asked. "I can't make her play."

"So you're just going to let her quit?" she asked.

"She's old enough to make that decision."

Palmer turned and stared out the window.

"May's at work right now," her mother said. "She'll be back around seven. You can either warm up something when you get home, or you can wait and have dinner with her."

"Fine."

"Don't get upset, Palm."

Palmer had every reason to be upset. Every reason in the world. And the fact that her mother didn't understand why made it even worse.

In Palmer's eyes, Brooks had given up everything and left her alone.

As she hung up her apron in the storage room after finishing her short evening shift, May's eyes fell on her name tag. It read *Lirpa*. She'd been wearing it for three hours and hadn't even noticed.

She pulled the apron back down and went into the shop. Nell was leaning against the counter, eating her dinner, which consisted of painfully pungent kimchi and large squares of wiggly tofu.

"What's this?" May asked, holding up the tag. "I just fixed it."

"It's April, spelled backward." Nell grinned, pinching up a clump of cabbage with her chopsticks. "Have fun finding the label maker again."

May tried to smile, because this was supposed to be funny. She returned to the storage room and deposited the apron. While she was there, she couldn't resist looking around for the label maker. It was no use. Nell had probably bricked it up in the wall or something. When she emerged, she found Pete leaning against the counter, already immersed in a chat with Nell. He didn't seem to mind having her talking into his face with her tear-inducing kimchi breath.

"Tech," Nell was rambling. "That's cool. I'm really into tech. Technical stuff is so important in theater. So many people don't realize that—they think it's all about the actors."

"Yeah," Pete agreed. "That's true."

Pete was wearing an open long-sleeve shirt over a T-shirt for Grant's recent production of *Brigadoon*.

"You do, what, lights?"

"Lights and sound," Pete replied. "Mostly lights. Some construction, too."

"I act," Nell said. "I did a lot of shows in high school. I've done some Shakespeare and some modern plays and some plays that my friends and I wrote."

"You wrote some plays?" Pete asked, looking impressed.

"Yeah." Nell nodded. "I had two years of playwriting classes in high school. I've written at least twelve or fifteen short plays and three full-lengths. They were all pretty experimental. We did them in alternative spaces. We did this kind of political play in the men's bathroom once. . . ."

"You didn't go to Grant, did you?" Pete asked.

"No." Nell laughed. "I went to the Albert School."

May turned around to roll her eyes. Pete stood up and wiggled his fingers at her.

"My girl Lirpa." Nell smiled. "I guess she's ready to go. You two have a good night."

There was something unbearably irritating about the way Nell said this. May gave her a stiff smile, then pushed Pete out the door.

"We're going to go parking," Pete said as he and May got into the car. "Let's just say it and get it out of the way. *Parking.* I know I feel better. How about you?"

"Where are we going to do this?"

"I was thinking here. You can just practice going in and out of spaces."

"Maybe we can do it on the other side of Pet Mart?" May offered, wincing. "I'd rather not have Nell as an audience."

They pulled around Pet Mart, on the far side of the parking lot, and switched positions.

"I heard Brooks quit softball," Pete said, moving his seat back and putting his Pumas up against the glove compartment.

"News travels fast," May said.

"Is that what you were mad about the last time you drove?"

"Probably," May said. "It's hard to remember anymore."

"Why'd she quit?"

"I don't know," May said, starting the engine and timidly backing up. "She's a mystery."

"That's kind of a big deal for her."

"No kidding."

"So she's not doing anything now? Is she working?"

"No," May said. "She's not doing anything. That's why I'm wearing her underwear right now."

Pete cocked an eyebrow.

"What, do you rotate?"

"Yeah." May smirked. "It's just something we like to do."

"If I guess what color they are, can I see them?"

"Just forget I said it."

"Give me one guess."

"Can you tell me what I'm supposed to do?" May asked.

"Pull into spaces, back out. We'll work on your turning angle."

May's turning angle was absurdly wide. She found herself heading into her space at a wild diagonal.

"So you don't know why she quit?" Pete asked.

"I told you, I don't know."

"A little less to the left," he said. "Here . . ."

As he leaned over to demonstrate, Pete snagged the waistband of her pants with one finger, pulling it down just enough to reveal the elastic of the famous underwear. Startled, May jerked away and in the process accidentally hit the gas. There was a great heaving under them. A grinding noise. And a heavy bump. May screamed and stopped the car.

"Oh my God . . ." May clutched at Pete's arm in panic. "What did I just do?"

"It's okay," he said, although his eyes had widened. "Hold on."

He was out of the car for about a minute, walking around the front and the back and taking a quick peek underneath. May sat perfectly still the entire time, like a rabbit, quivering and listening for signs of danger. Pete leaned in.

"You just . . . a concrete divider is there."

"I broke your car," she whispered.

"It's probably fine," he said. "This thing is a tank. We're just on top of it."

"*Probably* fine?"

"Here," he said, indicating that she should get out. "I'll do this."

As Pete eased the car over the divider, May took a look for herself, although she didn't know what she was looking for. There were no wires hanging down. There were no loose pieces of metal. Those seemed like good signs.

May quietly got in on the passenger's side.

"It's fine," Pete assured her. "We didn't even get started. Why don't you try again? Well, not *that*, but parking."

"I can't," she said. "Sorry."

May mused over what she should do for a finale as they drove home. Maybe she could tell him that when they'd taken pictures of him naked last year, her little sister had mentioned that she thought he wasn't very well hung. Of course, Palmer had no idea what she was even talking about, and they had no visual proof one way or another, but the mere suggestion that a thirteen-year-old girl found him inadequate would really make his evening complete.

"Forget it," she said. "Let's just forget all of this. I can't be taught."

"It was my fault. It wasn't anything you did. It's not—"

"Don't say it wasn't a big deal. Please. Just let it be. I screwed up. I am a screwup. Tell your mom you're not teaching me anymore because I drove your car up a wall. You're off the hook."

May could hear herself rambling but felt powerless to stop the rush of self-criticisms. Pete evidently knew that there was no point in trying to stop her either. He was being irritatingly patient, which only made her crazier.

"Camper!" she finally yelled.

"What?"

"Why aren't you saying anything?"

"What am I supposed to say?"

"That I suck!"

"You suck!"

It didn't make her feel better.

It took May a few minutes to realize that it actually hadn't been her fault. It had been Pete's. Instead of teaching her, he'd been his usual asinine self. But because May had been the one behind the wheel, she had mistakenly thought she was to blame.

She looked over at him slouching down in his seat. He glanced over.

"You're mad now," he said. "Aren't you?"

"A little."

"Thought so."

It was still early when they pulled back up in front of the Gold house. The garage door was open. Palmer was probably practicing out back.

"Look," Pete said, "we're good, right? You're going to try again?"

"I don't know."

"I shouldn't do stuff like that," he said. "It's just . . . old habit. Sorry."

He really did look sorry. And they were pretty much even since she *had* ended up almost destroying his car.

"Fine," May grumbled.

"Just tell me something."

"What?"

"Are you really wearing Brooks's underwear?"

May nodded and opened her door to get out.

"Why?"

"It's a little game we play," she said. "Sometimes we make out, too. Good night, Camper."

As Palmer lay in bed that night, she felt her heart jumping—hiccuping. She pressed her fingers to her neck and felt the irregular beat. Quickly at first, then a pause, then two hard beats at once. The sensation seemed to lock off her breathing for a moment. She sucked in air as powerfully as she could, and her heart staggered harder. By then the pressure was everywhere, blocking her nose and her throat, pressing down on her lungs. The dark in the room got darker. It throbbed.

Her hands scrambled for the bedside lamp. Unfortunately, the light only caused everything to glow a heady orange, which made the walls look like they were leaning in. She was unable to move from her position, unable to call out for fear of wasting all the breath she had left. She bent over and pulled the blankets to her abdomen. She concentrated on her breathing. Her chest hurt.

The fearless side of Palmer rose up long enough to tell the rest of her to ride it through. She tried imagining being on the field or being at school. Something with daylight, people all around her. She tried to imagine the most boring place to be— the back row of her algebra class, stuck in line at the supermarket. Sometimes those images were the easiest to pull up. Anything to distract herself, get her mind to a good place.

The feeling of dread was impossible to shake. It was like a stench that clung to her clothes. She knew from experience that this would last for at least an hour. These night attacks had started about a month after her father had died. At first they'd happened about once a month. But she'd had one once a week for the last three weeks.

She went down to the living room and switched on all the lights. She switched on *SportsCenter* and wound herself up in an afghan. The worst part was still coming—the feeling that the world was permanently screwed up. That this crippling fear would go right into her bones and stay there. That the afghan would suffocate her.

She kicked it off and wondered if she was crazy. Probably.

"Jesus, Palm," May said, appearing in the living room doorway a few minutes later and squinting at the television. "Could you turn that down?"

"I couldn't sleep," Palmer said. Though she felt like she should barely have been able to speak, her voice came out very loud.

"Fine. So you can't sleep. Does it have to be so loud?"

Palmer turned the television down a few notches.

"Did Brooks come home?"

Palmer shook her head mutely.

"Whatever," May growled. "If she oversleeps, she oversleeps. I'm sick of this."

May turned and went back upstairs, and Palmer pulled her blanket tighter. This wasn't working. Even the living room seemed like a bad place to be. The dark plaid sofa and the green carpet made her feel claustrophobic. The bobble-headed base-ball dolls on the top of the entertainment console seemed to be leering at her. And she needed more air. Someplace cooler. She would go get a flashlight and take a walk.

She threw her fleece on over her pajamas and headed out to the garage. As she was sliding alongside the Firebird to get to the shelves on the other side of the room, Palmer looked into the backseat. She barely noticed the car anymore, even though it took up most of the garage. There was something weird about it now. It seemed forbidden.

When she was little and couldn't sleep, her father would put her in the backseat, take the top down, and drive her around. Palmer would stare up at the sky, and before she knew it, she would realize that her father was carrying her up to bed.

She stared at the door and bit at her cuticles. No one had gone inside the Firebird since that day.

If it would help her relax, she didn't care. She carefully opened the door, released the front seat, and crawled into the back.

Even though the seat wasn't quite big enough for her to stretch all the way out, it was still large enough for her to be comfortable. She looked up at the black convertible top that stretched above her. It wasn't like before, when she would look up at the stars, but still, things didn't seem to be closing in as much. She breathed in and out slowly, taking long breaths and holding them in her chest. She ran her fingers along the stitching on the backseats that had always reminded her of the pattern on the front of a catcher's chest protector. Slowly she started to feel a bit better. She actually started to nod off.

The next thing she knew, there was a horrible grinding sound above her, causing her to jolt awake midsnore. The garage door was rolling back. Palmer crouched down, but Brooks was obviously going to notice the huge car door that was blocking her path into the house. Sure enough, Palmer heard the footsteps stop, and Brooks leaned down and peered into the back of the car.

"What are you doing?" Brooks said, smirking.

"Nothing."

"You're sleeping in the garage now?"

Palmer didn't answer. She would just wait for Brooks to lose interest and go away.

"You're getting freaky, Palm," Brooks said, tripping just a bit as she went up the two steps to the kitchen door.

When Brooks was gone, Palmer gave up on her idea. She went back into the house and curled back up on the sofa, keeping the television on mute.

At work the next night, Nell approached May as she was restocking the milk-and-sugar counter. May went right on working, stuffed sugar packets into their clear plastic box, even though Nell lurked there for a solid minute or so. She got close enough for May to get a good whiff of her clove shampoo.

"Did you want something?" May finally asked.

"What's your deal with Pete, Ape?"

"My deal? I don't have a deal with Pete."

"Yes, you do. You guys seem pretty tight."

"I've just known him for a long time," May said, pushing way too many napkins into the dispenser. "My dad and his dad were best friends."

"Were? Did they fight or something?"

"No."

"So they're not friends now?"

"They're friends," May said, not wanting to explain. "Is there a reason you're asking?"

"So if Pete's not your boyfriend, why does he always come here?"

"He gives me rides sometimes. That's all."

"So you don't have a boyfriend?"

It was a piercing question.

"Not at the moment," May said, reaching for another pack of napkins. She wasn't about to tell Nell that she had never had a boyfriend—but for some reason, she felt like Nell could sense that fact.

"I think that thing is full," Nell said. The napkin dispenser was now groaning from the pressure of May's overzealous packing. Nell's cool hazel eyes said it all: *You poor, sexually frustrated mess.* Yeah. She knew.

May stopped filling the napkin dispenser.

"I did this photography project once," Nell said, looking down at her nails. "It was a study on body markings. You know. Piercing, tattoos, stuff like that. But also natural stuff, like people who have extra skin somewhere or freckles. I like freckles. I liked your friend Pete's freckles. He would have made a good subject."

"He's got enough of them."

"You brought your bike today, didn't you?"

Automatically they both turned their glances out the window and focused them on the Brown Hornet, which was bathed dramatically in a pool of parking lot light. It was U-locked to one of the parking signs, and it slumped rather pathetically against the pole.

"So he's not coming to get you?"

"No."

"Oh," Nell said casually. "Too bad. Why don't you give me his number?"

May cocked her head, unable to accept what she'd just heard. Nell carefully pulled one of the napkins from the dispenser, produced a pen from her pocket, and pushed them over to May. May stared at them.

"You just said there's nothing between you guys," Nell said. "Right?"

May could only nod.

"Does he have a girlfriend?"

This was something May had not asked Pete, but it seemed very clear that he didn't. She shook her head.

"So . . ." Nell tapped the napkin.

It was true. There was no reason May could give for not handing over the number—at least, not one that made sense. She couldn't really say, "No, if you and Pete come together in any kind of romantic or sexual way, nature will rebel and the entire fabric of the universe will collapse. All will perish."

Nell was looking May right in the eye now. As calmly as possible, May wrote out a number she had known all her life. The first phone number she had ever learned, in fact, after her own.

She pushed it over to Nell.

As May was wheeling the Brown Hornet across the front lawn a half hour later, a car came up directly behind her. It pulled up so quickly that May actually shrieked and put her hand up to her chest, damsel-in-distress style.

"Sorry," Pete said, stepping out of his car. He was dressed all in black—black T-shirt, black jeans, black sneakers.

"Were you at a ninja club meeting tonight?" she asked.

"I ran the lights at a show. We have to wear all black."

"Oh."

"I got home early. You should have called. I could have driven you home."

May almost cringed. If Pete had taken her home tonight, she would have been able to witness Nell asking him for his number in person. That might have caused her to have a seizure.

"I don't mind riding," May said. "It's the only exercise I get."

"Exercise is good."

The black outfit made Pete look thinner and taller than normal. They'd always been the same height when they were younger, then suddenly one day he was six feet tall (even taller with the hair) and she was half a foot down. It was weird to have to look up at him all the time.

"My mom asked me to bring something over, and I saw you go past on your bike a minute ago, so . . ."

May eyed him skeptically as he went back to his car and pulled a shrink-wrapped case of dozens of ramen noodle packets out of the backseat.

"That's a lot of ramen," she said.

"I know," he said, looking at the package critically.

"Let me just put my bike inside and I'll take it."

May reached into her bag and pushed the remote control for the garage door. It squawked hideously as it rolled up on its track.

"I think that thing needs a little oil," Pete said, watching it rise. "Want me to do it?"

"You're not our servant."

May ducked under and wheeled the bike into the darkness. Pete followed with the noodles.

"Your friend called me," he said.

"Do you mean Nell?" May replied, trying to sound casual. "What did she say?"

"She kind of asked me out."

"Kind of?"

"Well, she did. She asked if I wanted to do something with her sometime."

"Oh," May said.

"I wanted to see if you were okay with it."

"If I'm okay with it? What does this have to do with me?"

"Well, you know her."

"I work with her," May clarified quickly.

"I was just wondering what you thought. You don't really seem to like her."

"Does that matter?" May asked.

"No, but . . ."

"Well, what did you say when she asked you?"

"I said okay."

May shrugged, indicating that the matter seemed settled.

"I haven't figured out what to do yet about the prom," he said. "It's in the first week in June."

There was a long pause while May elaborately secured the Brown Hornet. She hadn't seen this one coming. She should have, of course. Brooks had been talking about the prom. For some reason, she hadn't connected Pete to the idea, even though he and Brooks were in the same class.

"Who are you going to ask?" she finally said, having run out of things she could do with the bike.

"I don't know."

"Oh," May said breezily, slipping between Pete and the Firebird and making her way out of the garage. He followed her and waited again for the horrible groaning and creaking of the garage door to stop. He shifted a lot, moving the light-weight box from arm to arm.

"Are you saying you want to take Nell to the prom?" May asked. "Is that what I'm supposed to get from this?"

"Well, maybe. I don't know. Like I said, I don't really . . ."

Pete sighed loudly and rolled his head back on his shoulders. May relieved him of the load of ramen. He used his free hand to start pulling on the collar of his shirt. May didn't even know what they were talking about anymore. Whatever it was, though, it was making her ill.

"Just ask her," May said. "I'm sure she'd go, especially if you sneak up on her with that smooth crouching tiger move."

"Right," Pete said. "I thought you'd say something like that."

Palmer watched May and Pete talking through the blinds on the living room bay window. It was hard to tell what was going on. May was doing a lot of shuffling and staring at the ground. Pete looked happy but not as animated as usual, and he was carrying a big box of something.

Palmer had a great interest in Pete. Unlike May, she had always found him amusing. (She had never been the direct target of any of his jokes.) He was kind to Palmer, and he liked to make her laugh. Plus he had his own car, and he always seemed to have some cash.

Palmer watched as May took the box from Pete and turned back toward the house. She came into the living room a minute later.

"What were you and Pete doing?" Palmer immediately asked.

"Ballroom dancing," May said, setting the box of noodles on the recliner. Palmer examined the package.

"Are you guys going out or something?" she asked, digging her fingers into the shrink-wrap.

"That's sick, Palm."

"He's always here now. And he brings stuff."

"You're right," May said. "You caught us. We're dating. That's why he brought me all this soup."

May jogged upstairs. Palmer listened carefully. She could read her sister's mood from the sound of her walking above, since her room was right above the living room. May was particularly stompy tonight, dropping her bag heavily on the floor and then throwing herself onto her creaky bed.

Palmer knew she wasn't going to be able to sleep again tonight—she'd known this the whole day. To spare herself the trouble of having to find something to do to relax, she'd already come up with a plan: She was going to go through the boxes and bins she'd seen stuffed under her parents' bed.

She waited about half an hour for May to fall asleep (May usually read in bed for a while), then crept up to her mother's room. Her mother, Palmer noticed, wasn't as tidy as she used to be. The bed was unmade. A camisole and shorts were on top. A black bra hung from the bathroom door handle. A pile of dirty scrubs lay on the floor.

Palmer lifted the cream-colored dust ruffle and evaluated the stash. The first thing she pulled out was a red expanding file full of drawings, tests, report cards, and notes from each of the girls. Each pocket was marked with a name and an age. From Brooks, age eleven: three certificates from various sports, a drawing of a dinosaur, a math quiz that she got 100 percent on (a rarity). From Palmer, age eight: a handprint in brown paint that had been drawn on to look like a turkey, a Little League certificate, a Valentine's Day card. May, age ten: a science fair ribbon, a report on koalas, a poem about ice cream, and a carefully written note on heart-studded stationery that made a passionate but well-structured case for a family dog.

Other things were under there. A cigar box brimming with concert ticket stubs, a few pairs of cleats, some rolled-up posters in a tube. She was in the process of trying to pull these out when she heard a car drive up. She hastily shoved everything under the bed and quickly left the room.

There were voices downstairs, very low voices. It sounded like there might be a few people in the house. Palmer came down the dark stairs and slipped along the hall past the living room, heading back into the kitchen.

A figure was leaning against the refrigerator in the dark. It took Palmer a minute to realize that it was actually two people, Brooks and Dave. They were the same height, and when they wound around each other, they seemed perfectly matched. Dave was on the outside, and Brooks's back was pressed against the door. She had her arms down low inside his jacket and was pulling out his shirt. Dave was mumbling things to her, nuzzling his head into her neck, kissing her.

It wasn't like Palmer had never seen anything like this before—she'd just never seen anything like this in her kitchen. With her sister. Against the magnetized frames that held the photos of their cousins in Maryland. Dave was pressing his one palm flat against their fridge now. Brooks turned her head in Palmer's direction and opened her eyes. She jolted upright.

"Oh my God, Palmer," Brooks said, her face full of disgust. "What are you doing?"

"I heard something," Palmer said.

Dave eased himself back against one of the kitchen chairs and laughed.

"How long have you been standing there?" Brooks demanded.

Palmer was thankful for the dark. Her face was flushed with embarrassment and she suddenly felt perverted.

"Like a minute," she replied angrily. "Not even. I heard you come in. You're loud."

"Go away," Brooks said. "Go back to whatever it was you were doing."

"Fine," Palmer said. "Whatever."

Palmer was a little too spooked to go right back to her explorations. She went back into the living room and switched on the television instead, trying hard to quickly lose herself in *SportsCenter*. After a minute or two, Dave passed by the living room door and grinned at her on the way out. Brooks stalked past a moment later and went right up the stairs.

Palmer had to wait another twenty minutes or so for Brooks to go to bed before she could slip back into her mom's room to put everything back as carefully as she could.

On a bright, warm morning a week later, Brooks landed her fist
on her alarm clock. She was dismayed to discover that apparently she'd been eating paste all night. Her mouth felt like it
was full of it. There was a dull, grinding pain on the flesh of her
brain that sent shocks along her eyebrows. She slid one of her
legs out from under the blankets and sent it on an exploratory
mission to the floor.

Day? Probably a Saturday or a Sunday, since she was hung
over. No . . . it was Friday. The night before, she'd been at the
opening night party at the pool—the Memorial Day opening.

She wiped the film from her eyes and focused on the clock.
Seven-fifty. She was supposed to be at school in fifteen minutes.
She swung out of bed and felt the first full shock of cold air.
Everything hurt. Even the carpet hurt her feet.

The house was quiet. The sun coming in through the window was cold and white. May and Palmer's things were gone.
Her mom's keys were on the key rack. She could take the minivan to school. She opened the refrigerator and surveyed the
contents. The only thing that appealed to her was half a lemon.

Five minutes later Brooks stood in a hot shower, leaning
against the wall and sucking on the lemon. She tried to work up
the energy to reach her hands over her head to wash her hair.
That wasn't going to happen. The fragrance of her shower gel as
it got caught up in the stream overwhelmed her. The transition

from the warmth of the water to the cold air almost shattered her, and the rough towel grated her skin.

She went back into her room and grabbed a pair of jeans and a shirt from the chair next to her bureau. It made no difference to her what shirt it was. She put the clothes on, stepped into some sandals, and made her way downstairs to go to school.

There was a moment right between second and third period when Brooks thought she might be sick. She was walking past the art room, and a strong scent of spray mount came wafting out. Then she turned and looked at the putty-colored lockers, and the combined effect did her in. She ran for the nearest girls' room, where she spent ten minutes sitting in front of a toilet with her head resting against the side of a stall.

She delivered herself to study hall ten minutes late. The moderator was angrily fiddling with her laptop and didn't notice. Dave looked up in surprise to see Brooks hunched over, pale and sweaty. She put her head down on the table.

"From last night?" he asked quietly.

"Kill me," she said.

"Come on." Dave hoisted her up and grabbed her bag.

"I'm fine," she mumbled.

"Come on."

He took her up to the desk at the front of the room.

"I think she's sick," he said, pointing his thumb at Brooks's slumping figure. "Can I walk her down to the nurse's office?"

The moderator pounded on her enter key and glanced up at the two of them. Taking one look at Brooks's face, she nodded her assent, then continued slapping her disobedient machine.

Dave put his arm around Brooks's waist and eased her down the hall, joking with her the whole way. When they reached the door to the nurse's office, he put her bag over her shoulder for her.

"You'll be fine," he said, stroking back her long blond hair. "Tell them you have stomach flu. They'll send you home."

"Today's really bad."

"Drink some water. Take some aspirin."

"My dad died a year ago today."

She'd never mentioned much about her father before, except to convey the general information that he wasn't around.

He ran his finger along the line of Brooks's chin very softly. The sensation momentarily cut through the racking pain she felt. She set her head down on his shoulder for a moment, and he rubbed her back in small circles. She could have stayed like that all day, but he gently pulled her upright and looked her in the face.

"Go home," he said with a smile. "Sleep."

"Right."

He kissed her once on her lips and once on the forehead, much more gently than he ever had before. For a moment Brooks almost thought the sickness was worth the sensation. She looked up at him, and he gave her a broad smile, showing off the gap between his teeth.

"Go," he said, pointing at the door. "In."

"Okay," she said.

Dave started walking backward, watching her until she was inside the office.

"You all right, Palmer?"

Diana had pulled up to Palmer and was looking up at her

from the driver's seat of her car. The day was long over. Practice had been finished for half an hour. Everyone else was gone except Palmer, who was standing at the edge of the field, her bag over her shoulder.

"Yeah," Palmer said, eyeing the road. "I'm fine."

"Need a ride?"

"No." Palmer shook her head firmly. "My sister's coming."

"Brooks?"

"Yeah."

"You want me to call her?"

"No. She's coming."

"If you're sure . . ."

"I'm sure."

Palmer wasn't sure at all. Brooks could very well have forgotten. Brooks forgot everything. This wasn't the first time she'd been left waiting. Brooks's incompetence embarrassed her. She preferred to cover it up.

With a nod Diana drove off, leaving Palmer staring out at the empty brown field and the expanse of surrounding trees. The sky was heavy, prematurely dark. A wind was kicking up. She set her messenger bag down in the dirt along the side of the clubhouse and started digging through the contents, finally producing a small address book and a handful of change. Enough for two calls. There was a pay phone at the front of the school. It would take her ten minutes to walk all the way around. If Brooks came while she was gone, she'd be stuck. She jingled the change in her hand and stared up the driveway. Then she took out her algebra book and put it in her lap. Then she stared out at the road again.

Fifteen minutes later she was still staring.

No one was in front of the building by the time Palmer made her way around. Somewhere, deep in the bowels of the building, there were probably meetings or detentions going on, but outside there was only the phone, a concrete bench, the flagpole, and Palmer. She took one of the two coins, dropped it into the phone, and dialed her house. No answer. She dropped in the second and dialed the work number that May had given her. An unfamiliar voice answered the phone, and she asked for May.

"Brooks zoned," Palmer said when May got on the line.

"What?"

"She forgot about me."

She heard May sigh into the phone.

"Just stay where you are, okay?" May said. "Someone will be there for you soon."

"Who?"

"I'll figure it out. Just don't worry about it."

Palmer hung up the phone. Undoubtedly Pete would be sent, since he suddenly seemed willing to run or fetch or roll over at May's bidding. In response, May was going out of her way to make it clear that she didn't notice this—until, of course, she needed him to do something. It was an annoying little game they played. Even if he was being dispatched to pick her up like a FedEx guy, a ride home with Pete was still a good thing. He was one of the few people who might actually make her feel better today.

Palmer sat down on the bench and stared out at the road, waiting for Pete's car to turn into the parking lot.

*   *   *

As May hung up the phone, she noticed Nell had fixed her with a curious stare.

"Was that Pete?" she asked.

"Yes."

"Who called before?"

"My little sister."

"She's stuck at school?"

Nell seemed to have no desire to hide the fact that she listened to other people's phone conversations.

"Yeah," May said. "She's stuck."

"Pete's going to get her?" Nell asked. "You know, we went out on Wednesday."

No. May did not know that. However, this was probably the best day to get this news. Listening to the story about Pete and Nell's date—as nauseating as it was sure to be—would at least shift the focus away from her.

Not only was it kind of ironic that her father should have died over the Memorial Day weekend, it also made it easy for people to remember when it had happened. That morning it had seemed like everyone in homeroom was watching May out of the corners of their eyes. Linda had shadowed her all day, constantly asking if she was all right. Her English teacher had quietly mentioned that May was exempt from her homework for the weekend. The guidance counselor had pulled her aside to ask her how she was doing.

Today had reminded May, with shocking clarity, of what the first few weeks had been like last year. Constantly being watched. Constantly being asked if she was all right. Having conversations stop when she walked by. Facing that strange collage of forced smiles and concerned expressions at every single turn. Repeating the mantra "I'm fine" over and over again until it lost all meaning, and she had no idea what fine was anymore.

So this was really a perfect time for Nell to be her normal rambling self and allow May to fade into the background. Unfortunately, she decided to act completely out of character and paused and took a good long look at May's face.

"You look kind of weird, Ape," she said. "Are you sick?"

"No," May said, rattling a coffee mug full of tiny flags that sat by the cash register.

"Maybe you're a little toxic."

"Toxic?"

"From dairy. Your vessels could be clogged up."

"Vessels?"

"Dairy is harsh on the digestive system. So is meat. Do you know that it takes seven years for a piece of meat to leave your system? It rots in your body. Maybe you should do a cleanse. You should get some psyllium husk. . . ."

"Yeah . . . so you were about to say? About Pete?"

"Oh, right!" Nell smiled brightly and pulled herself up on the counter. "Pete collects movies, did you know that? We watched *The Fearless Vampire Killers*, which is just classic. We're really alike."

May doubted this but made no objection.

"And this you will not believe, Ape. He asked me to his prom. How hilarious is that? We didn't even have a prom at my school—we had 'The Collective Experience,' which was like an all-night thing with music and poetry readings and then we all went swimming at like two in the morning. So now I have to get a *prom dress* and *prom shoes* and a *manicure*, and all that. Seriously, how funny is this?"

"That's . . . funny."

"Know what's cool, Ape? Pete's got freckles on his eyelids. So when he closes his eyes, you can barely tell where they are. It's like they're camouflaged."

May suddenly felt a throbbing along her left temple and a pressing need to get out of Presto immediately.

"You know, I really don't feel well," May said. "I think I have to go across the parking lot to get some aspirin from the drugstore. I'll be right back."

When she arrived home four hours later, May was less than thrilled to see Pete's car sitting in her driveway, right behind the minivan. She looked at her watch. It was almost nine o'clock. He'd picked Palmer up over three hours before. It made no sense for him to still be here.

She dismounted, wheeled the Brown Hornet into the garage, and slipped in quietly through the kitchen. The first strange part was the silence. No blaring TV. Then the faint laughter. May followed the sound until she reached the doorway to the living room. She paused for a moment and listened. Palmer and Pete were talking. And laughing. Her appearance stopped them both cold.

"You're still here," she said.

"Oh . . . yeah." Pete glanced between Palmer and May. "We were just talking."

"Where's Brooks?" May said, looking up and around the room as if her sister might be clinging to the ceiling like a spider. "I have to kill her."

"She's sleeping," Pete said. "She seemed kind of sick today."

"Pete and I were talking," Palmer said suddenly. She looked at May with a decidedly unfriendly expression.

"Okay, then . . . ," May said. "I'm starving. I'm going to make something to eat. Anybody want some dinner?"

"We ate," Palmer said.

"We?"

"Pete and I."

"You went out?" May asked. "The two of you?"

"Yeah." Palmer almost looked defiant. "We went out. To the T.G.I. Friday's near the mall."

Pete was not contributing to this part of the conversation, May noticed. Instead he seemed to be asking himself whether or not the two sides of his body quite matched up. He looked at his hands side by side. Then he grabbed the zipper of his sweatshirt and began pulling it up and down.

May flicked her eyes in his direction and he glanced away.

"Okay . . . ," she said. "Well, I'll be in the kitchen."

A minute later, as she dug around the icy, uncharted territory in the back of the freezer, May heard someone come into the room. She retracted her head and peered around. Pete was standing in the kitchen doorway.

"You took Palmer to dinner?" she asked. "What, was she complaining about my cooking again?"

"No. She just seemed kind of lonely."

"Oh," she said simply. "That was nice of you. I'll pay you back for whatever you spent."

"Don't worry about it."

May disliked the thought of Pete giving them money, so she

left the freezer door open and reached for her purse anyway.

"No, really," he said, more insistently this time. "She was just upset because of today."

"Oh, right," May said. Pete pulled out a chair and sat down. May pried a frozen dinner from a pack of unidentifiable meat and shut the door.

"Brooks really looked kind of bad," Pete said.

"She was out last night."

"She looks like that a lot."

"She goes out a lot."

Palmer turned on the TV, and the kitchen wall began to shudder. May deposited the frozen lump on a baking tray.

"I got a call about this summer job I applied for," Pete said. "It would be really cool. It's at a golf course, just inside the city, about fifteen minutes from here."

"That's great."

May shoved the snowy brick into the oven. She could feel Pete's eyes on her as she did this.

"My dad . . . ," Pete said slowly, rubbing at his chin. "I don't know if you heard this, but he's sponsoring a bench at the softball field, the one over by the middle school. It'll have your dad's name on it."

"A bench?"

"I know," Pete said. "It's just a bench. And it's going to take them four months or something to install it—don't ask me why. But just so you know . . ."

"Thanks." May nodded.

"How are you?" he asked.

"Me? I'm fine."

"Are you guys going to be doing anything?"

"No," May said. "You know us, we've never been religious or anything."

"I thought you might have a dinner or a service or something."

"We're not a dinner-and-service kind of family."

May had nothing more to say about this. She looked down at the floor. There was a blotch of something dark and sticky by her foot.

"So Nell tells me that you two are going to the prom," she said.

"Yeah. I . . . you know. Asked her."

"I figured that."

Neither one of them seemed to want to push this subject any further, either.

"Monday still good for a lesson?" he asked.

"Monday's fine."

"I guess . . ." Pete looked down the hall. "I should go."

"Okay. Thanks again."

After he'd let himself out, May spread her books on the table. She hastily flipped through a four-page biology lab report that she had to complete. She felt like she had lived this moment a hundred times over—making dinner for herself in the middle of a messy, empty kitchen with a pile of homework on the table. Feeling the walls rumble from the television. An endless, deadly cycle.

"Turn it down!" she yelled to Palmer.

The volume went up.

Before, she could just as easily have walked into the living room and found her dad sitting on the edge of his recliner, yelling at the screen. Part of her almost wanted to try it to see if this was some kind of very long dream. Maybe he would be sitting there in the stretched-out navy blue T-shirt he always put on when he got home. He would laugh and apologize for "disturbing the professor," and he would turn it down. He always called her that—the professor. May could never tell if it was a joke or a compliment, but she assumed it was a joke because Brooks would laugh, and Brooks *got* everything their dad said, and May didn't. So it had to have been a joke.

She felt herself getting angry, like she wanted to go in and have an argument about something that hadn't been said with someone who couldn't possibly be there. But only insane people did things like that, so the argument twisted and stewed inside her with nowhere to go. She wanted to scream, but she just threw one of her pens against the refrigerator. It bounced off and rolled under the lip of the dishwasher. She felt stupid. She got up and retrieved it.

There was a burning smell coming from the oven. It needed to be cleaned.

And the volume just kept going up. For once, though, it had a useful effect. When it was sufficiently loud enough to cover her sobs, May sat down on the floor, put her head in her hands, and cried.

june

Firebird, golden
Gold family entrances associated with

1. Site of Brooks's conception. Occurred at the Vince Lombardi rest stop off the New Jersey Turnpike, just outside New York City, on the way to a game at Yankee Stadium. (Not something I asked to know. I overheard my dad talking about it to Mr. Camp at a picnic.)

2. Impromptu ambulance used to rush my mother to the hospital when she went into premature labor with me. My dad ran four red lights trying to get there and was eventually pulled over. The police escorted us the rest of the way. (I figure I can say "us"—I mean, I was there, right?)

In the past, the arrival of June had always been treated like a major holiday in the Gold house because June meant summer. June was when school ended and the Golds could turn themselves over entirely to the Baltimore Orioles and the summer leagues. A balanced meal suddenly consisted of hot dogs burned nice and dark on the grill, with a pile of fried onions and coleslaw on the side. Dinner was either in front of the television or out in the backyard, with the radio tuned to the sports station. There would be beer for the adults and fudge Popsicles or Mister Softie for everyone else. The Camps and various softball teammates of Palmer and Brooks drifted in and out, the phone rang constantly, May complained that she didn't have anywhere quiet to do her homework (until she got her ice cream cone), and a happy chaos reigned. The main concerns were how Baltimore was doing and when Brooks or Palmer was playing.

All of that had changed last year.

For a start, Mike Gold's funeral had been on the first of June— an overcast and unseasonably cold day. The service at the funeral home had been short and simple. Since his body had been cremated, there was no trip to the cemetery. There was an informal lunch in the back room of a small local restaurant, during which the Gold sisters sat in a corner, mute, ordering soda after soda and looking numbly out on the crowd of people, many of whom they barely knew. Their mother, who had been medicated by this point, made hollow conversation with whoever sat next to her.

Their father's parents had come out from California and stayed for the entire month. When that set of grandparents had gone, their mother's parents, the Dreijers, had come over from Holland for a week. The Camps made daily visits. It was strange to have this endless company—this steady stream of people who seemed hell-bent on distracting them all. Whenever Brooks tried to retreat to her room, someone would come knocking.

When Brooks finally got tired of sitting at home and returned to work at the pool in mid-July, her bosses gave her the easiest and most boring assignment—checking tags at the gate. People got quiet when they passed her. Even members of the pool who were complete strangers to her seemed to know that she was "that poor girl who had just lost her father."

This year, June came in on a decidedly more positive note. Brooks was concentrating on the details of her junior prom. It had taken a while for Dave to get around to asking her, but two weeks before, he'd finally done it. Casually, of course. In study hall.

Even though the Gold family budget couldn't really cover Brooks's expenses, destiny had already decided that she should go to the prom in a certain amount of style. Magically, people started coming forward with all kinds of items. A neighbor had recently been in a wedding, and she had a spare dress—satin, basic black, with removable spaghetti straps. A nurse who worked with her mom lent Brooks a choker. Another had the right size feet and an amazing pair of black heels. The nurse manager had a gift certificate for a free manicure at a local salon that she was never going to use, having permanently lost her thumbnail after getting her finger caught in a car door.

The topper was a two-hundred-dollar check made out to Brooks from their grandparents in California, who had correctly guessed that funds were running a little low. Of course, with all of the donations, this was just gravy. It went toward the limo, her hair, an eyebrow wax, a deluxe pedicure, ten minutes of shiatsu shoulder massage, and a black henna tattoo (the Chinese character for *party*) on the small of her back. She had just enough left over for all of the odds and ends.

Brooks had started reading fashion magazines to get ready. She'd ripped out an article called "The Ultimate Prom Preparedness List," which she tucked into the side of her mirror. (When May had seen this, she'd simulated vomiting. Brooks took it down and folded it into a notebook.) On the night before the prom, Brooks stopped into the huge drugstore across from Presto Espresso to do a little shopping.

She wandered the sterile aisles, examining the cotton balls and cold remedies. She picked up a box of medicine that Jamie swore cured hangovers. She grabbed bobby pins, dry-clear deodorant, clear nail polish, safety pins, a small pack of tissues—everything on her list. As she walked past the alcove near the pharmacy, something caught Brooks's eye. There, between the nonprescription eyeglasses and the incontinence supplies, were the condoms. Brooks stopped and stared at them for a moment. Then she turned her back on them and pretended to be deeply engrossed in the task of picking out baby formula.

Condoms were not on the prom preparedness list. But maybe they should have been.

The one thing that had been eating at Brooks recently was the fact that—no matter how obvious it was—Dave had yet to say that he was her boyfriend. Brooks had tried to bring the subject up, but it always seemed to fall by the wayside.

Brooks was a virgin. No particular reason—it was just that she hadn't seen the right opportunity yet. This, she realized, was the right opportunity. If she were ready at the prom, with Dave . . . it would be hard to evade the subject after that.

She turned back to the display and tried to figure out where to begin. There were about fifty different kinds— ribbed, thin, sensitive, flavored, colored, extra strength, non-latex, nonlubricated, spermicidally lubricated, extra pleasure, large. . . . After a quick examination, she grabbed the pack that seemed the most average—something that offered protection yet came wrapped in a green package that looked kind of fun (it featured a dancing cucumber). She shoved the pack under her other purchases and headed for the checkout.

There were two registers open at the front of the store and only one person waiting in line. As Brooks stepped behind, she saw that one of the cashiers was a girl from her Spanish class. It wasn't someone Brooks really knew, but still, she didn't want someone from school ringing up her stuff. She went to the back of the store, to the pharmacy line. There were eight people in this one, but Brooks joined it anyway.

"Are you waiting for a prescription?" the woman behind the counter called to her.

"Uh . . ." Brooks dug into her basket. "No."

"Then go up front. There's no line up there."

Brooks couldn't really demand to wait in the longest line, so she reluctantly turned and went back to where she had just been. Now Brooks was the only person waiting.

"I can take you."

Of course it was the girl from class.

The girl gave Brooks a glance and an I-know-you-slightly nod. Brooks nodded back and started unpacking her basket. Bobby pins . . . tiny hair spray . . . pack of tissues . . .

"You're in Keller's Spanish class," the girl said. "Right?"

"Yeah," Brooks said.

Nail polish . . . deodorant . . . morning-after effervescent medicine . . .

"Are you taking Spanish IV?"

The girl's name tag read *Tammy*. She didn't even know this girl Tammy. Why was she trying to get the lowdown on Brooks's academic future?

"I don't know yet," Brooks said.

The basket was empty now except for the condoms. She wondered if she should just drop them to the ground. Forget about them. Or come back later.

"I am," Tammy was saying. "I'm thinking about taking Keller again."

No, Brooks thought. Why should she care if someone she barely knew saw her buying something that she had every right to buy? Brooks reached in one last time and set the condoms on the counter, sliding them as far under the pile of stuff as she could.

"Except that I want to take AP history, which is at the same time," Tammy said. She wasn't even looking at the stuff. She reached over blindly, grabbed each item, and held it up to the scanner. Maybe she wouldn't even notice.

"Oh."

Everything but the condoms had been rung up. Tammy

looked down, as if to ask, "Is that all?" and spotted the condoms on the counter. If Brooks had blinked, she would have missed it, but Tammy shot her a curious look, scanned them, ran them over a separate sensor, and dropped them into the bag.

"Fifteen seventy-five," she said, not looking Brooks in the eye.

Brooks handed over her last twenty dollars of the two hundred. Tammy pushed back the change.

"See you in class," she said.

"See you," Brooks replied.

As she hurried out into the parking lot, Brooks made a mental note to herself: Avoid Tammy like the plague.

Palmer was on her way out of the locker room when she heard her name being shouted. She turned around to see her coach waving her into her tiny office, off on the far side of the gym. Palmer went over and peered into the room, with its mint-colored cinder block walls. Her coach, Mrs. Grady, was ducking in and out of various file cabinet drawers. Mrs. Grady never sat still.

"I want to ask you something, Palmer," she said, throwing a pile of manila folders to the ground.

"Okay."

"I'm running a July session this year," she said. "It's the whole month, four hours every weekday morning. I have a pitching coach come in for part of the time. We'll also be playing a few sample games for some scouts. It's very competitive. We're taking people from all over Pennsylvania, New Jersey, and Delaware. I'm not even taking too many people from our team."

Palmer tangled her fingers in a nearby volleyball net, wondering where this was going.

"I think you should come, Palmer. I think we could do some good work."

"When's the tryout?"

"You don't need to try out," Mrs. Grady said, dumping the contents of a very fat file into a recycling bin. "I'm accepting you."

Palmer didn't know what to say. This was almost too good. But camps cost money.

"I have to ask my mom," Palmer said. "I don't know if I can."

Mrs. Grady stopped file purging for a moment.

"I need an assistant," she said. "If you help out with the equipment and the paperwork, you can come for free."

"Free?"

"Do you want the job?"

Palmer nodded, trying not to look too eager. She didn't really succeed. She also didn't question why the coach seemed to know that money was a problem. That was fine. If it meant that she could go to the summer session, Palmer didn't care what she knew.

"So," Mrs. Grady went on, "if you want to, talk to your mom about it and let me know by the end of this week."

"I'll come," Palmer said.

"Check first. Make sure that you can."

"I'll come," Palmer repeated. "I'll check, but I'll be there. I'm just telling you."

"Good." Mrs. Grady nodded. "We start the first of July."

As she left the building, Palmer felt a lightness she hadn't experienced in a long time. Tonight she just might get some decent sleep.

The next morning May gazed miserably into her locker, trying to make some sense of the mosaic of self-stick notes that covered the door. Why did she write incredibly obvious and non-specific things like *study Tues.* or *bring book*?

"You're mad about something," Linda said as May yanked down three identical notes that read *paper due*.

"Brooks's prom is tonight."

"You're mad about Brooks's prom?" Linda asked.

"I'm not mad about her prom," May said, shutting her locker door with a loud bang. "I'm mad because she gets everything she wants. I work so I can buy a laptop and save some cash for college. Brooks does nothing, and people like *leap out of the bushes* to throw money and stuff at her."

"Bathroom," Linda said. "With me. Come on."

They turned into the bathroom by their homeroom door. Girls' had been built over a century before as a club for male students. The bathrooms were huge, intricately tiled places with historical plumbing and six inches of paint on the walls. May leaned against one of the old pedestal sinks and played with the cold water knob. Linda went over and sat on the high marble windowsill, pulling her long hair from behind her back and piling it on top of her head in a huge black coil. This was her thinking spot.

"So," she said. "The prom."

"I know what you're thinking," May said. "That's not it."

"I'm just asking. Could you like him?"

"Pete? He's *Pete*. . . ."

"Let me get this straight," Linda said. "Pete gives you driving lessons and he drives you around. He shows up whenever you need him and even when you don't. You want to know what this means?"

"Not really."

"You're in denial."

"I am not in denial."

Linda smiled, as if she had just heard a little voice in her head that was telling her a private joke.

"I am not in denial," May repeated. "Seriously. Pete is just a big-haired freak. He's like a brother to me. It's like asking you if you could date Frank."

"But he's *not* your brother."

"I said *like* a brother," May replied.

"Right," Linda said. "But Frank is *actually* my cousin, which makes it illegal as well as repulsive. You are not related to Pete in any way."

"After a while, it's almost like I am. He's like my common-law brother."

"You should work in an excuse factory," Linda sighed. "It doesn't occur to you that he's only dating Nell because you pretty much told him to? And that it's possible for him to date Nell and like you at the same time?"

"Stop. Seriously."

"You won't admit it."

"There's nothing to admit," May said. "He's teaching me to

drive because his mom made him, and he's going out with Nell because he feels like it. He was nice to Palmer because it was a serious thing. That's it. End of story."

Linda considered this as she reached into her bag and pulled out a small white candy, which she unwrapped and popped into her mouth.

"My grandmother keeps giving me this ginger candy," Linda said, her face contorting into an agonized spasm. "And I really hate it. It burns. But I can't stop eating it."

"Is that supposed to be some kind of parable?"

"No," Linda said, sucking in air to cool her mouth. "Do you want it to be?"

May turned the ancient tap on one of the sinks a bit too roughly, and water came gushing out and covered the front of her skirt. She brushed it away. The one good thing about her uniform was that it was made of indestructible polyester, impervious to stain or spill.

"It was always the big joke," May said, "when we were kids. Our parents always used to say that Pete and I were going to end up together. My dad said it all the time. He thought it was hilarious."

Linda fell into the wide-eyed silence that always cropped up whenever May accidentally mentioned her dad. It was a guaranteed conversation breaker. May was obliged to continue speaking so that Linda could see that it was okay to keep talking about the subject.

"Pete is that person who wiped his nose on my ruler in fifth grade," she went on. "I still can't eat bologna because of him. . . ."

"Is that a bad thing?"

"The point is," May said, "I just don't understand why Nell would date *that* guy."

"Because Pete's not that guy anymore."

"Quit it with the deepness."

"I'm serious," Linda said. "Things change."

"They don't change that much."

"Yes, they do," Linda said. "Are you saying that you're the same now as you were when you were eight?"

"I'm not talking about when I was eight. I'm talking about last year."

Linda made a thoughtful noise. May looked up at her.

"What? That's a Dr. Linda sound."

"Why did you give Nell the number?" Linda asked.

May shrugged.

"I had to."

"Had to? Oh, I get it. Nell's scary, impressive assistant manager's credentials got to you. You were blinded by her power."

"It doesn't matter," May said. "I don't even care."

"Yes, you do. You care a lot. Will you please stop saying you don't? It's annoying."

"I just think it's weird," May said. "I can't figure it out. Pete was the most annoying person I knew, and just as he was becoming normal, he gets together with the person who took his title."

"Okay, two things," Linda said. "One, don't try to figure out why people pair up the way they do. Perfect example: You know Dash?"

"Frank's girlfriend?"

"Right," Linda said. "Pep squad girl. Father owns a paper

company in New Jersey. Painfully dumb, but really good looking. She's got the hair and the scrawny body and the nose-job button nose—everything. And she's dating *Frank*? Four out of five experts would never have seen that one coming."

"Well," May said, "Frank's kind of smart. . . ."

"He has five snakes and he just dyed his hair purple," Linda said firmly. "He laminated his Mensa card. Dumb blond paper heiress—insane, snake-loving engineer. There's no logic behind it. Don't try to find any. And don't try to figure it out with Pete and Nell."

"Okay," May said, reaching up to pick at some flaking paint by the mirror. She looked at her reflection as she did so. She was scowling. She looked a lot like Palmer when she scowled—all chipmunk cheeks and round, maniac eyes. Very attractive.

"Second thing," Linda continued. "Don't get involved in the details of other people's love lives, because the details are always creepy."

"Trust me, I'm not getting involved."

"I'm not saying you would want to. I'm saying it might happen, and you have to avoid it."

"Huh?"

"Here's an example. Just last night Dash comes over to dinner. So I have to listen to her rambling on at the table for half an hour about how she's so excited to be eating actual Chinese home-cooked cuisine. We were having little crab cakes, which she obviously thought were dim sum fish balls or something. But I can let that go. She's from Jersey. It's a handicap."

Linda reached into her bag and popped another candy into her mouth.

"Anyway," Linda went on, waving her hand in front of her mouth again, "after dinner she tries to bond with me. She comes up to my room, sits on my bed, and tells me that she's been shopping. She pulls this pink silk gown out of her bag and asks me how I like it. This gown is about five inches long and covered in lace—it's disgusting. I don't want to see this. So I tell her it's nice, thinking she'll go away. But she just agrees with me and starts explaining to me how sexy it looks on her."

"We should get her together with Nell," May said. "They could start an I'm-comfortable-with-my-own-body club."

"It gets worse. Then she starts asking me if I think Frank will like it, as if I study my cousin's turn-ons. She was going to try it on and show it to me, but someone called her from downstairs and she left."

May wrinkled her nose in sympathy.

"But you see what I mean," Linda said. "People will try to open that window sometimes and give you a little look. Don't let them. Unless, of course, you have some personal interest in the relationship."

It was said innocently enough, but May understood what the pause meant.

"What am I going to do?" May asked, sagging against the sink.

"I don't know," Linda said. "Can you talk to Pete about it?"

"No." May shook her head. "It would be too weird."

"Then try not to watch," Linda said. "That's really all you can do."

*   *   *

That night May could barely be coaxed out of her room to take the obligatory photos of Brooks stabbing Dave Vatiman in the heart with a small boutonniere pin.

"Palmer!" her mom was yelling up the stairs. "Come down here and look at Brooks."

May sniggered as she laid the photos out on the coffee table. *Yeah, Palmer,* she said to herself, *come see the leaning tower of Brooks.* Brooks had mastered walking in her heels on the driveway, but the living room carpet was presenting a whole new challenge, and she was listing precariously to the left.

Palmer came halfway down the stairs and stared at Brooks, as directed.

"Doesn't your sister look great?" her mom prompted.

"Uh-huh." Palmer was chewing on something very loudly.

"Instamatic," Dave said, reaching for May's camera. "Cool. Can we take this? Do you have more film?"

"No," May said, automatically retrieving the camera and tucking it under her arm. She didn't know Dave that well, but her every instinct told her that she didn't want him getting his hands on her precious Polaroid.

"Isn't Brooks's dress great?" Her mom was still needling Palmer. "Doesn't she look nice?"

"Yeah."

May gathered up the photos and went into the kitchen. Brooks pigeon-toed behind her and cornered her by the refrigerator.

"We need a camera," Brooks said pointedly.

"Buy a disposable. You have the cash."

"I'm out."

"Well," May said, dropping the still-developing photos into Brooks's purse, "at least you have that nice tattoo."

Brooks hadn't actually mentioned the tattoo to May—May had heard her describe it over the phone. This silenced Brooks, and she did her funny little walk back into the living room, this time with an angry little hustle.

May smiled in a rare moment of complete satisfaction.

The feeling lingered up until the time May arrived at Presto Espresso, but it fled at the first whiff of elevator jazz she heard as she walked in. It didn't help that it was a gorgeous, warm Friday night in early June. And this was where she would spend it. The only good thing about it was that for the first time, she would work alone. There had been no one available to share the shift. At least she could get something done.

May spent an hour attempting to read *Pride and Prejudice* for her English class, but her attention kept drifting. She kept looking out the window or just staring into space. As she tried to turn her focus back to her book one more time, she noticed Pete's car pulling into the far entrance of the lot. Without any time to wonder what Pete and Nell were doing there, she dropped into a casual pose and tried to look as engrossed in her book as possible.

Nell flounced—and that really was the only word for it— out of the car and into the store, striking the skinny heels of her shoes hard against the red tile so that her every step could be clearly heard by all.

"Like it?" Nell said, twirling for May.

"It's great." May nodded. It *was* great. It was black and very long and clingy, run throughout with a gold threading. Nell had piled her hair on top of her head and tied it into a shaggy lump with a leopard print scarf. It was the kind of thing May could never, ever pull off.

"It's Betsy Johnson," Nell said proudly, coming closer so that May could feel the velvety material. "I got it online for forty bucks. Vintage."

"Wow."

"This," she said, holding forth her hand and revealing a silver bracelet that was linked to a silver ring on her middle finger with a small chain, "is my new slave bracelet. Like?"

"It's beautiful."

Pete came in quietly. He wore a slate gray suit, which May recognized from her father's funeral. It was probably the only one he had.

"You going to be okay by yourself here tonight?" Nell said, taking a sudden concern in the running of Presto Espresso. On any other day the roof could have caved in and she would hardly have noticed.

"I'll be fine," May said. "Nothing's happening here."

Pete saw Nell and May conferring.

"I'm going to"—he looked around—"go to the bathroom."

He sped off toward the back. Nell nose-whistled.

"I already traced a star on the side of his neck," she said.

"You what?"

"The freckles," Nell explained. "They make a star pattern on his neck. On the right side. I already told him that he should get the outline tattooed."

"Oh."

The rather eerie image of one of Nell's slender fingers playing along the side of Pete's neck leapt into May's mind. She could see it quite clearly. Nell leaning across the front seat of Pete's gray tank, her short, ruby-colored nail stroking the coppery freckles. Linda was right. Nell was already opening the window and letting the creepiness come pouring in. She really didn't want to know these things.

While May was musing, Nell jammed her hand down the front of her dress and busily adjusted her bustier.

"I have this wire that's making me crazy . . . ," she mumbled. "And the front keeps getting stuck on my . . . Ow. Ow. My rings are . . . Oh, I think I may be bleeding."

May struggled for something to say.

"I don't know if he really likes them," Nell managed as she rummaged around in her bustier.

"Likes what?" May asked as the horrifying image of Pete examining the knocker knockers leapt into her brain.

"Tattoos."

"Oh." May sighed. "Right. Tattoos."

"I'm totally caught here," Nell said as she pulled a napkin from one of the dispensers and plunged it down into the depths. "I'm seriously stuck."

Do not expect me to help you, May thought. *You are on your own.*

"This *always* happens." Nell groaned, rummaging and pulling like crazy now. "But with studs it would even be worse, you know? I . . . oh. Got it. Thank God."

She tugged the bustier up and arranged herself. Pete emerged from the bathroom just as Nell's performance was complete.

"You look nice," May said in her clearest this-is-a-sincere-yet-obligatory-remark voice. But he did actually look nice, even though the sleeves of the jacket were a bit too short. The gravity of the suit really made him seem adult, something she'd never thought possible with Pete.

Pete stared down at the suit, unbuttoned the bottom button, then quickly rebuttoned it. He must have seen the extra space at the ends of his sleeves in the process, because he jammed his hands deep in the jacket pockets.

"I guess we should go," Nell said. "You're sure you're going to be all right?"

"I think I'll manage."

"Here are my keys," Nell said, pulling a Hello Kitty key chain out of her bag. "And don't worry about doing the bank deposits. Someone will do them tomorrow."

"I never do them anyway. . . ."

"And if you have any problems, you can call Ann on her cell. Mine's going to be off."

With that, Nell skittered off in the direction of the door. Pete turned to follow, smiling a good-bye at May.

"Have fun," May said.

"We will," Nell said, grabbing Pete's arm and pulling him along.

May walked over to the window when they were far enough away and watched Pete's Cutlass disappear through the line of shrubs that separated the shopping center from the road. The parking lot was nearly deserted. A big white moon was just coming into view in a lavender evening sky.

It was only seven thirty. She would be here until eleven,

engulfed in the odor of overroasted coffee and the chill breeze of the air conditioner, guarding her empty tables and doing homework. May pressed her hand against the window and left a soft print that quickly faded away. She rubbed at the spot with the edge of her apron and stared across at SuperDrug. She remembered that whenever she'd go in there with her dad to pick up soap or bleach, he'd always have to buy something by the front counter, like a pack of mini–Snickers bars or some barbecue potato chips. Or they'd stop and get a double-dip cone from the ice cream stand ("they're only open three months a year"). There was always a reason, some little celebration, some splurge. He seemed to see every day as a special event.

May turned away from the window. This night was bad enough without dragging up any of *that*. She went back behind the counter. At the very least, she could use the time to try to search for the label maker and fix her name tag. At least that would be constructive.

The ladies' room in the catering hall was divided into two parts—the stall-and-sink room and the bizarre "ladies' parlor" area. This was overstuffed with silk flowers, plush pink carpeting, beaded glass light fixtures, and prints of shy ballerinas waiting to go onstage. There were two marble-topped mirrored makeup tables, a full-length mirror, and several chairs in this antechamber, inviting all users of the rest room to recline and breathe in the overwhelming fragrance of woodland rose potpourri and listen to the cascade of flushing toilets. Brooks and Jamie had taken them up on this generous offer several times this evening.

"Okay," Jamie said, shuffling through her red silk drawstring bag. "Anyone coming?"

Brooks cracked open the door and peered into the hall. Nothing but the lingering smell of sterno and a staff member pushing an empty coatrack into the lobby.

"No. We're good."

"We got Jack. We got Jim. Who do you want?"

"Jack," Brooks said.

"Jack." Jamie nodded, pulling a tiny bottle of Jack Daniels from her purse. "Here you go. I'll take Mr. Jim."

"How did you get all of these?" Brooks asked.

"My dad is a frequent flyer," Jamie said, breaking the seal on her little bottle. "Ready?"

Brooks unscrewed the cap and nodded. On Jamie's nod they tipped the small bottles back and sucked down the contents. Jamie quickly passed her empty over to Brooks, who had a disposable hand towel ready and waiting. She wrapped up the evidence and shoved it deep into a small pink trash can next to her chair, taking a moment to carefully rearrange some of the other discarded towels and tissues over it.

"Okay," Jamie said, taking another look in her bag. "So, Jim Beam I can do without a chaser, but I am not drinking straight gin. That's disgusting. Ooo . . . teeny, tiny Absolut vodka."

She held up a small bottle, grinned, then plunked it back into the bag.

"I swear to God I had a little Grey Goose in here, but I think Dave swiped it. Oh, well." Jamie rose unsteadily on her open-backed heels and turned to the mirror to rearrange her tight, Chinese-style red cocktail dress. Brooks watched her for a moment, then reached for her own evening bag and emptied the contents onto the dressing table.

"Look," she said.

Jamie looked down at the small pile of makeup, keys, and wallet. Brooks pushed the objects around until she revealed a small square of green plastic. Jamie laughed and picked it up.

"Did you just buy these?" she asked. She held on to one edge and dangled the three condoms from her fingertips.

"Yesterday."

"Are they for tonight?"

"I don't know," Brooks said, staring at them. "I was thinking tomorrow night, at the party, when we stay over at Dave's. Here."

She opened up her bag, and Jamie dropped in the condoms.

"Look at you." Jamie grinned. "All prepared."

"I don't know if I can get up," Brooks said.

Jamie reached over and presented her carefully manicured hand. Brooks accepted the help out of the chair.

Back in the main room, about half the people were on the dance floor. The others were huddled in conference around tables. The inseparable couples were in each other's laps. Brooks looked at one of the tables near the door. Pete was there, deep in the throes of telling some story, obviously. He had taken off his suit jacket and rolled up the sleeves of his shirt. He was waving his arms wildly at some girl in a tight black dress who was laughing hysterically.

For some reason, Brooks found the sight very amusing.

"Oh my God," Brooks said, pulling Jamie to a stop. "That's Camper."

"Who?"

"Camper. Peter Camp. Don't you know him?"

Jamie shook her head.

"He's s friend of ours."

"Who's he with?" Jamie said, leaning in close to Brooks. "Is that Ani DiFranco? All she needs are the dreds and maybe a little more body hair."

"I have no idea. I thought he was stalking May. I *have* to say something. Come with me."

Arm in arm, they approached the couple. Pete stopped his gesticulating.

"Pete!" Brooks screamed. "What's going on?"

Jamie laughed politely into her fist, as if coughing.

"We're sitting," he said. "What's going on with you, Brooks?"

"Who's this?" Brooks asked.

Nell narrowed her eyes a bit.

"This is Nell," Pete said.

"Nell. Oh, *Nell.*" This was much too loud. Brooks had lost her sense of volume. "You work with May, right?"

"Yes." Nell nodded. "You know her?"

"She's my sister."

"May's your *sister?*" Nell said. She carefully looked over the very tall, very blond, very drunk thing in front of her.

"Pete," Brooks said, throwing herself down in the empty chair on his other side, "have you seen Dave? We're looking for Dave."

Brooks dropped her head onto Pete's shoulder and began to laugh a loud, snorting laugh, grabbing the front of his shirt for support. Her head began to slide down, and she left a long smudge of black mascara across his chest.

"Who's Dave?" he asked.

Brooks picked her head up and smiled.

"You want a tiny Absolut?" she said. "Show him, Jamie. Show him."

"You're kind of falling out there, honey," Nell said sweetly, pinching the front of Brooks's dress and tugging it up an inch. "You might want to get off your hem."

Brooks looked down. Her dress was pinned under the leg of the chair, and it was pulling down the entire front.

"Come on," Jamie said. "Let's go find them."

"We have to go," Brooks explained as she stood up and steadied herself. Then, somewhat mysteriously, she added, "Good luck with everything."

"That's why I don't drink," Nell said as Brooks and Jamie stumbled off across the floor. "Nothing. No alcohol, no drugs. Not even taurine. Is that really May's sister?"

Pete nodded, watching as Brooks tried to regain a steady gait.

"That's really her sister," he confirmed.

The next day Dave's parents left town for a Jimmy Buffet Parrothead convention in Key West to drink tequila and sing "Margaritaville" for four days.

Brooks had spent the day in bed, recovering from the prom and resting up for the evening. She'd worked out a cover story about staying at Jamie's, so everything was ready. In the late afternoon she showered and dressed, then tore through her closet looking for the most feminine outfit she owned. This was tricky, since she mostly wore jeans and T-shirts. Of these, she chose the most flattering. She finally chose a blue baby tee that just hit her waistline and her darkest jeans, which made her legs look even longer than they already were. It wasn't that much of a switch from what she normally wore, but it was a nice combination.

She used some of the makeup she'd purchased for the prom. Brooks never wore makeup, so the sensation of having stuff on her face was a little distracting. She could smell the foundation (it reminded her of glue) as she rubbed it into her skin with her fingers. She applied a bit of the blush, then stood back to check the effect. It wasn't even noticeable. She tried again, streaking the brush along her cheekbones up past her eyes.

She took the condoms from her prom purse and considered them, unsure of where they should go. In the end she put two of them in the front pocket of her backpack. The third one went in the pocket of her jeans, in case she couldn't get to her things when she needed them.

As she came down the stairs, Palmer glanced over and grinned.

"Hey, Ronald," she said. "Blush much?"

Brooks ran back up and practically sanded down her cheeks. The force of her rubbing only made them redder, until she couldn't tell what was natural and what was cosmetic. After a minute, though, the redness faded, and Brooks was satisfied with the result. Her eyes stood out more. Her lips were pink and slightly wet looking, which was exactly the effect in the ad that had prompted her to buy this lipstick in the first place.

Brooks stayed in her room until Fred arrived at seven to get her. He was on his way back from a beer run. It was a strange sensation, riding along with Fred, making idle conversation over his stereo, knowing what was about to happen to her tonight. This was it. She would walk in a virgin and out—not so much.

Dave lived in a massive new house in a development by the mall. A dozen or so speakers shook the thin, new walls. The noise echoed down the newly paved street of mostly vacant houses. The ground actually had a pulse. There were cars in every available space along the entire length of the road.

"I guess people are here," Fred observed.

He parked on the next street and didn't seem to worry about being caught carrying two cases of beer to the house. It was crowded already. Some of the people Brooks recognized; many, she didn't. Fred squeezed through a crowd by the door, hoisting the cases over his head. He continued on through the living room, straight out to a back porch. Brooks was on her own. There was nothing for her to do but go in and wander around until she found Dave or Jamie.

She'd been to Dave's a few times before, but it was a big enough place that there were many parts of it she hadn't really seen. There was something strangely impersonal about the inside of the house. Brooks felt as though if it were destroyed during the course of the night, Dave could just pick up the Pottery Barn catalog and have it back in order within a day.

Every room had its own wonders. The tarp from the swimming pool was stretched over the living room floor, and a keg sat in the middle. There were flaming Dr. Pepper shots on the enclosed porch. The blender was going in the kitchen. A bit of towel stuck out from under one of the bedroom doors where the potheads had barricaded themselves. There was a girl in a vintage eighties prom dress standing on the back deck and shouted the name Gary into a cell phone.

Brooks wound her way down to the furnished basement. It was very dark, and the music was mellow and guitary. There were a few candles burning. This was a more refined group. People sat in all corners of the room, close together, talking. Jamie was there, sprawled out on a piano bench, sipping from an enormous round glass of blue liquid. She was perched above a group of what looked like college guys in retro-chic nerd gear—sweaters, T-shirts, thick glasses—and they were all talking in very deep and sober tones about some band that Brooks had never heard of.

Jamie had taken the opportunity to pull out all the stops. Her black hair was chiseled sleekly behind her ears, she had long drags of black eyeliner carefully smudged around her eyes, and she wore tight black pants made of some leather-pleather-vinyl-plastic-wrap amalgam.

Brooks looked down at herself. So tall, so plainly dressed. Her muscles, though still well developed, had melted a bit since she'd given up her daily workouts. She did have some glitter on her T-shirt, and she was wearing makeup . . . but it wasn't the same. Jamie had a perfect, barely tinted glaze on her lips; Brooks's were a childish pinkish red. And she still had a backpack on her back.

"You look great!" Jamie said. "Sit down! Drink." She pressed her glass into Brooks's hands. Brooks studied the glass. Jamie didn't even drink unfashionably.

"I found that in a cabinet in the dining room," Jamie explained.

Brooks nodded, taking a sip of the blue liquid. It was a harsh combination. All raw alcohol.

"I've been here since five. Dave's here somewhere," Jamie said, waving her hand and indicating the entire house. "He's making the rounds."

As if on cue, Dave strode in with a bottle of Johnny Walker Red in his hand. He had kept his tuxedo from the night before and was wearing the jacket and shirt with a pair of jeans. He hadn't shaved, so his face had a shadowy cast. Seeing Brooks and Jamie, he gathered them up, one under each arm.

"My ladies!" he said. "Come with me."

Brooks and Jamie headed off on the parade route with Dave, and it soon became apparent to both of them that he had started early. He leaned on them heavily, and he kept accidentally knocking the bottle into Brooks, where it made contact with her clavicle with a hollow thump. Jamie was too small to offer any support, so Brooks ended up doing the lion's share of the work.

He dragged them from group to group, all people Brooks had never really met before. He did most of the talking, since these people regarded Brooks and Jamie as bits of human architecture. They exchanged amused glances across his chest and passed the bottle back and forth. They wound up their tour by kicking a few people out of the master bedroom and dropping onto the bed. It was covered in a thick, obviously expensive, and very ugly comforter. Brooks put her backpack down to the side and threw her legs up on the bed somewhat gracelessly. Try as she might, she still moved like a jock. Jamie stretched out as well. Dave reclined between them.

Brooks tried to meet Jamie's eye to signal her to leave. Jamie leaned heavily against Dave and wrapped her arms around his chest. Brooks leaned on his other side and crossed her legs in his lap.

"What do you say?" he asked, drawing them both in to his shoulders. "We're all here. . . ."

"You have to be kidding," Jamie said with a laugh.

"Worth a try." He shrugged amiably.

Brooks smiled at both of them but was a bit confused as to what was going on. Jamie was clearly out of it—she had buried her face in Dave's neck and seemed to be going to sleep. Dave rummaged around in his pocket.

"Okay," he said. "Let's play a game."

"I like games," Jamie said, her muffled voice taking on an affected little-girl tone.

"Me too," Brooks said, surreptitiously grabbing one of Jamie's fingers and tugging on it, trying to get her attention.

Dave held up a quarter.

"Jamie is heads. . . ." He balanced it on his thumb. "Brooks is tails. Here we go. . . ."

He flicked the quarter into the air, then slapped it down on his wrist.

"Heads!" he said.

And with that, he passed the Johnny Walker to Brooks and rolled over on top of Jamie. Within seconds they were fully engaged.

Brooks sat there for a moment, holding the bottle, trying to process what she was seeing. She had just been lost in a quarter toss. She stared at her reflection in the television, took a sip of the Scotch, and then quietly slid off the bed. She watched the two of them for just a moment before leaving, waiting to see if this was some kind of joke or if they would try to stop her. But they were both too busy.

She set the bottle down on one of the dressers and left the room. Outside, everything still pulsed. Brooks walked back downstairs. A large guy with a goatee was sitting on the sofa with a bug sprayer at his feet. He regarded it proudly, like it was his pet. As Brooks passed, he held up the nozzle invitingly.

"Close your eyes and open your mouth," he said.

Brooks eyed the sprayer doubtfully.

"It's okay," said a girl who was now suddenly standing beside Brooks. "I did it. It's good."

The girl seemed like a bit of a Gap victim, a walking, talking display of khakis and white cotton shirt. But she seemed somewhat sober and certainly sincere. It was enough of an endorsement for Brooks. She leaned down and closed her eyes, and a fast shot of grain and juice washed down her throat.

"Good?" he asked.

She nodded. He looked pleased.

"More?"

She nodded again and received another spray. Thanking him in a thick voice, Brooks continued across the room and out the French doors onto the patio. She pulled a beer from the outside cooler and sat down at the empty wrought-iron umbrella table to collect her thoughts. Somewhere, deep in the back of her mind, she knew that she was devastated by what she'd just seen. It should have torn her apart that he was lying on top of Jamie right now, and that Jamie had been so willing, and that this had all happened *right in front of her.*

But she was just drunk enough to momentarily accept this as part of the reality of the party. Instinct told her that if she drank more, it would become less and less of a problem.

Brooks drained her beer and began peeling off the label.

Suddenly the girl in the prom dress who had earlier been making her repetitive appeal to Gary threw herself down in the chair next to Brooks, put her head down into her hands, and started sobbing uncontrollably. She looked up for a moment and saw Brooks staring at her.

"I hate him!" she screamed. "He said he would call!"

Presumably this was Gary she was talking about. Not that Brooks really cared. Her brain was too busy making mental movies of what was going on in the bedroom.

"I waited," the girl continued, dribbling rivulets of eye

makeup soup all over her dress. "But he didn't call, and he wasn't picking up, and he was on the phone with her the whole time, and—"

"Shut up," came an annoyed male voice from somewhere on the opposite side of the patio.

"You want me to shut up?" the girl asked.

A chorus of affirmative noises. The girl threw a knowing glance at Brooks. Brooks held up her hands to the group, indicating that she had no connection to the matter.

"Okay." The girl sniffed angrily. "Okay. I'll shut up. I won't say another word. I'll just . . ."

With that, she started slamming her cell phone into the wrought-iron table. Everyone else on the patio backed away from their corner.

"Fountainhead's doing it again," Brooks heard one guy mumble as he retreated behind the grill.

The girl made a low, animal-like grumble. She started banging other bits of the table to try to make more noise. She beat the phone on the chairs and on the hollow umbrella pole. Then she started a little chant to her own rhythm.

"This . . . is . . . me . . . shutting . . . up . . . this . . . is . . . me . . . shutting . . . up. . . ."

"I have to go," Brooks explained to her, quickly getting up. The girl was too absorbed now to care whether Brooks was there or not, and she said nothing as Brooks headed for the patio doors.

Sprayer Guy was happy to have a repeat customer.

"It's good, huh?" he said as Brooks took another hit of the punch. She nodded, swallowing hard. The alcohol burned her throat this time.

"Tell your friends!" he called to her as she walked away.

Brooks made her way through the people on the basement floor, the people on the stairs, the people in the upstairs hall waiting for the bathroom, down to the bedroom door. She had made a decision. She would see what was going on.

The bedroom door was closed. She put her hand on the knob and leaned her head against it, trying to hear what was going on inside. Everyone else in the hall was being too loud—laughing too much. She couldn't hear anything. She gently tried the knob.

It was locked.

She was surprised to feel her eyes filling with warm tears.

Brooks backed up and leaned against the opposite wall. She looked down at herself again—the jeans, the stupid T-shirt. Her hair smelled like smoke and her lipstick had eroded. She suddenly wanted out of this place, to get away from all of these people.

"Hey . . ." A girl had grabbed Brooks by the arm and was pointing to the bathroom. "Where's the puking sink?"

"What?"

"The *puking . . . sink?*"

The girl kept falling forward, almost hitting her head against the wall.

"It's in there," Brooks said, pointing at the bedroom door and walking away. "Just keep knocking."

While this was going on, May was at the wheel of Pete's precious Cutlass Ciera, headed right for the center of Philadelphia, which loomed on the horizon, like Oz. She wasn't happy about this, nor did she mean to be here.

It had probably been a mistake to leave her house in the first place, as she was intently studying for her finals. She had taken over the kitchen completely over the course of the last week, writing papers, making flash cards, shifting from subject to subject. But she did have a lesson scheduled with Pete for that night, and she felt like she needed a short study break. He'd shown up and made the observation that highway driving was easier than driving on little roads—that the lines of traffic were neat and well divided and all you had to do was go straight. That had sounded good to May, so she'd agreed to turn onto I-95 and try to go a few minutes up the road.

What Pete apparently hadn't taken into account was that it was eight o'clock on a glorious Saturday night in June. The sun was just setting over the skyline, the air was balmy, and thousands of people were racing toward the downtown area. May found herself surrounded by tailgaters and weave-arounders who trapped her on the road, forcing her to drive all the way downtown. Or at least, that was how it seemed to her.

"Okay," Pete said. "This turns into an exit lane. We'll loop through the city and turn around."

"Loop through the city?" May cried. "Are you nuts?"

"It's either that or keep driving forever," he replied. "Besides, you just got off."

May looked up and found, to her horror, that he was right. She was on a ramp now, about to merge with fast-moving traffic on the Vine Street Expressway.

She screamed.

"Just keep right," Pete said firmly. "You're fine."

May turned the wheel hard to the right, and an angry honking came from behind her.

"Uh . . . that's okay," Pete said, glancing from back to front quickly. "Maybe use the mirror next time. Good. Now. Merge."

"What?" she said, stepping on the brake. More honking.

"No!" Pete yelled. "Go! Go! Now!"

May stepped on the gas and the Cutlass narrowly slipped in front of a truck and into the right-hand lane of the expressway.

"Okay," he said, wiping his brow and pointing straight ahead. "First exit. Right up there. Turn."

This resulted in a near-death experience on a hairpin turn that wound 270 degrees and landed them on a tightly congested road near City Hall.

"Okay." Pete sighed. "We can stop. I'll look for a parking space."

"No, we can't!"

"Why?

"There are too many cars coming for me to stop!"

"Just find an empty space—"

"Shut up! I'll figure something out," May mumbled.

They drove deeper into the city, into historic downtown Philadelphia, where the streets were as wide as twin beds. Cars were parked all along the side of the road, making it difficult for her to pass through. She gripped the wheel with such force, she felt as though she might snap it to pieces, like a pretzel.

May looked at the lunchbox-size spaces between the cars on the side of the road. She looked in the rearview mirror and saw the endless stream of cars behind her. All she could do was drive on and on, deeper into urban traffic hell, onto streets that she imagined only got smaller and bumpier and had even more trolley tracks to catch the wheels on and more drunken bystanders wandering into them.

And this had all been Pete's idea. He sat there, in his bright red T-shirt, his hair wild in the intense humidity, the fringe around his face almost covering his eyes—like some overgrown talking rag doll that spouted nonsense about driving when you pulled its string.

"Come on," he said. "There are two spaces right there. Just pull over and I'll do the rest."

"I won't fit."

"Yes, you will."

"*No, I won't*. Have you seen this car? It's about fifty feet long. Just shut up for a second, okay?"

Cars were now crowding her out on her left. Why were people trying to make these streets into two lanes? She screeched in anguish.

"All right," Pete said, speaking slowly, "at the next red light, put the car in park and I'll slide over and drive."

"The light's not long enough for that!"

He leaned back against his seat and put his hands over his eyes.

At the height of her despair, May had a burst of inspiration. She knew, from the occasional trips she took into the city with her parents, that there were parking garages where attendants parked *for* you. It would be expensive, but it was better than crashing the car or running someone over.

"Look in my purse," she gasped. "In my wallet. Open it up. See how much money I have."

He gingerly picked up May's straw purse and poked around inside.

"Three bucks," he said.

On her right May saw a sign with a big *P* on it and an arrow pointing left. She made an abrupt turn onto one of the narrow, cobblestone streets that she feared so much. There, in the bottom of some kind of warehouse, was the opening of a garage. She pulled the car up to the attendant and came to a jerky stop. She laboriously rolled down the window with a shaking hand.

"Do you, like, park the cars for us?" she asked.

"Yeah," the man said, ripping a ticket in two and putting half under a windshield wiper.

"Okay." May nodded. "What do I do?"

"You get out."

May reached for the door release.

"Park," Pete said quickly, his hand flying for the shift.

"Oh. Right. Sorry." May slipped the car into park, collected her bag, and exited. Pete was already standing off to the side, looking a little weary.

"So," May asked the man, "how much?"

The attendant, who was gazing at May with unconcealed disgust, pointed at the huge wall sign with the times and amounts.

"Do I pay now or—"

"When you come back."

"Oh, right." She laughed. "Because that's how you'll know how long I've been gone. Okay. Great. Thanks."

So what if her pride was shot? Her sense of relief at being out of the car was immeasurable. She suddenly understood those stories of ship captains who dropped to their knees and kissed the sand once they hit shore.

"What are we doing?" Pete asked, looking down at her through his curly fringe. He was slouching a little more than usual.

"I have to go find an ATM to get some cash," she said.

"Why didn't you say so? I have some cash. Let's just get the car back."

"No," May said as she started walking briskly. "I'm not borrowing."

"Come on." Pete groaned. "Don't get like that."

"It's your fault we're here."

"*My* fault? You wouldn't park!"

" 'Straight line on 95!' " May mimicked. " 'It's like the *easiest thing in the world*.' "

May walked ahead, and Pete followed, somewhat grumpily. The area was fairly desolate since all of the office buildings, squares, and historical sites in the area generally emptied out at five or six. There seemed to be a thousand shadowy nooks behind trees, low brick walls, and deep doorways. Independence Hall loomed up on their right.

Okay, maybe this *was* her fault. But it wasn't so bad.

"Look!" She held up her hands. "Free field trip."

"Uh-huh. Maybe America's first ATM is in there."

"Look, I'm sorry, okay?"

Pete stared up at the side of Independence Hall and attempted to whistle. All that came out was a strange sputtering sound.

"They have blinds in the windows," May said, stopping and pointing up. "That seems wrong."

Splutter.

"I was just trying to keep your car in one piece. You can't blame me for that."

He switched over to humming.

They walked around Independence Square, which was filled with construction equipment. One lonely park ranger stood against the barricade that surrounded the area. He turned orange, red, and purple as the huge spotlight that sat on a tall building just beyond Independence Hall threw its light down on him. At the end was the Liberty Bell pavilion, a small glass structure that housed the world's most famous defective noisemaker.

"Remember coming here in grade school?" May asked as they looked across the square at the building.

"Yeah. I think we went about twelve times."

"I always thought they'd keep it someplace bigger . . . and look at this," she said. "It's a *shed*. And it's just a bell. It feels like such a rip-off."

"It *is* kind of a rip-off."

"Then why does everyone get so excited about it?" she asked.

"I have no idea."

"A lot of things seem like that," she said. "They build you up and build you up, and it's . . . a bell in a shed."

They examined the bell and its housing critically.

"So," May said, giving him a sideways glance, "speaking of big buildups, you haven't told me about the prom. Was it good?"

"It was all right."

"So are you and Nell *dating* now or something?"

"I don't know." He shrugged.

"How do you not know something like that?"

"We might go out again," he said. "But I haven't really dated anyone since Jenna."

"Jenna?" May said, throwing him a puzzled look. "You dated Jenna? Jenna Cazwell?"

"Yeah. All last fall."

Jenna Cazwell was an unrelentingly perky girl with huge boobs and an amazing singing voice. She had been in May's elementary and middle school classes.

"How did I not know this? How did that happen?"

"We worked on some shows together." Pete shrugged again. "Things happen when you do shows. And we liked a lot of the same stuff—same bands, same shows, same movies. She was really into movies, like me. Really specific stuff, too. Like we both like bad shark movies. She had *Jaws 4* and *Deep Blue Sea* on DVD. She even had *Shark Hunter*."

"Jenna Cazwell collects *shark movies*?" May said. This seemed about as likely to her as finding out that Jenna collected human bones.

"I know. I couldn't believe it either. She seemed perfect— but she was so—"

"Chestually blessed?" May offered.

Pete was wise enough not to reply to this.

"Jenna always reminded me of a stewardess," May said coolly, "with that creepy smile. And she was kind of dumb."

"Yeah, well, we're not all geniuses."

"What's that supposed to mean?"

"I didn't get a 200 on the PSATs like you did," he said,

looking just a little irritated. "I mean, I didn't think she was dumb."

"Two-oh-five . . . ," May mumbled automatically before catching herself. "It doesn't matter. So what happened?"

Pete didn't reply right away.

"We kind of . . . stopped calling each other."

"You stopped calling each other? That's it?"

"Kind of," he said, pulling on his watchband.

"That's weird."

"It happens that way sometimes," he said.

"God," May said, finding herself inexplicably annoyed by this new knowledge. "You're like crush boy. Nell, Jenna, Diana . . ."

She started walking again, a little faster this time. There was a strong horsey smell here, which was emphasized by the heat. May picked her way through the numerous knee-high concrete thumbs that had been planted all along this stretch of sidewalk, presumably to keep cars from crashing into the square, or maybe just to make life *that much* more difficult for people searching for ATMs in a historical zone. "That's not a lot," he said. "It's just that someone's there, so you date them."

May raised an eyebrow. She wasn't sure what this meant, but he seemed to be *saying something*.

"What about you?" he asked.

"What *about* me?"

"Do you . . . like anyone? I mean, you never mention it."

"All-girls' school." She smirked. "It's not happening."

"What about work?"

"It looks like you're already dating Nell. That totally breaks my heart."

He stopped moving for a moment. Pete was one of those people who had to freeze completely when he was turning something over in his mind.

"It's so hard for me to share her with anyone," she clarified quickly. "Come on. I guess we should be looking for the ATM."

Brooks managed to bum a ride home from the party, and she arrived home at the pathetic hour of nine o'clock. Only Palmer was home when she got there, and she was glued to the television as usual. Brooks sat alone at the kitchen table in the dark, looking down at May's books and notes, which were spread everywhere. She felt the dryness setting in. She needed hydration. She got up, threw open the refrigerator door, and eyed the empty water-filter pitcher.

"Does that thing *always* have to be empty?" she muttered. "Is it the *law*?"

There was nothing cold enough to drink. There were a few cans of warm soda, but the ice cube trays were also empty. She got some water from the kitchen tap, but it seemed to make her throat even scratchier. Her stomach was tumbling lightly now. She knew this was only a sign of the turbulence to come.

The Dave and Jamie movie was still playing on all screens inside her head, and now, as she thought about it, it was all getting weirder. She had shown Jamie the condoms. She had told Jamie her plans for the night. And what had Jamie done? Vamped herself up in bondage pants and planted herself in Dave's lap. In fact, Jamie had moved in before Brooks could do anything.

Jamie had screwed her over. She had done it intentionally.

Brooks drummed her fingers on the table. Then she got up and started pacing the kitchen. Her head was going to explode.

A glint across the room caught her eye. The key to the Golden Firebird hung from the key rack on the kitchen wall. The pewter key ring embossed with the logo, the key with the three colored triangles at the top . . .

She knew why no one had touched the car. It had never been said, but it had never needed saying. It was Dad's car. The car was where it had happened. The car was frozen in time—left, like a museum exhibit, commemorating the worst moment in all of their lives. Through the warm haze of grain punch, beer, insecticide, and whiskey, Brooks saw the absurdity of this. Dad wouldn't have wanted the Golden Firebird kept that way. He had loved that car, and the thought of it rotting away would have made him miserable.

It was her *duty* to take it out.

She grabbed the key, then lunged in the direction of the garage door.

The long fluorescent lights blinked on in segments and sizzled a bit before lighting completely. There it was—all dull, heavy gold, a beast from a different time. There was the black vinyl top. The headlights that reminded her of frog eyes. The huge backseat where she and May used to sit and have kicking wars.

As she approached the car, she had the weird sensation of breaking through an invisible barrier, like an electrical dog fence. The shock was internal, very deep. It repulsed her and charged her at the same time. The Golden Firebird had been waiting here for a long time, wanting to take her wherever she wanted to go. It had been sleeping.

Brooks crossed around to the driver's side. The door was unlocked. She opened it slowly but waited a moment before getting in. This was *the place*. The actual spot where he had passed from living to dead . . .

She couldn't think about it that way. Besides, years of athletics had hardwired one fact into Brooks's brain: On the field, you don't hesitate. You decide, and then you do. So she had decided, and now she had to act. If she stood there and thought about it all night, nothing would ever happen.

She dropped down into the driver's seat. It was very far back. (Her dad had been six-foot five, after all.) She reached around the side of the seat and found the crank that moved it forward. The inside of the car seemed a bit strange to her now, after an absence of a year. It was a world of cream-colored vinyl. It had ashtrays and a bench seat. Nothing aerodynamic or sleek about the inside of this monster. The radio was ancient, ridiculous. Nothing digital. Huge knobs for the lights. Cold bits of metal. There were some things of her father's on the floor—his gym bag, a plastic container that must have held his lunch, a newspaper. She used her foot to push them a little farther under the shadow of the dashboard.

Brooks looked at the key in her hand and the outstretched wings of the embossed Firebird on the key chain. Her father had always told her it was good luck to touch the key chain, so before games she would always "pet the birdie."

She stroked it once and put the key into the ignition.

Nothing.

She tried again. Still nothing.

Luckily her father had at least taught her something about

the car. She got out and reached under the front bumper for the hood release, then popped it to have a look. The problem was, fortunately, one she'd been taught how to identify—corrosion on the battery terminals.

When she looked up, Palmer was standing in the doorway. She didn't speak.

"What?" Brooks spat. "I'm fixing the car."

"Why?"

"Because," Brooks said, as if the point were self-evident, "it's got stuff on the battery."

"Why are you fixing it now?"

"Go watch TV."

Palmer didn't move.

"Or just stand there," Brooks said. "I don't care."

Palmer stood there. Brooks retrieved a can of cola from the supply shelf. She cracked it open and poured the contents over the terminals.

"Why are you pouring soda into the car?" Palmer asked. Her round face was pulled into a very dark scowl. Her hair was pulled up in a lopsided ponytail. She cocked her head, as if it were weighed down by the imbalance.

"I told you already," Brooks said, leaning down and keeping her eyes on the battery. "Go take a shower or something."

"I took a shower. . . ."

Brooks grinned as the corrosion bubbled away. She closed the hood and jumped back into the driver's seat. After waiting a moment she tried the engine again. This time there was a growling, grumbling noise. The engine seemed to be in the process of deciding whether or not it was going to fully engage.

Brooks felt it rumbling under her, alternating between a steady purr and a dying cough. Suddenly there was a familiar if alarming smell, and a steel gray cloud of fumes came seeping up from the back. Life rippled through the Firebird, and the engine became loud and steady.

"Okay," she said, wincing, "I'm never drinking that again. . . ."

"What are you doing?" Palmer shouted over the engine.

"Nothing. Go back inside."

"You're drunk."

"I'm fine," Brooks shouted. "Go inside!"

After snapping on her lap belt, she took hold of the thin steering wheel, adjusted the rearview mirror, and slowly began backing the Firebird out of the garage. The wheel turned stiffly, and the sheer length of the car's back end was intimidating. You could *feel* this car.

Palmer stood in the open doorway of the garage, watching her go.

When Brooks started down the road, the acceleration pushed her against her seat. The Firebird seemed to despise low speeds, and it became easier to drive whenever she went a little faster. No wonder her dad had felt so manly driving this thing.

She reached for the radio dial and switched it on. The signal was weak, just long silences broken by deafening crackle. Single words boomed out of newscasts. Jolting snatches of songs. Frustrated, she gave the knob a hard spin and got a weird range of feedback. She held the car steady on the road with one hand as she worked the tuner furiously with the other. Scratches of noise—blips. A little more pressure from one finger . . . carefully. It required absolute precision, like safecracking. Minute turns now. Microscopic.

A horribly loud *whooping* sound filled the air. Brooks jumped back and let go of the dial. Punishing static noise blasted through the car. She slapped at the knob to turn the thing off. As she did so, she caught a swirling vibration of light out of the corner of her eye and jerked her head up and looked into the rearview mirror. There was a police car just a few feet behind her, and it was the one making the unpleasant sound.

Pete drove on the way back from the city. As if trying to exact some revenge for what he'd been put through on the ride through the city, he spent the entire return trip talking like Yoda. He seemed to enjoy watching May flinch with every "Annoyed you look" and "Irritating you, am I?" After the first fifteen minutes she got the impression that he wasn't even doing it consciously anymore—that he had just gotten stuck and couldn't stop himself.

"Hear me can you?" Pete asked as he turned off 95.

May flicked him on the shoulder with her finger. Pete switched on the radio and adjusted a nickel that he had taped to the face of the dial.

"Works this does. Ask me why do not."

May concentrated on the music until they pulled up in front of the house and he spoke in a normal voice.

"That's weird," he said.

"What is? Talking like a human?"

"Palmer's out front."

Sure enough, Palmer was sitting on the low, flat step in front of the screen door. May felt her nerves tingling. There was something very not right about this. Palmer got up and walked over to meet the two of them.

"Brooks," she said.

"What about her?"

"She took the car."

"What?" May shook her head, not understanding. "Mom took the car."

"No," Palmer said, pointing to the empty garage. "The Firebird."

May got out of Pete's car and walked to the garage as if to prove to herself that the Firebird was really gone. She stood in the space that it had occupied for the last year. The void was weird, almost mesmerizing. The garage was suddenly huge.

"Where did she go?" May asked.

"She said she was just going to get some Gatorade."

"She took the Firebird for Gatorade?"

"She poured soda into the engine, too," Palmer added, pointing to the case of generic cola on the shelf behind May.

"Probably for the battery," Pete said, coming up behind them and looking around for himself.

Both Palmer and May turned and stared at him as if he had suddenly started speaking in Portuguese.

"Coke can loosen things up," he explained. "Get rid of buildup on the battery nodes."

"How long has she been gone?" May asked.

"About two hours."

"Two hours?"

"She was drunk," Palmer said. "I'm pretty sure."

May exhaled heavily and paced the room. She plucked a

canister of WD-40 from one of the shelves and shook it violently, listening to the little metallic rattle.

"I can go look for her," Pete offered. "Drive around."

"There's no point," May said. "Two hours. She could be anywhere."

She continued to walk around the room, seemingly looking for something that would explain it all—where Brooks was, why she had committed this insane act of treachery. Something that could put the Firebird back just as it was, just as it had been for the last year. But nothing was there but half-used containers of car cleaners, a few tools, some rags in a bucket, some shelves of old junk. Palmer lingered by Pete's side, keeping about a foot away but moving whenever he moved, as if he were a magnet pulling her around. She looked at him searchingly, but since he had no explanation either, he could only shrug.

"Okay," May finally said, "I'll give her another half hour. Then I guess we can drive around and look. She's probably over at Dave or Jamie's or something. . . ."

A car approached the house. It pulled in behind Pete's Cutlass, under the heavy shadow of the Starks' oak tree. May could see that there was writing on the door and sirens on the roof. A large man in a dark uniform got out of the front seat.

"No," May said, almost to herself. "There's no way. . . ."

Palmer shot off in the direction of the car. May and Pete followed, almost cautiously. With every step the scene came into clearer focus, and May's fears were confirmed. The car was a police cruiser, and Brooks was being unloaded from the backseat. She had no handcuffs on. Her makeup was smeared.

A husky officer was standing by the door, watching May and Pete approach and basically ignoring Palmer.

"Are you her brother?" he asked Pete.

"No." Pete shook his head. "I'm—"

"I'm her sister," May offered, pulling herself up straight. "What's going on?"

"Your mother is on her way," he said. "Is your father home?"

"No. He's . . . no. Not home."

"She's been processed," the officer went on. "Will you both be here until your mom gets home?"

By both he seemed to be indicating May and Pete.

"Yes." May nodded. "I will. . . ."

The officer looked to Pete.

"Sure," Pete said. "I'll be here."

"All right. Here are your forms." The officer passed Brooks a number of pink and white papers. "Call that number on Monday morning."

Brooks took the papers silently.

"Where's the car?" May managed to ask. "Our car?"

"It's at the police lot," the officer explained. "One of your parents can get it out tomorrow. I circled the address on that yellow sheet there."

"Right," May said.

"Wait here," he said to Brooks. He walked back around and got in his car, leaving the door hanging open. He spent a few minutes talking into his radio. All four of them stood silently, listening to the muffled codes and chatter from inside the car. Brooks stared at the ground. Then the officer climbed out and leaned over the roof.

"We're good," he said. "You'll stay here, Brooks, with your sister and—"

The "and" was Pete. Palmer was still invisible.

"Okay," Brooks said.

"Remember what I told you."

"I remember."

"Okay."

Without another word, he got back in his car and pulled away.

"What was that?" May asked, even though she felt like she probably already understood.

"I'm going in," Brooks said.

"It's a DUI." May sighed. "Isn't it?"

"I'm going in," Brooks repeated, heading toward the house. Palmer trailed along behind her.

When they were gone, May looked around and saw curtains being drawn back discreetly in the house across the street. The Stark boys were standing in their screen door, unabashedly staring. Once again, she realized, the Golds were the neighborhood show. She walked over to Pete's car and slid down the side to the ground, leaning against the tire, where she couldn't be seen. Pete came over and stood with her, pushing his hands deep into the pockets of his long army green shorts.

"It had to be a DUI," May said. "She gets that look when she's drunk. Kind of glassy."

"Is she drunk a lot?"

"A couple of nights a week."

"What do you mean by a couple of nights a week?"

"Two, three. Maybe more."

"Does she have some kind of problem?"

May stared at Pete as if she didn't understand the question. Asking her if Brooks had a problem was kind of like asking her if rain was wet.

"Does your mom know?"

"I don't think so," May said. "Brooks leaves after she goes to work."

"Did you ever tell her?"

"My mom's got enough problems," May said, picking up a twig and snapping it into several small pieces. "What am I supposed to do? She hates working nights as it is. Do I tell her that Brooks gets wasted all the time and that Palmer stays up all night watching TV? Great. She can feel even worse."

"She's going to know now."

"This is just what Brooks is like," May said, her exasperation growing. "Everybody knows it. You know it. My mom knows it, but she doesn't want to deal with it. Besides, no one yells at Brooks. Probably not even this time."

May listened to the cicadas chirp for a moment and stared at the yawning space in the garage, the spot where the car had been.

"I must sound pathetic," she said.

"What?"

"It's just that this is it. This is my life. I go to school, and I go to work. Someone has to be the good one, you know? I'm the good one. Which pretty much means I'm the boring one. No boyfriend. No life. Nothing."

She exhaled deeply and turned to look at him. She noticed that his nose was just slightly crooked. It had been broken twice when he was younger—once when he'd played Superman and tried to fly down the steps and again when he'd ridden a shopping cart through the grocery store parking lot like a skateboard. He had a personal understanding of stupid behavior and its consequences.

"I'm fine with it," she continued. "It sounds really sad now, I know, but I have a plan. College. I can do fun stuff in college, when I don't live here. I just have to get in and get a scholarship."

"So you can't have fun now?" he asked.

"I have fun," May clarified. "I just don't have as much fun as some other people, like Brooks. And Palm's happy as long as she's playing softball. She doesn't even notice anything else."

"I don't know," he said. "Palm always noticed things. She's really aware of stuff—what people are doing."

"Well, yeah. She listens in on conversations when you don't want her to. But she's still a lot like Brooks. She's clueless. Like she'll spill her soda everywhere and just stare at it. It doesn't occur to her to wipe it up. Things don't *occur* to my sisters because it was always different with them. My dad would yell at me for taking too long in the bathroom, but if Brooks burned the house down, that would be okay. He'd probably get some marshmallows or something. Everything she did was great as far as he was concerned. Brooks was like the son he never had."

As she was speaking, May felt herself getting angrier and angrier. The Firebird's absence was starting to give her an actual ache. She pulled her knees tight into her chest. It was a minute or two before she noticed that Pete was holding her hand. It wasn't a dramatic gesture. He was sitting cross-legged, leaning forward on his elbows, looking at her. It took her another minute still to realize that she didn't mind and that it actually made her feel a bit better. She didn't, however, want to call attention to the fact, so she just went on as if she was unaware of it.

"Anyway," she said, "I just wanted you to know that I'm consciously pathetic. It's all part of my plan. My escape-to-college plan."

"You're not pathetic," Pete said, somewhat unexpectedly. May didn't know what to say to that. A silence settled over them for a few minutes.

"I'm sorry you had to be here for this," she said. "Sorry for the drama."

She felt his grip on her hand tighten slightly.

"What is this *processing*?" she said. "'She's been *processed*.' I guess that's police-speak, but what the hell does it mean? She's not cheese."

May heard a car spinning around the corner. They both looked up and saw the minivan racing toward them. She casually took her hand from Pete's, as if sitting in the driveway holding hands was something she did every day, then rubbed her face and got up.

"Here we go," she said.

"I guess I should leave."

Before Pete could make his getaway, however, the minivan screeched to a stop in front of the house. May's mom, clad in pink scrubs, raced across the lawn. She went right to the opening of the empty garage, looking as confused as May had been. Pete froze in his tracks, looking unsure about his next move.

"We can get the car in the morning, Mom," May said quietly. "And she's been processed or whatever."

Her mother didn't answer—not in English, anyway. Whenever May's mom got really mad, she started speaking in rapid-fire Dutch to herself. She never told anyone what she was saying, but May was pretty sure that it was some seriously unrepeatable, melt-the-paint-off-the-walls swearing. The Dutch was flying freely now, all *j*'s and hocking sounds.

Pete backed up a few feet and gave May an I'm-going-to-go nod.

"Pete." May's mom finally noticed that Pete had been there the whole time. "This is . . ."

She shook her head and paced in the driveway.

"What happened?" May asked cautiously. "What was she arrested for?"

Before she could answer, Palmer came down and joined the group.

"Brooks is in her room," she reported. "I think she's still pretty drunk."

With the Dutch still trailing from her lips, their mother headed inside with a determined stride.

"You're still here," Palmer said, staring at Pete.

"I was leaving." He walked around to the driver's side of his car. He gave May another nod, and she acknowledged this with a nod of her own. Palmer observed this silent exchange, then watched as Pete drove away.

"What were you guys doing?" Palmer asked, cocking her head like a little kid.

"Talking."

"About what?"

"What do *you* think?"

"You guys were holding hands."

May felt her face flush.

"God, Palm," she said, heading for the door. "What's *with* you?"

"Well, you were," Palmer replied to her sister's retreating figure.

When May had gone inside, Palmer stood for a minute on the lawn and looked up at the house, wondering why all activity always seemed to stop whenever she came near.

Brooks's sentencing took place late on Tuesday afternoon, in the middle of a torrential downpour. She sat in the court, carefully dressed in a turtleneck (May's) and a pair of khakis. The room, to her surprise, was just a small, plain space in the middle of a huge office building. It had no windows, and everything—the walls, the judge's bench, the seats—was made of the same dark wood. No imposing columns or marble, no paintings. Her mother sat next to her, stony faced.

The memory from the bedroom still stung her, even now, as she faced the bench. She could still see their reflection in the dark television—the three of them. Dave rolling over so easily, Jamie so willingly. The last two days at school Dave had been amazingly evasive. He didn't even show up to study hall. Every time Brooks saw Jamie, she had somewhere to be, immediately. She'd never had much to say to Fred, and the rest of Dave's friends were strangers to her. So she was alone.

A bailiff came in and ordered them all to rise.

The judge walked into the room, and then they all sat down. She took a few moments to shuffle through some papers in front of her.

"Brooke . . . ," the judge read. "No. Brooks? Is it Brooks, with an *s* on the end? Is this right?"

The stenographer paused. Brooks and her mother nodded.

"*Brooks* Gold," she repeated.

Brooks steeled herself, then walked to the small podium that the bailiff pointed her to.

The process took little time. Charges were read. When asked, she pled guilty to underage drinking and driving under the influence, as the family attorney had advised her to do. She hadn't thought you were just supposed to plead guilty. On television everyone always fought or entered some crazy reason that all the evidence has to be thrown out. But Brooks had nothing to say in her own defense. She'd been speeding. They'd done a Breathalyzer. She was underage. End of story.

The judge was not going to care that she'd just seen her boyfriend cheat on her from two feet away—with her best friend. It didn't matter that she hadn't hurt anyone or that she'd just wanted to take the Firebird to get something to drink. That it had been hard to take the Firebird, but she'd done it. She'd liberated it. Now anyone could drive it. May had even taken it for a test run to the store with her mom.

Nope. The state of Pennsylvania did not care about any of that.

Her license was immediately revoked for the year. She was remanded to a counselor who would evaluate her substance abuse. She would be referred for treatment. She was fined three hundred dollars. She was directed to check in with the court clerk on her way out.

Brooks had known this was coming; the lawyer had advised her that this was the likely sentence. It meant no driving until November, so the summer was shot. All the money she'd earn at the pool would pay for the fine and the treatment. She could deal with that, but Dave and Jamie . . .

The judge banged her gavel. At least that seemed authentic and final.

May watched the rain that flooded the parking lot outside of Presto.

"So I was on top of him, right, and then we heard the door open. . . ." Nell paused. "Do you know how Pete's house is laid out?"

May nodded, defeated.

"Okay, so we hear his parents, and they're coming up the stairs. Then we remembered that I'd hung my shirt on the doorknob before we shut the door, so my shirt is like hanging in the hallway, like a flag. . . ."

For the last half hour Nell had been pouring out every clinical detail of the events of the previous night. Apparently quite a bit had happened since the conversation she'd had with Pete on Saturday, during which he hadn't even seemed sure that he'd see Nell again. Whatever pet theories Linda had had about Pete holding out for his one true love . . . they were out the window. Pete was waiting for nothing.

May didn't particularly need this news right now. For three days she'd been listening to the wailing and crying and slamming doors that had echoed through the house since Brooks's arrest. In the last two days she'd been dragged through her German, history, and trig finals and had finished her English paper on three female British novelists. She still had to finish getting ready for the most terrifying exam of all: the biology exam, which she would be taking in the morning. She'd barely gotten any sleep. And now she knew the unabridged biblical truth about Nell and Pete's relationship.

In short, she was in hell.

"So Pete completely freaks out. He jumps out of bed and puts his boxers on. . . ."

Sheets of rain battered the windows. May wanted to run out into the storm, swinging something large and metallic over her head until the lightning got her and frizzled up her brain, wiping all of this information away forever.

". . . and jumps for the door and just manages to grab the shirt. It was hilarious. Can you imagine his mom catching us like that?"

"No," May answered honestly.

"It's good that you're so cool about this," Nell said. "I mean, it bothers some people to hear about their friends dating. Some people get so weirded out."

"It's fine," May said as she watched the pansies in the flower box outside getting crushed by the torrent. "Why would it bother me?"

Later that night May bunched herself into a corner of her bed and tried to imprint the following sentence into her head: *The Krebs cycle, also known as the citric acid or the tricarboxylic acid (TCA) cycle, is the second of three steps involved in carbohydrate catabolism.*

"He said he'd call when he could, but it's been three days . . . ," Brooks was saying.

For the past year Brooks had more or less shut May out of

her personal business. She had chosen this moment to break her silence, as her exams weren't for another week—not that May was expecting her to do much studying then, either. She had stationed herself at the foot of May's bed and had been talking nonstop for the last fifteen minutes.

The Krebs cycle, also known as the Dave-has-not-called cycle, is the second of three steps involved in my going insane if she doesn't shut up. Oh my God . . .

"Three days," Brooks went on, rocking back and forth slightly. "What does that mean? Three days? What do you think I should do?"

"I don't know," May said, keeping her eyes trained on the page. "Call him, I guess."

"You think I should?"

"Um, yeah. Sure."

"It's that thing with Jamie," Brooks mumbled, chomping at her nails.

"What?" May asked.

"I didn't tell you about that."

May gripped the edge of her book. One more tangent and she would definitely go down a full grade.

"Brooks," she said with a sigh, "I do care. I really do. But do you see this?" She held up the book. "I am going to be up all night. I have an exam at nine in the morning. Could we maybe talk tomorrow?"

Brooks looked shocked, as if she'd just been slapped.

"God, you're so selfish."

"*I'm* selfish?" May shook her head. "You didn't just say that."

Brooks slid off the bed without comment and stalked out of the room, slamming the door behind her.

When May emerged from her room two hours later, she saw Brooks sitting on her bed, listening to her CD player and staring at the wall. (Brooks had blue-and-white-striped wallpaper, which, though much cooler than May's pink ponyland paper, gave her walls the unfortunate appearance of bars on a jail cell.) Brooks looked up as she passed, and May felt obligated to stick her head in.

"Did you call him?" May asked after Brooks slipped off her headphones.

Brooks didn't reply.

"Are you okay?" May asked. "What happened?"

"I called Jamie," Brooks said, her voice raspy.

"What did she say?"

"They're dating now."

"Dave and Jamie?"

Brooks nodded and pushed the advance button on her CD player a few times.

"I'm sorry," May said, running her finger along the edge of the door frame. "What happened?"

"Jamie says that he and I were never dating," Brooks said. "Not officially."

"Not officially? What does that mean?"

"We never said it. *He* never said it." Brooks smirked. "It wasn't official. So it was okay for him to sleep with Jamie."

"Dave slept with Jamie?"

"That's what he said."

The logical side of May's brain was sending her urgent

messages, telling her that she didn't have time to stop and talk to Brooks right now, that it was partially Brooks's fault that she was so behind. But the sight of her sister slumped up against her headboard, her hair hanging limply over her shoulders, looking as defeated as May had ever seen her—it seemed bad enough to merit taking a few minutes away. May came over and sat at the foot of Brooks's bed.

"Do you want anything?" May asked quietly.

"No."

May heard a gentle plunking sound. She glanced over to see water dripping down into a trash can in the corner of the room.

"Your ceiling's leaking again," she said, looking at the yellowing spot that the water was coming from.

"Why do you think I put that there?"

She was cranky as ever, but May could see tears welling up in Brooks's eyes. She got up and moved to where Brooks was sitting. Aside from the funeral and when they were small, May had never seen Brooks cry. It was a little bizarre. May reached out to put a hand on her sister's shoulder, but Brooks turned to her with a decidedly unfriendly expression.

"Just go, okay?" she said.

"I was just—"

"Go."

"Fine," May said. She felt a little stung. Only Brooks could make her feel bad for something like that.

Brooks put her headphones back on and May got up and left. Back in her room, the television roared up from below. May rubbed her eyes and kept reading.

*   *   *

May took a minute to buy herself a soft pretzel and a soda for breakfast from a cart on the corner of Thirty-fourth and Chestnut, right around the corner from school. It was a sharp, crisp morning with a bright blue sky. Because she had only slept for a couple hours the night before, she was overtaken by that strange trembling and hyperawareness that comes from pulling an all-nighter.

She saw Linda coming down the street from the direction of the subway. She looked just as exhausted as May. She had on her thin, rimless glasses instead of her contacts, and she walked quickly, pulling her sweater tight against her chest.

"You sleep?" Linda asked as she approached May.

"An hour and a half."

"I think I slept two," Linda said, accepting a piece of May's pretzel.

"Brooks was having a crisis," May explained as they walked down Walnut through the throngs of Penn students hurrying to their morning classes.

"About her court thing?"

"No. About her boyfriend. That guy Dave."

"What's going on with him?"

"He dumped her," May said. "And she has to go for counseling, starting tonight."

"Not a good time to be Brooks," Linda said, reaching for May's soda and taking a long sip. "You're still coming over to my place afterward, right?"

"I'm thinking about moving in."

"Fine by me," Linda said. "I could get rid of Frank that way."

*   *   *

The biology exam was twenty-two pages long and included five diagrams and three essay questions. May worked until the very last minute, furiously scribbling out her final sentences. It was an extensive, somewhat painful test, but May had known all of the material. The only problem was time. If she'd had four or five hours to finish it, she would have been a lot more content.

Linda stumbled up to May's seat.

"I think I just got my Ph.D.," she said.

Dazed, they headed out of the building, toward the subway.

Linda's house, one of the only ones on the block built after 1776, was in a small gated area called Independence Mews. Each floor had only one or two rooms. The kitchen and laundry room took up the whole basement level. The living room (with the wood-burning stove that May loved) was on the first floor. The bedrooms were on the next two floors. Everything was cozy and compact.

Since they were both completely exhausted, they headed right up to the third floor, where Frank and Linda's rooms were.

"Is Frank here?" May said quietly as they passed his door. She had never actually seen Frank—he was kind of like the Easter Bunny to her.

"No," Linda said, pushing open her door. "He's doing some kind of big experiment with gasoline today. Maybe he'll blow himself up."

Though it was extremely tiny, Linda's room always awed May. One of her walls was a bright violet, and the other three were cream. Her slender window was guarded by purple blinds, and a large round paper shade covered the overhead light. The bed was in a metal frame and covered in a thick cream-colored duvet. Aside from her desk chair, the only place to sit was in a pile of multicolored cushions in the corner. Linda set herself down in these.

"I'm seriously going to die," Linda said. "You can take the bed. I'll be fine here. I sleep here all the time."

Linda leaned back on the cushions. May kicked off her shoes and climbed up the metal rungs. Linda's cream-colored duvet was very thick and soft, and May sank into it appreciatively.

"So," Linda said, "it's over."

This should have filled May with elation, but for some reason, it didn't. School gave her life some structure. She didn't want to think about another long summer stretching out in front of her.

"Have you seen Pete?" Linda asked.

"Not since Saturday," May said, burrowing into the thick folds. "But I've heard about him. Ask me how much I've heard."

"You sound bitter," Linda said, propping herself up. "You got details, didn't you?"

"Kind of."

"Bad?"

"I feel . . . unclean."

"Unclean? Or jealous?"

"The weirdest part is that I got this feeling like it wasn't even the first time," May said. "He's been dating her for what, not even a month? I mean, what the hell?"

"He's sleeping with her? Who told you? Pete or Nell?"

"Nell."

"Are you sure she's not lying?"

"I don't think so," May said. "She described the inside of his house."

"They had sex inside his house?"

"Maybe we should talk about this later," May said. Before, when she'd found this out, she'd just thought it was weird. Now that the exam was over, the facts were starting to sink in, and they were immeasurably depressing.

"May?"

"Yeah?"

"You're bummed, aren't you?"

"Kind of."

May rolled to the side of the bunk and looked down at Linda.

"The other night," she said, "when Brooks got busted—Pete stayed with me. He sat with me and . . ."

"And?"

"Well, he just held my hand. But it was weird. It felt kind of huge."

"Huge?"

"Yeah," May said, hanging her head over the edge. "Sucks, doesn't it?"

"No," Linda said. "He likes you. You like him."

"If he likes me so much, why is he sleeping with a girl I work with?"

"It could be that he thinks he has no shot with you."

"I guess that's one way of handling rejection. . . ."

"Think about it," Linda said. "Before you knew that he dated this other girl and that he was sleeping with Nell, you never seemed to think of him like he was a guy. Now you seem to. So maybe it's good."

"Good how?" May grumbled, rolling onto her back and propping her feet against the ceiling. "Good for making me feel jealous and pathetic?"

"Talk to him."

"And say what?" May asked. "I can't compete with Nell. I'm not ready for that yet."

Linda fell silent. May listened to the traffic passing by out on Locust Street.

"If it really bothers you, maybe you should stay away from him for a while," Linda suggested. "I mean, if you're not going to do anything about it, why torture yourself?"

"Stay away?" This hadn't occurred to May before. "I'd have to stop the lessons."

"It sounds like you're almost ready anyway."

"Maybe you're right," May said, closing her eyes. "Maybe I need to do this one on my own."

Palmer was completely alone in the house that night. She didn't mind. She planned on taking advantage of that fact to conduct her most thorough examination of her mother's room yet—she was going to do the top shelves of the walk-in closet.

She started by carefully removing her mother's shoe boxes and sweaters, arranging them on the floor exactly as they'd been set up on the shelf so she would be able to put everything back as it had been. As she had expected, she hit a gold mine. There were yearbooks, photo albums, a heavy crate of vinyl records. She spread herself out on the bed and took a long look through everything.

The most interesting items could be found in the photo albums. These were early ones, from when her parents had started dating. She spent a good two hours paging through them. There was her mom in leather pants and ripped shirts and Halloween-like makeup; then there she was in her nursing school uniform, looking demure. There was her dad, with the same goofy face he made in every picture—his huge eyes popping open and the strange grin that obscured his bottom teeth. There he was with his college roommate Richard Camp at a toga party. There he was, eighteen years old, posing in front of the Firebird, which he had just purchased.

These pictures fascinated Palmer. The idea that her parents had had lives before she and her sisters had come along—totally different lives—was hard for her to believe. The pictures had been taken in front of bars, in dorm rooms, in hallways at parties. Her dad with a beer in one hand, his other arm wrapped all the way around her mom's tiny waist. She could see the slow change as she flipped through. Her mother cut back on the makeup; her father grew a little larger. There were pictures of them in cutoff jeans and T-shirts (her mother's pregnant belly proudly popping out) getting Brooks's room ready. Then there was May, with the head of red hair she'd been born with. And then the picture labeled *Me and Peach*. That was her father holding her when she'd just been born. She looked incredibly tiny in her father's arms; he practically had her resting in one of his hands.

After a couple of hours, Palmer started packing up. As she replaced the items on their shelf, she realized the shoe box she was holding was very heavy. She took off the lid. Inside she found a bronze canister, shaped like a vase. In small block letters along the bottom was an engraving that read *Michael Scott Gold.*

For a moment Palmer thought she'd found a strange trophy. Then it hit her. These were the ashes.

Time stopped moving for Palmer for about ten minutes.

Palmer took the canister from the box and willed herself to walk over and set it gently against the pillows on her father's side of the bed. She stared at it. She couldn't put it back, not up there in a shoe box in the back of the closet. It was impossible.

No. She had to take care of the canister. It was her job now.

She hurriedly replaced all of the other items in the closet, including the empty shoe box. When everything was as it had been before, she plucked the canister up and quickly took it to her room.

Without the burden of having to study, May had no problem sleeping in on the first few days of the summer. She had to be at Presto at three, so she lay in bed until eleven, basking in the cool breeze from her clickity oscillating fan.

When she came downstairs, she found her mother sitting at the table in a pair of black running pants and a black T-shirt. There was a box of doughnuts on the table. May eyed them. Her mom must have picked them up on the way back from dropping Brooks off at the pool for work. Her mother never bought doughnuts unless she had something unpleasant to tell them.

"Doughnuts?" she said. "Okay. What's going on?"

"Well," her mother said, casually piling up a stack of laundry detergent coupons, "the Starks offered us something."

"One of their boys? Say no. We don't have any Ritalin to give them."

"Their RV. It turns out they rented a spot at a campground in Ocean City, Maryland, for a few days, starting on the first of July, but they can't use it."

RV? May's mind tried to connect these letters to an object, but the only thing she could come up with was one of those extremely large trailers.

"A what?"

"Like a Winnebago. They keep it at Bonnie's mother's house."

"But that's so soon," May said.

"I know."

"I have work," May said, sitting down with her coffee. "Brooks has work, and she has her alcohol awareness classes. And Palmer has her softball camp. We can't go then."

"You can take off. Brooks can take off, and we can work around her class schedule. Palmer can miss a few practices."

"But why?"

"We need to spend some time together," her mother said, peering at the coupons. "I think we need to regroup a little."

"But we've never been camping," May said slowly, taking a chocolate doughnut from the box. "I mean, we don't even know *how* to camp."

"I know how to camp. I went camping when I was younger, and your father and I used to go."

"You used to *camp*?"

"Sure." Her mom nodded. "Why do you seem so surprised?"

"How did you keep your hair spiky in the woods? Did you have to use maple sap or something?"

"It wasn't that spiky. And I just used to tie it back under a bandanna."

"Punk-rock nurse in the wild, using her hair to trap small animals . . ."

"New wave, not punk," her mother corrected. "Anyway, you'll love it. We'll camp right on the beach."

"We're going to park a huge RV on the beach?" May asked. "Won't it . . . sink?"

"The park is next to the beach. It's paved."

Palmer passed through the kitchen and grabbed a doughnut

from the box. She was about to leave, but her mom caught her by the sleeve of her shirt.

"What?" Palmer growled.

"Just explain that it's a family emergency," her mom said to May.

"But it's *not* a family emergency."

"What's not a family emergency?" Palmer yawned and took a bite of her doughnut.

"Going to Maryland in an RV," May said.

Even Palmer couldn't ignore something like that. "Mwhuh?" she replied as she chewed her doughnut.

"On July first," May added.

"Mhwha?"

"To Maryland! They have crabs there!" their mom suddenly jumped in, as if the presence of crustaceans would transform the prospect of spending days trapped together in a parking lot into a living dream.

"Mom," May said, "RVs are enormous. They're like houses. How are you going to drive something like that to Maryland?"

"It'll be fine," Mom said. "They explained everything to me. And it's gorgeous. They took me through it. It has a bathroom, and a shower, and a TV, and everything."

"That's when my summer session starts," Palmer finally said. "I can't go."

"I'm not asking you, I am telling you. We need some time together, and we are going. It's up to each of you to get yourselves ready to go."

"I'm supposed to take the driver's exam . . . ," May said.

"You'll take it when we get back. Or take it before you go. It will be fine."

Palmer leaned against the counter, chomping furiously on her doughnut. When she was finished, she left the room without a word.

Palmer stalked into the backyard. It wasn't a great idea to go and exercise with a fat doughnut still sitting in her stomach, but she had to do something.

She bent her knees just slightly and hung herself down over her toes until she could easily straighten out her legs and put her palms on the ground. The grass was already dry and warm, and there was a fat bee buzzing around nearby.

She knew perfectly well that the girls who got on the professional teams, the Olympic teams, and the good college teams all went to camps and had personal coaches. She was way, way behind. Her dad had known all about this. You needed to be serious about it; otherwise, you were just another girl with a pile of worthless school trophies and a few pictures in the sports pages in the yearbook. Brooks's entire dresser was filled with trophies—what had they gotten her? Now the only thing Brooks did was lifeguard at the pool. It was pathetic.

As she hung upside down, she saw her mother coming out the back door with her cup of coffee in her hand. Palmer gracefully moved her right foot back into a lunge and pretended not to notice her.

"Do you have a second, Palm?"

"No," Palmer said, reversing her feet and stepping back with her left.

"You seem mad."

Palmer deepened her lunge and concentrated on stretching out her inner thigh.

"It's only a few days. And I thought you liked the beach."

"I start summer session then," Palmer said simply.

"You'll only miss three days."

"We play our first game for the scouts on the sixth," Palmer said.

"We'll be back by then."

"But I won't have time to get ready!"

"It's just a game," her mom said. "You know how to play. You'll be fine. Then you can start the session on Monday."

"Why do we have to go now?"

"Because that's when the Starks have the space," her mother said. "They're doing us a favor."

Palmer shook her head. Her mom just didn't get it.

"I'm going to go run," she said.

"Our lives don't revolve around softball, Palmer," her mother said, irritation creeping into her voice. "I'm sorry if this doesn't fit your schedule the way you'd like, but that's not the only thing we have to consider."

Palmer walked away from her out of the yard. As she passed through the house, she saw May still sitting at the table.

"I don't really want to go either," May said.

"It won't hurt you," Palmer spat. "You'll just miss work."

She continued on her way to the front door and headed out to the street.

The day before the trip May was in the basement, staring down into a laundry basket full of her sisters' dirty underwear and listening to the rhythmic thumping of the load she had just put into the dryer. There was a heavy fabric softener smell in the air, and she realized that she had forgotten to clean out the lint trap.

It was nine o'clock at night, and she'd just gotten off an eleven-hour shift. To compensate for the time she would be gone, May had managed to squeeze in fifty hours at work over the last four and a half days. Technically, this wasn't legal, but she'd managed to quietly swap out with people on the side. She had only "officially" been there for thirty-two hours; the rest of the time she'd entered someone else's work code into the cash register. During her absence some of her shifts would be covered in the same way.

The overtime meant that even if she'd wanted to, she'd had almost no time to see Pete. She hadn't even spoken to him in almost two weeks. He had called several times, but she'd never called back.

The idea, of course, was that this separation was going to make things easier for May. In reality, it made things much worse. She'd found that it was becoming harder and harder to listen to Nell talking about him. There was no way to deny it. She missed him, and not being around him was weird.

She stared at the bits of broken elastic zinging up from the waistband of one of Brooks's blue thongs.

"Why I am doing this?" she suddenly said out loud. "This is Brooks's job."

She grabbed the basket, marched up the basement steps, and went into the living room, where Palmer and Brooks were silently watching a baseball game. She dropped it to the floor.

"You do this," she said.

"What?" Brooks said, not looking over.

"This is your job," May said. "You do it."

"We've already done our stuff," Brooks said, turning to May. "We had to clean out the garage and get all of the dishes and chairs and beach stuff ready. We're done."

"But this is *your job*, remember? I've been doing it for weeks because you haven't."

"Like I said, I'm done."

"Well . . ." May kicked the basket in her direction. "I've done the first two loads of stuff. Now I guess it just depends on how much you want underwear for the next five days."

She walked away, feeling a strange adrenaline rush. She went upstairs to her room, closed the door, sank down on her shaggy rose-colored carpet, and picked up the phone. Before she could think it over, she dialed Pete's number. He answered and was clearly surprised to hear her voice.

"I have to get out of here," she said. "Seriously. Can you—I mean, are you around?"

"I'm here," he said. "I can. I was supposed to meet Nell after work, but . . ."

"Oh," May said quickly. "Never mind."

"But it's not a big deal. I can get out of it. You sound kind of burned out."

"I am," May admitted. "I just need to not be here."

"Sure," he said. "No problem. Give me fifteen minutes?"

May got off the phone.

She changed into her favorite T-shirt, a blue camouflage print. She squirted on some freesia body spray and let her hair down. Maybe it was the light (or the lack of it, since the blinds were down), but May actually liked the way she looked tonight. She pulled her hair around her chin. With her widow's peak, this gave her face a heart shape. The blue shirt made her eyes seem even greener.

Brooks and Palmer were still watching the baseball game when she went back downstairs. The laundry still sat in the middle of the room.

"Where are you going?" Palmer said, glancing over at May.

"Out."

Brooks and Palmer watched in amazement as May sailed out the door.

May was waiting on the front step when Pete pulled up. The humidity had frazzled his hair a bit, and he was wearing his standard-issue cargo shorts and a T-shirt that read I Ate the Whole Thing!

"I called you," he said as she got into the car. "You haven't called back."

"Sorry," May said. "It's just been a weird couple of weeks."

"Oh."

"Can we just go away from here?" May asked. "Can we just drive?"

"Sure." He nodded, pulling back on the road. "Anything wrong?"

"Just stir-crazy. And I have to go away tomorrow."

"Away?"

"Camping on the beach for a few days. I'll be trapped with Palmer and Brooks."

"I have an idea," he said. "I think you'll like it."

They drove for about ten minutes. May noticed that they were heading for the edge of the city, to the northeast. The houses got closer together as they approached the city line. There was a high wall of fence and trees. Pete pulled into a hard-to-spot opening, which led to a vast, empty parking lot.

"What is this?" May asked as Pete stopped the car in front of a small white building. She then noticed a line of white golf carts next to the building, just behind a cyclone fence. "Is this where you work?"

"Yup." He nodded. "The world's crappiest golf course."

"What do you do here?" she said, looking through the fence at the expanse of shadowy lawn.

"I'm a cart boy, but really I'm sort of an unofficial greenskeeper. I mow lawns, dig holes, collect the pins at night. And I sometimes accidentally lose control of the carts and chase golfers into the rough. Stay here a second."

He walked up to the door of the building and let himself in. A minute later he appeared on the other side of the fence. He unlocked the gate from the inside, let her in, and locked it again. He walked to the first parked cart and pulled off the seat, revealing the engine underneath.

"Here's another lesson," he said, pointing at the mess of

parts. "This is the governor. It regulates the speed. And this is how you disengage it." He produced one of the tiny scorecard pencils from his pocket, pulled back a spring, and jammed the pencil in as far as it would go.

"Now this," he said, replacing the seat, "is a much-improved golf cart. Hop in."

"Won't people get upset?"

"This is a public golf course. No one cares. My boss definitely doesn't. Come on."

With a quick look around May carefully got into the cart.

"Aren't there cameras or anything?"

"Nope."

"Or guard dogs?"

"No. It's really simple. Accelerator. Brake. Wheel. Put your foot on the brake."

May did so. Before she knew what was happening, Pete put in the key and started up the engine.

"That switch by your leg flips it from forward to reverse," he said. "You have to come to a full stop before changing direction, or it'll make a really ugly sound."

May nervously glanced down by her leg.

"Drive wherever you like. Just be careful not to go too fast on the declines, especially near the water. Not that that even matters much. It's only a foot deep. But you might flip the cart."

"What?"

"And don't push the brake too hard, or it will switch to an emergency brake. If that happens, just tap it again and it should release."

"Oh my God . . ."

"Okay," he said. "Go!"

"What about you?"

"I'll be right behind you," he said, pulling the seat off the next cart. "Go on."

The thing was chugging underneath her. She put her foot on the accelerator, and the cart started rolling forward. Though there were a few floodlights scattered around the perimeter, they barely illuminated the ground. She saw some slight dips, bits of sand and grass, but mostly just murk. Pete shot past her a moment later and waved her on. She hit the accelerator and the cart rumbled along a little faster.

Puttering through the dark at ten miles an hour wouldn't be exciting to some people, but to May it was kind of like having a private amusement park. Sometimes she trailed along behind Pete, and sometimes she just drove off whichever path she liked and he would come along and find her. Then they would race for a minute.

After about an hour, when she felt she'd had enough, she rode up next to him.

"How do I stop it?" she yelled over.

"What?"

"You said if I hit it too hard, it would turn on the emergency brake! So I don't know how to make it stop!"

He stopped his cart and jumped out. Then he jogged alongside her and hopped into her cart.

"Excuse me," he said, reaching over her and putting his foot on the brake and his hands on the wheel. This meant that he was somewhat on top of her, which was a weird sensation. The cart eased to a halt. He turned off the engine and retracted himself.

"Sorry," he said.

"No. Thanks. I would have been riding around all night."

"Or until it ran out of gas," he said, putting his feet up on the dashboard (which was also the hood). May followed suit and gazed around at the course.

"Your hair is getting longer," she commented.

"Oh, yeah. I haven't cut it in a while. I know, it's—"

"It looks good. You should keep it." She nodded.

"You like it this long?"

"Well, it was longer when we were kids, but then it just made you look crazy."

"And it doesn't now?"

"You still look crazy. But it suits you. You don't scare me as much as you used to."

"You thought *I* was scary?"

"You *were* scary," she said. "You're *still* scary. You're just not *as* scary."

"Me? You used to flick me on the head with a pencil every time I looked at you."

"Self-defense."

"No, it wasn't." He laughed. "You were *always* trying to kick my ass."

"You must be thinking of Brooks."

"No. That was you."

They were shoulder to shoulder now. She could actually feel his heart beat by leaning against him. There was something comforting about being here—it was open, yet it was dark and quiet. Nothing they said here would be heard by anyone.

"Are you mad at me?" he asked.

"What do you mean?"

"You know what I mean."

May slapped a mosquito on her leg and flicked it away. She didn't reply for a moment. She didn't know what she was feeling.

"I'm not mad," she finally said. "I think it's really weird that you're dating Nell. I know both of you. It's just weird when two people you know are together. And I've known you forever. . . ."

A bat flew out of one of the trees next to the course and zipped past them. May jumped. She was edgy now, and a deep curiosity was burning inside her.

"Was Nell the first?" she asked.

"First?"

"First person you slept with."

"Um . . ." Pete stared around at the dark trees. "No. There was Jenna."

"Oh." May nodded.

Okay, it really bothered her. It was like she'd swallowed a drill, and it was boring a hole through her insides. Now she felt like she was somehow way too unsophisticated for him—for Pete, *her* Pete. The whole thing was just humiliating, and it hurt.

"Great," she heard herself saying. "Good for you. Go, Pete."

Pete kept unbuckling his watch, taking it off, and putting it back on again. His face was serious.

"With Jenna, it was kind of weird," he said. "She had a lot of problems. Her parents put a lot of pressure on her. I know she looked really happy all the time, but she was on antidepressants."

"Jenna was?"

"She used to have to talk to me or be with me all the time.

She was always really emotional, constantly, but especially after we would—"

He grabbed his mouth, as if he had just caught it speaking out of turn without his knowledge. He thoughtfully drummed his long fingers against his lips, debating how much more to say.

"Have sex?" May asked.

"Right."

"Intense."

"Yeah."

"So what happened? You said you stopped calling each other."

"*We* didn't stop calling each other," he said slowly. "It's just that she always needed me. Always. And if you have sex with someone and then they always start crying afterward, you start to wonder about yourself. It's sort of not what you hope for."

May caught herself smiling at that, even though it didn't seem appropriate.

"So we didn't stop calling each other—I stopped calling her. I didn't know what to say to her anymore or what to do."

In the last minute or so, it seemed like the world had utterly transformed in May's eyes. The perfect Jenna Cazwell was depressed. Pete had done something a bit cruel, but also pretty understandable. His confession lifted her sinking spirits. She felt the spasm in her stomach relax.

"It sounds like a dick move," he said dejectedly. "I almost told you before, when we were in the city. But I thought you'd hate me, you know, more than usual."

"I don't hate you. You're Camper. Nobody hates Camper."

"That's not true." He laughed mirthlessly. "I'm pretty sure Jenna does."

"But I don't," May said. "I know you're a nice guy. I mean, your mom makes you teach me how to drive and you don't even—"

"My mom never asked me," he said.

"What?"

"I lied."

"Why?"

"I don't know," he said. "Seemed like it might be a good thing to do. So I just offered."

It hung in the air between them for a moment.

"Why did you make up the part about your mom?" May asked.

"You looked suspicious, so I decided to say that my mom had asked me to. Sounded like something that could happen. Are you mad?"

The one thing May knew at that point was that she was definitely not mad. Instinctively she reached out to ruffle his hair to reassure him. She always whapped at his curls when they were kidding around. This time, though, instead of just giving the outer curls a quick shake, she actually let her fingers sink in. His hair was very soft, almost like baby hair. She could feel his surprise at the contact. He sat up a bit straighter.

She continued pulling her fingers through his hair, right down to the nape of his neck. His skin was cool, and she dragged her hand along it casually as she pulled her arm back. She pressed her fingers down into the soft fabric of his cotton shirt. A strange tingling spread through her body.

It seemed to turn her brain back on.

"We should probably drive back," she said, withdrawing her hand. "It seems kind of late."

Pete didn't get up right away, so she gave him a gentle push out of the cart.

When they pulled back up to May's house, they stared at the RV in the driveway. All twenty-six feet of it. Longer, actually, since the Firebird was latched onto the back. So more like forty feet. The chain holding the Firebird on seemed way too small, and the mess of wires and lights would be impossible to disentangle.

"So that's it?" Pete said.

"Yep." May nodded, getting out of the car. "Want to see?"

It was very dark inside the RV. Shadowy mounds covered the sofa, the table, and the floor. There was a light smell of mold in the air. May found a tiny battery-powered camping lamp on the counter and switched it on. It emitted a feeble glow.

"See this?" May said, grabbing a dish from the kitchenette sink. "We stopped using these dishes when I was five. All of this other stuff is just junk we haven't gotten around to throwing away. It's like we're taking a trip in a garage sale."

She sat down on one side of the bench-style kitchen table. Pete shut the door and sat on the other side of the table. May could barely even see him over the pile.

"This isn't going to work," he said. "I'm coming over."

"Okay," May said. "See you when you get here."

Pete came over to May's side and joined her on the bench.

"This stuff reeks," she said, cringing. "It's probably been baking in here all night. It's going to be unbearable tomorrow."

She reached up and pulled a box down from the top of the pile.

"Operation," she said, feeling the thick dust under her fingers. "We used to play this."

"I remember," Pete said. "I think I swallowed some of the pieces."

"That's right. I dared you, and you did it. What did you eat?"

"Definitely the Adam's apple. And the butterfly from the stomach. Maybe the funny bone."

"God." May laughed. "You would do anything. Brooks and I used to sit and think stuff up to get you to do. I'm glad we didn't kill you."

"You wouldn't have learned how to drive."

There was something very deliberate about the way he said it.

"Right," May said. "I guess you can't complain about having to teach me, you know, since—"

"I wasn't complaining. Like I said, I wanted to."

"Oh. Well, thanks. It's been . . . good. It's kind of weird not wanting to kill you. Much."

"Yeah."

They were shoulder to shoulder now, the box between them.

"This box is so filthy," May said. "Did I get dust all over you, or . . ."

And that's when it happened. It was almost too dark to see Pete's face distinctly, but May saw a shadow coming closer. Her first instinct was to brace herself in panic when she felt Pete's lips trying to find hers (he missed at first, catching her nose). But then she found herself reaching up to his face and wrapping her arms around his neck, and in a moment she was leaning back against the window. Pete was leaning into her, and she was sliding farther down on the bench.

And the panic was gone.

july

Vomiting on Gold family vacations
a brief history of

1. Mike and Anna Gold drive Brooks [age six], me [age five], and Palmer [age three] to Williamsburg, Virginia. Brooks throws my Barbie out of the Firebird on I-95. As cosmic retribution, she is seized by car sickness and hurls into a shopping bag from Baltimore all the way to the Virginia state line.

2. The next year the Gold family joins the Camp family for a trip to Florida. I get a very serious case of sunburn while riding in the back of the Firebird on the way there—one so bad that it causes me to barf non-stop. I spend two days in the motel being cared for by my mother while everyone else goes to Disney World. Pete brings me back the stick from his Mickey Mouse Popsicle as a present.

At seven o'clock the next morning, dressed in the same blue camouflage T-shirt, May carried a laundry basket full of food to the RV. She gazed down the length of the behemoth before climbing in. Even at this hour, it was already hot. The air was heavy and wet. When she stepped inside the RV, May felt herself explode in perspiration. She set the basket down and started loading up the kitchenette counter. Spaghetti. More spaghetti. Taco shells. Cereal. Ziti. Peanut butter.

It was going to be a starch fest.

When she was finished, she turned and stared at the spot where she and Pete had been the night before. The Operation box was on the floor. May quickly moved to pick it up, as if it were somehow incriminating. Once she'd picked it up, though, she was flooded with emotion. She held the box as if it were a love letter.

"What are you doing?" Palmer greeted her, pushing in with a waterproof sleeping bag.

"Nothing," May said, tossing the box back onto the stack. "This fell."

"Whatever. Move."

Palmer managed to knock over most of the groceries May had just piled on the tiny counter. She shoved her way back into the bedroom, which was one tiny space with two small beds. There was what looked like a large curtained shelf right above these beds; this was really yet another bed. This "room" was where the three of them would be sleeping (Palmer had already been assigned the shelf-bed). Brooks had brought her bags down the night before, and her things alone took up most of the tiny space. May had thrown hers on top.

"Where is my stuff supposed to go?" Palmer whined. "You guys took up all the space!"

"Snooze, you lose. We got down here first."

"I'm moving this crap out."

"You can't. Mom's sleeping on the pullout couch. You can't put it there."

Assorted grumblings from Palmer as she climbed over the bags.

"Where's my bed?" she yelled.

"Behind that curtain."

May heard the curtain being drawn back and Palmer's groan.

"How's it going?" Their mom was at the door, travel mug in hand, beaming over the entire disaster site.

"Palmer's complaining," May said.

"Uh-huh," she said, walking away from the door and toward the cab. "Make sure all of that stuff is secure. We're leaving in half an hour."

An hour and a half later, when Brooks had woken up, when the dishes were finally done, and the map had been reconsulted, the four Golds were ready to go. As she climbed inside the RV, May took one last quick glance at the huge load they were towing behind them—the Firebird dangling off the back like an uncontrollable tail that could wipe whole lanes of traffic clear off the road in mere seconds.

"We're going to kill everyone," she whispered to Palmer.

"Shut up," Palmer replied.

The driver's seat was the only uncluttered space, so the girls each had to find themselves a place to sit. Brooks was stretched out on one of the bench seats at the table and was already trying to go back to sleep, even though she'd only been in the RV for thirty seconds. Palmer nestled amid the sheets and towels on the sofa. May got the passenger's seat, which was completely surrounded by bags. She had to tuck her legs up.

"Listen to this," their mom said as she started the engine. "The Starks told me that all we need to do is fill a big container with hot water, our dirty clothes, some detergent, and a rubber ball or a sneaker. Then we stick it on the back of the RV, and it bounces around while we drive. It acts just like a washing machine. We can try it on the way back if you want."

She's lost her mind, May thought.

It took six hours for them to get there. Palmer and Brooks slept for most of it. Their mother listened to talk radio. May put her headphones on her ears and stared out the window. She didn't want to be going on this trip. It was so strange—for years, all she'd wanted to do was get away from Pete. Now the thought of being separated from him was more than she could take.

May replayed the scene from the night before in her mind. She would find that the memory worked well with one song, so she'd play it over and over until she got bored and had to search out a new song. Then the scene would come alive again, with different nuances. It was one thing to know someone in a sitting-across-from-them kind of way; it was another thing entirely to lie on top of someone. Everything she knew about Pete was different now.

Of the many varieties of pathetic she had been in her life, May was proud that she had never slipped into the I'm-obsessed-with-my-boyfriend kind—although this was largely due to the fact that she had never had a boyfriend. Now, she realized, she was already slipping into the behavior. She was going to be like one of those pathetic girls who had to call their boyfriends on their cell phone every two minutes, except that she didn't have a cell phone. Maybe she would start writing things like MG + PC = TRUE LOVE 4 EVER on her note-books. Then the transformation into Totally Pathetic Girlfriend would be complete.

Then again, she thought, she shouldn't be premature. The one useful life lesson that Brooks had taught her was that you shouldn't assume someone was your boyfriend without solid evidence. But this was Pete. And she knew Pete. And she felt pretty certain that was what he was thinking—that he should be her boyfriend.

She replayed the scene several more times, looking for clues on this subject.

After about four hours the memory started to wear a bit, so she tried to distract herself by reading the RV camping guide-book that she'd found in a pocket on the side of her seat, trying to get a sense of what was going on. Anything was better than looking up and seeing the trail of destruction she was sure they were leaving behind them.

"Okay," she read aloud, "gray water means the water from

the shower and the sink. And black water . . . oh God . . ." May put the guide down. "They have actual bathrooms there, right?"

"I'm not sure," her mom replied.

May sank lower in her seat.

When they arrived at the park, it took twenty minutes for their mom to steer around the narrow roads to get to their space. It took three people to guide them in, but the ride finally came to an end. Their mom hopped out, strangely energetic.

"We have to hook up the water," she said, "and the electricity, and I think maybe the air . . . or that might be with the electricity. I'll have to ask. Go down and look at the ocean. It'll take a few minutes."

"Where is it?" May said, looking around the lot.

"It's the ocean. You should be able to find it." She strode off in the direction of the park director's trailer, which they had passed (and, May would have sworn, hit) on the way in.

"I'm staying here," Palmer said, sinking down into a chair.

Brooks and May walked off without her and promptly got lost in the tangle of tiny roads. All the trailers looked pretty much identical to theirs, so they couldn't get their bearings. The same kids rode past them on their bikes four and five times in a row and started giving them strange looks.

"Maybe we should ask someone," May finally said.

"We're standing next to the ocean, but we can't find it," Brooks explained. "Imagine what that's going to sound like."

They kept walking in circles until Brooks spotted a small path lined with railroad ties that they hadn't noticed before.

They followed this through another campsite, this one filled only with tents, until they found themselves walking on some sand. They followed the sandy path to an inlet and the inlet to the ocean.

"There it is," May said. It was a beautiful view—a gorgeous, clean beach surrounded by a wall of enormous rocks along the inlet. People fished from these. Since it was getting late, people were starting to take down their umbrellas and chairs and head back to the park.

"Well, here we are," Brooks said. "Want to go back?"

On the walk back, they discovered that the entire trip actually took three minutes, not the forty they had spent getting there in the first place.

"We're going to starve," Palmer greeted them.

"What?" Brooks asked.

"Something's wrong with one of our cables or something. We have no electricity."

May and Brooks looked up at the dark windows of the RV.

"Mom's seeing if she can borrow one from someone else. She's going around to all the other trailers. We're supposed to find the grill. It's in one of these things." She pointed to the small hatches at the base of the RV.

"Don't we need keys for those?" May asked.

Palmer squinted at one of the hatches.

"Yeah."

"Did she leave the key?"

"No."

"The water's running, right?" May asked.

"No. We didn't have some kind of hose."

"Well," Brooks said, sitting down at the picnic table. "Who's having fun?"

The cables and hoses couldn't be found before dinner, so plans were made to take the Firebird back to town to pick up some fast food. But as May had anticipated, her mother didn't know how to detach the car from the complicated system of chains and lights that held it to the RV. Some neighbors came over and showed them how to do it.

It was almost eight o'clock before they were finally able to get out. They brought back a bag of hamburgers and drinks and waited for the man with the cables and hoses to arrive. The rest of the night was spent attempting to hook everything up.

By eleven they had electricity and water, but—despite the hours of sleep that most of them had gotten in the car—everyone seemed too tired to care. They all decided to use the bathhouse instead of the slightly frightening bathroom (especially since they weren't entirely sure that they had connected the water supply to the correct feed line, and the consequences if they had made a mistake were too dire to even imagine).

Washed, groggy, and annoyed, the Gold sisters piled into their "room." The beds were only a foot apart, and Palmer kept climbing in and out of her shelf, stepping on May and Brooks's pillows and heads.

"I don't get it," May said, trying to settle herself in her bed. "Mom said she'd been camping before. She said she and Dad used to go all the time."

"That doesn't mean anything," Brooks replied. "Remember

how she used to tell us that when she went to Amsterdam to see Aunt Betje, they used to like to go for coffee all the time?"

"So?"

"Dad told me that in Amsterdam a coffee shop is where you go for pot."

"Oh . . ."

"Mom smoked pot?" Palmer leaned down from her shelf.

"Mom did a lot of things," Brooks answered. "I think what she meant was that she and Dad went camping, and Dad put everything up."

"Makes sense," May said. "She doesn't lie. She's just—"

"Mom smoked pot?"

"It's legal there," Brooks said. "Go to sleep."

"Dad never told me that," May said.

Brooks turned her back to May and switched off her overhead light. May followed suit. A moment later something soft fell over her nose and mouth.

"Could you keep your socks up there, Palm?" she said, removing the sock from her face.

A hand came down and clawed up the sock. May closed her eyes and went back to the place in her mind where she and Pete were always kissing, and she stayed there until she fell asleep.

As far as May was concerned, the days at the beach were just days she had to kill as painlessly as possible so that she could get back home. She stretched out on the sand with her chemistry book (she'd already purchased her textbook for the next year, as was recommended for advanced students), trying to absorb the periodic table. When she couldn't focus on that, she tried to work through her pile of required summer reading books for English, all of which she'd checked out of the library and brought with her. About ten pages into *Frankenstein* she flipped over on her stomach and fell asleep. She accompanied Palmer to a batting cage and watched as her little sister stunned everyone by hitting every single ball with astonishing ferocity. She walked along the strip of shops in town with her mom and tried to work up an interest in coral necklaces and knickknacks made from painted seashells. She played cards with Brooks under the awning of the RV.

But her brain was filled with Pete. He walked into her every thought—all freckles and frizzing curls. When she walked past the old-fashioned photo place, she imagined them getting their picture taken. (He would look cute in one of those gangster outfits.) At night she counted up in her mind the dozens of secluded spots on the campground and the beach where they could be together.

On the third night her mom and Palmer decided to get

some dinner and go to a movie. Their selection held no appeal for May or Brooks, so they were dropped off at the boardwalk along the way. It wasn't quite dark out, and the crowd was still mixed. There were groups of elderly people and adults with kids, but the first of the night crowd had also arrived, taking their positions in front of the arcade or at the beachfront bars.

"I feel like a twelve-year-old." Brooks sighed, leaning against the boardwalk rail, looking out over the sand. "I hate getting dropped off."

May was gently pressing on her sunburn, watching the white fingerprints appear and disappear under the pressure. The time on the beach had fried her beyond recognition.

"What do you want to do?" Brooks asked. "Or are you just going to do that all night?"

"I might," May said. She leaned against the rail and put her back to the ocean to watch the slow boardwalk tram chug along at three miles an hour. "Why do they need a train for something called a board*walk*? Doesn't that kind of defeat the purpose?"

Brooks kicked a crab claw in the direction of an overflowing trash can and took a deep breath. The smell of beer and buffalo wings wafted over from the restaurant across from them.

"What have we got?" she asked May. "Two hours until their movie is over?"

"Something like that," May replied, making a happy face of white splotches on her thigh. "We can go back whenever we want. We can just walk."

"I guess we could go down to the rides," Brooks said, squinting at the brightly lit amusement pier, about a quarter mile up from where they were standing.

They walked along past the T-shirt shops with the throbbing speakers and the endless food stands. Brooks stopped and bought a soda. May bought a small bag of candy fruit slices.

"Palmer told me that you and Pete were in the RV for almost an hour the other night," Brooks suddenly offered as they continued toward the pier.

May almost choked on her orange slice.

"I was . . . showing him . . . it."

"*Were* you?"

"You know what I mean."

"Actually, I do," Brooks said.

May saw no point in trying to deny anything. Brooks would see right through her.

"Want me to shut up?" Brooks said.

"That's an option?"

"Come here," Brooks said, pulling May off to the side and taking a large Coke bottle from her bag. It was filled with a clear liquid.

"What's that?"

"Vodka."

"Are you nuts?" May said. "Where did you get this?"

"I had a bottle left over from before. Come on, we're on vacation. And I'm not driving. Neither are you."

"You can't have this! You've already been arrested."

"No one is going to find out," Brooks said. "Look around. We're on the board*walk*. We're *walking*, not driving."

May threw up her hands and walked over to the rail. She stared out over the sand. Brooks followed her.

"Come on," Brooks said. She smiled. It was an approving

smile, one that warmed May's heart. Brooks never smiled at her unless she had something horrible caught in her teeth or some piece of damaging information against her. "We've never gone out together."

This was a first—Brooks was actually trying to include May in something. Normally Brooks's idea of bonding with her sisters was shooting straw wrappers at May's face and snickering with Palmer.

"You have to be kidding," May said.

"What else are we going to do tonight?" Brooks asked. "Come on. It'll be fun. And I'll shut up about Pete."

There was something in Brooks's tone that warmed May. She really did appear to want to spend some time with her and include her. Brooks wanted to *party* with her. As much as she hated to admit it, she had always longed for this kind of approval from Brooks.

And really, what else *were* they going to do? Drinking might make the time go by a little faster.

May reached over and took the bottle.

"All right." Brooks nodded encouragingly. "This is how this works. You take a long sip from the bottle, then you gulp it fast and take a drink of the soda right away. It's got to be fast—the soda washes away the taste."

May sniffed the contents of the bottle and eyed the sweating soda cup.

"Okay," May said. "But you have to promise to keep quiet about Pete."

"My lips are sealed," Brooks said.

*   *   *

An hour later—was it an hour? May wasn't sure. Anyway, they were playing Skee-Ball.

May had always been the queen of the arcade when they were kids. She could roll those hard wooden balls down the lane, catch just the right amount of bounce, land them right in the middle rings, get loads of tickets. It was her one athletic skill.

Of course, she'd never tried the game after sucking back a huge bottle of extremely cheap vodka and Tang. Some of May's Skee-Balls made it into the rings, but many more made their way into other people's lanes, and she decided to leave after getting a few dirty stares. She wandered out of the arcade and into the crowd, past the Tilt-A-Whirl and the haunted house and the giant slide.

She looked out over the beach to the water. Kites. A whole lot of kites tethered to rails of the boardwalk, to poles in the sand, to . . . nothing? May hung her head over the rail and looked in wonder at the dark space below her, then she swung her gaze up to the kites. There was one kite in particular, an enormous dragonfly, that held May's attention as it cut through the air. It made crisp noises to demonstrate—just to her, she felt—that the air was there and real and tangible. You could slice into it with a soft piece of cloth and it would make a sound like a knife sliding into an apple.

The wind that propelled the kites blew strands of her hair into her mouth when she opened it, so she had to spend a few seconds extracting them from between her teeth.

"That's it," she said aloud to no one. "I'm going to do it. I'm going to call him."

After making this pronouncement, it took her a few minutes

to find a phone. It took a few more still to figure out how to make a collect call, even though there were clear instructions. But her trying paid off, and she heard Pete's mom answering the phone and taking the call.

"Hi!" she screamed.

"May?" Mrs. Camp seemed surprised to hear from her. "Are you okay?"

"Hi, Mrs. Camp! It's May! Is Pete there?"

"Um, hold on, May."

Some noise as Pete was found. May picked some chipping paint off the wall behind the phone.

"May?"

"Can you hear me?" she yelled. "Should I speak up?"

"No!" Pete yelled back. "No. I can hear you."

"Okay!"

"What are you doing?" he asked. "Is everything all right?"

"I'm on the boardwalk! I wanted to talk to you."

"Okay."

The dragonfly swooped down to the sand, then tore straight up again, dipping and swerving.

"It's just that . . . there's been a lot going on, you know?" May inhaled deeply and took in some of the warm salt air, the fragrance of hot fries, lemons from the lemonade stand, a sugary odor that floated on the cold blasts from the air-conditioning vent of the candy shop.

"Right . . ."

"Okay." She sighed. "So listen. The other night."

Silence as May watched a kid feeding cotton candy to a dog. The dog got confused when the candy stuck to his nose. He tried unsuccessfully to wipe it off with his paw. May considered setting down the phone to go help him.

"Are you still there?"

"Listen," May said, snapping back to the conversation, "I want to know if you're . . . mad at me or something."

"*Mad* at you?"

"Because now you might have some trouble. The whole Nell thing. I mean . . . I just wanted to call and say thanks."

"For what?"

"I mean, since my dad . . . It's all been so weird since then. Since we have, like, no money, and my mom has no time . . . You should break up with Nell."

Now the silence was on Pete's end.

"You should really, like, dump her and date me instead," May heard herself saying, all confidence. "I'm not as irritating. I mean, I'm irritating, but I'm not as bad as she is. And you know me better. Wouldn't that be funny? I mean, we've already hooked up, so we're good."

"We broke up," Pete said quickly. His voice was so bright that May could hear the smile coming through. For a moment she was confused.

"Who, you and me?"

"No. Nell and I."

"Oh . . ."

The meter in her brain clicked once or twice, signaling May that she'd probably said enough.

"I have to go," she said suddenly. "Okay? I think that's great. Cool. Okay. Gotta go now. Hey, Pete, I love you!"

There was a pause during which Pete should have said

something back, but May didn't hear anything. She assumed that he was gone, hung up the phone, and swaggered off back down to the boards. That was good. It was good that she'd had a talk with Pete. All she wanted to do now was let the warm ocean air run along her skin, let the breeze push her hair from her eyes, and walk around with people.

Brooks . . .

Her sister's name drifted through May's consciousness, but there was no urgency accompanying the idea of Brooks. Brooks was somewhere in this crowd, and if she walked around, sooner or later she would find Brooks or Brooks would find her.

She went down the steps to the beach and walked along the cool sand. The ocean was dark and thin and rolled off like a carpet until it hit the horizon. May walked toward it, noticing a strange, tumbling feeling inside, as if her stomach had switched into cement mixer mode. It all went south very quickly. May was down on her knees within a few minutes, gripped by a hideous wave of nausea.

Sand gets cold, she thought. *Cold sand seems to stick less.* Maybe the coldness of the sand could prevent vomiting. If she just focused on the coldness of the sand and nothing else, maybe, just maybe, she might not vomit.

Cold sand, cold sand, cold sand, cold sand . . .

Nope.

Her back arched, her insides convulsed, and nothing came up but air. She clawed into the sand. Nothing to grip.

She was alone, as alone as she could ever get, shuddering on the sand, looking out over the sea, in the realm of jellyfish and ghost crabs and rogue tidal waves and wayward Jeeps racing along the beach and potential rapists hiding under the board-walk—and she was in danger of just generally dying, unseen and unheard. Everything, including the entire ocean and hori-zon, was spinning.

I'm just drunk . . . , she told herself. *I'm not dying.*

She curled herself up into a ball, put her head on a pile of damp seaweed, and tried to breathe evenly and rest.

It took Brooks about fifteen minutes to realize that May was no longer in the arcade. She had been mesmerized by a group of guys trying to master Dance Dance Revolution, and when she'd managed to rip her gaze from their efforts, May had been long gone. At first she was unconcerned, thinking May had stepped out for air. But when May wasn't waiting outside or standing at one of the booths nearby, it began to dawn on her that she might have a problem on her hands. She looked down at the mile of boardwalk, the surrounding beach and water that bordered them on one side, and the entire shore town that was right at their heels. May could be anywhere in the mix.

She cased the boardwalk, walking at first, then loping into a slow jog. She was slightly drunk, so each step seemed to bounce her high, and all of the lights bounced up and down with her. She went all around the area, up one side and back down the other, peering in every shop, every arcade, every ride, every lit-tle offshoot. When the search of the pier turned up nothing, she went down to the sand. She looked under the boardwalk and the pier, then started combing the beach. The run on the sand was a slightly harder one, especially considering that there was a good amount of punch still sloshing around in her stomach. It was a smelly night at the ocean. The air was heavy with salt and decaying seaweed.

She found May a block or two away, sitting between six tethered kites, staring out at the water. Brooks sat down in the sand next to her sister. May smiled and coughed. Her eyes were badly bloodshot.

"I *didit*," May slurred.

"That's great, May," Brooks said, rubbing her temples. "Now, do you think you can walk?"

"Warlk?"

"Walk. Can you stand up and walk?"

"I can walk," May said, angrily smacking Brooks on the arm. *"Shuddup."*

May lay back against the sand.

"No, no," Brooks said, tugging her back up. "No. Stay up. We're going to walk."

Brooks reached under May's arms and pulled her little sister up. Even though May was shorter and lighter and even though Brooks was very strong, May was total deadweight. It was a hard trudge over the sand. May's head rolled senselessly on her shoulders, and she mumbled nonsense at Brooks the entire way.

"It's all right, May," Brooks said over and over as she led May to the sidewalk. "You're doing fine."

It took about four blocks before May's feet actually started to move in rhythmic steps—but it was still a plodding, Frankenstein kind of walk. As they made their way along, a Toyota Tercel full of guys slowed next to them. The car was equipped with a subwoofer so powerful that two alarms went off as it passed. An Eminem wannabe in a bandanna and an Abercrombie and Fitch hat leaned out of the open window.

"Your friend need a ride?" he asked, smiling.

"No," Brooks said, dragging May along.

"Ri—"

"Shut up, May."

"She can sit on my lap," he said as the car slowly followed them along. "I got room for both of you."

Brooks ignored him.

"Come on," said the guy, leaning far out now, reaching for May with outstretched arms. "She likes me."

Brooks switched positions with May and increased their pace. May groaned.

"You don't like me?" The guy leered. "Your friend does. She's looking at me."

"Look," Brooks said, reaching deep into her pocket, grabbing her thick stick of zinc oxide, and pulling it out as if it were a canister of spray, "Feminem, how about you keep driving before I pepper-spray you?"

There was a roar of laughter in the car, and Brooks heard the word, "Dykes!" screamed from somewhere inside. The guy pulled himself back in, spitting on the ground near Brooks's feet before they skidded off. Brooks heaved a sigh and slipped the sunscreen back into her pocket.

"Jackass," she mumbled, continuing to steer May back in the direction of the camp.

"*Wooo*, Brooks is tough. . . ."

"Please, May. Just walk, all right?"

When they got to the convenience store halfway to the camp, Brooks set May down on a bench for a moment.

"Stay here," she told May firmly. "Got it?"

May's chin slumped down on her chest. She wasn't going anywhere. Brooks ran inside and bought a bottle of water and a bottle of Gatorade. Even though she was barely in the store for a minute, May had thrown up on the ground by the bench by the time she came out.

"Oh God," Brooks said, pulling her up and forcing some of the water down her throat. Tears of confusion were running down May's face. Her skin was damp.

"Come on," Brooks said, stroking back May's loose, damp hair. "Almost there."

May slumped, and her eyes began to close. There was no way she could walk any more. Brooks sat down on the bench next to her sister and looked at the passing traffic in despair. There was only one solution she could come up with. May would need to be driven, and that meant getting the Firebird, which was at the movie theater four blocks away. She didn't have the key, of course, and wasn't legally able to drive it. But she *was* sober now.

"May," she said, very clearly, "I want you to stay here. Got it? *Stay here.* I'm going to come right back. Don't move from here, and don't talk to anyone."

May had slipped out of consciousness. Brooks managed to get her up and pull her over to the side of the store, which at least kept her out of sight from the road.

Brooks stood up and pulled each heel up to the back of her thigh, stretching out her muscles. Four blocks. She could do four blocks in just a minute or two. With one final look at May, she took off.

The sidewalks were crowded with people headed up to the boards. She cut across the parking lot of a run-down hotel and headed down an alley parallel to the main road. Her arms pumped hard and even, and her footfalls were steady and fast. *One, two, three, four*—over a broken boogie board. Around a discarded cooler. Past three Dumpsters behind a pizza shop.

It took very little time for her to reach the theater, but once she was there, she faced another problem. Generally speaking, movie theaters didn't let people in unless they had money for a ticket, which she didn't. So she would have to get creative.

The guy at the door was about her age. He didn't look too inspired by his job.

"I need your help," Brooks said, running up to him.

"Huh?"

"Our car is in the lot, and my mom and little sister are inside. My sister's medicine is in the car, and I have to get the keys. Could you please let me in?"

He stared at her doubtfully. She wondered if she had alcohol on her breath. Then she remembered that vodka didn't have an odor.

"Look," she said, reaching into her pocket and pulling out her worn tiger print wallet. "Here is my wallet." She unsnapped it and handed over her worthless driver's license. "Here is my ID."

She held the card up to her face so that he could see that the image matched the reality.

"You can keep this. Keep the whole wallet. I will be in there for less than five minutes, I promise. I just need the car keys."

"I need to ask my manager."

"I have no time," Brooks said. "You have all my money. You

have my ID. I'm not trying to sneak in. Who leaves their wallet?"

The guy looked at the wallet.

"Please . . . ," she said, leaning in.

"Okay," he said. "Five minutes."

Brooks tore off down the hall. It was a little place, with only four screens, so the theater was easy enough to find. But since it was a holiday night, the room was packed. And, of course, the scene she walked in on seemed to be a suspenseful one—two people staring at each other significantly—so the place was dead quiet. She squatted down almost to a crawl and sneaked down the middle aisle, snooping on each row from a dog's eye perspective. Using this method, she finally found her mother and Palmer sitting about five seats into one of the front rows.

Palmer noticed her first and wrinkled her brow in confusion. Brooks tried to pantomime keys, but that had no effect. So she decided to try the whisper-down-the-lane method.

"Could you tell that girl I forgot my wallet," she whispered to the first guy in the row, who was staring at her strangely. "Can you ask them for the keys?"

He passed the message, though somewhat grudgingly.

Palmer turned and looked Brooks in the eye. *You are so lying,* her gaze said.

When her mother looked over, Brooks turned her pockets inside out, showing that she had no wallet. Then she pointed out, hoping this would signify the parking lot. She tried the key pantomime again. Her mother looked hesitant.

"Tell them I'll meet them out front when it's over," she said.

There was some shushing.

Once again the message was passed. Finally the keys were

passed back, but not before Brooks got a strange look from her mother and one final, withering gaze from Palmer.

Out in the lobby, Brooks ran up behind the guy at the door and threw herself over his shoulders.

"You're my guy," she said, plucking the wallet from his hands. "I'll remember you forever."

She kissed him on the cheek and ran out the door to the parking lot. She found the Firebird toward the back. She checked her watch. Nine-ten. The movie would be over in half an hour. She started the engine and pulled onto the road.

Her desire, of course, was to drive as quickly as possible. But her suspended license and the heavy traffic kept her crawling along. It took her five minutes to drive four blocks to the store. May was still there, thankfully, but lying on her side. Brooks loaded her into the backseat, which she lined with some bags she found in the trash, just in case May threw up again.

It took another ten minutes to drive back to the camp. The air was full of the smell of ocean, burning wood, butane, and barbecue. Normally it would have been pleasant, but any one of those odors might very well cause May to hurl again.

One of the neighbors, who was passing by with his dog, stopped as Brooks dragged May's limp figure out of the backseat.

"She okay?" he asked.

"Oh," Brooks said casually as May nearly slumped to the ground. "Yeah. Fine. Too much sun."

He looked doubtful but moved on. Brooks set May down on the tarp in front of the camper. May managed to get on all fours and crawl over to the picnic table. She put her head down on one of the benches and stopped moving.

"Why don't you try to be sick again?" Brooks suggested, making her voice cheerful, as if this was something fun May should do for old times' sake. "You'll feel better."

Something incomprehensible.

Brooks looked at her watch. No time for this. Her mother and Palmer would be out of the movie within minutes. She grabbed one of the beach blankets that was drying on a chair, pulled May up again, and walked her around to the back. There she spread out the blanket and set May on it. May immediately curled into a fetal position and passed out.

Traffic again on the ride back to the theater. Brooks beat on the steering wheel in agony. She got there with just two minutes to spare, only to find that someone had taken the parking space.

"No," she said, feeling everything drop out from under her. "No . . ."

Lacking an option, she parked a few spaces over and hoped that no one would notice. Then she jumped out of the driver's seat and sat on the back bumper as if she'd been waiting there for ten minutes. Her mother appeared to notice nothing amiss when she came out, but the look on Palmer's face clearly showed that she knew something was up.

"So, I got back down there," Brooks said with a laugh, "and May decided she was tired. So she went home."

"She walked home?" her mom said, concerned.

"Yeah. I think it was all the sun. She said she wanted to go back and take a cold shower."

Even Brooks was staggered by the speed of her own lie. Palmer eyed the parking space.

"We should get back, then," her mom said.

As they rode back to the camp, Brooks felt herself hitting the wall. She was exhausted in every way. All of the confusion and adrenaline had worn her out. And her mind kept replaying the moment she couldn't find May on the beach. She saw herself looking out at the water, not knowing if her sister had wandered drunkenly into the surf. It wouldn't go away.

May obviously wasn't around and waiting when they got back, so Brooks had to continue the act by jumping up and going to the bathhouse to check on her. She walked over, wandered around for a second, stared at the wet toilet paper on the ground, and returned with a false report of May's well-being.

"Well," said her mom, yawning, "I'm heading in. I'm beat."

Both Palmer and Brooks received a kiss on the forehead. After she went inside, Palmer scowled at Brooks suspiciously. Brooks could feel her skin breaking out in goose bumps.

"What?" Brooks asked, trying not to look nervous.

"What are you doing?"

"I'm sitting here."

"Want to go to the batting cage?" Palmer asked.

"Not really."

"I can't go by myself."

"Palm, why don't you watch TV or something?"

Palmer fell silent for a moment, picking at a rip in the plastic tablecloth.

"I may just sleep out here," Brooks said, faking a long yawn. "Everybody keeps saying you can see shooting stars."

The idea that Brooks would spend a night at the beach staring at the sky was extremely implausible, but she acted on it, grabbing one of the beach towels and spreading it out on the ground. Palmer couldn't seem to make anything of her motives and soon gave up and went inside. Brooks had to wait almost two hours for Palmer to go to bed before she could move her charge. This stirring caused May to be ill once again, after which she wanted to walk around the park to work off some of the dizziness. By three in the morning, Brooks was finally able to tuck her in and fall into her own bunk in exhaustion.

"So May's drunk?" said a voice from the shelf-bed above her. "That's a switch."

Brooks rolled toward the wall and put her pillow over her head.

"Happy Fourth of July!"

At ten in the morning May's mother threw open the flimsy piece of plastic that served as their bedroom door. Blistering sunlight poured in. May's head was revolving slowly. Pain was everywhere.

"Palmer and I are headed to the beach," her mom said, pulling her large plastic beach bag over her shoulder. "Want to put on your suit and come?"

"No . . ."

"Okay. See you later, sleepyhead."

May pulled her sleeping bag over her head for protection.

"How are you feeling?" Brooks said, standing in the sunlight, looking disgustingly tall and healthy, her blond hair loose. May felt like a small, gnarled sewer creature, something that recoiled from the light.

"Drink this," Brooks said. She held a Gatorade out to May. May struggled with the cap, so Brooks opened it for her and passed it back. May's thirst was overwhelming, and she drank the whole bottle in about a minute. Brooks took it from her, disappeared for a moment, then returned.

"Take these," she said, holding out two pills and a glass of water.

"What are they?"

"Medicine."

Okay. May could deal with medicine. Didn't matter what kind, really. She took the pills. She decided to experiment with standing up. Maybe she would feel better that way. She pulled herself out of the bed and into the living area. She didn't remember coming to bed. She had glimpses . . . walking, being outside on the ground. She was covered in bug bites.

"What happened last . . . ?" But as soon as she started the question, it started coming back in flashes and spurts. Brooks and her bottle. The arcade. The sand. The phone.

"Oh my God," she said.

"What?"

May put her hand over her mouth. Brooks dove into the cabinet and quickly produced a large plastic popcorn bowl. She shoved this under May's chin, but May brushed it away. Her problem wasn't physical.

"I need to go back to bed," May said, heading into the bedroom and slamming the door. It bounced back open.

"What?" Brooks asked again.

"You should really leave me alone," May said. "You should go as far away from me as you can."

May spent the majority of the day sleeping in fitful bursts. All of her movements were tailored to find the exact position in which her stomach would stop heaving and the flashes of pain would stop running through it. She kept sliding around on her slippery sleeping bag, which covered her tiny bed. Her pillow always seemed to be in the wrong place. One minute she'd be hot and sticky, her sunburn throbbing, and in the next second a shuddering chill would ripple through her.

When she hadn't emerged by three in the afternoon, her mother returned to examine her. Fortunately for May, her symptoms mimicked the sickness that resulted from excessive sunburn. She was smeared in aloe vera, forced to drink bottles of water and take a few aspirins, and told to stay out of the sun as much as possible for the remainder of the trip. May was fine with all of this except for the aloe, which made her shiver even more.

It took until evening for May to find the strength to get up and eat a little dry cereal for dinner. She was sick of being in the tiny bedroom, so she agreed to come along and watch the fireworks. Gingerly she pulled on a pair of running pants and a sweatshirt and slunk along behind her mother and sisters to the boardwalk. They got four Orange Juliuses and found a prime piece of railing to stand along, not far from where May and Brooks's escapade had started the night before. Just the smell of the beer was enough to almost cause May to relapse.

"Isn't this nice?" their mom said, throwing her arms over May and Palmer's shoulders.

Palmer shot May an angry look, which May didn't even feel like analyzing.

The fireworks began popping over the water, and the crowd started the obligatory oohing and aahing. May's brain was elsewhere. The illness had filled her mind with morbid thoughts, and now everything she'd been experiencing for the last few days took on a different cast. She was thinking about the word *love*. That much she could recall from the nightmarish montage of barfing, crawling, walking, and rolling around on the ground. She had used the full "I love you" construction. Not even "love ya!" or "I totally love you!"—either of which might have meant she wasn't serious. With every boom in the sky, she heard the word.

The air grew a bit cooler, and she leaned into her mother's fleece pullover. Her mother gave her ponytail a gentle tug.

There was another thing that was even harder to grasp, and she wasn't sure why this hadn't dawned on her before: They had cheated on Nell. Or Pete had, but she had definitely been a part of it. She was definitely in the middle of things now—she was the *other woman*. The more she thought about it, the weirder and more wrong it got.

For May, this was a very disturbing transition from a pleasant fantasy to a harsh reality, like a rude awakening in a horror movie—one of Pete's favorite devices, which he had explained to her several times. It went like this: Some indestructible serial killer slays half the high school. Then in the end, right after the massacre, the only surviving character wakes up on a sunny morning. All the blood is off the walls. The severed head is no longer sitting on top of her dresser. She looks around with an expression of infinite gratitude and says, "It was all a dream. . . ." At that moment the killer pops out of the nightstand wearing her deceased boyfriend's football jersey and wielding an ax. Everything goes black, but you know she is *so* dead. . . .

That was what it was like for May. Just without the ax.

"What do you think, guys?" her mom enthused. "Pretty good spot, huh?"

May numbly watched another explosion on the horizon.

"It's going to be a shame to have to go back tomorrow," her mom went on. "It's been great being here, all of us. But back to reality, I guess . . ."

May had been home all of an hour, and she'd spent most of it sprawled on her bed with her legs flipped over her head, yoga style. This was her thinking position. She assumed it in times of crisis to encourage blood flow to her brain. All it was doing for her now was making her stare at her calves close up. She needed to shave.

The phone rang, jarring her meditative flow.

"May!" Palmer screamed up the stairs. "It's Camper!"

She wasn't ready for this conversation yet.

"Hey," he said as May got on the phone. She could hear the smile in his voice. "I was wondering if I could drop by. Are you busy, or . . . ?"

"We're . . ." May glanced around her room for something she could be doing but came up with nothing. "I'm burned. Really burned. I'm covered in aloe. I'm sticking to my sheets. It's gross."

"You always look good."

Every alarm in May's head went off.

"No, I mean I'm in pain. I feel a little sick. You know what it's like when I get burned."

"Right," Pete said. "Want me to bring you something? Ice cream?"

"I was going to try to go to sleep."

"Oh," he said. The disappointment in his voice was clear.

"But it's only because I have the test in the morning. I have to try to be able to move and not be too swollen."

"Need a ride there?"

"My mom is taking me. I think she feels obligated since she didn't teach me."

"Afterward?"

"Oh," May said. "Yeah. Sure. Come by."

She cringed at her obvious lack of romantic suavity.

"I've really missed you," he said eagerly. "We should talk. You know. Maybe tomorrow. Or now, if you felt like it. But if you're tired . . ."

"We should," she replied, trying to sound equally as excited. "But we should do it in person."

"Sure," he agreed quickly.

The line went quiet.

"You're tired, huh?" he asked.

"Yeah. I guess I should sleep."

"So I'll see you tomorrow?" he said. "Around noon?"

"Great. See you tomorrow! Bye!"

May hung up quickly. She was pretty sure that there had been a real possibility that he was going to hang up with an "I love you," and that would have caused her to take a running leap out of her window.

May slid off her bed and pulled out the flat drawer along the top of her desk. She reached into the space underneath, retrieved an envelope, and shook out the contents. Seven Polaroids fell out. The famous Peter Camp photos. They'd had great plans for the pictures at the time that they were taken. They were going to post them online. But in the confusion that followed, they'd been put away and forgotten.

May arranged them on the desktop and turned on the light. They really were very blurry. Still, she could see enough. She could see that he had been much skinnier last year; he'd developed muscles recently. It appeared that he had very few freckles on his back. The "good butt shot" was not only an excellent photo, but it revealed a really good butt as well. The much contended issue of size was still impossible to resolve, however, even when she squinted and held the photos up to her desk lamp.

She put the photos back into the envelope quickly. She sometimes had the strange fantasy that her father could see her whenever she was doing something embarrassing, as if the dead watched the living like they were the cast of a reality show. And as on a reality show, no one would want to see the boring, virtuous parts. The bits when she was studying or when she got to work five minutes early, May was sure these were edited out. But the sight of May hunched over a photo of a naked Peter Camp—that would be included.

"I need sleep," she said to herself, crawling under the quilt. "I'll know what to do tomorrow."

Palmer sat on her bed, staring at the bronze canister. It was the first thing she'd wanted to see when she got home. She felt weird being away from it now. She didn't like leaving her dad alone in the house while they went to the beach. Using the corner of her pillowcase, she wiped away the smudges her fingers had made.

Though she was glad she'd found it, having the canister presented some problems. One, she didn't necessarily want to be its keeper. That seemed like a scary, eternal responsibility. The second was that now that she'd found it, she'd lost her desire to go through the house at night. That had been her only occupation, and now it seemed to be gone.

It had been all right at the beach, sleeping in close quarters with everyone, having Brooks and May right there with her. But now that she was home, Palmer was afraid. She was going to have to go back to the horrible feeling of waking up in the middle of the night unable to breathe. And she would have nothing to do but sit and wait until she finally managed to drift back to sleep—and that sometimes took hours.

This was not the time to be sleepless. She was already behind the other players at the camp because she'd missed the first days. The thought of games rarely made her nervous, but tomorrow she'd be playing with strangers. They'd probably be girls a lot older than she was, most of them the best players from their schools. And there might be scouts in the crowd.

She leaned back on her bed and hung her head upside down over the side. She counted her trophies. There were twenty-one, all lined up on the special shelf her dad had put up above her dresser. When her head filled with blood, she pulled herself upright and looked at the canister again. She needed to do something with it, or she was going to go crazy.

It suddenly dawned on her—May. She would tell May what she had done, and May would have a good answer. Even if she had gotten wasted over the weekend, May was still the responsible one.

Palmer slipped off her bed and went down to May's door. She knocked once, then let herself in. May was sitting in bed, reading a book.

"Could you wait for me to say, 'Come in,' for once?" May asked, looking up in annoyance.

Palmer shifted from foot to foot. How did she explain this?

"What did Pete want?" she asked. The second the words were out of her mouth, Palmer realized her mistake. She had blown it.

"You have to stop it, Palm," May said, sitting up on her elbows. "Stop watching everything Pete and I do."

"I'm not—"

"I'm really tired," May said, putting down her book and reaching over to turn out the light. "I have this stupid test in the morning. Would you please let me sleep?"

Palmer felt like she was going to cry. She wanted to tell May what she had sitting against the Orioles pillow on her bed. She wanted to tell her about her nights of prowling, and the horrible pain in her chest, and the terrible fear.

"Please, Palm." May groaned. "Go."

There was just something about her that annoyed people, that made them ask her to leave. Not knowing what else to do, Palmer turned and went back to her room.

Since she'd been practicing in Pete's car, May decided to take the Firebird for her exam. It was a little more similar in feel and in size than the minivan. Now that she was here, though, she wondered if it was way too old or too weird for the exam. Maybe you needed a car that didn't look like it had been stolen from the Smithsonian.

Her new examiner, a stern-looking man with a crew cut and raw red circles under his eyes, seemed much more interested in the car than in his examinee. He walked around it, inspecting it minutely.

"Firebird 400," he said, throwing open the door and taking the permit he was meekly offered. "Sixty-seven, right? Someone in the family a car buff?"

"My dad."

"He do the restore?"

"The what?"

"Okay." He glanced at the permit. "*May-zee.* Maize-eee. Mayzie? Give me your hazards while we're here."

As May demonstrated all the requested functions, she felt more like a model demonstrating a car in a showroom than someone taking the driver's exam. Her examiner even wanted to see the latch that released the convertible top.

"All right," he said, satisfied that she knew the controls. "Let's get moving."

One thing became immediately clear as May started moving the car forward—Pete had prepared her well for this. The lessons had helped, but what really boosted her confidence was the fact that she'd had so many nerve-racking experiences in the car with him. Nothing the examiner could do really rattled her. Even when she struck an orange cone on the serpentine and caused it to wobble or when she was clearly going too slowly on her thirty feet in reverse, her nerves remained steady right to the end of the course. She was actually shocked at how easy it was.

"Congratulations," the man said, checking off some boxes on his form. "Pull over in front of the building."

"I passed?"

"Yes," he said, handing her back her card and a form. "Take this inside. And tell your dad he's got a nice car here."

"Sure." May nodded, pulling into the directed spot. "I'll tell him."

It took only a few minutes to have the permit verified. When she came back out, the examiner was gone and her mother was sitting in the passenger's seat, grinning broadly. May got into the driver's seat.

"I saw you go in," her mother said. "I thought that seemed like good news."

She leaned over to give May a hug. She smelled vaguely of hospital, even though she'd showered since she'd been there last.

"You have no idea how relieved I am," she said.

"Relieved?" May asked, giving her mother a sideways glance. That wasn't quite the reaction she'd been expecting—not immediately after she passed the test, anyway.

May started the car and carefully backed out of the space. It took her almost a full minute to do this, as she stopped for every car that came down their row. She overshot her turn leaving the parking lot and almost ended up on the shoulder on the opposite side of the road. Okay, maybe the state of Pennsylvania had made a mistake—but too late now. She wasn't giving them the license back.

"Palmer has a game this afternoon," her mom said. "I'm leaving for work at six, so if you could take her, that would be great."

"Sure."

"And if you could run to the store . . ."

"Can't I be normal and celebrate for a second?" May asked. She could hear the irritation in her voice.

Her mom flashed her a quick look.

"I mean, could you wait maybe five minutes before laying the jobs on me?"

"I'm just—"

"Brooks didn't get a list of chores when she got her license," May found herself saying. "She went to a game. She had a cell phone."

"What are you saying?" her mother asked.

"I'm saying Brooks actually did stuff, had fun. I got my license because I had to. It's always been about Brooks. You let her do whatever she wants."

"Don't exaggerate." Her mother pried a few stray M&M's from the well near the shift.

"So why is Brooks practically in rehab now?" May spat. "She was like that for months, and you didn't say a word."

"If I had known . . ."

Maybe it was because she was in the driver's seat now, but May felt a sudden urge to say exactly what she thought.

"How could you *not* know, Mom? How could you not know that your own daughter was out about every other night, wasted out of her mind? Didn't you guess something was up when she quit the team? Or what about the fact that she was hung over and half dead the rest of the time? What about her grades? What are *they* like?"

Her mother put on her sunglasses and stared out the window.

"Dad liked her best," May said. "You like her best. Why can't you just say it?"

In her frustration May almost ran a red light. She skidded to a stop several feet past the white line. The nose of the Firebird stuck out into traffic. She couldn't back up because cars had come up right behind her. People wove around her to get by, some honking in annoyance as they passed.

"You're too far up," her mother snapped.

"Like I didn't notice that."

Neither of them spoke again for the rest of the ride. Once they were in the garage, her mother left the car, slamming the door behind her.

Palmer was immediately on May's heels the second she walked into the house.

"What did you do?" Palmer asked, her voice low.

"We had a fight," May replied, rubbing her temples. She pushed past Palmer and went into the kitchen, but Palmer followed her.

"Mom's *upset*."

"I know." May threw open the fridge and cursed at the empty water pitcher. "Can you leave me alone for a second, Palm?"

"What did you do?"

Palm was clenching her jaw and glowering down at May.

"I didn't do anything," May spat. "I passed my test, okay? That's what I did."

May heard a car pull up in front of the house. Pete. She hurried to the front door to check. The Cutlass was in front of the house, and Palmer was still at her back, yapping like a dog.

"You did something to her!"

"Not now, Palm! Go away!"

Palmer stomped upstairs.

May examined herself in the mirror. Her eyes were slightly red. She had her sunburn, which was almost fading into a tan and looked sort of nice against her dark blue tank top. She reached up and pulled out the twist tie that held her hair back in a knot and gave her head a good shake. Her hair was kind of bumpy and strange looking from being pulled up when it was still wet, but May decided to tell herself it was attractively wavy. She had no problems at all lying to herself in desperate situations.

She peered through the glass at the top of the door and saw Pete marching across the front lawn. He was casually but carefully dressed in long green khaki shorts and a black short-sleeve button-down shirt. His clothes even looked ironed. His hair seemed to be carefully dried and even kind of . . . arranged. His arm was tucked behind his back.

She opened the door. As he got within a few paces, he broke out into a huge grin. May clenched her hands into fists to keep them steady.

"You *are* burned," he said.

"Oh." May looked down at herself and remembered her excuse from the night before. "Yeah. I scorch."

He swung his arm around and presented her with three Gerber daisies. May pushed open the door and stepped outside to take them. They were vividly colored—red, orange, and yellow.

"I got these . . . ," Pete said. "I knew you were going to pass."

"What's this?" May said, even though they were obviously flowers.

"There's only three of them," he said, almost apologetically.

"They're great. Thanks."

"Are you all right?" he asked. May turned away and headed for the garage.

"I'm fine," she said quickly, wanting to get away in case her mother came downstairs. "Let's go . . . out here. We can sit in the car."

They sat down in the front seat of the Firebird, leaving the doors hanging open.

"So, I passed," she said. "Finally. Amazing."

Neither of them could think of anything more to say about the test. May looked down at the cream-colored vinyl seat. Traces of fabric softener fragrance wafted off Pete's shirt.

"So, your call," he began. "The other night. Did you mean what you said?"

May stroked the flower petals and found herself unable to speak. Her entire attention was on the fact that Pete's hand had fallen on her far shoulder, and this time he wasn't going to tap on it and make her turn the wrong way. He had gotten closer to her. His face was just inches away from hers. There was no question what was supposed to happen next.

Pete kept talking, his words coming more quickly.

"Because for a long time I've really . . . I like you a lot. Obviously."

All of Pete's attributes, which had seemed so appealing just a short while before, took on a threatening quality. His hair was too curly. His nose, too small and well formed. He had gotten too tall. His lips seemed especially ridiculous. They could be the most perfectly formed lips on the planet and still look like some very disturbing instruments when viewed up close for over a minute.

He slid closer to her. The hand that had been on her shoulder was now cradling the back of her head.

"Pete . . ."

Oh God, his head was even at an angle. He was ready. It was like a crowded elevator full of emotions had just risen to May's head and gotten stuck there. They were all banging around, making her feel like she was going to explode.

"Just wait." She put her hands up against his chest and pushed herself back. "Just stop, okay?"

Pete stopped moving entirely.

"What?"

"I don't want to do this, okay? It's weird."

"What's weird?"

"This!" she yelled. "Us!"

He seemed confused.

"You called and said you loved me."

"I was drunk. Brooks got me drunk. I didn't know what I was doing."

"You weren't drunk before you left."

She couldn't deny that one. She couldn't think, period.

"What about Jenna?" she asked, wondering where her words were coming from. Pete almost jumped to his side of the seat.

"What about her?"

"It just seems kind of weird to me, now that I think about it," May said. "Why you broke up with her."

Pete's eyes seemed to get bloodshot instantly. His brow lowered, and the freckleless spot between his eyes turned a bright crimson. Bizarrely, May's impulse was to make him mad. *Be vicious.* That was the only message she was getting.

"What about Nell?" she asked. "You just cheated on her, then you dumped her."

"Nell was . . . I explained this to you. What are you saying?"

"I just wanted to learn how to drive," May went on, "and you . . ."

Were nice. Helped me. Made me laugh.

". . . completely took it the wrong way. And you didn't even care what you did to her. Is that what you do? You just stay with someone as long as you feel like it? I mean, are you just going to screw me and dump me?"

May never used the word *screw*, not in that sense. The word left a hard taste in her mouth.

"Screw you and dump you?" he repeated incredulously. His voice had gone a bit hoarse.

In the silence that followed, May could hear the Stark boys gleefully using each other as lawn dart targets. Their breathless screaming drifted up over their house, through the open garage door, and passed into the Firebird.

It was hard to do, but once you made Pete angry, he stayed angry. There were times when they'd fought as kids that he'd cut May dead for days until they had made up. But those times were nothing compared to the anger she saw in him now. Now she saw a much bigger, scarier emotion. He wasn't the little boy who used to ride over to her house on his bike anymore—he was a fully grown guy.

He turned to face forward. His chest was rising and falling quickly. May leaned back and looked out her side of the car. She couldn't understand why she was so very calm when this horrible thing was exploding all around her. She actually felt a strange sense of relaxation.

When Pete left a minute later, she decided not to turn to watch him go, even though something inside her was yelling at her to follow him. Quickly. To get out of the car and catch him and stop this insanity.

That was impossible.

She sat, staring at the tool shelf. She heard Pete's car pull away.

Brooks came down into the garage and set a bucket of freshly washed dishes on one of the shelves.

"Nice one," she said, and headed back inside.

May was sitting against her bed, staring at the phone on the floor. She'd been in the process of reaching for it for an hour, wanting to call Pete but having no idea what to say—or what her voice might say, since she was apparently possessed by demons who did all her talking for her.

Brooks pushed open her door without knocking.

"It's time for Palmer's game," she said.

May shoved her star-spangled flip-flops on her feet. As she walked down the hall, Brooks followed her.

"You're coming?" May asked.

"Moral support."

"Since when have you given that out?"

Palmer was already sitting in the back of the car, silently examining her glove. Brooks hopped into the passenger's seat.

"You have a lot of problems, you know that?" Brooks said casually as May backed out of the garage. "Seriously. I think you need a psychologist."

"Not now," May said flatly.

"Really. I think you do."

"Well, when your rehab guy has some free time, maybe he can see me."

"Both of you," Palmer said from the back. "Shut up."

"What you did to Pete was cold."

"Okay," May said, backing out onto the road a bit more aggressively than necessary. "I don't think you're far enough along the twelve steps to start criticizing me. Wait until you get your sixty-day chip or something."

Palmer slammed her fist into her glove a few times.

"At least I'm not a user," Brooks continued.

"I guess you haven't used me or used Mom. I mean, we really love paying for all of your screwups. It gives us a reason to live."

"You're both retards," Palmer mumbled, but neither May nor Brooks could quite catch what she'd said.

"He's been great to you," Brooks said. "He'd do anything for you. And you treated him like crap."

"Look," May said, "I'm sorry that I didn't meet someone classy, like Dave Vatiman. . . ."

Another jab. Maybe it was the driver's seat, May reasoned. Maybe it did something to her—made her evil. But Brooks didn't seem to notice the remark.

"That's my point. You could at least be *nice* to him."

"You have no idea what you're talking about," May broke in. "He's Pete. He's an idiot. He'll get over it."

Even as May said it, she winced a bit. Why did she say these things?

Because she was crazy. Because she was a zombie.

They rode the rest of the way in silence. May brought the car to an abrupt stop in front of the clubhouse. Palmer was the first out. She pulled her things out of the backseat briskly.

"See you after," May said.

"Yeah," Brooks said over her shoulder. "Good game."

Palmer didn't answer them. She walked off to the clubhouse. May and Brooks got out of the car.

"You know what?" Brooks said, looking her sister up and down. "You deserve it. You deserve to be weird and miserable."

"Thanks," May said, walking off toward the bleachers.

Seventh inning. Three to two in favor of this team of strangers Palmer found herself pitching for. She was perspiring. This was a game she could have played better. Three obviously incompetent batters had gotten past her—girls she could have struck out with her eyes closed on any other day.

She just needed to get through this. To get home and go back to bed.

Playing always took her mind off things, but today her head was still buzzing. She was exhausted—she hadn't slept much. May had argued with her mother and left her crying. May had argued with Pete about something, and Pete had gone away. May had gotten drunk at the beach. She was used to Brooks doing these things, but now even May was falling to pieces on her. But this wasn't the time or place to think about that.

Palmer squared herself off and faced the batter, putting both of her feet on the pitcher's plate. She gripped the ball with both hands.

Then it hit all at once, without warning. The nighttime panic was here, now. The strange heartbeat, the tunnel vision. Her arms didn't work. She couldn't throw. She couldn't move. She curled her knuckles up along the stitches of the ball. It was the only recognizable sensation.

The girl at bat straightened up impatiently. Palmer tried to calm herself, but she knew that she was rapidly approaching the ten-second mark, which was the maximum amount of time she was allowed between taking her position on the pitcher's plate and beginning her pitch. The batter crowded the plate, sensing her nervousness.

Palmer had to do something.

In one smooth gesture she stepped forward, wound her arm, and released the ball. She closed her eyes. It was a solid pitch. She could see it moving in her mind—how it arced, how it slowed. The batter, confused, would move in even farther. But then it would curve and go right back toward the plate, picking up speed. And if the girl didn't move away . . .

Palmer closed her eyes right before the ball hit the girl's helmet with a sickening thud.

*   *   *

Brooks had risen to her feet a moment before the impact; her instincts had told her that something was wrong with the pitch. Palmer had waited much too long. She watched the batter stagger and fall, and her team and coaches came running. There was confusion in the bleachers and on the field. Cell phones were pulled out. A few people leapt down and ran to the fallen girl. Palmer turned and ran off.

"What's going on?" May said.

Brooks was already climbing down the bleachers in pursuit. May scrambled for her purse and trailed behind.

Palmer disappeared around the clubhouse, toward the parking lot, so Brooks increased her pace. Even though she was a little out of shape, Brooks was still an excellent runner. Palmer was fast, but she could keep up with her. She followed her through the parking lot and watched her duck behind the Firebird. When Brooks jogged up a few seconds later, she found Palm sitting on the ground, curled up into a ball.

"Go away," Palmer said in a low voice.

"What happened out there?"

"I said *go away.*"

"Are you all right?"

There was heavy breathing coming from behind them. May had just caught up.

"Palm, you should really go back there," Brooks said. "Go back and explain."

Palmer screamed. Not an angry scream but a painful, high-pitched, unbroken wail. Brooks remembered screaming like that when she was a little child, so hard that she felt her throat might bleed. It carried across the parking lot. It drew the attention of everyone in the entire area. If her desired effect was to scare Brooks off, it worked. But May stepped forward and sat down on the ground in front of Palmer. Palmer scrunched her face together in what was probably an attempt at a threatening expression, but May didn't move.

"What's going on, Palm?" she said.

"It keeps happening," Palm said through clenched teeth.

"What does?"

"The thing. Where I can't breathe."

"Can't breathe?"

"It happened out there. Things get dark."

May reached out and rubbed Palm's knee.

"Do you want to go home?" she asked quietly.

The knee rubbing seemed to subdue Palmer. Her face relaxed, and she gave a heavy nod, like little kids do when they're upset or tired. May looked up at Brooks, who was surveying the activity in the distance with a dark expression.

"I don't know if we should," Brooks said. "They're going to want to know what happened."

May was already getting out her keys.

"I don't care," she replied. "Let's get her out of here."

Palmer locked herself in her room the minute she arrived home. It was stuffy and overly sunny. At least the scary, closed-in feeling was going away fairly quickly this time, probably because it was daytime and people were around.

She didn't want to think about the pitch. She couldn't think about the pitch. Not yet. Her brain was already too loud and crowded with stuff. Until she solved the problem of the urn, nothing was going to be right again. It sat there on her bed, gleaming in the sunlight that came through the blinds. She dropped down on the bed and stared at it.

"What do you want?" she asked it, hoping that by asking the question aloud, she would get some kind of magical inspiration. But the urn just slipped a bit to the right. Palmer straightened it, then lay back and stared at the ceiling.

Her life was over. She was so out of the camp. And if they kicked her out of softball, Palmer would die.

No. She could fix it. She could explain to them.

The attacks were coming in the day now. Now she really was a crazy person.

She would fix that too.

The urn . . . She just had to figure out what to do with the urn.

She just had to *calm down*.

She closed her eyes and tried to imagine the happiest place she could. Camden Yards. Definitely. Cheese dog in one hand. First inning. They hadn't taken their trip to Camden Yards this year. She had missed it.

Yesssssss . . .

The idea came as a sudden rush. Every detail was there, as if her brain had already written the plan and she had stumbled upon it. First she had to see if it was possible. She had a season schedule card pinned to her corkboard. She checked. The timing was perfect.

She looked at the urn. This was going to be hard, but she had to do it.

*   *   *

When Palmer crept downstairs a half hour later, Brooks and May were sitting at the kitchen table, holding conference over an assortment of dry crumbs, self-stick notes, and random pens. Brooks was methodically sticking and unsticking a Post-it to her forehead. May was chewing on a mechanical pencil with her back teeth, like a dog trying to tear the knobby end from a rawhide bone.

Palmer stood right outside the doorway and listened.

"It was an accident," May was saying. "Accidents happen. And those helmets are really strong. Aren't they? I mean, they look strong, and they have that flap over the ear."

"The girl's probably all right," Brooks said, putting one of the Post-it notes over her eye. "That's not it."

"Then what is it?"

"It wasn't an accident."

"What are you talking about?"

"She was head-hunting," Brooks said simply.

"She was what?"

"She aimed for the girl's head to knock her away from the plate. It's a really illegal move, but it happens."

"You're saying Palmer hit her on *purpose*?" May asked.

"I don't know. I saw her face. Something was wrong. Maybe the sun got in her eyes or something. . . ." Brooks pulled off her Post-it eye patch and started nervously folding it into the shape of a small hat.

"This is pretty bad, isn't it?" May said.

"It could be."

Palmer couldn't listen anymore. It was time to act. She strode into the kitchen, causing her sisters to lurch in alarm. Without giving them a chance to say anything, she gingerly removed the urn from the bag and set it on the table between them.

"I found it in Mom's closet," she said. "It was in a box. A shoe box."

May and Brooks said nothing. It was clear that they immediately knew what the thing was, and it seemed to affect them in the same way that it did Palmer. They flinched away from it, yet they had to look at it. Palmer took advantage of their silence to keep talking.

"I just figured it out," she said. "We didn't go to Camden Yards this year. So we have to take him. There's a home game tonight. It starts in an hour. We have to leave soon."

This concept didn't seem to click in May and Brooks's minds as quickly as it had in hers, because they looked up at her as if she'd just sprouted wings and a beak. Then they exchanged a long, puzzled look.

"You want to go to Camden Yards?" Brooks asked. "Now?"

"Right."

"And take that?" Brooks pointed to the urn but didn't look at it.

"Uh-huh."

"And do what?"

"Take him to the pitcher's mound," Palmer said. "It'll be easy. We just—"

"Are you *nuts*? You just nailed some girl in the head with a ball, Palm. And now you want us to drive to Camden Yards to go to the pitcher's mound? What the hell is the matter with you?"

Palmer had been expecting an objection from May, but not from Brooks. And she didn't like being called nuts, either.

"Where do you think he'd like to be?" Palmer snapped. "In the closet or there?"

"I don't know," Brooks said, "but he probably wouldn't want *us* to be in jail."

"We won't go to jail. They're not going to arrest three girls."

"Wanna bet?"

"There are buses to Baltimore from the city," Palmer snapped. "I know how to get to the bus station. I know which train to take. If you guys don't come with me, I'll go on my own."

She would, too, even though the bus station bit was a lie. She knew it was somewhere downtown, and people got downtown by train. She could walk to the train station and ask someone there. It wouldn't be hard.

Brooks exhaled loudly and picked at a scar in the wood. Palmer gingerly lifted the canister back up and put it back into her bag. May still hadn't spoken. She was watching Palmer as she worked. Palmer reached into the front pocket of her bag and shoved a pile of cash into May's hand. May looked at the cash in surprise, then counted it.

"Where the hell did you get that from?" Brooks asked, gazing down at the money in amazement.

"I saved it."

Brooks, who never saved, just stared in awe.

"Eighty-five bucks," May said, holding up a crisp, unused twenty.

"We have money. You can drive." Palmer nodded to May on

that one. "We have the Firebird. It'll take two or two and a half hours to get there. Same to get back. We'll probably be down there for two hours, depending on how the game goes. Mom's asleep now, so she won't notice that we've even been back from my game. She'll be at work until seven in the morning."

Nothing else was said for the next few minutes.

"So, we're talking about eight or nine hours?" May finally asked.

"You're not really thinking about doing this." Brooks shook her head at May. "*You're* going to drive all the way to Baltimore? You?"

"I'm thinking about it," May said thoughtfully. "Yeah."

"Oh my God." Brooks put her head down on the table.

"What about this pitcher's mound thing?" May asked.

"Easy. Trust me. I've got it all figured out."

"If it's so important, why don't we just wait?" Brooks asked desperately, pulling her head up. "We'll do it later."

"No, we won't," May said, rising. "That's the point. We have to do it today."

"Why?"

"Because we won't do it on some other day, when we've had time to think about it," May answered. "I won't, anyway. And she means it. She'll do it by herself. So it's better to just go."

Palmer didn't mind being talked about as if she wasn't there this time. She could see that May *got it*. She was saying exactly what Palmer was thinking. There was an energy in the room that she hadn't experienced in a long time. Something good was happening.

May started going through her purse, making sure she had

everything she thought she needed. Brooks sat staring at the wall.

"Besides," May mumbled, "today's already completely screwed up. Why stop now?"

"Come on," Palmer said, leaning down and looking Brooks in the eye. "You know you have to. Think about it."

"How's Mom going to feel when she finds out the ashes are all gone?"

"She had them in a shoe box," May said. "It doesn't sound like she had too much of a plan for them anyway."

May seemed as determined as Palmer now, and one good thing about May was that she was hard to argue with. She was always the voice of reason, and if she was going, then the plan had to be a solid one. Plus with her red hair knotted back, her neat tank top and khaki shorts, her purse resting in the crook of her elbow, and her keys dangling off her finger—May looked mature. Brooks would have to buckle. She wouldn't be able to live with herself if she was too scared to do something May was willing to do.

"Onetime offer," Palmer said. "Come now or miss out."

Palmer could almost hear Brooks's brain whizzing. Her eyes flashed back and forth, as if an argument were going on inside her head. Finally Brooks looked down at the little paper hat she had made, looked at her sisters, then slowly rose from her seat.

"We better be back in time," she said.

"Trust me," Palmer replied.

One hundred miles is a long trip when you're going at a good pace—it was an agonizing trip at fifty miles per hour, especially for Brooks, who only slowed down to that speed to go through school zones and drive-through windows. It had been even longer since she'd been in a car with no air conditioning and no decent stereo, and the open windows meant that she was bathed in that heady fuel perfume that bellowed out of the Firebird's tailpipe.

She struggled with the map in her lap, refolding it until she had a manageable-size rectangle. They were passing through Wilmington, Delaware. She located the city along I-95 and worked out the distances. At the rate May was going, they had at least another two hours of highway driving ahead of them.

"May," Brooks ventured, "can you try to go just a little faster?"

"I could." May nodded. "But I'm not going to."

"Look, if you drive a little faster, we could get there and back by the time Mom gets off. She'll never know."

"We're going to need gas soon," May replied. "You pump it."

"Why aren't you listening to me?"

"Because," May said, ignoring the other drivers who were so tired of following her that they'd begun to weave around her, "I am trying not to panic. You do not want to see me panic. If I were you, I'd do everything I could to keep me from panicking."

"Can we at least put the top down?"

"No."

"Why not?"

"It makes my hair fly into my eyes. Then I can't see. Then we crash."

"I like the top down," Palmer chimed in from the back.

"That's nice," May said. "When you drive, you can feel free to take the top down. But I have to drive, so it stays up."

"God, you sound like Mom." Brooks groaned.

"I could probably drive," Palmer mumbled. "Better than you, anyway."

Brooks felt them lose some speed. May dropped down to forty-five miles an hour.

"You have to do at least fifty, May," she said. "You can get in trouble for going too slow, too."

"New rule!" May called out. "Everyone shuts up until we get through Delaware, or I slow down to forty."

Palmer banged the back of her head against the seat back a few times but said nothing.

"I think . . . ," Brooks began.

May decelerated again. Brooks shook the map at her.

"I think," she began again, "that we should stop for gas just below Wilmington."

May gradually took the car back up to fifty miles an hour. It rumbled contentedly as she stepped on the gas.

The sun was just going down as the Golden Firebird slipped into the tunnel that led under Baltimore Harbor. Palmer went on the lookout for signs, which May carefully followed to the huge complex of old redbrick warehouses and the banner-lined road in front of them. May turned into the first parking lot she saw, which was, of course, practically miles away. She had to let Brooks slide over and actually put the car into the tiny space that was available.

Camden Yards had always reminded May of Disneyland. It was very clean, with lots of flowers and trees, and the old brick buildings that surrounded it had large, distressed signs painted on them, carefully faded, with sort of an Old West feel. Even the stadium was made of red brick. She'd never approached it before with any kind of criminal intent. Its cheery wholesomeness made her feel guilty.

The game had already started. The music was flowing up and into the night air. Palmer gazed up into the glow of the high-intensity lights that illuminated the field and grinned.

"We only need the nine-dollar tickets," Palmer explained as she ran through the front plaza to the ticket booth. "Then we can just go down to the good seats. No one will stop us."

Tickets in hand, they stepped onto the concourse that ran the circumference of the stadium, a wide ring of concrete lined with concessions and souvenirs. Hot dogs and sodas and ice cream were all a crucial part of the game experience normally, but not tonight. Tonight it appeared to be all about running. Palmer cut ahead and slipped through one of the passages that led down to the seats along the field. May and Brooks had to hurry to catch up with her. There were no seats available, so Palmer squatted on the last step. From there, they were almost perfectly level with the field. It definitely seemed like a place where they shouldn't be waiting around.

"If anyone says anything to you," Palmer counseled her sisters, "say we're waiting for our parents. Say that we got separated, and this is the only place they know to look for us."

Brooks nodded at the wisdom of this.

"Bottom of the eighth," Palmer noted. "That's good."

May silently agreed with this sentiment. She was nervous to

the point of nausea. Brooks was trying to look determined, but May could tell she wasn't doing much better.

"They're going to win," Palmer said, pointing at the score-board.

She was right. The ninth inning moved fast, and the crowd exploded when the Orioles won. The music pumped, the screens flashed, popcorn flew in the air—and the three Gold sisters were considerably jostled as the stands started emptying out. They grabbed three vacated seats.

"We have to do it soon," Palmer said, raising her sun-bleached brows and looking over the field. She turned back to look down at May's flip-flops.

"Those are going to be a problem," she said.

"My feet?"

"Your shoes. Take them off."

May hadn't thought about the footwear issue. But she wasn't about to run barefoot across the field, so she left them on.

"All right," Palmer said, dipping her hand into her bag, "let's get ready."

She fiddled around inside the bag for a moment. May could see that she must have been going into the canister. A moment later she produced three small plastic zipper-locked sandwich bags, each full of a grayish substance that looked like coarse sand. Each bag held an amount about the size of May's fist. As Palmer passed the bags out, a man bumped into May and she nearly dropped hers.

None of this was real to May. Not the music pumping over-head, or the heavy breeze, or the residual smell of popcorn and beer.

"We go all over at once," Palmer said, eyeing the short divider that separated the stands and the field. It was only about three feet high. "Even you can jump this, May."

May looked up sourly.

"Have your bags ready," Palmer continued, "but be careful when you run with them. Run straight out to the pitcher's mound and open them up. Don't stop, no matter what happens. Then head straight for the wall over there, to the left of the Orioles' dugout. Go up the nearest steps and out into the concourse. If we get separated, we'll meet by the car. Ready?"

"What?" May asked, looking around in a panic and grabbing at her things. "No. No, I'm not."

"Then get ready. You should have put your purse in the trunk or something."

"Why didn't you tell me all of this earlier?"

Brooks straightened up and flexed her knees a few times.

"On my mark," Palmer said quietly. "One . . ."

"What if I fall?" May whispered. "I fall, like, at home. Just walking around."

"Two . . ."

"Don't fall," Brooks advised.

"Thanks a lot."

"Three!"

In various stages of readiness, the Gold sisters went over the wall.

It was a funny thing to be on an actual baseball field. It seemed much smaller than May had imagined it would be. And even though she'd seen the pitcher's mound before, in her mind it had been just a small pile of dirt. In reality the mound was crop-circle huge and rose up almost a foot at the center. Brooks and Palmer had gotten there within moments and were stopped, bags ready. As she approached them, Brooks grabbed her arm and the three pulled close together, leaning their heads in, creating a small sanctuary.

"Now!" Palmer said.

It only took a moment and it must have been invisible to anyone outside of their huddle, this trickle of dirt over a larger pile of dirt. A chalky cloud came up around their ankles. The pitcher's mound itself was kind of reddish, so the ashes stood out as three distinct piles. Palmer started mixing them in with her foot. Brooks and May automatically followed suit.

It was a strange feeling for May, grinding at the dirt. Not only was she literally burying her dad at a baseball stadium, she was doing it with a four-dollar pair of novelty flip-flops. She threw herself into the task, shaking out the very last bits in her bag and toeing them hard into the ground. She was so intent that she tried to brush Brooks off when she grabbed her arm and started pulling her. In that moment she understood what was happening. She felt his presence surround her. Her father. Then she realized that Brooks was trying to move her away from the three security guards who were quickly approaching them, speaking into walkie-talkies pinned to their shoulders.

"Oh, shit . . . ," was all May managed to say before she got the message to her legs that they should start doing their very best to propel her off the field.

Brooks and Palmer sprinted across the diamond at Camden Yards as if it was something they did every other day or so—even strides, backs straight, heads high, side by side. They turned to look for May occasionally and shouted back encouragement.

"Go, May!"

"May, *run!*"

"I . . . am . . . running!"

Thwack, thwack, thwack, thwack.

"No, RUN!"

"Oh . . . my . . . God!"

Thwack, thwack, thwack, thwack.

May's feet were striking the ground so hard that her head shuddered. The toggles of the flip-flops ripped into the skin between her toes. This was why Palmer had told her to take them off. There was probably no historical precedent for *anyone* running from the cops in flip-flops. She was in the vanguard of a whole new breed of idiot criminal.

Thwack, thwack, thwack, thwack.

The guards were catching up to her. Yelling for her to stop. As she struggled to force more air down her raw, windburned throat, she saw her impending arrest in an oxygen-deprived flash—the handcuffing, the fingerprints, the mug shot, the one phone call, the bitter and cold plastic foam cup of coffee, the good cop and the bad cop circling her ("Come on, what were you doing on the baseball field? We've been waiting long enough." "Aw, leave the kid alone, Joe. She'll tell us when she's ready . . . won't you, May?").

She thought about just stopping. Giving in to the creeping inertia that was weighing on her limbs. Giving in to the strain of holding on to her flip-flops with clenched toes. Giving herself up so that Brooks and Palmer could get away. She could take the rap. It would be the perfect movie ending—the others running away, only to turn back. . . . "Where's May?" And there May would be, standing in a pool of searchlight, surrounded by a throng of police, with a beatific smile on her face. They would know that she had sacrificed herself for them. A loving look would pass between them as May was dragged away to the sound of wailing sirens. . . .

But then she remembered—*she had the car key.*

This jolted May. Car. *Get to the car. Don't trip out of the flip-flops and die. Keep going.* She put her head forward and pushed harder. Her calves were burning, and the cutting sensation between her toes was almost unbearable. Left of the dugout . . . left of the dugout . . . Palmer and Brooks were at least leading her there; she realized too late that she hadn't been paying attention to which of the dugouts was the Orioles'. Then Palm and Brooks suddenly veered sharply to the opposite side— guards had appeared at their planned point of exit. May followed, not quite as sharply but with a wide turn to keep the flip-flops from flying off sideways.

A light, scattered clapping and cheering came from the remaining crowd left in the stands. May was almost tempted to swivel her head around to see if she had made a second appearance on the Jumbotron, but she couldn't take the time. Her focus was steady on her sisters, who had by now made it to the wall, where a few people were cheerfully helping them over. They glanced back at her, then disappeared into the crowd. Now May was alone, and some other guards were closing in on the point where they had just exited, trying to meet May.

So she zigzagged in another direction, this time cutting

across the alternating light and dark strips of grass to the wide dirt section between second and third base.

This had to be something out of a dream. It had to be.

May called up whatever reserves of power she had left in her body. She called up strength from the ground. She put it in her thighs. She put it in her calves. She was the greatest living example of what people mean when they say that someone "runs like a girl," but at least she was going faster now. She was getting off this field.

Thwackthwackthwackthwack . . .

The rail was in sight. The rail was closer. The rail was about ten more steps away, six more steps, three more steps. . . . She could almost touch the rail. . . . Her throat was so scorched with air that it no longer mattered how much it hurt. One more step . . .

A man lent her a hand to help her over and started laughing and asking her what she was doing, but she couldn't speak. She started right up the cement staircase, bobbing, weaving, and pushing her way through the crowd. She passed through the huge archway and found herself back in the main indoor concourse. It was all concrete and echoes in here, and the thwacking seemed painfully loud.

"Why . . . are . . . these . . . places . . . all . . . named . . . the . . . same . . . ?" she said, wheeling past the identical carts and shops. She ran past the pennant banners, the Russell Street exit . . . no longer even sure if anyone was after her. Maybe she should slow down, start walking? That way she would blend in.

No. Keep running.

Finally she saw the exit and tore off through it and kept

right on going, across the plaza, into the complex of parking lots, across a street. She looked for whatever signs or landmarks she could remember but found none. It was all just parking lot.

Then she saw Palm bouncing up and down in the distance, waving her in.

She didn't even care that Palm and Brooks doubled over with frantic laughter as they watched her run her strange, head-down, flat-footed run in their direction.

"The key!" Palmer was screaming. "The key!"

"I . . . know!"

Thwack, thwack . . .

"Get the key!"

"I . . . *know*!"

May's hand was already scouring the bottom of her bag, try-ing to hook a finger onto the all-important key. She found everything else. Wallet. Altoids. Millions and millions of Presto Espresso napkins, which went flying out and left a trail.

Bingo. Key.

"I got it!" she screamed, skidding up to the car. One of the shoes flew underneath, but she didn't try to retrieve it. (So they'd have Cinderella evidence as well. If they wanted to scour the East Coast trying to find the coffee-drinking girl with only one daz-zling and patriotic flip-flop, that was their business.) The adrena-line was causing her entire body to shake, so it was hard for her to coordinate her movements and get the key into the lock.

"May!"

"Shut up!"

She managed to control her hands just enough to unlock the driver's side door. She jumped in and unlocked the other side. Ignition. Where was the ignition? The key banged fruitlessly into the dashboard. Palm let out a high-pitched squeal that did little to calm May's nerves. Brooks reached over, grabbed her hand, and directed it firmly toward the ignition. The key slid into the slot, and the car roared to life.

"Drive!" Palm yelled.

Shift? Shift. Come on, May. Grab the shift. Her confidence growing, May threw the car into reverse and backed the Golden Firebird out of its parking space. *Shift again, May. Move it to* D. *Hit the gas. Go.*

The Golden Firebird pulled off into the balmy Baltimore night, leaving behind a star-spangled flip-flop, a fistful of crumpled napkins, and the contents of the bronze urn.

Hysterical laughter filled the car. None of them could stop. It wasn't necessarily a funny kind of laughter—it was a crazy, relieved kind of laughter. Palmer was flat on her stomach in the backseat. Brooks was doubled over, her head resting on the dashboard. May was hugging the wheel, barely able to breathe or see through her watery eyes. They were stuck in creeping traffic anyway, in a long line of cars trying to get back on I-95.

"I can't," May said between heaves. "I can't drive."

"Take the shoulder," Brooks said.

Normally May would never have taken a piece of advice like this, but all rules of her life were temporarily suspended. She steered the massive Firebird onto the shoulder of the road, then drove along slowly until she came to a small local road. She turned down this and kept going until she found a gas station with a convenience store attached.

Brooks filled the tank while May and Palmer went into the

store. May, ignoring the sign on the store entrance, kicked off her remaining flip-flop, put it in the trash, and walked in barefoot. They roamed the aisles, laughing and picking up a strange assortment of items: chips, Swedish fish, chocolate bars, minidoughnuts. When they dumped their selections on the counter, the clerk looked at them suspiciously.

"All of this food is for her," Palmer said straight-faced, pointing her thumb at May.

"I get hungry," May said.

"You're missing your shoes there," the man said, looking down at May's feet.

"Oh, right," May replied, as if just noticing this herself. "I ate them."

Once outside, they sat on the ground next to the Firebird and passed the bag around. They ate in silence for a moment, basking in sugar, fat, and impending doom.

"Do you think they know how to toe print?" May asked, looking down at the two raw and slightly bloody spots where the flip-flop toggles had cut into her skin.

"No." Brooks shook her head. "Probably not."

"Good." May stretched out her toes, and the stinging sensation from the broken skin shot up both her legs. She kept doing it anyway, trying to create as wide a space between the toes as she could. The pain almost fascinated her.

"They could check your shoes for DNA," Palmer said, shoving an entire peanut butter cup into her mouth.

"I'll tell them you made me do it."

Palmer shrugged and chewed.

"We should take the top down," Brooks said.

"Fine," May consented, still absorbed in her toe stretching. "Go ahead."

Brooks climbed into the front seat and flipped the switches on either side where the convertible top met the windshield. Palmer got up to help Brooks lower the top into the well. It was slightly stiff, but it came down without too much hassle.

"There," Brooks said as the interior of the Firebird was once again exposed to the open air. "That's more like it."

"So," May said, fishing around in one of the bags and pulling out a potato chip, "do we ever tell Mom we did this?"

Palmer was opening her mouth to reply, but Brooks beat her to it.

"No," she said.

"Don't you think she's going to notice?" May asked.

"Not if we just put the urn back," Brooks replied.

"Isn't it going to be a little light?"

"You think she takes it down and weighs it?"

"Do you know that she doesn't?"

"So we fill it with flour or something."

"She'll be able to tell the difference."

"You think she opens it up and looks at it?" Brooks said.

"Stop," Palmer said, coming over to stand in front of them. "You're ruining it. We did it, so just . . . stop."

May and Brooks fell silent. It wasn't an angry silence, either. For one of the only times in her life, May felt like she and her sisters were truly together, on the same page. But this time they had accomplished something enormous.

"You're right," she said. "We did it."

*   *   *

Brooks was sunk down completely in the backseat of the Firebird, submerged in a universe of vinyl, protected from the wind and bathing in the warm breezes. This was something that she had missed for a long time. Time moved differently here. Perspective changed. Even though she couldn't see where the car was going, she could watch herself moving quickly toward the moon. Billboards looked thin and straight, like redwoods. They seemed to be keeping time with a plane that flew overhead, probably in the direction of Philadelphia International.

Palmer was glorying in the front seat, hanging her arm over the side of the car. She took her ticket from her pocket and did as her father always used to do—she shoved it under the raised lock on the glove compartment. She examined the sight with satisfaction for a few minutes; then she watched May drive. May had gotten more relaxed. The road was fairly empty, and the route was straight and well lit. They were actually doing sixty.

"So, what did you do to Pete?" she asked.

"I don't want to talk about it," May said, tucking a stray piece of hair behind her ear.

"Why not?"

"Because."

"Those are the things that always come back and bite you in the ass," Palmer counseled.

May threw her a puzzled look.

"What things?"

"The things you try to avoid. You can never really avoid them."

Palmer was scary sometimes. May often suspected that she might have her own talk show someday.

"So what happened?" Palmer pushed again.

"We had a fight. Sort of."

"He tried to kiss her and she ripped into him."

"Thanks, Brooks," May said into the rearview mirror.

"De nada."

"Why?" Palmer asked.

"I don't know," May answered honestly.

"But he likes you. And you like him."

"I don't—"

"Yes, you do. Why do you keep saying that you don't?"

"Good question," came a voice from the back. "Especially since you made out with him all night before we left for the shore."

"What did you say to him?" Palmer asked.

"It doesn't matter," May said.

They drove the next five miles in silence.

"I screwed it up," May finally said. "I screwed it up really badly."

"So what are you going to do?"

"I don't know," May said, tentatively pushing harder on the accelerator. "I guess I'll figure something out."

Right before midnight the Firebird stopped just short of the driveway. The minivan was parked in front of the house. All three Gold sisters gazed at it in horror.

"Why is that here?" Brooks whispered, leaning forward.

"I don't know," May said, eyes wide. "Maybe she switched shifts."

"We can tell her we just ran out to the store," Palmer said. "We've got stuff."

"For six hours?" Brooks said.

"Okay," May said, "it's not so bad. Well, it might be for you, Brooks. . . ."

May heard a *thunk* as Brooks fell back hard against her seat in despair.

"We just need to have one consistent story. Where could we have been for that amount of time?"

"The mall?" Palmer suggested.

"The mall closes at ten."

"Okay," Palmer said, "we went to the mall, then to a movie."

After agreeing on the details, May pulled the Firebird into the garage. Their arrival was painfully loud, with the garage door squealing as it was opened and the coughing and growling of the Firebird engine echoing through the room. Immediately the door to the kitchen flew open. Their mother stood on the threshold. Her chest was actually heaving, like a volcano in those final, huff-and-puff seconds before an eruption.

"Oh," Palmer said. "Hi."

"Where have you been?"

The question echoed through the calm night air. It shook the garage. It vibrated between the houses. It caused a neighbor's dog to start barking. A car alarm also started going off somewhere in the distance, but that was probably unconnected.

"The mall?" May offered. "And then to a movie?"

"I got a call from the league. You hurt someone today, Palmer? Then you left?"

"That was an accident," Brooks said. "Bad pitch."

Normally Palmer would have jumped at Brooks's throat for

a remark like that, but she just sat now, staring dumbly at the dashboard.

"You have your license for half a day, May, and you do this? You take Brooks out? You keep Palmer out until midnight when she's hurt someone?"

May could tell that the fight from earlier hadn't been forgotten. She sighed and looked up at the steel garage door tracks in the ceiling.

"Just get inside," her mother said, disgusted. "All of you. And go right to bed. I don't even want to discuss this tonight. I'm—"

She stopped suddenly, her eyes frozen on a spot along the dashboard. May knew in that instant what she had seen, but it was too late to do anything about it.

Her mother reached into the car and plucked Palmer's ticket from under the glove compartment lock.

May was lying in bed, unwilling or unable to get out, even though it was after noon and a sweet breeze was coming in through her screened window. It seemed to be trying to reach her through the sheet she had over her head, to tell her that a perfect summer day was waiting outside. But May wasn't interested. She liked it where she was, under this soft, cool canopy dotted with the undersides of little orange flowers. If she could have, she would have stayed there all day. The adrenaline of last night had worn off, and there was too much ugly stuff outside that she had to face now. But she had to get ready for work, so she reluctantly rolled out of bed and went downstairs.

May's first surprise of the day was that her mother wasn't drinking coffee at the kitchen table when she got down there—but Mrs. Camp was. She rubbed her eyes. Yes. Definitely Mrs. Camp. Her long, pale orange hair, now streaked with a few gray wisps. Her freckled skin.

"Oh, hi, May," Mrs. Camp said, pretending not to notice that May was standing in the doorway wearing only a T-shirt and her underwear. "Your mom asked me to . . . stay."

"To stay?" May repeated, pulling down hard on the hem of the shirt and trying not to move too much.

"To keep you guys company today," Mrs. Camp said, smiling apologetically.

"Keep us company?"

"I brought some cinnamon rolls," Mrs. Camp said, pushing a large white bakery box in May's direction. "And I hit a huge sale on paper towels, so I brought some of those over."

May glanced over and saw a massive fifteen-pack of paper towels sitting on the floor by the stove.

"I'm just going to . . . put on some other things," May said. "Be right back."

May ran up the stairs and to her room, shutting the door tightly behind her. First, they had, in essence, a babysitter. This meant they were under house arrest. Second, their guard was Pete's mom, which definitely put a little salt in the wound. It was entirely possible that Mrs. Camp knew what May had done yesterday—and there was so much to know: she'd fought with her mother, spat on Mrs. Camp's son's declarations of love, driven to Baltimore . . . and that was just the public domain stuff. Wait till everyone found out about the criminal trespassing and the going into a convenience store with no shoes on.

But then again, she'd brought cinnamon rolls. Who brought cinnamon rolls for heartless juvenile delinquents, anyway?

After putting on a pair of pajama bottoms and pulling back her hair, May ventured back downstairs. Mrs. Camp was busy doing the crossword now, but she looked up on May's approach.

"Am I the first one up?" May asked, looking around. "It's almost twelve-thirty."

"Actually, yes." Mrs. Camp smiled. "You all must be tired."

Cowards, May thought. And they didn't even have half of May's problems.

"So," Mrs. Camp said, detaching a cinnamon roll from the

gooey mass for May, "I heard you passed your driver's exam."

"Kind of." She smiled, automatically looking over to the key rack on the wall. The key to the Golden Firebird was no longer hanging there. Mrs. Camp followed May's gaze.

"Your mom told me to tell you to take your bike to work," she said. "It's such a nice day out. It'll be a nice ride."

Okay. She knew that they were in trouble, but she gave no sign of knowing about what May had done to her son. Mrs. Camp chatted about a trip to North Carolina they were planning on taking, about her yoga class. . . . May stuffed down a cinnamon bun. An hour went by, and Palm and Brooks still hadn't shown their faces.

"I should get showered," May said. "I have to be at work soon."

"Go ahead," Mrs. Camp said, pulling a romance novel from her bag. "I've got lots to read. You can tell Palmer and Brooks to come down anytime they like."

"I'll tell them," May said. "I don't know what's wrong with them."

"Pete was sick this morning too." Mrs. Camp nodded.

May stiffened.

"Really?"

"He came in yesterday afternoon, after he stopped by here," she went on. "He just didn't look well. He went up to his room. I didn't see him this morning either. Maybe something's going around."

"Maybe." May backed out of the room. "I'll see if they're up. . . ."

*   *   *

When May cautiously pushed open the door to Presto Espresso that afternoon, she was immediately bathed in an icy gale from the air-conditioning vent above the door. Everything seemed off. The milk stand had been rearranged, and there were at least ten customers sitting at various tables. Nell was behind the counter, humming to herself and filling oversized coffee filters.

"Okay," May said to herself, and shivered. "This is creepy."

Nell glanced up from her filters and coolly examined May's sunburned figure.

"Who are all of these people?" May asked, walking behind the counter and punching in on the cash register.

"Some church group," Nell said. "Can you go and refill all the coffee bins?"

Refilling the coffee bins was a heavy, tedious job that involved pulling out twenty-pound bags of coffee beans from the back room and topping off an entire wall's worth of plastic bins. It required using the ladder, lifting, and repacking—and it was something that May and Nell never, ever did. There was a crazy guy named Craig who worked about once a week who seemed to live to do this job.

It took May an hour to finish. When she was done, Nell asked her to dust the wall of expensive, oversized mugs that they never sold, empty and clean the pastry case, and open a new shipment of supplies and stock the metal shelves in the storage room. These were the jobs they always did on a very occasional basis and never all at once.

So she knows, May thought as she cut open a cardboard box full of cans of sweetened condensed milk. *And this is how she's going to get back at me.*

At first that felt fine to May. She thought it would make her miserable day go by a little faster. Unfortunately, she also had time to think about Pete, and she replayed their final conversation in her head nonstop as she stocked shelves in the gray, windowless storage room with the fluorescent lights.

When May came out of the storeroom, it was almost seven-thirty. Nell went off on her half-hour break to go to the little health food shop up the road to get her dinner. May leaned against the counter and tried to relax. She could see the vivid sunset, an explosive orange and red and purple filling the sky.

It was altogether too much like the flowers Pete had brought her yesterday.

Pete—he was in her head. Every part of her brain that held a piece of information about him was firing simultaneously. She could smell his skin and his shirt. She could feel the weight of his arm over her shoulders. She could hear him laughing at one of his own jokes. . . .

She couldn't lose it—not here, with Nell. She had to keep a brave face.

Nell came back in a few minutes later with a tin container of adzuki beans, seaweed, and brown rice and set herself up at one of the tables with her food and her cell phone. May listened to her chomping away and cheerfully talking to one of her friends for the next twenty minutes about some amazing deal she'd found on a flight to Budapest. May made up little jobs for herself to keep her focus off Nell. She cleaned between the keys on the cash register with a coffee stirrer wrapped in a napkin. She scraped the buildup off the milk-foaming attachment on the cappuccino machine.

When Nell had finished her call and food, she stacked everything up and quietly came behind the counter and glanced over at May.

"Ann found out about what you did with your schedule," she said as she threw away her dish.

May's head jerked in Nell's direction at the sound of Presto's owner's name.

"She said you can finish your shift today," Nell went on breezily.

Finish your shift today. . . . May ran the words through her mind, trying to pull meaning from them.

"Are you saying I'm fired?" she managed to ask.

"Pretty much."

"How did she find out?"

"I told her," Nell said plainly.

"Why did you tell her?" May asked. "You've swapped shifts dozens of times."

"Pete told me what you did," Nell said. "He told me what happened."

"So you got me *fired*?"

"Right."

May felt slightly faint. She suddenly had a flash of how she wanted it all to end. She would dramatically take off her apron and hat, throw them on the counter, and walk to the door. At the last second she would turn and say, "I think what happened was that he realized how annoying you are, like how you never stop talking about yourself. I think that may have had a lot to do with it." Then she would open the door and step out. Before she was all the way gone, she would add over her shoulder, "But I'm just guessing."

The fact was, though, it didn't really matter anymore that Nell was irritating or even that she had just deliberately caused May to lose her job. May had disrupted something personal in Nell's life. Nell could have really liked Pete, and May had ruined that for her. The score seemed even.

But May did take off her apron and hat.

"I'd like to go now," she said.

"Fine." Nell shrugged. "You have to punch out and sign a form for your uniform."

May entered her employee code for the last time, then verified that she was returning one apron, one name pin, and one hat in good (as opposed to excellent) condition. Then she picked up her bag and headed for the door. At the last moment the guilt really started to kick in. She stopped and turned back to Nell, who had taken out a backpacker's guide to Eastern Europe and started to read.

"I'm sorry," May said. "I didn't mean for it to happen."

"Whatever, Ape."

"I just wanted you to know that it wasn't intentional."

"Fine."

There was nothing more May could say, so she opened the door.

"See you later, Ape," Nell said, turning back to her book.

"Later," May replied as she left Presto Espresso for the last time.

May coasted along her street. Even though the sun had just gone down, it was easily ninety-five degrees. Despite the heat, she wasn't ready to go home yet. She skidded to a halt at the mailbox at the end of her street to cool down and watched two little kids getting dragged along by a very eager Dalmatian.

The lightning bugs were already out in full force, looking like strings of insane, moving Christmas lights. May clasped one of the bugs in her hands, like she used to do when she was little and she and Brooks used to compete to see how many they could catch in a night. The bug wandered around her palm, not particularly concerned for its own welfare. When she opened her hand and let the bug go, it didn't seem to want to leave her. She had to blow on it to get it moving. Finally it took off from her palm and lingered around her head, flashing its little yellow taillight.

She turned her bike and rode around the corner and up the slight hill to Pete's house. The Camps' rancher sat in the middle of a fairly wild yard, with lots of trees. She stopped by the edge of the driveway, near the thick wall of shrubs that marked the edge of the property.

She could do something, or she could spend the next days, weeks, or months of her grounding picking lint out of the carpet and wondering.

Her hair was probably wild, and she was definitely sticky and rumpled. She knew she probably had perspiration marks under her arms, so she took care to keep them pinned to her sides.

She knocked at the Camps' door. There was a frantic barking from deep inside the house. A thumping as someone came down the steps. And then Pete was in front of her. His skin looked very tan against the white T-shirt he was wearing. He seemed tired.

"Can I talk to you for a second?" she asked.

"What are you doing here?"

"Look," she said, "this is your chance. If you want an explanation, you have to get it now. Or if you want to yell at me. Whatever."

It took him a minute to think this one over. He opened the door and came outside.

"So talk," he said.

"Do you guys still have the glider?" May asked.

"Yeah. Out back."

"Can we go sit on it?"

Pete looked at her in disbelief, then leaned his head back to stare at the sky.

"For privacy," she said. "So we don't have to stand in the middle of the lawn."

They made their way through the rakes, shovels, bikes, and spare pieces of wood that filled the narrow passageway that separated the garage from the house. The Camp yard was overgrown, with a slightly unstable picnic bench off to one side and a brick barbecue against the back fence. The honeysuckle bushes that they used to feast on as kids were still flourishing. The people next door were cooking dinner, and the air was hot and smelled of hamburger.

"God," May said, taking a deep breath, "we haven't taken out the grill in forever."

Pete knocked some spiderwebs and leaves from the glider with his shoe, then pointed at it. May sat down. Pete sat on top of the picnic bench a few feet away and fixed her with a steady glare.

She had no idea where to begin, but she had to say something.

"I don't know why I said all those things, but I'm sorry," she said. "I was insane."

Pete said nothing to this general apology. His expression remained frozen. A cloud of gnats descended on May's head. She waved them away, but not before getting a few up her nose. She had to snort them out. Even though she tried to do this in a very low-key way, it still wasn't exactly attractive.

She decided to try again.

"Look, I know how I've been. I was just afraid all of a sudden, and I started saying whatever I could. I know that makes me seem really weird and unstable. . . ."

She could have bitten off her tongue. Now it sounded like she was talking about Jenna again.

"Let's just forget it, okay?" Pete said. He got up, took a broom from the walkway, and started cleaning some leaves and dirt from a corner of the patio. "It was a bad idea."

"What do you mean? What was a bad idea? Us? Dating?"

"Right. So it's over. Let's just forget it happened."

"I don't think it was a bad idea," May said quickly. "I think it was a really good idea."

Pete didn't answer. He swept.

"If it makes you feel any better," she added, trying to get a response, "Nell just got me fired."

"Yeah, that makes me feel great."

"I don't know. I thought it might."

"Why would I be happy about that?" he asked, never once taking his eyes from his work. "Do you think it's my fault that she got you fired? Do you think *I* told her to do it as part of my plan to screw you over?"

From the way he'd said the word *screw*, May could tell that her words had definitely not been forgotten.

"No," she said.

"So what's your point?"

That corner of the patio had probably never been so clean.

May put her head down and told herself not to cry. This was not the time for that. This was the time to become a genius and say something amazing. Unfortunately, nothing was coming to mind.

"I don't know, Camper," she said. "I didn't really have a plan. I wanted to explain, but I guess I don't have an explanation."

"I guess you don't. Like I said, it was a bad idea. Can we drop it now?"

There was a swell of emotion building up in May. It was huge. It seemed to spread over every thought in her mind.

"Brooks didn't have these problems," she said, mostly to herself. "Why is that not surprising?"

Pete stopped sweeping for a minute and leaned into the broom, looking down at the supremely clean bricks.

"I mean, he liked Brooks the most," May went on. "Brooks was perfect. Palmer too. It was like they had a little club. Maybe if I played sports, it would all have been okay."

Nothing like another little attack of Tourette's to spice up a conversation, May thought. She really didn't seem to be in control of her own speaking voice anymore. Pete looked like he was about to say something (maybe call for help), but the patio door opened and his mom came out. He moved on to another corner of the patio.

"May?" Mrs. Camp said, clearly surprised to see her and even more confused by the weird silence that lingered between her son and May.

"I was just on my way home from work," May said. "I was giving Pete a message."

"Oh. Right. Does your mom—"

"No, I know. It's fine. I'm going home now."

"Okay."

Mrs. Camp looked between the two of them, then went back inside. Pete stood there with his broom, not moving.

"I'm kind of in trouble," May said. "It's a long story. I should probably go."

He didn't say anything.

May got up and walked back through the covered passage toward the front lawn. She tripped over the Weedwacker in her haste. It didn't matter. There was no reason why she should try to be graceful. She just wanted to get out of there as quickly as possible.

Out of the corner of her eye she saw Pete coming through the walkway. He came halfway down the driveway and stopped a few feet away from her.

"I'm sorry you got fired," he said.

"It's not so bad," May replied, grabbing her bike. "I won't have to smell that cabbage stuff Nell eats anymore."

Pete leaned against the Cutlass.

"Hey, Pete!" his mom called from the front doorway. "Can you start up the grill?"

"Um . . . yeah," he said. "Just a second."

His mom lingered by the door for a moment before disappearing back into the house. May could see her walking past the living room window. She was watching.

"You'd better go start the grill," she said.

"I know."

For the first time in the conversation, May saw a look on Pete's face that seemed somewhat familiar. He was staring off down the street, squinting just a little, wrinkling the top of his nose.

"Why'd you say all of that?" he asked.

"All of what?"

"That he didn't like you as much."

"Because it's true."

"No, it's not," Pete said. "Your dad never shut up about you."

"Trust me, okay?"

"How do you think I know all your grades and all your scores and stuff?"

"You do?" That was news to her.

"Yeah. He talked about Brooks and Palm sometimes, but it was usually about you."

"He never talked to me, though. Not like he did to them."

"Come on," Pete said. "You always used to get those little jokes he'd put in your lunch in grade school. Or we'd come over to watch a game and he'd be quizzing you and we'd have to wait."

"That's not the same," May said. She had no idea why she was having this conversation with Pete at all. Stuff was just coming out of her mouth faster than she could keep up with it.

"What's your problem?" he said angrily. "You get mad at people a lot. You think they're doing things to you. You're pissed at Brooks, at your dad, then you got pissed at me."

"I already said I was sorry. . . ."

She was crying, she noticed. There were tears running down her face. She wondered how long that had been going on before she became aware of it. Pete was just watching her now.

"Sorry," she said, sniffing and wiping her eyes with the back of her hand. "I'm stupid. I'm going to go."

She was about to swing her leg over the guy bar when another thought came into her mind. It flew out of her mouth in the next second, unchecked.

"Sometimes I feel like I've been waiting for someone to tell me when I can be normal again," she said. "I keep thinking I'll get a letter or something. Or a call. When does it happen?"

Pete looked like he wanted to walk toward her, but then he fell back against the car. The staring contest between them went on for almost a minute, and finally Pete exhaled loudly.

"It's okay," he said.

May could have been wrong, but it seemed—it *seemed*—like he was forgiving her.

She couldn't keep still any longer.

She ran up to him, stretched up onto the tips of her toes, and kissed him. It didn't matter to her that she looked gross, or that he might still be mad, or that his mom was clearly gawking out the living room window. At first he seemed startled. He stood up quickly. After a second or two, though, he wrapped his arms around her. May didn't know if it was a romantic embrace or just an attempt to keep her from losing her balance and falling backward onto the blacktop—and it didn't matter. Pete was holding her, and he was kissing her. She was getting his entire face wet in the process.

When they separated, the freckleless spot between Pete's eyes
was bright red. Before anything else could be said or done, May
grabbed her bike and hopped on. She waited until she was six
houses down to turn and see if he was still standing in the
driveway watching her.

He was.

She stopped for just a moment, and they caught each other's
eyes. Then he slowly started walking backward toward the house.
May couldn't see that well, considering that her eyes were still a
little blurry and he was far away, but it looked like he was smiling.

May arrived home to find Brooks, Palmer, and their mom
in the living room, freezing from the overfunctioning window
air conditioner that shot out small pieces of ice along with cold
breezes. Her mother was quietly crocheting a pale yellow baby
blanket. Obviously a gift for someone. Crochet was a new
thing for her mom. She had picked up the habit from some of
her friends at the hospital. May thought it seemed like a weird
activity for someone who used to go to clubs in outfits made of
black trash bags, but it did seem to relax her.

"You're home early," her mom said.

"It was dead at work," May replied, trying to look as casual
as possible.

"What's wrong with you?" Palmer said, looking May up and
down. May was sweating profusely. Her shoes were covered in
grass, her face was flushed, her eyes were red, and she was
breathing a little too quickly—not things typically associated
with a night spent at Presto.

"It's hot out."

May sank down on the floor. She immediately felt her energy leaving her, like the final, dying flickers of a battery indicator light sending those last-gasp warnings before blinking off. She had spent all of her emotions, and now she was going to slump on the floor and think about nothing. If she tried to analyze the Pete thing now, she'd go insane. As for her job, she'd think about it tomorrow. She'd definitely have the time.

Brooks flicked through the channels, trying to find something remotely interesting. Palmer didn't seem to care. She sat on the floor with her legs stretched out, looking content with everything—CNN, golf, a documentary on the evolution of the battleship, a Spanish soap opera. . . .

"Maybe we should get a movie," Brooks said.

"We have plenty of stations," her mom answered. "Find something to watch."

Brooks sighed and clicked away.

So this was how it was going to be for the next few weeks, May thought. They would all be like Palmer now—dumbly staring at the television, never speaking. She focused on a commercial for some kind of wonder spatula. Usually infomercials entertained her. She liked the way they would always show people who were apparently so incompetent that they couldn't flip a burger without putting out an eye or roll their garden hose without an ambulance crew on standby. That was why they needed product XYZ—they had very serious problems.

They were just getting to the part where they offered to send two wonder spatulas for the price of one if May called right now when Palmer suddenly spoke.

"We took Dad's ashes," she said. "Last night. We took them

to the field, to the pitcher's mound. That's what we were doing at Camden Yards."

From the way she said it, you would have thought that Palmer was just mentioning what she'd eaten for lunch. It was a very stealth move. May swung her head around and saw the old maniac gleam in Palmer's eyes, even though they were still steadily focused on the television. May looked the other way to find Brooks backing up in her seat, looking like she wished the recliner would swallow her up.

The only thing that could be heard in the next minute was the Starks' infrared bug zapper along the back fence.

May slowly turned to see how her mother was taking this news. Her hands were frozen midway through a stitch, and she was looking right at May. Not at Palmer, not at Brooks. Just at May. And her expression said it all very clearly: *Tell me what the hell Palmer is talking about.*

"We . . ."

That was as much as May could come up with. Palmer had just said it all. There was nothing to deny, nothing to add.

"We did it all together," Palmer said, picking up from there. The light was still in her eye, but she was balling up her fists and releasing them over and over. She was afraid. "He's gone. We did it. All of him is there, right in the middle of the field."

At the moment May expected the blowup or the violent outburst of Dutch, her mother simply stood up and left the room.

One in the morning and hot. Hot, hot, hot. A million percent humidity. A universe of hot soup. The clickity fan did nothing but push heat from side to side. On nights like this one, the

Gold sisters frequently camped out in the living room to bask in the air conditioning. But no one was down there tonight. They'd all scattered. Everyone was sweltering alone, in safety.

May had lived about three lifetimes in the last two days, so she wasn't too sure where she stood on Palmer's surprise announcement. On the one hand, she was glad not to have the secret hanging over her head. On the other, she was completely worn out. Brooks had freaked, completely. She'd screamed at Palmer. Palmer had just sat there and taken it. May had just wearily trudged up to her room in the middle of their fight.

For the last five hours she'd moved seashells around on her desk, stared at the wall, reorganized her bookshelf, and examined the cuts between her toes. She had nothing to get up in the morning for. Nothing to get ready for. Nothing to look forward to. She could stay in her room for the rest of the summer and count the ponies on the wall.

What she wanted to do was run out right now, in her boxer shorts and old T-shirt, and go to Pete's and sit on the glider. But she figured that she could only turn up at his house once a day looking scruffy and desperate.

This heat was going to kill her.

She needed something to drink. If she was quiet, she could go down to the kitchen without attracting any attention. Peeking out into the hall, she saw that all the doors were shut. There was no light coming from downstairs. She was safe. She crept along on her toes down the stairs and through the hall to the kitchen.

May was surprised to see her mother sitting at the table, looking strangely young in her bleach-stained scrub shirt and her ruffled, spiky hair. She had both of her feet on the chair, and her knees were drawn up to her chest. May almost tried to back up and disappear, but her mother had seen her. She nodded toward an empty chair.

"Sit down," she said.

May sat down. She was so stupid. She should have known better than to leave her room. Now she was going to go through this all over again.

"How did you get them?" her mom asked. She sounded exhausted, not angry, which was somewhat of a relief.

"Palmer found them."

"Was it Palmer's idea to take them to Camden Yards?"

"She was upset," May said, nodding. "She said she was going whether we went with her or not. So I drove there."

"So she wouldn't go on her own?"

"Yeah . . ."

Zap. Another bolt of purple light from the bug whacker shot through the room. Another bug moved on to bug heaven. May stared at the microwave clock for a moment until her focus gave and the numbers went fuzzy.

"Who took them to the field?" her mom asked.

"All of us."

"Didn't someone try to stop you?"

"They tried," May said. "We ran. We got away."

She couldn't really blame her mother for looking so surprised. It was still a little hard for May to believe that she'd successfully run away from a group of grown men. Her mom tucked her head between her knees and scrunched her lips together. She looked a little like Palmer when she did this.

"Sometimes I don't know what to do," she finally said. "I'm not like your dad. He always knew."

"Knew?"

"He knew how to talk to Brooks and Palmer. I don't. I always felt like I had more in common with you. I was just like you when I was sixteen."

"Right." May snorted. "Because I always wear fishnets."

"I was quiet," her mom said. "Shy. The hair, the makeup—that was me just pretending I wasn't. It was easy to fake it that way."

"You were faking it?"

"Sort of," her mom said, smiling slowly. "I liked some of it. But a lot of it was just trying to fit in. Your dad didn't have to try that hard. He never seemed to be afraid of anything. He was totally comfortable with himself and with everyone else. I liked that. I wished I could be like that. And he knew who I really was, even under all that makeup and stuff. He liked me."

There was something in her voice that May had never heard before. Her mom wasn't talking like a mom—she was talking like someone with a huge crush. It was the same kind of voice that May heard in her own head when she thought about Pete.

"What you said yesterday," her mom went on. "You were wrong. Your dad didn't like Brooks or Palmer best. They're a lot like him, so he understood them. But he could never believe that he helped make you. He thought you were amazing. When you got into Girls', he couldn't stop talking about it. He'd tell anybody he met about his May. You were always his May."

"Why didn't he tell me that?" May said quickly. "He always told Palm and Brooks how great they were."

Her mother leaned back and thought about this.

"I think," she said, "that he didn't know how. He tried. He was almost in awe of you, May. You're smart. You're mature. It was almost as if he thought he couldn't keep up with you."

Having just heard something similar from Pete, May couldn't help but feel ashamed. She couldn't even remember why she'd thought her father hadn't liked her. Now she remembered it all clearly—the way he'd managed to find the money for her school, the fact that she alone had been allowed to have the kitchen table for homework, and even how he'd called her "the professor." It all made sense now.

There was a noise by the door. May didn't have to turn around to know that Palmer was lurking somewhere in the darkness of the hall. She must have heard them talking. Evidently, her mom knew she was there as well.

"You can come in," she said.

To May's surprise, Palmer wasn't alone. She had brought Brooks with her. Brooks shot her a look as if to ask, *What's the damage?* May could only shrug.

"There's something I want to know," her mom said to the three of them. "Why didn't you ask me to come with you?"

The bug zapper claimed another victim in the ensuing silence.

"Wouldn't you have stopped us?" May asked.

"Of course I would have stopped you."

"That's why," May replied, puzzled.

Her mom nodded, as if this confirmed something she had been thinking.

"I never knew what to do with the ashes," she said. "I never believed they were really him. So I just put them away. You did a dumb thing. Something could have happened to you."

All the control she'd been keeping herself under dissolved all at once as she said that, as if the thought of anything happening to them was more than she could even bear to contemplate.

"You're good girls," she said, her eyes filling with tears. "You know that? You're in a lot of trouble, but God—you're really amazing girls."

The four Gold women slept in the living room together that night, with the air conditioner blasting. May's mother took the sofa, with Palmer splayed out all over the floor by her side. They were the first to fall asleep.

Brooks took the recliner. May claimed a patch of floor by the television and made herself a little nest of blankets and pillows to defend herself against the icy gale that was coming straight at her. She wriggled down into the plaid flannel depths of an old waterproof sleeping bag that she had opened up and wound around herself. The recliner groaned softly as Brooks shifted.

"It's either kill-you hot or kill-you cold," May whispered. "It's never just right."

"It's better than sleeping upstairs," Brooks whispered back.

May heard a tiny chip of ice rattle around before flying loose from one of the AC vents.

"What are you doing tomorrow?" Brooks asked.

"I don't know," May said, staring up at a moving shadow on the ceiling that was a car passing by. "My schedule's pretty wide open."

"Mine too."

Lots more shifting around coming from Brooks's direction. The footrest banged back into starting position.

"You want the chair?" Brooks asked.

"I'm good."

"I can't sleep here. Can I share those blankets?"

"Sure."

She made some room in her warm pocket to accommodate Brooks, who managed to completely destroy the careful arrangement May had set up. But Brooks also acted as a human shield against the blast, so temperature-wise things were more or less the same.

"Hey Brooks?" she whispered.

"What?"

"Do I seem different to you?"

"What?"

"More unpredictable? Not as boring?"

"What?" Brooks said again. But this time it was a softer "what?" A "what?" that meant yes to anyone who spoke Brooks.

"Thanks," May said.

"Go to sleep." Brooks gave a tug on the blanket.

May took the suggestion and closed her eyes. She knew she would wake up on the living room floor, still grounded and unemployed, with Brooks's hair in her face and no covers at all. But these things didn't seem as bad as they would have even a few hours before.

Within a few minutes, Brooks was snoring in her ear loudly enough to cover the thick, icy coughs of the air conditioner. This didn't bother her either. In fact, it was lulling, reassuring. Her eyes grew heavy. She was right at the point where the real world gets taken over by dreamy haze when she felt a bump as Palmer rolled over and joined them.

ACKNOWLEDGMENTS

Many thanks are due to Leslie Morgenstein, Ben Schrank, Josh Bank, and Claudia Gabel at 17th Street Productions, and Abigail McAden at HarperCollins. They are the reason this book made it to the shelf.

Jason Keeley, Karen Quarles, John Vorwald, Joey Sorge, Matt Zimmerman, "the real" Linda Fan, and Chris Blandino provided inspiration and information. The Fasslers provided the starting point. Joseph Rhodes committed an act of kindness simply out of the desire to help a writer.

I would be lost without the assistance of my friend and longtime partner in crime, Kate Schafer. And it was Jack Phillips who—among millions of other things—explained to me how to remove corrosive buildup from the nodes of a car battery.